JUDGE WHO SURROUND ME

THE OBAMA CHALLENGE

Rick,
Let's All be on the Same Page!

Barbara Bluefield

BARBARA BLUEFIELD

outskirtspress
DENVER, COLORADO

Judge Me By The People Who Surround Me
The Obama Challenge

v5.0

Outskirts Press, Inc.
http://www.outskirtspress.com

ISBN: 978-1-4327-8558-1

PRINTED IN THE UNITED STATES OF AMERICA

Dedication

I want to thank and dedicate this book to my husband Edward, and my parents Jim and Shirley. Our children Douglas and his wife Deena, Deanna and her husband Michael, Jim and his wife Sue, Larry and his wife Sue have given me the inspiration to put my thoughts into written words. To my sister Beverly and her husband Chris, brothers Jim, Gilbert, and Michael and his wife Debby thank you for listening to me and respecting my opinions.

This book is especially dedicated to our grandchildren; Gina, Tommy, Dougie, Tony, Grace, Elizabeth, Megan, Erin, Victoria, Anna, Justin, Sandy, Steven, Sean, Loren, Andrew, Madelynn, Julieanna, and Eddie. We are truly blessed with our great-grandsons Travis and Blake. I also want to dedicate this book to the young ladies that have become part of our family; Tammy and her daughter Rheilyn, plus Erin and her son Wyatt. In addition I want to recognize everyone at Eastside Teen Outreach and all the good things they do

I want all the children to select friends carefully. Find friends who share the ideals and morals your parents have instilled with you. Be proud of yourself and be proud of the people you choose to associate with. You are judged by the people who surround you.

Introduction

This book began by simply looking up information regarding the controversies that surrounded Barack Obama when he ran for office in 2008. There were rumors and comments made about his birth, his background, his community activism, and his friends. Some of the responses from his spokespersons just talked around the issues or just didn't make sense. I have learned that if a story doesn't make sense, there is always more to the story. This is an attempt to find the rest of the story.

It was my daughter, Deanna, who suggested I should put my research into book form. So I did. The information I discovered has fascinated me and I found out how much I did not know. The facts that seemed strange or interesting I sought out multiple resources to verify. Original sources were used whenever possible, but articles from left leaning, right leaning, domestic and foreign were used to document the information written about. Subjects I found interesting that related to the persons described within are included to clarify issues. All information was found on the internet.

I, of course, stated my opinions throughout the book; as you don't get to my age without forming opinions. You may not agree with me and that's okay. I hope you will do your own research to verify or debunk the information I gathered. I thoroughly enjoyed my journey as I learned about not only Obama's associations and their past; but also the history surrounding them. Follow me as I discovered the people and organizations that have shaped the life and opinions of the man that resides in the White House. I hope you will find the information as interesting as I did.

Contents

Section Five: President

CHAPTER 1

★ ★ ★ ★ ★

Judge Me

Judge me by the people who surround me. The actual quote from Barack's Presidential campaign in September 2008 was "Judge me by the people I surround myself with". This statement is based on an old adage and was apparently made to portray his honesty and integrity. However I took it as a challenge. There is another old adage 'birds of a feather flock together.' so I began to research his background and the persons he chose to surround himself with.

Obama's campaign promise was that his administration would be the most transparent ever. He repetitively made that promise, maybe as often as he said, "Let me be perfectly clear". This is a familiar phrase that parents often used with their children, normally before a lecture or threat of discipline. It usually ended with, "Do you understand me?" An example might be; 'Let me make this perfectly clear, you will get no dessert unless you eat everything on you dinner plate. Do you understand me?' Or, 'Let me make this perfectly clear; you may drive the car to the store, you may go with Jimmy and Janie, but not with Brutus or Lolita. You must be home by 8:00 pm and you must not leave the gas gauge on empty, or you will never be able to drive again. Do you understand me?' Would Obama's promise of transparency be as fulfilled as the empty threat of never being able to drive again? Time will tell.

So Obama told the nation to judge him by the people who surrounded him and promised to be the most transparent President ever. But I was curious about the controversy regarding his associates and the reported lack of documentation about his past. I discovered many documents about him, his family, and associates have been sealed, lost, or were questionable. What I found troubling, for a transparent administration, is the number of Washington appointments to positions of power which were being made without congressional inquiry or approval. The other thing that bothered me was his promise of change, but never an explanation of what he wanted to change, nor what the change was.

I decided to collect information about him, his family, his friends, plus his past and current associates. This was done to determine if the lack of transparency was connected with those who surrounded him. What I discovered was spider web type of connections that spanned generations. It was like deciphering the relationships of characters in a mystery novel. The plot of this mystery appears to be how he plans to "fundamentally transform America"; as he proclaimed on October 31, 2008. What is interesting how are many of the connections were based on political activism and community organizations.

While gathering information, I found that it was easier to comprehend what I was learning if I had a better knowledge about the different governing systems. A common denominator between those who associated with Obama was their political ideology. I investigated the differences and similarities of different theories of government, the methods of governing, and America's three largest political parties. I also researched information on the largest caucuses (sometimes called coalitions, conferences, or committees) of each party. I was surprised at how much I did not know. Therefore, before I begin in sharing what I learned about Obama's background and associations, I will explain the differences among governing ideologies and the political parties.

Judge me by the people who surround me.

SECTION ONE

★ ★ ★ ★ ★

Practical Knowledge

CHAPTER 2

★ ★ ★ ★ ★

Theories of Government and Political Parties

There are four main systems or theories of governing. These are Capitalism, Fascism, Communism, and Socialism. Each system has different economic policies and different regulations to control its citizens or allowing individual freedoms.

CAPITALISM is a social system that is based on the principle of individual rights and freedoms. It emphasizes the rights of individuals to choose where to live, to choose where to work, to own their own business, the right to worship as they want, and to own property. This system rewards ability and achievement, regardless of the social status of their parents or where they were born.

Capitalism is the dominant economic system in the Western world. This system allows for the production and the distribution of privately, or corporately, owned goods by contracts made by individuals or companies. The proceeds of production, whether manufactured or agriculture, remain with the individual or company that produced it. It is their decision to either reinvest or accumulate the profits. Proceeds are not mandated to be used to build castles, churches, or be redistributed to those not contributing their labor or resources. Pricing and distribution of goods are determined by the owners, not the government. In fact, Capitalism working at its best requires the market be free of government interference. People using their own investments of money and labor can prosper or fail. Underground markets are known to flourish when the government has outlawed such items as drugs, alcohol, weapons, and even prostitution.

> Walter Williams once wrote, "Prior to Capitalism, the way people amassed great wealth was by plundering, looting, and enslaving their fellow man. Capitalism made it possible to become wealthy by serving their fellow man."

FASCISM is a government system of central rule under a dictator. It controls opposition through terror and censorship. Fascism is very oppressive. Fascists control with the belief of supremacy of a national or ethnic group and the denial of equality to specific segments of the population. Human rights are not recognized and religion is often used to manipulate public opinion. The police often are abusive and have unlimited powers to enforce laws. Fascist governments directly or indirectly control the media and censoring of content is common. There is an insistence on obedience to a powerful leader. The government controls every aspect of national life.

> Jim Garrision warned, "I'm afraid, based on my own experience that fascism will come to America in the name of national security."

COMMUNISM is a form of government where the State plans and controls the economy. Government holds all the power, professing to make Progress toward a higher social order and all goods and services are equally shared. The Marxist and Leninist versions of communism advocate the overthrow of Capitalism either by revolution or by changing from within. Lenin believed that to operate in Capitalist countries you had to disguise yourself with misleading missions. Karl Marx supported revolution and stressed communal ownership. Under Communism the government owns all business and the government makes all decisions of production and distribution. The Communist social policy is all property belongs to the community and each person contributes and receives according to ability or need. All wealth is held in common. Marx believed that a new revolution is possible during or after a new crisis. If there are no natural crises, then he believed one needed to be created. It did not matter if the crisis was real or imagined. He so believed in this ideology that these words are engraved on his tombstone: 'WORKERS OF ALL LANDS UNITE.' The Communist Manifesto written in 1848, by Marx, separates people into two groups, the oppressed and the oppressor, it was also called the working class and the ruling class. The Manifesto states that if the following events happen then Capitalist countries will transform into Communism.

- Abolish property rights and confiscate all property
- Have a heavy progressive tax
- Abolish the right to inheritance

- Control media and transportation
- Control factories and agriculture
- Have equal pay for all labor
- Establish industrial armies (unions)
- Abolish the distinction between town and county with equitable distribution of population
- Free public education
- Combine education and industrial production

SOCIALISM is a social organization that demands that the ownership, the production, and the distribution of capital (land and property) belong to the community and not to the individual. Common welfare is achieved by the Socialist economic system. This means the government controls the production and distribution of goods, but not necessarily the ownership. Production of goods would be only to meet "human needs" and could end the need for buying and selling, or the need for money. There are some Socialist systems that will allow limited capitalism, if the government maintains a major influence. Some Socialists believe in destroying all private ownership of property. All Communists are Socialist, but not all Socialist are Communists. The basic difference between Socialism and Communism is that Socialism is a society ruled by workers and Communism is a classless society, ruled by the government.

> The Socialist slogan is "From each according to ability, to each according to needs".

FABIAN SOCIALISM is a strategy, or conspiracy, to take over a country and convert it. Fabians believe in collectivism, as do the Marxists, but it prefers stealth instead of bloody revolution. Their shield's design is symbolic of its tactics. It depicts a wolf in a sheep skin. I think we have all heard the adage "He's a wolf in sheep's clothing". The saying comes from the bible, written in the King James Version, Matthew 7:15; "Beware of false prophets, which come to you in sheep's clothing but inwardly they are ravening wolves".

Quintus "Fabius" Maximus Verrucosus Cunctator, the model of this strategy, was a dictator and a General in Rome. Fabius was at war with General Hannibal, from Italy, who had a superior military force. Fabius could not win in open battle but his city was walled and impenetrable. So he stayed behind his wall and kept an eye on Hannibal, refused to fight openly, then denied him reinforcements and supplies. Hannibal's men lost their enthusiasm to fight as there were no victories, had no supplies, and no morale. Hannibal lost.

Two of the founding members of the Fabian Society Socialist were activists Sidney and Beatrice Potter Webb. They wrote numerous books explaining the ideas they promoted. These books include the titles, "Facts for Socialists', 'History of Trade Unions', and 'The Cooperative Movement'. One charter member was George Bernard Shaw a well known playwright and novelist. He was a proponent of eugenics, saying the world would be improved by selective reproduction. He recommended that people should go before a board and justify their existence. Shaw also suggested a lethal chamber with a deadly, but humane, gas for people unfit to live.

H.G. Wells was another early member of the Society. He thought the Fabians were going in the wrong direction as he advocated for large pressure groups agitating for change. In 1911 he wrote the book 'The New Machiavelli" to portray the direction of the Fabian movement. He later resigned from the Society but stayed active in the Socialist movement. Wells advocated that both WW I and WW II should have been used as an opportunity to create a new world order. He was disappointed that the Fabians did not use the wars as an excuse to impose Socialism on the people.

Fabians believe in the Doctrine of Gradualism. This is a slow, unrelenting, and continuous transformation of society by gaining control of the universities, the media, political parties, and the churches. The doctrine allows those in power to control the message and to dictate what is said and how it is said. It is a non-aggressive way to get from here to there. 'There' being a Socialist society.

Gradualism is also the basis of Keynesian economics which is named after the late Baron J. M. Keynes a Fabian Socialist and author of "The End of Laissez-Faire." He advocated governments to enact regulations that would cripple private enterprise to the point that the Government had to take it over, rather than suddenly and overtly taking control. The idea is to gradually take control of all production and grow bureaucracy, while confiscating private ownership, and claiming to work toward "Full Employment". The desired result is to end free enterprise and then to control all resources so that people no longer have individual choices and are dependent on the government. High taxation is a method to controlling people and Keynesians believe controlled inflation is desirable as it limits personal spending. The combination of high taxes, plus targeted tax breaks, and inflation enables the government to redistribute wealth while assuring that the interventions will prevent economic depression and higher unemployment. Keynes actually advocated government control of the number of children each family should have.

> Thomas Jefferson said, "I would rather be exposed to the inconvenience attending to too much liberty that to those attending too small a degree of it".

Professor Rudolph J. Rummel teaches political science at the University of Hawaii. His latest book is titled: "Death by Government". He teaches the subject of 'Democide' a theory he created, which means murder by government. Democide is different from genocide because it is not the murdering of entire cultural groups. It is the elimination of groups which the government feels is a current political threat, or a potential future threat. Rummel states freedom is a basic human right and countries with a strong central government suppress human rights which lead to violence. The reaction to violence has too often been the elimination of the threat. His studies revealed that countries with the most personal freedoms had the least violence and was the cause of converting him from a Socialist to a Libertarian.

Countries are ruled by different styles of government based on the powers of the leaders and its citizens. The most common forms are Republics, Democracies, Oligarchies, Dictatorships, Theocracies, Monarchies, and Caliphates.

The United States was formed as a REPUBLIC. A Republic is a representative style where the citizens control the government. It has a Constitution and is ruled by laws enacted by a legislative body and approved by three branches of government. A Republic believes the judicial branch should interpret law; not create it. The founding fathers of the United States believed citizens have God given inalienable rights of life, liberty, and the pursuit of happiness. They believed in individual freedom, not government control of the people. They believed God bestowed these rights and it was not the role of the government to create man made rights. The founding fathers believed it is the government's responsibility to protect the rights of all citizens.

DEMOCRACY is a style of government that is directly ruled by the majority of people either by elections, polls, or in the extreme by mobs. The majority rule is absolute and unlimited. This rule is not appealable under the legal system. There is no consideration for minority opinions. The majority have the ability to bestow rights and create laws, then demand that the government follow their dictates. Laws may change as often as the opinion of the majority changes. The people have the ability to create laws that will benefit the majority at the expense of the minority.

An OLIGARCHY has a power structure where small segments of the citizens rule. This is by royalty, wealth, family ties, or the military. The leader has absolute control over the citizens. Often an oligarchy is achieved while a country is in transition between different government types. South Africa was considered an oligarchy while under apartheid because the minority white race ruled over the majority black citizens. Iran is considered to be an oligarchic republic as it is controlled by clerics and a Grand Ayatollah.

A DICTATORSHIP is ruled by a single group or person. There is no structure by laws or constitution and the dictator controls the legislature and judicial branches of government. If initially elected, the dictator will often cancel future elections, run unopposed, or have fake elections. Human rights are not recognized and dictatorships are often referred to as police states. Cuba is an example of a country ruled under a dictatorship

A THEOCRACY is ruled by the dictates of a religion and has a Supreme Leader whot is often considered to have a direct connection to God. The distinction between religion and governance is blurred. Saudi Arabia, Iran, and Yemen are examples of theocracies that are under Islamic or Sharia Law. Vatican City is the only Christian theocracy.

ISLAMIC SOCIALISM is an Islamic theocracy governed with Socialist political system. The principles of redistribution of wealth and central control are considered compatible with the teachings of the Qur'an. Libya was declared an Islamic Socialist county by Moammar Khadafy. Islamic scholar Ibnu Hazm stated, "It is permitted to have only one leader (of the Muslims) in the whole world".

A CALIPHATE is Islamic theocracy controlling countries under a single central controlling religious figure. The Muslim Brotherhood is an international movement with a goal of creating an empire from Spain to Indonesia. They believe corruption and poverty will be eliminated with 'social justice'. Their slogan is: "Islam is the solution". Incidentally, the Muslim Brotherhood has also targeted the United States with a type of grand Jihad. The plan is to destroy the country from within using various activist organizations. They cultivate members from students, the military, African-Americans, and prison inmates by instilling anti-American and anti-Israeli positions and viewpoints. Egypt elected the Muslim Brotherhood candidate as their new president in June 2012

A MONARCHY is when political power is given to a person; known as a monarch, king, or queen. They generally rule until death. Their successors are usually because of heredity. Countries called absolute monarchies (leaders with total control) are Oman and Brunei. Some countries have a constitutional monarchy where the Monarch has ceremonial functions and the people are represented by an elected parliament or legislature. The United Kingdom and Spain have constitutional monarchies.

As the United States was formed as a Republic, the people elect representatives in all branches of government locally and nationally. Persons running for office usually are identified by a political party. The three largest political parties are the Libertarian Party, the Republican Party, and the Democratic Party. The two major parties are the Republican and Democratic Parties. The major parties have caucuses (sometimes called committees, conferences, or coalitions) that meet to set agendas and support candidates.

The LIBERTARIAN PARTY, founded in 1971, is the third largest political party in the United States. This party advocates for personal responsibility, individual freedom, and minimal government interference. Libertarians believe:

- in the right to life
- in the right of speech and action with no censorship
- in the right to own property and oppose all government interference
- that people should be able to make free choices and take responsibility for the consequences of those actions

- the government should stay out of all personal relationships
- the only legitimate use of force is in self- defense or for the protection of property
- there shall be no laws requiring the licensing of, or restricting the use of, the ownership or sale of firearms or ammunition
- in a free and competitive free market without government interference
- in supporting a healthy environment and sensible use of natural resources
- that government should not control the pricing, the allocation, or the production of energy
- in no government subsidies to business or corporations
- in ending income taxes and the abolishment of IRS
- health care and education should be provided by the free market
- public services should be abolished and provided by charities or neighbors and friends.

Libertarians believe the government exists solely to protect the rights of life, liberty, and property. They believe all efforts to redistribute wealth or control trade to be improper in a free society.

Anti-slavery activists founded the REPUBLICAN PARTY, also known as the GOP (Grand Old Party), in 1854. At that time the pro-slavery agricultural southern states and the anti-slavery industrial north divided the country. The Republican Party was formed as a protest against allowing slavery, which was beginning to spread into the western territories. The GOP promoted higher education, banking, railroads, industry and cities, plus promoted free homesteads to farmers. Republicans believed the free market was superior to slavery. It was the Republican Party which endorsed the right of women to vote by proposing the 19th Amendment. The Democratic Party defeated the Amendment four times before being enacted in 1920. The first Republican President was Abraham Lincoln.

At the end of the 19th century the GOP stood for progressivism because during the presidency of Teddy Roosevelt so many regulations were imposed on businesses. All these regulations restricted business and were detrimental to the economy. Republicans changed their ideology to reflect the needs of the country. By 1920 Republicans developed into a party that was pro-business, supported conservative values, strong nationalism, and economic libertarianism. The Republican Party believes:

- the free market economy creates prosperity
- in low taxes and opposes the graduated tax system as they believe it penalizes those who create jobs and wealth
- the policy of private spending promotes better fiscal economy than government spending
- helping the poor is better done by charitable organizations, with the help of federal grants, than being run by government agencies
- that dependence on government programs weakens abilities and lessens self esteem
- that building a strong national defense and maintaining strong alliances will lead to peace and stability.
- in an effective and strong intelligence community.

The Republican Party governs by the Capitalist beliefs that equal rights, equal justice, and equal opportunity belongs to everyone; not special groups. They believe government must maintain sound money and a responsible economy. On national security, Republicans believe it is better to negotiate from a position of strength than a position of weakness. They believe world peace depends on a strong America.

The Republican Party has five Congressional subgroups generally referred to as caucuses. They are the Republican Senate Conference, the House Republican Conference, the Republican Study Group, the Liberty Caucus, and the Congressional Hispanic Conference.

The Republican Senate Conference differs from a caucus as decisions made are not binding on members. In 1925 it was resolved that no Senator was bound to any action taken by the Conference. Senators were free to act as was his or her judgment and notification was not required if they were to act differently. All Republican Senators are members of the Conference. The purpose of the Conference is to communicate the party's message to its members, the press, and to citizens.

The House Republican Conference has 242 members. The purpose of the Conference is to inform the media of Republican opinions and activities.

The Republican Study Group (or Committee) established in 1973 and has 170 members. It is a conservative group with the purpose of advancing a conservative economic agenda. They support less government, lower taxes, personal responsibility, individual freedom, strong families, civil liberties for all, and a strong national defense with secure borders.

The Republican Liberty Caucus supports the Constitution as the law of the land. They support individual rights and a limited government. This caucus believes in equal protection under the law, the right to bear arms, and the sole function of the courts is to interpret the law; not create new laws. They adhere to the idea that the Constitution limits federal government power; and powers not identified belong to the States or local government. They advocate phasing out subsidies which support businesses and special interests. Members want to repeal the capital gains and inheritance tax. The caucus supports a balanced budget, a strong national defense, and opposes a mandatory draft. Members also promote phasing out foreign aid. Their other function is to support Republican elections.

The Congressional Hispanic Conference was formed in 2003 in response to the debate over the nomination of Miguel Estrada to the U.S. Court of Appeals. Members promote policies that are of importance to the Americans of Hispanic or Portuguese heritage. The Conference supports free trade, tax relief, a strong military to defend against terrorism, faith based support groups, and education of choice.

The DEMOCRATIC PARTY is the oldest political party founded in the 1790's. It was formed on the principle that Americans should help the government to resist aristocracy and monarchism. They thought farmers exhibited the virtues of independence from the corruption of the cities and government policies. They strongly believed a centralized federal government should not violate State's rights. The founders of the party believed that a standing army and navy were dangerous to individual liberty. They stood in favor of economic coercion using embargoes and sanctions.

As with the Republican Party their current doctrines have dramatically changed. Democrats now support the following:

- government has the responsibility to care for citizens
- highly structured regulated markets
- strong gun control
- opposition of the death penalty
- women's right to abortions paid by the government
- people should share economic burdens and support welfare programs
- separation of church and state
- comprehensive energy and climate control
- reduction of energy consumption
- equitable judicial system that provide second chances and rehabilitation
- judges having the ability to make new laws by disregarding current laws and regulations; even when such laws were previously voted on by the citizens
- health care for all persons residing within the country
- removal of all obstacles to voting, including proof of identity
- immigration reform to grant amnesty to persons who have entered the country illegally
- creating jobs and rebuilding the infrastructure using green energy and technology with high speed rail and advanced car batteries

- a commitment to Social Security and Medicare
- the commitment to government paid education and job training
- ending all forms of discrimination

Democrats advocate for social justice, meaning that all persons are entitled to the same rights and services and are entitled to share all resources with redistribution. The party stresses two things; diversity and rights.

Democrats have been called the liberal party with a philosophy that citizens should look beyond self-interest and work toward the greater common interest. The preferred word is now Progressive. A Progressive is a very liberal Democrat.

The Democratic Party has six Congressional caucuses. These caucuses are the Blue Dog Coalition, the New Democrat Coalition, the Congressional Hispanic Caucus, the Congressional Asian Pacific American Caucus, the Congressional Progressive Caucus, and the Congressional Black Caucus.

The Blue Dog Coalition was established in 1995 after Democrats lost members in the House. They thought the party had shifted too far to the left. The coalition has 26 members. Blue Dogs are considered to be an independent voice for fiscal responsibility and accountability. The coalition attempts to find bi-partisan common sense solutions to issues. They try to find the middle ground between ideological extremes with different ideas. This group attempts to represent the moderate and conservative Democrats in the House. The Blue Dog Coalition had 53 members until the November 2010 election but membership was reduced because of loses in the election and retirement from Congress.

All Democrats do not look upon the Blue Dog Coalition favorably. Some Democrats have proposed running Progressive candidates against the Blue Dogs in elections. In fact, the Blue American PAC has run ads against Blue Dogs. Their argument is because these members don't promote the Progressive agenda the GOP could win those seats in Congress. Other Democrats don't agree, because they want to keep as many seats in Congress as possible. The Blue Dogs are free to vote as they want, 46 members voted for the Stimulus Bill and 28 for the Health Care allowing both Bills to pass.

The New Democratic Coalition was founded in 1997 and reorganized in 2005. Members state they are a moderate and pro-growth group that wants to modernize the Democratic Party and the country. New Democrats support expanded growth, fiscal responsibility, effective government, a secure home front, foreign trade, and a modern strong military. These members believe the Democratic Party platforms have wandered too far left for political viability. They believe in supporting Israel, increased defense spending, supporting NAFTA, and increased personal responsibility by reducing support for minority and welfare agendas. They are particularly focused on energy, financial services, health care, and trade.

The Senate New Democratic Coalition, formed in 2000, now has 39 members. They strive to provide a unified voice in the senate for Progressive ideas, mainstream ideas, and market based solutions to modernize the Democratic Party.

In May 2009 the Blue Dogs and the New Democratic Coalition met with House leaders to discuss the proposed Health Care Bill. They felt the Bill was too Progressive, didn't like the process, and had concerns about financing of the Bill. Both groups spoke out stating this Bill would result in a public insurance that would compete with private insurance. These two groups told the party leaders the Health Care Bill shouldn't be based on Medicare rules, it must pay for itself, and should be administered the same as private insurance companies.

The two groups had 122 of the 218 votes needed to pass the Health Care Bill. On March 22, 2010 the Bill passed 219 to 212.

The Congressional Hispanic Caucus was founded in 2003. Their aim is to promote policy of importance to Hispanic and Portuguese Americans. They support troops in war against terrorism, free trade, tax relief for small business and families, faith based initiatives, educational choice, and tax relief. Members advocate for agricultural and rural communities, civil and veteran rights, plus worker protection regulations. Members endorse better education and job training, renewable energy, improved infrastructure, and housing. They have 21 members.

The Congressional Asian Pacific American Caucus, which currently has 21 members, was established in 1994. Membership is non-partisan and bicameral, meaning the members can come from the House or the Senate. They promote equal rights for all Americans, not only Asian Americans.

The caucus advocates for advanced educational opportunities, hate crime legislation, economical opportunities, and legal protection for refugees and immigrants, plus support health care bills for minorities and veterans. Members also educate Congress on the history and concerns of Asian Americans and the Pacific Island community.

The Congressional Black Caucus was founded in 1971 with 13 members. There are currently 41 members, of which at least 20 are also members of the Congressional Progressive Caucus. Barbara Lee, the Chair from 2009 until 2011, was also a Chairman of the Progressive Caucus. The current Chair, and member of the Progressive Caucus, is Emanuel Cleaver. The mission of the Black Caucus is to free the black community of all disparities and to contribute fully in the community for the common good. They advance the global black community by developing leaders using information and educating the public about their policies. The Black Caucus strives to develop programs and research to address social, economic, and health disparities.

The Black Caucus leadership program works to increase the pool of black leaders in community based programs and public service careers. The program prepares students with the legislative tools needed to effect change in their communities. Promotion of economic development is an initiative to teach young people about credit and debt management which will lead to wealth and home ownership. Other programs teach healthy eating habits, diabetes control, and HIV/Aids training.

Issues the Black Caucus promotes are guaranteed child care to low income families and early education for all. They strive to improve student achievement, expanded college access, expanded after-school and summer programs as well as additional job training. Members strive to achieve lifelong education options for everyone. Economic issues include increased unemployment assistance and minimum wages indexed to inflation or to a percentage of median income. Universal government paid health care is a priority as is public housing reform and programs to prevent foreclosures.

Addressing global poverty, the Black Caucus supports the United Nations program Millennium Development Goals. The program has eight goals it wants to reach, most by 2015.

The first goal is to eradicate extreme poverty and hunger. They propose to halve the proportion of people who earn less than $1.00 per day. The second is universal education so all children complete primary schooling. The third goal is gender equality eliminating gender disparity in primary and secondary education. The fourth goal is improved child health care, attempting to reduce by 2/3 the mortality rate of children under age five. The fifth goal is maternal health aim is to reduce by ¾ the maternal mortality rate and achieve universal access to reproduction health care. The sixth goal is to combat HIV/Aids, malaria and other diseases. The seventh goal is obtaining environmental sustainability by integrating methods of sustainable development with the reduction of environmental resources. They want to reduce by half the proportion of people without safe drinking water and basic sanitation, plus improve the lives of at least 100 million slum dwellers. The eighth goal is global partnership, which addresses the needs of underdeveloped, landlocked, and small island countries. The aim is to develop non-discriminatory trading and financial systems and reduce the debt burden. The last goal is the availability of technologies in information and communications. As underdeveloped countries lack access to the World Wide Web and high speed internet connections the problem needs to be addressed and corrected. These goals will be paid for with funding from American taxpayers.

The largest caucus is the Congressional Progressive Caucus, formed in 1991, currently has 83 members. When founded this caucus stated its mission was to reflect diversity and strength of the American people and seek to build a more just and humane society.

Their current web site states that most people in the United States support Progressive policies on environmental regulation, health care, and guarantees of adequate food and shelter. It has four main objectives: peace and global security; energy independence and environmental sustainability; civil rights, civil liberties and human rights; plus public health, education and economic opportunity. The Progressive Caucus calls this

"The Progressive Promise-Fairness for All."

The Progressive Promise is very detailed and very goal specific. The first objective is for Economic Justice, Security, and Global Economy advocating universal health care for all. Then there is insistence on corporate and private business accountability and that Social Security benefits will be protected. The Promise wants investment in America to create new jobs by building more affordable housing, rebuilding schools and infrastructure.

The plan is to export more products, not jobs, by affirming the freedom of association and enforcing the right to organize unions. They also promote raising and indexing the minimum wage.

The second goal is to Protect Civil Rights and Liberties by sun-setting the expiring provisions of the Patriot Act which they claim will protect privacy from unbearable police power and government intrusion. To ensure civil rights and liberties, they plan to fight corporate consolidation of the media. Then they will work to enforce legal rights in the work place and eliminate all forms of discrimination.

Global Peace and Security, their third goal, is to be achieved by honoring and helping the overburdened international public, the military and civilian servants. To reaffirm engagement with the U.N. and other multilateral organizations, they want to rebuild alliances around the world. The Promise will combat hunger and infectious diseases worldwide, plus encourage debt relief to poor countries. They support the U.N.'s Millennium Goals for developing countries.

The final goal is the Advancement of Environmental Protection and Energy Independence by freeing the United States from dependence on imported oil by relying on renewable energy and technology. They state these measures will create at least 3 million new jobs, clean the environment, and enhance national security. The Promise advocates changing incentives in federal tax to procurement appropriation polices to speed commercialization of solar, bio-mass and wind power. The plan is to convert assembly lines to manufacture highly efficient vehicles, which they insist will enhance global competitiveness of the auto industry. They propose increased government investment in 'green buildings' with more energy efficient homes and businesses, and to link high efficiency standards in appliances to consumer manufacturing incentives.

The Promise states they are attempting to eliminate the threat of global warming by expanding other energy efficient transportation; including bicycle, bus, high speed rail, and magnetic levitation rail projects. Members want to pressure the public to encourage sustainable growth, ensure energy diversity, to protect workers and the environment by rewarding consumer conservation with taxes and/or fees.

The Progressive Caucus also has official positions on many issues. On Immigration Reform they want to grant illegal aliens a pathway to obtain legal status, citizenship, and promotion of family reunification programs. They want to ensure immigrants have access to higher education and to stop racial profiling. In a letter the Progressive Caucus sent to Obama on 6/15/2010, they wrote, "Immigration reform must not become a victim of electoral politics". The letter warned that if no immediate action is taken other States might take similar steps that Arizona did.

On the U.S. policy toward Iran, the Progressive Caucus wants to establish diplomatic dialogues to deepen relationships and have a cross cultural exchange with the Iranian people. They insist America will not enter into a pre-emptive war against Iran and will use military force only as a last resort. The Caucus also demands that no funds are to be used for covert actions that would cause regime change or military action. To ensure Iran's nuclear programs are peaceful there must be ongoing inspections and no diplomatic relations can occur unless enforceable international safeguards are in place. The caucus stated the U.S. must recognize the International Atomic Energy Agency (IAEA) and the United Nations to oversee the development of Iranian nuclear power. Finally, the United States must be obligated to the commitment to move towards full and complete disarmament.

The Progressive Caucus is quite opinionated on the subject of trade. Members support developing a new trade model based on democratic principles; meaning the people's objectives not the objectives of investors. Reforms should serve the people and societies and not the capitalists and not the corporations, with benefits distributed both within the United States and other national economies. Reforms should also exclude patents and data protection that obstructs public access to needed medications. Global markets which have been closed need to be opened, trade policies restricting U.S. exports need to be abolished, and U.S. businesses should be rewarded when investing and producing in America. Globally, they want to eliminate forced labor and enact rules that all nations need to protect labor's right to organize and bargain collectively. Trade rules must be required to consider the 'rightful' role of government to interact with citizens to set policies in the development and welfare of the community.

These programs and enforcement of all these regulations, nationally and globally, are to be subsidized for by the approximately 60% of American citizens that pay federal taxes.

At one time the Progressive Caucus did not hide their association with the Democratic Socialist of America (DSA), or that they openly agreed with their agenda. Originally, the Progressive web site was hosted by DSA. In 2009 the 70 members of the Progressive Caucus were also members of the DSA (as reported in the Socialist Party of America newsletter of October 2009). DSA policy is defined as Socialist reforms, which are a means to consolidate and control wealth…everything is regulated by the government… and they are organized around the principles of Socialist economic justice. Economic justice, as defined by the Socialist Party of America in 2009, is based on the conception of human rights and equality through progressive taxation, income redistribution, and property redistribution. Another DSA document, titled 'Electoral Politics as a Tactic -- Elections Statement 2000,' reports "the DSA recognizes that some politicians representing labor, environment, gays, lesbians, and communities of color may choose to run under Democratic auspices."

The DSA website (dsausa.org) has a description of their strategy under the section titled: Political Perspective of the DSA. Portions of the strategy states "through the control of the (U.S.) government by the Democratic Party coalition, led by anti-corporate forces, a progressive program regulating corporations, redistributing income, fostering economic growth and expanding programs could be achieved." It further states "today's social movements must be as global as the corporate power they confront". The statement ends with, "Democratic Socialists have a historic opportunity and responsibility to play a role in founding the next 'Left' and DSA is prepared to meet this challenge".

Norman Mattoon Thomas, a well known socialist and associate editor of 'The Nation' magazine, is noted for his prediction for America. He said, "The American people will never knowingly adopt Socialism. But under the name of 'liberalism' they will adopt every fragment of the Socialist program, until one day America will be a Socialist nation, without knowing how it happened."

Some members of the Progressive Caucus have publicly admitted that their programs are Socialist. Maxine Waters admitted this on May 22, 2008 when speaking at the House Committee hearing to Shell Oil CEO, John Hofmeister. "This liberal is about umm …umm…umm… socializing… um…um…basically taking over and the government running all of your company". On June 10, 2009, Congressman Brad Sherman stated that the Pay Czar is for "companies who are not in Capitalism, those are companies that took TARP." He further clarified this the following day by saying that "we have Socialism for some companies, we don't want Capitalism for the executives of those companies". Addressing the Senate on March 25, 2010, Max Baucus admitted Obamacare is a Socialist redistribution of wealth and an income shift to correct 'mal-distribution' of wealth. Then on August 23, 2010 Baucus took credit for 'essentially' writing Obamacare but stated he didn't read the bill because of all the statuary language.

I found it fascinating that the original proponents of the Republican Party were from the industrialized cities and communities that had opposed slavery and supported a large Federal government. Now they support States' Rights and a smaller limited government. Persons that typically support Republicans now live in rural areas or live outside large populated cities.

Then conversely, the Democratic Party originally represented the agricultural areas and they supported slavery. They distrusted big cities and the manufacturing industry. Now supporters want a large government involvement for social reforms and tend to live in large highly populated areas and cities, and support organized labor.

Judge me by the people who surround me.

CHAPTER 3

★ ★ ★ ★ ★

Leading Radicals

Obama and some members of his family or his associates and friends are sometimes referred to as Marxists or as Socialists. Many of these individuals have had training or have been exposed the philosophy by known activists.

There are four people who advanced the Socialist movement the most. They are the husband and wife team of Richard Cloward and Frances Fox Piven, the revolutionist Saul Alinsky, and Black militant activist George A. Wiley. These people developed strategies that are taught and used by community organizations across our nation. Their influence on our policies past, present, and in the future cannot be ignored.

SAUL ALINSKY was born on January 30, 1909 in New York. His Jewish parents escaped Russia to come to America while their son spent his life dedicated to destroying this country and converting it to Socialism. Barack Obama taught the Alinsky method of organizing. Hillary Clinton met with Alinsky while writing her thesis about him in college.

Saul Alinsky wrote several books, but is best known for the 1971 publication 'Rules for Radicals: A Pragmatic Primer for Realistic Radicals.' The book is dedicated to Lucifer. The first paragraph states, "What follows is for those who want to change the world from what it is to what they believe it should be."

Alinsky's intent is to destroy free market wealth, destroy Capitalism, destroy individualism, destroy the middle class, and destroy the United States. He advocated creating numerous organizations with the goal to seize power and give it to the people. "A Marxist begins with the prime truth that all evils are caused by the exploitation of the proletariat (workers or the poor) by the Capitalists." He stressed that the process to end Capitalism is by a revolution and then to reorganize as a new Socialist order.

He explained that real revolutionaries must disguise their radicalism by wearing suits and cutting their hair. They need to look respectable to infiltrate the system and work from within. The purpose is to penetrate existing institutions, universities, churches, and a political party.

Describing the role of an organizer; Alinsky states an organizer needs to build a power base with local organizations. These organizations can be made up with service groups, labor unions, students, and even corner gangs to create personal relationships. Personal relationships allow open discussions on any topic and the ability to identify or create problems. He believed change requires the disorganization of an old organization. Once dissatisfaction is identified, the organizer creates resentment and hostility while stirring up agitation until the people want conflict. The process is the purpose as "The end justifies almost any means."

The organizer is instructed to use a method called 'popular education.' These are active and deliberate actions meant to raise discontent and to get people to recognize their problems aren't individual, but are the grievances of a group. They teach group action is stronger than individual action. Then the group is motivated to accept whatever solution is agreed upon, or sometimes called "whipping up the mobs".

Alinsky describes the makeup of a good organizer. This person has the ability to listen and create issues. He has imagination, uses humor (either satire or ridicule), and has a personality of confidence. He is able to describe goals using words like liberty, equality, pursuit of happiness, peace, or for the common good. The organizer must look presentable and do or say whatever it takes to gain power. Simply stated the organizer's job is to "create problems or crises, rub raw the resentments of those involved, fan the hostility, and promote action".

The tactics to be used are well thought out and extensive. Here is a list of the tactics as he describes them.

- Power is not only what you have, but what the enemy thinks you have.
- Never go outside the expertise of your people.
- Go outside the expertise of the enemy. Look for ways to increase insecurity anxiety and uncertainty.

- Make the enemy live up to its own book of rules.
- Ridicule is man's most potent weapon. It is almost impossible to counter ridicule.
- A good tactic is one your people enjoy.
- A tactic that drags too long becomes a drag.
- Keep the pressure on with different tactics and actions.
- The threat is usually more terrifying than the thing itself.
- Maintain constant pressure.
- If you push a negative hard and deep enough, it will break through to its counter side.
- Pick the target, freeze it, personalize it, and polarize it.

Alinsky had this advice to organizers; use eyes, nose and ears. It is explained this way; use eyes if your groups is large by parading them for everyone to see. If the group is small, conceal the numbers and make a big noise. If the group is tiny, "stink up the place". "Do what you can with what you have and clothe it in moral arguments."

The basic formula is to organize, educate, agitate, aggravate, and act.

Hillary Clinton studied the Alinsky method when she wrote her college thesis titled "Alinsky's View on American Life", meeting with him three times. Hillary wrote "Saul Alinsky was an academic turned radical as he found American adversaries more interesting than America itself." She compared him to others who had been feared such as Walt Whitman, Eugene Debs, and Martin Luther King. She theorized this was because each "had embraced the most radical of political faiths - Democracy". She said Alinsky was crafting a fresh appeal to the potentially powerful middle class.

Saul Alinsky offered Hillary a job while she was attending Wellesley College in 1968. He was searching for competent liberals to move to Chicago and build grass root organizations for radical leftist causes. She declined his offer. Hillary recalled, "Alinsky said I was wasting my time, but my decision was an expression of my belief that the system could be changed from within." The Clintons had asked Wellesley to seal its copy of her thesis during Bill Clinton's Presidency.

Barack Obama taught the Alinsky method while employed at ACORN after receiving formal training of the techniques. He said his years of organizing gave him the best education of his life. Obama was praised by none other than L. David Alinsky, the son of Saul Alinsky. He said that Obama "learned his lesson well." "All the elements were present: the individual stories told by real people of their situations and hardships, the packed to the rafters crowd, the crowds chanting and using phrases and names, the on the spot texting and phoning to show instant support and commitment to jump into the political battle, the rallying selections of music, and the setting of the agenda by the power people." "I am proud to see that my father's model for organizing is being applied successfully beyond local community organizing to affect the Democratic campaign in 2008. It is a fine tribute to Saul Alinsky as we approach his 100th birthday."

'Rules for Radicals' methods are still used today. The book is recommended as a training tool and reading material for community organizations, unions, and even the teachers in your children's classrooms. The January 1, 2002 Wall Street Journal described SEIU union leader Andy Stern as a devotee of Alinsky. 'Rules for Radicals' is listed on the union web page of the American Federation of State, County, and Municipal Employees as a reference for training by their shop stewards. The National Education Association (NEA) had Saul Alinsky as a consultant to train their own staff. In fact, the NEA still suggests Alinsky's books for those involved in grass roots organizing. His books are recommended on their web site as a resource and guide book for those teachers who are union stewards (Associations Representatives) and for those who are contemplating taking actions in their communities.

The NEA summarizes the differences between Liberals and Radicals. "Liberals utter bold words, they strut, they study, and they sit. Radicals don't sit still with indifference because if a Radical sees an injustice they strike out with passion. Society has reason to fear Radicals because they are skillful at 'breaking the necks' of Conservatives. Liberals may simply follow, but Radicals take action when they see a social crisis by using power. Radicals fight privilege and power" (unless it is their own). The NEA review certainly appears to endorse this radical ideology.

The Midwest Academy that teaches the Alinsky method has many connections to Barack Obama. The co-founders are Heather and PAUL BOOTH. Paul Booth was a co-founder of Students for a Democratic Society (SDS). Many of the board of directors have worked with, or have been involved with, Obama during his political career. The directors are:

- Robert Creamer, Director – wrote the outline of the controversial health care bill while in prison, he is also the husband of Rep. Jan Schakowsky
- Cathy Hurwit – chief of staff for Jan Schakowsky
- Jackie Grimshaw – was on the Chicago Transit Authority board, political advisor to Harold Washington, and Obama neighbor
- Alicia Ybarra – training director for SEIU
- Jackie Kendall – helped develop and train at Camp Obama
- Nancy Shier - Ounce of Prevention, Director of Kids Education and Policy Project

RICHARD CLOWARD and FRANCES FOX PIVEN are a married couple who were both professors of Sociology and Political Science, both Socialists, both authors, and both political activists. Richard Cloward was born December 25, 1926 and died August 20, 2001. Frances Piven was born in Canada in 1932, came to the United States in 1933, and was naturalized in 1952. They are known for their strategy to create and manage a crisis.

They developed their ideas in 1965 after a six day riot in Los Angeles when police used batons to beat a suspected drunken driver. That November they wrote an article titled: "Mobilizing the Poor: How It Could Be Done." They personally circulated copies of the paper before it was published.

A magazine, 'The Nation,' published the report now titled: "The Weight of the Poor: A Strategy to End Poverty." 'The Nation' is the oldest continuously published weekly magazine in the United States and promotes a liberal-left ideology. Members of its editorial board include Tom Hayden, Barbara Ehrenreich, and Deepak Bhargava. The article was so popular the magazine sold an additional 30,000 reprints. The method was explained as taking action to overwhelm the welfare system by deluging the rolls with new recipients. They prophesied the government would not be able to afford the costs and the system would crash. This article was a blueprint promoting the use of "cadres of aggressive organizers" to utilize "demonstrating to create a climate of militancy". The group could use media campaigns, provided by left-wing journalists, to suggest "a federal program of redistribution" with a guaranteed living wage proposal.

Socialist Scholars Conference held a three day seminar during the second weekend of September 1966 in New York. Cloward gave a speech on September 10th titled: "Poverty and Powerlessness: Organizing the Poor and Can It Be Done?" He stated the poor could become such a powerful organization, that they could destroy the system, and create a financial crisis. Cloward estimated an additional $200 million from special grants could be obtained for the poor, just in New York City, with programs already in existence.

This obviously was not a strategy to help the poor but to use them as pawns to get the desired effect. Cloward described a plan where the poor would be used to create "irregular and disruptive tactics" to demand benefits. He also suggested the poor could be unionized. The union could be funded by demanding the welfare offices deduct 50 cents to $1.00 from the welfare grants to be diverted to pay the union. This union would then represent the recipients while they are making further demands for more money. This would become a very powerful organization he argued. "We have to help the poor to make claims; for this they will organize and act."

During this speech Cloward revealed he had been meeting with a national group every Wednesday for the past few months. He told the audience there would be a demonstration at city hall on Monday. On Monday the demonstrators were televised by NBC and CBS and the event was coordinated with 15 other cities. It was the beginning of the National Welfare Rights Organization (NWRO). Cloward and Piven enlisted George Wiley to lead this operation as he had a background in community organizing. Demonstrations grew across the country and was known as the Welfare Rights Movement.

Not content with their zeal to undermine the country with just welfare demands, they set their sights on controlling the voting and the electoral process. Stalin once said, "The people who cast the votes decide nothing. The people who count the votes decide everything." Realizing they could manipulate almost everything by advocating for 'the poor', they created Human SERVE (Human Service Employee Registration Voting and Education) with Hulbert James, a former NWRO organizer. Human SERVE developed the idea that "the poor" don't have the same opportunities to register to vote as other people. Therefore, they advocated voter registration to be set up in government offices such as Departments of Social Services and Vehicle Registration. This would allow persons signing up for welfare benefits and other services the ability to register to vote at the same time. Easy registration also eliminated the time consuming effort of going door to door, as now paid government employees would do the work.

Cloward and Piven recognized that poor people usually didn't vote, but if they did they normally voted Democratic. They believed this was a way to influence politicians who held similar Socialist views. Massive and multiple registrations would also create chaos and election results could be manipulated. President Clinton signed the National Voter Registration Act of 1993 with Richard Cloward and Frances Piven at his side. Now all States were required to provide voter registration at State agencies that provide driver licenses and welfare benefits. Known as the Motor Voter Act, this regulation requires public employees to offer the registrations to the public it serves.

Richard Cloward died on September 9, 2001. Attending the funeral with Frances Fox Piven was Barbara Ehrenreich, Cornel West, Gus Newport (all members of DSP), Howard Zinn, June Jordan, Joel Rogers, Tim Sampson (all activists), and DEMOS president Miles Rapoport

FRANCES FOX PIVEN a Distinguished Professor of Political Science and Sociology at City University of New York and is still an activist. In 1994 she was a founding member of the New Party and in 1996 a founding member for the Campaign for America's Future. Then in 1997 she joined the Democratic Socialists of America and in 2002 endorsed the organization STORM. The year 2008 was a busy year for signing petitions for Barack Obama and endorsing him for President with the group Feminists for Peace. In 2009 she was a signer of the Progressives for Obama website and served on the boards of two magazines 'Social Politics' and 'New Politics.' She also served on the boards of Center for the Study of Working Class Life, Left Forum and Wellstone Action (a training center for progressive leaders). She joined the Board of Directors of Project Vote for 2010-2011. Piven continues to write books and is the person who is responsible for the suggestion that people who are losing their homes should just refuse to move.

As the year 2010 ended she wrote an article for "The Nation" titled 'Mobilizing the Jobless'. She questioned why there were no angry mobs demonstrating for injustice. She wrote there was still time to demand more 'investments' in public-service programs, green technology, and other initiatives. 'Investments' is the new code word for taxes. She continued to state that mobilizing the diverse population (blue and white collar) of the unemployed might not be easy, but could be accomplished with good organizers at government service centers. Piven reminds organizers that the people must transform from being "hurt and ashamed to being angry and indignant". She explained the unemployed need to "stop blaming themselves" and "return their anger on bosses or politicians'. She promotes local actions that will spread and become destructive with strikes and riots. Piven wrote she is hoping for an American social movement (crisis) "from the bottom" to provoke action from the government (the top). Government actions normally create more regulations and restrictions on its citizens making them less free and more dependent which is the goal of Socialists. She must be real pleased with the "Occupy" movement.

GEORGE ALVIN WILEY is best known for founding the National Welfare Rights Organization (NWRO) and 'franchising" activist organizations. Born on February 26, 1931 to parents who were both involved in political activist activities. Wiley was well educated; obtaining his undergraduate degree at the University of Rhode Island in 1953 and his Doctorate in organic chemistry in 1957 from Cornell. He led a voter registration drive, in Virginia, while serving six months at ROTC. He earned his Post Doctorate Degree at UCLA. Wiley taught chemistry at the University of California/ Berkeley and at Syracuse University in New York. While teaching at Syracuse University, in 1960, he founded a local chapter of Congress for Racial Equality (CORE).

CORE began in 1942 by James Farmer as a non-violent protest group against racial inequality. These tactics were based on the tenets of Gandhi and Martin Luther King Jr. In the 60's, activists such as Malcolm X, Stokely Carmichael, and H. Rap Brown began influencing members. There was a split on which tactics would bring about the change they wanted. Some people tired of the small results using non-violent demonstrations. The Black Power movement became involved with the group in 1966. Roy Innis took charge in 1968. He believed in Black Nationalism but changed his mind not long after his son died because of gun violence. He became a conservative, backing both Nixon and Reagan in Presidential elections. Innis became an ardent member of the National Rifle Association and believed in the right to own guns for self-defense. Sadly, he lost a second son to gun violence in 1982.

In 1964 George Wiley became the Associate National Director of CORE. He stopped teaching and moved to New York City. After he was unsuccessful in his attempt to become the National Director in 1965, Wiley left. He started his own activist group Poverty Rights Action Center (PRAC) in Washington D.C. located near the Institute for Policy Studies. The Institute for Policy Studies is the country's oldest progressive think-tank. He stopped wearing suits and wore dashikis and grew an Afro. The PRAC doctrine was called creative disorder.

In 1966 Cloward and Piven were looking for an experienced organizer to lead a new group with the goal to increase the welfare rolls and demand maximum benefits. They wanted a person who would have credibility in the inner city Black community. They found George Wiley.

His first large demonstration involved cities across the nation starting with about 40 people marching 155 miles from Cleveland to Columbus, Ohio. In Columbus he joined approximately 2000 people with a demonstration. At the same time 15 cities were demonstrating simultaneously. This was the beginning of the National Rights Movement and the National Welfare Rights Organization (NWRO). Their slogan was, "Know your rights, demand your rights, protect your rights, link up with Welfare Rights".

NWRO had its best success in New York City as welfare cases increased by 50% in 1966. NYC Mayor John Lindsay had buckled under to every demand. By the early 1970's there was one person on welfare for every two persons working in private industry. In 1975 New York City declared bankruptcy.

Wiley held his first National Convention of the NWRO in late August 1967. He said, "If this country does not listen to poor people after what happened in Detroit and Newark and New Haven you haven't seen nothing yet." Demonstrations at welfare offices were often violent. Activists bullied social workers demanding to get what the law 'entitled' them to. They had sit-ins in legislative chambers, had mass demonstrations, school boycotts, and picket lines. Rocks were thrown, glass doors smashed, desks overturned, and telephones pulled out of the walls during protests. Between 1965 and 1974 welfare increased from 4.3 million to 10.8 million.

Funding for NWRO came from both the government and private philanthropists. Between 1968 and 1971 the organization received half a million dollars from the National Council of Churches. The Johnson administration promised them $435,000, but President Nixon put a stop to it and NWRO only received $106,000. However, they got free legal aid and free office space from local legal aid offices.

This still was not enough money to fund all expenses so Wiley created a business model based on Burger King and McDonald franchises which set up identical businesses and copy the same business practices. Each franchise pays a license fee plus a percentage of sales receipts to the parent company. What Wiley did was to train and encourage activists to organize and set up their own chapters of NWRO. Each chapter paid a fee and charged their new members for training to learn how to exploit the welfare system. The new chapters then could have their new graduates set up additional chapters and pay them. The franchises charged the welfare recipients' membership fees or dues for the privilege of having the NWRO demand the maximum benefits and "shake down" the local welfare office. By 1969 NWRO had a membership of 22,500 families and 523 chapters across the nation.

The leaders of NWRO began to turn on each other. White activists where being driven out of the leadership roles by the black extremists. Wiley was even attacked because of his middle class background. Some thought only the poor should be involved and only welfare recipients should have leadership roles in the organization. George Wiley resigned on January 1, 1972.

Then he started The Movement for Economic Justice, named because he believed that people were tired of the 'welfare' label. This organization reached across racial lines to build a coalition of senior citizens, the working poor, and the lower middle class. He said he wasn't abandoning his original mission he was 'expanding' it. Wiley believed that welfare was only one road to the goal of 'income redistribution'. He held the belief that real welfare was paid to airline companies, railroad companies, and other corporations. He was going to change that and give the money to the people. His new issues were national health insurance, consumer rights, housing rights, day care, and tax reform.

His efforts with Economic Justice ended before he saw any accomplishments. He died on August 8, 1975 in a boating accident. NWRO also folded in 1975. George Wiley's legacy continues as his radical "franchise chains" are still being used by organizations such as ACORN and many others. In fact Wiley mentored Wade Rathke, the former SDS founder, NWRO activist, and founder of ACORN. The George Wiley Center in Rhode Island organizes and trains poor people to advocate for changes on issues affecting poverty.

Judge me by the people who surround me.

SECTION TWO

★ ★ ★ ★ ★

Childhood

CHAPTER 4

★ ★ ★ ★ ★

Grandparents

I believe it is insightful to investigate a person's childhood background to understand how someone develops his or her core beliefs. So I decided to first explore Obama's family and mentors that helped to shape his life and goals. It was his maternal grandparents that he spent much of his time with, so I decided to begin with them. They are quite interesting; some speculate that they were Communists and others think they were connected to the CIA. The other option is that they traveled around the country in the search of better furniture stores for Stanley Armour Dunham to work at.

MADELYN LEE DUNHAM was raised by her parents Rolla and Leona Payne which Obama claims were strict Methodists (didn't believe in dancing, card playing, etc.) in Kansas. I found several reports that her father received royalties by leasing their property to Standard Oil Company and/or worked there as an accountant. There is also a report that the Payne family lived in a 'company house' with stacks of oil pipe in the back yard and the office where Rolla worked was only 100 feet away.

> Standard Oil was owned by John D. Rockefeller who also founded the University of Chicago, the Rockefeller Foundation, and helped to fund (as did J.P. Morgan) the Council of Foreign Relations (CFR). His son, John Jr. is recognized as the largest stockholder in Chase National Bank (currently J.P. Morgan Chase) and donating the land where the United Nations is located. David Rockefeller, son of John Jr., became the President of Chase Bank that has close relations with the World Bank. Three of the six World Bank presidents have worked at Chase Bank. David attended meetings with the Bilderberg Groups, was a Director of the Council of Foreign Relations, and in 1973 formed the Trilateral Commission.

Madelyn was known to be an honor roll student and appears to have been a spirited and independent youngster as she enjoyed going to big band concerts on the weekends in Wichita. This is where she met Stanley Armour Dunham. Obama says that Madelyn and Stanley secretly married on the night of her senior prom, but no record of the marriage has been located. She supposedly told her parents of her marriage after she graduated. Her brother Charles, a retired assistant director at the University of Chicago library, remembers that their father's first impression of Stanley was a guy with 'with black, slicked back hair and a perpetual wise-guy grin.'

STANLEY ARMOUR DUNHAM born on March 23, 1918. His parents were Ralph and Ruth Dunham, but he was raised by his maternal grandparents in Kansas. Ralph was an auto mechanic who worked in the tool department of Boeing Aircraft and owned the Traveler's Cafe in Wichita. After Stanley discovered his mother's body, from a reported suicide, his father abandoned him and his brother. Stanley was only 8 years old. Strangely; the local paper, in 1926, reported her death was caused by food poisoning the day after Thanksgiving. His paternal grandparents, Jacob and Mary Ann Dunham, ran a pharmacy out of their home until they opened Gem Pharmacy in 1928. Obama wrote in his memoir that Stanley was rebellious child and was kicked out of El Dorado High School after he punched the principal in the nose. He also wrote that his grandfather drifted about, taking odd jobs, and traveled by hopping railroad cars to Chicago, then to California, before returning to Kansas. Another report states he worked in the oil fields during the depression.

After Stanley married Madelyn, he worked as a furniture salesman and later joined the Army. Obama said his grandfather enlisted on December 8, 1942, the day after the Japanese bombed Pearl Harbor. There are other reports that say he enlisted on January 15, 1942, January 18, 1942, and June 18, 1942 at Fort Leavenworth. Accurate dates are hard to determine as Stanley's records were destroyed in a fire at the Military Personnel Records Center in 1973. The Associated Press reported Stanley was stationed state side for 1½ years at Baer Field in Indiana and in late July, six weeks after the Normandy Invasion, he crossed the English Channel and landed at Omaha Beach. The report stated that he was assigned to Patton's 3rd Army in February 1945 and discharged on August 30, 1945. This report admits that the story was pieced together from Air Force historical records as Stanley's records were unavailable. On June 5, 2009, Obama spoke in France at the 65th anniversary of the Normandy Invasion. He stated his grandfather was at Normandy Beach on

D-Day and marched across Europe with Patton. In his book, 'Dreams from My Father,' Obama wrote that his grandfather saw no military action. Details of his military service are confusing and conflicting. After Stanley left the service he returned to Kansas and worked in furniture sales.

Prior to Stanley joining the Army, Madelyn worked as a waitress. During the war she was employed at Boeing Company either working on the line or as an aircraft inspector on the B-29 airplanes in Wichita. I found reports that she attended classes at the University of Washington prior to being employed at Boeing, but other reports state she attended the University when the family lived in Seattle after the war. An interesting side note is that Boeing Company is a member of the Council of Foreign Relations (CRF) founded by Rockefeller. Boeing manufactured the B-29, which was the aircraft that dropped the atomic bomb on Japan.

The Dunham family moved to Berkeley, California and lived there for two years. Mr. and Mrs. Dunham were both working full time in Kansas when they decided to relocate. Little is known about them while in California; except both attended classes at the University of Berkley and neither attained a degree.

> Berkeley College with MIT, Cornell, and Harvard were the academic platforms used for training with the intent to turn Indonesia into a military government. Cornell and MIT made the contacts and Berkeley trained those who would seize power. The funding came from the Ford and Rockefeller Foundations.

In 1948 they moved again; to Ponca City, Oklahoma and lived there about two years. Stanley worked at a furniture store. He was known as being funny and friendly, as well as an expert in furniture and a good salesman. Stanley Ann attended local elementary schools from 1948 until 1951. Nothing is known about Madelyn during this time.

> Conoco Oil is the main industry at Ponca City. Marland Oil was the original oil company there but was the victim of a hostile takeover by industrial banker J. P. Morgan in 1929. The company merged with Continental Oil and became Conoco. Ponca City Airport is also known as a place that trained pilots during World War II and where Piper Cub airplanes were manufactured from 1946 to 1948.

Obama wrote that his parents lived in Texas and moved around the State.

Many records say the family moved to Vernon, Texas, and some mention Wichita Falls. The only record I could locate regarding the Dunham family in Texas was a school picture taken of Stanley Ann in 1951 when she was in third grade. School records show she attended 4th grade at Hawkins School in 1951 and went to the First Methodist Church in Vernon. Oil production was a major and growing industry in the 1950s in both cities. In 1950, at Wichita Falls, the Sheppard Air Force Base had just reopened. This base was a training facility for pilots and aircraft mechanics. The Dunham family returned to El Dorado, Kansas after living in Texas for about three years so Stanley could work at a furniture store and Madelyn was a waitress.

The family moved to Seattle, Washington in 1955 so Stanley could work at another furniture store. Stanley Ann attended Eckstein Middle School and Madelyn was the vice president and escrow officer of a local bank. I could not find any information how Madelyn acquired the expertise to switch employment from a waitress to bank vice president. Madelyn attended classes at the University of Washington. Some reports state she attended U. of W. prior to working at Boeing and later went to University of Berkley. Others report she attended the college when they lived in Washington, which seems more plausible. I was not able to find the dates she was enrolled at U of W. All reports state she never received a degree. Washington was a hub for U.S. Naval Intelligence and has a large Boeing Company presence in Seattle.

In 1956 the family moved to Mercer Island, Washington so Stanley Ann could attend Mercer Island High School. This school was known for their highly radical indoctrination and ties to the Communist Party. In fact, in 1955, school board member John Stenhouse testified before the House Un-American Activities Committee because he had been a member of the Communist Party. The philosophy classes at the school included the teachings of Karl Marx and the literature class included Margaret Mead's writings on homosexuality.

The Dunham's regularly attended church at East Shore Unitarian Church, which was referred to as 'The Little Red Church on the Hill.' The church was dedicated on October 20, 1955 with a membership that was dedicated to learning about the world and how it affected them. They sponsored debates like whether 'Red China' should join the U.N. Later the church supported Save the Children and participated in Viet Nam War protests. There are committees to work on problems in education, local politics, and racial discrimination. Political involvement was promoted by their members. The church's stated purpose is, "Values transcend our church, therefore, we nurture faith-filled leaders who transform the world". "Sharing our insights permits deeper commitment to each other and our greater community." "We believe, we act, we accomplish, we will change the world." Current adult classes at the church include 'The introduction to Unitarian Universalism' and 'Green Talks' discussing sustainability, green living, climate change, and earth justice. Unitarian Universalism is creedless and teaches from all religions, Buddhism, Judaism, Islam, and Christianity. During the summer of each year members celebrate Flower Communion. Each member brings a flower and puts it in a vase as a symbol that they are voluntarily participating. A prayer is said and the flowers are blessed. The vase of flowers represents the diversity of the members as each flower is different and unique. The vase of flowers represents the community and at the end of the ceremony each person selections a different flower to take home.

After Stanley Ann graduated from high school in 1960 she and her mother moved to Hawaii to join Stanley who had obtained a job at a better furniture store. Madelyn found work at the Bank of Hawaii and became the vice president in 1970. The promotion was considered very unusual because at that time women and whites were considered minorities and were discriminated against.

> The reason that whites were discriminated against is because they represented the repression, the loss of independence, and the loss of their native culture by foreigners. Hawaii was first discovered in 1778 by Captain Cook. At that time the island had a population of approximately one million people and they were self sufficient. The influx of foreigners brought contagious diseases that reduced the population to 88,000 within the next 50 years. The history of Hawaii is one of influence and domination from Russia, France, England, the United States, and Christian missionaries. In 1894 they declared themselves independent as the Republic of Hawaii, but in 1898 the United States made Hawaii a colony and called it the Territory of Hawaii. When they voted to become a State the islands was composed of only 15% native Hawaiians, the other 85% were Americans and foreigners. Then to add insult to the injustice, the President appointed governors and judges without a vote from the Hawaiians affected.

Madelyn worked in the loan department and ran the escrow department prior to promotion to vice president. She retired in 1986. Madelyn also volunteered at the probate department of Oahu Circuit Court. At this position she had access to information of deceased people including birth records and social security numbers.

> An investigative reporter and prior member of Department of State, Wayne Madsen, suggested that Madelyn's work in the escrow department links her with the CIA. He states the Bank of Hawaii was a financial vehicle known for sending funds to CIA operations in Asia and in the South Pacific. The operations included the Indonesian Lippo Group, the American International Group, the Commerce Bank of Cook Islands, the Bishop Baldwin Rewald Dillingham Wong (BBRDW) Ltd., and more. Madsen believes this financial operation was the idea of retired CIA official Ray S. Cline.

In 1960 Stanley Ann started classes at the University of Hawaii. At the university she met Barack Obama, Sr. and became pregnant. Madelyn worked at the bank to help with college expenses.

Madelyn and Stanley became part-time caretakers of Barack Jr. when Stanley Ann returned to Hawaii from Seattle in 1963 to reenroll at the University of Hawaii. In 1967 Stanley Ann and Barack Jr. moved to Indonesia with her second husband. Then, in 1971, little Barack returned to Hawaii to be raised by his grand-parents while their daughter remained in Indonesia.

The Dunham's regularly attended the First Unitarian Church of Honolulu with their grandson. This church was a sanctuary for draft dodgers and had strong links to SDS (Students for a Democratic Society) the radical group led by Bill Ayers. The SDS publication, 'The Reach,' was distributed to draft dodging activists, had information about the Unitarian Church. Unitarian Principles as described on the current web site sound much like communist doctrine and not religious doctrine. 'The Principles' state they have "The goal of world community with peace, liberty, and justice for all." They add, "Humanist teaching connects us to heed the guidance of reason and the results of science and warn us against the idolatries of mind and spirit." The church promotes liberal policies and collective justice rather than a religious dogma.

Meanwhile, Stanley found a friend in a committed Communist Frank Marshall Davis. They drank, smoked pot, and played cards together. Stanley often visited the 'red light' district as Barack Jr. later wrote about in his book. Stanley died in 1992. Much of Stanley's history has been difficult to find. The FBI admitted they had a file on Stanley, but stated that it was destroyed in 1997. One can only speculate why the FBI had a file on him (or why it was destroyed). It might be because they suspected him of communist activities. Then it could be because the FBI and the CIA at that time distrusted each other and the FBI was spying on him because they suspected him of being connected to the CIA.

Stanley Armour Dunham has some other history that is interesting. Stanley was photographed at the airport with Obama Sr. at the 1959 welcoming ceremony when he was airlifted to Hawaii by a CIA sponsored program. Stanley moved to Hawaii prior to his wife and daughter arriving at the island. It was Stanley who was instrumental in getting Obama Jr. into the prestigious Punahou School. The application to Punahou School, which may have contained a birth certificate, is missing. Obama wrote that through "Gramp's boss" it was arranged for him to attend the elite private school. Obama was told by his grandfather, "through the contacts I made at Punahou would last a lifetime, that I would live in charmed circles and have all the opportunities that he never had". Is that prophetic, wishful thinking, or did he know something?

Stanley Ann is reported to have died in 1995 from cancer. Her mother cared for her during her last days. Madelyn remained at the apartment where she lived most of time she lived in Hawaii.

It was widely published that Madelyn Lee Dunham died on November 3, 2008. However a reporter discovered that this may not be true. According to an unnamed person who worked at the coroner's office, Madelyn actually died on October 21st, two days before Obama left the campaign to visit her. The informer stated that Madelyn's remains were cremated on November 24th. The reporter stated that Obama and his sister demanded that the reports be falsified. Additionally Madelyn would have had her 89th birthday on October 26th and her son did not visit her.

A memorial service was held for Madelyn on December 23, 2008 at the First Unitarian Church. Following the service Obama and his sister scattered her ashes in the Pacific Ocean.

Judge me by the people who surround me.

CHAPTER 5

★ ★ ★ ★ ★

Mom

"The values she taught me continue to be my touch stone, when it comes to how I go about the work of politics." This is an Obama quote about his mother. His mother certainly led an interesting life while traveling extensively, mostly in Southeast Asia.

STANLEY ANN DUNHAM was born on November 29, 1942, but the question is where. It is widely reported that she was born at Fort Leavenworth, but sometimes in Wichita, Kansas. Recently a birth certificate has surfaced stating that Stanley Ann was born in the city of Sedgwick at the Saint Francis Hospital. On the certificate her mother's name was spelled 'Madeline' and her father's occupation was listed as a corporal in the Army.

She moved about the country as a child with her parents. Her parents once relocated so she would attend a specific high school. That school was Mercer Island High School that had a reputation of being connected with Communist teachings. One hallway was known as 'anarchy alley' because of the far left teachers and classes. The current web site indicates it is still a liberal campus, with emphasis on 'green' lifestyles. Stanley Ann was tagged as an "intellectual rebel", said to be very observant and had an ironic sense of humor. Her father would drive her and her friends to basketball games and she would be embarrassed with his loud boisterous cheering. She was known to watch foreign films at an art theatre in Seattle and liked the coffee shops in the University District. Stanley Ann was not known to date while she attended high school and was remembered saying, "I don't have to date and get married to have a baby." The day after she graduated she left with her mother and flew to Hawaii to join her father who had already moved there.

She started classes at the University of Hawaii on September 26, 1960, six weeks late. She met Barack Obama Sr. in a Russian language class in the

East-West Center, and then dropped out of college in December. She reportedly got married in February 1961. A marriage license has never been located.

A complication to this story is that Barack Obama Sr. was already married and had a wife and children in Kenya. Young Barack was reportedly born on August 4, 1961 and the birth was announced in two local newspapers. The address listed in the announcements was 6085 Kalanianole Hwy. Barack Sr. lived at 625 11th Ave. and there is no evidence that Stanley Ann ever lived there. By some accounts her parents lived at 2277 Kamchameha and never lived at the Kalanianole Hwy. address. Other reports state the Dunhams did live at the Kalanianole address. A certified sealed birth certificate was not produced during the campaign for President. The Obama web site displayed a certification of live birth that some persons found questionable. Some called it a fake. The document presented is not acceptable proof of birth for a passport, a driver's license, or tax reductions under Hawaiian law. A certification of live birth is not the same as a certified birth certificate. A certified birth certificate lists the parent's names, date and time of birth, and the location where the child was born. Hawaii revised Statue 338-178 states upon receiving an application the director of the health 'shall' issue a birth certificate if verification is received that the legal parents have resided in the Territory or State of Hawaii for a year previous to the birth of the child. The Statute does not state that location of the birth of the child needs to be verified. Obama Sr. arrived in Hawaii in 1959 and Stanley Ann moved to Hawaii in June 1960, although her whereabouts after February 1961 have been questioned.

The lack of verifiable documentation of Obama's birth in the United States had produced a variety of theories about his birth. Many of these theories indicate Obama does not resemble his father. One theory is Frank Marshall Davis fathered her child. This comes about because of nude pictures resembling Stanley Ann that were taken at somebody's home with a Christmas tree in the background. Another picture of her at the same location has a record player and what appear to be jazz records in the background. Mr. Davis, a friend of Stanley, had written books about his vast sexual escapades including young children and his hobby was photography. It has been suggested that the pictures were taken at his home.

Another theory is that she was pregnant when she left Mercer Island, possibly by Malcolm X who had been the Seattle area. There are pictures showing similar physical appearances between Malcolm X and Obama. Then another suggestion is that Stanley, who enjoyed going to the red-light district in a black community, fathered a child in Hawaii and his daughter was put in the position of raising him. The theory is that Obama Sr. was given some incentive to acknowledge parenting the child and the whole story is a sham.

If Obama had been fathered by Dunham, Davis, or even Malcolm X his natural born status would not be in question. However, his often told colorful past would prove to be total fiction.

There are those that accept the idea that Obama Sr. is the father but there is a controversy as to where Jr. was born. This is because the lack of information regarding the whereabouts of Stanley Ann after she got married until the next time she was seen; which was in the State of Washington in August of 1961. This is a mystery. Some people believe the child was born in Hawaii, but neither hospital has acknowledged that Obama Jr. was born there, nor have any hospital employees recalled the birth. At a much later date Obama said he was born at one hospital and his sister said he was born at the other.

There is a theory that he was born in Kenya. A schoolmate of Stanley Ann recalls a conversation in which she said her husband is going back to Kenya in the summer of 1961. There is speculation Stanley Ann went with him and gave birth over there. It is probable that airline officials would not allow somebody late in pregnancy fly back to Hawaii from Kenya. Years later Obama's Grandmother Sarah said, during a telephone conversation with an interpreter, that she was present when Obama was born in Kenya. Later, she changed the story. It could mean that the grandmother was in Kenya and Obama was not, or she was told to change her story. This was during the Presidential campaign when there were several challenges about his eligibility. There is evidence that Stanley Ann had a passport in 1961, because INS has paperwork for a later renewal and the original paper work is not available. In Obama's book "Dreams" he relates how his mother wanted the three of them to 'return' to Kenya some day as a family.

Several newspapers have referred to Obama as being Kenyan born, including the Kenya Sunday Standard, The Ghana Times, and the Nigerian Observer. During the 2004 Illinois senate debate, Alan Keyes stated that Obama was not a natural born citizen. Obama's response was, "So what? I'm running for Illinois Senator not the presidency." In October 2008 at Harvard Town Hall Forum, Olara Otunnu (President of Uganda Peoples Congress) referred to a statement by Ali Mazrui, a Kenyan historian about Obama. The statement was about how odd it was that a Kenyan and member of the Lou tribe could become the president of the United States before a Lou tribe member would be president of Kenya. Then the fact that Michelle Obama has referred to Kenya as Obama's home country has made many people believe that Obama was born in Kenya. A certified copy of a Kenyan birth certificate of Barak Obama was obtained in 2009 by Lucas Daniel Smith. He mailed a copy of the document to each member of Congress in September 2010.

Another theory is that Stanley Ann went to Canada to give birth. This idea has merit as the first time Stanley Ann was seen after Obama's birth was when she was in Seattle in August of 1961. She was with her child while applying for classes at the University of Washington. Stanley Ann began classes in Washington on August 19th, only 15 days after she gave birth to her son. Seattle is near the Canadian border and it seems unlikely she would fly across the ocean with a newborn to Washington from Hawaii or Kenya.

Somebody notified the Department of Health in Hawaii about the birth of Obama. The unanswered question is who. Of course hospitals notify the department; but they also take the word of relatives. The answer to the location of Obama's birth has never been proved. What I find interesting is that not one hospital employee has ever come forward stating that they remember Obama being born as it wasn't a common occurrence in 1961 for a white woman to give birth to a black child. Plus with all the attention given to the question of where he was born, I would think somebody would want the attention of being able to verify they were present at the time. But not one hospital employee has done so, not an admittance clerk, a nurse, or any other employee who would have come in contact with him as a newborn infant.

Finally on April 27, 2011 Obama announces he is releasing his long form birth certificate. This was done after Donald Trump,a potential 2012 Presidential candidate, had received so much publicity asking why Obama was refusing to produce it. When he announced its release Obama called the attention about his place of birth silly and was now releasing it because he had more important business to be concerned about. Polls had shown that 38% to 45% of voters did not think he was born in the United States and was therefore not eligible to be President. Several States had also been considering enacting legislation that persons running for office must provide verification of citizenship prior to having their name put on the State's ballots. The long form birth certification he provided indicated the same address as the birth announcements in the local Hawaii newspapers in 1961. His mother's race was listed as Caucasian, while his father's was African instead of Negro. African is not a race as not all Africans are of the Negro race. This did not stop all the speculation regarding his citizenship which had been questioned since he first campaigned for office. Photoshop experts have stated that the document was altered. They have a process that can separate the document into layers to determine when each line was incorporated into the paper. It is their contention that there are four layers and the information written was 'doctored'. A lawsuit has been filed stating the document has been changed and is not authentic.

The birth certificate, even if authentic certainly hasn't quieted the people who contend he is not natural born citizen. They state a natural born citizen is a person born in the United States and both parents are citizens of this country.

Stanley Ann attended the University of Washington in the fall of 1961 while her husband attended college at the University of Hawaii. She returned to Hawaii after Obama Sr. left to attend Harvard. Incomplete paperwork of a divorce decree has been discovered attesting to a divorce in 1964. I have seen no documentation that child support was ever requested or received.

In the spring of 1963, Stanley Ann returned to the University of Hawaii campus and its East-West Center to work on her Bachelor's Degree in anthropology. The Federal Government established the East-West Center in 1960. The Center received over $13 million plus $1million in 'grant-in aid' from the State Department. Grant-in aid is a term used to describe funds that are granted for specific projects. The East-West Center has long been associated with CIA activity. It was the CIA that sponsored the students that flew in to study at the University of Hawaii and was how Barack Obama Sr. came to the Hawaii. This is probably why there was a celebration at the airport that Stanley Armour Dunham (the furniture salesman) attended when Obama arrived, as it was the first airlift. The East-West Center has continued its relationship with the CIA to this day. It has expanded its campus for training and recruitment. As recently as February 2010, activists protested the University's involvement with intelligence agencies. The East-West Center current web site boasts that over 50,000 people have used their program and many currently hold positions of leadership worldwide.

It was at the East-West Center that Stanley Ann met Lolo Soetoro in another class. Lolo was 32 years old and had arrived in Hawaii on August 18, 1962 on a CIA project. Stanley Anne was only 20 years old at that time. He studied for his Masters Degree in geography there until his visa ended June 20, 1965. Her divorce from Obama Sr. was finalized on March 20, 1964 and she reportedly married Lolo on March, 15, 1965. She is now known as Ann Soetoro. Lolo was deported in 1965. For two years Ann attempted to get Lolo to be able to come back to the United States, but was denied each time. She attained her Bachelor's Degree in 1967. Ann renewed her passport (it appears that her original passport was probably approved around 1961 but records of it are unavailable), packed up Obama Jr., and moved to Indonesia to be with her husband.

Ann's passport forms show two different dates and locations where she married Lolo. One date is March 15, 1965 at Moloka, Hawaii and the other is March 5, 1965 in Maui, Hawaii. Lolo's paperwork, when trying to return to the United States, has a marriage license attached but not a marriage certificate verifying a wedding took place.

Upon arriving in Indonesia, Ann worked at the American Embassy in Jakarta teaching English. This embassy also housed a large CIA station and satellite systems. The U.S. Agency for International Development (USAID) was a major cover for CIA activities. Shortly before Ann arrived in Indonesia General Suharto had ousted Sukaro in a coup. Anyone suspected of supporting Communism faced death; it was a very tense time.

Lolo Soetoro registered Barack at the Fransiskus Assisi Catholic School in Jakarta on January 1, 1968. He was registered as Barry Soetoro, an Indonesian and religion was Islam. This brings up the question as whether Lolo adopted Barack either in Hawaii or in Indonesia. Under the Muslim religion if your father was Muslim so are the children. Barack Obama Sr. was Muslim as was Lolo. To attend public school children must be citizens and dual citizenship is not recognized in Indonesia. The Assisi school was a private school and I do not know if citizenship was required for attendance. Approximately two years later 'Barry' did attend a public school called Besuki Primary School. No records of adoption have been discovered, but there has been speculation that he was because he was using a different last name.

Ann moved to Yogyakata, Java reportedly to study the village's industries, especially blacksmithing. Her studies became a basis for a doctoral dissertation she completed in 1992. She left Barack in Jakarta to attend school while she was in Java.

On August 15, 1970 Ann gave birth to Maya. She was named after American poet Maya Angelou. Lolo was becoming more westernized and Ann was involved in the Indonesian life style. This was at a time when the military was stronger in the streets. Students were required to attend indoctrination classes and had to profess loyalty to the State. Criticism was not tolerated. Ann packed up her children and returned to Hawaii in 1972.

Ann again attended classes at the University of Hawaii from the fall of 1972 until the fall of 1974. She was working towards her Masters Degree in anthropology.

> Barack was enrolled at Punahou which is a very elite expensive college prep school and the largest private school in the United States. The current admission requires students to pass an achievement test or have a high SSAT testing. The current yearly cost of admission is $17,800. I don't know what the cost was in 1972 but I'm sure it was as costly. The school has a Mission Statement which includes a section on Spiritual Development and Individual Independence stating the school "promotes the sense of responsibility and interdependence with their schoolmates, their community, and their world." The school stresses global community and sustainability. The Chapel Program offers community service programs, character education, and worship related experiences consistent with Christian principles. They "seek a quest for meaning and a call to make a difference in God's world."

In 1975 Ann and Maya went back to Indonesia while Barack remained in Hawaii with his grandparents. Ann returned to her field work in Java. Her observations brought her to the conclusion that the underdeveloped countries were a result of a scarcity of capital. She believed the allocation of capital was a matter of politics and not culture. The New York Times ran a quote from anthropologist Clifford Geertz: "The aim of anthropology is the enlargement of the universe of human discourse". This appears to be the philosophy of Stanley Ann Dunham Soetoro.

Records indicate Ann attended classes in the spring of 1978 and the fall of 1984 at the University of Hawaii. Information shows the Ford Foundation employed her in1981 to travel throughout Southeast Asia as an International and Cultural Development Program Officer. She was working with women and their employment with the Regional Southeast Asia Office in Jakarta. Ann was really an international banker involved with micro-financing in connection with the United States Agency for International Development (USAID). One of her overseers was Peter Geithner the father of Timothy Geithner who is the current Secretary of Treasury.

The Ford Foundation hired Peter Geithner to oversee the programs that Ann developed.

> Micro-financing helps to develop an economy by allowing people to establish an ability to earn income. Small loans are given to those living in poverty to start a business. The people who secure the loans typically have no collateral, no credit history, or steady income.

In 1980 Ann gets divorced and starts using the name Ann Dunham Sutoro, changing the spelling of her last name. Divorce papers were finally released in 2008 or 2009. The divorce decree does not list the date of marriage. The document does state that the couple had one child under the age of 18 and another child over age 18 that was still dependent on his parents because of education. The fact that Barack was referred to as one of their children has added to the speculation that he was adopted. If he was adopted then he would have been an Indonesian citizen. No adoption papers have ever been released.

In 1984 Maya returns to Hawaii and goes to school at Punahou, the same elite school that her brother Barack attended. Maya graduates in 1988. Her mother came with her to attend classes at the University. Ann later returns to Indonesia to continue her work with the Ford Foundation. The Ford Foundation is highly connected with the CIA. The CIA uses foundations as a way to transfer funds to agency projects and covert actions without the recipient knowing its source. The cooperation between the CIA and the Ford Foundation has been ongoing since the 1950's.

Her work has her traveling all over Southeast Asia. As an international banking consultant, she traveled to Ghana, India, Thailand, Nepal, Bangladesh, and China. In 1986 she was the consultant for Pakistan. She monitored funds for the Asian Development Bank and trained credit officers. This work continued for five years. Stanley Ann lived at the Hilton International Hotel for the five years she was in Pakistan. This is where, it was reported, that Obama stayed when he went to visit her in 1981. In 1988 she was employed at the Bank Rakyat of Indonesia, the country's largest bank. She continued working with the practice of micro-financing making loans to women. The concept of loaning money to persons with no steady income or credit history is the same practice that Fannie Mac and Freddie Mac used. It was the same practice that caused our mortgage melt down in the United States.

> One problem with the story of Barack traveling to Pakistan to visit his mother is that she was living in Indonesia at the time. What actually happened was that he traveled to Pakistan after visiting his mother and sister. He stayed three weeks in Karachi, Pakistan with college friends, Hasan Chansoo and Wahid Hamid. His travel itinerary included a trip to India. It was later reported he actually stayed with the family of Muhammadaian Soomru, an internationally known professional banker. Soomru became the acting President of Pakistan after Musharraf resigned in 2008.
>
> The other problem with this story is that Pakistan was under martial law at the time. There was a travel ban for all U.S. citizens. Non-Muslims were not allowed into the country; unless they were sponsored by their Embassy for official business. So the question is, what passport did he use to travel? It couldn't have been an American passport, so people wonder if he had and used an Indonesian passport. If he had an Indonesian passport that would mean that his nationality was Indonesian and not American. This question has not been answered and a passport has not been provided.

In 1992, Ann completed her thesis titled: "Surviving the Odds: Village Industries in Indonesia." She received her PhD. in Anthropology on September 9, 1992. In late1994 she had stomach pain and a local doctor in Indonesia diagnosed it as indigestion. Early in 1995 she went to New York City and got the diagnosis of uterine cancer which had spread to her ovaries. She moved back to Hawaii to stay with her mother until she died on November 11, 1995. There are no records that have been located that verify she was treated for cancer in Hawaii. The only report I could find that Obama saw his mother while she was ill was in a television ad for his health insurance bill when he said he visited her and she was more concerned about paying medical bills than getting well. There was no funeral and it is reported that her body was cremated. It has also been reported that there was a memorial service held for her at the University of Hawaii and her ashes were scattered into the Pacific Ocean. A Death Certificate was finally found and released one month before the Presidential election 2008 on a data base. The data base also indicated the information came from the government in California and from the same District that Nancy Pelosi represents.

Interestingly enough, a search of her Social security number in 2008 found that the number was still active to Dunham and listed two addresses in New York and one in Hawaii. It stated that Dunham was 66 years old, which is the age she would be if she is still alive. A white pages search was done for Stanley A. Dunham and the address that came up was the same address as the Ford Foundation in New York City. A further search of her telephone number found an identical match to the name of Scott Terkowitz. He is a dentist that was found guilty of professional misconduct in Virginia in 2004. In addition to that; the telephone number is a Verizon line. Verizon didn't have telephone numbers until 1996.

Some researchers came to the conclusion that she had additional aliases that were connected to either her parents or to her business ventures. These names include Kelly A. Dunham, Kelly A. Shipplock, Sandra Dunham, Sandra Lee Dunham, Susan N. Dunham, Stephen O. Dunham, and Scott Dunham. Another item came to my attention is her Social Security number is also reportedly assigned to another person living in Washington State, who was born in Washington State and has a birth date of December 28, 1942. Fortunately, a copy of Stanley Ann's original Social Security application is on file. This is only of interest because of the controversy about Barack Obama having so many different Social Security numbers and of him using a number that was issued in Connecticut.

Judge me by the people who surround me.

CHAPTER 6

★ ★ ★ ★ ★

Fathers, Sisters and Mentor

Barack Obama Jr. had both a father and a stepfather that influenced his life. He also had a step sister, and possibly an adopted sister. One of his grandfather's friends became a mentor to him while he was growing up in Hawaii. All of his immediate family is deceased with the exception of his half sister Maya.

President Obama's grandfather in Africa was Onyango Obama who had at least three wives. BARACK HUSSEIN OBAMA SR. was born in 1935 to his father's second wife, Akumu, but raised by the third wife Sarah. They belonged to the Lou Tribe in Kenya. Onyango traveled widely when enlisted in the British colonial forces. During his travels he converted to Islam and changed his name to Hussein Onyango Obama. The Mau-Mau Rebellion started with a movement of Nationalists who wanted to over throw the British rule. He joined the Mau-Mau (which means get out- get out) as he was not happy with how the British treated Africans. The Rebellion was about becoming an independent nation and no longer a colony of England; the same as our nation's Revolutionary War. Hussein Onyango Obama was jailed in 1949 by the British and tortured for two years as he was involved in the Kenyan Independence movement. Grandma Sarah described the torture her husband received to Obama during his 1988 visit to Kenya.

In 1953 Barack Obama Sr. married his first wife Kezia, in a tribal marriage, sealed with a dowry payment of 14 cattle, while the fighting continued with the British. Obama Sr. was an anti-colonist, just like his father. In January of 1958 their first child Abongo, known as 'Roy, is born. In May of 1958 Tom Mboya, of the Lou Tribe, (and the General Secretary of the Kenya Federation of Labor) organized non-violent boycotts to protest colonial rule.

In 1959 Mboya went to the United States to persuade Americans to train

Kenyans. He wanted to educate people so the British bureaucrats could be replaced when independence was achieved. In September, Barack Obama Sr. arrived in Hawaii on Africa-Airlift, which was coordinated by the CIA. This is just one month after he learns that his wife is pregnant with his second child, a daughter named Auma. The Prime Minister and his father, the former Prime Minister, are related to Barack Sr. through marriage and are from the same Lou Tribe. Obama Sr. has status in his community.

The following year he meets Stanley Ann Dunham in his Russian language class at the East-West Center at the University of Hawaii. Stanley Ann is seven years younger than he is. Obama wrote in "Dreams From My Father" that his parents were married in February as his mother was pregnant. Barack Sr. had his own residence but there is no verification that Stanley Ann ever lived with him. Barack Jr. is born August 4, 1961 and Stanley Ann enrolls at the University of Washington, in the State of Washington, the same month. Barack Sr. continued his studies at the University of Hawaii and became a good friend with fellow classmate Neil Abercrombie. In May 1962 Barack Sr. was a featured speaker at a Mother's Peace Rally and he joined the ILWU (International Longshore and Warehouse Union) in their march protesting the Viet Nam War. He graduated in June of 1962, majoring in economics, and soon leaves to attend Harvard University in Massachusetts.

> Neil Abercrombie was Hawaii's State Representative from 1975 until 1979 and State Senator from 1980 until 1986. He was elected to the U.S. Congress in 1986 and was a member of the Progressive Caucus. The Democratic Socialist of America (DSA) endorsed his 1990 re-election bid for congress and he spoke at a DSA/PAC event in 2007. His wife is Nancie Caraway a member of the Feminist Commission of the DSA. During the 2010 campaign for governor, Abercrombie promised to provide proof that President Obama was born in Hawaii. He won the election and within a week of taking office his Health Director resigned and Abercrombie said he could not provide proof of Obama birth.

His divorce from Stanley Ann was finalized in 1964. Obama Sr. graduates in 1965 with a Master in Economics. While at Harvard he met a school teacher, Ruth Nides, who follows him back to Kenya. They get married and have two children, Mark and David. She eventually divorces him claiming he was abusive.

When Obama Sr. returned to Kenya he secured a job with an oil company. He later worked as economist at the Kenyan Ministry of Transport and then as Senior Economist in the Kenyan Ministry of Finance. Tom Mboya was assassinated in 1969 and Barack was fired by Kenya's President Jomo Kenyatta and blacklisted in Kenya. He began drinking heavily and was involved in a bad car accident that injured his legs. In 1971 he came to Hawaii to visit friends and saw his son. He continued to drink and had a second car accident that caused him to lose both legs. He fathered another son named George. Six months later he was in a third car accident and died. He is buried at his home village in Kenya near Lake Victoria. His brother, Sayid Obama, told a reporter that Barack Obama Sr. was wealthy in the Lou tribe.

LOLO SOETORO, Barack's stepfather, was born on January 2, 1935 in Bandung, West Java, Dutch West Indies. He was one of ten children living in Yogyakarta which was the Indonesian capital during the Indonesian National Revolution from 1945 to 1949 against the Dutch. Indonesia was a colony of the Dutch and they were fighting for their freedom. His father and uncle were both killed in the Indonesian National Revolution. When the Dutch lost, they burned the Soetoro family home and Lolo fled with his mother to the countryside. He earned a Bachelor's Degree in geography from Gajah Mada University in Yogyakarta, which is the oldest and most prestigious in Indonesia.

Lolo came to Hawaii in September 18, 1962 with the CIA sponsored Exchange Visitor Program. He attended the East-West Center at the University of Hawaii where he meets Ann. He marries her in March of 1965 and returns home in July after graduating with a Master's Degree. Indonesia was in a battle between Sukarno, leader of the Communist Party of Indonesia (PKI), and Suharto who was trying to over throw the government with CIA backing. Lolo was called back to fight; as all foreign students were called back to Indonesia at that time. Three months after his return there was a coup and Sukarno was thrown out of office. Two days later the PKI headquarters was burned down. Lolo served as a colonel in the Army of Suharto.

> Strangely enough, the East-West Center got a new Chancellor in 1965. His name was Howard P. Jones who had been the U.S. Ambassador to Indonesian from 1958 until 1965. He was in Jakarta when the CIA backed military planned to overthrow Sukarno. As Chancellor, he wrote an article for the Washington Post defending

Suharto's actions. The Embassy and CIA was housed in the same building in Jakarta.

Sukarno wanted to return and asked for unity and no vengeance, but it was not to be. Suharto became a dictator and there was mass murder of members of the PKI. The CIA started programs to 'win the hearts and minds' of the area. They concentrated most of their efforts in East Java where Ann did the majority of her work.

Lolo continued to work in the Army as a geologist in the Director General Office of the Topography Division. Meanwhile, back in Hawaii, Ann tried for two years for Lolo to get permission to return to America. During this time Lolo was probably conscripted to fight Sukarno. Returning to Hawaii was not allowed, so Ann packed up Barack in 1967 and moved to Indonesia. When Ann arrived the country was under military control.

Lolo registered Barack at a Catholic school as a Muslim named Barry Soetoro. It was common practice to sign up children with the same religion as their parents. A couple of years later Lolo became a government relations consultant for Mobil Oil Company. Mobil Oil is directly descended from Rockefeller's Standard Oil Company. He was the liaison between the oil company and the Suharto regime.

With the increased income, the family moved and Barry went to the public school. The principal of the school Tine Hahiyary recalls that Barry studied Mangaji, which involves reciting the Koran in Arabic. He said non-Muslims would not send their children to Mangaji classes. One former classmate, Emirsyah Satar (current CEO of Garuda Indonesia Airlines) said Barry was quite religious in Islam and only after marrying Michelle that he changed. Classmate Rory Aminis (current manager of Bank Mandiri) said Barry was a very devout Muslim. Other reports deny Barry practiced the Muslim religion

Under Indonesian law a student in a public school had to be a citizen. The country was under a police state at that time. Immigration officials and the police checked weekly at public schools to confirm citizenship compliance. Ann would have had to renounce her U.S. citizenship for their marriage to be recognized as legal. This country does not recognize dual citizenship and America must recognize this in accordance with the Hague Convention of 1930.

Maya was born on August 15, 1970. Ann was getting more involved in the native culture. Lolo was becoming more involved with Western culture and Indonesian corruption. The military and police were becoming more dangerous. Students had to attend indoctrination classes and profess loyalty to the State. Ann didn't want Barry to be influenced by Lolo so she sent him back to Hawaii to her parent's home in 1971. Ann left Indonesia with Maya in 1972 to further her studies in Hawaii. Lolo visited Hawaii but they never lived as husband and wife again.

Divorce papers were filed on August 20, 1980. Divorce papers stated the couple had two children. One child was under age 18 and the other over the age of 18 but still a dependent because of education. Maya would have been the child under age 18 and Barry the older child. No child support was requested.

Lolo remarried. His wife was Erna Kustina and they had two children, Yusuf Aji and Rahayu Nurmaida Soetoro. He died in 1987 from a liver ailment in Jakarta and is buried in South Jakarta.

Barack Obama's father and stepfather were both air lifted by the CIA to Hawaii to attend the University of Hawaii. Both were being trained so that they could return to their home countries, after the removal of the current rulers, to be part of the new government. The two men both met Obama's mother while attending classes at the East-West wing of the university that the CIA uses for training purposes. No verification of either wedding can be located (although divorce documents have) and neither of the men was requested to pay child support. I wonder why Obama's mother took so many classes at the East-West wing of the university. Perhaps the subject of anthropology is crucial to CIA operations, or the job is used as a cover occupation for its employees. I don't know, I'm not making any accusations, just wondering.

MAYA KASSANDRA SOETORO NG, Barack's half sister, was born in Indonesia in 1970. She has a Hawaiian birth record as does her brother. In Indonesia she attended Jakarta International School from 1981 to 1984 and was homeschooled by her mother. Maya attended the expensive Punahou School in Hawaii and graduated in 1988.

Maya attended school at Barnard College in New York and received two Master Degrees from New York University in English and secondary language studies. Maya attained a PhD from the University of Hawaii in international comparative education. She taught high school at La Pietra High School for Girls in Honolulu.

In 2003 she married Konrad Ng and has a daughter named Suhaila. Maya met her husband at the East-West Center when they were both students there. In 2009 she helped to get her mother's dissertation published as a book in which Maya wrote the forward. Maya and her husband are both employed at the East-West Center at the University of Hawaii.

During the month of April 2011 she was interviewed on television to promote her book. She was briefly questioned about her brother's place of birth. She responded that he had been born in Hawaii and wished all the talk about his birth would stop.

A woman who claimed to be Barack Obama's adopted sister died suddenly on February 26, 2010. Her name is HOLIYAH 'LIA' SOETORO SOBAH. That month Lia was talking to reporters about the upcoming visit of Obama to Indonesia and how excited she was to see him. The conversation was recorded and during the interview she repeatedly called her husband to tell him what she was saying.

Lia told the reporters that when she was 7 years old, in 1966, she ran away from home and ended up in the home of Mrs. Siti Bogor. Mrs. Bogor was the maid to Lolo and Ann Soetoro. Ann asked Mrs. Bogor is she could adopt Lia and the answer was yes. Lia said when she lived at the Soetoro home Maya had not yet been born.

She remembered being excited when Ann went to America to get Barry. Lia was disappointed when he came because the black boy could not speak Indonesian, but within about seven months they could communicate. She said Barry was 4 years younger than she was. She called Lolo and Ann by the names of Mr. and Mrs. Lolo and Eny. They called her Non for Nona and Barry called her Ma'am Non. She recalled that Barry went to school and got basic education in Jakarta and that they played, slept, and even bathed together. She said that after living with Lolo and Ann she was adopted.

Lia told the reporters Mr. Lolo became the manager at P.T. Pertamino. Lia had fun with Barry. She said he liked her sharing the bedroom at night and would be upset if she left the room while he was sleeping. So he got a long rope and tied her hand to it in her bed to his so she had to wake him up if she left. Barry liked to go to the summit and return with cakes that he shared. He also enjoyed climbing the mango tree in the back yard to pick mangos. She recalled that his birthday was near the time of the festival Agustusan. During the festival red and white flags were put on the sides of the streets and he liked that. Barry wanted red and white flags so he got them on his cake and put them in every room of the house.

Lia went to Hawaii in 1971 and stayed there for three months. She remembers having fun going shopping and to the beach with Barry. Her grandmother gave her a stuffed monkey and some clothes. (There is a picture of Lia with a stuffed monkey on the internet that was said to be taken at the Dunham home.) She was sad when she left and missed Barry. She claims she still has some of his belongings, including a blanket, to remember him by. She told reporters that she planned to give the monkey to Barry when he visited. She said it had so many good memories.

Lia also told the reporters she had received an invitation to go to the Presidential inauguration. She claims a white woman with glasses named Gelt asked her to attend. This person told her another woman of great status and means would pay her Rp600.000 to pay for her birth certificate and travel expenses. After she received the money she was told to wait for news of the final plans. It is not known if she attended.

Soon after the interview Lia died suddenly. No reason for death was stated. Maya has said that this is a fraud. However the Consulate General of the Republic of Indonesia has confirmed the relationship. Her obituary stated she was born in 1957, was married to Edi Sobah, and had three children. The obituary also states Lolo Soetoro and Ann Dunham Obama Soetoro adopted her. This is just another mystery that surrounds this family.

The other person who shaped young Barry was Frank Marshall Davis, who was introduced to him by his grandfather. Stanley Dunham picked Frank to be his grandson's mentor as he was black and believed Barry could relate to him.

FRANK MARSHALL DAVIS was born on December 31, 1905 in Arkansas City, Kansas. Frank's great grandmother raised him as he never met his father and his mother abandoned him at age two. He never forgot the terror he experienced when five white boys lynched him as a child. He attended two colleges in Kansas studying journalism, never graduated, but learned he had a passion for poetry while he attended school. In 1927 he moved to Chicago.

Frank was a Communist, a writer, a poet, and enjoyed jazz music. He was a member of the Communist Party USA (CPUSA) in Chicago and active in the Progressive movement. He was known for his poems that where pro-communism, anti-American, and anti-Christianity. Davis was also the author of hard core pornography. He published an autobiography, in 1968, called "Sex Rebel: Black" stating he was bi-sexual, a voyeur, an exhibitionist, liked bondage and group sex. He wrote about a time when he and his first wife had sex with a 13 year old girl for a period of time. He told of 'cruising' the parks in Hawaii, looking for couples or female tourists to have sex with. Davis also wrote a manuscript called "The Incredible Waikiki Jungle" where he said he specialized in sex during the time period of 1969 and 1976. He worked with a CPUSA front called American Committee for Foreign Births. This organization's goal was preventing deportation of foreign communists from America.

In Chicago, Davis worked for three different black owned newspapers. He wrote articles and short stories for magazines and began writing poems. Then in 1931 he moved to Atlanta to become the editor of the newspaper 'Atlanta Daily World' which became the largest successful black owned newspaper. He wrote about Social Realism which addressed racial justice in politics and economics, plus legal justice. It was in 1931 that he got interested in Communism. Davis moved back to Chicago in 1935 and met Vernon Jarrett (the father in-law of Valerie Jarrett a close friend to the Obama's and current White House Advisor) at the South Side Community Art Center. Frank and Vernon became good friends. They worked together at a black owned newspaper called 'Chicago Defender' and at the Citizen's Committee to Aid Packinghouse Workers a communist front group. Davis was also the editor of the communist publication 'Chicago Star'.

At this time he met Harry Bridges, a member of CPUSA and first president of the union IWLU, at the Abraham Lincoln School where Davis taught a jazz history class. Harry Bridges was later involved with IWLU in Hawaii. The Abraham Lincoln School was formed in the 1930's as a training center by the Communist Party USA. One faculty member, and friend of Davis, was Earl Durham who worked to elect Harold Washington as mayor of Chicago. While in Chicago, Davis was involved with many communist and subversive groups such as the American Youth for Democracy, National Federation for Constitutional Liberties, and the National Negro Congress.

He started a photography club and was a member of the CPUSA group American Writers.

Davis moved from Chicago to Hawaii in 1948 because of increased communist repression. He arrived with his second wife Helen Canfield who he met in his photography studio. She was a white socialite from Chicago and was actively involved with CPUSA. They had five children while in Hawaii.

He went to work for the 'Honolulu Record' a newspaper controlled by IWLU. It was here he met Jack Hill, the local president. Jack Hill had previously been convicted for conspiracy to overthrow the government. The IWLU Book Club promoted books authored by Saul Alinsky (who developed community organizing in Chicago and wrote "Rules for Radicals"), Carl Marzani (imprisoned for concealing Communist Party membership while member of OSS), Howard Fast (communist convicted for contempt and won the Stalin Peace Prize), and Victor Perlo (CPUSA Marxist economist, who while working for the U.S. government at the War Production Board supplied information to the Soviet Union). Davis wrote a weekly column called "Frankly Speaking". In an article "Free Enterprise or Socialism", published January 26, 1950, he wrote that he hoped the economy would brew a perfect storm to allow change of America into a socialist country. What was needed, he said, was to first trash the free enterprise system and then argue to change to something else. The idea is to act quickly and gain support before the people understood what the change was. Davis was upset that large companies like General Motors made large profits and felt the government should take control and operate the country's major industries.

Davis has been called a bohemian libertine who drank heavily and loved jazz. He was Stanley Dunham's good friend. They met after Dunham and his family moved to the island. The pair was known to drink, smoke pot, play scrabble, crack jokes, and argue together. Davis was also known to sell marijuana and cocaine from a 'Chicago style' hot dog cart near his home in the 1970's. An unnamed source claims he used to buy "8-balls" from Davis' cart. (An 8-ball is 1/8 ounce of cocaine) He said he would see a kid that was 14 or 15 years old called Barry and an older man named Stanley with Frank when he was purchasing drugs. He thought Stanley was Barry's father. He said he made his first purchase in 1975 and "8-balls" cost $300.00. Barack admits he used marijuana and cocaine while in high school.

His home was near the University of Hawaii with his porch only two feet from the sidewalk. He wrote in "Living the Blues" this permitted him to meet many students from the college. He said sexual relations between the "brothers" and "sisters" with the white students were common. Davis wrote "I permitted young white girls to sleep overnight on my floor. I saw no signs of racial hang-ups; these were all members of the Now Generation associating with whom they liked and color be damned."

The FBI had a file on Frank Marshall Davis that was over 600 pages long. What is known about this report is the FBI followed Davis from 1943 to 1963. The report mentions the FBI found Davis taking numerous pictures of the Hawaiian coastline with telescopic lens with no definable subjects. Most reports of Davis said he came to Hawaii to get away from Chicago, others believe he was assigned by the Communist Party to go to Hawaii. The islands were a strategic area with the United States Defense Department. He died in 1987.

Frank Marshall Davis is certainly a very interesting character. Maya told the Associated Press that her grandfather saw Davis as "a point of connection, a bridge if you will, to the larger African-American experience for my brother".

Judge me by the people who surround me.

SECTION THREE

★ ★ ★ ★ ★

Young Adult

CHAPTER 7

★ ★ ★ ★ ★

College and Community Organizing

Barak Obama attended Occidental College from 1979 to 1981. No college records including application, financial aid, and grades have been released. There was an e-mail posted on the internet stating that Occidental College released records indicating Obama attended the school on a Fulbright Scholarship using the name of Barry Soetoro. Fulbright Scholarships are only offered to foreign students; however the e-mail was later dismissed as an April Fool's joke.

There are no pictures of Obama are in the yearbooks, but several students and professors remember him. In his book "Dreams" Obama wrote that he smoked marijuana and used cocaine but became afraid he would become a 'pothead' or 'junkie'. Some of his friends recall him smoking 'pot', smoking cigarettes, and drinking beer, but none remembered cocaine use. His roommate Paul Carpenter said he was an athlete, very bright and had a "funky" red fiat. A good friend Vinai Thummalapally remembers him playing basketball, jogging and studying. Thummalapally, who lived with Obama in 1980, said his friend wanted to work in public service and help the disadvantaged. Another roommate, Robert McCrary thought he was cocky and arrogant, while friend Margot Miffen recalled he was unpretentious, down to hearth and somewhat reserved.

Obama was remembered for discussing his political beliefs. Classmate John Boyer recalls discussions regarding the ideology of such people as Friedrich Nietzsche (philosopher who challenged Christianity and morality), Sigmund Freud (atheist who developed psychoanalyst treatments and promoted cocaine use), and Jean-Paul Sartre (a Marist philosopher and political activist). John Drew, another classmate, said that Occidental College was a prestigious school that had many Marxist professors. He remembers Obama as an ardent, committed radical Marxist who wanted a revolution of the working class to overthrow the ruling class in America which would convert this country to Socialism. He recalled the time Obama and Hasan Chandoo (Obama's roommate) picked him up in a BMW and went to a restaurant where they smoked, drank and discussed the ideals of Marxism. Obama stated wealthy people exploited other people, America was the enemy, and the Soviet Union was misunderstood. Drew believes Obama is aware that taxing the rich will harm the economy and is committed to redistribution of wealth.

A junior professor of political sciences who was denied tenure, Lawrence Goldyn told "The Southern Voice" (a gay newspaper) that he mentored Obama. Goldyn designed and taught a class on sexual politics and mentored gay and heterosexual students. He said he contributed to Obama sorting things out and focusing on what he wanted to do. When asked if he was disappointed about Obama's lack of support for gay marriage, he responded that he was sure that his former student was supportive of gay rights. He added that he understood that the country is not ready for that discussion during an election and Obama would devise a way to address the subject.

During his second year at Occidental Obama became active in social activism. He was involved in a campaign to encourage Occidental from investing funds in companies which did business with South Africa. Obama joined Students for Economic Democracy (SED) which was founded by Tom Hayden (founder of Students for Democratic Society SDS) and Jane Fonda. The mission statement for SED is: "Economic democracy means that ownership and control will be spread among a wide variety of public bodies: city, state and federal governments, churches, trade unions, cooperatives and community groups, small business people, workers, and consumers". On February 18, 1981, Obama gave the opening speech at a SED rally in Coons Hall at Occidental organized by Hayden. In the book "Dreams", he wrote the rally was led the Black Student Alliance and SED where white students dressed in military uniform went on stage while he was talking who had to be dragged away. This incident was staged for impact on the audience to make a point.

In 1981 Obama traveled to Pakistan and India on spring break with roommate Hasan Chandoo (aka Hasan Chandio) and friend Wahid Hamid for about three weeks. Some reports state that he traveled during the summer but that would be in the middle of monsoon season and I believe that would be doubtful. He first stayed with the Chandoo (Chandio) family; one of the largest landowners in Pakistan. Later he was the guest of the Honorable Ahmad Mian Soomro and stayed at his Muhammad Ali Society residence.

Soomro took him partridge hunting in Jacobabadon. Partridge hunting is a symbol of good hospitality. Soomro, a Pakistani Sindhi, was Prime Minister of Pakistan from November 2007 until March 2008 and later became acting President in 2008 when Musharraf resigned. Soomro is an internationally known banker and instrumental in establishing micro-credit banking in Pakistan. He said somebody asked him to "watch over" Obama during this visit but will not name that person without getting permission. The Obama campaign stated that the travel included a stay at Hyderabad India, but did not state where he stayed or who he visited.

Pakistan in 1981 was under martial law, was on the United States banned travel list, and non-Muslims were not welcome unless their embassy sponsored them for official business. Several people have questioned how he could have traveled to Pakistan as he would not have been able to use a United States passport and how he had the funds to travel there. Other travelers to Pakistan in the spring of 1981 were Zbigniew Brzezinski and Osama bin Laden. Brzezinski was arming the radical Muslims, the mujahedeen, and using the CIA to create instability to provoke a war between Afghanistan and the Soviet Union. He was creating what he called an 'arc of chaos' with the intent of giving the Soviet Union their own 'Viet Nam' type war they could not win. The other goal of destabilization of the area was to ensure access to the oil reserves. The person he met was Osama bin Laden who had connections with the Muslim Brotherhood.

Obama decided to transfer to Columbia University in New York in 1981. He met up with Sohale Siddiqi, a friend of Chandoo and Hamid, who he met in Los Angeles while attending Occidental. Siddiqi described in "Dreams" as Sadik a Pakistani who smoked marijuana and snorted cocaine when the two of them shared an apartment. Siddiqi, who was not a student, said he liked to party while Obama wanted to study and the friendship became strained.

As with Occidental, all of his college records at Columbia are sealed and there is no picture of him in the yearbook. Obama wrote in "Dreams" that he studied political science specializing in international relations spending much of his time in the library studying. He wrote he was involved with the Black Students Organization and continued to be involved in anti-apartheid activities. Brian Connolly, spokesperson from Columbia, confirmed that Obama graduated without honors in 1983.

In 1981 Zbigniew Brzezinski returned to Columbia University as a professor and the head of the Institute of Communist Affairs. There is speculation that Brzezinski mentored Obama as a CIA agent in Asia and Obama did not attend the college. Television network MSNBC located professor Michael Baron who said he taught Obama and recalls a paper that Obama wrote. Baron claims the subject was about nuclear negotiation and arms reduction with the Soviet Union. Unfortunately Baron no longer has a copy of the paper as he lost it. Obama may have met and/or attended classes with Professor Edward Said. Said, a friend of Bill Ayers and Khalid al Mansour, is an ardent spokesperson for pro-Palestinian causes. He later became a friend of Obama in Chicago.

The lack of any information about his years at Columbia prompted three different news agencies (Wall Street Journal, FOX News and the New York Times) to search for any student that remembered Obama while he was at the college. They were not able to find anyone who recalled knowing the person who would become the next President of the United States.

In 1983 and 1984 Obama attended the Socialist Scholars Conferences in Manhattan. These were marketed as a tribute to Karl Marx and how America could be transformed by undercover socialism. The purpose of the conferences was to promote community organizing without using the label of Socialism. This was during the time that Harold Washington, Obama's political idol, was elected as Mayor of Chicago. Socialists envisioned Harold Washington's election as a first step to encourage the Democratic Party to lean left. The belief was this would occur by polarizing the country along class lines, the 'haves' and the 'have-nots'.

Persons attending the conferences included Francis Fox Piven, Peter Dreir who advocated combining community organizations into a national movement and later worked with Obama's presidential campaign and James Cone a black Liberation Theology advocate. Cone was Reverend Jeremiah Wright's theological mentor and a member of the Democratic Socialist of America. After the 1984 conference Cone went to Cuba with Reverend Wright. Wright and Cone supported the Cuban social system and believed it was a system that the United States should follow. There is speculation Bill Ayers also attended the conference as he was attending Bank Street College nearby.

After graduation Obama went to work for Business International Corporation (BIC), a publishing firm and consulting company that assisted American companies doing business abroad. BIC is closely associated with the CIA. Obama does not mention the company by name in his memoir "Dreams" other than to state he looked for work to pay off his college expenses. He does state that he wore a suit and tie, plus had his own office and secretary. Co-worker, Dan Armstrong says Obama "embellished" the story. Armstrong says the atmosphere was informal and mostly staffed by young people making modest pay. He said the "employees called it high school with ash trays". He maintains the only person who had a secretary was the vice president in charge of Obama's division. Obama's supervisor, Cathy Lazere, remembered him as being very mature and bright. It has been reported that BIC paid his college tuition at Columbia. A member of the White House Press Corps has admitted that they have been told that no questions about Obama's years at college or his employment at BIC would be allowed.

Journalists at BIC were sometimes employed as non-official cover (NOC) on assignments around the world. Obama was a researcher in the company's financial services division. At BIC he wrote articles for two of the company's publications; 'Financing Foreign Operations' and 'Business International Money Report'. The high foreign debt of Latin American countries was closely monitored by BIC, as was the movements of Sandinista government in Nicaragua. During 1983 and 1984 this country was being fed the propaganda that America would be adversely affected by the 'communist threat' in Central America.

BIC is known for its Roundtable conferences also called Business International Roundtable. The company has been linked with the Ford Foundation and the Joseph P. Kennedy Foundation which funded the CIA Airlift Africa project. BIC worked with USAID in the 1960's to conduct "reconnaissance missions" in Indonesia and Thailand that involved support of a venture capital company. This is during the time frame that Obama's mother was employed by USAID

During the 1960's BIC was also involved with the CIA in domestic issues. James Kunen was a Columbia University student when he got involved with Students for a Democratic Society (SDS) who later wrote a book "The Strawberry Statement". He was part of the group that started a riot and took over the university in 1968. He describes how a person from BIC came to their strategy meeting for the upcoming 1968 riots in Chicago. He offered to finance the demonstrations telling "us to make a lot of radical commotions so they can look more in the center as they move to the left". He says they 'tried to buy up a few radicals...and decide how our lives are going to go". "These are the guys who wrote the Alliance for Progress and "are the left wing of the ruling class". He claims the money to finance the riot was coming from Esso (the Rockefellers).

Robert Gibbs, the White House Press Secretary, informed reporters in February of 2010 that no questions regarding Obama's employment at Business International Corporation were allowed.

The following year Obama left BIC and was employed by the New York Public Interest Research Group (NYPIRG). NYPIRG is a non-profit, student directed, environment and government reform organization which trains students in activism. NYPIRG currently has 20 college campus sites; each office has one full-time staff organizer and many student volunteers. In 1985 Obama became a full time organizer at the City College in Harlem. As an organizer he educated and mobilized student volunteers while convincing them about the importance of public projects. At NYPIRG he was trained in advocacy skills, public speaking, and how to structure campaigns. He worked on issues of mass transit, increasing voter participation, support of higher education, and the benefits of environmental justice. He is cited for contributing to the rebuilding of New York's mass transit system and overseeing voter registration at City College. He drove students to Washington D.C. to lobby for the Higher Education Reauthorization Act and led a letter writing campaign to public officials to provide funding for higher education. He led a protest against a municipal trash incinerator and raised awareness on the benefits of recycling in New York. Currently NYPIRG is advertising to hire students and recent graduates to work (or volunteer) at their community outreach program. The positions are described as an opportunity to fight for environmental preservation and social justice by fundraising and organizing citizens into a powerful political voice.

> Dr. Thomas Sowell, sociologist from Stanford University, "What does a community organizer do? What he does not do is organize a community. What he organizes are the resentments and paranoia within a community, directing those feelings against other communities, from who either benefits or revenge are to be gotten, using whatever rhetoric or tactics will accomplish that purpose."

In 1980, Gregory A. Galluzzo and Mary Gonzales created an organization called United Neighborhood Organization of Chicago (UNOC) after leaving the Industrial Areas Foundation (IAF) founded by Saul Alinsky. UNOC is a service organization of community leaders and local priests using Alinsky strategy to create a power base and address local issues. Their primary issue was helping illegal aliens obtain amnesty and citizenship. In 1982 the pair decided to create their own activist group Gamaliel Foundation. The couple needed to find an activist with experience in community organizing. They found JERRY KELLMAN from the Calumet Community Religious Conference (CCRC) in the south Side of Chicago. Kellman trained Galluzzo and Gonzales to become better organizers, and in exchange they supported his work which enabled Kellman to concentrate on forming his own group named Developing Communities Project (DCP).

The GAMAMALIEL FOUNDATION is an umbrella group of church based community organizations which empower the poor to push for economic redistribution. The organizers do not appear to be radical, they dress in conventional clothing, and press for common sense solutions. They advocate collective action for public programs. They talk about social change to create a more democratic society. Funding comes from Catholic Campaign for Human Development, the Bauman Family Foundation, the Carnegie Corporation, the W.K. Kellogg Foundation, Public Welfare Foundation, and the George Soros funded Open Society Institute.

It was decided that Gamaliel needed a black organizer to relate to the residents on the South Side of Chicago, so ads were put in newspapers across the country. In 1985 Obama answered an ad Jerry Kellman submitted in the New York Times looking for a community organizer. After the interview Kellman gave him $2,000 to purchase a car to move to Chicago plus a $10,000 to $13,000 per year salary (minimum wage at the time was $3.35 per hour or about $8,000 per year). Obama wrote about Kellman in his book, “Dreams”, but Kellman was renamed Marty Kaufman. Kellman called MIKE KRUGLIK to teach Barack the Alinsky method of organizing. Both Kellman and Kruglik had been trained at the Industrial Areas Foundation (IAF), a training center founded by Saul Alinsky. The DCP was split into three areas, Obama directed the South Side of Chicago, Kruglik to direct the Suburban Action Conference, and Kellman led in Northwest Indiana. Galluzzo was appointed as Obama’s consultant.

The WOODS FUND supplied $36,000 to start DCP. The Woods Fund was founded by the Woods family that owned a coal company. The coal company supplied power to the Commonwealth Edison. The CEO and President of Commonwealth Edison was Thomas Ayers, father of Bill Ayers. Ayers was a friend of Mayor J. Daley. Daley formed the organization Chicago United after the 1968 riots. The Chicago riot was organized, in part, by Students for a Democratic Society (SDS), the Bill Ayers radical group. Tom Ayers was on the Chicago United Board. Mayor Harold Washington asks Tom Ayers to set up an educational reform program. Tom Ayers contacts the Woods Fund. The Woods Fund has two purposes that it supports; community organizing and the creation of public workforce developing policies. Tom Ayers formed Alliance for Better Chicago Schools (ABCS) financed by the Woods Fund. Bill Ayers (SDS and Weathermen Underground) helped organize ABCS and he **was the contact person for ABCS**. Tom Ayers remained active with the project. Obama worked on school reform at DCP. DCP was a member of ABCS

This can be stated another way. Educational reform was wanted. Two foundations provided seed money to community organizations to agitate the citizens to demand change. In this case it was the Woods Fund and the Wieboldt Foundation. (The Wieboldt Foundation's mission is to fund grassroots community organizations to empower the local neighborhood residents.) The neighborhoods demand the change, but have no plan. However there already was a plan, but the activists now believe that they instigated it. The people who had the plan use the demands of the manipulated citizens to get more money (from other foundations or taxes) for themselves and for the program they designed.

In this situation ATT, Chicago Community Trust (Tom Ayers), Joyce Fund, and McArthur Foundation came together with the Community Renewal Society (Tom Ayers) where the plan was designed and enacted. The people with the money (and the plan) used the activists (and its neighborhood residents) to create the demand for a new program which gave them more power over the people. Chicago School Reform Act became law late 1988 which requires Local School Councils and abolished local school boards. The school system now has a program called Designs for Change. Currently, Designs for Change provides workshops and runs elections for Local School Councils. Members of the Local School Councils need no experience, no formal education, and citizenship is not required.

So it is possible, or probable, that Barack Obama met and knew both Tom and Bill Ayers while he worked at DCP back in 1985. I think probable, as Bill Ayers was the contact person for ABCS who gave the grant money to DCP for school reform activist activities.

Obama's work with DCP was widely recognized as the Times wrote, "Obama's task was to help the South Side residents press for movement". They also quoted Madeline Talbott, the leader of Chicago ACORN, "He got people to vote with their feet". "At one time…she initially considered Obama a competitor", the article continued; 'but she became so impressed with his work that she invited him to help train her staff." National Review Online stated, "Part of Obama's work, it would appear, was to organize demonstrations much in the mode of radical groups like ACORN". Obama wrote in "Dreams", "Change won't come from the top, I would say. Change will come from mobilized grass roots. That's what I'll do. I'll organize black folks. At the grass roots. For change." He stayed with DCP until 1988 when he was admitted to Harvard Law School.

Mike Kruglik, years later, worked at Camp Obama training supporters in the Alinsky method during the Presidential campaign. Jerry Kellman also helped form ACORN that Obama was connected with when he returned to Chicago.

> Admission to Harvard Law School is very competitive as the school only accepts 555 students out of approximately 7,000 applicants. The current annual cost to attend is about $35,000. Applicants must submit transcripts of all academic work; submit two letters of recommendation, and a personal statement. All applicants must take a Law School Admission Test (LSAT). Admissions officers consider grade point averages, plus the letters and test scores; or admission can be based on ethnicity, cultural background, and life circumstances. It is not known how Obama had the finances to pay for college as his college records are sealed.

A person who helped instruct Barack in the Alinsky methods at DCP was JOHN McKNIGHT a professor at Northwestern University. McKnight worked with the militant group Nations Peoples Action. They were known to bus hundreds of angry protesters to the homes of business and government leaders demanding 'justice'. This group has intimidated families and destroyed property in their mission. McKnight is also a former director of ACLU. McKnight wrote a letter of recommendation for Obama to Harvard.

Another person who claimed to recommend Obama to Harvard Law School was attorney Perry Sutton (who represented Malcolm X and the Black Panthers) a media mogul for black owned radio stations. He was a Manhattan Borough President for 12 years and a mayoral candidate for New York City in 1977. Mr. Sutton was interviewed for a television show in March 2008. He stated he was introduced to Obama by Dr. Khalid al-Mansour about 20 years ago. Sutton claimed that al-Mansour asked him to write a letter of recommendation, which he said he was glad to do. Mr. Sutton said that al-Mansour was raising money for Obama's schooling.

DR.KHALID AL-MANSOUR was born Donald Warden and changed his name when he became a Muslim. He was a friend of Bill Ayers when he was a Black Panther before he changed his name. Al-Mansour is a Muslim, Black Nationalist, strongly anti- Israel, and business partner to Perry Sutton. He was a mentor to Black Panthers' Huey Newton and Bobby Seale. It is not known how Barack Obama met al-Mansour, but he did give a speech at Columbia University when Barack was a student. Al-Mansour is a friend of Obama's former instructor Edward Said from Columbia. He is also an advisor to Saudi Prince al-Waleed bin Talal and attorney for OPEC. Prince bin Talal is the man who sent Rudi Giuliani the $10 million check after 9-11 when the Twin Towers were brought down. Giuliani returned the check. Prince bin Talal also sent Harvard a check for $20 million for Islamic studies.

Barack Obama denies this story and says he does not know al-Mansour. It has been reported that the Obama has never claimed a tax deduction for student loans on his income tax forms.

Barack didn't seem to have close friends at Harvard claiming he was a loner when he attended there. A professor who does remember him was Charles Ogletree. He stated Obama was a smart student who had a thirst for knowledge. He said Obama often participated at the Saturday School Program that Ogletree started for minority students. He mentored both Barack and Michelle who had attended Harvard earlier.

CHARLES OGLETREE was the attorney who later represented Professor Gates who was a participant in the "beer summit' with Obama and the policeman that arrested him. In another high profile case Ogletree represented Anita Hill who claimed that Supreme Court nominee Clarence Thomas had sexually harassed her. Professor Ogletree has ties with the Black Panthers. He edited a Black Panther newspaper called 'The Real News' and attended most of the trial of Black Power activist Angela Davis. In 2000 he was a member of the Reparations Coordinating Committee and served as their co-chair. This committee intended to bring a law suit to obtain reparations for descendants of slaves. Charles Ogletree has remained friends with Obama.

It was revealed in March 2012 that Ogletree hid video of Obama supporting Professor DERRICK BELL at a rally held at Harvard. Obama is saying, "Open your hearts and minds to the words of Professor Derrick Bell.' Derrick Bell was the first tenured black professor at Harvard and a known racist.

He is remembered for saying "I live to harass white folks" Obama assigned books by Bell to his students at the University of Chicago.

Another professor that knew Obama at Harvard is LAURENCE TRIBE. Tribe recalls that Obama approached him with a request to be his research assistant. Obama helped him write an article explaining the connection of physics and constitutional law. Then he helped to write a book on abortion. Obama also took his class in constitutional law. In February 2010 Tribe was appointed to the Justice Department as Senior Counselor for Access to Justice. He worked on a project titled Access to Justice Initiative and traveled across the country to find areas where the justice systems could be improved. In October 2010 he sent a letter to Obama regarding Sonia Sotomayor about her Supreme Court nomination. He wrote, "Bluntly, she's not as smart as she seems to think she is, and her reputation for being a bully could well make her liberal impulses backfire and simply add to the fire power of the Roberts/Alito/Scalia/Thomas wing of the court". In November he announced he would leave his position due to of medical conditions connected to a benign brain tumor. He returned to his teaching position at Harvard.

At the end of Obama's first year he was elected President of the 'Harvard Law Review' a prestigious journal Harvard produces. There are no known articles or editorials that Obama wrote for "The Review", but this might be because his primary function was to edit articles that were submitted for publication. He is known to have written a letter to the President of Harvard stating "as someone who has undoubtedly benefited from affirmative action programs during my academic career…" Students and professors have said he was an eager listener and gave the impression he agreed with everyone. It was also noted that his speeches had more style than substance. There is very little information about his friends or acquaintances while at Harvard.

Several Harvard professors have been appointed to positions in the Obama administration. The list includes Larry Summers (Director of National Economic Council), Cass Sunstein (Director of Regulatory Affairs), Elizabeth Warren (Special Advisor to Secretary of Treasury of the Treasury Department on Consumer Financial Protection Bureau), and Elena Kagan (Supreme Court Judge).

Judge me by the people who surround me.

CHAPTER 8

★ ★ ★ ★ ★

Michelle

MICHELLE OBAMA has not only been a big influence on his life, she became his wife. Michelle LaVaughn Robinson was born on January 17, 1964 to Fraser Robinson II and Marian (Shields) in Chicago. Her father worked at the city's water plant and was the Democratic precinct captain in the South Side of the city. Her mother was a homemaker until Michelle completed high school, and then became employed as a secretary for Speigel's catalog store. Her brother Craig graduated from Princeton University in 1983 and is the basketball coach at Oregon State University. Michelle and her brother were very intelligent young students as they both skipped second grade. They lived in a second story apartment above the home of her aunt on Chicago's South Side. She had great-great-great grandparents on both sides of her family that were slaves

> Barack Obama's family also has history with slavery. Generations ago his mother's family owned slaves as reported in old census records and his father's family most likely participated in slave trade. Tribes in Kenya have a long history trading ivory, wood, and slaves with the Arab Muslims. Warring tribes would sell their prisoners; and it is reported the Muslims actively agitated conflict to cause the wars. The Luo Tribe, as well as surrounding tribes in the area, were involved in this trade.

Michelle attended Whitney Young High School graduating in 1981 as Salutatorian. Her classmate and still close friend is Santita Jackson. Santita is the oldest child of Jesse Jackson and brother of Jesse Jackson Jr. She currently has her own radio talk show, sang at the Obama wedding, and is the godmother of Malia. Michelle said that she knew the Jackson family very well as she spent much of her time at their home.

After high school she attended Princeton. While at Princeton she wrote her thesis titled, 'Princeton: Blacks in the Black Community.' It was about racial assimilation and racially insensitive practices at Princeton citing there were only five black tenured professors at the University. She said she was surprised that so many blacks choose to assimilate into the American melting pot. For research she sent out 400 questionnaires but received only 90 replies. She started her thesis by stating she was influenced by the definition of black "separationism" by Stokely Carmichael's 1967 book, "Black Power: The Politics of Liberation in America." Stokely Carmichael was a violent Black activist in the 1960's. She finished her paper with: "I had hoped my finding would help me to conclude that despite the high degree of identification with whites as a result of educational and occupational paths that black Princeton Alumni would still maintain a certain level of identification with the black community. However, these findings do not support this possibility."

She spent much of her time at the Third World Center, an organization for minority students at the University. In 1981 the student population was 1,141 students and only 94 were black. This most likely inspired her to write her thesis about her experiences on the campus at Princeton. Michelle graduated with a Bachelors Degree, cum laude, in 1985. She majored in Sociology and minored in African-American Studies.

After graduating from Princeton, Michelle entered Harvard Law School. She participated in demonstrations demanding more minority students and professors on campus. Michelle worked at the Legal Aid Department helping poor families with issues such as housing and evictions. One friend she met has followed her to the White House. This is Jocelyn Frye who is Michelle's policy and projects director and is on Obama's domestic policy team. Frye is married to Republican consultant Brian Summers. Michelle graduated in 1988 with a Juris Doctor Degree. Michelle passed her bar exam on her second try and obtained a law license for the state of Illinois.

Michelle got a position at Sidley Austin law firm in 1988. Sidley Austin is one of the oldest law firms in the world, the 6th largest in the United States and the 9th largest in the world. They are known for their securities practice and international trade practice. It has been reported that she may have interned there in the summer of 1987. Michelle did marketing and intellectual property practice handling transactional, anti-trust, and other matters. An interesting person also employed at Sidley Austin was Bernardine Dohrn, the wife of Bill Ayers. This couple formed the SDS domestic terrorist group in the 1960's. Bernadine had passed her bar exam but was denied a license because of her criminal past. Howard Trienens, a close friend of Tom Ayers, hired Bernadine. He admits that the firm often hires friends.

In 1989 Barack joined Sidley Austin as a summer intern and Michelle was assigned as his mentor. It is widely reported that he asked her out several times before she agreed to go on a date with him. On their first date they went to the movies to see 'Do the Right Thing' by Spike Lee and were embarrassed when they ran into somebody from work as they wanted to keep the date a secret. At the end of the summer Barack left to go back to Harvard and Michelle continued working at the law firm.

The year of 1991 presented many changes for Michelle. First her father died in March. As a young man he enjoyed boxing and swimming but was diagnosed with multiple sclerosis when he was about 30 years old. Even as the disease got worse and he needed two canes to walk he went to work to support his family. He was a role model for both Michelle and her brother Craig.

Then she got engaged to Barack Obama. They went to dinner to celebrate his passing the bar exam. Then dessert was served. The waiter brought the dessert and a tray with a one carat ring in a box. Barack asked if she would marry him and she said yes.

Later that year she interviewed for a position at Mayor Richard M. Daley's' office with Valerie Jarrett. Jarrett was impressed and offered her the job immediately. Michelle said she wanted to think it over and asked Jarrett to meet Barack. He wanted to know who was going to mentor Michelle and watch over her. So that night the three of them had dinner to discuss the position. After dinner Jarrett asked, "Well did I pass the test?" Michelle accepted the position.

I found this to be quite odd. Michelle applies for a job and is accepted. However, before taking the position her fiancée interviews the potential employer to see if she is the appropriate person to employ his future wife. The interview takes place at dinner outside the office of the employer, but the "employer" questioned whether or not "she" was acceptable. It appears to me that it was Barack who was deciding if the position Michelle was applying for would benefit his career. It would be interesting to find out what was discussed at the dinner table.

Michelle was an assistant commissioner in the city's Office of Planning and Development. Her job duties included addressing infant mortality, after school activities, immunization programs, plus possibly helping to trouble shoot for companies having problems with city bureaucracy. She accepted the starting salary of $60,000 which is reported as a large decrease in wages from her previous position at the law firm. The average wage in the United States in 1991 was $21,811, so the public service position paid approximately three times the national average. Barack was earning $12,000 at the time as a community organizer.

In 1992 (or 1991) she traveled with Barack to Kenya to meet his family before they got married. His Uncle Sayid (Said) Hussein Obama told reporters about this visit of his nephew and Michelle. He said Barack helped Grandmother Sarah carry vegetables to the market and Michelle would help the women carry water from the stream. Sayid reported that Barack enjoyed the local food and tried to learn some of the Lou language. Neighbors were quite surprised as Barack he got up early and jogged. Grandmother Sarah was very pleased Barack followed the African tradition of asking the family's permission to get married. Barack is very popular in the areas near Nyangoma- Kogelo where the family lives. The people follow the news about him and even name their oxen after him, as they have done in the past to honor Kenyan leaders.

Then in November 1992 she married Barack at Trinity United Church by Reverend Jeremiah Wright. She said her husband didn't promise her riches but their life would be interesting. Santita Jackson was the maid of honor and the best man was Malik, Barack's half brother. Her brother Craig walked her down the aisle as her father had passed away. Attending the wedding was her mother, Marian Robinson, Barack's mother Ann Sutoro, and his grandmother Madelyn Dunham. Michelle had a traditional ring while her husband had an intricately designed gold ring from Indonesia. Family in attendance included Auma Obama (Barack's half sister) and Rabbi Caper Funnye Jr. (Michelle's first cousin once removed). Friends that attended included Sohale Siddiqi (classmate of Barack at Occidental and roommate in New York), Muhammad Hasan Chandoo, and Wahid Hamid (Barack's friends from Occidental and companions on his trip to Pakistan in 1981), and Vinai Thummalapally (former classmate at Occidental, bundler for the presidential campaign and current Ambassador to Belize). Guests also included Loretta Augustine Herran, (Developing Communities Project leader), Cindy Moelis (Director of the President's Commission on White House Fellowship), and Penny Pritzker (a billionaire who was the financial chair of the presidential campaign). The reception was held at the South Shore Cultural Center.

The year of 1992 was a very busy year with travel to Kenya and getting married. It's a wonder that Barack had time to be employed as a Lecturer at the University of Chicago (he became a Senior Lecturer in 1996, was never a Professor and never received tenure), be involved with ACORN's Project Vote, and be on the founding committee of Public Allies.

In 1993 Barack left the board of Chicago's Public Allies. Michelle Obama left Mayor Daley's office, after 18 months of employment, and was hired to the newly created position of Executive Director for the Chicago Office of Public Allies. The Board of Directors consisted of three friends who had worked for Mayor Daley; Valerie Jarrett, Cindy Moelis, and Yvonne Davila.

Public Allies is a non-profit organization which identifies and develops the next generation of leaders from young people between the ages of 18 to 30. They are recruited from colleges, housing projects, and youth centers. Public Allies teach and develop skills for future careers in public sector work and community organizing skills. Public Allies promotes diversity and inclusion, and discourages working in the private corporate community. They are proud that 80% of their alumni have careers in public employment or are engaged in civil work to achieve social change. This organization believes social change always comes from the acts of many, and not the inspiration of a few, as when citizens come together they can advance the 'public good.' The first chapter was founded in Washington D.C. in 1992 so the Chicago chapter was active very early in the history of Public Allies.

Some critics of the organization describe Public Allies as government funded re-education camps and others call it boot camps for radicals. 'Investor Business Daily' stated that 'when not protesting, they staff AIDS clinics, hand out condoms, bail criminals out of jail, and help illegal aliens and homeless get welfare." Those that volunteer for this program receive $1,800 per month plus paid health and child care expenses. In addition there is a $4,725 award that can be used for student loans or for future educational costs.

Michelle Obama gave a speech on May 12, 2009 at a Corporation for National and Community Service event. She said this organization allows young people to pursue a career in public service and to invest in service. "This is a concept that is now a part of this culture." She stressed that now "all youth can serve, not just those who have the luxury of being wealthy". Michelle continued to say, "National Community Service is a link between government, non-profits, foundations, community organizations, and 'social entrepreneurs'." She further stated, "The President is counting on you to take this vision and make it a reality".

Barack Obama uses Public Allies as an example of how to create a national service group for the youth of this country. He calls it Universal Voluntary Public Service. This program has an estimated cost of $500 billion. Somehow, voluntary or trial government programs never seem go away but grow. Obama said, "We have got to have a civilian national security force that is just as powerful, just as strong, just as well funded as the military." I wonder why and what does a civilian national security force do? Or what is it meant to enforce?

Public Allies is government funded through Ameri-Corps and donations from George Soros (billionaire currency speculator and liberal activist), David Geffen (an openly gay billionaire in the movie and music industry), HUD, Fannie Mae, and Sallie Mae. Michelle claims working with Public Allies was the happiest time of her life.

Then, in 1993 Michelle Obama and Paul Schmitz became the original members of Asset Based Community Development (ABCD) at Northwestern University. John McKnight and Jody Kretzmann led ABCD. John McKnight was the person who trained Barack Obama in Alinsky tactics when he first became a community organizer. CEO Paul Schmitz said, "Michelle developed an unparalleled network of young activists". The purpose of ABCD was to train community organizers to change negatives into positives and then create a congregation centered coalition. The core principles of ABCD are:

- Knowledge is relational
- There is no immaculate perception
- Language is a moral choice
- Affirmative stories can be used to stretch the collective imagination
- Learning ABCD "language" is mandatory before you are allowed to use it

A great opportunity came in September of 1996 when she became the very first Associate Dean of Student Services and the Director of the University of Chicago Community Service Center. This is another position created for Michelle.

During this time Barack was the executive director of the Faculty-Student Committee on Volunteers (at the University of Chicago) that was chaired by Harold Richman. Richman recommended starting the University Community Services Center. This was happening just as Barack was about to be elected as State Senator in Illinois and he leaves the Committee on Volunteers. Michelle is then appointed as the director of this newly formed organization which was created with the help of her husband. Her new title was Dean of Student Services of University of Chicago Medical Center. The purpose of the organization includes developing an off campus federal work study and obtaining volunteer referrals. Her position involved promoting staff diversity and minority contracting. Another responsibility was to expand service opportunities for the students in the surrounding communities. This appears to coordinate with her position at Public Allies.

It was her responsibility to create workshops and training curriculum. She set up monthly discussions groups with topics of interest to the students. In 1997 she invited four guests to speak on juvenile delinquency; two of the four speakers were Obama and Bill Ayers. One of her volunteer projects for the students was to join the Obama for Senator Campaign.

In 1997 she got an additional position serving on the National Board of Directors of Public Allies. That's a lot of pay checks. In fact it totals to approximately $500,000 per year. This doesn't include the fact she sat on and got paid for sitting on the boards of the Chicago Council of Global Affairs and the University of Chicago Laboratory Schools.

So Barack Obama created a job for Michelle at the University of Chicago. She recruited volunteers for the community organizations that she and her husband were involved with and recruited volunteers for Barack's campaign. The University of Chicago promotes community service, but does it also hope to have influence with funding from a Senator?

I did not find that money was funneled to the University of Chicago while Obama was a State Senator, even though he became the Chair of the Health and Human Services Committee in 2003. He did promote granting $1 million for a pavilion for the University of Chicago Medical Center, but funding was denied. As U.S. Senator he got through a $2 million grant for brain trauma research of the military that was to be used exclusively for this

University. Then in 2009, the University of Chicago received $42 million for medical research from the 'stimulus package'.

Malia Anne Obama was born on July 4, 1998 and her sister Natasha (Sasha) was born June 7, 2001. Their parents do not give them birthday gifts, but do give them lavish parties or sleepovers. They do not receive Christmas gifts from their parents either. Santa Claus does give them 'seasonal gifts'. Barack Obama told 'People Magazine' in 2008 that they don't give their children these presents because they must learn "limits".

This reinforces speculation that the Obamas were not Christian. Muslims do not celebrate birthdays as it represents that another year has decreased. Those who believe the Obamas are Muslim cited the fact that the Obamas celebrated a non-religious Christmas at the White House. Spokesperson, Desiree Rogers, said that there was discussion as whether or not to have a nativity scene at the White House. The theme for Christmas was "Reflect, Rejoice, and Review". It was also noted the National Day of Prayer was canceled and they had a gala celebration of Ramadan.

In 2002 Michelle left her position of Associate Dean of Student services and in 2005 was promoted as University of Chicago Hospital's executive Director of Community and External Affairs. She got a large pay increase with her promotion. In 2004 her salary was $121,910 and was increased to $316, 962. This included a onetime signing bonus and a onetime mandatory payout from a terminated retirement plan. Working with her was Valerie Jarrett and Susan Sher. The year 2005 was also the year Barack became a U.S. Senator and she became a director on the board of Treehouse Foods. As a director she was a member of the Audit Committee and on the Nominating and Corporate Governance Committee of the Board of Directors.

Her time at Community and External Affairs wasn't without controversy. The University of Chicago Hospital is a non-profit corporation that receives large tax breaks in exchange for providing charity care. Michelle created the Urban Health Initiative (UHI). The purpose of UHI was to redirect and limit non-critical visits to the emergency room of Medicaid and uninsured patients. This would free up space for the well insured patients and more complicated health care. The program was criticized by some community organizations as 'dumping." These actions were criticized by a physicians' group called the American College of Emergency Physicians (ACEP). ACEP said "dumping" is illegal under the Emergency Medical Labor and Treatment Act. Community based health clinics increased but was said to be substandard and delivered inadequate treatment. However, patients were told they could have "free" shuttle service to and back from clinics.

David Axelrod was hired to promote the Urban Health Initiative. He used normal tactics to direct the community away from using the emergency room at the hospital. He utilized focus groups, branding, targeting, religious leaders, and the media with editorials to get out the message. Axelrod left UHI in 2007 to direct Obama's run for President.

One of the largest minority contracts involved Barack's employer and campaign contributor Robert Blackwell. The business Blackwell Consulting Services received a $650,000 grant for computer services. In March 2009, UHI was canceled and was put under review because of the many complaints that the hospital was in violation of the Federal Emergency Medical Treatment and Active Labor Law that prevents patient dumping.

In 2007 Michelle resigned from the board of Treehouse Foods. Treehouse Foods is a major supplier of Wal-Mart and Barack was criticizing the company's labor practices.

Michelle gave an opening speech at the Democratic convention on August 25, 2008. Her speech was designed to introduce her family and their values to the voters. She said she, and Barack, were raised with the same values which meant "that your word is your bond". She said that when they were dating Barack introduced her to his work of community organizing. Michelle told the audience about the time he stood up and said the words that stayed with her ever since. "He talked about the world as it is and the world as it should be." She continued thanking people who worked toward their dreams and continued, "All of us are driven by the simple belief that the world as it is just won't do…It's a belief Barack shares". Near the end of her speech she said, "We committed ourselves to building the world as it should be."

These words support Barack's statement on February 5, 2008, "We are the ones we have been waiting for". Then four days later, "Our time has come… Change is coming to America."

On January 9th, 2009 Michelle resigned from Community Affairs and Valerie Jarrett and Susan Sher left with her to join the White House staff. On January 14th the position of Vice President of Community and External Affairs was abolished.

As the First Lady at the White House, she began supporting the Health Care Bill by promoting healthy eating and exercise. The program "Let's Move" was announced by her with Kathleen Sebelius, Director of Health and Human Services, and Surgeon General, Regina Benjamin. "Let's Move" is a national obesity initiative directed primarily toward children. It is designed to become a coalition between the government, the community, the schools, the doctors, and the parents.

Michelle began advertising the "Let's Move" program across the country. She's been to pro baseball and football camps talking to children. Television shows she has been on include the Iron Chef, Larry King Live, and Sesame Street. Health fairs have been visited and she is advertising "Let's Move" in coordination with the Disney Company.

The Grocery Manufacturing Association, which represents over 300 food, beverage, and consumer products, had a visit from Michelle. She told the Restaurant Association that Americans are "programmed" to enjoy sugary, salty and calorie dense foods through advertising. They were told she wants to see smaller portions, less butter and less cream. She wants them to help "reprogram" personal tastes by serving more of "what we should have and not what we want". Michelle warned that voluntary efforts to reduce fats and calories are insufficient and too slow, and may mean more government intervention.

While in Alexandria she announced the city had already received $40,000 since 2009 to develop a plan to reduce obesity. The money came from a Stimulus Plan grant. The City of Baltimore has created a Food Policy Task Force. Is this the Food Police? I wonder how many cities and towns across the nation are taking 'Stimulus" money to tell us what to eat.

"Let's Move" is a $400 million program focused on healthy living with a goal of bringing down childhood obesity to 5% by the year 2030. The program has 70 recommendations directed toward the federal government, local leaders, private business, public schools, and parents. "Let's Move" list of suggestions include:

- Learning what effect state and local taxes have in the influence of calorie dense foods – (taxing 'unhealthy' food may be a reality in the near future)

- Supply economic inducements to increase the production of healthy foods – (more taxes)

- Improve federally funded early childhood programs – (more taxes)
- Educate parents – (federally funded?)
- Restaurants serve smaller portions and healthier options – (food police)
- Mandate restaurants & vending machines display calorie counts - (food police)
- Self regulation or federal regulation of the food and beverage industry advertising to children- (food police)
- Entertainment and media limit the licensing of popular characters to only healthy food and beverages - (controlling business decisions)
- Doctors monitor children's BMI – (more data for medical computers to be monitored by new Health Care Program)
- Health care providers provide counseling on dietary intake -- (more data to be monitored)
- Increase funding to public schools to improve nutritional education – (more taxes)
- Improve federal funding for public school lunches & breakfasts – (more taxes)
- Have school gardens (schools are closed during the growing season in most areas of the country)
- Promote recess and exercise breaks at public schools – (dictate school programs)
- Build schools where it is easy to use bicycles or to walk to school – (loss of local control of school and building decisions)
- Have businesses incorporate and encourage exercise breaks – (dictate business decisions)

How far government intrusion in personal decisions will get is still to be determined. The Little Village Academy public school in Chicago has decided that students cannot bring lunches from home unless they have a doctor's note. The school principal has decided that the cafeteria food is more nutritious than what parents can make at home. Therefore, unless a child has a medical condition that the school determines is sufficient enough to require a lunch packed at the child's home they must eat what the school prepares. For students that do not meet the qualifications for a free lunch the parents must pay $2.50 for each child every day for their meal. If a child will not eat the healthy food that is prepared at school they will go hungry. Then there is the New York City health commissioner who had an office party. The employees were told they could only drink water or low calorie beverages, could eat no fried food, and their bread had to be thin sliced whole wheat. San Francisco has presented a bill that fast food restaurants cannot include a toy in fast food meals that have more than 500 calories.

"For the first time, the nation will have goals, bench marks, and measurable outcomes that will help us tackle the childhood obesity epidemic; one child, one family, and one community at a time." A quote by Michelle Obama as she explains the benefits of "Let's Move".

Obviously she believes that parents are not capable for the decisions on how and what to feed their children. Then, as the health commissioner in New York City has shown, adults also are not capable of deciding what they can eat and must have a government official dictate what they can eat at an office party. How far will the people allow government to dictate their lives when they are told what we can eat (for our own good of course) before they rebel. If a vegetarian is put in charge of deciding our food choices, will we be told we can no longer eat meat? The question seems outrageous, but is it?

The First Ladies' clothing and style have been analyzed, admired, and criticized since Jackie Kennedy. It may have gone back longer than that but I'm not old enough to remember. Michelle is no different. She has been fashion conscious since she was young. As a teenager she purchased a Coach purse with the babysitting money she earned. Her style of clothing has been described as conservative, savvy, jock preppy, and fashionable. Many of her outfits are sleeveless to feature her much admired well toned arms. The media often mentions her wardrobe while covering her vacations.

Vacationing has been a large part of Michelle's life since moving to the White House. Beginning in 2009 until the fall of 2010 she has vacationed in

New York, Paris, Montana, Wyoming, Colorado, Arizona, Chicago, several trips to Martha's Vineyard, Hawaii, North Carolina, Los Angeles, Niagara Falls, Maine, Florida, Camp David, and Spain. Rules for vacations by the President and his family require them to reimburse for travel based on commercial rates and personal expenses. This does not include the actual cost of Air Force One or the First Lady's airplane. Nor does reimbursement include the cost of housing, food, and travel expenses of the Secret Service and additional security.

The most controversial trip was to southern Spain in August 2010. Michelle, with Sasha, went with a friend and her daughter. They rented 60 rooms at the five star hotel Marbella Villa Padierna. So this trip definitely had many more than three people traveling with her. Of course there is the Secret Service, the journalists and other media; but I would think that the media would arrange their own accommodations. The trip took place during her husband's birthday (he was vacationing in Chicago) and during the height of the national discussion about a mosque being built on a site that had been damaged on 9/11. There were pictures of her visit to King Juan Carlos and Queen Sofia, the beach she relaxed at, and even her trip to Granada to see the Alhambra Palace. This is a beautiful building built by Muslims when they last ruled Spain. The architecture and fine details tell the story of the tragedy of the return of Christianity. The media concentrated about the trip's cost (approximately $80,000 per day plus about $160,000 for air transportation) and the sensitivity of traveling abroad when so many people have lost jobs in America. What wasn't discussed was her trip to a mosque. The media was aware of her itinerary as she was photographed going to the mosque and reporters describing her apparel. She was wearing an expensive black and white off the shoulder blouse.

The Great Mosque of Granada is the mosque Michelle visited with her daughter Sasha. The mosque was build with some of the same controversy as the proposed mosque in New York. It was built in 2003, but the land was purchased in 1981. The people of the town had been opposed to the construction but "came around"; the initial resistance was explained as the people had a lack of knowledge about Islam. The mosque is a beautiful building built incorporating the designs from the Great Mosque of Cordoba. The building has a garden, a prayer hall, a library and conference rooms. It was financed by the Islamic countries of Libya, United Emirates, Malaysia, and Morocco. At the opening ceremony, in 2003, the spokesman for the Great Mosque of Granada said; "The mosque is a symbol of a return of Islam among Spanish people..." "It will act as a vocal point for the Islamic revival in Europe". I wonder if her non-publicized excursion had any connection to the Cordoba House to be constructed in New York City.

What the media ignored was not only where she went, but who was also in Spain at the same time. What wasn't mentioned was that Jesse Jackson Jr. was also in Marbella while Michelle was visiting. He stayed at a private home and not at the Villa that got so much attention. While he was there he met with Prince Salman bin Abdul Aziz, the Governor of Riyadh, and the brother of King Fahd of Saudi Arabia. The media in Spain reported that Michelle met with these men during her vacation. I wonder if it is coincidence that the day after she returns from Spain the United States announced plans to sell F-15 fighter jets to Saudi Arabia.

As mentioned Barack was in Chicago and his activities did not create much media attention while his wife was on her trip. He visited an auto plant and went to three fund raisers. One of the fundraiser was for Alexi Giannoulias who had the Senate seat that Obama previously had. The Giannoulias family owned the former Broadway Bank that loaned Tony Rezko $22 million for development projects and over $27 million to mafia members Michael "Jaws" Giorgano and Demitri Stavropoulos. Alexi Giannoulias was the senior loan officer when this loan was approved to run businesses such as a nationwide prostitution ring. Down the street (close-by anyways) Rod Blagojevich was on trial for attempting to sell this same seat.

This is the same week that Barack was having his Ramadan Dinner called Iftar. This is a meal that is eaten after dusk to break the day of fasting. At this dinner the President said, "But let me be clear...I believe that Muslims have the right to build a place of worship and a community center in Lower Manhattan". He further stated, "Muslims have contributed much to American life." He was telling America that he supported the building of the Cordoba House in New York. The Cordoba House is named for a city that Muslims conquered in 700 A.D. There was a second Iftar dinner held on September 7th for young Muslims, hosted by Hillary Clinton.

> This is the second Iftar that Obama hosted. The very first State Dinner hosted by the Obama administration was an Iftar on September 1, 2009. In his dinner speech he noted again how much the Muslim community have contributed to this country. (He never mentioned, in either speech, their contribution of bringing over the slaves they purchased from the tribal leaders in Africa so many years ago or terrorist activities against the American citizens). He

also voiced his support for the mosque that was proposed to be built in New York City at the Twin Towers site which many citizens opposed. The dinner for the Indian Prime Minister Singh, it was famously crashed by Michaele and Tareq Salahi, was also called the first State Dinner of the Obama administration. However that dinner was on November 24th, so it was the second first State Dinner, it does get very confusing.

Michaele and Tareq Salahi are a well known socialite couple from Virginia. Tareq previously sat on the board of the American Task Force for Palestine. The vice president and founder of the organization AYFP was Palestinian activist Professor Rashid Khalidi. Khalidi is a friend of Obama and PLO spokesperson. AYFP has ties to Hamas and Saudi Wahhabists. Tareq also runs a charity polo event called Courage Cup, and have frequent parties and wine tastings at their home. The couple is also known for not paying their bills and Virginia is looking into how charity funds were spent. Their home was in foreclosure and their car was repossessed..

The Bravo film crew brought the Salahi couple to the White House and filmed them as they entered the party. They were hoping to promote themselves for a reality television show. They claim they had e-mail correspondence with the Defense Department requesting an invitation. A marine announced them as they entered the event. The party crashers were discovered because Michaele put the event on her Facebook page. She must enjoy the company of famous people as she has a collection of pictures of her with other celebrities on Facebook. She has since left her husband and is dating guitarist Neal Schon from the band Journey.

This was not the first time that Obama met Michaele and Tareq. He is pictured with them at 'Rock The Votes' awards on June 9, 2005 when he was a Senator. In 2009 Hillary again had a second Iftar dinner that she hosted by video and again targeted the younger generation. President George W. Bush began having the Iftar dinners in 2002. It was an attempt to convince Muslims that this country was at war with terrorists and not a religion.

Michelle campaigned across the country during the 2010 elections. She urged people to vote for Democratic candidates so her husband could continue the agenda he started. Her campaign against childhood obesity also continued with an invitation to students from local schools to help with the fall harvest from the White House garden. Unfortunately, the soil from the garden has levels of lead because previous gardening at that location used sewage sludge as fertilizer.

Michelle, as honorary chair of the President's Committee on the Arts and the Humanities (PCAH), awarded groups for programs contributing to their communities with the arts. PCAH is a program that promotes the use of art to improve communities, a vehicle to learn about and celebrate cultural diversity and traditions, and to combine public and private support for the arts. PCAH is composed of tax funded groups from National Endowment for the Arts, the National Endowment for Humanities, the Institute of Museum and Library Services, and Sundance Institute founded by Robert Redford.

As the year 2010 ended Michelle left for Hawaii for vacation before her husband could join her which cost the tax payers additional money. Her vacations during 2010 were estimated to cost taxpayers $10 million. In 2011 she began her vacationing with a ski trip to Vail and in 2012 her first vacation was skiing in Aspen. Her new campaign is to give tax breaks to breast feeding mothers. What else will she become the expert on and tell the American people how to live their lives? Perhaps she is on fact-finding missions during all of her travels.

Judge me by the people who surround me.

CHAPTER 9

★ ★ ★ ★ ★

Rev. Jeremiah Wright and Friends

The summer of 1990 Barack Obama worked as a summer associate at the law firm of Hopkins and Sutter in Chicago. He also took the time to go to Los Angeles to take an eight day training course in the Alinsky method of organizing.

The year 1991 was also a busy and exciting time for Obama. First he graduated from Harvard, then moved to Chicago and joined a church. He got engaged to Michelle and started to write his book "Dreams from My Father: A Story of Race and Inheritance." Obama got an unexpected job offer in Chicago before he graduated which he declined. Then on December 17, 1991 he was admitted to the Illinois Bar.

> In 2008, he voluntarily retired his law license as a formal complaint had been received regarding Obama falsifying information on his license. Obama stated that he had used no other names, which was false as he had also been known as Barry Soetoro. Then question #33 asked if he had any outstanding tickets, which he answered negatively, when in fact he had at least 17 unpaid parking tickets during the years of 1988 to 1991. After a person voluntarily retires his license the Illinois Bar Association will not take any action. As Andy Martin said to CitizenWells on September 21, 2008, "They can't punish someone who has resigned, which is why so many corrupt lawyers in Illinois resign before they are disbarred."

David Brint, vice president of Rezmar, read a newspaper article about Barack Obama as president of the Harvard Law Review prior to his graduation. The article said that he was interested in low income housing, so Brint called Obama to ask him if he would be interested in working for Rezmar. Brint arranged for Obama and Tony Rezko, the owner of Rezmar, to meet. Obama declined the job offer, but the two men and their wives became friends. The couples would socialize or go out for dinner and even took a trip to Lake Geneva, Wisconsin together to visit at Rezko's home.

'Free South Africa' was the sign in front of Trinity United Church in 1988 that lured Obama into the church one Sunday. He was looking for a church he felt comfortable with as the people in his community kept asking him what church he belonged to. 'Audacity to Hope' is the sermon he identified with that kept him coming back. This is the sermon that inspired Obama's title of his second book "Audacity of Hope". Rev. Wright said it was the intellectual discussions they had between two college educated individuals that made them friends.

REVEREND JEREMIAH WRIGHT was born on September 22, 1941. His father was a Baptist minister and his mother a highly recognized teacher and vice principal. He attended Central High School in Philadelphia graduating in 1959. For two years he went to Virginia Union University and was a member of a Zeta Chapter fraternity called Omega Psi Phi, Inc. Then, in 1961, Wright joined the Marines, assigned to the 2nd Marine Division; attaining the rank of Private 1st Class. He enlisted with the Navy in 1963 and was trained as a cardio pulmonary technician. He was part of a medical team that tended to President Johnson in 1966 after his surgery. In 1967, Wright attended Howard University in Washington D.C. studying English. He completed his Bachelor Degree in 1968 and his Masters Degree in 1969. Then he went on to earn a Master's Degree at the University of Chicago Divinity School. Wright competed his schooling at United Theological Seminary in Dayton, Ohio and received his Doctor of Ministry Degree in 1990. He studied with Samuel DeWitt Proctor who was a mentor to Martin Luther King Jr. Reverend Wright boasted in his church bulletin that he had a Master's Degree in the area of Islam in 19th century West Africa. Wright has seven honorary Doctorial Degrees. He is married to Ramah Reed Wright and they have five children. During the years of 1970 to 1975 he received a Rockefeller Fellowship. This grant is from the Fund for Theological Educations through the Rockefeller Foundation. The fund's mission is to support future pastors, and those that teach them, to renew the church and to serve the "common good".

Wright was a professor at numerous schools and a member on many Boards of Directors. When he became the Pastor at Trinity United Church of Christ in 1972 there were 250 members and only 90 of them were active participants. In 2008 he had the largest church with over 8,000 members in the mostly white United Church of Christ denomination. While at Trinity, Wright began 'Minister in Training (MIT) classes that are based on Black Liberation Theology that was started by Professor James Hal Cone.

> LIBERATION THEOLOGY started in the late 1960's in Latin America. It's based on Christian faith with an interpretation reflecting the suffering, the struggles, and the hope of the poor. The Catholic Church was the primary influence in the colonization of Latin America. Based on a proclamation of Pope Alexander in 1492, colonists felt it was their duty to spread the Catholic faith. The hierarchical structure in the communities began to resemble the Catholic Church that inhibited social mobility and democratic societies. Protestant missionaries began coming to Latin American countries, secularization was growing, as was the spread of communism. The Catholic Church lacked the number of clergy needed to serve the poor and the people believed the Church was involved in creating an unjust society. Revolutions started and the people grew militant. The Church wanted to unite everyone from peasants to professionals with income redistribution. They believed this could be achieved peacefully with discussions among the privileged.
>
> Theologians realized that the Church should not be influencing societies between Socialist and Capitalist governance. They began to rethink the idea of interpreting the Bible from the viewpoint of the poor, as they were doing using Liberation Theology in their mission work. Years ago Cardinal Joseph Ratzinger, the current Pope Benedict XVI, was concerned about the infiltration of the Catholic Church by Marxists through Liberation Theology. He spoke to Pope John Paul II about his concern, telling him that wherever the Marxist ideology of Liberation had been instituted a total lack of personal freedom developed. He may have realized the dangers because as a youth living in Germany he had to join the Hitler Youth Corp. He knew from personal experience that doctrines of supremacy based on race or nationality is dangerous. Ratzinger understood that Liberation Theology was a Marxist doctrine simply dressed up as Christianity. Cardinal Ratzinger was and is a very educated and knowledgeable man and recognized the techniques could be used to undermine his religion.

BLACK LIBERATION THEOLOGY is a humanistic doctrine of teaching the gospel to reflect the black community struggles under white oppression. The doctrine states white Christianity emphasizes individualism and divides the world into the sacred and the secular, the public and the private, and is committed to an idea of life in the world as it is to come. Black Liberation is based on life in the present and salvation is a physical liberation, not a spiritual one. Some associate Christianity with slavery not spirituality. The Muslim religion has a growing presence in the black community. Islam has a reputation of living what is preached, stressing discipline and personal integrity; while some Christians are observed drinking and partying after Sunday services are over. Muslims claim Islam was the original faith of Africans and Christianity was imposed on them as slaves. Some Muslim ideology has seeped into the teachings of Black Theology.

> Black Liberation perceives Satan as the power in the world that enslaves and demeans human beings. Black Liberation doctrine teaches the most evil and demonic experience a black person can endure is racism. Spiritual messages get little attention and Jesus is relevant in his role of an emancipator of the poor. Those who do not agree with Black Liberation Theology believe it is a doctrine that manipulates bitter black people with feelings of hopelessness and jealousy to rebel against white people, Orientals and the rich. They think it encourages black people to separate from the rest of American society and discourages people from working hard and being self reliant.
>
> James Cone wrote several books describing the tenets of Black Liberation Theology, the most well known are "Black Theology and Black Power", "A Black Theology of Liberation," and "For My People: Black Theology and the Black Church." He was highly influenced by Malcolm X, Black Power, and Martin Luther King Jr. during the civil rights movement. Cone interprets the gospels as Jesus helping the poor and the oppressed. He believes that God is not a concept for all people, but only to those being persecuted. In the 1969 book "Black Theology and Black Power" he wrote, "The time has come for white America to be silent and listen to black people." Other quotes from Cone include, "Marxism as a tool of social analysis can disclose the gap between appearance and reality; thereby helps Christians to see how things really are". Another quote, "Black Theology will accept only the love of God which participates in the destruction of the white enemy. What we need is the divine love as expressed in Black Power, which is the power

of black people to destroy their oppressors here and now by any means at their disposal." More quotes; "Together, black religion and Marxist philosophy may show us the way to build a completely New Society" and "Capitalism is economic slavery imposed on black Americans by whites". Cone is also quoted as saying, "I don't see any in (Obama's) book or in the (Philadelphia) speech that contradicts Black Theology. Obama simply sanded over the radical edges".

Cone writes and speaks frequently about 'hope' and calls it 'hope theology'. He is a contributing editor to Sojourners Journal that was founded by Jim Wallis, the current religious advisor to Barack Obama.

New members of Trinity United Church take a class that teach Black Theology. After completion of the class each person walks down the aisle and kneels before the cross to make a commitment to his faith. Obama describes this experience in June 2007, when he said; "I walked down the aisle, kneeled before the cross, and heard God's spirit beckon me. I submitted myself to His will, dedicated myself to discovering His truth, and carrying out His works."

The classes the new members take teach the Black Value System:

- Disavowal of the Pursuit of "Middleclassness".
- Pledge to make the fruits of all developing and acquired skills available to the Black Community.
- Pledge to Allocate Regularly a Portion of Personal Resources for Strengthening and Supporting Black Institutes.
- Pledge Allegiance to all Black Leadership who espouse and embrace the Black Value System.
- Personal commitment to embrace the Black Value System.

Education of members continues by teaching the commitment of the church:

- A congregation committed to ADORATION.

- A congregation preaching SALVATION.
- A congregation actively seeking RECONCILLATION.
- A congregation with a non-negotiable COMMITMENT TO AFRICA.
- A congregation committed to BIBLICAL EDUCATION.
- A congregation committed to CULTURAL EDUCATION.
- A congregation committed to HISTORICAL EDUCATION OF AFRICAN PEOPLE IN DIASPORA. (ancestral homeland or people separated or scattered from their ancestral homeland)
- A congregation committed to LIBERATION.
- A congregation committed to RESTORATION.
- A congregation working toward ECONOMIC PARITY.

Trinity United and Reverend Wright have many connections with Muslims and the Muslim religion. Wright is a friend of Louis Farrakhan who had his picture on the cover of the church's magazine 'Trumpet'. He traveled with Farrakhan to Libya in 1984 and met with Col. Muammar Khadafy (also spelled Khadafi, Qaddafi, Gadafi, and Gadafy). In 2008 Wright stated, "When (Obama's) enemies find out that in 1984 I went to Tripoli to visit (Khadafy) with Farrakhan a lot of Jewish support will dry up quicker than a snowball in hell". Wright has repeatedly stated Farrakhan will be remembered as a great leader of the 20th and 21st century. Among the persons who organized Farrakhan's 1995 Million Man March in Washington D.C. was Rev. Wright, Al Sharpton, and Barack Obama. Wright was scheduled to speak at the March, but couldn't get to the podium in time. Obama reflecting on the March said, "There was a profound sense that African American men were ready to make a commitment to bring about change in our communities and lives". It's been reported that Khadafy even called Farrakhan to congratulate him for his successful demonstration. In November 2007 Farrakhan received the 'Reverend Dr. Jeremiah A. Wright Jr. Lifetime Achievement Trumpeteer Award.

Wright received national attention when excerpts of his inflammatory sermons became public. On September 16, 2001, after the 9/11 attack, he said, "We have supported state terrorism against the Palestinians and black South Africans and now we are indignant because the stuff we have done overseas is now brought right back to our own front yards. American's chickens are coming home to roost." He preached, "Blacks should not sing God Bless America, But God Damn America." He calls this country the "US of KKK." "When Minister Farrakhan speaks, Black America listens." He described Jesus as, "a poo black man fighting the tyranny of white oppressors".

Books and copies of Wright's speeches are in the library of his church. When the public began questioning Obama about it, as he had been a member of the church for over 20 years, he claimed he never heard the statements the media published. Obama had previously praised Wright earlier as his mentor and spiritual advisor. After the media first exposed the sermons Obama defended his pastor stating, "I can no more disown (Wright) than I can disown my white grandmother." Then he cut ties with him and removed him from the African American Religious Leadership Committee of his presidential campaign. His said, "I vehemently disagree and strongly condemn the statements that have been the subject of controversy".

A confused Barack Obama said, "I don't think my church is actually particularly controversial."

This is actually understandable because this is the only Christian church he has ever been a member of. When Obama attended the Unitarian Church they honored the environment and social justice. At Trinity United Christian Church the emphasis seems to be about racial justice, plus censoring the white race, the Jewish religion, and the wealthy. Members identify with the oppressed and demonize oppressors.

In February 2008 Wright retired from Trinity United Christian Church. The church took out a $1.6 million mortgage for him and a $10 million loan as a line of credit. His retirement home is quite large at 10,340 square feet and a four car garage. It has four bedrooms, the master bedroom has a whirlpool, and there is an elevator, a butler's pantry, plus an exercise room. The house also a spare room that will become either a theater room or will have a pool. The house is built in a gated, mostly white, community in Tinley Park.

I remember an old saying; “"Do as I say, not as I do”.

Wright wasn’t ready to leave the limelight. He gave a speech on April 27, 2008 at the Detroit chapter of the NAACP. The theme of his talk was “A Change is Gonna Come”, and he spoke about racial differences. This is the topic that Obama was trying to avoid. This trip was sponsored by the American-Arab Anti-Discrimination Committee. This group is openly pro-HAMAS and pro-Hezbollah. Its chapter is headed by former Islamist terrorist Imad Hamad. Hamad is a suspected member of the Marxist-Leninist terror group called Popular Front for the Liberation of Palestine. For two years the U.S. Immigration and Naturalization service tried to deport him due to terrorist connections.

The next day he spoke before the National Press Club. “This is not an attack on Jeremiah Wright. This is an attack on the black church.” Wright defended himself, dismissed Obama’s criticism, and as a joke, said he would consider the office of vice president. As for Obama, Wright said, “Politicians say what they say and do what they do because of electability.”

Judge me by the people who surround me.

CHAPTER 10

★ ★ ★ ★ ★

Project Vote and Rezko

In 1992 life for Obama had many new beginnings. This is the year he got married to Michelle after their trip to Kenya. He took a part time job as lecturer at University of Chicago and worked for Project Vote. Then Obama took a trip to Bali. In 1993, he hired on with the Law firm of Davis, Minor, Barnhill and Galland.

Obama became a part-time lecturer at the University of Chicago Law School in 1992 and remained there until 2004. He has been called a professor but never attained that status, per Marsha Ferziger Nagorski the Assistant Dean for Communication and Lecturer of Law. He only taught one class from 1992 to 1996. When he became a Senior Lecturer he taught three classes. He was always a part-time employee. After 1996 he did teach classes that professors normally do, but he never had any research obligations which are required by professors. The University gave him a fellowship and an office to write his book, "Dreams from My Father".

The Governor of Illinois, Jim Edgar, refused to accept voter registrations mailed in by postcard without identification. ACORN approached Obama to represent them in a lawsuit and he accepted. He won the case. Illinois appealed and lost the appeal in 1995, and Barack Obama was the lead attorney on that case too.

In 1992 Sandy Newman, the founder of PROJECT VOTE located in Washington D.C., decided to start a chapter in Chicago. He came to the city looking for an activist to run the project and after asking at different activist organizations he kept hearing the name Barack Obama. At that time Obama was working with community groups on the West Side of Chicago and writing his book which was under contract. Obama decided he would put his other work aside and accepted the offer. In April Obama became the Director of the Chicago chapter of Project Vote. He worked there for seven months and achieved more than Newman ever expected. More new voter registrations were collected in Chicago than any previous Project Vote leader in the country. Obama had 22 steering committee members to help him. These members included Rev. Wright, Fr. Pfleger, Madeline Talbott, (leader of Chicago ACORN) and her husband Keith Kelleher (the leader of SEIU Local 100).

> Project Vote is a national non-partisan, non-profit 501(c) (3) organization with the mission to empower, educate, and mobilize low-income, minority, youth, and other underrepresented voters. They develop state-of-the-art voter registration systems and get-out-the-vote programs. The developer of Project Vote is HEATHER BOOTH. Heather Booth is the co-founder of Midwest Academy that teach activists the Alinsky method of organizing. She is also the wife of Paul Booth the co-founder of Students for a Democratic Society (SDS). With the help of service and community organizations, they have registered over 5.6 million people in low-income and minority communities since 1994. Project Vote attempts to enforce and expand public policy which increases access to voting. The organization investigates and, if they deem necessary, take legal action to protect the rights of voters. The Public Agency Registration Program works with Project Vote and DEMOS to give technical assistance and document non-compliance with voting laws.
>
> Project Vote is an arm of ACORN and the program has had numerous problems with fraud. This is an obvious result of not requiring identification when registering or voting. Project Vote registers persons to vote, turns in the registrations by mail, and the newly registered voters can return the ballot in the mail. States have limited powers to clean out the voter rolls of individuals who are deceased, have moved, or are felons. These registrations are referred to as 'phantom voters'. In 2000, Indiana stated that their voter rolls had 'hundreds of thousands' of these phantoms voters. In 1998 one Project Vote contractor, a single mother, was caught completing over 400 registrations herself. She used fake names and non-existent addresses or addresses of businesses, even empty lots. Project Vote dismissed the numerous cases of fraudulent registrations as the result of a "few bad apples".

Obama's strategy was to set up a network to obtain the maximum number of registrations. He set up block captains, trained them, and then trained 700 deputy registers. He started a media campaign that saturated the air waves with the black owned radio company Brainstorm Communications. Newspapers ran editorials and minority owned McDonald restaurants allowed registers on site. Brainstorm Communications donated thousands of dollars to the project, as did various unions and the Clinton/Gore campaign drive run by Bobby Rush.

Over 150,000 new registrations were obtained from mostly black and low income minorities. For the first time in Chicago, the 19 primarily black voting wards had more voters registered to vote than the 19 primarily white wards. Carol Mosely Braun was elected to the U.S. Senate as a direct result of the newly inspired and energized voters. Politicians in Chicago definitely took notice of the increase of voters and the influence these voters had.

It was not only the politicians that took notice. One person who noticed was Johnnie Owens who left Friends of the Parks to join Obama at DCP. Others included Jean Rudd the executive director of the Woods Fund, which was the first foundation to underwrite Obama's work at DCP, and Madeline Talbott a leader of ACORN.

> PROJECT VOTE, an ACORN subgroup, was involved in 1996 in an activity called Teamstergate. Teamstergate was a conspiracy to embezzle money from the Teamster treasury. These monies were then laundered through organizations and returned as part of a re-election fund for Teamster President Ron Carey. Persons involved with the money laundering include AFSCME president Gerald McEntee, SEIU president Andy Stern, AFL-CIO president John Sweeney, and UMW president Richard Trumka.

After getting married to Michelle, the couple went to Bali for either several weeks or several months depending on the report. Obama had received an advance in 1990 from Poseidon, division of Simon and Schuster, an amount between $125,000 and $150,000 to write his book. The book was to be titled "Journeys in Black and White" and was due on June 15, 1992. A booklet promoting the book was discovered by Andrew Breitbart's Big Government. The booklet stated "Barack Obama, the first African American president of the Harvard Review was born in Kenya and raised in Indonesia and Hawaii." Soon after he got married, Poseidon canceled the contract and requested the money back as the book had not been written. The Obama's claimed poverty and his agent, Jane Dystel, was able to get him an advance of $40,000 from Times Book, a division of Random House. The couple went to Bali in 1992 or 1993, to get away and to have time to write. The book, "Dreams from My Father", was published in 1995.

Then in 1993 Obama took a job with Davis, Miner, Barnhill, and Galland. The law firm represented developers, primarily non-for-profit groups sometimes known as slum landlords. Obama told Miner, when interviewing for the position, that he was more interested in learning the political lay of the land than in the job itself. This is apparent as he worked for the firm from 1993 until 2004 and handled only 30 cases. In fact, he had total billable hours during that entire time of only 3,723 hours. A full time job of 40 hours per week is 2,080 hours in a single year. JUDSON H. MINER (who hired Obama) was a former classmate of Bernardine Dohrn, in 1967, at the University of Chicago. Miner and Dohrn were both members of the Anti-Vietnam War Campaign. He was also the legal counsel for Mayor Harold Washington. Obama wanted to learn from Miner how Washington was able to play the political field to get elected as mayor.

What he learned is that Washington depended on grassroots organizations to have voter registration drives (he brought in over 100,000 registrations) and get-out-the-vote volunteers. He ran with the message, "Together We Can Make a Difference". The Democratic party had three primary candidates; two were white and Washington was black. The white voters evenly divided their votes between the two white candidates and the black voters voted exclusively for Washington, giving him the majority. After winning the Democratic primary he went on to win the election.

ALLISON DAVIS left the law firm in 1998 when he invested in government subsidized low income housing projects with Tony Rezko. They also built upscale homes in the Kenwood neighborhood of Chicago. All legal work for their joint venture was done at his former law firm now called Miner, Barnhill, and Galland. Mayor Daley was helpful in getting them favorable deals and they grew to become Chicago's top developer. It was also helpful that he had been appointed by Daley to be on Chicago's Planning Commission. While Davis was employed with the law firm he was a member of the Woodlawn Preservation and Investment Group which was connected to Rezmar Corp. Davis was also a fund raiser and had contributed to Mayor Richard Daley, Governor Blagojevich, and Barack Obama. Davis was appointed to serve on a state pension board that controls billions of dollars in 2004. He was appointed by Blagojevich with the recommendation of Rezko. Then in 2005 Davis and Robert Vanecko (Mayor Daley's nephew) started DV Realty to redevelop neighborhoods. They requested, and received, $68 million in retirement funds to invest in their company that planned to upgrade properties near the proposed, but failed, 2016 Olympics site. They lost over $1.5 million of the retirement funds but Davis and Vanecko are guaranteed about $8.4 million in management fees before 2015. A grand jury investigation was started to determine how the pension funds got invested in DV Realty. Davis was also part of the Governor Blagojevich pay-to-play trial listed as individual BB.

ANTOIN 'TONY' REZKO was born in Syria in July 1955 and moved to Chicago after graduating from college at age 19. He earned his undergraduate and Master's Degree from Illinois Institute of Technology Center in the late 1970's. Rezko later designed nuclear power plants for an engineering company and designed roads for the Illinois Transportation Department. He got into the real estate business by buying empty lots, developing single family homes, and investing in fast food restaurants; mostly in low income black neighborhoods. Rezko made money rehabilitating low income housing with government grants. He financially backed politicians that helped him get grants.

In 1983 he was approached by Jabir Herbert Muhammad to support Harold Washington in his run for mayor. Jabir was the manager of Muhammad Ali, the boxer, and son of the late leader of the Nation of Islam, Elijah Muhammad. In 1984 Rezko worked for J.H. Muhammad's company called Crucial Concessions. Rezko obtained food contracts at the beaches on Lake Michigan and at South Side parks after Harold Washington become mayor. He also became the executive director of the Muhammad Ali Foundation and was able to travel around the world getting endorsements. In 1997 he obtained the Panda Express Restaurant at O'Hare Airport with a minority set aside program. In 2005 it was discovered that Muhammad was a front for Rezko and he lost the contract. Then in 2008 Muhammad sued Rezko stating Rezko dealings caused Muhammad to be swindled out of his home and business.

In January 1989 Rezko joined Daniel Mahru and founded a real estate developing and restaurant holding company named Rezmar Corporation. They were able to make deals to rehab 30 buildings, or a total of 1,025 apartments, with over $100 million in tax dollars and bank loans. Neither Rezko nor Mahru were responsible to repay these monies. Rezmar contributed $100 toward each project but received 1% interest as general partner to hire a management company. They contracted Chicago Property Management that just happens to be owned by Rezko and Mahru. Rezmar also got almost $7 million in development fees. In 1998, when his company's value was $34 million, Rezmar began purchasing land and old factories in Chicago, turning them into upscale condominiums, and invested in restaurant franchises. He was named the Entrepreneur of the Decade by the Arab-American Business and Professional Association.

Rezko was very good at picking political winners. He donated $117,650 and bundled over $1.44 million to Blagojevich's political campaigns. Patricia Blagojevich, Rod's wife, made over $38,000 as Rezko's real estate agent. After Blagojevich became governor Rezko made recommendations to have his family and business associates assume state appointments. One of his associates, Stuart Levine was charged with demanding kickbacks.

Rezko first met Obama in 1990 or 1991 when he offered Obama a job. Although Obama turned down the job, he did take a position at the law firm Rezko used for his legal work in 1993. In 2003 Rezko held fund raisers and contributed $14 million towards Obama's Senate campaign. In 2005, Obama bought a home in the Kenwood District of Chicago for $1.65 million. It was $300,000 below the asking price, but it was the highest offer on the property. The property owner had an adjoining piece of property that he wanted to sell at the same time, but the Obama's could not afford both properties. Mrs. Rezko, on the same day, put an offer on the adjoining property for the listed price of $625,000. Both properties closed on the same day as required by the seller. Obama has insisted this was not a coordinated effort; but it is one heck of a coincidence. At some time in 2006, Obama purchased a 10 foot strip of adjoining land from Mrs. Rezko for $104,500. Mrs. Rezko then sold the remaining property to Michael Sreenan, a business attorney for her husband, for the amount of $575,000. Sreenan has listed the property for sale for an amount of $950,000 to $1.5 million.

It might be another coincidence, but it was only 23 days before Obama purchased his mansion that Rezko was wired $3.5 million from Nadhmi Auchi. Obama met Auchi about one year before at a dinner in honor for Auchi hosted by Rezko. Senator Emil Jones also had the honor of being a guest at the affair. Later that year Rezko held a reception for Audi that both Barack and Michelle attended. Auchi is a billionaire global arms dealer who smuggled arms for Saddam Hussein. He duped the United Nations in the Oil for Food program and smuggled arms into Iraq. The Pentagon said he was involved in fraud and prevented further entry into the United States. The Pentagon also stated they had credible evidence that Auchi was attempting to bribe foreign governments and individuals to change public opinion about America invading Iraq. At Auchi's request Rezko had lobbied to have his visa reinstated.

Obama estimated that Rezko contributed between $10,000 and $15,000 toward his Senate campaign and that he received approximately a quarter of a million dollars between 1995 and 2004. Obama has returned and/or donated to charity some of the money he received from Rezko and his associates. On October 13, 2006 he returned $11,500. On June 1st, 2007, he donated to charity $5,000, on June 7th he donated $16,500, on June 25th he returned $3,500, and on December 14th he donated another $5,000. On January 19th, 2008 Obama donated $40,350 to charity and on the 29th an additional $70,000.

Rezko's investments in Panda Express and Papa John's Pizza restaurants expanded each year. In 2002 he had acquired 26 restaurants in the Chicago area, 15 in Wisconsin and 7 in Detroit, Michigan. He received part of his financing for these projects from GE Capital. But in 2001 Rezko was getting behind in his payments and changed the name of Papa John's to Papa Tony's. He also got into several partnerships with the Iraqi businessman Nadhmi Auchi; this included a project worth $130.5 million. Rezko was put in jail in 2008 for failing to reveal he received $3.5 million from Auchi.

In 2006 he was charged, with Stuart Levine, in an extortion scheme called Operation Board Games. The two men attempted to extort millions of dollars from businesses that were trying to do business with the Illinois Teachers System Board and the Illinois Health Facility Planning Board. Rezko was found guilty of 6 counts each of wire and mail fraud and 2 counts each of corrupt solicitation and money laundering. He also had an arrest warrant issued in Las Vegas for passing bad checks and failing to pay $450,000 in gambling debts. Plus another casino filed a complaint regarding an additional $331,000 in gambling debt.

MARILYN KATZ is a good friend and poker playing buddy of Judson Miner. She is the owner of MK Communications, a public relations specialist, and registered lobbyist with the city of Chicago. Katz met Obama through her connections with the law firm.

She has close ties to Carl Davidson, Tom Hayden, Bill Ayers, and Bernardine Dohrn, as they were all founding members of SDS (Students for Democratic Society). She has known Ayers since he was 17 years old and is still his friend. Katz took an active part in the 1968 riots during the Democratic Convention in Chicago. During the trials of the Chicago Seven an undercover policeman testified that Katz was head of SDS 'security' during the riots. She showed her group a new weapon which was a ball of nails sharpened on both ends and either welded or soldered together in the middle. Testimony was that Katz gave instructions that these weapons could be used to throw or to put under car tires. During the riot Tom Hayden told the demonstrators, which numbered from 10,000 to 15,000, to move out of the park so that if they got gassed, the city of Chicago would get gassed. The group used tactics that caused the police to use force (gassing and use of batons) in front of the media and got national attention.

Katz continued her activist activities. She was a founding member of the New American Movement (NAM) in 1972. The mission statement included, "We admire and draw inspiration from many accomplishments from the Russians, Chinese, Cuban, and Vietnam revolutions…as representing, on balance, very positive steps forward in human history…we deeply value Lenin's contributions to revolutionary theory and practice and his treatment of nationalism and imperialism". The Movement ran schools teaching Marxism. Through the NAM organization, in 1977 or 1978, she started the pro-abortion group Reproduction Rights National Network. NAM merged in 1982 with Democratic Socialist Organization Committee to form the Democratic Socialists of America.

Somehow she went from a radical terrorist to a respected businesswoman. In 1983 she started her business MK Communications and has many Chicago accounts as her clients, these include:

- Chicago City Colleges
- Chicago Law Department
- Chicago Department of Aviation
- Chicago Department of Environment
- Chicago Department of Housing
- Chicago Department of Human Services
- Chicago Department of Planning and Development
- Chicago Department of Public Health
- Chicago Department of Public Works

- Chicago Department of Streets and Sanitation
- Chicago Intergovernmental Affairs
- Chicago Special Events
- Chicago Park District
- Chicago housing authority

In 1996 Mayor Daley laid off city workers but gave Katz, and other PR firms, 5 year contracts that paid as much as $5 million each. MK Communications has had many other clients including:

- ACLU
- Amnesty International
- Chicagoans Against War and Injustice
- Harold Washington '83 – '87 and his mayoral campaign
- Lloyd Doggett '84 senate campaign
- Human Rights Watch
- Illinois Campaign for Choice
- Illinois Coalition Against the Death Penalty
- The publication 'In These Times'
- MacArthur Foundation
- Mother Jones
- National Committee Development Initiative (for Rockefeller Foundation)
- UAW Local 719

- UNICEF
- Project Vote
- Habitat
- Joyce Foundation

In 2002 with friend, another SDS founder, Carl Davidson she began a new organization named Chicagoans Against War in Iraq (CAWI). This is the group that organized the event where Obama gave his 2002 anti-Iraq war speech. In 2003 CAWI, with other groups, trained 200 people to register voters.

Katz is the contact person for Chicagoans Against War and Injustice, and is on the United for Peace and Justice (UFPJ) Steering Committee. The UFPJ, with other groups, coordinated the Hamas supported Gaza Flotilla on May 3, 2010.

She is now working at the White House as a member of the Obama Administration National Finance Committee.

While employed at Miner Barnhill and Galland, Obama represented a case filed by ACORN on September 17, 1994. The case 'Buycks-Roberson v. Citibank alleged that Citibank was denying loan applications to minority applicants while approving similar loans to white applicants. The case was settled out of court. The case was based on the 1977 Community Reinvestment Act (CRA) created by President Carter. Clinton's administration threatened to vigorously enforce CRA against banks and mortgage lenders that didn't approve loans to minorities with poor credit history. Banks therefore approved the loans and sold them to Freddie Mae and Freddie Mac as they continued to loosen credit standards. On September 17, 2007, at NASDAQ, Obama said he thought giving loans to people who couldn't afford them was a good idea. He believed that by spreading the risk over the country, and the world, it would reduce the risk. This may be part of the plan of redistribution of wealth he campaigned on. Therefore, it means that persons who pay their own bills also get to pay the bills for those people who don't, by paying increased taxes.

Judge me by the people who surround me.

CHAPTER 11

★ ★ ★ ★ ★

Ayers and Dohrn

The Woods Charitable Fund was originally established in 1941 in Lincoln, Nebraska by Frank and Nella Woods. They advocated for the equal rights of minorities. The fund has evolved to advocate for welfare reform, affordable housing, quality public schools, against race and class disparities in the juvenile justice system, and for a tax policy used as a tool to reduce poverty. They support increased funding to public schools and wealth redistribution.

The WOODS FUND of Chicago was established in 1993, the same year Obama became one of its Board of Directors. He stayed on the board until 2002. William "Bill" Ayers, former SDS and Weatherman, served on the board from 1999 to 2002. Howard Stanback served on the board from 1994 until 2005. Stanback was connected to New Kenwood LLC that was founded by Tony Rezko and Obama's former employer Allison Davis. The fund allocated money to three main programs.

- Community organizations; financing the formation of grassroots organizations, staffed by volunteers, with goals to shape public policy with activism.

- Arts and Culture programs; financing those that combine artistic endeavors with left-wing activism.

- Public Policy programs; financing projects that aid low income individuals and families to achieve higher standards of living.

During the time that Obama was on the Board of Directors large grants were allocated to many organizations including the following:

- TIDES Foundation

- TIDES Center
- Gamaliel Foundation – Obama was former consultant and trainer for this foundation's Alinsky system of organizing
- Chicago Jobs Council
- Chicago Annenberg Challenge - founded by Bill Ayers and Obama was the first chair and president
- AGAPE Youth Development
- Center for Community Change
- Arab American Action Network (AAAN) – founded by Rashid Khalidi, friend of Obama and former PLO member
- Community Justice Initiative Center for Law and Human Services
- Grassroots Collaborative
- Center for Economic Justice
- Chicago Coalition of the Homeless
- Trinity United Church of Christ – Reverend Jeremiah Wright
- Chicago Rehabilitation Network
- Association of Community Organization Reform Now - ACORN
- Neighborhood Rejuvenation Partners – benefits Rezko and Davis
- National Center on Poverty
- Northwestern University Law School's Children and Family Justice Center - where Bernardine Dohrn works
- Midwest Academy – trains activists and organizers, founded by Heather and Paul Booth. Paul Booth is co-founder of SDS

This is just a sample of some of the organizations that the Woods Fund granted money to. One example of the amount of grants issued is the organization ACORN which received $190,000 between the years of 2000 and 2002. Many of these organizations made political campaign donations to Obama in later years.

The Woods Fund is the first known connection that Obama and Ayers had a relationship. Obama had previously tried to diminish the ties they have, but this is not the only board they both served on. During the ABC News Democratic Primary Debate on April 16, 2008, with George Stephanopoulos, the subject of Bill Ayers was brought up. Regarding Ayers, Obama said, "This is a guy who lives in my neighborhood, who's a professor of English in Chicago, who I know and who I have not received some official endorsement from. He's not somebody who I exchange ideas from on a regular basis. And the notion that somehow as a consequence of me knowing somebody who engaged in detestable acts 40 years ago when I was 8 years old, somehow reflects on me and my values doesn't make much sense." Hillary Clinton responded, "I also believe that Senator Obama served on a board with Mr. Ayers for a period of time, the Woods Foundation." Then Obama replied, "President Clinton pardoned or commuted the sentence of two members of the Weather Underground, which I think is a slightly more significant act than me…serving on a board with somebody for actions that he did 40 years ago".

WILLIAM 'BILL' AYERS was born December 26, 1944 in Glen Ellyn, a suburb of Chicago. His father is Thomas Ayers the former chairman and CEO of Commonwealth Edison, chairman of Northwestern University, and the Chicago Symphony. Bill attended public school as a child, but went to a prep school for the last two years of high school at Lake Forest Academy. He attended the University of Michigan and earned a Bachelor of Arts Degree in American Studies.

In 1965, Ayers heard a speech by Paul Potter, the President of SDS. Potter asked the audience this question, "How will you live your life so that it doesn't make a mockery of your values?" That year Ayers got involved in his first picket line against a pizzeria that refused to seat black customers. He was first arrested at a sit-in at a draft board and spent ten days in jail.

Ayers' first teaching job was for preschool students in a church basement called Children's Community School. The teaching method involved no grades or report cards, and encouraged cooperation not competition. The students called their teachers by their first names. When he was 21 years old he became the director of the school. The school closed in 1968 due to lack of funding. The children were not learning to read.

His known first girlfriend was Diana Oughten who was an active member of SDS and then joined the Weatherman with Ayers in 1969. In 1970 she died when the nail bomb she was making detonated destroying the building, killing two other friends, and two escaped alive. The bomb was designed to kill army officers at Fort Dix New Jersey. Oughten was identified by a fragment of her finger. This happened in a Greenwich Village townhouse in New York City.

Bill Ayers became very active with the New Left and SDS, becoming its leader in 1968 or 1969. He belonged to a sub group called the Jesse James Gang. In 1969 the Weatherman took control of SDS. Bill first met Bernardine Dohrn in 1967.

BERNARDINE DOHRN was born Bernadine Ohrnstein on January 12, 1942 in Milwaukee Wisconsin. Her father changed the family name when she was in high school. She was raised in Whitefish Bay, an upper middle class town near Milwaukee. Bernardine graduated from Whitefish Bay High School as a member of the National Honor Society, the treasurer of a Modern Dance Club, a cheerleader, and editor of the school newspaper. She attended Miami University for one year and then transferred to the University of Chicago where she earned a Bachelor of Arts Degree, with honors, in Political Science. In 1967 she graduated from the University of Chicago Law School with a Jurist Degree. After graduation she moved to New York to work at the National Lawyers Guild.

In the late 1960's Dohrn joined and became the leader of Revolutionary Youth Movement (RYM) a division of SDS. In 1969 she published a 16,000 word manifesto called "You Don't Need a Weatherman to Know Which Way the Wind blows". The stated goal of the manifesto was world communism with the destruction of U.S. imperialism and achieving a classless world.

Bernardine Dohrn was very busy in 1969 and she got arrested a lot too. In January she was at the University of Washington and a speaker during a Cuba teach-in (She made a return trip in 2007). Then in May she spoke of plans to attack college graduations across the country. In June, at a SDS conference, the RYM led a disruption that led to the SDS collapse. The RYM was then called Weatherman and Dohrn continued to be a leader. She traveled to Cuba in July and trained in guerilla fighting. She was met by Dr. Quentin Young when she returned and he debriefed her. In August she was arrested for possession of drugs in Chicago. The charges were dismissed as the judge said the police conducted an illegal search.

In September she was again arrested at an anti-Viet Nam rally during the Davis Cup tennis tournament. Later that month she was arrested in Chicago at a demonstration in support of the Chicago 8 trial. Then on October 9th she was again arrested during the Days of Rage. On October 31st a grand jury indicted 22 people for their involvement of a trial of 8 men that rioted during the Democratic Nation Convention in 1968. Dohrn was one of the 22 people indicted. In December 1969, after actress Sharon Tate and two of her friends were murdered by the Charles Manson clan, Dohrn said, "Dig it! First they killed those pigs and then put a fork in the pig Tate's belly (Sharon Tate was 8 months pregnant), Wild!" Years later Bill Ayers wrote that those words were meant to make a political statement, they were meant to agitate and inflame, it was really a joke, a stupid and tasteless joke. He said that Bernardine had tried to explain but reporters at the time dismissed her. Weatherman members began greeting each other with their fingers spread apart to symbolize a fork.

The Days of Rage was planned for months, but didn't go as planned. What was planned was a National Action centered in Chicago for four days in October 1969, from the 8th through the 11th. Leaflets were handed out by day to students of high schools and colleges. The school campuses had graffiti painted on them at night. On October 5th a statue commemorating police who had been killed in 1886 was dynamited.

On the 8th only about 800 protesters showed up, but Chicago had 2000 police ready. By the evening the protesters dwindled to about 300. At about 10:30 that night Jeff Jones, John Jacobs, and David Gilbert led the group through the affluent Gold Coast neighborhood. Protesters broke windows of cars, homes and businesses. The mob wore motorcycle and football helmets, but the police were armed and had night sticks they aimed at necks, legs, and groins. The police also had tear gas; they had a very large amount of tear gas. After about a half hour there were 28 police injured, 6 protesters shot, many were injured, and 68 people were arrested.

On October 9th, Dohrn and about 70 females met at Grant Park with a plan to raid a draft board. The Governor announced he had called in 2,500 National Guard so the Weatherman called off that protest. Several peaceful rallies were led by Mike Klonsky and Noel Ignatin in front a court building, a factory, and a hospital. The Weatherman group discovered a police informant in their group who was then severely beaten up.

The next day about 300 people showed up to march through a business section of Chicago called The Loop. They moved quickly and got through the police line. The group smashed out the windows of cars and stores. The police were ready, moved faster than was expected, and sealed off the protesters in about 15 minutes. About half of the group was arrested. On the final day few were left to break more windows before the protest ended.

The protest cost the state of Illinois and the city of Chicago $138,000. There were 287 members of the protest arrested and most of the leaders were jailed. The organization paid $243,00 to cover the cost of bail. The Black Panthers disassociated the Weatherman group for fear of increased police oppression. The Weatherman did not show up in court in March 1970. On April 1st the Chicago Federal Grand Jury indicted 12 members on conspiracy charges to riot; including Bernardine Dohrn. Dohrn and Ayers, plus others, went underground. The group is now called the Weather Underground.

While the pair was 'underground' they lived in 15 different states and had at least a dozen aliases. They reportedly got married. They did have two children. Their first son Zayd Osceola Dohrn was born in 1977. He was named after a Black Panther who was killed in a shoot-out with police. The middle name is in honor of a Seminole chief who sheltered runaway slaves. Their second son, Malik Cochise Dohrn, was born in 1980. Malik is a Muslim name to honor Malcolm X.

They were very busy during the years they lived 'underground.' The pair declared war on America, wrote books, and bombed buildings. They were not individually involved with each bombing, but the Weather Underground was and they were the leaders. Ayers described Weather Underground movement, "Kill all the rich people. Break up their cars and apartments. Bring the revolution home; kill your parents, that's where it's really at."

In May 1970, Dohrn sent an audio tape to the New York Times declaring war against the United States. She said, "If you want to find us…we'll be making love, smoking dope, loading guns. Guard your planes, guard your colleges, guard your banks, guard your children, guard your doors."

Nobody can deny that Dohrn didn't warn the country of their intent. For the remainder of the year the following happened:

- February 13th – Bombed parking lot of Berkeley Police Department
- February 16th – Bombed the Golden Gate Park branch of San Francisco Police Department, one policeman killed, others injured
- March 6th – 34 sticks of dynamite found in 13th Police District of Detroit Michigan
- March 30th – Police find bomb factory on Chicago's North Side
- May 10th – Bombed National Guard Building
- June 6th - a letter was sent taking credit for bombing the San Francisco Hall of Justice. There was no explosion. Months later the unexploded bomb was found by workmen.
- June 10th - Bombed the New York City police headquarters
- July - Bombed the New York Bank of America and the same day a US Army base in San Francisco was bombed
- July 23rd - Federal arrest orders were issued
- September 12th - the group helped Dr. Timothy Leary escape from California Men's Colony prison and then arranged travel for him to Algiers. They charged $25,000 for this service. Leary was well known for promoting the use of LSD to young people. In 1974 he was arrested again, but got a lighter sentence as he decided to co-operate with the FBI.
- October 8th – Bombed the Marin County California Courthouse
- October 10th – Bombed the Queens New York traffic court building
- October 14th -- Bombed the Harvard Center for International Affairs

In October Bernardine Dohrn was put on the FBI's 10 most wanted fugitive list. FBI Director J. Edgar Hoover stated that Dohrn was the most dangerous woman in America.

The bombs continued in 1971:

- March 1st - Bombed the United States Capitol

- April – Police find bomb factory in San Francisco

- August 29th - Bombed the Office of California Prisons

- September 17th - Bombed the New York Department of Corrections in Albany

- October 15th – Bombed William P. Bundy's office at the MIT Research Center. Bundy was former CIA and Foreign Affairs Adviser to Presidents Kennedy and Johnson

Then in 1972 Dohrn was seen with Jane Alpert in the Golden Gate Park in California. Alpert was in hiding. She had bombed eight government and private businesses within three months in 1969. She was never a member of the Weatherman group. There was only one bombing attributed to Weather Underground that year:

- May 19th – Bombed the Pentagon

In March 1973 troops left South Viet Nam and the Draft ended. These reasons could no longer be used as excuses for bombing buildings, but the bombing continues.

- May 18th – Bombed the 103rd Police Precinct in New York

- September 28th – Bombed ITT in both New York and in Rome, Italy

In 1974 a book was written called "Prairie Fire – The Politics of Revolutionary Anti-Imperialism". It was signed by Bernardine Dohrn, Jeff Jones, Billy Ayers, and Celia Sojourn. Celia Sojourn is pseudonym for several unnamed individuals. The book was dedicated, in part, to Sirhan Sirhan who killed Robert Kennedy in 1968. Robert was the brother of President John F. Kennedy. The book admits they are a guerrilla organization and that they are communists. Written in the book, "Our intention is to disrupt the empire, to incapacitate it, to put pressure on the cracks". The bombing did not stop:

- March 6th – Bombed Department of Health, Education and Welfare in San Francisco
- May 31st – Bombed the office of California Attorney General
- June 17th – Bombed Gulf Oil Pittsburg headquarters
- September 11th – Bombed Anaconda Corporation (part of Rockefeller Corporation)

In March of 1975 the group released the first edition of a new magazine called 'Osawatomie.' In September an article appeared stating, "We are building a communist organization…We must further study Marxism–Leninism within the Weathermen Underground Organization." In July from the 11th to the 13th, the Prairie Fire Organization Committee held its first national convention to formally create a brand new organization. The bombings continue:

- January 29th – Bombed the State Department
- June 16th – Bombed Banco de Ponce in New York (a Puerto Rican bank)
- September – Bombed Kennecott Corporation a copper company

Dissention between members was beginning in 1976. Kathy Boudin, who lived through the NYC bomb factory that blew up in 1970, and others wanted to join the Black Liberation Army. The Black Liberation Army is a division of the Black Panthers. Ayers and Dohrn, plus others, want to surrender. Some members do start to surrender.

- In 1977 a plan to bomb California Senator John V. Briggs office is discovered and five members are arrested.

Then in 1978 Bill Ayers, Bernardine Dohrn, and Kathy Boudin move from California to New York City. Bernardine works as a waitress and is employed at a children's clothing store. Bill gets a job as a baker and then works in a children's day care center. In 1979 identifications of customers from the clothing store are stolen. The identifications are used to get drivers licenses and to lease trucks that were used in the 1981 Brink's robbery.

In 1980 the groups splits up, Kathy Boudin joins the May 19 Coalition and Campaign for Economic Democracy (CED) a division of the Black Liberation Army. May 19 is the birthday of Malcolm X, Ho Chi Minh and Kathy Boudin.

The New York Times, on November 27, 1980, report that Bernardine Dohrn has been seen in the area. On December 3, 1980 both Ayers and Dohrn surrendered, not in New York, but in Chicago where Bill's father, Tom Ayers, lives. Richard Daley was the Attorney General at the time and "cut them a deal". They paid their bail, got a court date, and two days later flew to Florida to visit with Dohrn's family for the Christmas holidays. When they returned to Chicago, they paid Bernardine's $1,500 fine and she received 3 years probation for her activity connected to the "Days of Rage". All other charges had been dismissed because of government misconduct; an illegal wire tap. They then returned to New York City and Ayers returns to his employment at the child day care center.

> TOM AYERS, February 16, 1915 to June 8, 2007, was CEO and past President of Commonwealth Edison. He was also known as the Godfather of Illinois Politics. He served as Chairman of the Board on the following organizations; Northwestern University, Erikson Institute, Bank Street College in New York, Chicago Symphony Orchestra, Chicago Community Trust, Chicago Urban League Community Renewal Society, (funds Trinity United Church), Chicago Chamber of Commerce and Industry, Chicago United, Leadership Council for Metropolitan Open Communities Dearborn Park Corp, Chicago Council of Economic Education, Chicago Public Education Fund, Commercial Club of Chicago, and Vice President of the Chicago Board of Education.
>
> Other Boards he sat on were; Sears, G.D. Searle, Chicago Pacific Corp., Zenith Corp., Northwest Industries, General Dynamics, First National Bank of Chicago, Chicago Cubs and the Tribune Company. He definitely had connections in Chicago.
>
> Tom Ayers once said, "It all starts at the basics, elections and grassroots, in order to be working from inside the establishment and not fighting from the outside." Arnold Weber, former President of

> Northwestern University said, "Those offices are not just honorary or for social distinction. It's for the power."

In September 1981, Bill Ayers enrolled at Bank Street College to study early childhood education. His father is on the Board of Directors at this college in New York.

On September 21st, the Weather Underground is involved with the bombing of Springboks South Africa Rugby League office. Then, on September 26th, acid was thrown at a policeman, blinding him, at JFK Airport. Connection to the May 19 Coalition was suspected in this incident.

New York City was in the news across the country in October 1981 when Weather Underground friends succeeded in a Brink's robbery that killed two police officers and the Brink's guard. The Black Liberation Army robbers took $1.6 million before they were gunned down the police. All this took place at Nanuet Mall within 20 miles of Boudin's apartment. Boudin was captured as she fled on foot. Within three days all the others were apprehended with the exception of one who got shot and died while police attempted to arrest him.

In October 1981 the Ayers/Dohrn apartment, Kathy Boudin's apartment, and Obama's apartment are all in the same New York City neighborhood. At that time Obama stated he lived on West 109th Street which was less than a mile from Boudin's apartment on West 98th street and about 16 miles from Ayers reported 1980 address. However, the New York telephone directory listed Obama living at 339 E 94th Street from 1981 through 1985 (even though he has stated he moved at least 5 times while living in New York). This is 11 miles from the Ayers/Dohrn residence.

With the exception of Boudin, most involved received sentences of three consecutive 25 years to life. Boudin's father was an attorney and retained a friend who got her sentence reduced to 20 years or life. She was granted parole and released in 2003.

When Boudin was arrested her parents decided they were too old to take care of her son Chesa, born August 21, 1981. Ayers and Dohrn took custody and adopted him.

> An interesting note: during the sweep for the Brink's robbery suspects, JEFF JONES and his girlfriend Eleanor Raskin were

arrested. They were not involved with the robbery but were arrested for unlawful flight to avoid prosecution after the police found bomb making material in their Hoboken apartment in 1979. Ayers and Dohrn obtained custody of their 4 year old son Thai while they were in jail. Jones and Ayers were good friends while working together in the Weather Underground. Jones and Raskin got married one week before their December 17th court date hoping to get leniency. They did. Jones got probation and community service at a hospital emergency room and at a children's day care center. Jeff Jones now is the director at the George Soros' funded Apollo Alliance which wrote the Obama $787 billion Stimulus Bill (TARP).

Isn't it strange that these two people who have been connected to bombing, terror, and death; living in hiding for over 10 years, would get custody of children?

In May 1982 Dohrn was sentenced to jail for 7 months. She had refused to testify in court regarding Boudin and the Brink's robbery. She was cited for contempt on May 19th, Boudin's birthday. On December 23rd Bernardine is released from jail.

At sometime during 1983 Bernardine obtained employment at Sidley Austin law firm at the New York office. Howard Trienens, manager partner at Sidley Austin, told the Chicago Tribune he arranged to have her hired as a favor for his friend Tom Ayers. Dohrn passed her New York bar exam in 1984, but was refused a license to practice because of her background. In 1985, Bill Ayers transfers to Columbia University.

Ayers graduates from Columbia in 1987, the couple and their family move to Chicago. Bernardine transfers to the Chicago office of Sidley Austin. Ayers begins his work with, and is contact person for, ABCS which is connected to Obama's employer DCP.

In 1988, Dohrn leaves Sidley Austin and begins work at Cook County Public Guardian. Public Guardian is an office that acts as guardians of disabled adults and for children who are abused or neglected. This is the same year that Michelle Robinson (Obama) becomes employed at Sidley Austin, although she may have interned there the year before. Barack interns there the following summer. In 1989 Ayers became a full professor at University of Illinois. Mayor Harold Washington dies and Richard M. Daley becomes mayor.

In1990, David Axelrod and Rahm Emanuel were working together as strategists for Mayor Daley and Valerie Jarrett was hired to work for the Mayor. After she meets Barack she hires Michelle to work for the mayor in 1991. Bill Ayers is working on Mayor Daley's project of reforming Chicago's schools (ABCS). Barack Obama is working for DCP under ABCS.

Dohrn starts work at Children and Family Justice Center at Northwestern University in 1991. Ayers told David Horowitz during an interview, "Guilty as hell. Free as a bird. America is a great country." Obama does associate work at Davis, Miner and Barnhill law firm. Judson Miner was a former counsel to Mayor Washington and a 1967 classmate of Dohrn at University of Chicago. Attorney Davis complains that Obama spends a lot of time writing his book on his laptop with his feet on the desk. Obama joined the law firm in 1993 and later joins the Woods Fund. The Woods Fund was the source of his $2000 car and job at DCP. Davis went to the Woods Funds to request funding for a project he and Rezko wanted. Obama approved the funding.

On December 17, 1993 Bill Ayers begins to put together a grant proposal for $49.2 million from the Annenberg Challenge to form the Chicago Annenberg Challenge (CAC). The money was to increase the funding for Local School Councils. This was part of the 1988 reform that Ayers with ABCS and Obama with DCP worked on. The grant proposal was submitted in June 1994 and a ceremony for the approval was on January 23, 1995. To obtain the grant $49.2 million had to be matched by both private and public funding. Private funds came from pre-existing grants from the MacArthur and the Joyce Foundations (Barack Obama joined the Joyce Foundation during the summer of 1994.) Public money came from pre-existing funding with the 1988 Reform and pre-existing Chapter 1 Funds for anti-poverty programs. Obama was selected as the founding Chairman of the Board for the Chicago Annenberg Challenge. Bill Ayers was one of the 5 members of a panel that chose the Chairman

Therefore, in 1995, Ayers is awarded the Chicago Annenberg Challenge of $49.2 million to promote his original educational reform experiment. He requires funding from the Joyce Foundation that has Obama on its Board and then he selects Obama as the Chairman of CAC. So Obama votes each year at the Joyce Foundation to grant funds to the CAC where he is the Chairman of the Board.

The money was spent, but the schools did not get the funds. Instead, the schools were mandated to participate with external partners; and the external partners got the money. These were far left groups like ACORN, South Shore African Village Collaboration, and Dual Language Exchange. Proposals for money to be spent on math or science were denied, but Ayers' project 'Small Schools' was funded. This project was designed for children to confront issues of injustice. Funding also went to train teachers in this method. There was training for the parents to teach them how to advocate for their children. The money went to DCP.

In Ayers' book, "Teaching Toward Freedom" education "is to teach against oppression, against America's history of evil and racism, thereby forcing social transformation."

Over $110 million was spent with CAC funding. There were no discernible positive results. If the children did not benefit from all this spending, somebody must have made money and/or gained power and influence. Results that benefit the children may not have been the real reason for the grant, but having your name on many Boards of Directors does make for an impressive resume.

"Dreams From My Father: A Story of Race and Inheritance" was finally published late in 1995. The book describes Obama's childhood and his struggles in finding his identity. At the end of the book he marries Michelle. Time Magazine stated it was "the best written memoir ever produced by an American politician". Quote from "Dreams;' "To avoid being mistaken for a sellout, I chose my friends carefully. The more politically active black students, the foreign students, the Chicanos. The Marxist Professors and the structural feminists and punk-rock performance poets."

There has been speculation the book was actually written by Bill Ayers. It was noted that the writing style and wording closely resembled Ayers' book "Fugitive". The writing style also does not match Obama's second book, "The Audacity of Hope". The notion that Barack did not write "Dreams" was also written about in a book about the Obamas by Christian Anderson. The title of the book is "Barack and Michelle: Portrait of an American Marriage." Anderson wrote that Michelle suggested to Barack that he get help from their friend Bill Ayers. The deadline for the book was coming due and the first deadline had already been missed. Barack had taped interviews with his relatives, many notes, and a partial manuscript. All this material was given to Ayers. Christian Anderson has written many books including books about George and Laura Bush, Bill and Hillary Clinton John and Jackie Kennedy, plus many more.

In October of 2009, Bill Ayers had an unexpected meeting with Anne Leary. Ms. Leary was at the Reagan Airport in Washington D.C. in the Star Bucks Restaurant. Bill Ayers was also getting coffee. After taking a picture, Anne Leary introduced herself as a conservative blogger. To her surprise he told her that he wrote the book "Dreams" because Michelle asked him to. Ms. Leary responded that he probably edited it heavily. He again told her that he wrote it. He then said if she could prove it they could split the royalties. To this she asked why she should believe him as he was a liar. He walked away.

Late in 1995, Ayers and Dohrn had an open house to introduce Obama to the Hyde Park neighborhood when he decided to run for Illinois State Senator. Senator Alice Palmer was there and so was Dr. Quentin Young.

Bill Ayers wrote a book in 1997 titled, "A Kind and Just Parent: The Children of Juvenile Court." Michelle held a panel discussion so Ayers could promote his book and one of the other speakers was her husband Barack. In the December 21st issue of the 'Chicago Tribune', Senator Obama wrote a review of the book' "A searing and timely account of the juvenile court system and the courageous individuals who rescue them from despair". Ayers received enough attention with his book that Chicago named him 'Citizen of the Year.'

Ayers wrote another book in 2001 titled, "Fugitive Days; A Memoir". In the 'Chicago Magazine' a picture of Ayers was taken standing on the American flag taken for an August interview. The book was published on September 10th, the day before the attacks on the Twin Towers. He was interviewed on 9/11 by the 'New York Times', "I don't regret setting bombs" and "I feel we didn't do enough". He said his actions were meant to end the Viet Nam war. He told the Chicago Tribune "We weren't terrorists." He explained that terrorism was being done by the United States in the country of Viet Nam. Professor Ed Said wrote a blurb endorsing the book saying, "For anyone who cares about the sorry mess we are in, this book is essential, indeed necessary reading."

On April 19-20, 2002, a conference was held and sponsored by The Center for Public Intellectuals" and the University of Illinois-Chicago. The mission of the conference was to create an engaged civil society working toward social change and fostering coalitions. It was a celebration of ideas and the roles intellectuals play in society. Three of the speakers included Bill Ayers, Bernardine Dohrn and Barack Obama.

A going away party was held in 2003 for former PLO radical Rashid Khalidi and his wife Mona. The pair created the Arab American Action Network (AAAN). In attendance at the party was an anti-war group Not In My Name, Anti-Israeli advocate and founder of The Electronic Intifada, Ali Abunimah and ex-Weathermen Ayers and Dohrn. Keynote speakers giving testimonials were the Mayor and State Senator Obama. Khalidi told the crowd to help support Obama in his run for U.S. Senate.

In September 2008, Ayers and Dohrn visited Cuba with two of Obama's supporters, Janice Misurell-Mitchell and W.J.T. Mitchell. The trip was reported in the winter issue of 'CUBE Ensemble' newsletter by Misurell-Mitchell. The pair went there "as part of a conference on 'useful art' or art that involves social activism."

In an October 2008 'Investor's Business Daily' editorial, "Operating underground Ayers's Weathermen aligned closely with Castro's Cuba, which aided Marxist terror groups". "Some Weathermen on the run found asylum in Havana, others like Mark Rudd were trained by the KGB there." A report from Cuba's General Doctorate of Intelligence (DGI) states that the DGI created a group called the Vencermos Brigades to recruit persons that may someday have a position in the United States government. When the Weathermen went underground the DGI continued communications with them. Ayers had plans to take over the government of the United States by re-educating citizens in a new way of thinking. When undercover agent, Larry Grathwohl, asked Ayers what would happen to committed capitalists Ayers responded that they would be eliminated. He said he sat in meetings with 25 people, mostly graduates from Columbia University, who were attempting to determine the logistics of eliminating 25 million people.

'Investor Business Daily' also reports that Ayers is involved with the education system of Venezuela. It reported, "Ayers sits on the board of a Venezuela government think-tank called Miranda International Center, focused on bringing a Cuba-style education to Venezuelan school children." "Some say Ayers had a role in 2007's effort to give Chavez total power in Venezuela." The article reported on what Ayers said about Chavez at the Bolivarian Revolution, "We share the belief that education is the motor-force of revolution…I look forward to seeing how he and all of you continue to overcome the failing of capitalist education…"

On August 12, 2009 Cliff Kincaid of Accuracy in Media wrote about two books authored by Chesa Boudin. Chesa Boudin was

> the child that Ayers and Dohrn adopted after his parents were imprisoned for their involvement in the killing and robbery of the Brinks truck in 1981. The two books are titled 'Gringo' and "The Venezuelan Revolution: 100 Questions 100 Answers." Boudin is a Rhodes Scholar.
>
> Chesa Boudin wrote about working for Chavez in the Presidential Palace and how he is an advocate for Chavez in the United States. Boudin stated his parents, Bill and Bernardine, traveled to Venezuela in 2006 to celebrate Chavez's "Socialism of the 21st Century". They addressed the "World Education Forum" at a conference called "Bolivarian Education and the Overcome of the Capitalist School".
>
> Boudin wrote that before each presentation the PBS documentary "The Weather Underground" was shown. The documentary is a romantic depiction of the terrorist group that targeted police stations and killed police officers. Boudin writes, "People of highly developed political analysis saw in the film...hopeful examples of internal resistance to American Imperialism." He continued that in May 2005 his parents were invited to give talks at universities and cultural centers. Boudin would interpret for them as they gave talks to stir up violence and hatred against the United States.

During 2009 the pair traveled doing book signings on their new book "Race Course: Against White Supremacy" and giving talks about the peace movement, the election and what more can be done. At one book signing they were questioned about when to start getting violent because change wasn't coming fast enough. Dohrn responded violence is used when other alternatives are exhausted. C-SPAN did a three hour Book TV show on June 7th with him as part of the "In Depth" series of conversations with noted American Authors. In March, Ayers and Dohrn opined about Hillary being a white supremacist in an article they wrote for the 'Monthly Review'. They complained that her words, and the words of others, were code words related to race. Words such as "blue collar", "working class", "mainstream" referred to white, while words as "untested" and "symbolic candidate" referred to black. They continued that questions regarding Obama's faith, patriotism, and his mysterious past contributed to a "carnival atmosphere".

It was an exciting time for the pair in late December 2009 and early January 2010. Ayers and Dohrn joined Jodie Evans of Code Pink and other activists in the Gaza Peace March. Approximately 1300 activists from 42 countries showed up in Cairo with the intent to cross into Gaza, meet with HAMAS, join 50,000 Palestinians, cross Gaza, and meet at the Israel border.

This did not go quite as planned. The group had letters from Congressman Andre Carson (on Congressional letterhead) and Senator John Kerry (on Senate letterhead) requesting that Egypt cooperate with the Gaza Peace March trip. Egypt was not so eager when confronted with the activist group. They were not going to allow passage because many of the group did not want to cooperate by giving identification and reasons for entering their country. Egypt said they had the right to approve or deny entry to their land. This caused the activists to do what activists do, which is to demonstrate. The police then put people in pens or did not allow them to leave their hotels. The police were not gentle. Bernardine got to sit in a pen for at least 4 hours. Jodie Evans met with Suzanne Mubarak, the wife of Egypt's President, and got an agreement to allow 100 members of the delegation to go into Gaza. Egypt got to pick the 100 people. They selected those who did not provoke the police, or who expressed that they wanted to go for peaceful reasons, and were willing to provide identification.

This caused many people to get upset. They felt it was all or nothing. Some of the 100 who were on the bus got off to express solidarity with those who were not chosen. Dohrn was selected to go. Others were chanting outside the bus "All or None…All or None", Dohrn got off the bus. When the bus left there were 87 people crossing into Gaza. At the border HAMAS detained them and put them in the HAMAS owned Commodore Hotel. They were not allowed to leave on their own and could have no contact with the local Gazans. The activists were put on a bus, given a "devastation tour." and nobody got off the bus. Then they were forced to participate in the HAMAS organized march to the Erez crossing. No Palestinian women were allowed to march and none of the activists complained.

Those that didn't get to go to Gaza were not happy. They already learned the Egyptians did not have a problem using excessive force. One Free Gaza participant wrote how they spent 10 days having demonstrations, hunger strikes and media events. Some activists were detained to their hotel. Others planned to demonstrate at the Egyptian National Museum, but it had to be done covertly. They broke up into small groups and pretended to be tourists. The security was tight and they knew they couldn't enter as a total group. When a secret code was issued they all converged together for a demonstration. The police rushed in and stopped the group within 15 minutes.

Rashid and Mona Khalidi backed the Gaza Peace March. Rashid told Amy Goodman of 'Democracy Now', on January 16, 2009, that he was in Cairo two weeks prior to the interview but did not state he took part in the demonstrations. Ali Abunimah, friend of Ayers, Dohrn, and Obama, with his group Electronic Intifada did attend and were very active participants.

While the demonstrations were taking place in Egypt and Gaza there were over 200 demonstrations occurring in the United States. The following is a list of George Soros funded organizations that were involved in the organization of the demonstrations in the United States, Gaza or both.

- Progressive Democrats of America - Members; Rep. Maxine Waters, Rep. John Conyers, Rep. Lynn Woolsey, Rep. Barbara Lee, Tom Hayden (SDS), Jodie Evans (Code Pink), Medea Benjamin (Global Exchange).

- Movement for a Democratic Society - Members; Rashid Khalidi (U.S. Campaign To End The Israeli Occupation), Carl Davidson (SDS), Tom Hayden (SDS), Alan Haber (SDS), and Bernardine Dohrn.

- Global Exchange - Medea Benjamin, Marilyn Katz (SDS), Van Jones (former Green Czar, STORM).

- Alliance of Community Trainers (ACT) and Root Activist Network Trainers (RANT) - Founded by Starhawk (Movement for a Democratic Society), Juniper, and Lisa Fithian.

- International Solidarity Movement - Founder Huwaida Arraf (Free Gaza Movement and US Campaign to End the Israeli Occupation).

- Interreligious Foundation for Community Organization (IFCO) also known as Pastors for Peace - Funding organization for Not In Our Name and Women's International League for Peace and Freedom.

- Center for Economic and Social Rights - Funding organization for US Campaign to End Israeli Occupation.

- US Action - Founders Paul and Heather Booth (SDS), members include Dr. Quentin Young (Obama's doctor) and Robert Creamer (convicted of multi-million dollar embezzlement and husband of Rep. Jan Schakowsky).

- Movement for a Democratic Society - Bernadine Dohrn (SDS), Carl Davidson (SDS), Tom Hayden (SDS), Alan Haber (SDS), Mark Rudd (SDS), Jeff Jones (SDS and Apollo Alliance) Starhawk (ACT and RANT) and Rashid Khalidi (Movement for a Democratic Society).

- The New Party reorganized as Working Families Party - Members include Hillary Clinton, John Edwards, Barack Obama, Andrew Cuomo, and Bertha Lewis (ACORN).

Ayers and Dohrn found a new cause with the Muslim Brotherhood sponsored Free Gaza Movement. They were both involved with the organization of the pro-HAMAS, anti- Israel Free Gaza Flotilla on May 31, 2010. The two boats from the United States were called the Challenger I and the Challenger II, both were yachts and neither carried any humanitarian supplies just protesters and activists. Not all the boats contained cargo but they all had journalists as passengers. The Challenger II had mechanical problems that was suspected to be sabotage and could not continue. The passengers were transferred to the ship MV Mavi Marmara. The Challenger I had a steering problem, but was repaired, and was able to join the flotilla. The incident ended in violence when Israel boarded the Turkish ship and were ambushed.

The Muslim Brotherhood announced in 'The Global Brotherhood Daily Report' on February 14 and March 8, 2011 that it planned another flotilla at the end of May 2011. The plan was to have 15 boats and over 1,000 passengers, including the media, charity workers, politicians, and activists from over 20 countries.

During the second week of June 2011, and after several delays, the Gaza flotilla gathered in the ports near Athens, Corsica, Corfu and Crete in Greece. The Turkish ship 'Mavi Marmara' was not sent as Turkey and Israel were attempting to mend their relations. Some ships needed repairs and the activists blamed Israel of sabotage. Greece did not allow ships going to Gaza to leave their ports. The U.S. boat, 'The Audacity of Hope' defied the ban but was stopped by Greek authorities. The captain was detained, charged with a felony and released four days later. For about two weeks approximately 300 activists were in Greece trying to decide what to do. They practiced what to do if arrested by the Israelis, gave news conferences holding "Free Gaza" signs, and chanted phrases such as "Exist to Resist". Meanwhile Greece offered to transport any relief aid to Israel, Israel has agreed to deliver it to Gaza, and Palestinian President Abbas had agreed to accept. Activists returned home declaring victory as they brought media attention to their cause.

The cause may be more publicity than substance. On July 1st a pro-Palestinian group called Gish stated that "Gaza does not really need more aid, and the Gaza flotilla would be better off taking exports out of Gaza" and the flotilla detracts from the real issues. Israel must continue to protect itself from its enemies as it intercepted a ship in March and found 50 tons of Iranian weapons concealed among bags of lentils and cotton. The Canadian Red Cross states that shipments of food and clothing is not the accepted method of delivering aid, because of the high costs of transport, and locally purchased food and clothing are more effective and culturally accepted. Israel delivers over a thousand truckloads of aid on a weekly basis. In 2010 Gaza opened up a new mall with merchandise from international companies including food, clothing, toys, etc. The 'London Times' reported in 2011 about the construction of a multimillion hotel that is a symbol of the rebirth of the coastal strip. The 'Times' reported that store shelves are well stocked because of the Hamas-run farms. The report states the farms were "developed on land vacated when thousands of Israeli settlers were removed by their Government six years ago, are providing the impoverished population with fresh fruit and vegetables.

Bill Ayers retired from the University of Illinois on August 31, 2010. He went before the board and asked for emeritus status and was unanimously denied. Emeritus status is a title of privilege that allows for continued access to university facilities and is rarely denied. The chairman of the board was Christopher Kennedy, son of Robert Kennedy, who was 4 years old when his father was killed. Kennedy gave an impassioned speech stating that he in good conscious could not vote for a person who wrote a book that was dedicated in part to the man that murdered his father.

Looks like Ayers will have to use the public library for any further research. Actions do have consequences.

Dohrn is employed as an Assistant Professor of Law and is the Director and founder of Children and Family Justice Center at Northwestern University.

Both spoke at the Green Fest in Washington D.C. on October 23, 2010. Dohrn complained the United States is still a "hegemonic" (dominant) power even in economic decline, but that its military strength is still a super power in the world.

Sounds like she thinks that is a bad thing!

Ayers told the small crowd that they need to focus on "community power". He said that education is a human right and he puts his faith in the United Nations Declaration of Human Rights. Not the Declaration of the United States; the United Nations!

Dohrn said the people have to learn to live differently. (She must have been talking to Michelle Obama again.). The crowd began asking questions about their past. Dohrn and Ayers got agitated and avoided answering. This may not last long.

The Phoenix Task Force still has an active case in the bombing of the San Francisco Police Department that killed one officer and left another partially blind. The task force consists of the FBI, the Department of Justice, and the San Francisco Police Department. At the America Survival Inc. Conference held in Washington D.C. on October 21, 2010, former FBI Larry Grathwohl spoke in detail about underground investigations with the Weatherman when he infiltrated the group. He stopped his investigation when many of his 'comrades' got arrested and his identity became known.

When Grathwohl infiltrated the group Ayers told him, "It was a success. But it's a shame when someone like Bernardine has to make all the plans, make the bomb, and then place it herself. She should only have to do the planning." Another FBI agent, Max Noel, said in the bomb factory he investigated there were many books and pamphlets about Marxist and Leninist information, but no anti-war information. Grathwohl wants to use modern day forensic procedures such as DNA, or fingerprinting the insides of gloves, to gather more evidence.

Grathwohl has requested Congress to create a committee to investigate some of the old terrorist's cases. He says that some of remnants of these old groups are still active today and are promoting Islamic terrorism. He argues that many of the terrorists have never had to testify under oath. Grathwohl is asking Congress to bring them in to testify, “no matter what high or influential positions they may currently have”. The people he is referring to are Bill Ayers, Bernardine Dohrn, Jeff Jones, and Mark Rudd.

Concern has been expressed that the Department of Justice under Eric Holder may protect these terrorists. Holder previously assisted President Clinton with the pardon of two Weathermen. Also of concern is the relationship with Obama as his first political fund raiser was in the home of Ayers and Dohrn, plus all his other connections with them in Chicago. Grathwohl is pursuing this as a matter of conscious and for the security of the United States. Ayers and Dohrn have maintained connections with Marxist leaders and Marxist activists. Their adopted son Chesa Boudin works with Chavez who has connections with Iran. Grathwohl stresses that these former Weathermen most likely have information that could be useful to protecting the security of the United States, and they need to testify under oath.

Judge me by the people who surround me.

CHAPTER 12

★ ★ ★ ★ ★

Joyce Foundation & Woods Fund

Obama joined the JOYCE FOUNDATION in 1994. He must have had an excellent resume or connections as he became the Chairman of the Board the same year. He remained on the board until 2002. Valerie Jarrett is on the board and became the Chair in 2002 and is still a board member. The mission of the Joyce Foundation is to protect the natural environment of the Great Lakes, reduce poverty and violence in the region, to ensure people have access to good schools, and create decent jobs. The foundation creates public policies and support efforts to reform the system of election campaigns.

Obama made many friends while on the Joyce Foundation and attempted to 'improve' public policies. While he was on the board the following actions were approved.

To improve education $1,968,710 was granted to Small Schools, a Bill Ayers project. John Ayers, (Bills brother) received $761,100 for his program Leadership for Quality Education. A $1.5 million grant was approved to redesign five high schools Bill Ayers proposed and $525,000 given to the University of Illinois College of Education to assist a network of small schools. The Annenberg Challenge program just makes the money multiply for certain projects.

The Joyce Foundation actions on gun control attempted to be far reaching. They financed anti-gun grass root organizations. This is a list of some of the organizations funded: Freedom States Alliance, Legal Community Against Violence, 50 Caliber Terror, Ban Handguns Now, License to Murder, Newspaper Loop Hole, and Red Flag Campaign.

The really innovative approach was to influence future Supreme Court decisions. When judges don't have past decisions to base their decisions on they use law review articles. These are usually written by law students and are voluntarily published for no pay. So the foundation decided to write their own reviews. They gave Chicago-Kent Law Review $84,000. The Law Review promptly published an entire issue in which all articles were anti-individual rights to own arms, undermining the Second Amendment. Chicago-Kent hired Carl Bogus be the editor. Bogus was the director of Handgun Control Inc. and a member of the Joyce Foundation Violence Policy Center. He solicited anti-individual arms rights articles from law students and offered $5,000 per article. Professor Randy Barnett, of Boston University, volunteered to write in defense of individual right to bear arms and was refused. He was told, 'Sometimes a more balance debate is best secured by an unbalanced symposium."

This plan almost worked. In Texas, a case was decided by quoting the Chicago-Kent Review 8 times. It was reversed by the Court of Appeals. Another case, Heller v. D.C. was upheld using the Chicago-Kent articles. It went to the Supreme Court. Washington D.C. lost in a 5/4 decision. Dissenting judges all cited the Chicago-Kent Review. In 2002, $400,000 was used to establish a Second Amendment Research Center as a think tank, headed by anti-gun advocate Saul Cornell from Ohio State University. The Ohio State University magazine 'Making History.' reported the purpose of the research center was to affect future Supreme Court decisions.

The most ambitious endeavor was to create a framework that would make millions with the enactment of future legislation. It was the creation of Chicago Climate Exchange (CCX) with over $1 million in grants. Richard Sandor is the founder of the company. Two months before founding CCX, Sandor joined the board of directors of Intercontinental Exchange (ICE).

In 1990, Sandor gave an interview to the Wall Street Journal. He said, "Air and water are no longer the free goods that economics once assumed. They must be redefined as property rights so that they can be efficiently allocated".

Interestingly, CCX is the only voluntary, legally binding green house Cap and Trading system for all six emissions and off-set payments in North America. London based Generation Investment Management (GIM) purchased a large part of CCX. GIM was founded by Al Gore and three Goldman Sachs executives; David Blood, Mark Ferguson and Peter Harris. GIM and the Goldman Sachs company each own 10% of CCX. Paula DiPerno was on the Joyce Foundation board when they agreed to the CCX grant. She soon left Joyce and joined the executive team of the new company designed tax green house gases.

This company was expected to gross $10 trillion each year if Cap and Tax passed. Franklin Raines, the head of Fannie Mae, used Joyce Foundation funds to buy technology to measure and manage carbon. The patent was approved the day after Obama was elected President. Fannie Mae, a mortgage holding company, holds the patent. The CCX director of the board is MAURICE STRONG. Strong was the former U.N. secretary of General Kofi Annan until the Iraq's oil-for-food scandal forced him to leave. He currently lives primarily in China. He is a former director of the Rockefeller Foundation and member of the Bilderberg Group, the Trilateral Commission, the Council of Foreign Relations, and the Club of Rome. Strong was in charge of the U.N. Environmental Programs and set up the Kyoto Protocol.

Cap and Trade was to attach a monetary value to waste by-products. This would allow carbon speculators to make more money with the massive redistribution of wealth.

The EPA stated that if Cap and Trade didn't get passed they may have to use the Clean Air Act to force greenhouse gas reductions. This is not the favored method by those who want regulation. The reason is the EPA would have to write the regulations and start a permit program that is mostly administrative and creates extensive paper work. Then they would need to phase in permits for large companies between 2011 and 2013, and smaller companies in 2016.

Jay Rockefeller asked how EPA would determine the Best Available Control Technology (BACT) for new projects. There are no standards and nobody actually controls greenhouse gas emissions now. He asked how the EPA would establish BACT standards for all companies. It was admitted that EPA had no idea how this would be accomplished. This is why promoters of the bill, that would control us with greenhouse taxes, want the Cap and Trade passed because it can be implemented immediately. The structure has already been planned.

The CCX is a company designed allow some people to make a lot of money at the expense of the rest of us. Now that the Environment Protection Agency has declared that greenhouse gases is a health emergency a crisis has been identified. The CCX has supplied the structure to manage the crisis. However CCX ceased to exist in December 2010 when it was sold to Intercontinental Exchanges. Sandor who started CCX with $1.1 million made $98.5 million with the sale. Al Gores's MIG company had shares valued at $18 million.

This leads to the next Joyce Foundation grant, the Shore Bank. Shore Bank was facing bankruptcy. It made money with micro loans but lost money on sub-prime loans. Shore Bank was known for making loans based on the green technology used by the lenders. A private rescue bail out was arranged with the Joyce Foundation when so many banks were being closed by FDIC. The Joyce Foundation and some Wall Street companies funded Shore Bank because this was the institution that would be designated as the "banking arm" of CCX. Co-founders of Shore Bank are:

- Jan Piercy - the Wellesley College roommate of Hillary Clinton

- Mary Houghton - a close friend, and co-worker from the Ford Foundation, of Stanley Ann Dunham Obama Soetoro; aka Ann Sutoro. (Obama's mother worked in banking, securing micro loans in Indonesia)

- Ronald Grzywinski – friend of Jimmy Carter

Former Vice President of Shore Bank was Bob Nash the deputy campaign manager of Hillary's presidency run and was on the Board of Chicago Law Review with Obama and Ayers. He was also on the Obama White House transition team. The Director is Adele Simons a close friend of Valerie Jarrett; both of them sat on the board of the Chicago Civic Organization. One board member is Howard Stanback who sat on the board of the Woods Fund with Obama and Ayers. He had been employed by New Kenwood with Tony Rezko. The other board member is Van Jones, the former Green Jobs Czar, who resigned when his Marxist past became public.

Obama is quite helpful to his friends and very good at making new friends and acquaintances. He has learned how to spread the wealth with them all. Unfortunately for his friends not this time, because the Shore Bank failed in August 2010 despite large investments. The bank did not survive the investigations of its policy of lending for "green" loans (borrowers had to make a commitment to be "green") or for making questionable investments as it did when it donated $1 million to set up a financial institution in Kenya. The Urban Partnership Bank has replaced Shore Bank; but some of Shore Bank's board members were able to stay. The new chairmen are David Vitale (past president of First National Bank of Chicago) and former White House Czar of Education Arne Duncan.

In 2009 the Joyce foundation granted $200,000 to start an Emerald Cities Collaborative. This is a national coalition of unions, labor groups, community organizations, social justice advocates, socially responsible businesses, and elected politicians. Emerald Cities has a goal of greening central cities and creating a "new vital economic sectors". JOEL ROGERS will lead this program. Joel Rogers is known for his ties to Apollo Alliance, the organization that wrote the stimulus bill, and Center of Wisconsin Strategy (COWS). The Chairman of the Board is Gerry Hudson the executive vice president of SEIU. Other board members are associated with the following organizations; Bronze Investments, AFL-CIO, Community Action Partnership, Service and Conservation Corps, Public Housing, Enterprise Community Partners, Green For All and many more.

> Joel Rogers said, "I hope you all realize that you could eliminate every power plant in America today and you can stop every car in America. Take out the entire power generation sector and you still would not be at anywhere near 80% below 1990 goals."

Some of the more recent pursuits of the Joyce Foundation is the Media Access Project (MAP) and Net Neutrality. The MAP group is working to reform media by mandating what they call localism and diversity policies. Privately owned radio and television companies would have to change their programming to meet new regulations if these rules become law. The Soros funded Open Society and other left-wing foundations help to fund MAP. Robert McChesney's organization Free Press is closely associated with this program. The other endeavor is Net Neutrality with government regulations which will allow the internet to be considered a public utility. Since other utilities are taxed, I wonder if future internet usage might also be taxed. Just wondering.

Judge me by the people who surround me.

CHAPTER 13

★ ★ ★ ★ ★

Chicago Friends

In 1995 Obama was installed as the founding chairman of the CHICAGO ANNENBERG CHALLENGE (CAC) which funded many of Ayers' educational projects. He was the chairman until 1999 and stayed on the board until 2004. Records of CAC are not available.

Stanley Kurtz, from the National Review, contacted the Richard J. Daley Library at the University of Illinois, in 2008, where the CAC records are being stored. He was assured that he would be able to see the 132 boxes containing 947 files of material. He was told, by telephone, that any material he wanted the library would copy for him in the Special Collection section of the library. However that did not happen. He was barred from seeing the records because the library did not have a "signed deed of gift" which means a legal right to make the material available. One month after Kurtz reported his inability to obtain records regarding CAC, the Obama campaign sent him a letter. The correspondence was sent to assure Kurtz that Obama and Ayers had only occasional contact while at CAC and Ayers had nothing to do with Obama being hired. They added that the CAC is currently being run through the Chicago Public Education Fund in coordination with the Chicago Public Schools CEO Arne Duncan (former czar) and the Mayor.

Bill Ayers coauthored the proposal for the winning $49.2 million five year grant for the Chicago Annenberg Challenge in 1994. The grant was awarded in 1995 when Obama was on the founding board and elected as the founding president. The Annenberg Challenge grant required matching funds and some of the funding came from the Woods Foundation that Obama chaired. The Chicago School Reform Collaborative was also formed in 1995 and Ayers was the founder and founding co-chairman of this group. The Collaborative was the advisory and operations arm of the CAC. The Collaborative also directed CAC's program content. Both men were known to speak at both organizations during board meetings. The CAC funded some of Ayers' educational programs.

Barack Obama did make the time to help organize the Million Man March for Marxist and racist Louis Farrakhan. Obama, Reverend Wright and Charlie Rangel worked on this project.

LOUIS FARRAKHAN was born May 11, 1933 as Louis Eugene Walcott. His mother taught him about justice, equality, and the struggle for freedom. As a young man he was a singer, dancer and a violinist. He changed his name to Louis X in 1955 when he joined the Nation of Islam which was founded by Elijah Muhammad. Muhammad declared all Muslims involved with the entertainment business had to quit or get out of the Temple. Louis believed the teachings had the ability to uplift and reform without the use of entertainment so he stopped those activities. He changed his name again, to Louis Farrakhan.

Farrakhan is now the National Representative of the Nation of Islam (NOI). There are over 120 mosques and study groups throughout America, Europe, and Africa devoted to NOI. He started a newspaper and wrote a book about his beliefs. The Nation of Islam wants complete freedom and equal justice. They want a separate state or territory for all persons who are descendants of slaves to be provided by former slave masters. The land they want must be fertile and rich in minerals. In 1985 he began the POWER concept. This is the same year he received a $5 million interest free loan from Libyan leader Muammar Khadafi.

He has a long history of biased racial comments and views on whites, Jews, and gay people. He has called whites the anti-Christ, blue-eyed devils, and skunks of the planet. Judaism has been referred to as a gutter religion and Jews as bloodsuckers. Farrakhan denies that Jews have a rightful claim to their religion or their homeland. He has argued that the Jews were involved with slave trade and that they control the government, the entertainment and financial industries.

Farrakhan has an annual Savior's Day Convention. In 1995 the convention was held in Chicago. Khadafi spoke via satellite to the attendees stating he would be willing to provide weapons to a black army in the United States to destroy "white America".

Farrakhan said he had a vision in September 1995 of being abducted by aliens in a UFO during a radio interview in 2005. He claims he was beamed up into a small craft and transported to a larger one. He heard the voice of Elijah Mohamed telling him the joint chiefs of staff were planning a war.

He later realized that the war would be against Libya and he went there to warn Khadafi. The Nation of Islam believe in UFOs and refer to them as the "Motherplane" or the "Wheel". The belief is that the Wheel was constructed in Nippon (Japan), is made of tough steel, and cost $15 billion in gold to build. The Wheel can stop and travel in all directions at great speed. Farrakhan claims there are 1,500 small wheels contained in the mother wheel which is one mile by a half mile in size. He believes the Wheel will destroy the Earth on the Day of Judgment.

He organized (with help of Al Sharpton, Rev. Wright, and Obama) the 1995 Million Man March in Washington D.C. where he spoke about atonement. Farrakhan said he was inspired by the negative image of black men connected with violence and drug use. He also spoke of the real evil in America being white supremacy. Rev. Wright was scheduled to speak on the topic: "Prayer for Hope". Gay men were not invited to the Million Man March. After the event Khadafi telephoned Farrakhan to congratulate him on his success and offered to work with him and unite their efforts.

In 1996 Farrakhan said "God don't like men coming to men with lust in their hearts like you should to a female. If you think that the kingdom of God is going to be filled with that kind of degenerative crap, you're out of your damn mind". He refers to gay black men as "race traitors". "Wicked Jews" are blamed for promoting homosexuality. He preaches that all non-black races are the result of a prehistoric breeding experiment on Patmos Island by Dr. Yacub, who was exiled there by the original black Eden in Mecca. White people are the "newest people" he explains and will rule for a time, but a new world is coming. The new world will not have white supremacy and black inferiority.

Farrakhan has a history with violence. In the 1960's Malcolm X revealed that Elijah Muhammad impregnated several teenage girls. Farrakhan became enraged over the Malcolm X disloyalty. He was quoted in a newspaper 'Muhammad Speaks', "Only those who wish to be led to hell or to their doom will follow Malcolm. The die is set, and Malcolm shall not escape... such a man is worthy of death." Ten weeks later Malcolm X was killed by three gunmen that had connections to NOI.

In 1984 Washington Post reporter, Milton Coleman, wrote that Jesse Jackson referred to Jews as 'Hymies' and NYC as 'Hymietown.' Farrakhan was not pleased with the article and threatened Coleman, "One day soon we will punish you with death".

In 1996 a Tehran Newspaper quoted him, "God will destroy America by the hands of Muslims....This is an honor God will bestow upon Muslims." After the September 11, 2001 attacks he wrote to President Bush offering advice to meet with spiritual leaders of various faiths for counsel. Farrakhan also said that America did not have any proof that the attacks came from Osama bin Laden or al-Qaeda as America had lied before and there is "no guarantee they're not lying now". In 2005 Farrakhan accused President Bush of ordering a New Orleans levee to be dynamited to cause floods to kill black people. He claimed it was an attempt to wipe out a large population of black people.

Threats and intimidation continue; in June 2010 he sent a three page letter to leaders of 16 Jewish organizations demanding reparations for African-Americans. The letter states, "This is an offer asking you and gentiles who you influence to help me repaying people for the damage that has been done by your ancestors to mine". Enclosed were two books detailing evidence of Jews inflicting economic harm on blacks and involvement in slavery. Morton Klein, President of Zionist of America, is afraid of violence. He claims that every week Farrakhan men wearing bow ties distributed messages named "The Final Call". Klein has asked Obama to condemn these actions. Abraham Foxman, national director of the Anti-Defamation League, was hoping the people of the black community would be courageous and ask Farrakhan to stop.

On September 21, 2010 Farrakhan met and had dinner with the New Black Panthers and Iranian President Ahmadinejad. Ahmadinejad was in New York as he gave his speech at the United Nations suggesting the United States orchestrated the September 11, 2010 terrorist attacks in New York.

The Nation of Islam has been strengthening ties with the Church of Scientology. Farrakhan wants to improve the literacy rate among blacks and end drug use. In 2010 he was urging black people to take the future in their own hands. He said, "Ain't nobody going to do something for us; we're going to have to do it for ourselves" in a speech on atonement, reconciliation and responsibility.

During the Presidential campaign Farrakhan compared Obama to Wallace D. Fard Muhammad, the founder of his religion. He said that because both had black fathers and white mothers, that Obama would be a savior and had referred to Obama as a messiah. He said, "the Messiah is absolutely speaking" when Obama talks and "Barack Obama to me, is a herald of the

Messiah. Barack Obama is like the trumpet that alerts you something new, something better is on the way". However Farrakhan became quite upset that Obama would be part of a coalition of nations that attacked Libya in March 2011. He said, offering advice to Obama on a radio interview (WVON-AM on March 16, 2011), "You can't order him to step down, and get out—who do you think you are, that you can talk to a man that built a country over 42 years, and ask him step down and get out? Can anybody ask you? Well, well there's a lot now (that are) going to ask you to step out of the White House, because they don't want a Black face in the White House".

In 1995 ALICE PALMER was the Illinois State Senator. She and her husband Edward 'Buzz' Palmer are very active with communist activities. In 1980 they were invited to attend a celebration of the Grenada Cuban/Soviet led revolution by Maurice Bishop. In 1982, they started a newspaper 'Black Press Institute" that collected articles and editorials from black owned newspapers across the country and reprinted them. Years later Palmer was proud that their newspaper influenced decisions of the Democratic Black Caucus.

In 1983 Palmer began a series of travels to the Soviet Union and Soviet bloc countries including a trip to Czechoslovakia to attend the World Peace Council's Prague Assembly. That year she became an executive board member of Communist Party USA. In 1985 she traveled with other black American journalists to the Soviet Union, East Germany, and Czechoslovakia. When she returned she said, "We came back feeling that we could speak very well about the interests of the Socialist countries in promoting peace." She spoke of and praised the concept of "central planning".

Palmer was elected into the International Organization of Journalists (IOJ) in 1986. The IOJ is another Soviet front operation and linked to the International Department of the Communist Party. The International Department, with the help of the KGB, use groups such as IOJ and World Peace Council, to influence the policies of other countries. Palmer wrote an article in BPI titled, "An Afro-American Journalist on the USSR" which was printed in the Communist Party USA newspaper, 'People's Daily World.' She praised the USSR that guaranteed jobs, education, housing, plus health care, and was striving to improve all the programs. She wrote that these services were attainable because all industries were controlled by a central government authority. She continued, stating the Soviet system focuses on groups and not on the individual. "They say it is the people together—not the leading privileged individuals–who make the nation happen."

Alice Palmer was elected as Illinois State Senator in 1990. A special election was held in 1995 to fill the vacated U.S. Congressional seat due to the resignation of Mel Reynolds. Reynolds resigned because of a sexual scandal involving an underage intern. Palmer announced that she was going to run for that seat and declared that she was not seeking re-election to the Illinois Senate. She had a 'Friends of Alice Palmer' group to support her election; the list included Barack Obama and Tony Rezko. Palmer was so sure of being elected to this new position that she announced her successor Barack Obama and attended his fund raiser at the home of Ayers and Dohrn. In the meantime, Obama publicly announced his candidacy at the Ramada Inn Lakeshore, the same place that Harold Washington announced his run for mayor. She lost the special election to Jesse Jackson Jr.

Palmer then scrambled to get enough signatures submitted to be included for the State Senate election. She collected 1,580 signatures on her petition for re-election that was submitted on December 18th, the last day to file. On January 2, 1996 the Obama committee began to challenge the validity of the signatures on her and the other candidates' petitions. It was determined that 2/3 of Palmer's signatures were invalid, which made her 200 signatures short of the 757 signatures needed. The Obama team also challenged enough signatures of the other candidates to remove them as well making Obama the only Democratic candidate. Obama went on to win his first political office.

In the 2008 presidential election Alice Palmer supported Hillary Clinton.

DR. QUENTIN YOUNG attended Obama's first fund raiser when Palmer introduced Obama to Chicago political operatives as her successor at the home of Ayers and Dohrn. Quentin Young was born in 1923 and joined the Young Communist League as a teenager. During the 1960's he was the personal physician of Martin Luther King Jr. and was active in anti-war and civil rights movements. In 1964 he co-founded the Medical Committee for Human Rights. In 1968 he was called to testify before the House Un-American Activities Committee to state what he knew about the Chicago riots at the Democratic Convention in August of that year. He was accused of being a member of Bethune Club, an organization of Communist doctors in the Communist Party USA.

In 1970 Young became associated the Marxist organization New American Movement (NAM). NAM and the Democratic Socialist Organization Committee later combined to form the Democratic Society of America in 1982. Then in 1972 he led a delegation to Communist North Viet Nam, during the Viet Nam war. Later that year Young became the chairman of Cook County Hospital, a position he held until 1981. In 1980 Dr. Young founded the Health and Medical Policy Research Group which advocates for single payer health care. In 1983 he was on the board of directors of Illinois' branch of the Americans for Civil Liberties Union (ACLU). He was co-founder, with Peter Orris, of the Physicians for a National Healthcare Program. Orris was a SDS leader at Harvard College in the 1960's, a leader of the Doctors Council of SEIU, and he traveled to D.C. on June 25, 2009 to rally for healthcare reform.

Dan Cantor held a NEW PARTY funder raiser in 1992 at the home of Quentin Young. That same year the doctor became a member of the board for the Illinois Public Action; the executive director was Robert Creamer and the program director was Creamer's wife, Rep. Jan Schakowsky. Also in 1992 Quentin Young, his wife Ruth, and Bernice Targ Weissbourd joined the Chicago Committee to Defend the Bill of Rights. In 1997 he joined the board of directors of Citizens Action of Illinois.

Activist, Mike Soto gave testimony in 1970 regarding SDS student rioting in Chicago. He testified about Dr. Young, "He is the movement doctor. He has taken care of me at times…He is also an abortionist doctor, takes care of abortions. I was given medicine by him without prescriptions, shots and things like that."

In 2005 Earl Durham, Bernice Targ Weissbourd, Quentin Young, Reverend Wright, and Alice Palmer got together at the Chicago Area Friends of the Student Non Violent Coordinating Committee to celebrate the civil rights movement of the 1960's. Earl Durham was a friend of Frank Marshall Davis, Obama's mentor in Hawaii. Bernice's son is Robert Weissbourd the founder of RW Ventures and a past executive at Shore Bank. At Shore Bank, he worked to strengthen Chicago neighborhoods and community organizations. During Obama's presidential campaign Robert Weissbourd was the chair of Obama for America's Urban and Metropolitan Policy Committee and was a major campaign bundler. In the Chicago world everybody knows everyone.

Dr. Quentin Young is an expert guest on WBEZ, Chicago Public Radio and on Tuesday mornings he hosts his own show "Public Affairs". Dr. Quentin Young is Obama's neighbor, friend, mentor, and personal physician for the last 20 years.

During Obama's run for the Illinois senate seat Obama joined the NEW PARTY. The New Party was established in 1992 with the aim of taking power and burrowing from within. The strategy is to use 'electoral fusion.' Electoral fusion is having a candidate run for office under two or more parties and using the combined number of votes as the candidate's total.

The New Party was founded by DSA member Daniel Cantor with professor and political activist JOEL ROGERS. The first meeting took place at Joel Rogers' home in Wisconsin with the following people:

- Sarah Siskind – Joel Rogers' wife, Obama colleague at Minor, Barnhill and Galland, and ACORN attorney
- Sandy Morales Pope – Union activist
- Wade Rathke - ACORN and SEIU
- Zach Polett – National director of ACORN and former director of Project Vote
- Steve and Jon Kest – both active with ACORN
- Steve Cobble – Institute for Policy Studies
- Harriet Barlow – Institute for Policy Studies
- Barbara Dudley - Greenpeace
- Gary Hudson - DSA and SEIU
- Gary Delgado – Applied Research Center
- Sam Pizzigati – DSA and Institute for Policy Studies
- Tony Mazzucchi – Institute for Policy Studies

New Party goals included full public funding of education, universal voter registration, and proportional representation. The party wanted the "democratization" of banking and financial systems that included popular elections for those who are in charge of the banking system. New Party members wanted guaranteed full employment with a shorter work week. They promoted a "social wage' including healthcare, child care, vacation time, lifelong access to education and a progressive tax system.

As published in 'New Ground 42' in 1995, "New Party political strategy is to support progressive candidates only if they have a concrete chance to win". "Candidates must be approved by New Party political committee." "Candidates must sign a contract with New Party. The contract mandates that they must have a visible and active relationship with New Party." The three Democratic candidates the Chicago chapter endorsed and won were Danny Davis for U.S. House, Patricia Martin for the Cook County Judiciary, and Barack Obama for State Senate.

In 1997 the Supreme Court, in a 6/3 decision, in the case Timmons v. Twin Cities Area New Party stated that fusion is not a constitutional protected civil right. Electoral fusion remains legal in Connecticut, Delaware, Idaho, Mississippi New York, Oregon, South Carolina and Vermont. New York is the only State that electoral fusion is still practiced. The New Party dissolved soon after the Supreme Court decision.

On September 24, 2010 the FBI raided the home of Stephanie Weiner and her husband Joseph Isobaker. Both were former leaders and activists in 1998 with the New Party in Chicago. They were being investigated by the Joint Terrorism Task Force and suspected of terrorist activities. FBI agents spent 12 hours and retrieved 40 boxes of evidence from their home. Neither was arrested on that day, but were scheduled to appear before a grand jury. The grand jury requested receipts to the Arab American Action Network (AAAN), the Popular Front for the Liberation of Palestine, and the Revolutionary Armed Forces of Columbia (FARC). The subpoena requested all items related to trips taken to Jordan, Columbia, Syria and Palestine. The grand jury was scheduled for October 5th but Weiner and Isobaker held a press conference instead. They said they will not cooperate with the FBI. Weiner and Isobaker are anti-war activists. Weiner teaches at Wilber Wilbright College and Isobaker is a professor at the University of Illinois. Isobaker is also the SEIU leader of Local 73 with 24,000 members.

The home of Hatem Abudayyah, the executive director of AAAN, was also raided in Chicago that day. AAAN was founded by Obama's friend Rashid

Khalidi. AAAN was an organization that received grants from the Woods Fund while Obama was the chairman of the board. Then six homes were raided in Minneapolis. All the people whose homes that were raided appear to have a connection with the Freedom Road Socialist Organization. Each person is vowing not to cooperate with the FBI in the grand juries and is invoking their 5th Amendment Rights.

The United States of America is a great country. Activists who spend so much of their energy in an effort to tear down this country will use their 'right' not to witness against themselves. They seem so proud of themselves as they march, chant slogans, and even intimate others; but hide from expressing themselves to the authorities. Actions do have consequences. If they are proud of their actions they should be proud to tell everyone what they do and say.

The AAAN website reported on their 15th Anniversary Banquet and Fundraiser held on December 12, 2010. The keynote speaker was Helen Thomas, an Arab American who was raised as a Christian in the Greek Orthodox Church as a child in Detroit. The subject of her speech was "Justice for Arabs". Thomas is a former member of the White House Press Corps. She was the first female officer of the National Press Club and worked with the Press Corps for 57 years. She retired on June 7, 2010 after some inflammatory statements. She was asked for a statement on Israel and her response was, "Tell them to get the hell out of Palestine". She was questioned about her remarks in October and admitted that her answer was controversial, but it was "exactly what I thought". The Arab American National Museum in Dearborn Michigan, a suburb of Detroit, announced on August 3rd 2010 that they are attempting to raise $30,000 to have a statue of Thomas in the museum. It was announced the day before her 90th birthday.

Judge me by the people who surround me.

CHAPTER 14

★ ★ ★ ★ ★

ACORN

Barack Obama is elected Illinois State Senator. One of his most ardent supporters was ACORN. The mission statement of ACORN:

> The Association of Community Organizations for Reform Now (ACORN) aims to organize a majority constituency of low-to moderate-income people across the United States. The members of ACORN take on issues important to their communities whether those issues are discrimination, affordable housing, quality education, or health services. ACORN believes that low-to moderate-income people are the best advocates for their causes, so ACORN's members act as leaders, spokesmen, and decision makers within the organization.

ACORN grew out of George Wiley's National Welfare Rights Organization (NWRO) which used confrontational tactics to remove eligibility restrictions for welfare. Where NWRO attempted to overwhelm the system through welfare, ACORN attempts to overwhelm the system from multiple fronts. Social rights goals that ACORN advocated for are regulating banking, housing, welfare reform, voting registration, living wages, education, and support labor related causes. ACORN has used the same type of "in your face" tactics as NWRO. They have been known to burst into city council meetings, bring in busloads of angry protesters to the family home of a mayor, overtake bank lobbies, and other hostile demonstrations.

Housing and home ownership has been a cause from the beginning. The Community Reinvestment Act (CRA) of 1977, enacted under President Carter, was meant to revitalize unstable neighborhoods by encouraging home loans. ACORN used CRA regulations to demand that banks make loans to persons that had no credit or work history; disregarding normal banking standards. This has led to the mortgage melt-down which caused the financial crisis the United States is facing today.

In the 1980's squatting camps began by ACORN encouraged people to move into vacant houses. Then, in 1982, they established tent cities in national parks. ACORN harassed banks and lending institutions into lending money for home improvement and mortgages to people without credit and stabile employment, using CRA as its banner. In fact, in 1991, ACORN took over the House Banking Committee hearing room for two days to bring attention to their position. In 1995 Obama represented ACORN in a lawsuit that resulted in an increase of lending institutions approving risky loans. ACORN Housing Corporation was established to aid persons who were not eligible to obtain mortgages because of poor or non-existent credit. The Housing Corporation is funded by taxes but that money also gets funneled to other ACORN sister organizations. As an example, in 2007 Housing Corporation received $5,205,527, then it loaned $119,509 to ACORN and paid $496,615 to Citizens Consulting Inc. (CCI), which is ACORN's accounting arm. The Housing Corporation also granted to the American Institute for Social Justice $3,803,948 used to train young community organizers to agitate for 'social justice'. In 2008 ACORN received an increase in funding in the amount of $25,050.939.

Another tactic that ACORN uses is to pick out a targeted area and form a housing collective. The collective applies pressure on the community to supply funds for ACORN to take charge of renovating and managing abandoned or destroyed buildings for poor tenants. The money goes into ACORN bank accounts. The poor are made to invest 'sweat equity' or free labor in the renovation before they move in and receive title to the home or apartment. ACORN keeps title to the land. When a person moves out they must sell the building back to ACORN at cost, not at market value. The more homes or buildings ACORN rehabilitates the more land the organization accumulates.

In 2009 undercover tapes made by journalists, James O'Keefe and Hannah Giles, dressed as a pimp and a prostitute were broadcast on television. They went to several ACORN Housing Corporation offices across the country from Washington D.C. to California. They told ACORN that they wanted to secure housing to open a house of prostitution and were going to illegally bring in very young girls from El Salvador to work there. Employees of ACORN offered to help them obtain housing, plus advice to avoid IRS audits and the police. They told Hannah to list her profession as a freelancer or a performing artist. They offered advice on how to hide their money, by depositing small amounts into bank accounts and to bury the rest in the back yard. The undercover journalists were also advised to report their $8,000 per month income as $9,600 per year instead of $96,000 on IRS forms.

I suppose this is "working together for social justice and stronger communities".

The 'living wage' movement started in 1994 advocating for wages based on the poverty level for a family of four. Advocates argue having a 'living wage' in urban cities will lift working persons into the middle class. What this program has actually does is eliminate jobs and that hurts the poor. Over 140 cities have adopted the 'living wage', but often exempt unionized businesses. Wal-Mart has been attacked by ACORN as it pursues the local "living wage" movement. Wal-Mart has sought urban areas to locate their stores as they recognize that the residents need to have a place to shop with a diversity of products at reasonable prices. When Wal-Mart locates a store in urban areas they always have more people applying for jobs than they can hire. Where Wal-Mart has located other national chains tend to locate offering the residents more choices. However ACORN continues to battle this big-box store as it resists unionization. ACORN even started an affiliate named Wal-Mart Alliance for Reform Now (WARN), its legal name is Change Wal-Mart Now.

In 2007 Michelle Obama left Treehouse Foods because of its connections to Wal-Mart during the Presidential Campaign. (Barack had been critical of the company over wages they paid their employees). But now she is embracing Wal-Mart and teaming up with the company in her "Let's Move" program. Wal-Mart will promote healthier food and provide better food choices in "food deserts". Michelle has promoted Wal-Mart's commitment with "Let's Move" and Wal-Mart banners.

ACORN knows that requiring business to pay more for wages discourages companies to locate in those communities. Companies that can't afford the additional costs go out of business or relocate elsewhere. Those companies that agree to be unionized provide income from union dues for the unions.

What is odd is that ACORN sued to so they could be exempt from paying the minimum wage in California. The organization requires a 54 hour work week, with no overtime pay, and they attempt to circumvent work safety requirements. ACORN even fights the unionization of their own employees. In a 1995 court case ACORN argued that paying minimum wage would endanger its mission because it would have to hire fewer workers.

Is this social justice? Or is it 'Do as I say, not as I do?'

Voter registration drives led by ACORN under its affiliate Project Vote have been found to be largely fraudulent with multiple identical signatures and non-existent addresses. Training manuals for Project Vote were found to give detailed instructions that condoned and even supported illegal activity to obtain signatures. Employees were required to meet registration targets to keep their jobs. Obama worked for Project Vote in 1985 and later helped train ACORN organizers. A list of some illegal or questionable activities:

- 1986 – Missouri -12 ACORN employees convicted of voter fraud
- 2003 – St. Louis Missouri - only 2,013 out of 5,379 ACORN registrations were legal
- 2004 – Minnesota – at a traffic stop over 300 registrations were found in a trunk that were over the 10 day requirement of delivery
- 2004 - Michigan - Detroit Free Press reports that "overzealous" ACORN campaign workers register non-existent people
- 2005 - 4 ACORN employees register 3,000 fake signatures
- 2005 – Virginia - 83% of ACORN submitted registrations are fraudulent
- 2005 - Missouri - 30 workers sit in a fast food restaurant and complete 1,500 fraudulent registrations from out of date voter lists
- 2006 - Missouri - 1,492 fake registrations are submitted in St. Louis and the State estimates that between 20,000 and 35,000 registrations are fake
- 2006 – Ohio - ACORN gave cash and cigarettes for completing voter registrations. One person admits to completing forms 72 times
- 2007 - FBI reports that ACORN is working for the Democratic Party
- 2008 – Indiana - 4,000 ACORN voter registrations thrown out

- 2008 – New Mexico - over 1,100 ACORN fraudulent registration given to prosecutors

- 2008 - Texas - Harris County throws out 10,000 ACORN registrations

- 2008 - Pennsylvania - 57,435 registrations thrown out

- 2008 - Nevada - ACORN registrations include members of the Dallas Cowboys

- 2008 - ACORN registers 1,315,037 voters.

- 2008 – the Obama campaign gave ACORN $832,000 for get- out-the-vote efforts in key primary states. The initial reports indicated the money was for staging, lighting and sound, but reports were changed when the Pittsburg Tribune-Review discovered the truth.

ACORN tried to get away with voter fraud in Florida during the 2000 election between Bush and Gore. The organization was behind the selection to recount in Miami-Dade Counties. This was a district that had an all Democratic canvassing board; as the entire State was not recounted. A room was selected that was too small to allow reporters or Republican observers in to watch the recount. It was decided that only hand selected ballots by the canvass board would be part of the recount. This prompted Republicans and Cuban-Americans to pound on the door and demonstrate outside the building. The media attention was nationwide and caused the canvass board to stop its illegal plan. Wade Rathke remarked, “We allowed conservatives to steal pages from our playbook and do actions on us in Dade County.”

After all this evidence, Democrats still wanted to provide funding for ACORN and even gave them the job of hiring census takers in February 2009. However, as the New York Times reported on September 11, 2009, the Census Bureau cut its ties with ACORN because it is an organization “that Republicans accuse of fraud” and has caused concern in the general public.

Funding for ACORN comes from various sources with about $7 million from dues paying members. Other sources of money come from government funds and grants, unions, charity organizations and corporate foundations.

- Government funds and grants
- Department of Housing and Urban Development - HUD
- Environmental Protection Agency – EPA
- Justice Department
- Internal Revenue Service – IRS

Unions

- Service Employees International Union – SEIU
- Illinois Home Care Workers and Home Children Providers – this Chicago SEIU affiliate also pays rent to ACORN
- Change to Win labor federation
- Food and Commercial Workers Union
- United Federation of Teachers

Charity foundations

- George Soros' Open Society Institute
- Bauman Family Foundation
- Charles Stewart Mott Foundation
- Corporate foundations
- JP Morgan Chase Foundation
- Ford Foundation
- Ben & Jerry's Foundation
- Bank of America Charitable Foundation

- Citigroup
- Bill and Melinda Gates Foundation

Funding is also given to Project Vote separately from ACORN and other affiliates.

- Tides Foundation
- George Soros' Open Society Institute
- Rockefeller Fund
- Vanguard Charitable Endowment Program
- Bauman Family Foundation
- Omidyar Network Fund
- Carnegie Corporation of New York
- HKH Foundation
- Stephen M. Silberstein Foundation
- Barbra Streisand Foundation
- Ben & Jerry's Foundation

Funding given to ACORN Housing Corporation separate from ACORN and other affiliates.

- JP Morgan Chase Foundation
- Bank of America Charity Foundation
- Annie E. Casey Foundation
- PNC Foundation
- Wachovia Foundation

ACORN received money from its affiliate American Institute for Social Justice in the amount of $4,952,288. American Institute for Social Justice received additional funding.

- George Soros' Open Society Institute
- Rockefeller Brothers Foundation
- Rockefeller Family Fund
- Marguerite Casey Foundation
- Sandler Family Supporting Foundation
- Bill and Melinda Gates Foundation Trust
- Needmor Fund
- McKay's Foundation
- Walter and Elise Hass Fund
- Wood's Fund of Chicago

With all the millions of dollars that ACORN received from government grants, dues paying members, unions, and foundations you would think they could at least pay their taxes. On March 10, 2008 a tax lien was put on the headquarters' property in the amount of $547,312. Then on March 14th an additional $132,997 was added to the original amount in overdue taxes. CCI owes $400,000 in back taxes to the IRS.

In 2008 ACORN had over 400,000 members in the United States, Mexico, Canada, Argentina, and Peru. Money from dues totaled over $7.2 million per year, plus they received government funding from approximately 300 affiliated organizations. ACORN had a $40 million budget in the year 2000. ACORN was set up as a 501©4 non-profit lobbying organization which allows the group to endorse political candidates. Project Vote was set up as a 501© 3 non-profit tax exempt charity which cannot endorse candidates.

All money going to ACORN first goes to Citizen's Consulting Inc. (CCI), which distributes the funds to all of ACORN's affiliates. The 300 affiliated organizations shift money between the different groups so keeping track of the money is practically impossible. CCI is a private non-profit organization in Louisiana, but never requested tax exempt status. Because CCI is not tax exempt it does not have to disclose its financial data. CCI shares the same address as ACORN and the building is listed for sale. However, the tax liens against the building exceed the value of the building and therefore cannot be sold. CCI not only does all of ACORN's, and its affiliates, financial business it also handles HUD, HHS, and the Dept. of Labor. Dale Rathke (brother of Wade) is known as a financial guru; and was the head of CCI from 1999 to 2001.

WADE RATHKE (former SDS member) is co-founder, with Gary Delgado, of ACORN. Wade Rathke is also a co-founder of TIDES, the Chairman of the TIDES CENTER, a co-founder of SEIU, and chairman of the AFL-CIO Organizer Forum. Wade Rathke was originally an activist under George Wiley's NWRO, but left when Wiley was being criticized for using too many white people in his organization. So he left and started the Arkansas Community Organization for Reform. This is the original ACORN before it became a national organization. Rathke enlisted civil rights activists and trained them in the Alinsky method of organizing.

He is remembered in Springfield Massachusetts for his demonstrations at the welfare office with NWRO members going through the offices and intimidating the employees. During the demonstration he stood on desks demanding benefits and threatening not to leave until all welfare was approved. In October 1969 he held a sit-in at the welfare office, with 300 demonstrators, the same day as a anti-war demonstration was planned with 2000 participants. The anti-war demonstrators met Rathke's group at the welfare office and a riot with rock and bottle throwing erupted. The city had a curfew for three days.

In Arkansas Wade Rathke's first mission was to obtain furniture for families. The Governor was persuaded to set aside a furniture fund for the poor. Rathke located a warehouse and thousands of people obtained furniture. ACORN's reputation grew rapidly with its first success. The organization went national and its headquarters moved to New Orleans in 1978. In 1977 he co-founded the TIDES Foundation with Drummond Pike. He formed the United Labor Union Local 100 in 1980 that four years later merged with Service Employees International Union (SEIU).

ACORN continued its mission of social justice as the organization continued to grow. Wade kept close control over ACORN while trying to give the impression that it was run democratically. It was discovered in 2001 that DALE RATHKE, Wade's brother and financial guru, embezzled almost $1 million dollars from ACORN. This information was not shared with the board nor was it reported to the legal authorities, but put on the books as a loan to CCI. Dale was quietly removed from CCI but continued to receive a salary until 2008. The embezzlement was leaked to the press in May and Dale was fired. The board fired Wade Rathke in June. Wade explained the reason he did not disclose Dale's misdeed was because of the word embezzlement. He stated that he didn't want his enemies to use the word as a weapon against ACORN. He said the family would repay the missing $948,607, but Drummond Pike from the TIDES Foundation personally repaid the money.

Wade Rathke was not only fired but was told he could have no further involvement with ACORN. However, he remained the chief organizer of ACORN International Organizing Committee which has been renamed the Community Organization International. This organization has chapters in Argentina, Canada, Dominican Republic, Honduras, India, Kenya, Mexico, and Peru. Now Rathke is involved with another organization called International Dialogue. He posted a message on their web site, in October 2010, announcing they were going to have a meeting in Egypt in the September of 2011. Egypt was going to have their elections in September prior to the fall of Mubarak in March. Rathke was the contact person for this trip. The group planned to discuss leadership transitions being challenged by the Muslim Brotherhood. He was attempting to find people to attend that represented community organizations and unions.

He is still the chief organizer of a SEIU local in New Orleans, still the publisher of the magazine 'Social Policy' which is published 4 times each year, and still on the board of the TIDES Foundation. Wade continues to control the Hospitality, Hotel & Restaurant Organizing Council (HOTROC), which received $58,654 in 2008 from ACORN.

In September 2009, Congress voted to stop all federal funding because of all the evidence of fraudulent registrations from non-qualifying voters. Plus there was the embarrassing video tapes that became public of ACORN helping to obtain mortgages for and helping to establish a brothel.

ACORN filed a law suit in November of 2009 stating that Congress took action to deny funding which amounted to a conviction without a trial. Federal

Judge Nina Gershon on March 10, 2010 agreed with ACORN that Congress had acted without proper judicial review. However the 2nd Court of Appeals overturned the ruling. The Court of Appeals stated that federal funding is a privilege and not a right; therefore Congress had the ability to stop funding.

On election day, November 2, 2010, ACORN and 6 affiliates filed for Chapter 7 bankruptcy. The organization listed assets as $115,000 and debts totaling $4.1 million. In 2008 ACORN had revenue totaling $46.2 million, in 2009 revenue of $16.3 million, and only $1.6 million in 2010.

On November 9, 2010 government auditors stated that ACORN should repay $3.2 million for federal funding they received during 2004 and 2005. They had received grants to remove lead from homes and it was determined that the cost they charged was unreasonable. The audit stated some of the monies were spent inappropriately. HUD is investigating.

ACORN stopped operating in March 2010.

Project Vote has not stopped operating, and only 6 affiliates filed for bankruptcy out of almost 300 known affiliates. In fact, Project Vote received $14,635,000 in grants and contributions in 2010. This affiliate stayed under the radar for the 2010 election and plans to use these funds for the 2012 election.

The current chief of the organization, Bertha Lewis, continued to send out mailings asking for solicitations. The House Oversight and Government Reform Committee reported that Bertha Lewis is still consolidating power and accumulating assets. It is estimated that there is still $20 million deposited in 800 banks; plus the affiliates have about $10 million. ACORN is regrouping and is renaming itself. Some of these groups and affiliates are being renamed:

- Colorado Progressive Coalition
- Florida Consumer Action Network (FCAN)
- Jobs with Justice
- Michigan Forward
- Missouri Pro Vote

- Ohio Voices
- Wisconsin Voices
- Alliance of California for Community Empowerment (ACCE)
- Affordable Housing Centers of America – the former ACORN Housing Corporation
- New York Communities for Change
- Missourians Organizing for Reform Empowerment (MORE)
- Community Organizations International (COI)
- New England United for Justice in Massachusetts
- Arkansas Community Organizations
- Pennsylvania Neighborhoods for Social Justice (PNSJ)
- Pennsylvania Communities Organizing for Change (PCOC)

ACORN may have closed its doors, but its buildings are still standing. The Washington Post has reported that ACORN had tax exempt status, but more than half of the money was not used for charity. The majority of funds went to other affiliates, used to lobbying, and for political activity. Millions of dollars were funneled through ACORN and it's inconceivable to me that people will voluntarily walk away.

On November 2, 2010 (election day and the day ACORN filed for bankruptcy) Louisiana state officials raided the New Orleans headquarters of ACORN. Computers and files were seen being taken out of the office. Bertha Lewis was in the process of moving the headquarters to New York, so it is presumed that officials wanted all material connected to the embezzlement case to be collected before the move. It has been speculated that the embezzlement amount may be closer to $5 million.

MADELINE TALBOTT was the leader of the Chicago ACORN chapter when Obama was in Chicago. She first met him when he led Project Vote and originally thought he was a competitor. Talbott was so impressed with his skills that she asked him to train her staff. Talbott is often mentioned as being a mentor to Obama.

Talbott is well known for her involvement with subprime lending and intimidating banks. She is proud that she lead her group to get banks to make risky loans, even though the banks got there "kicking and screaming". Obama trained the staff that used the intimidation tactics on the lending institutions. He was hired to represent them in the case Buycks-Roberson v. Citibank. The case ended in a settlement agreement and Fannie Mae agreed to buy the mortgages. Talbott said, "If this pilot program works it will send a message to the lending community that it's OK to make these kinds of loans."

Another other issue that Talbott is remembered for is her insistence in a 'living wage.' She coordinated her disruptive direct action attacks with SEIU. The mayor and the Chamber of Commerce were against a 'living wage' law as they argued that it would hurt small business in Chicago. During a meeting to discuss the issue in the City Hall, Talbott was insistent that she attend with other ACORN members even though she was told there was no room. So, of course, she knocked over the metal detector and the table it was on, and her cohorts backed the police to the door. She was handcuffed and arrested for mob action and disorderly conduct. 'Living wage' is now the law not only in Chicago, but also in Illinois. The current federal minimum wage is $7.50, in Illinois it is $8.25, and in Chicago it is over $11.00.

Michelle Obama complains about food deserts in inner cities with the high price of food. I would think the high cost of wages just might be part of the reason. I have no scientific data to support my theory, just common sense.

Madeline Talbott claims that Obama was never her employee, but he did support her financially through the Annenberg Challenge and the Woods Fund when he was on both boards. A report from the Woods Fund states that Obama was very aware of the tactics Talbott and ACORN used. The report indicates the problem of securing funds from foundations and donors for organizations that use intimidating and radical tactics can scare off even liberal donors. The report continued that because the Woods Fund claims to be non-ideological it "enabled the Trustees to make grants to organizations that use confrontational tactics."

Action Now is using the building that previously housed ACORN. In March 2008 Talbott locked ACORN out and took over the office. She is the lead organizer for the new grassroots organization Action Now. Its mission "is to organize working families and strengthen their voices on issues of racial, social, and economic justice". She is busy working on several new programs such as preventing foreclosures, working with the teacher's union, and increasing the minimum wage.

When Wade Rathke left ACORN, BERTHA LEWIS was named the new director. She had led ACORN in New York since 2007, founded and co-chaired the New York Working Families Party, and is a long time activist. In 2007, 'Crain's Magazine' named her one of a hundred of the most influential women of New York. The fate of ACORN was sealed when the video tapes from the undercover journalists was made public.

On September 2, 2009 Bertha Lewis made an appointment to visit the White House on Saturday the 5th. She was given a staff tour, which is much nicer and more personal than a normal group tour. This was five days before the damning video tapes were released to the media. The White House stated the Bertha Lewis who visited wasn't the Bertha Lewis from ACORN, but for security concerns will not identify who this Bertha Lewis is. They have also stated the visits of Malik Shabazz, Jeremiah Wright, and Bill Ayers that have shown up on White House logs are not the familiar names connected to the Black Panthers, Trinity United, or Weather Underground. When Obama was asked by George Stephanopoulos from ABC about the ACORN controversy he responded, "Frankly, it's not really something I've followed closely. I didn't even know that ACORN was getting a whole lot of federal money".

On March 23, 2010 Bertha Lewis told NPR, "we're not dead yet". She went on to say that they got somewhat smaller but they will "transform" into a "leaner and meaner group". Then on March 25th at a Young Democratic Socialist meeting she said, "Any of these groups that say I'm young, I'm a Democrat, and I'm a Socialist it is all right with me". She added that the group needed to fear the Tea Partiers as they "might round them up in the middle of the night and put them in internment camps". On May 25th she was arrested at an immigration rally in New York. She was demonstrating against the Arizona immigration law and for open borders.

In June she announced plans to start a new organization called Black Leadership Institute. The main priority is to bring Black immigrants and African-Americans into the immigration reform fight. She laments that Latinos have made an impact and the black community needs to get involved.

The former ACORN office has been renamed New York Community for Change (NYCC). John Kest, the former New York director of ACORN, is the director and the staff remains the same, but less in number. Kest remains on the staff of the Working Families Party that ACORN started

NYCC has an ambitious agenda. They still work to elect progressives into office and campaign for a living wage. Now they plan to union organize supermarket and car wash employees. The organization is concerned about foreclosures, so NYCC scheduled meetings with Bank of America, Citibank, HSBC, JP Morgan Chase, and Wells Fargo to demand they speed up efforts on mortgage mediation. The organization threatened to pull union pension funds from the banks if the lending institutions didn't cooperative. They also threaten to post videos on YouTube of angry foreclosed people removing their money from the banks.

As if this were not enough, NYCC has plans to go after landlords that they determine are discriminating against subsidized Section 8 tenants. Then the organization plans on getting an additional 2,250 subsidized housing units built in Forest City Ratner that ACORN began. If the Forest City project goes through as originally planned, the organization will obtain funding to manage the housing units. The United Federation of Teachers is giving NYCC $33,000 per month to support progressive campaigns and to help organize a union for home based child care workers. There is also a campaign to stop a Wal-Mart store from being built in Brooklyn, citing the company does not pay a living wage and discriminates.

Black Leadership Institute and NYCC will work in tandem as one is classified as a 501(c) 3 and the other as a 501(c) 4. This allows one organization to promote candidates and the other to collect funds to get out the vote. This is patterned like the ACORN affiliates that got into trouble.

The names have changed, but the people and the agenda have stayed the same. The organizers cite lofty progressive goals, take the money, and use people as pawns. Unfortunately, the pawns don't know that they are expendable and may actually believe in whatever cause they are fighting for. After all, NYCC is committed to promoting social and economic justice.

Judge me by the people who surround me.

CHAPTER 15

★ ★ ★ ★ ★

Muslim Friends

An Arab community fund raiser held on May 15, 1998 was hosted by Ali Abunimah, founding member of AAAN and co-founder of Electronic Intifada. Professor Edward Said, the keynote speaker, and his wife were seated at the dinner table next to the honored guest Barack Obama and his wife Michelle. Obama may have been a student of Said at Columbia University.

This fund raiser was to commemorate the 50th anniversary of Nakba (also spelled Nakbah), the translation means catastrophe. It was on this date in 1948 that the Palestinians state they were driven from Israel, the day after the creation of Israel. Yasser Arafat declared this date to be Nakba Day in 1998 and millions of people participate in marches and other events on that day.

EDWARD SAID (pronounced sigh-EED) taught at Columbia University from 1963 until his death in 2003. He obtained the title of University Professor in 1992, which is the highest ranking professor status. He has lectured at over 100 universities and his teachings have influenced Middle East studies throughout the country.

He wrote many books but is most known for the book titled "Orientalism". Orientalism is an idea he created. It means that the West have false impressions of the East which is a form of racism or prejudice against "Arabo-Islamic" people. He argued that the West created caricatures of the Arabs as being either oil partners or terrorists, and have not looked into the culture of the people.

Said was an ardent supporter of Palestine and was very involved in efforts to create a Palestinian statehood. He was a member of the Palestinian National Council from 1977 to 1991. He left because he felt that Arafat was too moderate and disagreed with the Oslo Accord, which was a negotiated settlement. He said that Israel is an illegitimate colonialist state that preys against blameless Palestinians.

The book "Orientalism" was also a memoir of his childhood. He wrote he was born in 1932 in Jerusalem, his parents were both Palestinians, and his father was a U.S. citizen who fought in WW I with General Pershing. As a Protestant Palestinian, he wrote that he was "raised as a Christian wrapped in a Muslim culture". He claimed his family moved in 1947 just before the mass eviction and fled to Cairo, Egypt and lived as exiles. Said wrote that he was a trouble maker in school and his parents sent him to a boarding school as a teen in Massachusetts.

It was later discovered that all the details of his youth Said described were not true. He was born in Talbiya, an affluent Arab quarter of Jerusalem. This was because his mother had a bad experience with the health care system in Egypt where her first son died at birth. The family had lived in Cairo for a decade and returned there after his birth. The family home he described was actually owned by family members. The family rented the second story to the Kingdom of Yugoslavia for consulate use and the first floor to a Jewish philosopher named Martin Buber. His father was a successful businessman and the family lived in luxurious apartments. Said studied at exclusive British schools in Egypt and attended an expensive American prep school as a teen.

Eight days after 9/11 he signed a published statement titled "Justice not Vengeance". The statement said, "military response will not end terror", but it "would spark a cycle of escalating violence". Other signatures included Mike Farrell, Danny Glover, Michael Lerner, Bonnie Raitt, Gloria Steinem, Martin Sheen, Harry Belafonte, Ruby Dee, Barbara Ehrenreich, and Ossie Davis.

Edward Said called United States foreign policy an "Israelization" and called the Bush administration "American Taliban". He is quoted saying, "most people in the Arab world are convinced –because it is patently true— that America has simply allowed Israel to kill Palestinians at will, with U.S. weapons, and unconditional political support in the U.N.". Said also criticized Islamic terrorists stating, "First I am secular, second, I do not trust religious movements; and third, I disagree with those (Hamas and Islamic Jihad) movements, methods, means, analyses, values, and visions".

Said was on the advisory committee of American-Arab Anti-Discrimination

Committee with Noam Chomsky, Ramsey Clark, Angela Davis, and Pete Seeger. He served on the advisory board of Middle East Children's Alliance and was also on the board of trustees of MIFTAH with Rashid Khalidi.

RASHID KHALIDI was born in 1948 in New York. His father was a Saudi Muslim of Palestinian descent born in Jerusalem and his mother was a Christian Lebanese American. They got married in a Unitarian Church in Brooklyn where Rashid attended Sunday school. His father worked at the United Nations and had a high security level position which allowed him to be involved with high level discussions on Middle East policy. These discussions were often talked about at the dinner table and Rashid learned at an early age that often what the media reported was distorted. As a child he attended the United Nations School. In 1970 he received his Bachelors Degree at Yale, where he was a member to the secret Wolf's Head Society. He earned his PhD at Oxford University.

Khalidi was a full time assistant Professor of Political Studies and Public Administration from 1976 until 1983 at the American University of Beirut. He was a research fellow at the Institute for Palestine Studies and taught at Lebanese University. Khalidi was in Beirut during the Lebanon War as an official at the Palestine news service for the PLO called WAFA. Khalidi denies that he was ever a member of the PLO. He was a professor at the University of Chicago from 1987 until 2003, and was the director of the Center of Middle Eastern Studies and the Center for International Studies. Khalidi is a member of the National Advisory Committee of the U.S. International for Peace in Middle East, which is a national organization of Jews, Christians, and Muslims. He is a member of the Board of Sponsors of the Palestinian Israel Journal, a founding trustee of the Center for Palestine Research and Studies, and is a member of the Council of Foreign Relations (CFR).

In 1986 Khalidi wrote the book 'Under Siege and PLO Decision' that was dedicated to Yasser Arafat. He called a two state solution an impractical "utopian vision" and gave a tribute to the anti-Israeli fighters. He wrote that Israel is "a state that exists today at the expense of Palestine".

Rashid is married to MONA KHALIDI and they have three adult children. In 2004 he told a reporter that one daughter was an archaeologist in Yemen and another daughter was attending a legal institute in the West Bank.

Mona also worked for WAFA in the English section of the newspaper. In

1995 Rashid and Mona, co-founded the Arab American Action Network (AAAN) in Chicago, which is a pro-Palestine and anti-Israel organization. This organization seeks to support illegal aliens with amnesty. The group attempts to empower Arab immigrants with community organizing, education, social services, and leadership development. AAAN believes Arabs are routinely mistreated in the United States and seek to remedy the injustice. Mona was the President until 2008 and remains on the board. The Woods Fund, where it is reported that Rashid served on the board with Obama, granted AAAN 20% of its yearly budget during 2001 and 2002. In 2005, Khalidi wrote a letter to New Mexico's Governor Bill Richardson about opposing illegal aliens obtaining driver's licenses stating these actions were a "bigoted attack on Arabs and Muslims". In 2008 Rashid said he never heard of the Woods Fund until he saw in on some blogs.

Khalidi and Obama met while they taught at the University of Chicago. Their friendship grew to the point that they and their wives began socializing. The couples shared dinners at the Khalidi home and the Obamas reportedly babysat for the Khalidi children.

During the 2000 Obama campaign for U.S. Representative the Khalidis held a fund raiser at their home. Rumor was the Hyde Park intellectuals were attempting to help Obama climb the political ladder. It was at the Khalidi home where Ali Abunimah, founder of The Electronic Intifada, met Barack Obama.

After the 9/11 Twin Towers attack in New York City, Khalidi condemned the news media for "hysteria about suicide bombers". He opposed the invasions in Iraq, even as he admitted "international terrorism has been sponsored by Iraq". He continued, "the invasion in Iraq had no legitimate justification and was the ideas of racist neoconservatives". Khalidi has called for reparations for the Iraqi people and is opposed to war in the Middle East. He was against the Gulf War in 1991 saying the public support for the war was "idiot consensus".

In 2003 Khalidi went to Columbia University to become the Edward Said Professor of Modern Arab Studies. A farewell dinner was held for him and the Obamas had the honor of sharing his table. Bill Ayers and Bernardine Dohrn were also in attendance. Obama gave a speech where he reminisced about sitting at the Khalidi table and Mona cooking dinner. He said they had many talks and Rashid "constantly reminding me of my own blind spots and my own biases". He continued, "It's for that reason the conversation, a conversation that is necessary, not just around Mona and Rashid's dinner table, but around this entire world." He added "Israel has no God-given right to occupy Palestine" and "there's been genocide against the Palestinian people by Israelis". Other speakers praised Palestine and panned Israel. Khalidi gave his support to Barack Obama for U.S Senate.

Khalidi had a 15 week teacher training program on Middle East politics at Columbian Middle East Institute. The training included statements which justified the jihad attacks against Israeli civilians. The New York Times reported the Saudis were "funneling tens of thousands of dollars" into the classes that brought attention to the program in 2005. The School Chancellor removed Khalidi from the teacher training program after the report was published. Khalid's influence continues as his books are frequently assigned as reading assignments and used as references for Middle East studies in college.

The second First State Dinner at the White House was widely reported as being crashed by two people who were not on the guest list and had no formal invitation. The couple was Michaele Salahi and her husband Tareq Salahi, who insist that they did not crash the affair as they were invited. They have ties with Rashid Khalidi. Khalidi was the Vice President of the American Task Force for Palestine and Tareq Salahi served on the board.

The Freedom Flotilla to Gaza that erupted into violence was financed in part by Movement for Democratic Society. Rashid Khalidi is on the board of directors and he is on the Advisory Board of the US Campaign to End the Israeli Occupation. Rashid and Mona participated in the appeal to fund the ship "The Audacity of Hope" for the second flotilla. The appeal was posted on UStoGAZA.Org and they were asking for donations to raise $370,000. Khalidi suggested the name, "The Audacity of Hope", which obviously refers to the title of Obama's book. He said that if the administration is troubled with the ship's name "it can simply insist publicly that Israel lift the siege". Khalidi stated he is not the organizer of this cause.

Khalidi supported the people in Tunisia, Egypt and Libya seeking a change in governance from dictators in the beginning months of 2011. He said the peaceful protestors were brave because they knew the leaders would use brutal force to subdue them. The young revolutionaries, he claimed, are very aware of world events, and they will know better than the dictatorial and oppressive leaders what they need to obtain their democracy and social justice. The young generation, he said, now has hope for a better life. He predicted the rebellion would "bubble over" in the Middle East from Morocco to the Gulf.

Since the beginning of 2011 the Middle East has indeed "bubbled over". Rebellion and the removal of the leaders of countries such as Egypt, Libya, Syria, Yemen, and others have dominated the news. It almost seems like he may have been part of the planning or he may be very psychic.

ALI ABUNIMAH is the co-founder, with Nigel Parry, of the Electronic Intifada, which is the internet portal for the Palestinian terrorist movement in the United States. He was born on December 29, 1971 in Washington DC to Palestinian American parents. His father was a former Jordanian diplomat and Ambassador to the United Nations. As a child he lived in the United Kingdom and Belgium. He received his Bachelor's Degree at Princeton and earned his Master's Degree at the University of Chicago. He continues to be a full time researcher at the university.

Abunimah is a pro-Palestinian activist, writer, and commentator on the Middle East and for Arab-Americans. He has written books and articles in many newspapers; and has been a guest on radio and television. Abunimah also lectures at colleges across the United States. The book he published in 2006, "One Country: A Bold Proposal to End the Israeli-Palestinian Conflict", rejects a two state solution. He states the Palestinian violence and terrorism are caused entirely by Israel because of "land confiscation" and "ongoing orgy of violence". He advocates for the complete destruction of Israel.

He's been on the board of AAAN, but is best known for his internet web site Electronic Intifada (EI). Abunimah co-founded the web site in 1991, which is an independent, not- for-profit internet publication with 501(c) 3 status. It publishes news and commentary regarding the Israel/Palestinian conflict from a Palestinian viewpoint. EI believes it can empower the collective and individuals to action by publishing information and analyst to activists, journalists, and the public. Critics of EI say it should lose its 501 (c) 3 status because information is not educational but inflammatory and is in violation of tax law. Critics also state that EI attempts to influence legislation.

Electronic Intifada (EI) operates under the Middle East Cultural and Charitable Society. EI receives funding from the International Solidarity Movement (ISM). ISM claims not to be an organization, but a movement that individuals, organizations, or groups can join that agree with dismantling the State of Israel. Other groups under this umbrella movement include 501(c)3 non-profits; Holy Land Trust, Middle East Fellowship, Middle East Children's Alliance (MECA),and AL-AWADA (or Palestinian Right to Return Coalition PRRC). Money raised by the non-profit charities is channeled through ISM and can then be funneled overseas.

ISM creates multi-layers of Anti-Israel groups to make the impression of mass movements. The coordination of several organizations makes it difficult to determine the centralized organization to investigate. If one organization is under scrutiny the others can then claim not to be represented by the actions of another. ISM use volunteers (mostly college students) to send to Israel pretending to be representatives of charities and then they interfere with anti-terrorist operations. ISM claims it receives no government funds, but depends on donations from people from all over the world.

The co-founders of ISM are Adam Shapiro and Huwaida Arraf. Arraf was an organizer and spokesperson for the May 2010 Freedom Flotilla. In 2002 Shapiro and Arraf wrote, "The Palestinian resistance must take on a variety of characteristics, both violent and non-violent... people will get killed and injured, but these deaths are no less noble than carrying out a suicide operation".

Ali Abunimah has interacted with Obama over the years at various functions in the Palestinian communities of Chicago. He said Obama often spoke at events to raise money for U.N. camps for Palestinian refugee camps. He remembers introducing Obama on stage for a fund raiser for the Deheisha refugees. Abunimah said Obama used to be very comfortable when speaking for and being associated with Palestinian rights advocates opposing Israeli occupation. He said Obama was "quite frank that the United States needed to be more even handed because it leaned too much toward Israel". "These were the kind of statements I'd never heard from a United States politician who seemed like he was going somewhere".

Abunimah recalled meeting with Obama at the Ayers 2000 political fund raiser. "I had a chance to really talk to him. He convinced me he was very aware of the issues and critical of the United States history toward Israel and the lack of sensitivity to Arabs. He was very supportive of United States pressure on Israel."

Abunimah also tells of a meeting they had in 2004 when Obama was running for U.S. Senate. He said Obama expressed that he was sorry that "I haven't said more about Palestine right now, but we are in a tough primary race. I'm hoping when things calm down, I can be more up front." Obama then told me "keep up the good work".

I question what Obama's real opinion of the Palestinian and Israeli conflict is. Does he relate to the view points of the Palestinians or was it the politically correct thing to do in Chicago? Did he really mean all the things he said or was it to get votes?

Abunimah went to Egypt as part of the Free Gaza movement in December 2009. He was not one of the hundred that were able to enter Gaza, so he held a demonstration instead in Cairo. He stated the demonstrators were surrounded by the police and some had their cameras taken. He said "Gaza is harder to visit than a prison…It is too bad we didn't get into Gaza, but the most important thing is that Al-Jazeera has carried it through the entire world".

He did not go on the Freedom Flotilla to Gaza in May 2010. However, when news of the conflict with the Israeli military became public, he was at a demonstration at the Israeli Consulate in Chicago the next day. On the day of the conflict Code Pink had the rally organized with buses to take people to the Consulate. They were calling, through the internet, for a militant and massive picket and demonstration. Abunimah was announced as the speaker for the event. On June 1st about 1,000 angry people were in the picket line chanting. There were dozens of demonstrations across the country on both May 31st and June 1st from Washington DC to San Francisco.

How many people still believe these demonstrations, with busloads of agitated people, are spontaneous events?

The EI was involved with the UStoGaza organization. One writer for EI is Ismail Khalidi, son of Rashid Khalidi, and one of the organizers is Najla Said, daughter of the late Edward Said.

There has been much speculation on whether or not Obama is a Muslim and where his priorities lay. He has maintained many friends who are anti-Israel and his religious mentor, Jeremiah Wright has voiced anti-Jewish sentiments. During the Presidential election the American Israel Public Affairs Committee (AIPAC) voiced concerns over Obama's loyalties even though he supported five AIPAC backed bills in the Senate. However some wondered if he was on a mission to change negative perceptions of him and the internet rumors that he was Muslim.

In "Audacity of Hope", Obama wrote, "I will stand with the Muslims should the political wind shift in an ugly direction".

Judge me by the people who surround me.

SECTION FOUR

★ ★ ★ ★ ★

Political Life

CHAPTER 16

★ ★ ★ ★ ★

Run for Rep

Illinois U.S. Representative Bobby Rush decided in 1999 to run against Richard Daley for mayor. He was defeated. Obama, and others, thought that Rush was now vulnerable and could be defeated when his term ended in 2000. Rush was first elected to Congress in 1993 and was well liked in his district. He was a Baptist minister, a veteran of the civil rights movements, and a founding member of the Illinois Black Panthers. His programs for meal programs and medical screening in the neighborhoods were much appreciated. Rush's campaign emphasized experience and the slogan; "Better Times are Coming".

Obama did not have the name recognition in the neighborhoods that Rush had. Journalists and reporters describe Obama's campaign as lack luster and failing to relate with the community. He was described as being stiff and sounding like a newscaster, or like he was reciting a political science thesis. He was called arrogant, placing himself above everybody else, always telling everyone he went to Harvard. There were rumors he was funded by the Hyde Park mafia, others felt he didn't relate and wasn't black enough as he wasn't descended from slaves. Some of the media thought his lack of enthusiasm was from embarrassment due to his lack of experience and his reputation as an ineffective legislator. When asked about his lack of experience Obama talked about his community organizing and helping to design programs from the ground level.

Obama said, "It's not enough for us to protest police misconduct without thinking systematically about how we're going to change practice". Rush said, "Protest has got us where we are today. Barack is a person who read about civil rights protests and thinks he knows all about it. I helped make that history by blood, sweat, and tears". Obama rambled, "Congressmen Rush exemplifies a politics that is reactive, that waits for crises to happen, then holds a press conference, and hasn't been particularly effective at building a broad based coalition". Rush responded, "He went to Harvard and became an educated fool. We're not impressed with these folk with these eastern elite degrees."

Congressman Rush won reelection and defeated Obama badly. A local newspaper wrote Obama "lost because he was a presumptuous young man challenging a popular incumbent". However Obama did make political friends and got fundraising experience. The local media was surprised and impressed at his transformation during the 2004 campaign for U.S. Senator. When Obama lost he began to take his work seriously and his aloofness was gone. He learned he needed to have an agenda and talk about issues he felt passionate about. His speaking was much more polished and he showed emotion. A reporter from the 'Chicago Reader' wrote, "He became a fight announcer, a preacher, and a motivational speaker all on the same platform".

One of the issues Obama became impassioned about is the redistribution of wealth. On September 6, 2001 he took part in a radio discussion on Chicago Public Radio, WBEZ.FM, about the civil rights movement and redistributive policies. He explained the inability of the courts to redistribute wealth by taxing those with more money at a higher rate than those with less money. He said, "One of the tragedies of the civil rights movement was that the civil rights movement became so court focused. I think there was a tendency to lose track of the political and organizing activities on the ground that are able to bring about the coalition of power through which you bring about redistributive change". Obama further explained that redistribution of wealth must be decided by the legislative bodies, "because that is what a progressive tax is about."

Obama must truly believe in redistributing other people's money as he has not been overly generous redistributing his own income. Per 2000 tax records he reported gross annual income of $240,505 and donated $2,350 to charity. In the tax year of 2001 his gross annual income rose to $272,759 and charity donations decreased to $1,470, which is less than $30 per week. For some reason in 2006 he donated $22,500 to Trinity United Church of Christ.

Abortion was a subject Obama spoke about on the floor in Congress during a March 2001 session. The issue was the Born Alive Infant Protection Act, which he argued against. Part of the bill defined what a "born alive" baby was. It was defined as a child that was independent of his mother, had a heart beat, was breathing, and/or could voluntarily move his muscles.

Obama argued against defining what a "born alive" infant was because it would encroach on the abortions rights of the mother. He explained that if child was defined as "born alive" he would have equal protection rights as an individual. When the issue came up for a vote, Obama voted 'present'. The issue came up again on Aril 4, 2002 and again he spoke against a bill that required a second physician available to perform life saving procedures to a child "born alive". This time he did vote 'No'. In 2003 the issue came up again, while he chaired the Health and Human Service Committee, and he was stilled opposed to the bill.

Did you know that Planned Parenthood, founded by Margaret Sanger, was designed to limit the population of undesirables? Sanger was a Marxist, member of the Committee of New York Socialist Party, associated with International Workers of the World (IWW), and associated with Emma Goldman, founder of the American Communist Party. Goldman mentored Roger Baldwin the founder of American Civil Liberties Union (ACLU). Sanger was also a nurse.

Sanger opened up a birth control clinic when it was still illegal for doctors to discuss birth control. After many arrests, and a public outcry, laws were changed. She started the American Birth Control League (ABCL). At their conference speakers talked about the "Black and Yellow" peril, sterilizing the unfit, and described eugenics as being humanitarian. Planned Parenthood Federation was organized in 1942.

Sanger believed in eugenics, the practice of improving the genetic composition of a population, by the sterilization of the "unfit". She believed it would be the salvation of the American civilization. Her advocacy of birth control was opposed by many Christians, but she blamed all opposition on the Catholics. She suggested in her magazine "Birth Control Review" that the "Catholic stock" was inferior to non-Catholic stock, the Unitarians, and Universal Freethinkers".

In 1939, with Dr. Gamble (of Proctor and Gamble) she started the Negro Project. They expressed concern that black leaders may come to the conclusion that their programs were designed as an extermination plot, so it was decided to put black leaders in positions that appeared to be in charge. Sanger said, "We do not want the word to go out that we want to exterminate the Negro population". They promoted the project as an economic betterment program and targeted black ministers.

The ultimate goal was to establish in Congress a Parliament of Population to improve the genetic pool. They wanted to stop medical care to slum dwellers, those dependent on taxpayers, and to those persons who were deaf, blind, unfit, feeble minded, or undesirable. They wanted boards where couples were granted permission to have children and to limit families to 2.1 children. In 1930 Sanger invited Nazi anthropologist Eugen Fischer to her home. His ideas were implemented in the extermination of the Jews in Germany. He is said to have inspired Adolf Hitler on his opinions of eugenics.

Planned Parenthood performs about 25% of all abortions in the United States. The majority of the clinics (78%) are in inner city black neighborhoods. They support homosexuality and advocate compulsory sterilization for those who already have 2 children. A Texas clinic had 6,000 patients and only 3 were referred for adoption in 1988. In 2002, Planned Parenthood performed 227,375 surgical abortions, claimed a total income of $288.2 million, and reported profits of $36.6 million. In 2008 they performed 324,008 abortions and received approximately $350 million in federal grants and had a profit of $85 million. Planned Parenthood is the main impetus behind the abortion and pro-choice groups.

In the fiscal year 2010 Obama ended funding for abstinence only programs and provided $178 million for comprehensive sexuality education. (Comprehensive sexuality education may include safe sex practices, sexual orientation, sexual pleasure, birth control, masturbation, and advocacy training against discrimination of lesbian, gay, bisexual, transgender and questioning persons.) The budget included $317 million for Title X family planning under the Medicaid program. Title X pays for contraceptive birth control, chemical abortions, birth control for teens, hormonal drugs, and sexual devices to teens with or without parental approval. Planned Parenthood receives both Medicaid and State funding. The organization also receives private funds and governments contribute to the International Planned Parenthood Foundation. Title X is administered by the Office of Population Affairs within the Office of Public Health and Science. Title X was established by Family Planning Service and Population Research Act of 1970.

Susan G. Komen for the Cure contributed $3.3 million between 2004 and 2009. United Way has contributed since 1970. However local United Way agencies are beginning to defund the organization. About 257 corporations stopped contributing because of boycotts and pro-life pressure. Many States are contemplating to stop, have begun to stop, or reduce funding because of their own financial problems. These States include California, New Jersey,

Florida Georgia, and Texas. Canada has considering defunding the International Parenthood Foundation. They told the G8 in 2009 that they would no longer fund overseas abortions. The International Planned Parenthood Foundation asked all governments to ensure that all children aged 10 and over, receive comprehensive sexuality education.

The American Life League did a review of Planned Parenthood reports and discovered that between 2002 and 2008 the organization received $2 billion in federal grants. But they only spent $657.1 million and that's $1.3 billion which is unaccounted for.

In 2008 two former employees turned into whistle blowers when they discovered the organization was over billing the federal government. They claim one affiliate in California paid $22,695 for birth control pills and fraudulently charged the federal government $918,084. Planned Parenthood denied the allegations and state their billing practices are permissible. The organization asked the court to dismiss charges, but the 9th Court of Appeal denied the motion. The attorney for the whistle blowers call it "ACORN-like corruption". There have been similar findings of fraudulent billing in New Jersey and in the State of Washington.

On October 2, 2002 Obama gave his anti-war speech on the Federal Plaza in Chicago just nine days before Congress authorized the invasion in Iraq. The rally was organized by Marilyn Katz and Bettylu Saltzman. The speech did not get much attention. The Chicago Tribune said they didn't cover it as they focused on Jesse Jackson. In the speech, he said he did not oppose all wars but did oppose "dumb wars". "What I am opposed to is the attempt by political hacks like Karl Rove to distract us from a rise in the uninsured, a rise in poverty rate, a drop in median income, to distract us from corporate scandals, and a stock market that has gone through the worst months since the Great Depression."

Saltzman met Obama when he was working on the black voter registration drive. She was very impressed with him and introduced him to the wealthy donors in Chicago and talked about him to political adviser David Axelrod. Obama was considering a campaign for U.S. Senate and wanted to work with Axelrod. He was concerned this speech could affect a future run for national office. An aide told him that if he wanted to get Axelrod as an advisor he should not disappoint Saltzman who asked him to speak at the rally.

During the Presidential campaign a 20 second spot of the speech was found at a local television station. The copy was grainy and the audio was poor. With Axelrod, Obama re-recorded the speech with a video of his image and scenes of war in the background. This video was released on the internet.

Judge me by the people who surround me

CHAPTER 17

★ ★ ★ ★ ★

Jackson and Jones Jrs.

Obama decided in 2002 to run for the U.S. Senate seat. He first spoke to Jesse Jackson Jr. about the Senate run. Jesse Jr. said he had no intention of running and became an early supporter. Emil Jones Jr. become his mentor after winning the election.

JESSE JACKSON JR. is the son of Reverend Jesse Jackson founder of The Rainbow Coalition and RainbowPUSH Coalition. Jackson Jr. was elected to the U.S. House of Representatives in 1995. Prior to being elected into office he was active with his father's organizations and political ambitions running for president. He actually gave his first speech at the age of five at the Rainbow Coalition. There was some controversy when he ran for office as it was discovered that part of his salary, while an employee at Rainbow Coalition, was subsidized by the Hotel Employee and Restaurant Employee International Union. Since being elected he has a reputation of never missing a vote.

He is a founding member of the Apollo Alliance.

Jackson Jr. was co-chair of the Obama presidential campaign and gave a speech at the 2008 Democratic National Convention. In December 2008, during the campaign, his father made some extremely negative remarks about Obama which he could not defend. Reverend Jackson said that Zionists would lose clout when Obama is elected and that Obama was acting white. The most publicized and controversial comment was that he wanted to "cut his nuts out...telling niggers how to behave" with moral lectures. He also called Obama a "half breed nigger". Jackson later apologized and stated his support for the campaign.

After the presidential election Jackson Jr. was caught in the middle of Governor Blagojevich's pay-for-play investigation for Obama's senate seat. He admitted that he was candidate #5 who offered between $1 million and $6 million for the senate seat. Later it was revealed that he was working with the federal investigation to verify that Blagojevich was willing to "sell" the seat. Previously, Jackson Jr. stated his wife was denied the position of Lottery Commissioner because he wouldn't give the Blagojevich campaign $25,000.

EMIL JONES JR. had been in the Illinois Senate since 1983 and became the Senate President in 2003. Obama asked Jones to help him in his bid to run for U.S. Senate. Even though Obama had voted "present" 129 times on previous legislation Jones agreed to support him. (Note that voting in the Illinois senate is done by pushing one of three buttons that are color coded. Green is for yes, red is for no, and yellow is for present.) Voting present is actually a no vote as only the yes votes can pass a bill. However by voting present there is no record of voting for or against any issue. First, Obama was given the position of Chair of the Health and Humans Services Committee. Then Jones directed to Obama most of the legislation that appealed to the local neighborhoods and grabbed media attention. During Obama's last year in the State Senate he sponsored 26 bills that passed.

Jones was first elected to the Illinois House of Representatives in 1973 and then to the State Senate in 1983. He retired in 2009 and nominated his son Emil Jones III to take his seat. Jones is an old school Chicago politician who knows how to block legislation of his opponents and pass legislation to those who contribute to him.

He has been criticized for using his position for helping his family and friends. A couple of months after he married his second wife, a state employee, she received a raise between $60,000 and $70,000. Governor Blagojevich had decided to reclassify the salary for some employees. Jones' son was able to secure a state position that wasn't advertised. A university got a grant for $4.5 million for computer work, and Jones' step-son and nephew found employment there.

When Obama left his Senate seat after winning the presidential election Blagojevich offered Jones the position. In return, he wanted Jones to steer the Senate to uphold a veto on a bill designed to prevent companies that did business with the government from making political contributions.

However, Obama called Jones and asked to let the Bill pass so Republicans wouldn't have any more dirt on Chicago politicians. Jones allowed the Bill to pass.

Not all of the Senators were pleased with the attention that Obama, with less seniority, was getting. Jones had a talk with them. When Obama asked Jones what happened, Jones replied, " I made them an offer and you don't want to know".

Judge me by the people who surround me.

CHAPTER 18

★ ★ ★ ★ ★

Christian Mentors

Obama was getting all of his ducks in a row for his next political move. He had already moved into the Hyde Park neighborhood which had a history of supporting progressive politicians separate from the Chicago Democratic machine. He worked on grant making foundations that supported his progressive friends and enabled him to enlarge his political base. He was known in the South Side as an organizer and worked closely with ACORN and their political machine for getting out the vote. He was working with the most powerful man in the State Senate. Obama also made relationships with the local churches. His connection to Reverend Wright has been well documented. Two other clergy he had relationships with are Reverend Michael Pfleger and James Meeks.

REVEREND MICHAEL PFLEGER is a Catholic priest at St. Sabina Church, which he calls a faith community, in Chicago. Pfleger met Obama when he was working at Developing Communities Project in the 1980's. They developed a friendship and Obama has called him a mentor. Pfleger is known for his community activism and is a close friend to Reverend Wright. He has invited people to speak at his church that hold some very un-Catholic positions such as advocating abortion. In 2003 he invited Harry Belafonte who criticized Bush for his pro-life beliefs. He also invited Louis Farrakhan to be a guest speaker in the church. Farrakhan has ridiculed the Pope and called Judaism a "gutter religion". Another guest speaker who has been to his church is the pro-abortion proponent Reverend Al Sharpton. Al Sharpton describes Pfleger as "a different kind of Catholic priest".

Pfleger has been arrested over 40 times for activist activities. He once had weekly demonstrations with Jesse Jackson in front of a gun store and threatened to kill both the store owner and legislators who supported the Second Amendment. Pfleger said he was going to "drag" the store owner out of the shop “like a rat” and “snuff him out”. He then threatened to “snuff out” the legislators. He was arrested for disorderly conduct. He has been arrested for defacing billboards that advertised tobacco and alcohol. During the Rev. Wright controversy, when tapes of his sermons were aired on television, Pfleger invited him to his church where he was greeted to a standing ovation.

Against the church’s policy he adopted three children Lamar, Beronti, and Jarvis. Jarvis was killed by gunshot in 1998, which probably influenced his views on gun ownership. Pfleger is an ardent supporter of Obama.

REVERND SENATOR JAMES T. MEEKS is another spiritual mentor of Obama. In fact, the evening after Obama won the 2004 Senate primary he attended bible study at Meeks’ church. Meeks has been the pastor of Salem Baptist Church since 1985. Starting out small it has grown to over 20,000 members with 10,000 attending weekly services. It is called a “Church Without Walls” and focuses on spiritual, social, and community outreach to serve and help others.

Meeks has made some racial remarks that made headlines. He accused a white police officer of racially profiling him during a traffic stop and said that white conservatives that don’t vote for him are “racists” and “house niggers”. He later apologized and asked Rainbow PUSH to advocate that African-Americans to stop using the word nigger. He also criticized “Hollywood Jews for filming the movie “Brokeback Mountain,” the film about homosexuality.

He has worked hard to improve his neighborhood. When he opened up a bible study he called a meeting with the local gang members. He told them that physical violence and graffiti on his buildings was not going to be tolerated. He then offered safe haven for anyone who wanted to quit the gangs and to help anyone who wanted to get a GED. Several did and he helped them obtain employment. When gun shots were heard during a worship service, he left the women and children in the church, and about 800 men went door to door looking for the source of the gun shots. Word got out that there were some mad men at that church. There has never been any graffiti.

He organized about 400 women, dressed in red and carrying roses, to go out between midnight and 3:00 a.m. to talk to prostitutes about their inner beauty and what they meant to their families and the community. When a drug house was discovered, he took the choir and about 250 people and sang songs for an hour outside the front door. The next day the people moved out. He gave a sermon about the evils of liquor and how liquor keeps people in poverty. Complaining they had 26 liquor stores on 19 blocks in their community, the congregation worked together to make the area free of the shops. Now the largest store is a Christian book store. All persons who lost work because of their actions were offered job training and income until they found other employment.

Once when a good friend and white pastor of an interracial church was about to have problems Meeks and his congregation stepped in to help. The other church had been leading peaceful protests outside an abortion clinic and Queer Nation threatened a noisy demonstration and to close down the church. Meeks and about 250 parishioners showed up, out numbering the demonstrators 10 to 1, and started singing. The crowd left.

Meeks is an ardent activist against the gay agenda and has been criticized for calling homosexuality an "evil sickness". He has opposed all pro-gay legislation. In 2007 the Southern Poverty Law Center named Meeks as one of ten leading black religious leaders in the anti-gay movement. Salem Baptist Church and the Illinois Family Institute partnered with Focus on the Family, Research Council, and Alliance Defense Fund on anti-gay issues. He is actively pro-family and pro-marriage. Once at the pulpit he offered to pay for up to 25 couples to get married, a small reception for each, and a night at a hotel. Seventeen couples got married at a group wedding ceremony and the church members donated gowns, jewelry, and flowers.

The other subject that Meeks is passionate about is education. When he found out that most third graders could not read at the grade level he offered tutoring classes on Saturdays for 8 weeks. He promised students who attended all 8 weeks would receive a personal computer. Members of the church volunteered time to do the tutoring and 300 students received computers. He is strongly in favor of school vouchers, as he believes that students in the inner city have the worse teachers. He said teachers in the inner city should receive additional wages and incentives to teach in those areas. The teachers' union opposed this suggestion because they believe all teachers should receive the same income. At a radio broadcasted RainbowPUSH meeting, he said that the teachers' union was a worse gang than any drug gang in the city.

Meeks was an executive vice president of RainbowPUSH coalition and considers Jesse Jackson a good friend. He says they don't agree on all issues as he his more conservative than his liberal friend. He is a member of Chicago's Gatekeepers, which is a network of interracial groups that work to erase the division between church and state.

He planned to run for mayor of Chicago when Mayor Daley left the position to spend more time with his family. Several of Obama's friends and associates also planned on running for that position. He wanted to address the city budget which was $655 million in the red. He was to work on issues that affect the entire community saying that both black and white people breathe air that should be clean and both black and white seniors want affordable prescriptions. He said, "If you live in a society and you only address the things that face your ethnicity you're not really concerned with social ills".

Obama's religious mentors have received criticism for racial comments. Wright and Pfleger seem to be similar with their activism and progressive issues. Meeks works with his parishioners to solve problems in a more creative and peaceful manner. Obama has looked to the churches in his neighborhood to coordinate with his idea of community organizing to attain social justice. He has said, "There is a lack of collective action among black churches" and criticized them for having food pantries and clothing drives when they would be more effective if they organized with direct political action. He has complained that many churches have fiery sermons but have no agenda. Obama is keenly aware that churches can be part a powerful political base.

Cathleen Falsani from the Chicago Sun Times interviewed Obama regarding his religious beliefs in 2004. She asked him what he believed. His response was all inclusive. "I am a Christian. So I have a deep faith. So I draw from the Christian faith. On the other hand, I was born in Hawaii where obviously there is a lot of Eastern influences; I lived in Indonesia, the largest Muslim country in the world between the ages of 6 and 10. My father is from Kenya, although he was probably most accurately labeled an agnostic, his father was Muslim, And I'd say probably intellectually, I've drawn as much from Judaism as any other faith." " My mother is a Christian…My grandmother was a Methodist, my grandfather a Baptist…my grandparents joined a Universalist Church". In Indonesia I went to a Catholic school, learned Catechisms by day…at night heard the prayer call".

Obama said he joined Trinity United Church of Christ in 1987 or 1988 and attended every week at the 11 o'clock service. He listed his religious mentors as Reverend Wright, Reverend Meeks, and Father Pfleger. When asked about Jesus his response was, "Jesus is a historical figure to me and he's a bridge between God and man with the Christian faith and one that I think is powerful precisely because he serves as that means of us reaching something higher".

Judge me by the people who surround me.

CHAPTER 19

★ ★ ★ ★ ★

Jewish Supporters

Obama continued to cultivate other influential people in Chicago as his supporters. These are some of the members of the Jewish business community he approached for support and their vast networks of friends.

LESTER CROWN is a billionaire who owns significant shares of General Dynamics (a military contractor). He also owns or owns shares in Royal Crown Cola, Marblehead Lime Company, Henry Crown & Company, Maytag, New York Rockefeller Center, Chicago Bulls, New York Yankees, hotels, and ski resorts. He is on the Board of Directors of General Dynamics, Northwestern University, Children's Memorial Medical Center, The Jewish Foundation, and The Jewish Theological Seminary. Crown is the chairman of the Board of the Chicago Council of Foreign Relations, the Commercial Club of Chicago, and the Chicago Council of Global Affairs. He is a major contributor to Jewish charities and the Aspen Institute. The board of the Aspen Institute includes these notable names, David Gergen, Madeleine Albright, Queen Noor of Jordan, Professor Louis Gates Jr., and Condoleezza Rice. This is a person who has connections.

Lester Crown was introduced to Obama by Newton Minow an attorney at Sidley Austin law firm. Minow was impressed by his new employee and told Crown that this was a person who was going places. Crown and his family have provided large sums of money to his campaigns. Lester's son, JAMES CROWN, bundled over $500,000 for the presidential campaign and personally with his wife PAULA CROWN, contributed $100,000 for the inauguration. SUSAN CROWN, Lester's daughter, was on the Board of Directors at Northwest Trust that gave the Obamas a discount mortgage for the mansion they bought with the help of Tony Rezko

When the public began to be troubled about Obama and his loyalty to Jewish interests, Crown sent out a large number of e-mails giving his support. He said Obama "is unyielding in defending Israeli security".

NEWTON MINOW was a partner in the Sidley Austin law firm from 1965 until 1991 and is currently a senior counsel at the firm. He has been active with the Democratic Party since he campaigned for President John F. Kennedy. He was appointed commissioner of the Federal Communication Commission where he was remembered calling television a "great wasteland". He created presidential television debates and is the vice chair of Commission on Presidential Debates. He is a founding member of National Museum of American Jewish History that opened November 14, 2010.

His daughter is Professor MARTHA MINOW at Harvard Law School. In 1988 she telephoned her father to tell him about a student he might be interested in for the law firm. This student had the ability to listen to arguments, restate differing points of view, and articulate a viewpoint that both could agree to. She told him his name was Barack Obama. When her father spoke to another partner to look into Obama he was told he had already been hired!

Obama has continued his friendship and has benefited with introductions to other people in the community, fund raisers, and political support. During the presidential campaign Martha Minow advised him on political issues. She has been appointed to vice chair of the Legal Service Corp at the White House and was considered for nomination for Supreme Court Judge.

ABNER MIKVA attended the University of Chicago law School after serving in World War II. He is a former State and U.S. Representative, a U.S. Court of Appeals Judge for the District of Columbia appointed by President Carter, legal counsel for President Clinton, and instructor at the University of Chicago. When Mikva ran for Congress in 1966 he was backed by Saul Alinsky. In 1969 he wrote articles for the newsletter 'Hyde Park Kenwood Voices'. Voices wrote articles for SDS, Vietnam War activists and other radicals. The publishers, David Canter and Don Rose, became mentors for David Axelrod.

In 1990 Mikva offered Obama a position as law clerk, which Obama declined stating he was going to Chicago to run for political office. Elena Kagan had been his law clerk previously. Mikva returned to the University of

Chicago after Clinton left office and became friends with both Obama and Kagan when the three of them taught there. He was a mentor for Obama and told him he needed to become a better speaker. His advice was to observe and study the speech patterns of preachers. In 1997 he founded the Mikva Challenge teaching youth to get involved in politics and creating local activism projects which students practice to improve schools and the community. Obama appointed his daughter, attorney Laurie Mikva, as board member to the Legal Service Corp at the White House.

PENNY PRITZKER a Hyatt Hotel heiress is the 204th richest person in the United States. She co-founded The Parking Spot which is the fastest growing off- site parking lot managing company. She is also the chairman of Chicago Public Education Fund that is the successor of the Chicago Annenberg Challenge. Pritzker was the chair of Superior Bank from 1991 to 1994 before she stepped down but remained a member of the board. The bank handled Mortgage Backed Securities otherwise known as subprime lending and the bank failed. Creative accounting hid loses while the bank paid dividends. The family agreed to pay $450 million over 15 years to cover costs of the closure, repay the FDIC, and cover some loses from customers who had deposits over the FDIC limit. Family members sued her and other family accusing them of looting the family trust.

Pritzker was named the National Finance Chair of the presidential campaign where she raised over $750 million plus $53 million for the inauguration. She had a fund raiser charging $28,500 per plate with Warren Buffet and Valerie Jarrett. Her brother Jay Pritzker was the National Finance Chair for Hillary Clinton. She was considered for the Commerce Secretary but didn't obtain that position because of her involvement with the collapse of Superior Bank. She currently serves on the Economic Recovery Board. Pritzker has argued against the Employee Free Choice Act, known as card check, with other billionaires including Lester Crown.

Her husband Bryan Traubert was named to the White House Fellowship. The White House Fellowship is for young people to get experience with government practices. It is a full time paid position that includes training, the ability to discuss policy with public and private leaders, and travel domestically and internationally. There were 28 persons named as Fellows. Other Fellows named include; Tom Brokow, General Wesley Clark, Tom Daschle, half-sister Maya Soetoro-Ng, former professor Laurence Tribe, and Michelle's friend and their children's godmother Eleanor Kay Wilson.

The Director of the White House Fellowship is Cindy Moelis, Michelle's friend who worked with her and Valerie Jarrett at Mayor Daley's office.

If the White House Fellowship is for young people to learn how the government operates, I wonder what the administrations definition of young is. And why does Tom Brokow, or the children's godmother, need to get paid to learn how the government operates?

LEE 'ROSY' ROSENBERG is a venture capitalist in real estate, private equity, and entertainment. He was the treasurer of American Israel Public Affairs (AIPAC), a pro-Israel lobbying organization, when he met Obama in 2002. The two have become friends and Rosenberg is an active supporter of Obama. Rosenberg introduced Obama to AIPAC where Obama told the members he was a "stalwart supporter of the Jewish state". During the presidential campaign Rosenberg was on the Finance Committee, advised on foreign policy in Middle East and Israel, and traveled to rallies. He spoke out about Obama being a friend to Israel to critics and to those who had questioned the candidate's positions. Rosenberg traveled with Obama to Israel after his election as senator, and is currently the President of AIPAC. He is friends with Rahm Emanuel and David Axelrod.

AIPAC is an organization with over 100,000 members that raise funds, advocate for. and provide resources for politicians. The group doesn't donate money directly to politicians but has the ability to provide relationships with powerful people. Members of AIPAC are Democrats, Republicans, and Independents. They have meetings with Congress to inform them of policies they endorse. They favor a two state solution, with a Jewish and an Arab the state within the territory of Israel. AIPAC lobbies for shared intelligence information between the United States and Israel, plus economic cooperation with Europe, Russia, and China. They endorse continued economic sanctions with Iran and offer suggestions about other countries that may harm Israel.

The lobbying group came under scrutiny in 2005 when two members were under a FBI investigation for passing top secret national security information to Israel. An analyst for the Pentagon was arrested for giving the data to AIPAC members at a luncheon meeting and was sentenced to 13 years in prison. Charges against AIPAC were dropped in 2009.

AIPAC holds an annual meeting each year in May. The group MOVE

OVER AIPAC planned in advance to disrupt the 2011 conference with the promise to expose the lobbying group and to begin a new foreign policy. MOVE OVER AIPAC is sponsored by CODEPINK, Interfaith Peace Builders, and the US Palestinian Community Network. Demonstrators did disrupt and heckle Netanyahu at the conference and later at the US Congress as he responded to Obama's demand that Israel return to 1967 borders. Helen Thomas, former White House correspondent, was asked to speak at the demonstrations, but declined because of concerns that she could become the focus of the news. She backs Move Over AIPAC ideals and wishes the group well.

ALAN SOLOW is a philanthropist, bankruptcy attorney, and community leader. He is a friend and supporter of Obama stating, "He (Obama) reached out to the Jewish community and the Jewish community has reached out to him". When Obama won the Democratic nomination for President, he stated that Obama would be the "first Jewish President". He maintained Obama's ties with Israel would be 'unshakeable". Solow was appointed in 2008 to chair the Conference of Presidents of Major American Israel Organizations. It is an umbrella group that represents 52 Jewish organizations established under Eisenhower as a pipeline for the President to learn about Jewish concerns. Later Solow criticized Obama's disagreement with Israel for legally building in Jerusalem, while not objecting to the illegal building done by the Arabs.

Solow's organization is not the only group concerned about Obama's actions towards Israel. The president of the World Jewish Congress also wrote an open letter to Obama in 2010 questioning his actions regarding Israel. He asked Obama to clarify his positions on Israel's legal building of homes, his rhetoric of Israel's lack of movement towards peace, his position on Iran, his position on Israel's borders, and his position on a two state solution with Palestine. The letter criticizes the deterioration of diplomatic relationship that is growing between the United States and Israel.

ROBERT SCHRAYER is another philanthropist from Chicago that Obama approached for support. Schrayer has been both the chairman and president of the Jewish United Fund/Jewish Federation of Metropolitan Chicago. He is known nationally for chairing the Jewish Community Relations Council; and internationally for being on the board of the Jewish Agency of Israel, and the American Jewish Joint Distribution Committee. Schrayer said he decided to support and raise money for Obama after a meeting that Obama requested.

DAVID AXELROD is the founder of AKP&D Message and Media that advises and represents progressive causes and candidates. He co-founded ASK Public Strategies which shapes public opinion and then manufactures public support. Axelrod promotes personality not issues. His campaign style has been called Astroturf organizing. The method is to create a grassroots or front group to promote either a product or a candidate. An example: When ComEd wanted to increase electric rates he created a group called Consumers Organized for Reliable Electricity. This group of supposed concerned citizens ran advertisements warning of the dangers of blackouts if rates were not raised attempting to get public support for rate increases. Sometimes the activists he recruits are uninformed and sometimes they are deceived. A journalist William Greider called this grassroots organizing "democracy for hire".

Axelrod has been interested in politics since he was 13 years old and sold Robert Kennedy campaign buttons. Axelrod has represented many political campaigns including John Edwards's presidential campaign and Harold Washington's mayoral campaign. He represented Barack Obama for his bid for U.S. Senate in 2004 and for President in 2008. He had a dilemma in 2008 as all the candidates for President had been past clients of his but he took Obama as his client.

When he was a child, his mother wrote articles for a radical magazine 'PM' that had Marxist and Communist connections. One journalist at 'PM' contributed articles for the magazine Negro Story, as did Frank Marshall Davis. Axelrod's mentors were Don Rose and David Canter who owned and edited 'Hyde Park Voices', a radical publication. Don Rose wrote a letter of recommendation for Axelrod when he applied for and got a job at the Chicago Tribune. Axelrod was a political writer for the Tribune for 8 years. Rose was a member of Alliance to End Repression; a Communist front to end the Chicago Red Squad. The Red Squad monitored Communist and radical organizations. Other members of the Alliance were Dr. Quentin Young, Rabbi Arnold Wolf, and Timuel Black, all supporters of the Democratic Socialist Party and friends of Obama.

Axelrod, with SDS members and Marxists Don Rose, David Canter, and Marilyn Katz, campaigned for Harold Washington's run for mayor. Katz introduced Axelrod to Obama in 1992. At that time Rose, Canter and Axelrod worked on the Moseley Braun campaign, while Obama and Katz worked on Project Vote registering new voters and energizing the vote that enlarged her voter base.

During the 2008 campaign Axelrod helped create the "Change" theme and worked to energize the younger voter to vote and donate money. He created a cult type figure, ignored Obama's Marxist associations, and promoted him like a Hollywood star with his picture on everything from mugs to banners. Obama's lack of experience and ability did not surface as grassroot groups chanted "Yes We Can". After the election, Axelrod went to Washington and was named Senior Advisor to the President. He helped to frame domestic policies from heath care to the stimulus bill. Axelrod said he does not create policy but helps decide what issues or images to push forward. He describes it as not being a policy maker but a protector of Obama's image.

David Axelrod left the White House and returned to Chicago in January 2011. He is working on Obama's 2012 presidential campaign.

Note: During the health care reform AKP &D earned $24 million from the drug industry through ads promoting the reform bill.

Barack Obama once said he picks his friends carefully. His connections to the radical, leftist, Communist, and Muslim associations has led to much speculation in the media. His friendships in the Jewish community have had much less exposure. I found it interesting is that he is able to communicate with each group on positions that they agree with, and has cultivated ardent supporters from all of them. Of course there are those who have expressed concerns that they are not confident of his positions, as they seem to shift according to the audience.

Judge me by the people who surround me.

CHAPTER 20

★ ★ ★ ★ ★

Senator Obama

A defining moment for Obama was when he spoke at the 2004 National Democratic Convention. He got national exposure and good reviews. The Democrats had looked at several governors for the honor of giving the keynote speech; including Jennifer Granholm from Michigan, Janet Napolitano of Arizona, Tom Vilsack of Iowa, Mark Warner of Virginia, and Bill Richardson of New Mexico. Meanwhile Axelrod and David Pouffe were lobbying the Kerry staff for Obama. Kerry heard Obama in Chicago and was impressed. The final decision was between Governor Granholm and Illinois State Senator Obama, a candidate for his first term as U.S. Senator. He was young, exciting, different, and he was selected.

The speech started as many of his campaign speeches did, introducing himself and his background. He then spoke of dreams; dreams of his grandparents, dreams of his parents, his dreams, and the dreams of the American people. The speech was an outline of his autobiography "Dreams from My Father". He then spoke about Kerry's valor, his beliefs, and his ability to unify the nations with a promise of a brighter day. He obviously had taken the advice to improve his ability to communicate at a higher level because the keynote address was a great success. This was allegedly the first time he used teleprompters which he is now uses on a regular basis. After the speech Obama was known across the country as he received so much positive attention by the media.

Obama won the Democratic Party primary and Jack Ryan was on the Republican ticket for US Senate. Three months later Ryan withdrew from the race because embarrassing details of his divorce became public. Alan Keyes became the Republican candidate just three months before the election. Keyes ran, and lost, on a platform defending traditional American and Christian values. He refused to call and congratulate Obama. He said, "I'm suppose to make a call that represents the congratulations toward the triumph of that which I believe ultimately stands for …a cultural evil enough to destroy the very soul and heart of my country? I can't do this." After the presidential election Keyes sued and was of one of 17 law suits claiming Obama was not constitutionally eligible to be President. Each law suit claimed Obama was not a natural born citizen and requested legal verification of birth. One by one, all the courts have refused to hear the cases and the dispute has never been decided.

Obama was supported in this election by unions including AFSCME, SEIU, and the Illinois Federation of Teachers. He had the support of Congressman Jesse Jackson Jr., Congressman Danny Davis, Congressman Lane Evans, and Congresswoman Jan Schakowsky. Obama also had the support of the Communist Party USA.

Congressman DANNY DAVIS is a Democrat and former New Party member and a member of Democratic Socialists of America (DSA). Davis was a candidate for the Mayor of Illinois until he withdrew his nomination on December 31, 2010. He joined Senator Reverend Meeks, who also withdrew from the mayoral race, to endorse Carol Mosely Braun.

Danny Davis is an interesting person. On March 23, 2004 Davis joined Reverend Sun Myung Moon in a religious ceremony in the Dirkson Senate Office Building. At the ceremony Davis, in white gloves, placed a jeweled crown on the head of Moon and his wife. They were declared the King and Queen of Peace. Moon founded the Unification Church and believes he is the Messiah and the Second Coming of Christ. He also owns the Washington Times, United Press International, and he contributes to politicians. Moon participated in Farrakhan's 1995 Million Man March.

In 2005, Davis took a seven day trip to Sri Lanka which was paid by the Tamil Tigers, a terrorist group. Davis preferred to call them freedom fighters. He spent most of the week in an area controlled by the Liberation Tigers of Tamil Elam. Davis claims he understood the funds for the trip came from an organization called Federation of Tamil Sangramsis, although he acknowledged he knew that they were associated with Tamil Tigers. After the trip, eleven members of the organization were arrested on charges of conspiring to funnel money, and arms (including surface-to-air missiles), plus bribery of public officials. One of the persons arrested was Murugesu Vinayagomoorthy, a friend of Danny Davis. He was charged trying to bribe an official from the State Department will $1 million to have the Tamil

Tigers pulled from the terrorist list. He was also charged with laundering Tamil Tiger money to pay for a trip of two individuals. This charge referred to the trip that Davis took.

The Sunlight Foundation discovered Davis paid his wife $10,543 to be his campaign treasurer in 2005 and 2006 from campaign funds. In 2007 he was ticketed for driving over the yellow line. Davis said that he was racially profiled and was pulled over for "driving while black". The ticket was eventually dismissed. In 2008 he was offered Obama's Senate seat by Blagojevich, but declined.

Congressman LANE EVANS paid a settlement of $185,000 in 2005 to the Federal Elections Commissions (FEC) for illegal transactions between the 17th District Victory Fund, Rock Island Democratic Central Committee, and the Evans Committee. The FEC determined that $200,000 came from labor union treasury funds, which is not allowed. The Victory Fund also spent $330,000 for get-out-the-vote activities which were too closely related to his campaign and contributions exceeded legal limits. Friends of Lane Evans Committee paid the fine. Evans served as a United States Representative for 24 years until 2007 when he retired due to Parkinson Disease. Evans is a founding member of the Congressional Progressive Caucus and a member of the Democratic Socialists of America.

Congresswoman JAN SCHAKOWSKY is a member of the Democratic Socialists of America. 'The Nation', a far left magazine, endorsed her nomination for Vice President in 2004. She endorses a public option health care program saying' "public option will inevitably lead to single payer health care" which will put private insurance companies out of business. She should know, as it was her husband Robert Creamer who wrote the outline for the health care plan while in jail for bank fraud of $2.3 million.

In 2007 she co-sponsored a bill to impeach Dick Cheney as Vice President. Schakowsky proudly boasts of her 100% pro-Israel voting record. Others have expressed concern because of her close connections to J Street, a PAC funded by anti-Semite George Soros. JStreet was established to counter AIPAC's advocacy for Israel to retain a strong military to secure their country.

Schakowsky was considered for Obama's Senate seat in 2008, but didn't get contacted before the pay-to-play scandal broke. She won reelection to Congress in 2010. During a debate with her opponent Joel Pollak she refused to condemn the Gaza Flotilla activists or to admit she was a member of the Democratic Socialists of America.

When Obama won the Senate primary in 2004, with 53% of the vote, people began to talk about him running for President at some time in the future. Obama then reissued his book "Dreams from My Father". He won the Senate election against Keyes with 70% of the vote.

Obama took his oath of office for US Senate on January 4, 2005, put his hand on his bible, and was sworn in by Vice President Cheney. He was accompanied by his wife and children, plus family from both Hawaii and Kenya witnessed the ceremony. In attendance was his AUNTIE ZEITUNI ONYANGO the half sister of his father.

She was in the United States illegally. Auntie Zeituni came to America in 2000 on a temporary visa. In 2001 she somehow received a Social Security card with permission to work. Her request for asylum was denied in 2004, but she ignored her deportation order. Meanwhile she is living in Boston, residing in public housing and claims to receive $700 per month disability payments. In May 2010 she was granted political asylum and has legal status. During an interview in September 2010 by WBZ of Boston she said, "If I come as an immigrant, you have the obligation to make me a citizen."

The swearing in ceremony was also attended by members of the House, the Senate, Supreme Court Justices, and other guests. One guest was DANIEL MUDD, CEO of Fannie Mae who spoke at the event. Mudd thanked Obama and referred to the Black Caucus as his "family". Fannie Mae and Fannie Mac were under investigation for fraud and corruption and he is thanking members of Congress! The Democratic Party had oversight of both companies which are privately owned, but government sponsored with an implicit guarantee they will not be allowed to fail, to underwrite and sell mortgages. Freddie Mae donated $126,349 to Obama's Senate campaign.

Late in 2004 Obama signed a book deal with a branch of Random House Crown Books to write three books. The first was 'Audacity of Hope', the second released in November 2010 is a children's book, 'Of Thee I Sing', and a third yet to be announced. The contract awarded Obama $1.9 million, which he received prior to being sworn in as United States Senator.

Because the contract was signed before he became a senator he did not have to meet congressional requirements of reporting and disclosure. He decided to invest his money in the stock market. Obama took the advice from friend, political contributor (approximately $50,000), and investor George Haywood to put his money in a blind trust with USB, an investment company. A blind trust is when an executor invests money without the owners prior input. Obama said this was done to prevent any appearance of conflict with his investments. Everything doesn't always go as planned. USB made two speculative investments from companies that contributed to his political campaign in early 2005 that did cause controversy. The first was for Sky Terra on February 10th a tech company owned by Jared Abbruzzese who contributed $10,000 to Obama's PAC. On that same day the FCC approved the company's bid to create a national wireless network. The second was for AVI BioPharma on February 22nd which was working on an avian flu drug. On April 23rd Obama co-sponsored a bill to fund research on the warning systems of and expanding research for avian flu. AVI BioPharma never asked for funding for its research on avian flu and never received funding on that project. It did receive funding later from the Department of Defense for research on Ebola, Marburg, anthrax, and ricin. In the fall of 2005 Obama learned of his investments, sold them, and left USB.

JARED ABBRUZZESE was found guilty in 2002 in a lawsuit alleging $9 million fraud. An appeals court over turned the verdict after the two parties agreed to an out of court settlement. In a related case there was a $5 million judgment filed against him. These cases involved Abbruzzese steering business to companies he controlled. In 2005 he was involved in an FBI investigation for paying New York Senator Joseph Bruno $200,000, plus $80,000 for a useless race horse, in consulting fees. At the time Abbruzzese had business interests with the state and was able to obtain $500,000 in public funds from Bruno for his company Evident Technologies. Bruno was indicted on eight counts of corruption and convicted on two counts of mail and wire fraud. He was sentenced to two years in federal prison, 3 years post release supervision, and pay $280,000 in restitution.

In April, 'Time' magazine named Obama as one of a hundred people most likely to influence the world. That month he wrote a letter to the Daily Kos asking them to tone down criticism on politicians that regularly voted progressive. "In order to beat them (Republicans) it is necessary for Democrats to get a backbone, give as good as they get, brook no compromise, drive out democrats who are interested in appeasing the right wing and enforce a more clearly progressive agenda". "Whenever they (Republicans) are wrong, inept, or dishonest, we should say so clearly and repeatedly."

On April 26th he gave a speech at the National Press Club about ending filibusters requiring less than 60 members. Obama strongly argued that the filibuster must remain at 60 members and not be reduced to 50. The filibuster was used to block nine of President Bush's appointments. Obama said the founding fathers of our country established the filibuster rules to protect the "minority from the tyranny of the majority".

In June, Obama bought his home/mansion with the help of Rezko. After the details of the transaction were made public he admitted it was a "boneheaded" decision.

Despite Obama's pledge to help the working middle class and support for unions, his voting record indicates differently. He voted on 9/15/05 to use foreign workers in the Katrina aftermath instead of using Americans to rebuild the city, in violation of labor laws, who lost employment because of the hurricane. On 6/29/06 he voted for the Oman Free Trade Agreement Implementation Act that sent jobs overseas to a country with no child labor or environmental laws. Obama is now opposed to Arizona's attempt to protect themselves against illegal immigrants, but in August 2006 voted to spend $1.6 billion to build a security fence on the Mexican border.

Very little was reported about Obama's trip to Israel in January 2006. Only one reporter accompanied him on this trip, his name was Chuck Goudie from ABC7 News. Others that traveled with him were Lee Rosenberg, Senator Evan Bayh, Senator Christopher Bond, and Representative Harold Ford. Obama visited the holy sites, went to the Yad Vashem Holocaust Museum, and flew over the country in a helicopter. He spoke of seeing a home destroyed by a Hezbollah Katyusha rocket and talking to the owner of the home. He visited Palestine during this trip and spoke with Mahmoud Abbas at his Presidential headquarters in Ramallah. Obama also spoke at the Jerusalem University and told the audience the United States has a strong commitment to Israel. This trip included visits to Iraq, Qatar, Kuwait, and Jordan.

In August 2006 Obama visited Kenya on a fact finding mission. His host was RAILA ODINGA who describes himself as a "close personal friend" of Obama and is a cousin. Odinga visited Obama in the United States three times; once each in 2004, 2005, and 2006. Odinga is from Obama's family Lou tribe and leader of the Orange Democratic Movement when he was on a campaign for President against incumbent Mwai Kibaki. While in Kenya Obama met with President Kibaki, spoke at the Nairobi University, and with Nairobi newspapers. He brought a professional film crew with him and parts of his speech at the University of Nairobi can be found on the internet. He spoke of the corruption in the current government and said "ethnic based tribal politics has to stop".

> A brief history of Kenyan politics. Kenya is 80% Christian (primarily Roman Catholic and Protestant), 10% Muslim, and the rest are indigenous religions. The two major tribes in Kenya are the Kikuyu tribe and the Lou tribe. Both tribes are primarily Roman Catholic although Obama's family are Muslim. Odinga was an Anglican and became a Born-Again Christian. He has four children, one son's name is Fidel Castro and a daughter is named Winnie after Winnie Mandela.
>
> In 1978 President Jomo Kenyatta, from the Kikuyu tribe, was elected President. He was opposed by Lou tribesman Jaramogi Oginga Odinga, popularly called OO. Kenyatta was a pro-American and OO was a pro-Soviet Union Communist. After the election OO was named Vice President. In 2002 Mwai Kibaki, from the Kikuyu tribe, won the election for President under the National Rainbow Coalition comprised of several tribes. Raila Odinga was on the ticket but felt slighted because he didn't get selected for positions that he felt were important. He started the Orange Democratic Movement with using orange as a color symbolizing opposition.
>
> He ran on a campaign stating that Kibaki was corrupt. Odinga's slogan was "Your Agent for Change" and campaigned promoting the installation of Sharia Law. On August 29, 2007 he signed an Evangelical Alliance of Kenya with Sheikh Abdullahi Abdi, the chairman of the National Muslim Leaders Forum, to support the 2007 elections. The agreement listed many objectives including that Kenya would declare Sharia Law as true law, the Commissioner of Police (who was influenced by heathens and Zionists) to be dismissed, and any Muslim charged with terrorism from Kenya would only go to trial in Kenya with government paid attorneys. When Odinga lost he called the election rigged and fraudulent. His

> supporters, carrying machetes, rioted, killed, raped, and burned homes and churches. Not one mosque was burned. It is estimated that 1,000 people were killed, 350,000 were displaced, and 800 churches burned. One church burned with families inside and all perished.
>
> Obama did not call Odinga and request he stop the rampage or to resign from the race. Instead he pressured the United Nations to push for Odinga to share the Presidency. Eventually Odinga was installed as Prime Minister so he is sharing in the leadership of Kenya. Now Kenya, with a population that is 80% Christian, has come under Sharia law and has established a close relationship with Iran.

While Obama was in Kenya the government said that Obama campaigned for Odinga and was called Odinga's "stooge". Odinga had t-shirts made with the image of Obama and Odinga printed on the front. Obama is well liked in Kenya, as they are proud that a person related so closely to their country is the President of the United States.

The trip, paid with tax money, was supposed to be a fact-finding mission to improve relationships of the United States and Kenya. However it has been alleged that Obama violated the Logan Act by attempting to conduct foreign relations without authority. In August 2006 the Kenyan Public Communication Secretary, Dr. Alfred Mutua, complained that Senator Obama "made extremely disturbing statements on issues…and on which he chose to lecture the Government and the people of Kenya on how to manage our country". In fact, there was a web site petition to impeach Obama for misrepresenting his mission to Kenya, misuse of his passport, and campaigning on foreign soil against a U.S. ally.

Although Obama denies that he actively campaigned for his cousin while in Kenya, verification of correspondence with Odinga proves otherwise. First Odinga received campaign funds totaling $950,000 from a group called Friends of Senator BO. Secondly, it was discovered that Odinga was instructed to correspond with Obama through the senator's aide Mark Lippert. In an e-mail dated 12/22/06 under the subject line "Let's share a dream!" he wrote the following note. "Hello brother, I will kindly wish that all our correspondence handled by Mr. Mark Lippert. I have already instructed him. This will be for my own security both for now and in future. Faithfully, Obama". Third, the Odinga campaign strategy called 'Executive Brief on the Positioning and Marketing of the Orange Democratic Movement & The People's President was uncovered and the source claimed it was shared with Obama's senate office. The document promoted class warfare by describing the Kibaki government an uncaring people and calling them Muthaiga Golf Clubbers. The document stirs up the emotions of the youth by exploiting class disparity. The strategy was ready to get them involved in violent demonstrations, especially if they lost the election. It had already been decided that in the event of a loss they would not admit defeat, but claim the election was fraudulent.

While Obama was on his tax paid trip he was able to enjoy visit his family's village. He also traveled to Djibouti and Chad.

The following are viewpoints that Obama expressed in 2006 that he probably wishes weren't documented.

On June 14th interview at CBS with Bob Schieffer regarding government paid drug coverage. "The worst of both worlds: we've got the price gouging of the private sector and the bureaucracy of the public sector."

On the Senate floor, "Raising the debt ceiling (Bush) shows a failure of leadership." "America has a debt problem and a failure of leadership.'

During a debate over the Military Commission Act of 2006, Obama stated that Khalid Sheikh Mohammed "should have a full military trial.'

After the midterm elections, "If President Bush is stubborn, refuses to take signals from the election that the people are looking for a different approach, then we could get bogged down and not make progress."

Judge me by the people who surround me.

CHAPTER 21

★ ★ ★ ★ ★

Running for President

An announcement was made on January 16, 2007, a few weeks after a meeting with George Soros, that Obama had formed a panel to explore a run for the President for 2008. Papers were filed to create an exploratory committee. The Senator announced, "The decisions that have been made in Washington over the past 6 years and the problems that have been ignored have put our country in a precarious place." On February 10th the announcement was made that he will run for President. Daniel B. Shapiro was selected as his political advisor and strategist. The announcement included the promise that lobbyists would not be welcome in his administration, "the lobbyist, the special interest, who've turned our government into a game only they can play. They write the checks and you get stuck with the bills...but we're here today to take it back. The time for that kind of politics is over. It is through. It is time to turn the page right here and right now."

DANIEL B. SHAPIRO worked as Obama's advisor while employed with Timmons & Company as a lobbyist. The Obama policy of lobbyists; "No political appointee in an Obama administration will be permitted to work on regulations or contracts directly and subsequently related to their prior employer for two years, and no political appointee will be able to lobby the executive branch after leaving government service during the remainder of the administration." Shapiro was appointed as Vice President of Timmons & Company in 2007. One of his major clients was API (American Petroleum Institute). He lobbied for them on agriculture, renewable fuel standards, greenhouse gas emissions, gas price gouging and regulation, defense, the stimulus bill, farm bill, and the IRS code relating to refineries. When questioned about Shapiro working as a lobbyist and advisor, the Obama administration said that Shapiro had worked as unpaid volunteer until August 11th and therefore did not violate policy. Other companies he lobbied for include Teva Pharmaceuticals USA, Inc., and Freddie Mac.

Shapiro officially joined the campaign in August 2008 and left Timmons. Prior to working for Obama he was a staff member of the House Foreign Relations Committee, was on President Clinton's National Security Council, and Deputy Chief of Staff for Senator Bill Nelson of Florida. He is a member of the Council of Foreign Relations. Shapiro served on the National Security Council in the Obama administration and was named Ambassador to Israel in March 2011.

Campaign speeches stated there would be no lobbyists in the White House. "They won't work in my White House", changed to "They are not going to dominate my White House "and "They are not going to run my White House." The truth is that lobbyists do work in the White House; the limitations are that they cannot work DIRECTLY on matters that they were involved with for two years prior to appointment.

ERIC LYNN, former pro-Israel lobbyist, was named on July 11th as an advisor on the Middle East and as liaison to the Jewish community. He designed an English/Hebrew web site to demonstrate Obama's commitment to his Jewish supporters. In 1998 he was a summer intern at AIPAC and worked and lived in Israel for one year. He advocates for Israeli causes and states that Israel must maintain a strong military for defense against Iranian supported Hamas and Hezbollah. Lynn is the Director of Special Envoy Affairs in the State Department.

Attempting to assure Jewish backers of his support, Obama spoke at AIPAC in March. He spoke about his commitment to Israel and spoke against Iranian President Ahmadinejad's nuclear ambitions. We said he would work to help both the Israelis and the Palestinians to obtain their own state and live side by side in peace.

CAMP OBAMA was established to train supporters to become organizers. Each trainee is taught to tell his or her own story, their own goals, and how it motivates them to vote for Obama. The personalized stories are meant to energize the volunteers and connect with the undecided voters. The trainees are taught to listen and then give feed back to influence a person's opinions. The camps which were organized across the country were run by professional organizers at churches, business offices, and college campuses. Each class had about 50 students, but class sizes ranged from 30 to 300.

Trainees were instructed how to canvass, use phone banks, raise funds, and create their own organizations or neighborhood teams. Information gathered was collected in a data base for future use. The sessions were typically 3 to 4 days long, free to the trainee, but did not include lodging or transportation. The better trainees became paid employees. The sessions included mock caucuses and the students learned to influence supporters of other candidates. Florida was considered a pivotal state. Camp Obama was credited with helping to create the estimated 230,000 volunteers and the 19,000 neighborhood teams to get-out-the vote in Florida alone.

Much of the funding for Camp Obama came from Obama's PAC at Hopefund Inc. He started his Hopefund 20 days after he was elected to the U.S. Senate. Donations to the fund can come from politicians or private donors. The stated purpose of the fund was to be used for candidates that were committed to "changing" America. PAC funds are meant to be used for "party building" and not for collecting favors. When Obama announced his candidacy for President he quit accepting donations, but by 2008 he had raised $778,642,047. This way he could say he was not accepting funds from PACs as the money had already been raised. Some candidates from the early voting states of Iowa, New Hampshire, and South Carolina received donations from the fund in the beginning of the campaign. There were complaints that the funds were going to some candidates that were supporting Obama in his campaign. The Federal Elections Commission did look into the legality of the fund, because soliciting donations for political favor is in violation of PAC regulations. Paul Ryan from the Campaign Legal Center said that sometimes activities don't pass a "smell test" but are legal under existing statutes.

ANITA DUNN was the communications and political strategist of the presidential campaign. She is a partner of Squier Knapp Dunn Communications that recently merged with its partner Knickerbocker to become SKDKnickerbocker which is a consulting firm for campaigns, causes, and corporations. Dunn previously worked as an intern under the Communications Department for the Carter administration. She was a political strategist for both Senators Evan Bayh and Tom Daschle.

Dunn first worked as PAC chief communications director for Obama For America. She was later appointed the Direction of Communications at the White House and trained Robert Gibbs for the position of press secretary. She was the person that started a campaign criticizing the Fox News Channel (FNC). She claimed FNC was a research and/or communications arm of the Republican Party and told CNN and Time Magazine, "Let's not pretend they're a news network". Robert Gibbs briefed the White House press corps while Dunn was meeting with people like Keith Olberman and Rachel Maddow from MSNBC, Maureen Dowd from the New York Times, Gloria Borger from CNN, Eugene Robinson from the Washington Post, and Gwen Ifill from NPR.

Dunn met with the President of the Dominican Republic to explain her strategy of electing an unknown politician with little experience into office like Barack Obama. This was at a conference that was held just eight days prior to Obama's inauguration. First, she bragged, they put emphasis on personality and built an image of personal appeal that would attract popularity. They emphasized what he was saying and not why he was saying it. The media was by-passed with the use of live long speeches and video as a way to control the message. Another way the media was controlled was Obama did not talk directly to reporters. She explained that rarely did they communicate with the press in situations they could not control.

At a high school graduation speech, she told the students her favorite philosophers were Mother Theresa and Mao Tse-Tung. Dunn claimed that she admired them because they both followed their own path; however she said little about Mother Theresa and raved about Mao. The speech was broadcast on television and she was demonized for admiring a man who, in 1966, had re-education camps and murdered millions of people who he believed opposed his views. After the controversy she suddenly left her position in November 2009, after just six months on the job. The administration said she would continue to provide advice. Since leaving the White House she has been a commentator for NBC, MSNBC, and CNBC. She joined Leading Authorities, a speaker's bureau. The president of Leading Authorities sent e-mails to their clients announcing that Dunn and Andy Stern, of SEIU, where available to be hired to give speeches. Dunn is married to Obama's personal attorney Bob Bauer.

BOB BAUER is a partner at the law firm Perkins Coie, is a campaign attorney, and chairs the firm's Political Law Group. He is a lobbyist for America Votes and the attorney representing Obama For America. In 2004 he represented Kerry's Presidential campaign and is the legal representative for America Coming Together (ACT).

> AMERICA VOTES was formed in 2004 to defeat President Bush. Its stated mission is to advance progressive policies and to expand access to the ballot. It calls itself "the largest grassroots voter mobilization in the country". It is one of four groups working together under the organization America Coming together (ACT) that was formed by George Soros in 2003. ACT was involved in many controversies during the 2004 election. They used felons to conduct door-to-door registrations, collecting personal information in several states; at least two of them had been convicted of murder and rape. Other canvassers had been convicted of assault, burglary, and drug charges. Some of the canvassers lived in half-way houses and later returned to prison. ACT maintained that convicted criminals deserve a second chance. Faulty voter registrations were found in several states. The problems were duplicate registrations, registrations using variations of the same name, dead people, and signatures that did not belong to the registrant. One nursing home resident in Ohio was registered by ACT, who signs her name with a shaky X, had a clear cursive signature when she registered. Also in Ohio Republican voters were receiving phone calls directing them to wrong polling sites and provided misleading information. In 2007 the Federal Election Commission fined ACT $775,000 for violation of federal campaign finance laws.

Obama waived the ethics rules for Bauer when he appointed him as White House Counsel in November 2009. The waiver states the law firm Perkins Coie will continue to represent the President on personal matters. This allows Bauer to remain Obama's personal attorney and represent the White House legal concerns.

Bauer has been Obama's personal attorney since 2004 and has defended him against multiple lawsuits questioning his "natural born" citizenship. Bauer called these lawsuits frivolous. He is the person responsible for the ban on releasing all personal documentation of Obama's background. It was reported on May 10, 2010 that Obama For America paid Perkins Coie $2,161,155.55. Of that amount $1,352,378.98 was paid after Obama's eligibility was in question.

Bauer was the general legal counsel during the Presidential campaign and for Obama For America that his wife directed. During the campaign he urged the Justice Department to investigate McCain and Palin when they asked that ACORN be investigated for election fraud. He said it "was an unholy alliance of law enforcement and the ugly form of partisan politics", and accused the Republicans of "trying to create doubt in the electoral process". While Obama was crusading for campaign finance reform Bauer was suing the Federal Election Commission on restrictions of "soft money". Prior the campaign Obama promised to use public financing if the Republican candidate did. Bauer was influential in Obama's reversal of that decision. Public financing requires much more transparency on how money is spent. Bauer also threatened several lawsuits over anti-Obama television ads that questioned the candidate's relationships with radicals such as Bill Ayers and his support from groups such as SEIU and ACORN. He also represented Obama during the Rod Blagojevich trial.

After the election, Obama For America was transformed into Organizing for America. Bauer was named general counsel for the new organization. Organizing for America is a grassroots group to support Obama's agenda. Volunteers are encouraged to call and make visits to town halls, to spread the message, and form neighborhood groups. They call this building from the bottom up. During the health care debates many of the angry loud crowds televised were from Organizing for America and similar groups.

In November 2009 White House Counsel GREG CRAIG left and Bauer was appointed to replace him. This the same month that Bauer's wife, Anita Dunn, left her position at the White House. Craig resigned after several decisions became controversial, including the closing of Guantanamo Bay, the decision to try Khalid Sheikh Mohamed in civil court, and the release of pictures of detainees that had been abused overseas. Craig has been involved with many high profile cases in the past. He represented John W. Hinckley Jr. in his trial for the attempted assignation of President Reagan and represented Senator Ted Kennedy during the rape trial of William Kennedy Smith. Craig was the attorney for the Cuban father of Elian Gonzalez in the custody case and represented the U. N. Secretary General Kofi Annan in the oil-for-food scandal.

One of Bauer's first ideas was to suggest that all Gitmo detainees be treated as a group instead of trying each case independently. This strategy titled the "Grand Bargain" would need new legislation to implement. In August 2010 he was assigned to be the Ethics Czar when Norman Eisen left the position. Bauer is the same person who fought against transparency of political campaign funds, accused McCain and Palin of voter intimidation for questioning voter fraud while sending e-mails to attorneys, law students, and other professionals to participate in Obama's Voter Protection Program.

He is now going to oversee ethics in the White House. I wonder what ethics he will enforce.

ROBERT GIBBS was Senator Obama's press secretary and an early supporter for the presidential campaign. Gibbs has been active with politics since he was a child. His mother took him to League of Women's Voters meetings and had him involved with voter re-identification work. He interned for Congressman Glen Browder and was press secretary for Congressman Bob Etheridge. Gibbs was press secretary for a short time on John Kerry's presidential campaign before working for Obama in 2004 advising him on politics and strategy. He believes his mission is to protect Obama and help to "shape the message". He is known as the "enforcer" for quickly countering disinformation; like the rumors of Obama being a Muslim during the campaign. There were rumors in the fall of 2010 he would leave the White House to Chair the DNC, which would give Obama an edge in re-election for 2012. He did leave but did not become the Chair of the DNC nor did he get the position at Face Book he applied for, however he is currently a campaign advisor for Obama. He will be remembered for some of his statements such as accusing Bush for using "cowboy diplomacy", asking political commentator Sean Hannity if he was anti-Semite, calling commentator Bill O'Reilly a bully, and stating the "professional left" were "liberal naysayers". He will also be remembered for cursing the First Lady as reported in a new book "The Obamas".

DAVID PLOUFFE, a partner with David Axelrod at AKPG Message and Media, was Obama's campaign manager, traveling press secretary, and communications director. He has been called the architect of the successful campaign using TV, radio, internet, and social networking. The campaign message was a promise of fiscal responsibly, post partisan politics, and an open and transparent administration with moderate views. When Solis Doyle joined the campaign in June 2008 Plouffe said, "Today we're adding to our leadership team so that we can reach even more Americans who share the belief that people who love their country can 'change' it." Plouffe became the Communications Director after Anita Dunn left. He is also an avid baseball fan, even sharing season tickets to the Washington National with Robert Gibbs.

In 2009 Plouffe wrote a book titled 'The Audacity to Win: The Inside Story and Lessons of Barack Obama's Historic Victory'. He asked Obama supporters to buy a copy of his book on December 8th of that year to "Beat Sarah Palin" in books sales for that day.

When Axelrod left in January 2011 Plouffe became the new Senior Advisor to the White House. His job is to remake the image of the Obama administration. Since assuming this position he has called cuts in spending "draconian" echoing Senator Harry Reid's ideas that children and seniors will be harmed. He went on Fox News Channel and told the interviewer, "Even your viewers" would want Washington to compromise on budget issues when the Democrat spending plans are explained.. In April, Donald Trump was making headlines about his possible for run for the Presidency as he questioned Obama's birth place. Pouffe said Trump "had zero chance" of being elected. However, before the month was over Obama sent a representative from Bauer's law office to Hawaii to obtain two copies of his long form birth certificate. With all of Obama's vacations in Hawaii he must have never had the time to pay $10.00 and pick up a copy himself. A copy of the long awaited birth certificate was put on the internet to quiet talk of his ineligibility to be in office.

JIM MESSINA was the campaign's Chief of Staff and after the election became Deputy Chief of Staff under Emanuel. Prior to working on the campaign he was Chief of Staff to Senator Max Baucus. He claims his biggest win was when, with Senator Harry Reid, he stopped President Bush's plan to partially privatize Social Security. He has been the point man for gay issues; gay marriage, gay rights, and with the Don't Ask Don't Tell repeal. Those who were pushing this agenda have criticized him for not acting fast enough on their issues.

Messina's main job is to fix problems. One of the first was the discovery the Treasurer nominee, Tim Geithner, didn't pay all of his taxes. He had a meeting with Max Baucus to get assurances that the tax issue would not be a problem with the confirmation. It wasn't. Geithner was approved.

It was Messina's job to help prepare Congressmen with talking points on the health care reform bill at town hall meetings; telling them they needed to convince those with insurance that they would not lose coverage. Congressmen were told to address groups like women and those who lived in rural areas that were more prone to endorse the plan. The other suggestion Messina gave was to make sure the town hall meetings were highly attended by their supporters.

In another effort to promote health care reform, Messina took part in making a deal with Pharmaceutical Research and Manufacturing of America (PhRMA) that Congress would not increase costs over $80 billion in exchange for their support. The President was telling the public that the health care reform would allow the government to renegotiate drug costs. PhRMA demanded that the administration publicly state that they would not pursue drug cost cutting measures, such as the importation of drugs from Canada, or they would withdraw their support. Some congressmen who knew about the large profits drug companies would receive were promoting the idea of cutting costs with importation of cheaper drugs. PhRMA had agreed to producing advertisements promoting the reform only with government guarantees of no further costs or rebates. PhRMA hired 165 lobbyists (the majority were former employees of the legislative or executive branches of government) and spent over $28 million to endorse the health care reform. The Obama administration finally admitted publicly to the deal which was made to PhRMA. No such deal was made with the health insurance companies. In April, Messina met with PhRMA, other leaders of other health care groups and organized labor to come up with a way to promote the health care reform bill. They created two nonprofit groups called Healthy Economy Now and Americans for Stable Quality Care for this promotion. The groups spent $24 million on advertizing and other expenses which was paid to AKPD, most was funded by PhRMA.

Messina does not tolerate grassroot tactics against his policies. In 2009 a group called the Campaign for America's Future started an action called 'Dog the (Blue) Dogs' with the intent to pressure the Blue Dog Democrats to support the Democratic budget proposal. Messina stepped in to stop them as the administration could handle the Blue Dogs better than they could.. He told them if they did not stop their campaign their leaders would not be invited to the weekly strategy meetings. The campaign stopped. He insists on total control of progressive groups and their message. He does not want them to insist on changes that are part of the administrations agenda.

Messina was connected to offering jobs for congressional candidates not to run for office against an incumbent that Obama endorsed. Andrew Romanoff had entered the primary race against Michael Bennett in Colorado. Messina wrote and e-mailed inquiries to Romanoff about three different job opportunities that may be available. Romanoff and Messina agreed that no specific job offer had been presented. This event was embarrassing as the offers became public the same week that Joe Sestak said Bill Clinton had indicated there might be positions available to him if he dropped out the primary against incumbent Arlen Spector.

Messina resigned in February 2011 to become the campaign manager for Obama's re-election. Robert Creamer, the former convicted felon and husband of Rep. Schakowsky, praised Messina stating he thought he would do a great job campaigning for Obama. Creamer cited that Messina was committed to progressive values and vision using grassroots methods. He continued that Messina knew the value of making people believe they are part of making history and being part of something big. William Daley was appointed Chief of Staff to replace Messina. He is the son of former Chicago Mayor Richard J. Daley and brother to John Daley, a former Illinois representative, and Richard M. Daley, the outgoing Mayor of Chicago. William Daley resigned January 9, 2012 and was replaced by Jacob Lew.

CASSANDRA BUTTS met Obama in the financial aid office at Harvard Law School and have remained friends. She is a registered lobbyist and attorney for the NAACP, senior advisor to the Millennium Challenge Corporation, and Senior Vice President, and registered lobbyist, of the Center for American Progress (CAP). CAP's President is John Podesta and is funded by George Soros. Butts was selected to observe the 2000 parliamentary elections in Zimbabwe. She had acted as senior political advisor to Richard Gephardt.

Butts worked with John Podesta on the transition team; but remained on the payroll of the CAP. The team had 77 days to put together a government staff of 7,840 appointees; including 1,177 which required Senate confirmation. Her assessment of Obama is, "people see in him what they want to see".

She was part of a controversial decision about not prosecuting the New Black Panthers Party (NBPP) members who stood outside a polling place on election day intimidating voters with night sticks and verbal taunts. The situation was videotaped and broadcast on television. The Bush administration filed suit prior to leaving office citing the NBPP had violated the Voting Act. Defendants did not show for court and a default decision was issued. Associate Attorney General Thomas J. Perrelli met with Butts several times regarding this case as it was pending final determination. Perrelli had case dismissed and told the judge not to prosecute. One of the defendants, Jerry Jackson, was a Democrat Polling Watcher, he was ordered not to have deadly weapons near polling places until 2012, but only in the city of Philadelphia. Evidently Jackson is free to intimidate at other polling precincts, just not Philadelphia and only until 2012. Later the NBPP released a video joking about the decision. The chairman of the group said, "You know we don't carry batons...PSYCHE! I'm just playing". He continued, the "Justice Department leadership changed into the hands of a black man by the name of Eric Holder." Attorney J. Christian Adams from the Department of Justice resigned over this case. He said he was not allowed to testify and stated the Voter Section told him that cases brought against black defendants for the benefit of white victims would not be pursued.

Butts left the White House in November of 2009 to work for the Millennium Challenge Corporation. The organization is a United States agency created to fight global poverty. Her resignation came soon after her boss Craig left. She continues to work with Podesta at CAP.

MELODY BARNES left her position as executive vice president at the Center of American Progress (CAP) in June 2008 to join the presidential campaign advising on domestic policy. Her title is Director of Domestic Policy Control. Previously, she was the director of legislation affairs for the Equal Opportunity Commission and assistant counsel to the US House Judiciary Subcommittee on Constitution Civil Rights and Civil Liberty. While on the Subcommittee she promoted the Voting Rights Improvement Act. She has been former board member of both Planned Parenthood and EMILY's List. EMILY'S List is an organization that promotes pro-abortion candidates (EMILY stands for Early Money is Like Yeast). Barnes was appointed to the transition team and appointed the Director of White House Domestic Policy Council in 2008. She created the 'Let's Move' program that Michelle Obama promotes with her anti-obesity project. Barnes is the chair of the Childhood Obesity Task Force that Obama created. In 2009 she married Marland Buckner Jr. the founder of Global Strategic Partners, former lobbyist for Microsoft, an aide to Charles Schumer, and Chief of Staff for Harold Ford.

JOHN PODESTA is the president of the Center for American Progress (CAP), former Chief of Staff for the Clinton administration, and co-chair of Obama's transition team.

> The CENTER OF AMERICAN PROGRESS (CAP) founded by George Soros is a progressive think-tank promoting the Obama political agenda. It has promoted the DREAM Act (citizenship for illegal aliens), Cap and Trade (taxing carbon emissions--the air we exhale when we breathe), repeal of Don't Ask, Don't Tell (allowing

openly gay persons to serve in the military), New START (reducing our nuclear arsenal while admitting that Russia will not allow on-site inspections). CAP promotes a progressive tax system and wants the Bush tax cut legislation to expire. The organization wrote an article supporting the building of the mosque in NYC stating, "Building this facility will strengthen America's fight against al- Qaeda".

The think-tank advocates changing the government and suggests that Obama can use his powers to by-pass Congress to implement his agenda.

CAP is a tax deductible 501(c) 3 organization. It started Progressive Media, a project that became Obama's "war room" for his policy agendas. Progressive Media is run through CAP Action Fund a 501(c)4 designation that can lobby and promote candidates. CAP Action Fund coordinates with Common Purpose Project that creates the acceptable messages that are forwarded to progressive organizations including Media Matters. CAP is also the parent organization for Campus Progress and the Enough Project. Campus Progress had its first annual conference in 2005 and Bill Clinton was a speaker. CAP has its own radio station that is used by Bill Press, Al Franken, and was used by the Air America Show. The organizations send out daily e-mails called the Progress Report, plus two blogs Climate Progress and Think Progress. This is another organization where funding appears to go in one pocket and recycles for multiple purposes. CAP funding comes from individuals, foundations, and corporations. Major contributors include Herbert Sandler, Peter Lewis, Steve Bing, and George Soros.

Notable names that have been on staff and policy experts include: Steven Kest (ACORN), Van Jones (former Green Jobs Czar, member of Apollo Alliance, and founder of STORM), Elizabeth Edwards (former wife of John Edwards), former Congressman Tom Daschele, Morton Halperin (director of Soros funded Open Society Institute), and David Halperin (founding member of Soros funded American Constitution Society).

Podesta was instrumental with the implementation of Executive Order 12958 that led to the declassification of 800 million classified papers. The order opened classified paperwork that was over 25 years old that did not violate national security. Podesta and Clinton wanted to obtain information on the Kennedy assassination, remote viewing, and UFO activity. They were especially interested in obtaining information regarding UFOs. Podesta has long advocated opening these files saying the public had a right to know. Information on Project Moon Dust and Operation Blue Fly have been identified as files that were requested. These were operations which identified the purpose of investigating and retrieving objects from UFO's. Podesta was not successful in obtaining more information. President Kennedy had also been interested in these records and wrote a letter to the CIA asking them to release files to NASA in connection with their projects. Two days later he was assassinated. The UFO community was excited when Podesta was selected to the transition team hoping he would have influence to open files. He had even been on Sci-Fi Channel requesting disclosure of UFO documents. But National Security continues to keep these files highly classified and closed. Wilbur Allen, former Air Force One engineer and friend of Podesta, takes photographs of UFOs with highly sophisticated equipment. He has taken pictures over restricted air space in Washington D.C. On a radio interview on May 21, 2010 (on Exopolitics) Allen said that Podesta asked him to stop taking photographs and videos as disclosure could "destroy society".

When Podesta worked under the Clinton administration he became known for a strategy known as "Project Podesta". The strategy allowed Clinton to enact unpopular policies by circumventing Congress. This was accomplished with the use of executive orders, presidential directives, White House directed lawsuits, vacancy appointments, and regulatory action against specific corporations. White House aide Paul Begala referred to this as "Stroke of the pen. Law of the land. Kind of cool".

Bush issued his own Executive Order 13292 that limited access to records that the Clinton administration opened. Obama issued his Executive Order 13526 expanding access, created a National Declassification Center, creating new standards for classification, and indicated that no records are to be classified indefinitely. However, Obama also issued an Executive Order 13489 that allowed incumbent or former Presidents the authority to block access of Presidential records. This was his first Executive Order and was issued on his first day in office.

Podesta took a temporary leave of absence from the CAP to work on the transition team. When the work was done he returned to his organization. After the 2010 elections Podesta began encouraging Obama to circumvent the Congress to advance his agenda. He urged Obama to use executive orders, agency management, and public-private partnerships, whatever it takes because he believes that is what the American people want. The "Podesta Project" has returned. Unpopular decisions include ordering a drilling moratorium and ignoring a court order to reinstate drilling, refusing to deport illegal alien students, ignoring a congressional subpoena to produce documents for the BATF regarding Project Gunwalker (allowing the smuggling of guns into Mexico), and others. Obama said he would ignore the 2011 budget that removed funding for four Czars, and Hillary Clinton told Congress Obama would ignore any resolutions they may make regarding actions in Libya.

RAHM EMANUEL was a supporter and part of Obama's inner circle during the presidential campaign. He strongly supports Israel. His father was a member of Irgu, a Jewish a paramilitary organization which is part of the Israel Defense Force. Irgu was active early in the 1948 Arab-Israeli war. In 1991 Rahm was a civilian volunteer in the Defense Force during the Gulf War. He is known as the "dancer" because he took ballet classes as a child and attended the Evanston School of Ballet. He also participates in triathlons. Emanuel has a Liberal Arts Degree and a Master' Degree in Speech and Communications. His brash manner of communicating has nicknamed him "Rahmbo". He is famously remembered for antics such as sending a rotting dead fish to a pollster he disagreed with and his use of strong "colorful" language.

Emanuel was an advisor and fund raiser for Mayor Daley before becoming an advisor and fundraiser for Clinton's presidential campaign. After the election, he was the Senior Advisor to Clinton, and is proud of his efforts in preparing the ceremony of the Oslo Accords. In 1999 he went to work in an investment banking firm and was able to make between $16 and $18 million in 2 ½ years, despite having no prior banking experience. Emanuel called his investment style "relationship banking". Others commented that he had a "golden rolodex" with of all his White House connections. The contacts he made while he was an investment banker contributed large sums to both his run for congress in 2002 and for mayor in 2011. In 2000, Clinton appointed him to the Board of Directors of the Federal Home Loan Corporation (Freddie Mac). When Emanuel was on the board Freddie Mac was involved in a scandal involving the manipulation of accounting books by showing profits for future years. These accounting tricks misled shareholders and increased bonuses for the board members. Freddie Mac was fined $3.8 million in 2002 and $585 million in 2003 due to the mismanagement of funds. This was also during the time period that Freddie Mac started subprime loans. Emanuel earned $320,000 for the 14 months he was on the board, plus later stocks earnings of $100,000 and $250,000. All Freedom of Information requests regarding actions taken while Emanuel was director have been denied by the current administration.

In 2002 he was elected as Illinois State Representative and a year later appointed to the Housing Finance Service Committee that oversaw Freddie Mac. He did not attend any meetings involving Freddie Mac to prevent the appearance of conflict of interest.

Emanuel co-authored a book in 2006: "The Plan: Big Ideas for America", that advocated for a required three month service program for all youth between the ages of 18 and 25. He called it "universal citizen service" and explained the participants would have basic training, perform community service, and learn "disaster preparedness". Although his proposal is mandatory service he insists it is not a draft. He also wrote about creating a "smarter military" and learning from our "mistakes".

In 2006 he stated that he would support Hillary Clinton for President, and then a year later Obama entered the race. Emanuel stayed neutral until he concluded that Obama was the presumptive nominee. During the primary race he said, "I'm hiding under my desk".

Obama offered him the position of White House Chief of Staff that he accepted. The National Jewish Democratic Council approved the choice. While Congress was contemplating the Stimulus Bill, Emanuel told the Wall Street Journal, "You never want a crisis to go to waste". He predicted this crisis could lead to reforms in energy, health care, education, and tax policy. As Chief of Staff, Progressives criticized him for being too conservative even though he was famous for his strong arm tactics. In September 2010 Emanuel announced that he was leaving the White House to run for Mayor in Chicago. He won the election on February 22, 2011.

Barak Obama won the Democratic nomination for President and the convention was held between August 25 and 29, 2008. Nancy Pelosi (Chair of the DNC) and Alice Germond (Secretary of the DNC) signed the Official Certification of Nominations on August 28th. Actually they signed two different versions of the Certification; one version was sent to 49 States and the other to Hawaii. The Certification which was sent to 49 States specifically says that the candidates for President and Vice President are legally qualified to serve under the provisions of the United States Constitution. The other one only states the candidates were nominated, it does not contain the wording about their legality to serve.

Judge me by the people who surround me.

SECTION FIVE

★ ★ ★ ★ ★

President

CHAPTER 22

★ ★ ★ ★ ★

Vetting for the White House

The election is over and Obama is elected President of the United States. Now it is time to fill positions in the administration. Will the administration be open and transparent? Will policies be moderate and bring people together? Who will Obama surround himself with?

VALERIE JARRETT is a long time friend and was appointed Senior Advisor for Public Engagement and Intergovernmental Affairs. Jarrett was born on November 14, 1956 in Iran to American parents. Her father, James Bowman, was on an American sponsored program and ran a hospital in Iran where she was born. She lived in Iran until she was 5 years old, moved to London for a year, then the family moved to Chicago. She spoke both Persian and French as a child. Her mother co-founded the Erickson Institute that worked with child development issues. Board members of the Institute included Tom Ayers and Bernardine Dohrn. Bill Ayers wrote about her in his 1997 book calling Bowman a friend and neighbor. In 1983 she married Dr. William Robert Jarrett, the son of Vernon Jarrett. Vernon Jarrett was a noted Black journalist that wrote articles for various papers praising known Communists. He had been a friend of Frank Marshall Davis, Obama's mentor in Hawaii. Her great uncle is Vernon Jordan, attorney, businessman, civil rights activist, formerly employed by the NAACP, friend of Bill Clinton and director at the American Friends of Bilderberg.

Jarrett was a practicing attorney from 1981 until 1984. Judd Miner, Obama's former employer, recruited her to work in Mayor Washington's Law Department. She continued to work in the Mayor's office under Daley and hired Michelle Robinson when Michelle was engaged to Barack. She has been a member and chairman of the board on the Chicago Stock Exchange, chair of the board of trustees at the University of Chicago Medical Center, trustee for the University of Chicago, a trustee of the Chicago Museum of Science and

Industry, and board member of USG Corp. She sat on the board of directors of the Woodlawn Preservation and Investment Center with Allison Davis (Obama's former employer) and Tony Rezko. She also sat on the board of directors for the Fund for Community Redevelopment and Revitalization that worked with Davis and Rezko. Housing projects by Davis and Rezko were substandard and violated many building codes. Jarrett was president of Habitat Company that managed many of Chicago's low income housing. Dan Levin is CEO of Habitat Company and is a cousin of Michigan Senator Carl Levin. One of the largest projects was Grove Parc Plaza that had so many violations that the Boston Globe called it "uninhabitable" and "unfixable". The buildings had collapsed roofs and major fire damage. It was so bad the federal inspectors rated the complex an 11 out of a 100 point scale. Davis was the developer of the complex and it was built with tax funding. A larger complex, Lawndale Restoration, was seized by the federal government in 2006. These housing complexes were in or near Obama's Senate District. In February 2009, Obama proposed a $1 billion Housing Trust Fund to rehabilitate housing in the poorest areas in the country.

Jarrett was on the presidential transition team and responsible for many appointments in the new administration. She recruited Van Jones as the Green Jobs Czar. Jarrett announced his appointment saying 'they' had been watching his career for a long time. He later resigned over much controversy. She pushed for the creation of a Diversity Czar at FCC that led to the appointment of Mark Lloyd. Jarrett also recruited Cass Sunstein who suggested the Fairness Doctrine. At the first Ramadan dinner she invited Jameel Jaffer, a Canadian who works for ACLU, who defends Islamic radical terrorists, and has sued the United States over tactics used in the war on terror. Jaffer is responsible for the release of pictures of prisoners from Gitmo, and other prisons, claiming torture and is currently suing to obtain detailed information on drones. He claims use of drones for targeting killing in war zones is illegal.

The proposed 2016 Chicago Olympics that Jarrett lobbied for had been planned to be situated at the Grove Parc Plaza which was designated to be demolished. If the Olympics had been approved for Chicago the city would have paid the owners for the property and would have paid to tear down the buildings. Habitat Company owns the property. Is that a coincidence? Perhaps this is why Jarrett needed an ethics waiver to work on the committee to bring the Olympics to Chicago.

The Obama administration has made more appointments, referred to by the media and others as Czars, than any other administration totaling 39. I was not able to confirm all the salaries for these appointments, but it seems they all receive six figure wages plus the cost of their office, staff, and travel expenses. When a person is appointed to an executive branch position they must get Senate confirmation with background checks and qualifications are questioned. These appointments by-pass Congressional confirmation and serve at the pleasure of the President. They make policy, without Congressional input or review, and have executive privilege. This means if brought before Congress for questioning they can refuse to answer or provide information. Czars are making policy for all Americans and they are not required to answer any questions.

Anthony VAN JONES was recruited to the White House by Valerie Jarrett and was appointed to work in the Council in Environmental Quality. His official title for the newly created position was Special Advisor for Green Jobs, Enterprise and Innovation, commonly referred to as the Green Jobs Czar. On August 15, 2009, at a Daily Kos Netroots convention, Jarrett told the audience, "We were so delighted to be able to recruit him into the White House. We were watching him…for as long as he's been active in Oakland." The White House web site announced his appointment stating he was responsible for starting the Ella Baker Center for Human Rights, Color of Change, and Green for All. The web site also mentions that he wrote the book, 'The Green Collar Economy'. The administration was aware of his background, his past activities, and his radical ideas.

Jones is a Yale educated attorney, environmentalist and activist. He started attending the ivy league university wearing combat boots and carrying a Black Panthers book bag. In April 1992, police officers were acquitted in a trial charged with brutally beating a man named Rodney King in San Francisco. This resulted in six days of rioting with 53 people being killed and thousands injured. Jones was an intern at Lawyers Committee for Civil Rights, volunteered to be a legal monitor during the riots, and was arrested. After spending a few days in jail all charges were dropped. Prior to the verdict he considered himself a political radical, after his arrest he considered himself a Communist. He was jailed with some very radical people, communists, and anarchists, which he tried to emulate after his release.

STORM (Standing Together to Organize a Revolutionary Movement) was founded in 1994 by Jones. It was an umbrella group of organizations such as SOUL (School of Unity and Liberations, a Marxist training organization) and POWER (People Organized to Win Employment Rights) based in Marxist theory. The purpose of STORM was to build a coalition of people from oppressed communities to lay a groundwork for a future revolution party. They attempted to build a consciousness that together people of color, and other underrepresented groups, could stimulate change from the bottom up. He started a hotline service, in 1995, called the Bay Area Police Watch for victims of police violence and provided a lawyer referral service.

In 1996 Jones founded the Ella Baker Center to document and expose unlawful activities of the police and to provide alternatives to incarceration. The organization addresses social issues, environmental issues, and inequality in under-represented oppressed groups. This was later expanded to include the green movement to provide employment opportunities for minorities. The Green Jobs Corps was founded to train youth in green related employment opportunities. California alone received $10 million in 2009 stimulus funds to train 1000 people in green technology to learn new jobs in renewable energy and green buildings. The Ella Baker Center received funding from the Soros' organization Center for American Progress.

On September 12, 2001 STORM, the Ella Baker Center, and other groups held a demonstration/vigil in Oakland mourning the victims of U.S. imperialism. Jones said, "Anti-Arab hostilities is already reaching a fever pitch as pundits and common people alike rush to judgment that an Arab group is responsible for this tragedy". STORM is responsible for demonstrations against the Iraq War coordinated with International ANSWER (Act Now to Stop War and End Racism) a front group for the Marxist-Leninist Workers World Party. Jones signed a 9/11 Truth statement asking for an investigation on Bush to determine if he had prior knowledge of the tragic event.

COLOR OF CHANGE is a web based organization to strengthen the voice of Black America he co-founded, in 2005, with James Rucker from the Soros funded organization Move On. Org. It is a 501(c) 4 non-profit lobbying group and there is Color of Change PAC. The internet is used to gather activists to protest for causes. They successfully lobbied the Congressional Black Caucus not to have a Democratic Presidential debate on Fox News Channel. The group also had a campaign urging advertisers to boycott the Glenn Beck Show on the same channel.

GREEN FOR ALL is a non-government lobbying organization Jones founded in 2007 with a mission to build a green economy seeking a government commitment to job creation and training for people from disadvantaged communities. The Soros organization Open Society Institute provides funding for Green for All, plus the organization receives federal funding through the Departments of Labor and Education. The Stimulus Bill (written by the Apollo Alliance which was founded by Weather Underground member Jeff Jones, no relation to Van) included $60 billion for green jobs. Van Jones was also the person who worked to get the Green Jobs Act passed in 2007, which authorized $125 million to train people for jobs in the green economy. In 2008 Jones wrote a book, "The Green Collar Economy" advocating the use of government funds and incentives to form coalitions with groups like the Apollo Alliance to create a massive populist movement demanding changes. He promotes "eco-equity" by steering green technology to low income and minority groups. The book received favorable reviews from Nancy Pelosi, Al Gore, and NAACP President Ben Jealous.

Jones is a founding director of the APOLLO ALLIANCE which wrote the stimulus bill that provided the money for Green for All. He advised the Workforce Development Institute instructing local and state governments, plus universities, how to apply for funds from the stimulus bill. Jones was also employed at the Soros funded Center for American Progress (CAP) which lobbies for progressive programming. They wrote bills that would receive tax funding for all their pet projects. How many pay checks did Jones receive just from Green for All, Apollo Alliance, Workforce Development Institute, and the CAP? He also sat on the board of directors for other organizations, including the Soros funded organizations Rainforest Action Network, Free Press, and Bioneers. He is part of the 1% the 'Occupiers' are protesting against; yet he fully supports the demonstrators. He stated the 'Occupiers' will get into politics and they will recruit 2,000 persons from that group to run for political office.

Van Jones resigned from his position at the White House on Labor Day 2009 after his radical associations and comments he made became public. Green for All should have no problem with finding funds as $500 million had already been authorized for "green jobs" projects in the stimulus bill. Since leaving the administration he has returned to both CAP and the Apollo Alliance. At CAP he works on the Green Opportunity Initiative and is the policy advisor for Green for All. In 2010 he was given a one year appointment to teach at Princeton University and received the NAACP President's Award for public service. At a Net Roots convention in April 2010 he stated that the businesses in the United States have plenty of money and the group should press Washington to have these businesses fund a new social structure in this country. He told this same group in July that Senator Kerry told him that

Congress planned to pass climate change bills during the 2010 lame duck session. (A lame duck session is the period of time after an election and prior to the new congressmen being sworn in.)

In 2011 at a Power Shift conference for young climate activists he called for them to "shift the power" and lead a clean power revolution. Jones has also become involved with an organization call the Pachamama Alliance that is pushing for the United Nations to give Mother Earth human rights referred to as "global environmental governance".

He has explained his 'green' philosophy at many different forums where he gives speeches. The following are some of his comments.

- "This movement is deeper than solar power...Don't stop there! We are going to change the whole system."
- "It is the violence and injustice of the U.S. Imperialism that has put the entire world in danger."
- "You gotta learn how to fight the war monger and the greedy capitalist developers."
- "White polluters and the white environmentalists are essentially steering poison into the people of colored communities' cuz' they don't have a racial justice frame".
- "I think it's more important to be a revolutionary, because a revolutionary proposed a more just order."
- "The green economy will start off as a small subset and we are going to push it and push it and push it until it becomes the engine for transforming the whole society".
- "I'm willing to drop the radical pose for the radical ends. People don't like hippies. People don't like Marxists or communists."
- You handled the top up, but it's also bottom up and inside out. So now your challenge...our challenge, is to take care of the bottom up part".

The last quote can be explained easily. The top down is the elected officials, who have a plan and structure for change. The bottom up is the activists demonstrating and using other measures to agitate for change. When the agitation becomes too uncomfortable for those in the middle, they will demand the government do something to stop the commotion. The structure is already assembled just waiting to take charge with more control, more restrictions, new laws, and more taxes.

Remember this advice; "Be careful what you ask for" and "Don't want anything in the worse way as that's probably how you will receive it".

MARK LLOYD was appointed at the newly created position of chief Diversity Officer at the Federal Communications Commission (FCC). He is also called the Diversity Czar. He is a former broadcast journalist at NBC and CNN and former vice president at the Leadership Conference for Civil Rights. Lloyd was also a senior fellow at CAP and a consultant for the Open Society Institute, both funded by Soros.

Lloyd wants to promote diversity by suppressing private ownership of broadcasting and instituting "localism". Localism is a term used to describe content of broadcasting in television and radio to reflect the segments of the population of each community. The programming would not reflect the listenership or ratings of each station but what the FCC determines should be aired. Private owned stations would be required to submit to the FCC regulations or pay fines up to $250 million or have their licenses denied. In addition, privately owned stations would be required to pay public broadcast stations monies to support the public non-profit stations like National Public Radio (NPR). This is redistribution of private profits and is intended to limit or shut down conservative and Christian television and radio stations.

Privately owned progressive radio stations currently have only 9% listenership while conservative radio has 91%. Private broadcast companies are in business to make profits and will air programming that people want to hear. The FCC had Fairness Doctrine regulations established in 1934 during the New Deal and stations were required to air both sides of debates. Then in 1949 the FCC demanded stations to have specific air time dedicated to public issue discussion to keep their licenses. The result was that radio stations dropped talk radio because of all the regulations and the mandatory public service programming limited debate. The Fairness Doctrine was eliminated in 1987 and talk radio came back and free speech was no longer being strangled. Conservative talk shows thrived as an alternative to liberal biased television, and liberal talk shows have struggled. Now the Progressives want to reinstate the Fairness Doctrine and call it "localism".

Under Lloyd's leadership the FCC wants guidelines, and "permanent" advisory boards made up of local leaders, to approve or deny licenses based on localism programming. Broadcasters are to determine all the different segments of each community and ensure that each segment receives programs that meets their needs and interests. Complaints regarding lack of diverse programming would be channeled to advisory boards to determine continuation of licenses. In a CAP report titled "Forget the Fairness Doctrine", Lloyd suggested that local activists should monitor and harass stations that don't promote their views. He wrote, "Community organizations should threaten licenses of stations with whom they don't politically agree, so if they don't want to be subject to criticism they should pay to support public broadcasts". In his 2006 book "Prologue to a Farce", "It should be clear by now that my focus here is not freedom of speech or the press. This freedom is all too often an exaggeration. At the very least, blind references to freedom of speech or the press serve as a distraction from the critical examination of other communications policies".

Speeches that Lloyd have given are also insightful for understanding how he wants to govern the FCC policies.

- "If our republican form of government is perishing because of communications – the infrastructure of that republic...We must build a confrontational movement to reclaim our democracy, a movement committed to active and sustained protest against the present order".

- "In Venezuela, with Chavez, is really an incredible revolution – a democratic revolution...The property owners, and the folks who then controlled the media in Venezuela rebelled...and then Chavez began to take very seriously the media in his country."

- "The other part of our proposal that gets the 'dittoheads' upset is our suggestion that the commercial radio station owners either play by the rules or pay".

- "We have really, truly good white people in important positions.

> And the fact of the matter is that there are a limited number of those positions. And unless we are conscious of the need to have more people of color, gays, other people in those positions we will not change the problem. We're in a position where you have to say who is going to step down so someone else can have power."

Funding for Mark Lloyd's position has been removed under a resolution in the House of Representatives in 2011. It is part of the Republican budget to reduce spending in Washington.

The FCC is not content with setting regulations for the air waves, now it wants control of the internet. A Soros organization Free Press lobbies for localism and is pressing for government control over the internet. Free Press founder ROBERT MCCHESNEY is a professor at the University of Illinois, director of a Monthly Review Foundation (a tax-exempt parent company of the Marxist publication Monthly Review), and host of the radio show "Media Matters" (he admits he has never had a conservative guest). The plan is to define the internet as a public utility, like the telephone, and to enact net neutrality regulations sometimes called 'open internet'. McChesney explained net neutrality, "At the moment the battle over network neutrality is not to completely eliminate the telephone and cable companies. We are not at that point yet. But the ultimate goal is to get rid of the media capitalists in the phone and cable companies and to divest them from control." "Instead of waiting for the revolution to happen, we learned that unless you make significant changes in the media, it will be vastly more difficult to have a revolution. While the media is not the single most important issue in the world, it is one of the core issues that any successful Left project needs to integrate into its strategic program." We need to do whatever we can to limit capitalist propaganda, regulate it, minimize it, and perhaps even eliminate it."

I wonder if these people stay up at night redefining our vocabulary. An organization called Free Press advocating for the Fairness Doctrine, net neutrality and open internet that is actually attempting to suppress free speech and open dialogue. It's the same mentality as those who support 'social justice' which in reality divides people into groups to be treated differently.

SAMANTHA POWER was a journalist and war correspondent for 'US News and World Report' and the 'Economist' prior to working for U.S.

Senator Obama as a senior advisor. She is known as an expert on genocide as a result of her Pulitzer Prize winning book titled "A Problem from Hell: America and the Age of Genocide". During an interview in February 2008 she explained she "got into journalism as a means to change the world". Power is the founding executive director of the Carr Center for Human Rights Policy at John F. Kennedy School of Government at Harvard Group as a political analyst. 'Time Magazine' published an article she wrote in January 2008 when she criticized Bush's policy with Iran. She suggested that Iran should have a voice and be part of the solution with the "Iraq quagmire". Power stated the United States should also insist that Iran address human rights issues in their own country. In a February 2008 interview with reporter Noah Pollak she stated, "To neutralize the support Ahmadinejad has domestically we need to stop threatening and get in a room with him... and then try to build international support for measures to prevent him from supporting terrorism and pursuing a nuclear program". During this same interview she was asked what the biggest challenge in foreign policy that Obama would encounter. She responded, "No long term peace in the Middle East is possible until we get some kind of modus Vivendi (agreement or treaty) in the Arab-Israeli situation".

She was part of the presidential campaign advising on foreign issues until she gave an interview on March 6, 2008. In the interview she called Hillary Clinton a monster that would stoop to nothing. That night Power apologized and the next day resigned. The very next day she joined the Soros think-tank The International Crisis Group (ICG). Other members of the board include Zbigniew Brzezinski and Robert Malley; both are Obama foreign advisors and both have views that are anti-Israel. She rejoined Obama in November to work in the State Department as a foreign policy fellow and was on the transition team. Hillary Clinton is the Secretary of State so their next meeting must have been quite interesting. In January 2009 she was appointed to the National Security Council as Special Advisor to the President and is the director of the newly created Office of Multilateral and Human Rights.

Her views on Israel have caused many Jews to be concerned. In 2002 she had an interview with Harry Kreisler the director of the Institute of International Studies at Berkley University. He asked her a hypothetical question on what her advice to Obama would be if she was his adviser regarding the Middle East. She responded that she would invest in a "mammoth protection force" for a new state of Palestine as she made a comparison of the "Israel situation" with Rwanda. Power has also complained that the United States foreign policy is to "defer reflexively to Israeli security assessments".

The founding executive director of the Carr Center for Human Rights was Samantha Power. The stated mission of the organization was to train people to be leaders in public service. The Carr Center advised on the policy of Responsibility to Protect also known as RtoP and R2P. Power gave an interview at the Harvard Kennedy School in 2007 stating America needed to change its foreign policies. She criticized Bush's actions in Iraq stating that he overstretched the military and caused the deficit. She continued to say the United States committed acts of torture, crimes against humanity and other sins in our conduct of the war. The doctrine of R2P was originated by the International Commission on Intervention and State Sovereignty. Power sat on the board with Arab League Secretary General Amr Moussa and Palestinian legislator Hanan Ashrawl. The United Nations World Summit adopted the principle R2P in 2005 with Resolution 1674 to commit support to protect human rights. In 2008 the Global Centre for Responsibility to Protect was formed with funding from Soros. Its function is to be the center for international governments to conduct and coordinate the application of the R2P policies to stop mass atrocities. UN Secretary General Ban said in February 2011 that the UN must protect people "from want, from war, and from repression" and use force if needed.

When demonstrations began in Egypt (crowds shown on television have been estimated at less than 0.01% of Egypt's population of 80 million people) the National Security Council debated which actions to take. What wasn't reported was that Egypt was moving in the direction of becoming a capitalist country. The currency had been devalued, more money was being invested, and its exports were starting to grow. In November 2010 Power met with the Egypt Working Group to discuss that country's political reform and move to democracy. Also not reported was that the leaders of Egypt's military were not in their country at the start of the demonstrations because they were in Washington with Pentagon officials. Their absence allowed for the rapid rise of violence and destruction which the media portrayed as being orchestrated by the pro-Murbarak populace.

Secretary of State Clinton, Defense Secretary Gates and National Security Advisor Donilon wanted Egypt to start a reform process and to assure them that the United States would stand by its ally. However Power argued against that tactic and suggested that Obama should demand Murbarak leave office. This caused concern for Israel because Murbarak helped Israel's security on the Gaza border. Obama eventually acted on Power's advice as he demanded Murbarak to leave.

The next conflict that got major media attention were the demonstrations in Libya. Power along with U.N. Ambassador Rice and Secretary of State Clinton pressed for military invention for humanitarian reasons. Power argued that this country could not stand on the sidelines when Khadafy was murdering people in his own country. The policy of R2P would finally find a place to be tested. Obama stated the United States would lead from behind and gave the mission to NATO. He stressed the mission was to prevent a massacre and to remove Khadafy from office, although he was not going to target him personally. Obama committed the United States military to fight, under foreign command, and not target the leader of the country they were sent to.

The policy of R2P has now been put into action and precedence has been set. What will come next? Could another country decide that the United States has committed an action under R2P and invade while demanding a change in leadership to a grassroots group that is making noise? Or what if a Palestinian demanding statehood charges Israel with military transgressions when defending itself from rocket attacks and petitions the UN to invade Israel? There has been speculation that R2P was created as a vehicle for the Arab countries to dismantle Israel.

Hillary Clinton has stated that she would serve only one term as Secretary of State and would resign if Obama was elected to serve a second term. There is speculation that Power will be approached to take that office because of her influence with Obama. Samantha Power is married to Cass Sunstein.

Judge me by the people who surround me.

CHAPTER 23

★ ★ ★ ★ ★

Regulations and Health

Some Czars were confirmed by Congress, but their background doesn't seem to have been scrutinized very carefully. Or perhaps the majority of Congressmen agree with the viewpoints of the people they approved. These next people have strong convictions about science and health care.

CASS SUNSTEIN was appointed, and confirmed by Congress, as director of the Office of Information and Regulatory Affairs, also known as the Regulation Czar. It is his responsibility to review and create regulations using cost based analysis. In this position he can affect every citizen in the United States and he has some very controversial views. This appointment allows him to make regulations without Congressional oversight or input. He has written numerous books, papers, and articles expressing his view points on many subjects. Sunstein wrote a book titled "Nudge" that advocates the government, or organizations, use and create situations to 'nudge' people to make desirable decisions or change behaviors. He wrote, "Once we know that people have some Homer Simpson in them, then there is a lot that can be done to manipulate them".

Sunstein believes there should be a Second Bill of Rights. He laments that those who wrote the Constitution did not include social and economic guarantees. He believes citizens should have guaranteed rights to employment, food, clothing, shelter, education, medical care, and recreation. The rights endowed by our Creator of life, liberty, and the pursuit of happiness are not sufficient for him.

> I wonder if everyone is ensured they will have food, clothing, shelter, medical care, and recreation why they would work or get an education. Of course, I suppose if someone didn't work Sunstein could pass a law so that the person would have to go to jail where all of the above is provided.

He is an animal rights activist and some suspect he may be a vegetarian. Sunstein has advocated for animals (wild life, pets, and livestock) to have legal rights to sue humans. At a 2007 speech at Harvard, he said that hunting for sport should be against the law. He also said he was against greyhound racing, using animals for testing cosmetics, and eating meat. Sunstein stated the treatment of livestock was "morally akin to slavery and mass extermination of human beings". Sunstein has strong opinions on how humans use and control animals. He believes decisions and actions towards animals must be based on whether the animal is capable of suffering. The example used was about rats and their ability to suffer. If they can suffer then their interests must be considered in determining how or "whether" they should be removed from houses.

Sunstein is against gun ownership. In a 2007 'National Review' article "The Most Mysterious Right" he wrote, "The Supreme Court is now being asked to decide whether the Second Amendment created an individual right to own guns. There is a decent chance that the Court will say that it does. Whatever the Court says, we have seen an amazingly rapid change in constitutional understandings—even a revolution—as an apparently fraudulent interpretation pushed by "special interest groups". He continued, "Even if the Second Amendment does confer an individual right, and therefore imposes limits on national gun control legislation, a further question remains. Does the Second Amendment apply its plain terms to the states? By its plain terms, the original Bill of Rights applies only to the national government. To be sure, most (but not all) of the listed rights are now understood to have been "incorporated" in the Fourteenth Amendment and made applicable to the state through that route. But is the Second Amendment incorporated as well?" Then in his book, "Radicals in Robes", "Almost all gun control legislation is constitutionally fine. And if the Court is right, then fundamentalism does not justify the view that the Second Amendment protects an individual right to bear arms". Then he summarized his beliefs, "My view is that the individual right to bear arms reflects the success of an extremely aggressive and resourceful social movement".

Sunstein believes in taxation, "In what sense is the money in our pockets and bank accounts fully 'ours'? Could we spend it if there were no public officials to coordinate the efforts and pool the resources of the community in which we live? Without taxes there would be no property. Without taxes, few of us would have any assets worth defending. It is a dim fiction that some people enjoy and exercise their rights without placing any burden whatsoever on the public. There is no liberty without dependency." He is not supportive of marriage, "Under our proposal, the word marriage would no longer appear in any laws, and marriage licenses would no longer be offered or recognized by any level of government". "Government would not be asked to endorse any particular relationships by conferring on them the term marriage".

> In his 1993 book, "Democracy and The Problem of Free Speech," Sunstein contemplates issues of free speech in the media. He states the problem is newspapers and broadcast media operate on the principles of profit and advertisers want a large audience. Then there is the problem of people listening to and reading subjects that they agree with and not being introduced to differing opinions. He wrote, "There must be pubic exposure to an appropriate diversity of view". (I wonder who will decide what an appropriate diversity of view must be.) Sunstein wrote, "Our speech market's relentless competition for viewers and listeners benefits neither society nor broadcast journalism." He continues, "Once we have broken up all interferences with the operation of the free market…our free speech problems will be solved". Therefore, Sunstein is against the principles of the free market where companies produce a product that people want and are able to make a profit. Then he wants to determine what people read and listen to. It appears to me he is concerned that the majority do not listen to, or read, the opinions that he agrees with. Sunstein does not say he wants to change people's opinions but only wants to nudge them in that direction.

Free speech and the internet are subjects that Sunstein has written about in many books and papers. The Regulatory Czar has advocated for an internet "Fairness Doctrine". He wrote, "the internet is a breeding ground for extremism" and produces what he calls 'cyberbalkanization.' He wrote that the First Amendment needs to be changed so that cyber free speech is more like a market place of ideas. Sunstein says the internet encourages people to only exchange ideas with those who have similar opinions. He prefers that legislation be enacted so websites are mandated to have links to sites with opposing viewpoints. He states, "A system of limitless individual choices with respect to communications is not necessarily in the interest of citizenship and self government." If limitless choices is not in one's best interest, he must want to limit those choices to those he approves of.

In his opinion the internet also has the ability to spread "conspiracy theories". Sunstein states that conspiracy theories are the result of what people hear or read and admits that some of these "theories" have been ultimately proven to be true. He says conspiracy theories contribute to the distrust of the government. So his idea for correcting the mistrust is for the government to infiltrate the groups with paid agents. The agents would pose as experts using "counterspeech" to discredit the theories. He suggests the agents could penetrate extremist group meetings, or go online and enter their social networks and chat rooms. Acknowledging that most groups would not trust a government agent he promotes the infiltration be undercover activities. His paper, "Conspiracy Theories" was written in January 2008.

Sunstein thinks personal e-mail should be monitored and he proposes a 'Civility Check' if the message appears angry. The internet would send a 'warning' that the e-mail is not civil. He even suggests having the ability to stop transmission of uncivil e-mail for 24 hours, at which time the person would need to resubmit the message. He must know that if the citizens realize their e-mail is being monitored for civility that all content is being monitored. This would certainly curtail personal use of the internet which appears to be his motive. That is quite a nudge! Who would determine what is civil and would any dissent of the government be determined to be uncivil?

WikiLeaks was in the news after it released secured information that may undermine national security. Wikileaks is a web site that that publishes information sent to them and the contributor's identity is kept confidential. However, Army Private Bradley Manning boasted about his involvement to a friend and the friend became a whistleblower. He was jailed Kuwait, put in solitary confinement Quantico, and later transferred to Fort Leavenworth pending his military trial. An article 32 hearing began in December 2011. Manning was considered for a 2011 Nobel Peace Prize.

The founder of WikiLeaks, Julian Assange was also imprisoned in England, not for releasing the information, but for consensual sexual encounters with two women in Sweden. He had been released to an estate of a supporter under police surveillance later to be released with an electric tag. England approved an extradition to Sweden, fined him and he continues to be on conditional bail. Assange released the information with the intent to create chaos under the guise of the public having a right to know. Mark Stephens, who does pro bono legal work for Soros' Open Society Institute, is Assange's attorney. Cass Sunstein wants to control the internet and there is some speculation ("conspiracy theory") that the Wikileak situation could be used to control or limit the internet. Sunstein wrote an article about the internet that included a reference to Wikileaks just as it was being formed and before the website issued any information. Therefore, he has been aware of the web site's ability to confidentially disseminate massive pages of information since its inception. The 'conspiracy theory' is that Soros funded the website with the intent to create the conditions that people would demand the government do something to prevent this happening in the future. This would make Assange a stooge in the grand plan to control the internet. Several Congressmen want Assange brought to trial for espionage against the United States, but I have doubts that these connections will become public in the main stream media.

Cost based analysis for government policies includes health care. Sunstein believes health care should be spent wisely based on life ages, not lives saved. He says everyone has a Value of a Statistical Life (VSL) based on age and pre-existing conditions. A person age 65 has a VSL of $2.7 million, age 40 VSL is $6 million, and age 10 is $11 million. He proposes that money spent on health care needs to take in consideration the value of the life in comparison with the money spent. Using life ages as a guide, less money will be used to save a life of an older individual than a younger one. Then a value is based on life ages saved instead of the number of lives saved. This is not age discrimination he argues, "because every old person was once young, and emphasis on life years does not discriminate against anyone". Disabilities also are a consideration, as money spent on a person severely disabled, that cannot provide substantial improvement, is not money well spent.

He also believes in routine removal of organs without consent. "The state owns the rights to body parts of people who are dead or in a certain hopeless condition, and it can remove their organs without asking anyone's permission". "It would save lives, and it would do so without intruding on anyone who has any proposal for life". These quotes are taken from his book "Nudge" and note that Sunstein did not even state that the donor had to be dead before the organs would be removed. He also asserts that the government must pay for abortions. In his book, "The Partial Constitution", he says that when the government pays for child birth but not abortions "It has the precise consequence of turning women into involuntary incubators".

Sunstein met Samantha Power while both were campaigning for Obama. One their first date he was asked what job he would want if he could have any job in the world. He responded that he would want to work in the White House as an administrator for information and regulatory affairs. The couple were married on July 4, 2008 and had a daughter on April 24, 2009.

DR. EZEKIEL EMANUEL was appointed as a Special Advisor for health policy in the White House Office of Management and Budget, also known as the Health Care Czar. He is the older brother of Rahm Emanuel. He believes in a voucher system of health care, to replace employer provided insurance, to be paid for by a Value Added Tax (VAT). Emanuel has written on methods to reduce health care costs and thinks part of the problem is the training doctors receive. He complains that medical schools train for thoroughness by attempting to look for all possible diagnoses. This leads to tests that will confirm or exclude diagnoses which he calls expensive and wasteful. He promotes rationing as a means to improve the quality and efficiency of the health care system. Emanuel has advocated for a two tier health care system which provides basic and discretionary services. Most people would be eligible for basic services, but it is not guaranteed for those persons who could not become 'participating' citizens. Some people would be eligible for both basic and discretionary services.

In the event that there is a scarcity of medical needs such as organs or vaccines he wants to use the complete lives system. Dr. Emanuel co-wrote "Principles for Allocation of Scarce Medical Interventions" explaining his positions. "The complete lives system discriminates against older people. Age based allocation is ageism …even if 25 year olds became a priority over 65 year olds, everyone who is 65 years old now was previously 25 years old. Treating 65 years olds differently because of stereotypes or falsehoods would be ageist; treating them because they have already had more years is not." "When completed, the complete lives system produces a priority curve which individuals aged between roughly 15 and 40 get the most substantial chances." "Allocation treats life years given to elderly or disabled people as objectively less valuable." This system "empowers us to decide fairly whom to save when genuine scarcity makes saving everyone impossible".

Dr. Emanuel believes that everyone should have health care by replacing employer based health insurance with vouchers as it will save money and tedious government paperwork. Rationing of services is only to be done if there is a scarcity of medical needs or services he explains, but the complete lives system gives structure when needed. In January 2011 Dr. Emanuel left this position to return to his prior employment the National Institutes of Health as the director in the Department of Bioethics.

JOHN HOLDREN was confirmed by the Senate as the Director of Science and Technology, or the Science Czar. He sits on the board of sponsors of the Federation of American Scientists which was founded by communists and Soviets spies including J. Robert Oppenheimer and Leo Szilard. Sitting on the board of sponsors with Holdren is Mark Ptashne whose father Fred Ptashne was a tutor at the communist Abraham Lincoln School in Chicago. Other former instructors at the communist school were Frank Marshall Davis and Bernice Targ. Frank Marshall Davis was Obama's mentor in Hawaii and Targ is a friend of Obama's personal physician Dr. Quinton Young.

Holdren is also a member of the Club of Rome. The Club of Rome is a think- tank with a mission to work on 'A New Path for World Development' through the environment (climate change), globalization, world development, social transformation, and peace and security. Holdren was implicated in the 2009 scandal called Climategate. Climategate was uncovered by a hacker in the records of the Climate Research Unit. He released over 1000 e-mails and thousands of documents purporting misconduct of the scientists in climate study. It exposed the scientists were colluding to present scientific information to support the claim of global warming and suppressing conflicting documentation. Some of Holdren's e-mails were hacked as part of this investigation.

He coauthored the book, "Human Ecology: Problems and Solutions" supporting the realignment of the economies of developed countries. The resources of developed countries, he argues, should be directed to the underdeveloped countries in a program called 'de-development". Holdren specifically named the United States as the country he wants to de-develop. He supports stopping all activities that are "frivolous and wasteful". Therefore, he supports the idea that by reducing the quality of life in successful capitalist countries will somehow increase the quality of life in poorer countries. He does not support the idea that underdeveloped countries could adopt a prosperous capitalist system and all nations could flourish and have the ability to purchase "frivolous" or perhaps fun products.

Holdren has published many books and articles about his views on climate change and population control. In 1971 he coauthored a text book warning about the new 'ice age' and the resulting disaster with insufficient agriculture to feed the world population. In his 1986 book, "The Machinery of Nature" he again warned about global cooling. He stated that human emissions of carbon dioxide would cause cooling to the extent it would reduce agriculture production. Then in another book published in the 1970's, and revised in 1977, he wrote that man made warming might cause a cooling trend that would affect food production so much that population control might have to be instituted. His last book titled," Ecoscience: Population, Resources and Environment", supports several methods of population control. One method is to put 'sterilants' into the drinking water. He cautions that the sterilizations used must not cause any unpleasant side effects and have no effects on "children, old people, pets or livestock". He also advocated for contraceptive capsules to be implanted into young girls that would need to be removed to get pregnant and reinstated after childbirth. He even suggested government boards to give permission to have children. He maintains that illegitimate children should be taken from the mother and given for adoption, or the mother would be mandated to get married, have an abortion or apply for adoption of her child through the courts. Persons who have more than two or three children could be encouraged to reproduce responsibly with abortions and sterilization. Holdren wrote that compulsory population control could be implemented under the existing Constitution. He further suggests a Planetary Regime under the United Nations to decide on the number of children each country may have and the creation of police powers to enforce the population numbers agreed on.

Holdren is now on the human caused global warming band wagon. He suggests making people change their life styles with "information barriers, tax barriers, financial barriers, and other perverse incentives". He does acknowledge that a 25% increase in a gas tax would be unpopular. Although he is not pleased that more regulations have not passed through Congress, he stated these measures may be enacted by the EPA with new regulations that won't need Congressional approval.

In December 2010 Holdren stated the Office of Science and Technology Policy received $18 billion in stimulus funds for research and over $100 billion for science and technology. He also reported that he increased his staff in the past two years from 45 to about 100 employees. He was given a deadline of July 9, 2009 to issue integrity guidelines for agencies and was unable to do that. Holdren explained the reason he did not meet his deadline was because the complexity of determining which details each agency should be able to decide individually and what should be mandated.

> It seems to me that Holdren wants to control the population and will use the excuse of global warming, a new ice age, or climate change to support his vision. Where carbons emissions once was the cause of global cooling, this same vapor (the one we exhale when breathing) is now the cause of global warming. This man is our Science Czar and I find his solutions to control population frightening.

KATHLEEN SEBELIUS is not a Czar but has a strong role in the implementation of health care policy. She was appointed as the Secretary of Health and Human Services (HHS) after the initial nominee Tom Daschle withdrew his nomination because he owed money to IRS. Sebelius had her own issues during confirmation when it was discovered she underpaid the IRS $8,000 by overstating deductions to charities, home sales, and business expenses. She stated these were "unintentional errors" and paid the money due to IRS.

Sebelius was the former governor of Kansas, former Kansas state representative, former lobbyist for the Kansas Trial Lawyers Association, and former Kansas State insurance commissioner. As governor she supported pro-abortion positions. One of her major political contributors was George Tiller, one of the few abortionists that performed late term abortions. He was murdered in 2009. Another political backer was Planned Parenthood who held fund raisers on her behalf. Sebelius is a Catholic, but the Vatican court has banned her from receiving communion because of her continued support for abortion, an action that is against the tenets of the church.

Global warming is a concept she endorses and she supports federal funding for wind energy. As governor she vetoed bills to allow concealed carry laws in her state, but the state Congress voted to over ride her veto. When an amendment was up for a vote in Kansas to outlaw same sex marriage she was against it, however the voters disagreed with her and voted it in.

As Secretary of HHS in 2010 she has 70,000 employees and had a budget of $860,000,000. It is her responsibility to oversee Medicare and Medicaid, plus implement the Patient Protection and Affordability Care Act commonly referred to as Obamacare. The 2,700 page bill mentions the word secretary almost 3,000 times. Examples of the many functions include the wording: "secretary shall establish, secretary shall promulgate regulations, secretary shall develop standards, secretary shall periodically review, secretary may raise rates, and secretary may act as deemed important. Section 4102 of the bill states, "The secretary shall develop oral healthcare components that shall include tooth-level surveillance" (meaning each tooth in the mouth must be looked at.) She will have to ability to determine "reasonable" rate increases to health care premiums.

The original Obamacare bill HR 3200 included Section 2561 stated the Secretary shall establish a national medical device registry to include Class II devices. Class II devices produce a radiofrequency that are implanted under the skin like they do with pet locators. The bill that passed HR 3590 did not have that language; but allowed the Secretary to implement electronic billing procedures. HR 4872 was an amendment to the passed bill that states the Secretary shall develop technology enrollment standards and protocols. Verichip is an implantable Class II device that has been approved in 2004 by the FDA.

Sebelius has been an ardent advocate for Obamacare. When popularity of the program was in decline she stated that people needed to be 're-educated'. When seniors received a $250 check she believed the money would encourage enthusiasm for the program. As secretary of HHS she has been called to testify before Congress a few times. In March 2011, she admitted that costs for Medicare and Medicaid had been counted twice. The $500 billion that was allocated for Medicare was the same money allocated to Medicaid, an accounting gimmick meant to confuse. The same money cannot be used two times. It would be like saying you had $30,000 for a new car, but you would spend the same money and also purchase a new truck. It can't be done, you either purchase the car or the truck, but no dealership is going to sell you two vehicles with the same money. Her explanation for the accounting gimmick was that was how it has always been done.

Also in March, she testified that Obamacare is not affordable unless everyone is mandated to purchase government approved health care insurance. Approximately 1,000 waivers to the mandate have been approved, many to unions such as the United Federation of Teachers, SEIU, and health care workers. In May 2011 she testified that the Republican proposed health care plan would cause cancer patients to die faster than Obamacare. The Republican plan endorses "premium support" for private health insurance plans and therefore the government would not bear the entire costs of health care. The Congressional Budget Office (CBO)stated this plan would reduce costs of providing care from the current 70% to 75% to approximately 32%. The plan has provisions for those who cannot afford needed additional medical care. Democrats have referred to the plan as a voucher system stating once a person uses the voucher there will be no further funding. Republicans deny that claim. The CBO has stated Obamacare will cost $2 trillion between 2014 and 2023, half supported by taxes.

These people will be instrumental with the implementation of Obamacare. What is troubling to me how the Health Benefits Advisory Committee of Obamacare will be formed. According to section 223, pages 111 to 112, of HR 3962 (Obamacare) the Advisory Committee will "recommend covered benefits and essential, enhanced, and premium plans. The Surgeon General will chair the committee. The current Surgeon General is Dr. Regina Benjamin who supports abortion rights. In addition there will be 9 non-government (federal) employees or officers appointed by the President. The Comptroller General will then appoint 9 members who are not federal employees or officers. Gene Dodaro, the current Comptroller General, also the head of Government Accountability Office (GAO), secured the 15 year appointment during the lame duck session in December 2010. Then the President may appoint up to 8 Federal employees or officers to the Advisory Committee.

Obama will have direct control over all the nominees, either by those he nominates and from his nominee for Comptroller General. The Chair will be the Surgeon General that he appointed. If the members of the committee share the views of the Czars listed above or of the HHS Secretary, the committee will be composed of persons who believe in the complete-lives system of health care and will be pro-abortion advocates. I wonder if anybody has conducted a poll of this nation to determine if these ideologies reflect the opinions of the majority of the population. I suspect there has not been a poll on these issues.

The Supreme Court decided that the health care bill was illegal under the interstate commerce clause. However, it determined the Federal government has the ability to tax. citizens. Therefore penalities and fines imposed are taxes and the health care bill is the largest tax increase passed in America's history.

Judge me by the people who surround me.

CHAPTER 24

★ ★ ★ ★ ★

Foreign Advisors

There have been numerous foreign policy advisors to Obama, during his campaign and since he took office. Reports state that he had over 300 advisors. Samantha Power and her views have already been reviewed in chapter 22. This is a review of some of his other advisors.

DAN KURTZER was an advisor during the campaign on Israeli/Palestinian policy. Many pro-Israel leaders are concerned as Kurtzer has views they disagree with. He has blamed Israel for the radicalization of Palestinians towards violence and came up with the term "land for peace". He blamed Israel for the failure of the Camp David talks and wants the United States to pressure Israel to make more concessions.

DAN SHAPIRO advised Obama during the campaign on Israeli/ Palestinian policy. He advocates for a two state solution and negotiations to bring peace in the area. After the election he became the senior director for Middle East and North Africa and is the current nominee to be ambassador to Israel.

PHILIP H. GORDON was an unpaid foreign policy advisor from the Soros funded Brookings Institution, a think-tank located in Washington D.C. He believes in talking with Iran with no preconditions. After the election Gordon became the Assistant Secretary in the Bureau of European and Eurasian Affairs. His main focus is to unite southeastern Europe (the Balkans) with the rest of Europe. Another priority is to restore a relationship with Russia.

IVO DAALDER was another foreign advisor from the Brookings Institution providing advice during the campaign and is now the Ambassador to

NATO. Daalder believes in talks and negotiations with Iran to establish a relationship. He thinks the United States should take a leadership role to reduce global warming, reduce nuclear weapons, and reduce poverty.

GAYLE SMITH was an advisor to Obama during the campaign, a senior fellow at the Soros funded Center for American Progress (CAP), and director of CAP's International Rights and Responsibilities Program. The Program's goal is "to establish 'responsibility' as a core progressive principle and promote a foreign policy that is committed to creating a safer and more equitable world for all". She is also the co-founder of Enough Project an organization to prevent genocide and crimes against humanity. It was a project of CAP to "promote peace, protect civilians, and punish perpetrators". She is now a senior director on Global Development Stabilization and Humanitarian Assistance in the National Security Council. She has announced a new program to combat AIDS called the Health Initiative, was part of a group of advisors to draft a report on unrest in Arab countries, and supported the invasion in Libya.

Smith has an interesting background. In the late 1970's she was a CIA undercover operative, working for the United States Agency for International Development (USAID), posing as a journalist when she joined a Marxist guerilla group called the Tigrayan Peoples Liberation Front (TPLF). She became a mistress to the leader Meles Zenawi and for about 10 years was the liaison between him and the CIA. After Zenawi overthrew the previous Ethiopian government in 1991 he became the Prime Minister and he holds that title today. Then Smith left Ethiopia and became the Chief of Staff at USAID where she oversaw CIA activities using the organization as cover. While in this position she was able to coordinate billions of dollars that enabled Zenawi to build one the best armies in Africa. Today Zenawi is considered one of the most brutal leaders in the world, accused of genocide and starving millions of Ethiopians. No humanitarian agencies are allowed in the country.

LAWRENCE KORB an advisor during the campaign is a Senior Fellow at CAP and a Senior Adviser at the Center for Defense Information, an organization that has received funding from the Soros organization Open Society Institute. Korb has written 20 books and many op-ed articles expressing his views. He often writes about reducing military funding, reducing military personnel, closing military bases overseas, and believes any military actions should be sanctioned by international organizations. He was critical of cuts to the United States Border Patrol because their function is vital to national security. Korb has praised the invasion into Libya because Obama got permission from the United Nations, took precautions not to harm civilians, and believes the action will appease Arab countries. Korb actively supported the removal of the policy of "Don't Ask, Don't Tell" and advocates for the release of Jonathan Pollard from prison. Pollard was convicted to life in prison for spying on behalf of Israel in 1987 when Korb was the Assistant Secretary of Defense during the Reagan administration.

JOSEPH CIRINCIONE the President of the Soros funded Ploughshares Fund was another advisor to Obama during the campaign. Ploughshares Fund's mission is to reduce nuclear weapons, oppose a missile defense system, and to redistribute military funding to humanitarian needs. Ploughshares is proud that the organization was instrumental the signing of the New Start program which canceled plans for a missile defense in Europe and the prevention of any stimulus money being spent on nuclear weapons. Circincione maintains that Iran is still 2 to 5 years away from completing any nuclear arms weapons. He supports diplomacy with Iran, rather than sanctions or military intervention, to convince the country to stop their nuclear program.

ZBGNIEW BRZEZINSKI supported Obama for President as early as August 2007 and was reported to be a campaign advisor in February 2008. On September 27, 2007 Obama said this about Brzezinski, "I can't say enough about his contributions to our country...somebody I have learned an immense amount from". In February 2008 Brzezinski took a trip to Syria organized by the RAND Center for Middle East Public Policy that was not coordinated with the American embassy. A representative from RAND stated that the trip was not meant to be covered by the press. He did meet with Syria's president Bashar al-Assad and other leaders of the country. Several members of RAND have connections to the Soros funded J Street. In November 2008 the Obama campaign denied that Brzezinski was an advisor.

As stated earlier Brzezinski was a former college instructor for Obama and former National Security Advisor to Jimmy Carter who encouraged and armed Osama bin Laden. He is also implicated in actions that led to the fall of the Shah of Iran and the rise of radical Islam. He founded the Trilateral Commission with David Rockefeller in 1973. Rockefeller approached him about forming the organization after Brzezinski's book "Between Two Ages: America's Role in the Technotronic Age was published. The following are quotes from his book;

- "The Technotronic era involves the gradual appearance of a more controlled society. Such a society would be dominated by the elite, unrestrained by traditional values. Soon it would be possible to assert almost continuous surveillance over every citizen and maintain up-to-date complete files containing even the most personal information about the citizens".

- "In the Technotronic Society the trend would seem to be towards the aggregation of the individual's support of millions of uncoordinated citizens, easily within reach of magnetic and attractive personalities effectively exploiting the latest communications techniques to manipulate emotions and control reason".

- "Society dominated by an elite whose claim to political power would rest on allegedly superior scientific know-how. Unhindered by the restraints of liberal values this elite would not hesitate to achieve its political ends by using the latest modern techniques for influencing public behavior and keeping society under close surveillance and control".

Brzezinski is a member of Council on Foreign Relations. This organization was formed to produce and disseminate ideas on foreign policy to policy-makers, students, journalists and other interested individuals. He has admitted that think-tanks such as the Council on Foreign Relations and the Trilateral Commission influence policy to benefit think-tank members. Many persons at these think-tanks are members or CEOs of media companies that never report what happens during the meetings of these organizations.

In 1995 the think-tank International Crisis Group (ICG) was founded by Brzezinski and George Soros with a stated mission to prevent and resolve deadly conflict. A member of ICG, Robert Malley (the founder of J Street) met with members of Hamas and later condemned Egypt's President Mubarak for not recognizing the Muslim Brotherhood. Another member on the executive committee of ICG was Mohammed El Baradei. El Baradei was the Director of International Atomic Energy Agency (IAEA) which announced that Iran's nuclear ambitions were legal. He is also the person who urged the Muslim Brotherhood to demonstrate in Egypt after they originally stated they did not want to be involved. Now El Baradei claims the Muslim Brotherhood is a peaceful group even though they created terrorist groups such as Hamas and Al Qaeda. El Baradei withdrew from the Egyptian presidential race in January 2012 because he stated that fair elections are not possible while the country is under military control. Other members of ICG include Javier Solana (formerly on the United Stated Subversive list), Sandy Berger (got caught stealing White House papers hiding them in his clothes), and General Wesley Clark (who once got fired from NATO).

Brzezinski promotes the idea of a one world order and created the term "global political awakening" to describe the greatest challenge of globalizing the political economy. In 2005 he wrote that "sovereignty now verges on being a legal fiction" while criticizing the war on terror as a demonization of the Muslim people. He explains that the youth in countries across the globe are turning to political activism "in a quest for personal dignity, cultural respect and economic opportunity in a world painfully scarred by memories of centuries-long colonial or imperial domination". "The central challenge of our time is posed not by global terrorism, but rather by the intensifying turbulence caused by the phenomenon of global political awaking". He has written that developed nations should create a new world order based on global governance under the direction of transnational elites. He presented this plan at a Bilderberg meeting in 1972 a year prior to creating the Trilateral Commission.

Brzezinski was President Carter's National Security Advisor. Carter advocated for global "human rights". At that time Indonesia received funds for military arms after they invaded and occupied East Timor. It was also during this administration that Iran held 52 American hostages for 444 days after Islamic militants and students supporting the Iranian Revolution invaded and took over the U.S. Embassy.

As a member of Council of Foreign Relations he created a task force with Robert Gates to develop a foreign policy with Iran. They concluded that Iran could play a "role in promoting a stable, pluralistic government in Bagdad (Iraq)". The task force was unable to determine if Iran was fully committed to developing nuclear arms, but concluded it was in the United States interest to engage with Iran diplomatically.

Many people call Brzezinski anti-Jewish. The fact that he reportedly told Obama in 2009 that the United States should tell Israel not to attack Iran does not dispel that idea. He added that if Israel were to fly airplanes over Iraqi airspace the United States should shoot their jets out of the sky.

MARK BRZEZINSKI, the son of Zbigniew Brzezinski, was an advisor during the campaign. He is an attorney specializing in international financial institutions. These institutions include the U.S. Export-Import Bank, the Overseas Private Investment Corporation, the World Bank, the International Finance Corporation, and the International Monetary Fund. Under the Clinton administration he was a director of Southeast European affairs and the Russian/Eurasian affairs at the National Security Council. During the campaign he praised Obama "because he takes a global approach to US challenges rather than a more conventional approach". He endorsed Obama's idea of "common security for our common humanity" in the areas of terrorism, climate change, and weapons of mass destruction. In November 2010 Obama appointed Mark Brzezinski to the J. William Fulbright Foreign Scholarship Board.

While Zbigniew and Mark Brzezinski were advising Obama during the 2008 Presidential campaign, Ian Brzezinski was advising the Republican nominee John McCain. Ian Brzezinski is Mark's brother. Ian is the head of a consulting firm called the Brzezinski Group that provides strategic advice and insight to both commercial and government clients. Ian is a registered lobbyist for the Brzezinski Group.

GREGORY CRAIG advised Obama during the campaign on national security and after the election became the White House attorney. He is famous for his defense in high profile cases. He defended John Hinckley Jr. in the assignation attempt of President Reagan, defended William Kennedy Smith on an assault charge, and represented the father of Elian Gonzales who was the 6 year boy in a custody battle between the father in Cuba and relatives in Florida. Craig was also the attorney that defended President Clinton during the impeachment trial.

It was Craig who was assigned the function of changing the previous administration's policies of interrogation and detention. It was Craig that drafted Executive Orders to end "enhanced interrogations, to suspend indefinite detention of detainees, eliminate military trials of detainees, and to set a one year deadline to close Guantanamo Bay prison. It was Craig that wanted to release pictures of terrorist detainees being abused. It was Craig that wanted Guantanamo prisoners brought to the United States for trial. It was Craig that wanted to release some detainees into the Virginia. Craig announced his resignation in November 2009. He was hired by Goldman Sachs in April 2010.

ANTHONY 'TONY' LAKE was a leading foreign policy advisor during the campaign and was considered for the positions of CIA Director and Secretary of State. Lake has worked with several presidents since 1969.

Lake started his career in 1962 when he joined the Foreign Service and became an assistant to Ambassador Henry Cabot Lodge from his assignment in Viet Nam. Then he became a special assistant for Nation Security Affairs with President Nixon but resigned in 1970 in protest to a Nixon foreign policy. The President had begun bombing raids in Cambodia to secure the Ho Chi Minh trail and to protect its government from being taken over by Pol Pot with his Khmer Rouge followers.

In 1975 the majority Democratic Congress, led by Senator Edward Kennedy, stopped funding to South Viet Nam and Cambodian governments and both countries surrendered to the Communists. Pol Pot set out to transform Cambodia in his image of an agrarian utopia. The transformation began with the destruction of memories of Cambodia pre-Pol Pot. All documents, books, and photographs were burned, all education (other than re-education) ceased, and religion was banned. People living in the cities were relocated (many with 24 hour notice) by foot to distant rural areas, separating families throughout the country. It was illegal to contact family members or even to show emotion. Persons caught engaging in illegal activities; that included sexual relations, crying, or even the suspicion of disagreement with Khmer Rouge rules were punished. Punishment usually involved torture before being killed; the most common practice of killing was repeated blows to the head. The population was turned into slaves growing food when many starved while working long hours with primate tools in concentration camps. The indigenous Cams were slaughtered. All persons from the former government were killed as well as any person that had an education. More than 1,000 mass graves have been discovered and an estimated 1 to 3 million people were killed under Pol Pot's regime.

In 1972 he joined George McGovern's campaign for president with a platform supporting the idea that the conflicts in Southeast Asia were the result of the "arrogance of American power". When Carter was elected in 1977, Lake was appointed as the State Department's Policy Planning Director. Lake supported foreign policy of majority rule, human rights and economic development. These policies led to the fall of the Shah of Iran to Khomeini, Ortega overthrowing the Nicaraguan government, and Mugabe becoming the leader of Rhodesia. When Bill Clinton was elected Lake was given the position as National Security Advisor. Lake was instrumental in the decision to allow Iran to arm the Islamic militants in Bosnia without notifying Congress, the Department of State, the Department of Defense, or the CIA putting American troops in danger. In 1995 Lake met with Abdulrahman Alamoudi, the director of both the American Muslim Council (AMC) and the Council on American Islamic Relations (CAIR), President Clinton and Vice President Gore. At that time Alamoudi was raising funds for Hamas and Hezbollah. Alamoudi is now in prison serving a 23 year sentence for those activities after his 2004 arrest. Clinton nominated Lake to head the CIA in 1996, but Lake withdrew when Republicans complained. He became the executive director of the United Nations Children's Fund (UNICEF) in May after Obama nominated him for that position.

JAMES JONES the retired four star General, former Marine commander, and a former NATO Supreme Allied Commander was appointed to the position of National Security Advisor in February 2009. From 2007 until his appointment he was the chairman of Atlantic Council. Members of the Atlantic Council include Henry Kissinger, Madeleine Albright, and Ian Brzezinski. Richard Holbrook and Susan Rice were also members who left in January when they secured positions at the White House. From several accounts Jones had a difficult time adjusting in his position as he didn't believe in working 16+ hours per day and expected to be in communication with the President on decisions. He was not part of the younger group of people that worked together to get Obama elected. At the February 2009 Munich Security Conference Jones stated, "As the most recent National Security Advisor of the United States, I take my daily orders from Dr Kissinger, filtered down through General Brent Scowcroft, who is also here. We have a chain of command in the National Security Council that exists today". James Jones resigned in October 2010.

TOM DONILON was on Obama's transition team and Deputy to NSA James Jones before replacing Jones as the National Security Advisor. Donilon has no military experience and was once a lobbyist at the law firm O'Melveny and Meyers. His only client was Fannie Mae. Then in 1999 he obtained the position of Executive Vice President for Law and Policy at Fannie Mae while continuing to be registered as a lobbyist. He left in 2005 just as Fannie Mae was about to be investigated and later fined for misstating their earnings between the years of 1998 to 2004. Donilon did not need a waiver to work at the White House as he last registered as a lobbyist in 2005.

Donilon's faced huge challenges in what has been termed 'Arab Spring' as countries in Asia and Africa had demonstrations and rebellions attempting to overthrow existing governments and create democratic societies. Arab Spring also brought an end to Osama bin Laden as he was killed in a raid in Pakistan in May. On May 15th he spoke at the Washington Institute for Near East Policy describing how the raid took place and assuring Israel that the United States was committed to their security. He spoke how the enemies of Israel were the enemies of the United States. On May 12th he met with Dr. Mahmoud Jibril the Transitional National Council's Executive Bureau of Libya. The White House announced that this was Jibril's first 'official' visit. Jibril came to request funds and supplies for the revolutionaries fighting for freedom and democracy.

Dr. Mahmoud Jibril spells his name numerous ways. He is also referred to as Mr. Jibril, Mr. Mahmoud Jibril El Warfally, Mahmoud Jebril, Mahmoud Gebril, Mahmoud Gibril, Mahmoud Jabril, and Mr. El Warfally. On the Founding Statement of the Interim Transitional National Council dated March 5, 2011 he is referred to as Dr. Mohamed Jebril Ibrahim El-Werfali and Dr. Mohamed Jebril.

Jibril received a degree in Economic and Political Science in Cairo University in 1975. In 1980 he received a master degree in political science and then in 1985 he earned a PhD in strategic planning from the University of Pittsburgh. While working on his doctorate he was employed as a professor at the university. He studied with professor Richard Cottam who was a CIA agent that specialized in studies of the Middle East, particularly Iran. The United Arab Training manual was drafted by a group that he led and later he managed leader training programs in Egypt, Saudi Arabia, Libya, UAE, Kuwait, Jordan, Bahrain, Morocco, Tunisia, Turkey and Britain. In 2007 he joined Khadafi and was the head of the National Economic Development Board to develop programs that promoted privation and other liberalized policies such as local business getting exemption from duties and taxes.

Somehow Jibril had the funds to travel the globe doing PR and raising funds for his group. He was in France in March when Libya country decided to recognize his group as the legitimate representative of that country. On May 5th he was in Rome attending a International Contact Group meeting with officials from many countries, including Secretary of State Hillary Clinton. The Contact Group agreed to pledge $250 million to his cause. He had previously met with the Contact Groups in Doha and London. Jibril asked that Khadafi funds (which have been frozen) to be given to him, he wanted oil revenues from their oil fields, he wanted heavy artillery, and wanted Khadafi's television to be jammed. It was Jibril that asked for no fly zones over Libya. Jibril explained, "What's taking place is a natural result of globalization that began in the 80's, a new cultural paradigm".

The Muslim Brotherhood had secret chapters in most towns in Libya. In March the spiritual leader of the Brotherhood told Arab leaders to recognize the National Libyan Council and to support the rebels with weapons. The leader of this group's fighting rebels is Khalifa Hifter who was once a leader in Khadafi's army until the two had a falling out. Hifter moved to Virginia about five miles from CIA headquarters about 20 years ago and has been supporting a large family with no known income. He was in Libya at the start of the rebellion. Wikileaks has provided information that the CIA has been planning the spontaneous revolt for years. Khadafi said the revolt was the result of al-Qaeda networks from al-Qaeda prisoners released from Gitmo prison and the West wanted Libyan oil.

Donilon's next challenge will come from Israel. On May 19, 2011 Obama gave a speech and in a strong tone stated that Israel was a friend of the United States, deserved their own land, and their own security. Then he said that Israel must give up land back to pre-1967 borders. This would put many religious sites, Jewish and Christian, in jeopardy as they would be under Muslim control. He decided that Israel must cede their land without even consulting the Prime Minister of Israel. He was demanding that Israel give away part of their land which would severely reduce their security. This must be how he celebrates Arab Spring.

Donilon's brother Mike is a counselor to Vice President Joe Biden. Catherine Russell, Donilon's wife, is Chief of Staff to Jill Biden.

DENIS MCDONOUGH replaced Donilon as the Deputy National Security Advisor and is a member of the Center for American Progress (CAP). He is a close friend and confident of Obama, even plays basketball with him. McDonough makes it his job to protect Obama's public image. He has been known to chastise those who have strayed from message or have not portrayed Obama in the most positive way. This includes the media, journalists, and officials. In April 2011 a reporter from the San Francisco Chronicle used her cell phone to record a group protesting Obama by peacefully singing “”We paid our dues…where’s our change”. The newspaper reported the White House threatened to ban that reporter from being a member of press print pool in the future. Not only that, threatened to retaliate against Chronicle and Hearst reporters if the banning of the reporter was disclosed. About a month earlier, an Orlando Sentinel reporter was given the assignment of White House pool reporter for a fund raiser that was to be attended by Joe Biden. He arrived before Biden but after guests had arrived. He was escorted to a closet that was guarded by a staffer until he was allowed out. The Sentinel did not report this incident until after it had been written about on the internet. On May 18, 2011 the Boston Herald was refused full access to an Obama 2012 fund raiser. The reason was the paper had previously put an op-ed with pictures of Mitt Romney on their front page instead of a story about Obama. A spokespersons for the White House responded, “My point about the op-ed was not that you ran it but that it was the full front page, which excluded any coverage of the visit of a sitting U.S. President to Boston. I think that raises a fair question about whether the paper is unbiased in its coverage of the President’s visits”.

In June 2009 Obama went to Cairo Egypt and gave a speech at a university calling for a partnership between the United States and Islam. After the speech McDonough was asked whether members of the Muslim Brotherhood had been invited to attend. His response was, “I can tell you that invitations have gone out to the full range of actors in Egyptian political society”. In March 2011 McDonough spoke at the All Dulles Area Muslim Society mosque in Virginia to reassure Muslims that America values include recognizing religious freedom and tolerance. He said, “Over the past two years, I-along with my White House colleagues-have benefited from the advice of many of your organizations through our Office of Public Engagement”. Mohamed Magid is the mosque’s Imam and the president of the Islamic Society of North America (ISNA). The INSA was listed as an ‘unindicted co-conspirator” in the Holy Land Foundation trial. They were found guilty acting as a charity that gave funding to the Muslim Brotherhood which financed Hamas. Documents at the trial proved the Muslim Brotherhood founded ISNA. CBS news reported that this mosque has a “longtime relationship and cooperation with the FBI.

SUSAN RICE was a foreign policy advisor during the campaign and later appointed as the Ambassador to the United Nations, a member of the cabinet, and part of the National Security Council. Her father was a professor of economics at Cornell University and governor of the Federal Reserve System. Her mother is an educational policy scholar and a member of the Brookings Institute. Rice attended New College, Oxford on a Rhodes scholarship where one of her professors, Sir Adam Roberts, was an expert on international humanitarian intervention. Sir Roberts advocated for global economic governance by the United Nations and for international law.

Rice has been described as hawkish on her views of using military intervention for humanitarian needs. Rice, Power, and Clinton advised using the military in Libya against the advice of Gates, Donilon, and McDonough. It is reported that she travels to New York each week and she stays in a penthouse at the Waldorf Astoria. At the United Nations, however, she has been largely absent stating she would rather socialize and negotiate privately. Rice missed the debate and vote to send Peacekeepers to Haiti, she missed the Security Council meeting regarding Israel and the ship to Gaza, missed the meeting when Iran was voted to the UN Women's Commission, and did not object to Libya being elected to the UN Human Rights Council. She did not attend the UN Security Council meeting when Libya's deputy ambassador asked for help because he could no longer work alongside Khadafi. Rice did not attend that meeting as she was in South Africa attending a discussion on global sustainability. She did return in time to vote to sanction Libya and to refer Khadafi to the International Criminal Court. When the vote came for a no fly zone in Libya, diplomats reported that the "Americans weren't involved".

Rice gave an interview with NPR Radio on May 19, 2011 the day after Obama gave a speech on the Middle East, and announced that he supported a two state solution for Israel and Palestine, with Israel losing territory. Asked about the administration's policy for peace and democracy in North Africa and the Middle East she responded, "We have a profound interest in supporting the democratic transformations that are underway in many states, which are just beginning in others. And we will support these democratic transformations with the full weight of our diplomacy, our political tools, our economic tools, our security tools as a top priority for U.S. foreign policy".

As I stated in the beginning of the chapter Obama had over 300 advisors on foreign policy. The people I profiled are just a small sample of the people who gave advice. Some were selected randomly from names I had not heard of before. All are interesting.

Judge me by the people who surround me.

CHAPTER 25

★ ★ ★ ★ ★

Security Matters

Now we know who offers advice on security matters. Next I researched those persons that implement the policies.

HILLARY CLINTON was appointed Secretary of State in the new administration after narrowly losing the election for President. She has been active in legal and political activities for her entire adult life.

She attended Wellesley College attaining a Bachelors Degree, with honors, in Political Science. Her final thesis was about Saul Alinsky, who she met and interviewed during her research. Alinsky was impressed with Hillary and offered her a job as a political activist and community organizer in Chicago. Hillary declined, deciding to work from within rather than working on the streets. The thesis was withheld from the public during her husband's Presidency by request of the Clintons.

From Wellesley she went to Yale Law School where she joined the Yale Review of Law and Social Action which is run by students and published quarterly. At Yale Hillary met Marian Wright Edelman, the founder of the Children's Defense Fund, and they became very good friends. Edelman is a well known advocate for children's causes. She supports Head Start, socialized medical care, and welfare programs. She also supports the idea of children's rights, including the right to sue their parents. Hillary wrote an article for the Yale Review titled, "Children under the Law". The article stated that the idea that families should be "private, nonpolitical units" was an antiquated notion. Marriage was compared to other dependency situations such as slavery or Indian reservations. Her solution was to "remodel" what a family was and allow children the right to sue their parents. Hillary interned at the Children's Defense Fund in 1970 and years later Edelman's husband, Peter, worked in the Clinton administration in Health and Human Services.

The highly profiled case of Black Panther's Bobby Seale was being prosecuted at that time. The Black Panthers were a radical, violent, revolutionist group which was part of the Black Power movement and were targeting police for brutality. They could also get violent with their own members. Bobby Seale was charged with torturing and killing a member of the Panthers suspected of being a police informant. Some Yale students joined violent demonstrations supporting the Panthers believing Seale would not get a fair trial. There is no evidence that Hillary was part on any of these demonstrations.

Hillary did closely monitor the trial for her civil rights professor, Thomas Emerson. Emerson was known for his ties to the Communist Party. It was in his class that Hillary first met Bill Clinton. While monitoring the trial, Hillary got to know the attorney for the defense from the law firm of Treuhaft, Walker, and Burnstein in California. The firm was well known for advocating for civil rights, defending draft dodgers, and other radical causes, plus its communist connections. Treuhaft had been called to testify before the House Un-American Activities Committee that labeled him one of the most "dangerously subversive" attorneys. Hillary was promoted to associate editor of the Yale Review. A special commemorative edition was produced about the Black Panthers that included cartoons of police depicted as pigs.

She moved to California during the summer of 1971 to intern with Treuhaft, Walker, and Burnstein. Bill Clinton went with her. The firm at that time was defending another Black Panther named Huey Newton. He was accused of killing a policeman in Oakland. Hillary says she remembers working on a child custody case during this internship.

After graduation Hillary failed to pass the bar examination in Washington D.C., but was able to pass the bar in Arkansas. Hillary moved to Arkansas with Bill. In 1975 they got married, but Hillary kept her maiden name. The year of 1976 was busy for both Bill and Hillary, as Bill was elected as Attorney General and Hillary campaigned for Jimmy Carter. Carter selected Hillary in 1977 to the board of Legal Services Corporation that provides legal counsel to the poor. She chaired the board in 1978 and was able to triple its budget in three years up to $321 million in 1980. In 1977 she also joined the Rose Law Firm. Her political connections, and connections to members of boards she sat on, were able to bring new clients to the firm.

Bill Clinton was elected governor in 1978 and the Rose Law Firm made Hillary a partner. One of Bill's first appointment was James McDougal as his economist. Hillary, on the advice of investment trader and legal counsel to Tyson Foods James Blair, invested in 10 shares of cattle futures. The cost of this investment is normally $12,000, but Hillary only had $1,000 in her account. The next day her investment made $6,300, 10 months later she made $100,000 and stopped trading. There is speculation that larger trades were made by another person and later shifted into her account. Meanwhile the Clintons became friends with James McDougal and his wife Susan. The two couples borrowed $203,000 to purchase 220 acres in the Ozark Mountains with the plan to build vacation homes; forming the Whitewater Development Corporation. The repercussions from this partnership lasted throughout the Clinton Presidential administration.

McDougal quit working for the government in 1980 when he purchased a bank and loaned Hillary $30,000 to build a model home for Whitewater. Two years later McDougal bought a savings and loan firm named Madison Guaranty. In 1984 the Federal Home Loan Bank Board issued a report that Madison had questionable lending practices and was unstable. The following year McDougal held a fund raiser to pay off Clinton's campaign debt and it was later discovered that money had been withdrawn from depositor's accounts for this cause. McDougal hires Hillary at the Rose Law Firm to represent him with his legal work and she got a $2,000 per month retainer. Susan McDougal at a later date testifies that all Whitewater records were given to Hillary Clinton in 1986 at the Governor's Mansion.

Meanwhile, James McDougal devised a plan to purchase 1,000 acres for $1.75 million, with plans to develop it into half acres parcels for double wide trailers. He borrowed $600,000 from his own Madison Guaranty bank and enlisted a part-time employee to borrow the rest in a non-recourse loan from Madison. A non-recourse loan means he has no obligation to pay it back. To hide these transactions he concocted several loans and transactions with other persons to confuse the bank regulators of the illegal activity. However, the regulators unraveled the mess and removed McDougal as president of Madison charging him concealing information, but he retained ownership. Hillary had been subpoenaed to provide her billing records for the investigation, but they got lost. (They were found in January 1996 at the White House.) In 1988 Hillary asks for power of attorney to sell remaining Whitewater lots to clear up bank obligations and requested the Rose Law Firm destroy all land contract files in connection with Madison. Madison was shut down in 1989, the federal government spent $60 million bailing it out, and McDougal was indicted for bank fraud. He was acquitted in 1990.

In 1992 Bill Clinton was running for President and the Federal Resolution Trust Corp was investigating the reason Madison failed. The referral to the Justice Department states the Clintons may have benefited from the illegal activity of check kiting at the bank. Check kiting is writing checks with no money in the account. The Clinton campaign issued a statement that they lost money in the Whitewater deal and the media didn't seem to investigate. Bill Clinton is elected President. Vincent Foster, from the Rose Law Firm, meets with McDougal on November 3rd and makes a deal for McDougal to purchase the rest of the Clinton's Whitewater shares for $1,000. McDougal borrows the $1,000 from James Blair and the loan is never repaid.

The story does not end here. In June Vincent Foster, as White House Deputy Counsel, filed Whitewater corporation tax returns which were three years delinquent. Foster confided to friends that he wanted to resign, wrote notes as an outline for a resignation letter, and set up an appointment with Clinton for July 21st. He was at work at the White House on the 20th when he walked out of his office, told his secretary he would be right back, and offered the other White House secretary Linda Tripp some candy. There are no videos of him leaving the White House or log books recording his exit. Several hours later he was found dead in a park near Washington D.C. His death was officially ruled as a suicide by shooting himself in the mouth.

Now the controversy over his death. The first witness claims there was no gun, but subsequent pictures show a gun in his hand that has no blood on either his hand or the gun. A gun shoot wound is later found in his neck. There is no gun powder on his hand, but there are burns on both arms indicating he was reaching towards a gun a close range when shot. The gun did not have Foster's fingerprints on it. The original photographs of the crime scene were lost or over exposed. The autopsy was performed earlier than originally planned and therefore police investigators were not present. The x-rays of the autopsy were lost. The keys to Foster's car that were not in his pockets before entering the morgue were found in his pocket at the morgue. The memory of his beeper had been deleted. No suicide note was found in his briefcase on the day of his death. A suicide note was found torn up, without his fingerprints, three days later in his brief case. White House aides began removing files and other material from Foster's office before the police started their investigation. There are other discrepancies with the gun, the bullets, exit wounds, blood on the body, no grass on his shoes, the position of the body, etc. The official record remains that Foster died as the result of a suicide. The Director of the FBI, William Sessions, had been fired the day before Foster died which led to a delay in the investigation.

In January 1994 Attorney General Jane Reno appoints Robert Fiske to investigate the Clintons involvement with Whitewater. Fiske says he will investigate whether Foster's suicide had any connection to the Whitewater affair. In March Webster Hubbell, the Associate Attorney General, was being investigated for bilking funds from the Rose Law Firm and was being pressured to cooperate with the Whitewater investigation. Hubbell resigned from the White House a few days later. He is eventually convicted of fraud and went to jail for 18 months. Further reports during the year indicate the Whitewater account at Madison received funds from other accounts, but the Clintons "had little direct involvement". There were 29 officials of the Clinton administration subpoenaed to testify at a congressional hearing about Whitewater. In August, Governor Jim Guy Tucker and the McDougals were indicted for bank fraud and conspiracy. During this same month, the U.S. Court of Appeals denied re-appointment of Fiske as Special Counsel citing the potential conflict of interest as he was assigned the job by Clinton's Attorney General.

In 1995 the Senate Banking Committee, which was dominated by Democrats, reported there were no laws broken with the Whitewater deals. Seven months later the Senate Special Whitewater Committee began hearings on both Whitewater and Foster's death. In August, James and Susan McDougal faced a grand jury on charges of bank fraud. The Senate Whitewater committee issues 49 subpoenas in October to federal agencies regarding involvement with the situation. In December former Rose Law Firm attorney and then current White House associate counsel, William H. Kennedy III, refused to release notes of a 1993 meeting between the President's attorneys and other officials regarding Whitewater.

In January 1996 Hillary's lost billing records from the Rose Law Firm, documenting her work for Madison, were found on a table in the White House residence. Hillary denies hiding the records, but was subpoenaed to testify before the Whitewater grand jury. In February Bill Clinton is told by a Federal District Judge that he must be a defense witness in the bank fraud case against the McDougals and Jim Guy Tucker. During the trial David Hale, the owner of a lending company, testified that Bill Clinton pressured him to make a loan to Susan McDougal in the amount of $300,000 in 1985. Jim Guy Tucker sentence of 4 years in prison was changed to home arrest and a fine of $319,000 because he was on a list for a liver transplant. Susan McDougal was imprisoned to 2 years for obtaining an illegal loan. She received further jail time for contempt because she refused to testify before a grand jury. The FDIC determined drafted real estate documents for Madison were used to "deceive" federal regulators in 1986. Bill Clinton is reelected at President in November. In December Susan McDougal goes to trial on charges of embezzlement of $150,000 and remains in jail.

Jim McDougal, in 1997, is given a reduced prison sentence of 3 years for bank fraud because he cooperated with the investigation of Madison. The investigation continued because Ken Starr, the special investigator, said he had "extensive evidence" of a possible obstruction of justice. The U.S, Circuit Court of Appeals determined that the White House must turn over subpoenaed notes taken at meetings with Hillary Clinton. The Supreme Court declines to take the case so the notes are given to Starr. James McDougal dies in jail of a heart attack, in March 1998, just a few months before he was to be released. Hillary is questioned, while being videotaped for 5 hours by Starr and his deputies. In June Susan McDougal was released from jail because of medical problems, but is still faced charges of embezzlement. In November she was acquitted of charges of fraud and embezzlement. Her legal troubles were not over because in March 1999 she went on trial for contempt and obstruction of justice and she continued to refuse to answer questions about Bill Clinton's involvement in illegal Whitewater transactions. At the trial testimony was presented that Hillary Clinton was going to be indicted in the case, but the draft for the indictment was never given to the grand jury. Susan's trial ends with a hung jury for contempt and an acquittal on the charge of obstruction. Finally in September 2000, the Independent Counsel reported there was "insufficient evidence" to bring criminal charges against the Clintons with the Whitewater deals. The investigation of Whitewater officially closes in January 2001 when Clinton leaves office.

The Independent Counsel was also investing Hillary Clinton's involvement in what has become known as Travelgate. Travelgate began in May 1993 when all seven members of the White House Travel Office where fired with the intention of being replaced with friends of the Clintons. Testimony showed that Hillary took interest in the Travel Office because she heard there was some financial mismanagement. Chief of Staff Mack McLarty testified that Hillary wanted the staff fired. This did not need to happen because the staff serves at the will of the President and could be given administrative leave at any time. The FBI was called to investigate allegations the Travel Director, Billy Dale, didn't use competitive billing, misused funds, and other charges. The staff was replaced by a travel firm that was based in Little Rock, Arkansas and the owners were friends of the Clintons. At the same time another friend wanted to start an air charter company out of the White House, he knew the Clintons because he arranged all the travel during the campaign. News of the firings made news and the media attention prompted the employees to be reinstated to other positions at the White House and the intended replacements where changed. Hillary denied having a role in the firings of the employees. The Independent Counsel found Hillary made "factually false statements", but failed to prosecute her because the evidence was inconclusive as whether Hillary 'knowingly' made the false statements.

The next scandal involving Hillary the Independence Council investigated was called Filegate. Filegate involved five main characters; First Lady Hillary Clinton, White House Counsel Bernard Nussbaum, Associate White House Counsel William Kennedy III, director of the White House Office of Personnel Security (OPS) Craig Livingstone, and his assistant Anthony Marceca. The OPS is responsible for keeping track of those employed at the White House, keeping their security clearances up to date and to give security briefings to new hires. The scandal was the 989 FBI security files of former Republican President Bush's administration had been requested and received. These actions were investigated by the FBI, the Government Reform and Oversight Committee, the Senate Judiciary Committee, and the Whitewater Independent Counsel with both Ken Starr and later by Robert Ray. Judicial Watch filed a class action law suit represented all persons who had their files illegally retrieved and reviewed by White House employees.

Craig Livingstone had been active in Clinton and other Democratic political campaigns. Nussbaum initially told the FBI that Hillary highly recommended hiring Livingstone for that position because she knew Livingstone's mother. Hillary, under sworn testimony, denied knowing or recommending Livingstone. Then Nussbaum told the Oversight Committee the FBI misquoted him as Hillary never recommended Livingstone's employment. Livingstone claimed Hillary hired him. A former Clinton staffer, in a sworn affidavit, said Hillary was responsible for hiring political staff and everyone knew Livingstone really worked for Hillary. Livingstone had one of the highest security clearances at the White House. Since no one took responsibility for his hiring the final report decided that the deceased Vincent Foster hired him. William Kennedy III hired Marceca. Marceca came from the Pentagon where he worked in the prevention fraud unit and was highly recommended from his former employer.

Filegate was discovered in 1996 because the Oversight Committee learned during the investigation of Travelgate that the White House had requested the FBI file of Billy Dale. The next day the committee received all the other

FBI files the White House had requested in 1993 and 1994. This started the investigation of Filegate.

Livingstone announced his resignation on his first day of testimony at the Oversight Committee. Marceca claimed receiving all the files was a bureaucratic snafu with no illegal motivation. He claimed the OPS staff was trying to rebuild records of permanent employees who remained working at the White House after Bush left office. Marceca stated the FBI sent him an out dated list with many names of people no longer employed including those who previously worked in high security positions, and members of the former National Security Council. The investigations concluded in March 2000, by Robert Ray, after the Clintons left the White House. He decided that there was no credible evidence of any criminal activity by any person in this matter.

Judicial Watch claims that the matter was not investigated sufficiently. They claim Attorney General Reno asked the Independent Council to wrap up the investigation in exchange of an agreement not to seek ethics charges against the Council. During the investigation sworn testimony was taken by witnesses that had not been subpoenaed, were not asked questions about Filegate, or information may have been just ignored.

Linda Tripp was a White House secretary that worked for the Bush administration and retained for the Clinton administration due to a request from Nussbaum. Nussbaum said he needed her as his executive assistant as she was a "substantive, savvy and experienced professional". Her desk was down the hall from the Oval Office. In sworn testimony for Judicial Watch she stated she saw "oodles" of FBI files in Nussbaum's office, saw documents with the Department of Justice seal, and saw Reno and Webster Hubbell often visiting his office. She also saw FBI files in Vincent Foster's safe, plus testified she saw the missing Rose Law Firm billing records in that safe. She did not know what they were at the time, but was able to identify them as the same records that were discovered in the White House residence by a presidential assistant. Tripp saw files, which were not personnel files, with the name of Clinger (in charge of the Oversight Committee), Dale, and others. She stated she voiced concern about these files to White House Counsel Bruce Lindsey and his response was, "That kind of talk could get you destroyed".

Tripp witnessed documents and boxes of files being removed from Vincent Foster's office immediately after his death. She also testified that Livingstone told her Mrs. Clinton hired him. The most damning testimony was that data from the FBI files was being uploaded into a White House computer. She was told data could be shared with the Democratic National Committee at the request of Hillary Clinton. Tripp's testimony stated a list of people connected to the Clinton administration who had died was left on her chair. She produced the document which included a note that appeared to be in Monica Lewinsky's handwriting. It said, "Linda, just thought you might find this of interest". A second, and longer, list in different handwriting, listed suddenly deceased people that were considered "troublemakers" to the Clintons. The lists showed up just before she was to testify what she witnessed regarding the appearance of Kathleen Willey after she left Clinton's office. Willey had alleged that Clinton groped her in his office. It appears the White House had grown concerned about Tripp's observations of the events that were happening near the Oval Office as she was transferred against her will to a public affairs basement office at the Pentagon in August 1994. Her boss, Kenneth Bacon, leaked information about Linda Tripp to a reporter which had been taken from her FBI file. The information stated that as a teenager she had been arrested for stealing; she was never convicted as the stolen items were put in her purse by the real thief. On her application for employment she said she had never been arrested. Days later 'New Yorker' magazine reported that Tripp lied on her employment application. Bacon apologized for not consulting the rules of the Privacy Act or consulting with attorneys before he "authorized the disclosure".

Another witness was Deborah Perroy, a National Security Council financial officer, who testified she saw two members of the Clinton administration (Manzanares and his secretary Dimel) examining FBI/CIA files in 1993 in a room on the third floor of the Old Executive Office Building. The files, which are usually kept in the safe at the CIA's liaison office, were being examined after normal office hours, and she stated they were making what looked like a list. She continued that when she walked into the room their reaction appeared that they did not expect to see her or that they were doing something they didn't want to be caught doing. She said Livingstone was hired by Hillary Rodham Clinton and Livingstone had "several meetings with Manzanares. Her statement was, "It was widely known at the Clinton White House that Hillary Clinton 'was running things' and was responsible for the hiring of political staff such as Livingston. Livingstone was really working for Mrs. Clinton as far as everyone knew and everyone dropped everything to accommodate Mr. Livingston's requests". Perroy resigned from her position soon after this incident. She was asked to return to her position, but refused. Then she was threatened that the administration would come after her "with false charges and allegations in order to smear my good name". She told them if the administration did that she would sue them and make public the information which she believed was "improper activities I witnessed". It was later learned that that Perroy's FBI file was requested on October 7, 1993 and then again on March 17, 1994. The second request was six months after she resigned and after she threatened to sue.

White House Counsel William Kennedy III gave a deposition for Judicial Watch. He admitted that there were stacks of the FBI files in his office, some on his desk and others on office tables. Upon questioning he admitted it was illegal for officials to disclose information kept in government files. When asked if he had reviewed the Republican FBI files he choked but refused to give a 'yes' or 'no' answer only stating he didn't believe he did. He also refused to answer any questions about conversations he had with Linda Tripp. Kennedy resigned in November 1994.

A report from a subcommittee of the Government Reform and Oversight Committee was written by Rep. David McIntosh. The report stated the $1.7 million centralized computer system at the White House was "used to advance the campaign fundraising objectives of the Democratic National Committee (DNC)." The conversion of government property for the use of the DNC constitutes a theft of the government property under 18 U.S.C.V. (sec) 641" and is a violation of the Hatch Act "which restricts government employee use of government property for political activities." The 54 page report stated, "The committee believes that the President's involvement in the conversion of the White House into a fundraising tool represents an abuse of power".

After the Independent Council ended the investigations Robert Ray was interviewed on the ABC show "This Week" by Sam Donaldson and George Will. Ray refused to answer the question as whether he interviewed Linda Tripp about her allegations that FBI records were uploaded onto the White House computers. Ray did admit that he did not speak with two whistle-blowers who testified at Judicial Watch that up to one million e-mails where suppressed and 457 disc drives had been hidden which contained information on Filegate and the other investigations. These witnesses testified that they were threatened by White House officials that anybody who talked about the e-mails or disc drives would end up in jail. Ray even admitted that the Republican FBI files were still at the White House.

On February 28, 1993, two days after the truck bomb detonated under the

North Tower of the World Trade Center, the Bureau of Alcohol, Tobacco and Firearms (BATF) raided the Branch Davidians in Waco Texas. The Davidians were a religious sect, led by David Koresh, which was suspected of practicing polygamy and child abuse. The BATF has no jurisdiction in cases involving polygamy or child abuse. The group supported themselves selling guns at gun shows. The BATF investigated them in 1992 when the local gun dealer telephoned Koresh on behalf of the BATF to ask questions. The agent refused to talk to Koresh directly. Koresh invited the BATF to their property, called Mt. Carmel or Mt. Carmel Church, to see their inventory and check their paperwork. The Davidians were known to carefully complete all legally required forms.

Instead the BATF showed up six months later with a search warrant and raided the building. The convoy that assembled at Fort Hood that morning had 80 vehicles, cattle cars and private pickup trucks hiding hundreds of agents, and three helicopters. The raid wasn't a complete secret though because the press knew about it and was there to document it. Koresh answered the door and gun fire started. Three minutes after the assault a member of the Davidians called 911 asking for help as they were being shot at. Four BATF agents died in the initial assault, and all four had been former bodyguards of Bill Clinton. Video of the raid show these agents were not shot by the Davidians, but by other agents shooting into the building from the roof.

At some point FBI agents joined raid on Mt. Carmel. The raid lasted for 50 days and ended with the building they resided in being burnt to the ground killing at least 76 men, women, and children. The fire started after a tank broke through the walls and the flammable CS gas that had been projected into the wooden structure ignited, the fire engulfed the building, and all persons inside died. The military and the national guard provided training, 9 or 10 Bradley tanks, 2 Abram tanks, 4 or 5 combat equipment vehicles, 3 helicopters, 1 surveillance aircraft (operated by Texas National Guard), advice and medical support. Some contend this operation was in violation of the Posse Comitatus Act which prohibits the military from participating in law enforcement.

It seems nobody wants to take credit for instigating the raid or ordering the final assault. Linda Tripp said that the entire assault was orchestrated from a crisis center set up by Hillary Clinton with Janet Reno, Wesley Clark and Vincent Foster. Tripp reported that Hillary called the final assault and had Foster make the call. Others have said Reno made the call. Dick Morris, a former Clinton advisor, claims Bill Clinton was in charge of the entire event and made the decisions. He further stated Reno told Bill Clinton that if he did not reappoint her as Attorney General she would report what really happened during the Waco massacre.

This whole episode reminds me of the words from the Charlie Rich song, "Nobody knows what goes on behind closed doors".

The Clinton administration must be relieved that the new UN policy of Failure to Protect was not in effect at that time. If it was; then foreign countries would have been able to decide that our government was firing upon its own citizens in violation of global policy. Those countries could then gather a group of other countries from NATO or the U.N. and demand the President resign while firing on and destroying our government buildings.

Hillary was named the director of a health care reform program which was proposed during the Presidential campaign. The media covered the reform bill which promised to provide universal health care through Health Medical Organizations (HMO), to be primarily paid for by employers, and would not cost the taxpayers much. The public was not convinced and the bill was never presented to the Congress for a vote. The Association of American Physicians and Surgeons sued the Clinton administration for crafting the health care bill in secret which is a violation of the "sunshine laws". The Clinton administration lost the case and the judge declared the Executive Branch of the government was dishonest with the court. She continued to advocate for passage of the State Children's Health Insurance Program (S-CHIP), the Adoptions and Safe Family Act, and the Foster Care Independence Act while he husband was in office. She is responsible for the creation of the Office on Violence Against Woman which currently has a $400 million budget and receives 19 federal grants.

As First Lady Hillary traveled to at least 82 countries, the most ever before her. Many of her trips were ceremonial and provided photo-opportunities for her and the people she met. The meetings she attended were primarily about women's rights, child care, health care and microcredit.

The Senator from New York announced in November 1998 he was retiring and would not run in the 2000 election. Hillary was encouraged to run for that position, but the problem was that she did not live in New York. The second problem was the Clintons were in debt. They owed $5 million in legal fees defending Bill with his Impeachment proceeding because he lied in court regarding his sexcapades in the White House, the Whitewater Scandal, and more. A house was found in Chappaqua selling for $1.7 million. Luckily for them their fundraiser put up $1,350,000.00 as security to the bank and the bank negotiated an adjusted rate mortgage for 5 years. This enabled them to only pay interest on the loan for the first 5 years. Hillary announced in February 2000 she would run for senator.

Congresswoman Nita Lowey had planned on running, but because Rudy Giuliani was the expected challenger the Democrats decided on Hillary. She also ran for Senator on the Working Families Party and the Liberal Party because New York is one of the few States that allow fusion; which totals all votes received by a candidate from all parties. The Working Families Party was formed by ACORN, unions, and other community organizations, plus has ties to George Soros.

In 2011 eight Democrats were charged with voter fraud in the 2009 Working Families Party primary for forging signatures on absent ballot applications. Four persons plead guilty to the charge and the trial of a former councilman and the Democratic County Elections Commissioner went to trail in January 2012 on the same charges. One of the persons that plead guilty stated that forging absentee ballots was a common practice.

She might have had another challenger but he died in an airplane in July 16, 1999. John F. Kennedy Jr. started a magazine called "George" with plans to use his magazine to uncover who really killed his father in 1963. He was also entertaining the idea of running for New York Senator in 2000 or possibly for President. The media reported that he had limited flying experience and the weather was poor at the time of the accident. However, Kennedy was a qualified pilot, the visibility was 8 miles and the winds calm. Forensic evidence led investigators to determine the airplane went down because of an explosion and broke up in mid-air. They determined that the explosion was caused by either a devise that was activated by the altitude, barometric pressure, or from a Particle Beam laser. There were 10 witnesses who saw the airplane explode. The National Traffic and Safety Board ruled the accident was caused by pilot error. Giuliani decided not to run for the office because of health issues and Hillary won the election against Republican Rick Lazio.

Upon winning the election she signed a book deal for $8 million dollars, signing the contract before she took office. Senator Clinton served on the following committees; Environment and Public Works, Health, Education, Labor, and Pensions, plus the Senate armed services. She sponsored 363 bills, but only 324 made it out of committee and 11 were enacted. One of her first issues was to abolish the electoral election process in favor of popular votes. Another issue she voted on consistently was against any tax cuts. During a speech before donors in 2004 she said, "Many of you are well enough off ...we're saying for America to get back on track...we're going to take things away from you on behalf of the common good". Senator Clinton favors persons that enter America illegally to be able to stay and enjoy the life of American citizens. She voted to extend time limits on illegal aliens, opposed a bill requiring applicants to provide legal identification (such as driver's licenses, State ID) to verify residency, and voted against a bill that would prevent convicted felons from obtaining citizenship. During Katrina she wrote to Homeland Security urging them not to deport illegal aliens found during the cleanup. Hillary originally voted to send troops to Iraq and later was against the war.

Hillary used her time as Senator to get involved with other activities. She stated she was one of the persons responsible in founding the Center for American Progress (CAP). She admitted she was involved in the establishment of Media Matters in 2007.

Media Matters is a tax exempt organization launched through CAP to monitor conservative media and promotes the "Fairness Doctrine". Media Matters not only monitors conservative media but targets them. They have a sub group called Drop Fox that actively targets not only the shows but the advertisers. Companies are threatened with boycotts if they continue to promote their products on the Fox News Channel. This group has targeted Orbitz, Netflix, Priceline, Best Western, Southwest Airlines, and Ocean Spray. They have targeted radio personalities Rush Limbaugh, Sean Hannity, Don Imus, Alex Jones, and Mike Savage. They wrote CNN complaining Lou Dobbs needed to go as he was undermining the station's creditability in 2009. George Soros in 2010 gave Media Matters $1 million to specifically target Fox News. Pat Buchanan believes Media Matters was the cause of him being let go from MSNBC. It has uncovered by the Daily Caller in February 2012 that Media Matters suggested they hire private investigators to look into the personal lives of Fox News employees searching for embarrassing information. The employees were not only the on-camera personalities but those behind the scenes as well. Media Matters is being investigated as whether they can keep their tax free status because of allegations of meeting regularly with the White House sharing information with the administration. The National Religious Broadcasters is also calling for Media Matters to lose their tax free status because the Daily Caller revealed the organization accepted funds to monitor and negatively report on religious broadcasting.

Another group Hillary was instrumental in founding with Soros is the Shadow Party. The Shadow Party started out as Shadow Conventions which were organized by Arianna Huffington of the Huffington Post. The conventions were held at the same city and the same time as both the Republican and the Democratic conventions in an attempt to draw media attention away from the major parties. The issues the Shadow Conventions endorsed were campaign reform, economic inequality, racism, and legalizing marijuana. After the conventions there was a session training attendees in community service. The Shadow Party began in 2004 with the express intent to defeat Bush's re-election.

The party is a network of grassroots organizations brought together under one umbrella. The McCain-Feingold Act changed how campaign funds are collected, dividing money into hard or soft money. This allows funds which normally went to the Democratic Party being sent to the Shadow party. Before McCain-Feingold the Democratic Party could divide funds between candidates, but now money such as union PAC funds have to designate a specific party and candidate. The Shadow Party now collects the money and divides it up according to their agenda. Eli Parsier (director from MoveOn.org) said, "Now it's our party. We bought it, we own it".

Hillary won reelection in 2006 despite her promise to increase employment in New York by 200,000 and the State lost 112,000 jobs. She even promised to raise taxes to restore government fiscal responsibility. In 2007 she campaigned to replace America's "ownership society" with a society based on communal responsibility and prosperity. She explained the American economy leaves it "up to the individual" which is causing the gap between the rich and the poor in our country. Hillary said, "I certainly think the free market has failed".

In January 2007, Hillary announced she was starting an exploratory committee to run for President stating she would not use public financing which would limit fund raising. By fall she was far ahead in all the polls, and she started her campaign with $14 million she had left over from her 2006 senate campaign. At the end of the year she accumulated $100 million, but somehow Obama had raised almost the identical amount. During the campaign she had some setbacks with campaign funds, having to return money that was raised illegally. Hillary returned $850,000 to Norman Hsu after it was discovered he was a fugitive for failure to return to court on a fraud conviction. Abdul Jinnah received $300,000 back for funds obtained illegally and other funds had to be returned to a front group of a terrorist organization called the Liberation Tigers of Tamil Eelam. Early in 2008 she was in debt and began borrowing from her and her husband's assets, but Obama continued to raise large sums of money. When she lost the election she was $22.5 million in debt, half of which was money she personally borrowed. The other problem she encountered was the media. She was not getting positive press as the media was praising Obama and reminding the public about her past. She complained, but it made no difference. After Hillary lost the election she endorsed Obama.

Obama appointed her to the position of Secretary of State. Hillary is the first former First Lady to become the Secretary of State or to hold a position in a President's Cabinet. Her primary concern as she travels the globe is hunger. Her travels have earned her the distinction of traveling more than any other Secretary of State. She presented her plan to reduce hunger worldwide with a program called Food Security Initiative at Bill Clinton's Global Initiative. The plan is to reform global agriculture to enable farmers to grow more food and have the ability to transport the food to cities.

In March 2009 she advocated to provide 20,000 extra troops in Afghanistan, and persevered against the wishes of some in the Obama administration. When the 2011 protests began in Egypt, she stated the Mubarak government was stable and advocated for a smooth orderly transition. Later she condemned the government for the use of violence against the protestors. When the demonstrations began in Libya she insisted that military intervention was needed. Some in the administration disagreed but she was able to get U.N. approval and the cooperation of other NATO countries. Then the administration went ahead without Congressional approval and assisted the rebels in their cause to overthrow the Libyan government. The problem was nobody explained to the American people who the rebels represent as there was obviously an organizing force that produced a unified front against their government.

With the 2012 elections around the corner there was speculation what Hillary will do. Some suggested she would run for President or replace Joe Biden as Vice President. She stated that she would not pursue any political office and she would not continue as Secretary of State for more than one term. There is a rumor that she wants to become the next president of the World Bank. I don't know what type of background a person needs to be the president of the World Bank. I would think a person would have a background in banking, finance, or economics. Perhaps a person would have the experience of running a large corporation, meeting payroll, or the knowledge of what is needed to produce something. Maybe the criteria is knowing the right people.

JANET NAPOLITANO was appointed to lead Homeland Security. She was first in the public eye when she represented Anita Hill who accused Supreme Court nominee Clarence Thomas of sexual harassment in 1991. Napolitano was responsible for preparing witnesses to testify before the Senate Judiciary Committee. The attempt to stop Thomas from getting on the Supreme Court was not successful as one of the witnesses for Hill changed her testimony after a recess conference with Napolitano. Two years later President Clinton appointed her to be the United States Attorney in the District of Arizona. In that position she was involved with the Oklahoma bombing investigation. In 1998 she became the Attorney General for Arizona and was elected Governor in 2002. She campaigned for stricter border control and improved education.

Controlling the border and illegal immigration are major concerns for persons living in Arizona and as Governor she had to face these issues. Actually she first got involved in 1984 when she defended the Southside Presbyterian Church for smuggling illegal aliens into the country and giving them sanctuary. She argued the Federal government could not infiltrate a church on a 'fishing trip' to discover illegal activity. Napolitano prevailed as the U.S. District Court stated that the "freedom of religion" does provide protection from certain government investigations. As governor she ordered State contracts must ensure that illegal aliens are not employed, stated she wanted to pursue persons that produced forged identification documents, and insisted the Federal government reimburse Arizona for the cost of imprisoning criminal illegal aliens. She even offered to send 12 Highway Patrol officers to help Immigration and Customs Enforcement (ICE) to help with cracking down on the smuggling of drugs and people. Napolitano said she worked with Mexico to decrease the illegal drugs and the "coyotes" that smuggled in undocumented people to the United States. She complained to and about Homeland Security regarding all the "red tape" and their lack of response to help "that is causing us to have an urgent situation in Arizona". As governor she concentrated on auto theft because it was connected to smuggling illegal drugs and people across the border. She also authorized 3 agents from the Department of Liquor License and Control to find those persons responsible for producing and distributing fake identification.

But actions speak louder than words. In 2004, Proposition 200 called Protect Arizona Now was on the ballot. This proposition made it illegal to receive public benefits or to register to vote if an individual was unable to provide proof of citizenship and to prosecute public officials who fail to report individuals who apply for benefits without documentation. Napolitano opposed the bill, but the voters approved it by 56%. Napolitano supported her attorney general decision that the law only pertained to discretionary state programs and not federally funded "entitlements" such as free school lunches and food stamps. In 2006 Arizona voted on measures regarding benefits for illegal aliens. They passed Proposition 300 which denied illegal aliens in-state college tuition, tax funded adult education, and childcare. Proposition 103 declared that Arizona recognized English as the State's official language. Both of these bills passed by 70% of the voters after both bills had been vetoed by Napolitano the previous year. Two other Propositions, 100 and 102, supported by 70% of the voters, denied bail to criminal illegal aliens and denied civil lawsuits for illegal aliens. Napolitano again opposed both these bills. Napolitano had always advocated on the position that the state should have a limited role dealing with border crossings. After the election, the Arizona Daily Star reported that she said the votes will not change how she deals with the issue in the next four years.

This what she said about illegal immigration, "My challenge is to devise a policy that makes Arizonans confident that some things are being done without going overboard and make it look like I'm 'tough', whatever that means". She is against what she calls "inhumane" restriction for illegal aliens. Republican Randy Pullen advocated for the immigration bills complained that Napolitano "talks a great story, but she believes in open borders. Every time we try to get something done, she vetoes it". In the 6 years she was governor she vetoed 180 bills that crossed her desk, more than any other in Arizona history. In 2007 Napolitano stated that the only way to deal with 11 million illegal aliens was to create a path to citizenship and she was against building a fence. She was critical of work site enforcement and refused to allow Arizona to comply with the Real ID Act. The Real ID Act was passed in Congress to create uniform ID cards.

One of the first things Napolitano did after her confirmation as Secretary of Homeland in January 2009 was to give a speech to Congress about her policies. She never used the words terrorist or terrorism. In March she gave an interview and was questioned as to why she did not use those words. She explained that she prefers using the words "man-made disasters" because "we want to move away from the policies of fear". Then in April she mistakenly stated that the attack of in New York City on 9/11 was caused by persons who entered the United States illegally from Canada. This upset the Canadians, so she upset them more with her apology. She stated she misunderstood the original question (that was clearly stated) and apologized. However she continued to talk, saying the problem with our northern border is that Canadians allow persons into their country that we don't allow in ours; inferring that they were lax with their security. The apology did not sit well.

April was not a good month for Napolitano as this is when she released her report titled; "Rightwing Extremism: Current Economic and Political Climate Fueling Resurgence in Radicalization and Recruitment". The nine page report was distributed to local police departments across the nation and each page begins and ends with the notation that the report is for official use only. The report singles out veterans, gun owners, those opposed to abortion or the lack of border control (and other government regulations,) plus white supremacists who are upset that an African-American was elected President as persons of concern. Suspicious activities include stock piling guns, ammunition, and food because of possible religious beliefs that the world is ending, or the government is leaning toward a one world government, fear of martial law, or detention camps. The report characterized right wing extremists as paranoid and believing in conspiracy theories and warns that the use of the internet brings these people together with ideas and methodology. The report continually stressed these people are capable of terrorist activities and destroying government property. The report also stated there is no current or specific information the groups mentioned are planning or coordinating such activity. On the last page, the report states that those persons who received the report need to report real or suspicious activity of rightwing activists to the Department of Homeland Security or to the FBI. The report caused an outrage especially to groups associated with our military veterans for being targeted as potential terrorists. Other groups complained that the police were given permission to investigate everyone because of their thoughts, ideology, and activities. Napolitano defended the report and said nobody was being singled out but later apologized to veteran groups.

Homeland Security released a report on leftwing extremists in January 2009. The report singled out anarchists, animal rights groups, and environmental groups as persons that have a history of destructive tactics. The report concentrated on potential cyber attacks and how it would affect us. This report also concludes requesting suspicious activity to be reported to Homeland Security or the FBI.

The year did not end well either, nor did it instill confidence in her ability. On Christmas a man attempted to blow up an airplane over Detroit with an underwear bomb. The detonator did not go off and the passengers, with the help of an attendant, subdued the terrorist. Napolitano went on the news talk shows bragging, "The system worked". The man's father had notified our government his son was radicalized, the bomb got on the airplane, he had a one way ticket to the United States, and he was not put on the no-fly list. She later admitted to CNN that the system failed.

In response to the Detroit incident Napolitano started the explicit body scanners and embarrassing and invasive enhanced pat downs at airport terminals. The pat downs involve touching breasts, buttocks, and genitals by Transportation Security Agency (TSA) employees. Pat downs can be done randomly and for all persons who opt out of using the body scanners. One man from California man decided the pat down was a sexual assault and told the TSA employee, "You touch my junk and I'm going to have you sued". A TSA official reported they were going to investigate the man and may fine him $1,000. The charge is leaving the airport security area without permission.

Napolitano said the pat downs are here to stay and may expand to other areas of transportation such as trains and boats. One train station in Georgia started using the enhanced searches 'after' the passengers reached their destination and 'got off' the train. Several States are seeking avenues to avoid the enhanced searches. Texas was first, but did not continue with the pursuit after the Federal government threatened to cease all flights into or out of the State. There is an opinion that States cannot overrule a Federal regulation. It may be difficult if not impossible for States to be exempt from the searches, but some people may get an exemption. TSA is considering exempting Muslim women in response to the Council on American Islamic Relations (CAIR) calling the searches invasive and humiliating. TSA is may allow Muslim women wearing religious head covers to be patted down from head to neck and then the women can check their own clothing. After the self-check of clothing TSA employees can do a chemical swipe of their hands. Then Mexicans may be able to apply for a "trusted traveler" status which will allow them to avoid some of the security procedures for 5 years. These persons will pay $100 to have a security check completed with information put on a data base that is to be checked daily. Unfortunately these exemptions are not being considered for American citizens; either adults or children. Rasmussen Reports states that because of Napolitano's response to border control with the invasive enhanced security policy her unfavorable rating among likely voters was only 47% in March 2011. Perhaps she hasn't convinced Americans that she is doing something and appearing "tough", whatever that means.

The Fourth Amendment of the United States Constitution states, "The right of the people to be secure in their persons, houses, papers, and effects, against unreasonable searches and seizures, shall not be violated, and no Warrants shall issue, but upon probable cause, but upon probable cause, supported by Oath or affirmation, and particularly describing the place to be searched and the persons or things to be seized."

ROBERT GATES as a child was a Boy Scout attaining the rank of Eagle Scout at age 15 and a honor roll student in high school earning all A's. He retired in 2011 as Secretary of Defense after a career of public service and academia, including 26 years in the CIA and the National Security Council.

Gates joined the CIA in 1966 but within the year was commissioned to the Air Force. He was an officer in the Strategic Air Command from 1967 to 1969. The Strategic Air Command promotes global security and deters attacks on U.S. vital interests. They are in charge of space operations such as military satellites, missile defense, intelligence, surveillance, reconnaissance, and combating weapons of mass destruction. He was also an intelligence officer at Whiteman Air Force Base in Missouri. After leaving the Air Force he returned to the CIA and to college. He graduated with a Doctorate in Russian and Soviet history in 1974. The same year he graduated he was appointed to the National Security Council, where he stayed until 1979 serving under Nixon, Ford and Carter. He then returned to work at the CIA. Gates was obviously doing a good job as he rose in rank until he became the Deputy Director in 1986. In 1989 he left the CIA to serve at National Security Affairs, first as the Deputy Assistant and left in 1991 as the Deputy in charge. Returning again to the CIA he became the Director.

Gates was investigated by the Independent Council in 1993 regarding his involvement in the Iran-Contra Affair in the 1980's. He was not indicted but chose to retire. From 1993 until 1999 he lectured at many colleges and wrote many articles for the op-ed page of the NY Times. Gates took the

Interim Dean position at George Bush Schools of Government and Public Service at Texas A&M university between 1999 and 2001. In 2002 he became the University President at Texas A&M and stayed there until 2006. In 2004 he co-chaired the Council on Foreign Relations task force on U.S. relations with Iran. His recommendation was to maintain direct diplomatic exchanges regarding their use of nuclear energy.

In December 2006 he was appointed the Secretary of Defense by President George W. Bush. Under Gates people who made mistakes or were ineffective soon found other employment. When it was discovered early in 2007 that there was neglect at Walter Reed Army Medical Center, the Secretary of the Army and the Army Surgeon General left. The following year the Secretary of the Air Force and the Air Force Chief of Staff left after a report of nuclear weapons mis-shipments. In 2008 he retained his position under Obama, but stated in March that he planned on retiring before his term was over. He continued the troop withdrawal in Iraq which began under the Bush administration, and implemented the troop surge in Afghanistan in 2009. He had regular meetings with Secretary of State Clinton regarding policy and procedures. In February 2010 he lifted the ban regarding women serving in submarines and began preparing the troops for the repeal of "Don't Ask, Don't Tell". In August he announced his 2011 retirement. Gates had always been aware of costs and made suggestions on how to reduce military spending and effective ways to shift costs. He advocated reduced spending for conventional warfare and increased spending on special forces and new technology.

In March 2011 he visited both Israel and the West Bank. Gates supports a two state solution with Israel and Palestine and cautioned Israel to use restraint in retaliations from the Palestinians. He continues to stress diplomatic solutions and sees this, even with all the disruptions in the area, as a time for opportunity to move on bold solutions toward the two state solution. Gates gave his last speech on June 1, 2011 stating that NATO had turned into a 2 tiered alliance with some nations taking only 'soft' humanitarian tasks, while other nations took the 'hard' combat missions. He continued that some pay the price and bear the burdens while others enjoy the benefits of security without the risks. He complained that some nations were happy to let American taxpayers assume the burden as the European nations were reducing their defense budgets. Gates warned that the day may come when American may hesitate because the returns from NATO is not worth the cost. He argued against American military involvement in Libya but got overruled by Summers and Clinton.

LEON PANETTA was appointed Director of the CIA in February 2009 and became the Secretary of Defense on July 1, 2011 replacing Gates. Panetta was elected to the U.S. House of Representatives from California in 1976, re-elected nine times, and voted the Democratic party line 90% of the time. He was primarily concerned with budget issues, civil rights, education, health, the environment(especially marine life), and the prevention of drilling for oil off the California coast. The last four years Panetta was in office he chaired the House Budget Committee.

On foreign issues he supported Marxists; voting no on the Mutual Defense Treaty with Taiwan, voted for most favored status to the Soviet Union, voted to give up control of the Panama Canal to the pro-Soviet Panama government, and voted to give aid to the Sandinistas in Nicaragua. He supported Ortega in Nicaragua and other Soviet and Cuban backed Marxist groups in Latin America. Panetta was active with the Institute for Policy Studies (IPS).

IPS was a front group for the Communist Party and as one congressman said in 1977, "IPS is an organization designed to neutralize America as a world power by crippling foreign and domestic intelligence". Former Congressman Larry McDonald said "IPS is a consortium of Marxists pressing for revolutionary change in American domestic and foreign policies through a variety of tactics". The International Intelligence Study stated that IPS manipulates and controls the media attempting to influence public opinion against the military, economic and political programs. They portray the United States as an aggressive colonialist and imperial power, attempting to isolate us from allies and to discredit nations that cooperate with them. IPS mission is to destroy or weaken the United States intelligence agencies, especially the CIA, and to expose intelligence personnel. The magazine 'American Opinion' wrote in 1983 that IPS supports dramatic cuts in defense spending while increasing spending for social programs. Panetta was listed as one of the members that put together IPS's 20 year anniversary celebration with Senator Chris Dodd and Representative Tom Harkin. One of the founders of IPS was Richard Barnet the speech writer for President Carter. IPS receives funding from George Soros.

In 1984 Panetta read into the Congressional Record his praise of Lucy Haessler who was an active member of Woman's International League for Peace and Freedom (WILPF). WILPF was a front group for the Communist Party of the Soviet Union that defended the Soviet invasion into Afghanistan and was opposed America's ballistic missiles in Western Europe. Panetta praised her as a peace activist that organized anti-war campaigns and hoped she would continue.

Bill Clinton appointed Panetta, in 1993, as the Director of Office Management and Budget. He was responsible for designing the budget plan that resulted in a balanced budget. Clinton appointed him as Chief of Staff in 1994, where Panetta said he established order where there was no order before.

The Panetta Institute for Public Policy was started in 1998 with his wife Sylvia. They are both directors and when Leon is not in public office he profits from speaking fees. In 2008 he earned $700,000 in speaking and consulting fees. The Institute, a not-for -profit organization, had $16 million in revenue in 2009 but the sources of the revenue are not published (or I didn't find it). The Institute is a study group and educational organization that sponsors lectures and has internships. Classes teach how the government works, lectures on government policies, and trains on politics. Students are selected by the presidents of California State Colleges and are provided an internship to work in Washington with a California Representative. The Institute is located at the California State University Monterey Bay, established in 1994 with the help of Panetta, at the former Fort Hood that was closed by Bill Clinton. The Panetta Institute has opposed holding terrorists as prisoners in Guantanamo Bay.

Obama nominated Panetta as Director of the CIA and he was sworn in February 19, 2009. During the confirmation process Panetta said he would improve intelligence on al-Qaeda, Iran, Iraq, Afghanistan, North Korea, and on cyber threats. He promised to work closely with Congress. The first controversy came on May 14th when Nancy Pelosi claimed the CIA lied to her at a briefing in September 2002 stating she was never told enhanced interrogation had been used. She claimed she was only told it was legal but was not informed until February 2003 about its use. Republicans asked her to provide proof of the misinformation she claimed and how and when she voiced her concern on the procedure of waterboarding. Pelosi gave a news conference on May 23rd but refused to answer any questions about her allegations that CIA lied. On May 15th Panetta wrote an e-mail to the employees regarding the situation. The e-mail stated. "Let me be clear. It is not our policy or practice to mislead Congress. That is against our laws and our values. As the agency indicated previously in response to congressional inquiries, our contemporaneous records from September 2002 indicate officers briefed truthfully on the interrogations of terrorists, describing the enhanced techniques that had been employed".

In May 2010 his top deputy, Stephen Kappes, retired after working at the agency for 30 years. There was speculation that the departure was because of Attorney General Eric Holder's insistence on the continued investigation on enhanced interrogation. Kappes had a major role with operations since the 9/11 attacks in 2001, oversaw the drone attacks in Pakistan, and started the talks in 2003 with Khadafi which eventually led to Libya ending its program on weapons of mass destruction. When asked to describe what victory in Afghanistan was Panetta replied, "Our purpose, our whole mission is to make sure Al Qaeda never finds another safe haven from which to attack this country". While at the CIA he was in charge when over 1,000 al Qaeda members and terrorists were captured or killed. He was also in charge when Osama bin Laden was killed. After the mission was completed Panetta wrote John McCain a note telling him that the information needed to defeat bin Laden came from many sources including enhanced interrogation.

GENERAL DAVID PETRAEUS replaced Panetta in September 2011. Petraeus was a four-star general in the Army serving for 37 years. He retired from the military before taking on his new assignment. He has a distinguished record of achievement during his years of service to our country. In the recent years he has been the Commander of International Security Assistance Force, U.S. Forces in Afghanistan, and U.S. Central Command. He has been the Commander General for the Multi-national Force in Iraq, at Fort Leavenworth, and at the U.S. Army Combined Arms Center. Petraeus has been called the world's leading expert in counter-insurgency warfare.

After Petraeus gave a report to Congress on 'The Situation' in Iraq in 2007 stating the conditions had improved after a surge of troops. MoveOn.org then started an ad campaign against him. MoveOn.org called him General Betray Us and said he was lying about the situation in Iraq and "cooking the books for the White House". Their ads were very controversial, both criticized and condoned. Rudy Giuliani called it a character assassination. Joe Biden said ad went "overboard" but the points were "valid". Hillary Clinton said, "I don't condone anything like that, and I have voted against those who would impugn the patriotism and the service of the people who wear the uniform of our country". Bill Clinton said those who criticize the ad, primarily Republicans, as "disingenuous and are demonstrating feigned outrage". The Senate passed an amendment condemning personal attacks on the "honor and integrity of General Petraeus" which was supported by all 49 Republican and 22 Democratic Senators. Hillary Clinton and Chris Dodd voted against the amendment. Joe Biden and Barak Obama did not vote.

Obama said the vote was a "stunt" and "by not casting a vote, I registered my protest against these empty politics". The House of Representatives passed the amendment 341 for and 79 against. MoveOn.org removed the ad and all references to Petraeus on June 23, 2010 right after Obama nominated him as the U.S. and NATO commander in Afghanistan.

Petraeus continued his command of Afghanistan until his retirement in September, as he was in charge with the removal of troops from that country. He was in favor of a slow moderate reduction through 2012, an opinion shared by Hillary Clinton and Robert Gates, of about 3,000 to 5,000 in 2011. However Obama decided to remove 10,000 troops.

JAMES CLAPPER, the current Director of National Intelligence (NI), is a retired Lieutenant General of the Air Force after serving our country for 32 years. NI was formed in 2005 as a recommendation from the 9/11 Commission which oversees 16 intelligence agencies. He is the 4th Director of NI and the 2rd appointed under the Obama administration (there was an additional acting director, David Gompert, who lead the agency between the time Dennis Blair left in May 2010 and Clapper was confirmed in August). Clapper worked in intelligence after his military retirement starting as Director of the Defense Intelligence Agency (DIA) from 1992 until 1995. He began his work there after the collapse of the Soviet Union and was in charge during Operation DESERT STORM. From 2001 until 2006 he directed the National Geospatial Intelligence Agency (NGIA). The mission of this agency is to map, chart, and obtain imagery and geophysical activities on, over, or beneath the earth's surface. The NGIA most recently was applauded for the information used in the May 5, 2011 raid in Pakistan that resulted in Osama bin Laden's death. In 2003 Clapper stated the weapons of mass destruction in Iraq were transferred out of the country to Syria and other surrounding nations. From 2007 until 2010 he was the Under Secretary of Defense for Intelligence.

Between his appointments in government positions he worked at different firms doing business for intelligence agencies. In 1995 Clapper was an executive director for the defense company Booz Allen Hamilton. This company collects digital information from e-mail, court records, credit cards, and medical records with a program called Total Information Awareness. The government paid them $63 million from 1997 until 2003 when Congress shut down the program because of public outrage. In 1998 he joined SRA International with the position of Intelligence Program Director and the company was able to get grants from I-Q-Tel. I-Q-Tel was an agency run by the CIA which was investing in technology companies. SRA designed NetOwl software that is able to recognize words and information. SRA has contracts with the Department of Defense, Homeland Security and Department of Health and Human Services.

When Clapper worked at NGIA he awarded a 15 year $2 billion contract to a company in Alaska named NJVC to build a precise computer system and the company never did that type of work before. However it had the start-up funds provided by earmarks from Senator Ted Stevens. Clapper also expanded the commercial satellite program and gave contracts to three companies that shared $1.5 billion. One of the companies was called ORBIMAGE that was in bankruptcy, but the $500 million dollars allowed them to purchase one of the competitors. The other company was called Space Imaging which was later renamed GeoEye Inc. Clapper went to work for GeoEye in 2006. By 2007 that company's gross revenue was up 22% and profit up 57% when income from NGIA increased by $29.9 million. He also worked for a few months in 2006 and 2007 at Detica DFI, a company involved with cyber security. Their web site states they develop, integrate and manage information and intelligence solutions. In 2007 Detica DFI was one of eleven companies awarded a share a 5 year $250 million contract.

As Director of National Intelligence he was interviewed in December 2010 by Diane Sawyer from ABC News. He was questioned about the 12 terrorists who had been arrested earlier that day in Great Britain. He was unable to answer her as he had no knowledge of the event. In February 2011 he testified before the House Intelligence Committee about the Muslim Brotherhood. He said, "The term Muslim Brotherhood is an umbrella term for a variety of movements...has decried al Qaeda as a perversion of Islam...has no overarching addenda, particularly in pursuit of violence".

> The Muslim Brotherhood is the largest and oldest Islamic group whose slogan is "Islam is the solution". Their goal is to have the Qur'an as the only reference to control the family, the individual, the community, and the state; using violence to achieve their goals. The Muslim Brotherhood took part in Egypt's revolution in 2011. However they were not popular with that country's youth so they renamed themselves the Freedom and Justice Party. The Muslim Brotherhood is actually a movement and not a political party, but members do form political parties. The Freedom and Justice Party is just the newest. The most well known is Hamas in the West Bank

> and Gaza. The Muslim Brotherhood had been outlawed in Egypt because it is against their law to have a religious political party. Prior to Arab Spring Egypt stated our State Department labels them as a 'potent political and religious force'.

A spokesperson from NI later that day clarified that Clapper did know that the Muslim Brotherhood was not a secular organization.

Clapper, in March 2011, said that Khadafi would prevail in Libya at the Senate Committee of Armed services. At that same meeting he failed to mention Iran and North Korea as nuclear powers that could be a potential threat to our country. Perhaps he just forgot.

Judge me by the people who surround me.

CHAPTER 26

★ ★ ★ ★ ★

Transition Economic Advisory Board

When Obama announced his Transition Economic Advisory Board it appeared to be an eclectic list of names. The first name that I recognized was Michigan's governor JENNIFER GRANHOLM, the State with the highest unemployment rate, and a revenue short fall of approximately $500 million despite numerous tax increases. The other Michigan native was former congressman DAVID BONIOR who took a trip to Iraq on behalf of Muthanna Al-Hanooti, an executive director of CAIR, who was later indicted for spying for Saddam Hussein. Bonior is noted for filing 75 ethic charges against Newt Gingrich, of which 74 were declared bogus and the final charge was eventually determined to be unfounded. The other politician was ANTONIO VILLARAGIOSA, the mayor of Los Angeles which is a sanctuary city for illegal aliens. Villaragiosa was under investigation on ethic charges for accepting tickets to events with a value totaling $50,000 to $100,000.

WARREN BUFFET and RICHARD PARSONS from Time Warner were named to the board. Buffet is an investor, a philanthropist and the richest person in the world. He supports higher taxes for wealthy persons. Parsons was a lawyer who took a position at Dime Bank when it was in financial trouble. He restructured the bank and it is now profitable. Then he was hired at Time Warner when the company was having problems after acquiring AOL. Parsons is recognized as the person who made changes that made the acquisition profitable.

ROEL CAMPOS and WILLIAM DONALDSON both had previously worked at the Securities and Exchange Commission (SEC). Campos as commissioner at SEC was a liaison in the international community. Obama appointed him to the President's Intelligence Advisory Board in January

2010. Donaldson as chairman at SEC was known for his consistent advocacy for more regulations.

LAURA TYSON was a chief economist in the Clinton administration and advisor to Obama during his campaign. In an August 2008 interview with PBS she described her views on how to improve the economy. She favored a second stimulus plan that would give States funds to counsel people facing foreclosure on their homes and to provide a $1,000 check as a tax rebate to help with increasing energy costs. She favored spending more money on community colleges plus spending an additional $10 billion per year on a preschool program for all children under the age of five. She also advocated for a government incentive program that she estimated would cost "hundreds of billions of dollars" to promote green technology, suggesting some of this funding would come from a cap and trade system which would price carbon.

> Carbon dioxide is the gas animals, including humans, exhale and plants use to build bio-mass that creates oxygen that animals breathe in. Levels of carbon dioxide are naturally higher during the winter and fall in the northern areas when plants are dormant and lower in the spring and summer, as plants absorb the gas when they are green. Carbon is the 15th most abundant element in the earth's crust and the 4th most abundant in the universe. Carbon is the soot after a fire and the lead in your pencil and is the source of limestone, marble, coal and diamonds. Combined with hydrogen it creates refrigerants, lubricants and plastics. Crude oil is 84% carbon and 14% hydrogen.

ANNE MULCAHY was appointed to the transition team had been named one of America's Best Leaders by U.S. News and World Report, named CEO of the year by Chief Executive Magazine, and was hailed as the person that saved Xerox from going bankrupt after an accounting scandal. She was the vice president and on the board of directors at Xerox while the accounting practices that defrauded investors took place. Mulcahy restructured the company by eliminating 3,000 jobs and removing retirees' benefits for future employees and for those that had been retired for the prior 10 years. Her income at Xerox, in 2008, was over $11 million including her salary, bonus, and other compensation. The accounting scandal that took place at Fannie Mae occurred when she was on the board. She was on the audit committee, and on the compensation board when they were committing accounting irregularities that ensured executives received maximum bonuses. She was instrumental in changing Fannie Mae's CEO Franklin Raines severance agreement so that when he left he received approximately $30 million in stocks and a yearly pension of over $1 million for the rest of his life. Fraud charges against her were dismissed but investors complained the audit "failed miserably". She resigned from the board a few days prior to federal regulators releasing the report of the multibillion dollar fraud.

After leaving Fannie Mae, Mulcahy joined the board of Citigroup and was appointed to the audit and risk management committee. While at Citigroup their stock dropped from over $50 per share to less than $4. Pension funds were lobbying to have the audit committee removed. While on the compensation committee the company paid out over $5 billion in bonuses after reporting a loss of $28 billion and accepting TARP funds totaling $45 billion. She currently sits on the boards of Target Corporation, Johnson & Johnson, and the Washington Post. Mulcahy is the Chairman of the Board of Trustees at Save the Children Federation, a non-profit organization with a mission to create lasting change to children worldwide.

ERIC SCHMIDT was CEO of Google and the 136th richest person in the world when selected to be on the transition team. He advised Obama that the "easiest way to solve all the problems of the United States at once, at least in the domestic policy, is by a stimulus program that rewards renewable energy and, over time, attempts to replace fossil fuels with renewable energy". He was later appointed to the President's Council of Advisors on Science and Technology (PCAST).

Schmidt has been busy promoting green technology particularly endorsing a smart grid system to keep track of energy usage. In February 2009 Google announced a new product called Google Power Meter saying it will become a platform for energy usage in the home. This appears to be an extension of Clean Energy 2030 that has a target to "wean the United States from its dependence on fossil fuels within 22 years." This plan wants the federal government to spend $4.4 trillion to subsidize renewable energy. Schmidt explained the plan to get 100% of power generation with green power and replace half of the automobiles with plug-in hybrid vehicles. In April 2011 Schmidt stepped down from the position as CEO to become the board's Executive Chairman. In February 2011 Schmidt stated he was "very very proud" that Google executive Wael Ghonim helped to organize the protests in Egypt. Google set up a system to circumvent the government's communication blackout. It set up a "speaktotweet" system that gave people the ability to call a specific telephone line and leave messages that would be forwarded by tweeting.

At a meeting of the world's top internet leaders which convened prior to the G8 Summit in May 2011, French President Nicolas Sarkozy wanted to establish a set of rules to govern the Internet. Schmidt disagreed saying, "Is there a technological solution...that can work globally, and move very quickly?" "Because we'll move more quickly than any one of the governments, let alone all the governments". Schmidt is a member of the New American Foundation with Jonathon Soros.

WILLIAM DALEY was the brother of Chicago's then current mayor and his father had also been a mayor of the city. He has been a lawyer, lobbyist, banker, and worked in the Clinton administration as the Secretary of Commerce. In that position he enabled the passage of the Free Trade Act. He was appointed Chief of Staff at the White House in January 2011 even though he is against the health care bill.

PENNY PRITZKER, also from Chicago, was an early endorser of Obama for President and held fund raisers for him. She is the CEO of Hyatt Hotels and the 204th richest person in the world. Pritzker was connected to Superior Bank of Chicago that was taken over by FDIC because of inaccurate record keeping with sub-prime loans. The accounting practices of the bank resulted in many depositors losing money.

ROBERT RUBIN had been an Assistant to the President for Economic Policy in the Clinton administration and directed the National Economic Council. In 1995 he was appointed the Secretary of the Treasury. Rubin was one of the people who convinced the Commodity Futures Trading Commission not to regulate over-the-counter credit derivatives even though he later wrote that he thought the derivative market was risky and many people may not understand that. When he was Secretary of the Treasury the Glass-Steagall Act was abolished. This Act was a banking regulation that separated commercial and investment banking. In 1999 he joined Citigroup, but unfortunately many of the reforms he suggested almost brought the company to bankruptcy and many shareholders lost up to, or more than, 70% of their investments. He was named in a lawsuit by investors as one of the executives that sold shares of the company at inflated prices without sharing the risks involved. While at Citigroup he earned $17 million plus received $33 million in stock options. In 2006, at the Brookings Institute, Rubin founded the Hamilton Project which promotes their vision of how to create a growing economy. He was named the co-chairman at the Council of Foreign Relations in 2007.

ROBERT REICH is a professor teaching public policy at Goldman School of Public Policy at the University of California, Berkley and a former professor at Harvard. He is a political commentator of several television shows on NBC, MSNBC, and CNBC. He is on the board of Common Cause; a lobbying organization "committed to progress in the struggle for social, economic and environmental justice for all". Reich has written 13 books, gives lectures, and has his own blog where he shares his political views.

Reich regarding Obamacare, "I am going to try to reorganize it to be more amenable to treating sick people…particularly you young healthy people… you're going to have to pay more." "If you're very old, we're not going to give you all that technology and all those drugs for the last couple of years of your life to keep you maybe going for another couple of months. It's too expensive, so we're going to let you die". "I'm going to use the bargaining leverage of the federal government to force drug companies and insurance companies and medical suppliers to reduce their costs. What that means, less innovations, and that means less new products and less new drugs on the market which means you are probably not going to live much longer than your parents". Reich on income distribution, "Expand the Earned Income Tax Credit – the wage supplement for lower income people, and finance it with higher marginal income tax on the top five percent". On the stimulus plan, "the stimulus plan will create jobs repairing and upgrading the nation's roads, bridges…and kick-start alternative, non-fossil based sources of energy, new health care information systems, and universal broadband Internet access…". If construction jobs go mainly to white males who already dominate the construction trades… many people will be shut out. People can be trained relatively quickly for these sorts of jobs. I suggest…stimulus funds require contractors to provide at least 20% of jobs to long term unemployed, at least 2% of project funds allocated to training…buildings trades apprenticeships which must be fully available to women and minorities". Then he opines that Obama should use an executive order to make government contractors disclose political contributions and ban companies that receive government contracts from making political contributions. Examples he used were Lockheed, Northrop Grumman, Blackwater, Raytheon and General Dynamics. He did not voice any concern about funding from unions, health care companies, pharmaceuticals, green technology, or computer companies. He believes when federal spending reaches the debt ceiling that it should just be raised.

ROGER W. FERGUSON, JR. is an economist, the President and Chief Executive Officer of Teachers Insurance and Annuity Association – College Retirement Equities Fund (TIAA – CREF), which is financial services company and provides retirement benefits primarily to persons in academic, medical, government, research, and cultural fields. Ferguson was previously employed at the Federal Reserve System as a Vice Chairman and member of the Board of Governors. He was appointed to the Board by President Clinton and reappointed by President Bush with a term to expire in 2014. At the Federal Reserve System he was Chairman of the joint Y2K Council, chairman of the Group of Ten Working Party (G-10), Chairman of the Committee on Global Financial system, and Chairman of the Financial Stability Forum. Ferguson resigned in 2006. He sits on several not-for-profit boards, including the New American Foundation think-tank with Eric Schmidt. He is also a member of the international Group of Thirty with Paul Volcker and Lawrence Summers.

PAUL VOLCKER is an economist who was a director of financial analysis at the Treasury Department in 1962. He became the Deputy Under-Secretary of Monetary Affairs in 1963, and then after a temporary absence, returned in 1969 as the Under-Secretary for International Monetary Affairs. In 1971 he was involved with suspending gold convertibility with the dollar. The dollar value now keeps its value based on the confidence of the United States government. Volcker was the president of the Federal Reserve Bank of New York from 1975 until he was appointed as Chairman of the Federal Reserve in August 1979.

He served as Chairman of the Federal Reserve during the Carter and the Reagan administrations. Carter appointed him during the financial crisis of his administration that endured high interest rates, high inflation and high unemployment. The inflation rate increased 4.9% during the first year of his administration. The inflation rate when Volcker took over was 11.8% and rose to 14.8% in March 1980. The high interest rates were referred to as

"Volcker Shock" and they did end the depreciation of gold. When Reagan was elected tax rates were cut and business regulations eased, then the inflation rate dropped to 3.2% by the end of 1983. Reagan reappointed Volcker in 1983 and he remained in that position until 1987 when he was replaced by Alan Greenspan. In 1974 the unemployment rate was 5.6%, and climbed to 7.1% in 1980. The unemployment rate went as high as 9.7% in 1982 but was reduced to 5.5% in 1988.

Volcker is a founding member of the Trilateral Commission and a member of the Bilderberg Group. In 2006 he became Chairman of the Board of Trustee of the Group of Thirty which is an international group that analyzes issues of global financial markets, foreign exchange, and advocates global clearing and settlement. Clearing and settlement involves all activities from the beginning of a transaction, including any modifications, until the contract is paid.

Obama named him the chairman of his economic transition team and later the chairman of the Economic Recovery Advisory Board. His proposal for bank reform became known as the Volcker Rule and was initially backed by Obama. The plan states banks must either be a savings and loan or an investment institution, but not both. Banks which are not investment institutions cannot trade or invest in speculative stocks or hedge funds. Nor can they invest in privately owned government backed deposits of stocks, bonds, equity funds, etc. that could benefit the company. Volcker believed that putting limits on banks would create financial stability. What he was suggesting was to return to the regulations of the Glass-Steagall Act which was eliminated in 1999. Those opposed to the Volcker Rule believed it would create chaos with banks closing and/or merging. Tim Geithner and Larry Summers opposed the Volcker Rule, although they agreed that banks ability to invest in risk taking opportunities needed to be contained. Geithner argued that banks needed to keep more capital in reserve even though it would reduce potential profits. The Volcker Rule would also reduce Geithner's power as the Treasury Secretary. Banks and investment companies that gave large campaign contributions were against Volcker's suggestions and eventually the plan was watered down enough to be ineffective.

Volcker also stated that increased taxes were needed to reduce the deficit. He was in favor of a value added tax (VAT) and a carbon tax. He resigned from the position, which Obama created for him, in January 2011.

This is the team of people that Obama brought together to develop this country's economic policies. The stated goals where to determine how to spend the extra $700 billion stimulus funds, how to create jobs, and how to extend unemployment insurance as the unemployment rate was at a staggering 6.5%. The group also had the mission to find a way to avoid mortgage foreclosures, help out the auto industry, and provide relief for the middle class. I tried to find the economic team's final report, advice, or suggestions and was not successful.

Judge me by the people who surround me.

CHAPTER 27

★ ★ ★ ★ ★

Money Men and Woman

Not being able to determine what the economic transition team recommended, I decided to research the people instrumental in implementing the Obama economic plan.

BEN BERNANKE started at the Federal Reserve System as a board member in 2002. He is known for his description of Great Moderation (improving and controlling the monetary system) and coming up with his Bernanke Doctrine. The Bernanke Doctrine describes a Kenyesian type economic plan he believes will stabilize the economy. Kenyesian economics is using government regulations to create policies and enact laws that will affect the economy instead of relying of the market place. The doctrine advocated the printing of money to increase the money supply and devalue the dollar, lower interest rates down to 0% to generate inflation, control corporate bond yields by accepting bonds as collateral and lending at 0%, and to purchase U.S. companies with the newly minted money.

The Federal Reserve System (sometimes called the Federal Reserve or shorten to the Fed) is this country's central bank. It was created by Congress in 1913. The Fed is composed of 7 Board of Governors (each appointed by the President and approved by Congress to serve 14 years terms), the presidents of 12 regional banks, and the Federal Open Market Committee (FOMC). FMOC is composed of the Board of Governors and the regional banks. Their responsibility to conduct our monetary policy, supervise banks, keep the financial system stabile and provide financial services to banks, the government, and foreign institutions. The decisions made at The Fed don't need to be approved by Congress or the President, even though there is Congressional oversight. Therefore the Fed is both private and public. Most central banks create their nations currency, but the Department of Treasury is the agency that creates the money that the Fed is responsible for.

President Bush appointed Bernanke as Chairman of the Federal Reserve in 2006 and he was re-appointed in 2010 under the Obama administration. As Chairman he is on the Financial Stability Oversight Board that controls the Trouble Asset Relief Program (TARP). Bernanke is also the Chairman of the Federal Open Market Committee that creates the monetary policy for the Federal Reserve. In January 2009, before Obama's inauguration, Bernanke stated the world needed to work together to solve economic problems. Co-operation between nations was essential, he explained, to create a healthy sustained economic recovery. He blamed the housing crisis and subprime mortgage delinquencies for causing "extraordinary stress" on the global economic problems. Bernanke was very optimistic the $800 billion stimulus plan would give a "significant boost" to the failing economy.

He started to manipulate the market with what is called Quantitative Easing (QE) which is monetizing the debt, or using our own money to pay off our own debt. The way this was done was money was created electronically (virtual money) and used to purchase securities (bad debt) with a "check" that the sellers would deposit into their own accounts. Then what is suppose to happen is the banks use the deposit funds for loans to individuals and businesses which is then, in theory, going to create inflation. Inflation was the desired outcome to combat deflation caused by a decrease in spending caused by declining home prices, the loss of 401k balances, and the fear of future loss of income and assets.

Bernanke and Secretary Treasurer Paulson approached Congress with an emergency request for funds to save financial institutions with the Troubled Asset Relief Program (TARP) in September 2008. The Fed previously allowed the Federal Reserve Bank of New York to provide AIG with billions of dollars to prevent the institution from going bankrupt. During the month of September Lehman Brothers filed for bankruptcy and Merrill Lynch was sold to Bank of America. Realizing more money was needed to shore up banks and prevent an economic collapse, the two men argued that large amounts of money needed to be released to purchase troubled assets in the mortgage market. The housing bubble burst and subprime mortgages were going into default in record numbers.

The Troubled Asset Relief Program (TARP) was approved by Congress on October 3, 2008 giving the Department of Treasury more power than it ever had before. The Treasury now had the power to purchase or insure any financial instrument they determined was necessary to promote financial security. TARP is actually a "revolving purchase facility" with the first release of $350 billion on October 3rd. The program allowed the Treasury to release additional funds after sending a report to Congress. Congress has 15 days to decline any request, if no action is taken the requested amount is automatically released. In November Paulson announced that the focus of TARP had changed from purchasing troubled mortgages to providing "capital injections" to troubled financial institutions.

In November 2008, the Fed announced it would purchase $100 billion of debt incurred by Fannie Mae, Freddie Mac and the Federal Home Loan Banks plus $500 billion to Fannie Mae, Freddie Mac, and Ginnie Mae for mortgage backed securities. This was the beginning of QE1. Then in January 2009 the Fed stated it wanted to purchase long-term Treasury debt as they projected it would improve private credit markets and increase further mortgage backed (sub-prime) securities. In March 2009, the Fed expanded the mortgage backed security purchases to $1.25 trillion and spent $300 billion on long-term Treasury debt. QE1 ended in June 2010 and it did create paper profits and the stock market stabilized. Banks did not extend more private or commercial credit than it did before QE1 (it decreased) and commercial loans were not guaranteed to be invested in the United States. Personal spending did not increase as people conserved in the event of further increased costs. The price of gold and other metals increased as faith in the government and the stability of money decreased. Bernanke spoke of the increase of core inflation. Core inflation is not the same as the Consumer Price Index. Core inflation does not calculate the increase or decrease of food or energy costs that each individual faces each day. It only calculates items that do not fluctuate wildly like rent, education and services such as medical services.

QE2 started November 2010 with the purchasing of about $75 billion per month (or $3.5 billion per day) of treasury bonds until June 2011. The expectation was this virtual money, which is not backed by production, would create low inflation and full employment. In May 2011 the unemployment rate was about 9% and the costs of food and gas continued to rise. The unemployment rate includes those persons receiving unemployment benefits. It does not include those people whose benefits have expired, those working part-time jobs because they cannot find full- time employment, those on welfare or living off friends and relatives, or recent graduates looking for work. The stock market has stabilized again, but experts disagreed if the end of QE2 would have no effect on stocks or whether they will suddenly lose value again. Gold is at an all time high at over $1,700 an ounce. Thus discussion as to whether a QE3 will be needed in the near future and how long can this manipulation, also called Macroprudential Economics, can continue.

TIM GEITHNER was named the Secretary of the Treasury by Obama and he assumed the office on January 26, 2009. Before assuming that position he was the president of the Federal Reserve Bank in New York.

Geithner spent most of his childhood overseas, living in Zimbabwe, Zambia, India, and Thailand. He attended high school at the International School Bangkok and went to college at Peking University and Beijing Normal University before graduating from Dartmouth College. At college he studied Mandarin and Japanese languages, Asian studies and government. Geithner earned a Masters Degree in international economics and East Asian studies in 1985 from John Hopkins University's School of Advanced International Studies. His maternal grandfather, Charles Moore, was an advisor to President Eisenhower and the vice president of the Ford Motor Company. His father, Peter, was employed by the Ford Foundation as director of "microfinancing" in Indonesia. Ann Dunham Soetoro, Obama's mother, developed the microfinance program in Indonesia that Peter Geithner supervised. Peter Geithner is a board member of the National Committee on U.S.-China Relations serving alongside Henry Kissinger.

After graduating from college, Tim Geithner obtained employment at Kissinger and Associates from 1986 to 1989. Kissinger and Associates is a highly secretive international consulting company founded by Henry Kissinger, Brent Scowcroft, and Lawrence Eagleburger. This firm starting working with the Bank of Credit and the Commerce International (BCCI) in 1986. The BCCI has known connections with drug trafficking and international money laundering operations for the CIA. In fact, the CIA, DIA, and the NSC all used BCCI as their private bank and secretly owned First American and Bank of America. One of Kissinger and Associates clients was Banco Nationale del Lavaro that a congressional investigation discovered had issued over $4 billion in loans to Iraq which allowed Saddam Hussein to purchase weapons used to attack Kuwait in 1990.

After leaving the consulting firm, Geithner went to work at the U.S. Treasury in the International Affairs division until 2001with Robert Rubin and Lawrence Summers. During this time he wrote the International Monetary (IMF) program for Indonesia. The IMF loans funds to countries that are experiencing financial troubles on the condition that they follow IMF policies.

Indonesia was not in debt; in fact the country was producing a growth rate of 7% for the previous 21 years. The country was growing and the banks were lending to private businesses, however the banks did not have the capital to back the loans. They had a bank crisis of private debt not government debt. Businesses began to fail, and the IMF plan brought in billions of dollars as a "bail out" in the form of a loan to stabilize the debt and encouraged massive government spending. This policy did not work because the money was quickly devalued and in 1998 the country lost over 13% of its GDP. Lending interest rates increased up to 50%, unemployment rose drastically, millions were suddenly impoverished and violent riots erupted.

Then he joined the International Monetary Fund (IMF) as Director of the Policy Developmental and Review Department until 2003. In 2002 he became a member of the Council on Foreign Relations and served as a Senior Fellow in the International Economics department.

Next, in 2003, Geithner became the president of the Federal Reserve Bank of New York and was the vice chairman of the Federal Open Market Committee. One of his endeavors was attempting to reduce the amount of capital a bank needed to continue operations. It was the lack of sufficient capitol that caused the Indonesia financial collapse. It was his responsibility to oversee Citigroup, manage its risk management, and make sure it had enough capital to cover potential losses at the time it was investing in subprime mortgage, hedge funds, and purchasing other financial firms. What he did was reduce restrictions that eventually led to Citigroup receiving a $52 billion bailout.

AIG insures financial firms against losses in the mortgage based secured loans. When the housing bubble burst those firms were cashing in on their contracts but AIG did not have the funds to pay them. Failure of the banks and AIG to receive those funds would have caused them to go bankrupt. On September 15, 2008 Geithner set up a meeting with several banks; including Goldman Sachs, Morgan Stanley, and Bank of America to discuss setting up fund to bail out AIG. The banks refused the private bailout of AIG. Geithner then authorized the New York Federal Reserve to save AIG and began lending them billions of dollars for the next two months. Finally, he went to the government and requested a Federal bailout.

The Fed had another option it did not use. They could have given AIG a short term loan and announced to the lending institutions that AIG was pending bankruptcy. This would have induced those institutions to settle for less money as it would also save those firms legal fees fighting against a discounted amount. At this time AIG had contacted banks looking for a settlement. However, when the Fed gave money to AIG and AIG paid the banks, the banks received 100% and took no loss. AIG had planned to inform their investors where the funds had been paid to, but it was later discovered that the Fed told them to withhold that information. The government was giving AIG a $185 billion bailout while the information was being withheld. In December AIG announced that 168 employees were going to be paid bonuses in the amount of between $92,000 and $4 million per person. The bonuses were renamed retention payments. A spokesperson from AIG stated that Geithner was not party with the withholding of information as he did not get involved with the AIG account after he was nominated for Secretary of the Treasury on November 24th. Geithner claimed he had no knowledge of the retention payments prior to the AIG announcement.

Confirmation hearings found that Geithner did not pay $42,782 in Social Security and Medicare taxes owed during the years of 2001 and 2002. He did not plan to pay all these taxes as the statute of limitations had run out for those years. Then a 2006 IRS audit found that he did not pay an additional $17,230 in taxes owed for tax years 2003 and 2004. Only when he was approached about the possibility of being nominated for the position of Secretary of the Treasury did he file an amended tax return for 2001 to 2006 and paid his past due taxes. Geithner was charged $15,000 interest on the unpaid taxes but was not assessed a fine for late payment. He made the payment for the back taxes on November 21st.

He has a history of problems filing with the IRS. He finally filed in 1996 for his household employees Social Security taxes for the years 1993 to 1995, miscalculated his employees Medicare taxes in 1998, and did not file forms for his employees during 2003 and 2004 until he received notices from IRS and Social Security. During the confirmation hearings Senators went through 30 pages of reports that documented his tax errors. Errors included deducting summer camp fees as child care expenses during 2001, 2004, and 2006, improper business deductions, deductions for charitable contributions on ineligible items, and citing his personal utility expenses as deductions. Geithner said these mistakes were unintentional as he used Turbo Tax to complete his tax filings. When questioned about why he waited until November 2008 to pay back taxes he replied, "I did not believe I was avoiding my liability…would never put myself in the position where I was deliberately not meeting my obligation as a taxpayer". Congress approved his appointment as Secretary of the Treasury.

In his new position he was in charge of TARP that had been approved by Congress in October. He had worked with Bernanke and Paulson to determine how the first $350 billion would be distributed and determining which banks would be rescued and which would not. During the confirmation hearings Geithner said his plan was to reform TARP to protect taxpayers and to be more transparent. In February he announced that the remaining $350 billion should be distributed as follows; $50 billion for mortgage loans, $100 billion to guarantee assets and bank securities, $100 billion to purchase distraught assets, and $100 billion for capital injections to banks. He also stated he was going to test banks (stress test) for stability and set up a public/private investment firm with a projected cost of $500 billion to $1 trillion. Then he planned to set up a consumer and business lending institution with an estimated cost of another $1 trillion. Geithner stated a foreclosure prevention plan needed to be implemented and small business and community lending initiatives needed to be created.

All of this spending occurred while the $878 billion stimulus bill, officially called America Recovery and Reinvestment Act, was being passed. The stimulus bill promised to save or create 3 to 4 million jobs. The money was for shovel ready infrastructure projects, a smart electric grid, green energy projects, local governments, etc. Keith Schneider in the 'Apollo News Service' from the Apollo Alliance wrote the policy in the Stimulus Bill was inspired by their proposals in what he called The New Apollo Program and the Apollo Economic Recovery Act. He quoted Phil Angelides, a former chairman and treasurer from Apollo Alliance, "The recovery bill represents the focused work of labor, business, environmental and social justice organizations who developed a clear strategy about where the nation needed to go, and worked together to achieve it". The Apollo Alliance membership includes several of Obama's friends, including radicals Van Jones and Jeff Jones. Obviously this Stimulus Bill was in the works for a long time just waiting for the opportunity to spring it on the public. Remember it was Rahm Emanuel that said, "Never let a crisis go to waste".

The bank's stress test results were to be released in May, but it didn't need as much fanfare as it got. When Geithner announced the stress tests the Dow Jones dropped 1,700 points. So then he said that none of the 19 banks being tested would be allowed to fail, as they were "too big to fail". The results showed that the banks had enough capital to continue operating, but Geithner decided that 10 of the banks could use extra funds. Smaller and community banks closed at record levels and now 5 banks control 50% of the banking system. From January 2008 to June 3, 2011 a total of 239 banks were closed by FDIC. By comparison, only 27 banks failed from January 2000 to December 2007. Geithner spent billions of tax payer money to save his favorite banks, the banking industry has been centralized, and many community banks are gone.

Using TARP funding the Home Affordable Modification Program (HAMP) was created in March 2009. HAMP was expected to help up to 4 million homeowners to prevent foreclosures with loan modifications. Modifications could lower interest rates, lower payments with the loan being extended for a longer time frame, or restructuring the loan to reduce payments with a balloon payment at the end. Yet just over 630,000 people were able to get permanent modifications through HAMP, but over 2 million people got loan modifications through banks outside of HAMP guidelines. HAMP was rife with problems, people got approved but their payments never got credited so they got further foreclosure notices. People complained that paperwork was not completed correctly, timely, or got lost. HAMP did not help many homeowners, but it did help the large banks. The program allowed continued payments to the banks delaying foreclosures which are costly to the banks and allowed accounting entries to show profits and/or income. Geithner calls HAMP a success.

One of Geithner's first assignments was to go after tax cheats. He was to "crack down" on companies which used tax loopholes to avoid paying taxes on foreign earnings. Geithner took this assignment seriously saying that his personal experience (not paying taxes while employed at IMF?) would allow him to "slip in unnoticed to spy on evildoers". Actually he could stay closer to home to find tax cheats. Charlie Rangle paid $10,000 in back taxes, failed to report assets, and failed to report rental income. Kathleen Sebelius owed $7,000 in back taxes, Sen. Al Franken owed $70,000 in back taxes, and Sen. Claire McCaskell owed $287,000 in back taxes. Then there is Tom Daschle who withdrew his nomination for a Cabinet position because he owed $100,000. He actually said in 1998, "Make no mistake, tax cheaters cheat us all, and the IRS should enforce our laws to the letter". In 2008 it was determined that 447 employees from the House and 231 employees at the Senate did not pay their taxes. The employees from the House owed over $5.8 million in back taxes and the employees from the Senate owed over $2.46 million. Did you know that in early 2010 a bill was put forth to make government employees pay back taxes or lose their jobs? Did you know that the Chair of the House Oversight and Government Reform subcommittee said this legislation would cause federal employees to lose their jobs and was against the bill? This bill did not pass.

During the confirmation hearings Geithner said the Obama administration would use all diplomatic tools available to convince countries like China to stop manipulating their money which caused an unfair export balance with that country. China sent a message that they "noted" Geithner's speech. They were not happy as they had stopped devaluating their money when the economic crisis began. On June 1st 2009 he was at Peking University to give a speech to the students. Geithner was in China to assure them that the value of their holding of U.S. bonds would not be devalued because of our country's deficit. A student asked, "How safe are Chinese investments in the United States debt". Geithner replied, "Very safe". The students laughed.

At a Senate Hearing in February 2011 he was questioned about Obama's proposed budget that would increase interest payments from $187 billion to $844 billion. He responded, "Senator, absolutely, it is excessively high interest burden, it's unsustainable." "You're absolutely right that with the president's plan, even if Congress were to enact it and even if Congress were to hold to it and reduce those deficits to three percent of GDP over the next five years, we would still be left with a very large interest burden and unsustainable obligations over time".

Geithner testified before the Senate Foreign Relations Committee on March 3, 2011. He predicted the United States dollar would remain the world reserve currency. On March 17th it was reported that in March 2009 both China and Russia wanted the IMF to issue a "super-sovereign reserve currency" to replace the dollar. This would make the IMF the world's central bank. The IMF does have its own currency, called the SDR, but it was not convertible. In September the SDR was made convertible with a plan to use it as the world's reserve currency. IMF stated they plan to start printing trillions of the SDRs. The report mentioned that in March 2009 Geithner said Washington was "quite open" to the gradual development of a global reserve currency as proposed by the Chinese. Did Geithner tell the truth in March 2009 or March 2011?

On May 9th Geithner spoke at the U.S.-China Strategic and Economic Dialogue and said, "The reforms we must both pursue to meet these very different challenges is to lay the foundation for a new growth model…with a more market based economy, and a more sophisticated financial system. And we each recognize that our ability to work together is important to the overall health and stability of the global economy. On June 3rd it was reported the China had dropped 97% of their holdings in United States Treasury bills. It also decreased it ownership of short term government securities to

$5.7 billion in March 2011 from $210 billion in May 2009. This is important because Treasury bills have a lower interest rate than long term bonds. As of March 2011we owed China $1.7 trillion in short term Treasury bills that must be paid before the end of March 2012. If debt is not paid then they can be turned into longer term bonds, with higher interest rates, if we can find a buyer to purchase them.

On May 25, 2011 he gave an interview predicting the economy will face another crisis after it recovers from the recession. However, he believes the future economic crisis will be milder than the one that ended in 2009.

Geithner chairs the Committee on Payments and Settlement Systems of the Bank for International Settlement at the G-10, and is a member of both the Council on Foreign Relations and the Group of Thirty. His wife Carole Sonnefeld has been active with the Soros funded group Common Cause.

LAWRENCE "LARRY" SUMMERS became the Director of the National Economic Council in January 2009. He had been employed at Harvard University and worked many years at the Treasury Department. In 1982 Summers worked for a year at the Council of Economic Advisors (CEA). The CEA is an agency in the executive office of the President and its function is to provide advice on domestic and international economic policy.

He became a tenured professor of economics at Harvard University when he left CEA. After working on the 1988 Dukakis for President he was hired by the country Lithuania in 1990 to advise them on their new economy. In March 1990 Lithuania declared independence from Soviet rule and in February 90% voted for independence and banned the communist party. Because of severe economic hardships, soaring unemployment and inflation, the communist party was voted back in 1992. But now the country has begun to improve as the ruling party broke away from a central planned economy to a free market. I was unable to find much of the advice Summers gave Lithuania, only that the economy got so bad that the suicide rate rose dramatically. The Summers plan demanded that Lithuanians needed to endure an austerity period of at least 10 years in which they should accept a lower standard of living. He advised they should advertize globally that they have an educated work force with high standards that were willing to provide labor for less than those in South Korea were being paid.

In 1991 Summers went to work at the World Bank as their Chief Economist and held the position as vice president of Development Economics. In December 1991 the Soviet Union broke up and the World Bank came to help. The World Bank and the International Monetary Fund (IMF) are two separate organizations, both created by John Maynard Keynes. They have similar functions to help developing countries and often work together. The Keynesian economics policy of central planning, plus government intervention and manipulation, is named after Keynes.

The Russian Privatization Plan was created by Harvard Professor, and Summers friend, Andrei Schleifer with a group of other Harvard professors and graduates called the Harvard Institute for International Development (HIID). Schleifer worked closely with Harvard graduate Jonathan Hay. Hay became the senior legal advisor and had control and power over policies and contractors. HIID was also comprised of radical liberal reformers who were being trained to take leadership positions in the new government. The USAHIID/ Harvard program received funding from Soros' Open Society Institute. They worked with the World Bank under the pretext of converting the country to a market oriented economy. Their experiment lead the country into a deep recession, unemployment went from 2% to 40%, privatized government property went to favored persons, and Russia assets were plundered. Russia's GDP dropped 50% and hyperinflation went up 2,500%. On top of this Hay set up a mutual fund, using USAID funds, called Pallad Asset Management for his girlfriend Elizabeth Hebert in Russia. Hebert, Hay, and Schleifer, using tax funding, started a private consulting firm. The first client was Schleifer's wife Nancy Zimmerman. Zimmerman operated a hedge fund, trading in Russian bonds out of a HIID office. The United States government finally sued stating the Russian government reform operation was rife with conflicts of interest. Results; Schleifer was fined $2 million and Harvard fined $26.5 million.

Summers said he was most proud of his work at World Bank for promoting education for girls and starting an annual health report. What he is most remembered for is his memo advocating putting toxic waste in low income countries. He stated that there are under populated countries in Africa which are under polluted. His reasoning was there would be less lost revenue in those countries for illness and in mortality costs in the low income countries. And yes, the Russian market economy collapsed in 1998.

Summers left the World Bank in 1993 and went to work at the Treasury Department where he quickly rose up the ladder. Started as the Undersecretary, in 1995 he became the Deputy Secretary, and was confirmed in 1999 as

Treasury Secretary. Ken Lay from Enron sent a congratulations letter upon his confirmation addressed to "Dear Larry". Summers responded, "I'll keep my eye on power deregulation and energy market infrastructure issues". He did. Summers refuted the idea that companies like Enron were manipulating the energy market that was gouging customers and he fought against regulations. Summers stated the 1990's was the time that "important steps" occurred to deregulate sections of the economy in financial services. He was one of the persons who were responsible for repealing the Glass-Steagall Act. The repeal allowed banks to make risky investments in security markets that had previously been illegal. Summers was one of the persons responsible for blocked regulations in the derivative market. His actions were opposed by Brooksly Born, the Chair of the Commodities Futures Trading Commission. Summers called her and accused her of risking a financial meltdown because she was proposing more transparency in the derivative market.

In 2001 Summers became the president of Harvard University and resigned in 2006 prior to a second no confidence vote. He angered many professors with his management style and arrogance. His comment suggesting that women did not succeed in science and math might be due to "innate" differences from men angered many professors. Summers' decisions to change Harvard culture, changing the curriculum, and designing a new campus angered others. After hearing from Harvard's governing corporation and friends questioning is ability to lead, he resigned. The university did negotiate with Summers to have a professorship which allows him to teach in any department. As president at Harvard he managed to change their investment and endowment strategy. He wanted to comingle operating cash with endowment funds to invest in risky stocks, bonds, hedge funds and in the private equity market. He wanted to invest 100% of their funds in these markets, but agreed to 80%, against the advice of the university's financial officials. The result was Harvard lost large amounts of money including $1.8 billion of their operating cash. Harvard lost 27% of the $37 billion endowment fund, paid $500 million to get out of the interest rate swap deals, issued $1.5 billion in bonds to obtain needed cash, and had major budget cuts and layoffs.

In October 2006 Summers joined D.E. Shaw, a hedge fund management firm, and left in 2008 when he was appointed as Assistant to the President for Economic Policy and the Director of Economic Council. He was a spokesperson for the firm and did private consultations for overseas investors. While he was at Shaw he worked 100 days and was paid $5.2 million.

During 2008 Summers had 40 speaking engagements and was paid $2.7 million, many paid for by Wall Street firms that were in financial trouble. Many of these speaking engagements occurred while Summers was advising Obama about the global financial crisis. Obama was using hedge funds to purchase troubled assets from banks and other financial firms.

In his new position at the White House he is a key economic decision maker. Paul Volcker was at odds with Summers. When Volcker criticized Summers for not getting advice from other economists Summers stopped inviting Volcker to White House meetings. Other economists wanted more stimulus funds to be spent on infrastructure which Summers dismissed wanting the bailed out companies to get tax cuts. He was criticized for accepting perks from companies that received stimulus money and asked Senator Chris Dodd to remove the cap on executive wages for those firms. Summers resigned from his position at the end of 2010 to return to Harvard where he can teach students his theories and ideas about the economy that don't seem to work. Summers has been on the board of the Brookings Institution, a member of the Council on Foreign Relations, the Trilateral Commission, and the Bretton Woods Committee.

CHRISTINA ROMER was named to chair the Council of Economic Advisors. She and her husband, David, are professors of macroeconomics (New Keynesian economics) at the University of California/Berkeley. He writes textbooks on the subject and they both research the subject, often together. Christina has done extensive research of economics and the cause of the Great Depression. Her research brought her to the conclusion that interest rates are a major cause of fluctuations in the economy. Low interest rates, she maintains, encourage companies to invest in growing their business and hiring more employees, which in turn provide more tax dollars. The increase of employees creates more spending and low interest rates encourage more spending, the building of more homes, and the creation of more jobs. Recession, she determined, was the result of high interest rates. She came to the conclusion that unemployment benefits and more social programs reduces incentives for people to find employment. She also found that each 1% increase in taxes lowers the GDP by 3%.

Romer embraces Keynesian economics, she was an assistant professor to Summers, and endorsed the $878 billion stimulus. She co-authored the recovery plan from the 2008 recession and the jobs creation policy. One of her main objectives was to reduce the unemployment rate that was at 7.7%

in January 2009 and she believed the stimulus would keep the unemployment under 8%. She argued that without the stimulus the unemployment rate would go over 9%. Some of her ideas were at odds with others at the White House. She agreed with Summers that the administration needed to focus on reducing the unemployment rate and not concentrate on the deficit. Peter Orszag, the Budget Director, agreed with Geithner as the two argued the administration needed to reduce spending to be more in line with tax revenue. They believed a reduced deficit would bring about long term economic growth. They thought the stimulus would only bring about a short recovery, while Romer believed the stimulus was the medicine needed to fix the economy long term. Obama signed a $13 billion jobs bill that was much less than Romer wanted.

When Romer left the administration in September 2009 the unemployment rate was at 9.5%. The Romers left Washington D.C. returning to University of California/Berkeley to continue teaching New Keynesian economics. Romer gave an interview in May 2011 and shared her ideas about the economy. She said she would encourage a $50 billion stimulus bill for infrastructure and fund more money to education and research. Another idea she has is to reduce payroll taxes for both employees and employers, as reduced costs to employers encourages more hiring. She was disappointed that the Quantitative Easing ended as she believed it should have continued until it got the desired result. Even though she believes in additional stimulus spending she says the deficit must be reduced. She explained it this way, "We should be rearranging spending at the same time we're dialing down".

AUSTAN GOOLSBEE replaced Romer as chair of the Council of Economic Advisors. He has been part of the Advisors since he took a leave of absence as a professor at the University of Chicago in 2009. He is a professor of economics and has done research on the internet, government policy, taxes and on behavioral economics. Goolsbee is the former host of History's Business on the History Channel and has been on the Daily Show and the Colbert Report.

Goolsbee has some interesting ideas. He has suggested that employers automatically enroll employees into a 401k plan, which the employee must de-enroll to opt out. He thinks the IRS should sent out completed IRS forms to persons that claim standard deductions so taxpayers only need to sign, date, and return. Goolsbee believes in something called Creative Job Destruction. This is the idea that if a job is shipped overseas a better job will appear because of technology and innovation. He advocates for increased investment in education because persons with degrees earn more money than those that don't. His studies found that those who pursue higher degrees earn even higher income, thus if everyone had a degree incomes would be higher for everyone. Lastly, he has stated that 60% to 70% of people face no impact from international competition in their jobs. Goolsbee is a fan of Keynesian economics and helped write the $878 billion Stimulus plan.

On June 6th Goolsbee announced his resignation and his return to teaching at the University of Chicago. As he left he said the economy is improving citing the creation of approximately 140,000 jobs each month. Unfortunately, there needs to be 250,000 new jobs each month to stay even with people losing employment and others entering the job market. He was pleased the unemployment rate was only 9.1%, as the rate was projected to be 9.3%. So Austan Goolsbee will join other economists and return to teaching to train our youth in his vision of economics.

His wife Robin Winters is a consultant at McKinsey and Company. McKinsey and Company announced on April 11, 2011 that the Department of Health and Human Services created a new medical group called Accountable Care Organizations, or ACOs. ACOs is a new way of financing and delivering Medicare with a "Shared Savings Program" set up much like HMOs. Medical providers will be able keep 50% to 60% of the money they save in medical costs for the first two years. It is expected that giving providers monetary rewards will encourage innovation and keep costs down. I'm sure that these monetary rewards will not encourage medical providers to keep costs down by providing less service especially since no medical provider would sacrifice services to keep money in one's wallet. Medicare beneficiaries won't actively enroll in ACOs, but will be assigned to the program. The providers must inform their patients when they have been assigned to ACO and that claims will be documented to determine if the provider will profit from them. Medicare patients will have the ability to opt out of the program (at least in the beginning). The McKinsey report states that ACOs might present some potential legal and tax complications, but several federal agencies have indicated they would "relax certain antitrust regulations for ACOs".

PETER ORTZAG was named the Director at the Office of Management and Budget. He was not new to the White House as he was the Senior Advisor at the Council of Economic Advisors and Special Assistant for Economic

Policy in the Clinton Administration. After he left the White House, in 2000, he became a columnist at 'Bloomburg View' and the 'New York Times'. He is also a senior fellow at the Council on Foreign Relations and was a consultant at McKinsey and Company. At the Brookings Institution he co-founded the Hamilton Project with a goal of determining how to grow the economy and ensure that all persons are "profitable". The Hamilton Project states everyone can obtain prosperity by encouraging economic growth. First, it must be determined what areas of the economy cause growth and secondly public investment (taxes) must be put into these areas. The third statement says these goals are "realistic", but "requires government and citizens to adhere to Hamilton's recommendations". Orszag also co-authored a publication at Brookings titled 'Saving Social Security'. The plan is simple, first taxes are increased gradually and benefits gradually reduced over the next 75 years. Persons who are determined to be able to pay more will pay more.

Obama announced Orszag's job was to eliminate jobs and programs which are not needed and to craft an effective budget. Orszag immediately advocated for both the Stimulus Bill and the Health Care Reform Bill. There appears that not everyone agreed with each other when discussing budgets. Orszag wanted the Bush tax cuts to remain at least temporarily, which angered Rahm Emanuel, and wanted to lower the budget deficit. Orszag had been accused of leaking information discussed at private meetings.

Peter Orszag left the White House in July in 2010. He got a job at Citibank as the vice chairman of Global Banking earning between $2 and $3 million each year. Citibank had received a bailout of $45 billion. Citibank is where Clinton's Treasury Secretary, Robert Rubin, found employment after he left the White House.

JACOB LEW replaced Orszag to lead the Office of Management and Budget. How ironic is it that Orszag left the White House to work at Citibank and Lew left Citibank to work at the White House. Lew worked in the Clinton Administration from 1993 until 2001. First he was the Special Assistant to the President where he crafted AmeriCorps as a national service initiative and helped design the unsuccessful health care reform called "Hillarycare". He then joined the Office of Management and Budget becoming the Director in 1998.

After leaving the White House Lew found employment at New York University as a professor and Executive Vice President for Operations. In 2006 he joined Citibank, first as the Chief Operating Officer of Citi Global Wealth Management, and then in 2008 directing Citi Alternative Investments (CAI). CAI invested primarily in hedge funds and private equity. Hedge funds are unregulated risky speculative investments that are not sold to the public; normally equities, bonds and commodities. Private equity companies are not traded on the market but purchased directly. Often the companies are distressed with large debt, which the purchaser plans to improve the prospects of the firm and eventually sell at a profit. Just before Lew left Citibank he received a bonus of $950,000, right after Citibank received their $45 billion bailout.

Lew doesn't believe deregulation caused the financial crisis against the prevailing view of the Obama administration that wants to increase regulations. Perhaps Lew's perspective on regulations is being heard. Obama announced in January 2011 that he signed an executive order asking the federal government to do a review of existing regulations "that stifle job creation". However the executive order exempts some agencies such as the Securities and Exchange Commission, the Federal Communications Commission and the Federal Reserve. Obama's announcement came days after the House Oversight and Government Reform Committee issued a report stating 43 new business regulations resulted in business costs of over $28 billion and the loss of thousands of jobs.

In February Lew testified before the House Budget Committee regarding the Obama proposed 2012 budget as the debt of the United Stated was growing to 100% of its Gross Domestic Product (GDP). Lew characterized the budget as a down payment towards the growing debt and acknowledged the proposed budget will not reduce the deficit in either the short or middle term. The budget, Lew explained, will reduce the deficit $1 trillion reduction in 10 years. This would be accomplished by implementing a non-security spending freeze for 5 years and reduced spending at the Pentagon by $78 billion, also for 5 years. The proposal includes the creation of an Alternative Minimum Tax (ATM) which limits tax deductions from persons in the high tax bracket. He emphasized there must be continued investments (taxes) in education, innovation ("visionary goals of clean energy"), clean energy, and infrastructure. There is also a provision to eliminate tax breaks to oil, gas and coal companies. Lew is adamant that the debt ceiling must be raised as the Republicans are demanding that any increase of the debt ceiling must be met with equal spending reductions.

Lew wrote an article in February about Social Security. He claims Social

Security is self financing, explaining that when more taxes are collected than needed they are put into a trust fund. The trust fund is converted to Treasury bonds, which are backed by the United States government, and the fund has a surplus that is growing. He continued to state the fund has enough resources to continue for the next 25 years even though fewer taxes were collected in 2010 than were paid out.

These are the people and their economic philosophy that are developing the economic policy. They share many of the same Keynesian economic policies that have not worked in the past in many countries.

I am not an economist, however, I think to grow jobs our country needs more manufacturing. We need to make stuff to increase our GDP. If we buy the stuff we make not only will that produce revenue but increase jobs. Persons who make stuff want to make good stuff so that they will have repeat customers and referrals from happy customers. People who make bad stuff will go out of business because they will have no customers. It was the manufacturing plants that saved us in World War II after Pearl Harbor because they quickly were able to produce tanks, jeeps, and other equipment needed to win the war. Now we have empty buildings that used to make stuff, and we have an enemy that has declared they want to destroy us. How will we be able to manufacture, quickly, equipment we may need in the future with only a service industry? Government employees need to stop making regulations, and time consuming paperwork, so industry will grow here. That is my unscientific opinion.

Judge me by the people who surround me.

CHAPTER 28

★ ★ ★ ★ ★

Misc. Friends

I spent time researching those persons at the White House who will affect health care as it is a concern to many, many of which have come to believe health insurance is a right. They believe it is a right that should be paid by the government. Others believe the government should provide a safety net and others believe health insurance is a product that that should be purchased to guard against future expenses, just like people purchase life insurance, home insurance and car insurance. All insurance is purchased by deciding the cost of insurance versus the amount one wants to insure. That is why I spent so much reviewing the ideology of those that will influence what type of coverage, under universal care, will be allotted to us.

The next people I researched were those that Obama chose to protect our country against aggressors that want to do harm to our people and our country. Will they protect our borders and our laws or do they have another agenda? Will they pursue our enemies and terrorists? Maintaining our national security must be the number one priority for the President. Did he select persons who are dedicated to that cause?

Finally I pursued the background of those chosen to protect our country's financial security. The majority believed in Keynesian economics, the idea that everyone should share equally without everyone contributing equally. They express the idea that it is fair that everyone have a house whether they worked and saved for their home or they didn't. I wonder how many people realize that people receiving government aid get free cell phones. Look at your next telephone bill; the universal connectivity fee is a tax that pays for others to have free phones. What is the incentive to work and save if those who don't are given, free to them, not only necessities but luxuries? There will always be the elites who are exempt from sharing. Do we want our country controlled with Keynesian policies or do we want our country to hold to the idea of Capitalism, where persons work to provide for themselves both necessities and luxuries?

Now I will examine other friends and persons Obama has chosen to associate with or put in office that affect us. Some names are regularly in the news and others are not.

ERIC HOLDER was sworn into the office of Attorney General, head of the Department of Justice (DOJ), on December 1, 2008. The DOJ is responsible for enforcing the law and administering justice. It is divided into nine divisions. The DOJ oversees several agencies including the FBI, U.S. Marshall Service, BATF, Bureau of Prisons, Drug Enforcement and the Office of the Inspector General. In 2010 DOJ had 111,993 employees and a budget of $27.7 billion; almost half for law enforcement.

While attending Columbia University, majoring in American history, he felt a need to help youngsters that were less fortunate than him and joined Caring Black Men. This organization helps and mentors minority youth and he volunteered his time taking children on trips in the city. It was at a Caring Black Men fund raiser where he met his wife Sharon Malone. After graduating from Columbia University he joined the Justice Department in the Public Integrity Section where he worked from 1976 until 1988. The Public Integrity Section, part of the Criminal Division, combats political corruption at all levels of government for elected and appointed officials. President Reagan nominated him for the position of Associate Judge of the Supreme Court in the District of Columbia, a position he held until 1993. In that position he heard cases from murder to school truancy and the number of black defendants troubled him. Holder told the Washington Post, "if you are a person who's concerned about the black community to see what ought to be the future standing before you charged with some sort of criminal offense". He continued, "Racism is alive and well in this country, but that doesn't excuse or justify the acts of the people who come before you".

In 1993 Bill Clinton chose Holder to be the U.S. Attorney for the District of Columbia. In this position he created the Domestic Violence Unit, supported strict enforcement of hate crimes, and revitalized the Victim/ Witness Assistance Program. He also developed Operation Crossfire a program to get guns away from criminals. Then in 1997 Clinton nominated him as Deputy Attorney General working under Janet Reno. During the confirmation hearing he gave this opinion regarding the death penalty, "I am not a proponent of the death penalty, but I will enforce to the law as this Congress gives to us.". Holder was the first person from the DOJ to write a legal brief that authorized the CIA to send alleged terrorists to Egypt for interrogation and torture. This process called extraordinary rendition (sending person to another country for interrogation) is sometimes called "torture by proxy". In 1995 the CIA kidnapped a member of a terrorist organization in Croatia and flew him to the United States. Holder concerned there were legal problems holding him here spoke to Bill Clinton. Holder made the arrangements to have the man flown to Egypt where he was put in a crate, tortured and executed by the Egyptian authorities. In 1998 he allowed two members of a terrorist group captured in Albania to be sent to Egypt to be tortured and executed. Torture in Egypt is severe. Typically prisoners hang from all four limbs and electric nodules are placed on their nipples, genitals and feet. Egypt was paid by the CIA to perform their torture program.

Clinton pardoned or commuted 456 persons while he was in office, the most ever. On his last day in office he pardoned or commuted 140, there were so many that it was referred to as Pardongate. Holder was involved the Clinton extending clemency to 16 members of the terrorist groups Armed Forces of Puerto Rican National Liberation (FALN) and Popular Boricua Army often referred to as the Macheteros. These groups were pushing for nationalization against the American colonists. To get their message out they used violence. FALN was responsible for 72 bombings and 40 incendiary attacks in the United States resulting in 5 deaths, 83 injuries and over $3 million in property damage. The Macheteros in Puerto Rico attacked the military and the police causing the death of a Puerto Rican police officer and several U.S. servicemen. They infiltrated the Puerto Rican Air National Guard and were able to blow up 11 airplanes and inflicted over $45 million in damages. They also robbed a Wells Fargo armored car in Connecticut. Both of these organizations were organized by Fidel Castro's secret police. After the men were captured and imprisoned, the reign of terror ended in Puerto Rico and in the United States, with the exception of a few random acts. The original request for a pardon was completed in 1996, but the DOJ declined. In 1999 Holder requested a new set of paperwork be made with DOJ approval, but again they resisted. So Holder told them to rewrite the pardon application with a neutral "options memo" which allows the President to issue a commutation without doing so against the DOJ's wishes. On August 11, 1999 Bill Clinton granted clemency to the terrorists and they never requested the commutation, nor did they renounce the violence. They were released against the advice of the FBI, U.S. Attorney Office and members of the families that were killed. Even Congress was outraged voting to condemn the commutation in the Senate 95 to 2 and the House 311 to 11.

Holder was instrumental in determining the Clinton pardons at the end of his term. One of the controversial pardons was for Marc Rich who was indicted in 1983 on 65 counts of defrauding the IRS, mail fraud, tax evasion, racketeering, defrauding the Treasury, and trading with the enemy in an oil deal with Iran while that country held American hostages. He fled with his partner, Pincus Green, to Switzerland and was known to spend the next 17 years traveling in France, England, and Finland avoiding arrest. Marc Rich hired attorney Jack Quinn, a former Clinton White House counsel, to take his case. When Holder was contacted regarding the pardon he advised Quinn to "go straight to" the White House and the "timing was good". This is not normal procedure as pardon applications are supposed to be vetted by the DOJ. One month before Clinton's term was to expire; Quinn took the pardon papers to the White House. On Clinton's last day in office he signed the pardon for Rich and Green. It probably didn't hurt that Denise Rich, Rich's ex-wife, donated over $1 million to Democratic causes including Clinton's Presidential Library and Hillary's senate race.

On the last day, with Holder's help, Clinton commuted the sentences of two Weather Underground members, Susan Rosenberg and Linda Evans. Both were in prison for charges including the bombing of the Capitol, the Brinks robbery where two officers and a security guard died, possession of 740 pounds of explosives, bombing the Naval War College, using fake I.D. to purchase weapons, bombing the Navy Yard computer Center, bombing an Israeli aircraft company, bombing the FBI, and other offenses. Clinton also pardoned Susan McDougal from the Watergate scandal, his half brother Roger Clinton on drug charges, and former U.S. Representative Melvin Reynolds. Reynolds was in prison convicted on charges of sexual assault and sex abuse of a 16 year old campaign volunteer, solicitation of child pornography, and 15 counts of bank fraud. He ran for office again after the pardon but lost to Jessie Jackson Jr. Another former Representative from Illinois who was pardoned that day was Dan Rostenkowski who was convicted on mail fraud after a two year investigation that Eric Holder led. Other noted cases were Dorothy Rivers who plead guilty of stealing $1.2 million from Rainbow/Push, Samuel Morison, an intelligence professional convicted of espionage and theft of government property, and former CIA Director John Deutch involved in a security scandal.

After the Clinton administration ended Holder worked at the international law firm Covington and Burling. The firm advises multinational companies and is noted for its pro bono work. The pro bono work is in the areas of civil rights, gay rights, police misconduct and environmental law. Their largest pro bono case in 2007 was representing detainees from Guantanamo Bay spending 3,022 hours on litigation that year. As Attorney General he has not recused himself of matters relating to Guantanamo as he said he didn't perform any legal work on that matter. He did recuse himself from matters relating to the Swiss bank USB AG as he did represent that company. USB AG was sued by the United States for conspiracy in U.S. tax fraud.

In 2004 Holder spoke at the American Constitution Society about his ideas. He said "This nation must be convinced that it is a progressive future that holds the greatest promise for equality and the continuation of those policies that serve to support the greatness of our people". On conservatives he stated, "The hallmarks of the conservative agenda include social division, mindless tax cutting and a defense posture that does not really make us safer". He returned in 2008 to speak about his opinions of President Bush, "our needless, abusive, and unlawful practices in the war on terror have diminished our standing in the world community". Holder continued, "I never thought I would see the day when a Justice Department would claim that only the most extreme infliction of pain and physical abuse constitutes torture, and that acts that are merely cruel, inhuman, and degrading are consistent with U.S. law and policy. He also advocated for the closing of Guantanamo Bay. I think he must have forgotten his role in the Clinton administration when he determined it was legal to send suspected terrorists to Egypt for torture that ended in death.

Before attaining the position of Attorney General Holder was an advisor during the Obama campaign and helped to vet appointees to the new administration. In January, before Obama took office, the DOJ filed a lawsuit against the New Black Panther Party for violating the 1965 Voting Rights Act. Members of the New Black Panther Party were at a Philadelphia polling station dressed in paramilitary uniform, one had a nightstick, shouting racial slurs and intimidating white voters. One man yelled, "You are about to be ruled by the Black man, cracker". The incident was videotaped and broadcast on national television. A former civil rights attorney stated it "was the most blatant form of voter intimidation I've ever seen". One of the defendants, King Samir Shabazz, said the activity was part of a nationwide effort. In May the DOJ dropped the case for lack of evidence. Shabazz was ordered to never brandish a weapon at another polling place (in Philadelphia) in the future and nobody received jail time as all other claims were dismissed. Holder said of the incident, "To compare what people enduring in the South in the '60's...to compare what people subjected to that with what happened in Philadelphia...I think does a great disservice to people who put their lives on the line for 'my' people". Later the Civil Rights Commission also dropped the case because of lack of evidence. If they missed the video on television they could have watched it on YouTube. One career employee and attorney at the Voting Rights Section of DOJ resigned because not only did the department dismiss the case, but refused to let him testify at the Civil Rights Commission. He was told to ignore the subpoena he received from the Commission regarding the New Black Panther Party case. It was frustrating because not only was dismissing the case wrong, but the case was won because the defendants refused to cooperate and did not show for the hearing. Just before sentencing the DOJ dropped the case. As for evidence Adams said, "It doesn't get any easier than this. If this doesn't constitute voter intimidation, nothing will". He also said, "We abetted wrong doing and abandoned law abiding citizens".

On April 1, 2009 Holder dismissed 7 felony charges of lying on financial disclosure forms that Senator Ted Stevens had been found guilty of. The dismissal vacated the conviction and this was not an April's Fools day joke.

The next controversial thing Holder did was announce to New York City, in November 2009, that he decided to hold a civil trial of Khalid Sheik Mohammed and four other terrorists in their city. Mohammed had already admitted his guilt in coordinating or planning the 1993 World Trade Center, in 1995 a failed plot to bomb 12 airplanes in flight and to kill Pope John Paul II, the failed Millennium Plot in 2000, the failed shoe bomb plot on Flight 63 in 2001, the 2002 nightclub bombing in Bali, the 2002 failed plot to attack the IS Bank tower in L.A., the death of journalist Daniel Pearl, and of course the attacks on America on September 11, 2001. Holder did not inform Congress of his decision, apparently believing the Congressional branch of government didn't need to be informed. Holder maintained the civil court system would be the best place to hold the trial, not military tribunals. A civil trial would ban any evidence obtained under duress or coercion and these defendants had endured enhanced interrogation. However Holder insisted there was enough untainted evidence to deliver a guilty verdict and expected a death sentence. A civil trial would also require that a Miranda warning would have been issued upon the time of arrest as a criminal and these individuals were captured as enemies at war. These individuals were detained at Guantanamo Bay in Cuba and would have to be transported into the United States.

Of course not everybody agreed with Holder's decision. The NYC Mayor, Police Commissioner, and other authorities stated that the cost of the trial and security would be too expensive. Senator Schumer disagreed with the decision and decided he did not want the trial anywhere in the State of New York. Surrounding States did not want the terrorists brought there for trial either. Congress, including many Democrats, voiced its displeasure with the decision. Family members of those that died voiced opposition as did many people in the United States that these terrorists would be treated as common criminals instead of enemies of war. David Beamer, father of Todd Beamer on Flight 93 said, "Our enemies must be thrilled, we are willingly handing them an opportunity to inflict economic harm in New York City, keep their cause in the headlines, gather new intelligence, create new terror strategies, stimulate recruiting, celebrate new found rights, and foist a fresh round of pain and suffering upon their victims".

Holder continued to argue for a civil trial and Obama called the opposition a "classic jam job". Supporters of his decision, in the legal profession, that believed the Obama administration policies were too close to the Bush policies. They wanted Holder to allow lawsuits by persons who had been subjected to extraordinary rendition. They probably did not know that the reason Holder did not was because he would have to admit he was the person who determined that process was legal. Finally, in April 2011, Holder announced the plan to hold these terrorist's trial in the United States in a civil trial has been reversed and will be held as a military tribunal. The decision came soon after Obama lifted a freeze on new military trials. Holder was obviously not happy with the decision, stating his hands 'were tied' by "unwise and narrow restrictions".

On April 23, 2010 Arizona Governor Jan Brewer signed into law a 10 page bill which allowed police to verify residency for individuals suspected of being in the country illegally. On April 30th the law was amended that the individual had to be in the act of committing a crime or suspected of a crime before residency verification was requested. The bill came as a result of Arizona being the home of 460,000 illegal aliens with increased violence, crime, and murder. Holder held a press conference on April 27th stating the DOJ may bring suit regarding Arizona's law saying that it might be subject to abuse, siphon federal funding, and may replace federal law. He went on talk shows to express his concerns, demonstrations and boycotts against Arizona began, but national polling found that 60% to 70% of American citizens and Arizonans favored the law. Holder testified at a House Judiciary Committee hearing on May 14th stating the Arizona law might lead to racial profiling. Then he admitted he had not read the law but had glanced at it and planned to read it before deciding if it was constitutional. He even said that he came to his opinions from newspapers and television reports. Holder did sue Arizona and and the Supreme Court made the decsision on 6/25/2012 that Arizona could check for status. However they stated it was the Federal government function to enforce the law. On that same day the Obama administration announced they will not help Arizona arrest illegal aliens unless they meet the federal guidelines. The administration also stated that they are rescinding previous agreements with Arizona officiers to enforce immigration laws.

On February 23, 2011 Holder officially announced the DOJ would no longer defend the Defense of Marriage Act (DOMA). He stated Obama read his recommendation and has agreed that DOMA fails to meet the standard of non-discrimination toward sexual orientation and is therefore unconstitutional. Holder said that since both agreed with the interpretation Obama ordered the DOJ not to defend the statute.

The investigation of DOJ and BATF program "Fast and Furious" also called "Gun Walker" started in 2011 by Rep. Issa and the House Oversight and Government Reform Committee. The story began early in 2009 when Holder and Hillary Clinton made efforts to enact new gun laws by stating 90% of rifles used by Mexican drug cartels came from the United States. This was not true. The majority came from Central America or from arms this country sold to the Mexican military. At this time the BATF began ordering gun dealers to sell arms to suspected smugglers. BATF agents were upset as they watched smugglers take arms into Mexico and asked that this program be stopped. On December 14, 2010 U.S. Border agent Brian Terry was killed by a "Fast and Furious" AK-47 that "walked" into Mexico. Two weeks later a BATF agent became a whistleblower stating the purpose of the program was to increase the amount of guns recovered in Mexico to justify new gun control regulations. Supervisors at BATF began threatening whistleblowers in January. On January 30th the Mexican press reported on the scandal stating their Attorney General began an investigation into the matter and may bring charges against U.S. officials. On the same day Senator Grassley offers protection of whistleblowers and starts an investigation. Twelve days later 12 BATF agents offer to help.

On March 16, 2011 Rep. Issa asks BATF to answer questions and produce documents, based on information and documents obtained from agents. On the 23rd Obama went on the Mexican network Univision and said that neither he nor Holder had any information about the program. Four days later a high ranking retired BATF agent said he protested the program repeatedly, but got the response that the policy was approved by high levels at both BATF and DOJ. April 1st BATF refused to provide requested information and Issa issued subpoenas. On the 9th Issa reports he is getting help from the BATF Phoenix office. Officials at BATF warned on the 20th there will be charges of contempt of Congress if requested information is not received. Holder testifies on May 3rd and 4th that he had no information about Fast and Furious or Gun Walker, and neither did his Assistant Attorney General. On the 4th, CBS News reported they had copies of documentation which conflicts with Holder's testimony.

It is reported on May 16th that Congress is interviewing BATF agents and gun shop dealers. On the 17th Phoenix BATF office gets new management and Issa reports he has proof the program started in Washington. On the 19th a DEA agent reported that 50 to 60 AK-47s from Fast and Furious were obtained at a drug raid in Phoenix. A retired BATF agent told a news reporter that the drug cartels are promoting more corruption in the United States than in Mexico. He stated he obtained the name and location of the killer of Brian Terry, but was told to ignore that because it wasn't necessary as other agencies were working on the matter. That is when and why he quit working for law enforcement. A September 2010 report was found and reported on May 24th, stating "strategies that address firearm trafficking to Mexican cartels have been developed and released by the White House and the Department of Justice. It is essential that ATF efforts support strategies promoted by the White House and the Department of Justice".

A report that a .50 BMG weapon from Fast and Furious may have been used to shoot down a Mexican helicopter. Issa announced on the 5th that he would hold public hearings during the summer and he believed the program was approved at "the highest level" as he got cooperation from the field and none from Washington. The next day it is confirmed the helicopter was shot down by this program's weapons and the following day it is reported the hearings will investigate obstruction of justice by the Obama administration. On the 9th Mexico finds a large cache of "Gun Walker" weapons including the .50 BMG rifle that shot down the helicopter. On the 10th it is reported there is an audio recording of BATF agent telling a gun dealer he must sell weapons to a known trafficker against his objections. Issa began reporting that the DOJ is stonewalling and accuses the Obama administration of conducting a cover up of links between the DOJ and gun control organizations. The Obama administration leaks news that Acting Director of BATF Ken Melson would be leaving on the 17th on the same day a Gun Walker AK-47 was used to kill a Mexican lawyer. On the 20th ABC network airs a special about Brian Terry and links the story to gun regulations. ABC, NBC and NPR are not airing information regarding the investigation, only CBS and FOX are. On the 23rd Melson states he does not want to step down because he doesn't want to be the "fall guy", but he had not been given permission to speak before Issa. It is reported on the 27th that Melson will testify as Obama continues to state that Holder did not authorize the "Fast and Furious" program. During 2010 3,000 people were killed in the city of Juarez, Mexico and 150 Mexican law officers and soldiers have been shot. The "Gun Walker" weapons not only killed Brian Terry also but ICE Special Agent Jaime Zapata. It has been determined that over 2,000 weapons have been sold under this program. The Obama administration has released the name of Andrew Traver as the nominee to head BATF. Traver is from Chicago and is an advocate of more gun regulations and is against gun ownership by private citizens. Holder continues to stonewall the investigation. On 6/19/2012 Holder met with Issa as Issa threatened to charge Holder with contempt of Congress for failure to provide subpoenaed documents. Holder suggested that Issa accept some additional paperwork Holder felt was appropriate with a brief discussion and drop proceedings. Issa declined stating Holder had until the morning to provide documents.

Holder shows up with a Presidential Executive Privilege to prevent providing further information. The committee then voted to hold Holder in comtempt of Congress. Members of the committe want to fi nd out how Executive Privilege can be approved if the President is not involved in the investigation. The House of Representatives voted 255 to 67 in contempt of Congress and 258 to 95 on civil contempt charges.

This certainly is not the transparency promised during Obama's campaign. Especially troubling is that this event is happening while another investigation is starting regarding the leaking of top national security information from the White House. Holder offers to have his Department investigate the leaks. Some are not confident that Holder who is withholding information in Fast and Furious will find the person responsible for the serious leaks from within the White House.

JEFFREY IMMELT chairman of General Electric (GE) was appointed as the new Jobs Czar on January 21, 2011. Officially he chairs the new White House Economic Group otherwise known as the new Council on Jobs and Competitiveness with the mission of coming up with ideas to create new jobs. The panel is made up of 26 company leaders including Ken Chennault from American Express and Dick Parsons from Citigroup. On February 9th he was appointed to the President's Economic Recovery Advisory Board to find ideas on how to fix the economy. Immelt has held many positions at GE including the former head of GE Medical Systems. GE is an international company that makes many products and owns NBC and MSNBC. He also served on the board of the New York Fed from 2006 until April 2011.

Immelt became the head CEO of GE in 2001 and since then GE's shares dropped from $60 per share to $19, and has had shareholders protesting over the left leaning coverage of its news broadcasts. Between 2009 and 2010 GE received $24.9 million in stimulus payments plus an additional $5 million in contracts paid with stimulus funds. During that time GE reduced their American work force by 18,000 employees and some of those employees used to make light bulbs. Since Immelt took charge he changed the company by selling half of its portfolio and invested in alternative energy and health care. For example, in November 2010 Obama traveled to India and announced it would purchase $750 million worth of steam turbines from India's Reliance Power company that are manufactured by GE. In January 2011 he signed deals with China, in China, for gas turbine engines, coal gasification plants, developing high speed rail for the United States, and supplying avionics for a new airline. Concerns have been raised that the gasification and avionics deals could provide China with new technology.

Obama's goal is to provide universal health care and GE is lobbying to get the buy-in program. Obama wants to reduce CO2 emissions and GE makes CO2 scrubbers. Obama wanted Cap and Trade and GE owns GE Capital that could sell carbon credits and then GE could also sell the CO2 scrubbers to those same companies. Obama wants alternative energy and GE makes alternative energy products. The company builds solar panels, windmills, hybrid locomotives, fuel cells, lower emission aircraft engines, mercury filled light bulbs, and water purification products. Obama computerized health care records and GE has a computer system to do that.

Immelt's committee came up with a plan to create more jobs. They suggested vocational training for manufacturing jobs in the new economy, converting buildings to be energy efficient using green materials, allowing the government to back small business loans, and encourage tourism.

KEVIN JENNINGS was appointed as the Safe Schools Czar, officially assistant deputy secretary for Safe and Drug Free Schools, in the Department of Education. He is an openly gay activist that founded the Gay Lesbian and Straight Education Network (GLSEN). GLSEN targets children in grades 7 through 12 giving conferences on alternate life styles that teaches sexual practices that some call deviant, hand out supplies such as a "fisting" kit, and booklets that can answer questions such as "is it polite to spit or swallow". Suggested reading lists are handed out with titles such as "Passages of Pride" and "Queer 13" with sexual content has been called shocking. In 2010 he took part in introducing Bill 4530 that would require normalization of homosexuality, transgenderism and cross-dressing in the class rooms. In June 2011 he announced he was leaving to lead a non-profit group called "Be the Change".

ANDY STERN was appointed by Obama to be a member of the National Commission on Fiscal Responsibility. When appointed he was the president of Service Employees International Union (SEIU) the second largest union, the largest is National Education Association (NEA). During the Presidential campaign, Obama said at a SEIU meeting, "Your (SEIU) agenda is my agenda". He also stated that he consults with their union before debating on immigration or health care issues.

SEIU was part of AFL-CIO when Stern was elected as president in 1996, and one of his first demands was that members must devote 5 working days towards political action activities and all support must be for the Democratic Party. Tactics used to recruit new members were tough and many times violent. They used boycotts, pickets, and used the media to promote negative campaigns against companies. In 2004 SEIU spent $40 million of union dues on organizers to defeat the re-election of Bush, plus an additional $25 million on get out-the-vote programs and voter registration. In 2005 John Sweeney from AFL-CIO decided to use $37 million dollars designated to back Democratic elections, while SEIU and the Teamsters wanted to use more funds for initiatives to increase membership. Stern tried to block Sweeney's re-election, but failed so SEIU (and the Teamsters) separated from them. Stern got involved with the Soros funded Shadow Party which bankrolled Kerry's presidential campaign through a loop hole in the McCain-Feingold Act. Stern also sat on the board of the Soros funded America Coming Together and started writing blogs for the Huffington Post. In 2006 he wrote a book, "A Country That Works" advocating unions as a force to promote progressive social reforms or wealth distribution through social programs, universal health care, etc. The book's publication prompted an investigation by the FBI in 2010. Stern received a retainer fee of $175,000 that he kept. Then he used SEIU member dues to fact check the book, promote the book, and then SEIU purchased thousands of the books.

After he separated from AFL-CIO he really began using the training he received at the Midwest Academy, the school run by former SDS members Paul and Heather Booth, which taught Alinsky rules for organizing He brought many small unions together to form a mega union. SEIU and ACORN (the George Wiley styled organization designed to overwhelm the welfare system) joined forces. Stern and SEIU partner up with ACORN. ACORN trains SEIU members in radical disruptive organizing tactics while some ACORN and SEIU offices share the same building. SEIU pays ACORN up to $4 million a year to organize protests. SEIU wants to unionize Wal-Mart employees. ACORN forms groups to protest Wal-Mart with names like Wal-Mart Alliance for Reform Now, Wake-up Wal-Mart, and the Wal-Mart Organizing Project. ACORN runs Project Vote and SEIU has voter registration drives.

SEIU members are health care related (nurses, aides), property services (janitors, security guards) and public services (government employees). Many people they represent are women, minorities, and immigrant groups with low wages, but usually lower than what SEIU pays the demonstrators. The prime groups they represent are government employees, 40% of membership are now public servants. This group of people rarely strike; the dues are taken from their tax paid wages, and are then spent to elect more government employees. Alinsky must be proud of the system that takes tax money to be spent to promote more taxes to undermine the government.

During the Presidential campaign Obama vowed to paint the nation purple. Purple is the color of the shirts SEIU wear to identify themselves during their activist activities. In January 2008 Obama said, "I've been working with SEIU before I was elected to anything. We organized homecare workers…we organized registration drives. That's how we built power on the South Side of Chicago and now the time has come to do it all across this country. We are going to paint the nation purple with SEIU". I wonder if this is the civilian organization that will be the "volunteer" or mandatory service Obama has envisioned as national service for our youth.

Stern was the most frequent visitor to the White House visiting 22 times between January and July 2009. If he was lobbying for his causes he did it illegally as he is not registered as a lobbyist. On April 2, 2009 Stern gave a speech praising Obama's new American economic plan" of "shared prosperity". He said, "Clearly, government has a major opportunity to distribute wealth...through tax policies, through minimum wages, through living wages...social benefits". Stern stated he supported a global government. In October a spokesperson from SEIU announced the union was "cutting all ties" with ACORN just as the investigation of $5 million in stolen money by Dale Rathke started.

Obama appoints Stern, an Independent Advisory Council member of ACORN, as a member of the National Commission on Fiscal Responsibility and Reform in February 2010. In April 2010 Stern resigned from SEIU. He left the union $85 million in debt and their national pensions funds at a critical level of being underfunded by 65%. Local SEIU pension funds were in worse shape. Stern, however, left with a lifetime pension and health care in a 102% funded plan. While members he represents are sent letters warning that their pensions are underfunded he does not have to worry. So Obama appoints him to create a plan for fiscal responsibility for our nation. He demonstrated how he redistributes wealth with the union he led.

Siga Technology announced Stern joined their board of directors on June, 21, 2010. Siga produces agents to combat bio-warfare pathogens. Stern was given 35,000 shares of stock. On May 13, 2011 Siga was awarded a $2.8 billion no-bid contract for small pox vaccine. Siga's stock price rose significantly the next day. The contract is now under investigation by the House Oversight and Government Reform Committee.

In April 2011 Stern wrote an article for the Huffington Post complaining that our Constitution is out-dated. He states the checks and balances were a great idea when it was written but is inefficient now in the global economy.

CRAIG BECKER was appointed to the National Labor Relations Board (NLRB) in March 2010 as a recess appointment because he could not get the votes needed to be approved in the House. Becker was general counsel for both the AFL-CIO and SEIU. The role of the NLRB is to prevent or remedy unfair labor practices by both employers and unions, interpret the NLR Act, and supervise union elections. The problem is Becker does not believe employers have a right to be heard in an unfair labor practice case "even though Board ruling might indirectly affect their duty to bargain". He believes opinions of employers and employees are secondary to union goals. Becker said, "Just as a U.S. citizens cannot opt against having a congressman, workers should not be able to choose against having a union as their monopoly bargaining agent". Becker has refused to recuse himself from decisions involving companies which he has had past involvement with.

RICHARD TRUMKA bragged that he has conversations with the White House every day and visits 2 to 3 times each week. White House records as of February 2011 show he visited 46 times and Andy Stern visited 58 times. Trumka was appointed to the Economic Recovery Advisory Board in February 2009. He was opposed to welfare reforms and supported the single payer health care plan. In February he was appointed to the council on Jobs and Competitiveness. He recommends an increase in gas tax to pay for infrastructure.

Trumka is the president of the AFL-CIO. He started with the union in 1974 when he was a staff attorney for the United Mine Workers and was elected as president in 1982. The UMW was known for their violent activist activities. During a protest in 1993 members vandalized homes, fired gun shots at a mine office, and trapped 93 workers in an underground mine when they shut off the power. A non-union worker was shot in the head; the widow sued the union which finally settled out of court for years later. No disciplinary action was taken against the person who shot the gun. Trumka's response was, "If you strike a match and put your finger in, common sense tells you you're going to burn your finger". In 1994 Trumka was honored at a Eugene Debs' Award Banquet. Eugene Debs was the founder of the Socialist Party of America. In the mid 1990's Trumka refused to testify at an investigation, taking the Fifth Amendment, of a Teamster's money laundering scandal.

In 2010 Trumka admitted why he enjoyed unionizing, "I got into labor movement not because I wanted to negotiate wages, but because I saw it as a vehicle to do massive social change to include lots of people".

JIM WALLIS is Obama's personal religious advisor. He is much like Reverend Jeremiah Wright as he believes in Liberation Theology. This the belief that the Bible teaches people should be liberated from unjust economic, political, and social conditions with the demand for "social justice" and with the redistribution of wealth.

Wallis grew up in a evangelical family in Detroit, Michigan and attended college at Michigan State University. At college he became a leader for SDS (the Bill Ayers radical group) and participated in demonstrations against the Vietnam War. He continued his involvement with the anti-war movement and his behavior almost got him removed from Trinity Evangelical Divinity School he attended after leaving Michigan State University. While he at the seminary, located near Chicago, he founded the magazine 'Post-American' which advocated for government managed economies and for wealth distribution. The magazine endorsed anti-capitalism and criticized American foreign policy.

In 1971 he established the commune Sojourners Community in Rogers Park, Illinois where people lived together sharing belongings and finances. When the commune disbanded in 1974, he moved the remaining followers to an inner city community in Washington D.C. These people combined their income and assists to set up a network of social outreach programs while living together in common houses. Wallis renamed his magazine 'Sojourners'. People in the commune advocated to transform America into a socialist nation and were told to "refuse to accept (capitalist) structures and assumptions that normalize poverty and segregate the world by class". They attacked our foreign policy, denounced American imperialism and promoted the Marxist revolutionary movements in the Third World. Followers established a worshiping community and organized events on the behalf of peace and justice. Wallis criticized refuges that left Vietnam's communist regime, stating they were leaving to support their consumer habits and because they were greedy capitalists as it was too hard for them to live under a dictator. His group supported the communist Sandinistas in Nicaragua and a Marxist terror group in El Salvador called FMLN. The Sojourn community is now an intern community, where persons are hired for a year to live together as part of an internship experience. Interns learn to combine evangelical Protestant beliefs with "social justice" priorities. Wallis wrote in his book "Agenda for Biblical People" that the United States is "the great power, the great seducer, the great captor and destroyer of human life".

'Sojourners' currently has over 100,000 readers in both print and electronic publications. While Wallis says he is bi-partisan, his magazine continues to oppose American domestic and foreign policies and advocates for more and more government intrusion with policies and regulations affecting people's lives. In 2005 he said private charity was insufficient to reduce poverty and "social justice" would only be achieved with government redistributing the wealth. He said that charity given voluntarily falls short of "Biblical Justice". In 2005 he organized religious activists to block the entrance to a congressional office building in an attempt to stop a vote on a Republican backed plan of spending cuts. He was arrested with his cohorts for this action in the Capitol rotunda in front of an 8th grade class studying civics. Wallis has been arrested at least 22 times for his actions of civil disobedience. In 2006, during a radio interview, he was asked if he was calling for redistribution of wealth. His answer, "Absolutely, without any hesitation. That's what the gospel is all about".

When Obama was elected Wallis told The Washington Times that his prayers had been answered. In April he was selected to sit on the White House Advisory Council on Faith-based and Neighborhood Partnerships. It seems strange to me that a 62 year old man who has spent his adult life time opposing everything American and praising everything Marxist is the President's spiritual advisor and sits on a national advisory committee advocating his positions. Wallis once said, "The monologue of the religious right is finally over and a new dialogue has begun".

Judge me by the people who surround me.

CHAPTER 29

★ ★ ★ ★ ★

George Soros

GEORGE SOROS has been mentioned many times for funding organizations connected to persons associated to Obama. He is an atheist, a billionaire, credited for developing hedge funds, an investor, and is known as the man who broke the Bank of England. He is a major figure in Human Rights Watch, Council of Foreign Relations, the World Economic Forum, and the Club of Rome. Soros is an advocate for democratic ideals that he supports internationally through his philanthropic organization Open Society Foundations (OSF), which is active in over 70 countries. He boasts he has contributed over $8 billion to support free speech, expose corruption, improve education, remedy poverty, and supporting human rights. This is what he says about himself, "I have always harbored an exaggerated view of my self-importance, to put it bluntly I fancied myself as some kind of god or an economic reformer like Keynes, or even better, like Einstein". He also said, "I am a kind of nut who wants to have an impact".

When he was born in Budapest, Hungary to non-practicing Jewish parents in 1930 his name was George Schwartz. His father Tivador had escaped prison in Russia where he had been held during World War I and recognized the changes of anti-Semitism and growing Fascism in his country. He knew he needed to do something to save his family and friends before it was too late. Tivador was an advocate of Esperanto which is an invented international language intended to unite cultures across the globe, foster peace and understanding, plus minimize nationalism to a singular country. He picked the name Soros because not only was it a palindrome but he liked the significance of the definition of the word. The word soros in Hungarian means 'next in line' or 'designated successor' and in Esperanto means 'will soar'. Tivador not only changed the name of his family, but changed the name and background of others in his community as well. To those who could afford to pay he charged a fee, to those who could not he did it for free. The Soros family, and most of the people who followed his advice, were able to leave the country and were not captured to be tortured or killed.

Nazi Germany occupied Hungary in 1944 and young Soros went to work at the Jewish Council. The Jewish Council established by the Nazis was actually very anti-Jewish. Soros was given the task to handout deportation notices. He showed the list to his father who instructed him to deliver the notices but to tell the people not to report as requested. The next year George was living with an employee of the Ministry of Agriculture as either his godson or grandson. At least once Soros went with him as he completed an inventory of the belongings of a Jewish family that escaped the country. He said he did not feel guilty because he was only an observer. Other reports state he actively partook in the looting and removing Jewish belongings for the Nazis. Soros describes this period of his life during both the Nazi and the later Soviet occupation as "an exhilarating adventure". He says the experience gave him "an appetite for taking risk", learning how to cope with it, and "exploring the limits of the possible".

Soros went to England in 1947 to live with his Orthodox Jewish uncle. It is not known how he was able to escape Hungary while it was under Soviet occupation as he would have had to go through multiple check points. In England he attended the London School of Economics, which taught Keynesian economics, and obtained a Bachelor of Science in Philosophy. The London School of Economics was founded by Fabian Society members Sidney and Beatrice Webb, Graham Wallas, and George Bernard Shaw. Soros studied under a philosopher named Karl Popper who considered himself a 'critical-rationalist'. Popper wrote the book "The Open Society and Its Enemies". After graduation he worked at the merchant bank Singer and Friedlander. A merchant bank deals in international finance and loans to large companies.

Soros moved to New York City in 1956 and secured a job at F. M. Mayer as an arbitrage trader which involves trading financial instruments such as stocks, bonds, and currencies. He later worked as an analyst at Wertheim and Co. where he developed his theory of reflexivity. Reflexivity is the idea that a person's bias is the root of their reality. Their reality shapes a person's thinking and this thinking creates their reality in a continually ongoing cycle even if their reality is not based on fact. He says he uses this theory as a basis for his financial dealings. Soros believed he could make money with investing using his theory on Wall Street but he needed training on how the market worked. His plan was to make $500,000 which he believed was enough to support him as he wanted to be a philosopher and author. Soros then went to work for Arnold and S. Bleichroder who had connections with the Rothschild family in 1963. Within 10 years he was the vice president of the firm. In 1967 he convinced the firm to set up an offshore investment hedge fund company called First Eagle. He must have done well as two years later they set him up with a second company named Double Eagle. Regulations prevented him from running the company as he wanted to, so he left in 1973.

He had already started Soros Fund Management with Jim Rogers in 1970 with the help of wealthy investors including the Rothschild family. The hedge fund company evolved into the Quantum Fund and it did very well. In the first 10 years the funds had a return of 3,365% . Hedge funds are unregulated pools of money from very wealthy investors that are aggressively managed. Minimum investments are typically $500,000 to $1 million and typical investors are foundations, pension funds, university endowments, and wealthy investors. The Quantum Fund (also referred to as the Quantum Group of Funds), later called the Quantum Endowment Fund, is based at Curacao in the Netherlands Antilles and in the Cayman Islands. The Netherland Antilles is a very busy transshipment region for drugs from South America destined for the United States and Europe. Soros denies his company is involved in illegal drugs or other criminal activities. By not locating in the United States the company can avoid public scrutiny and the IRS. Soros is not on the board, but is an adviser from the Soros Fund Management office in New York City. If he is questioned about the company he can state he is only an advisor and avoid giving any answers. Regulations on hedge funds mandate a maximum of 99 investors, and none of his investors are American citizens. Soros and six managers each split 15% of the annual profits, plus he receives 1% as an adviser fee, so it is easy to see how his income rose dramatically. The Open Society Fund was founded in 1979 with his own income to aid Hungarians and others in Eastern Europe. In 1980 Rogers left the firm.

The first Open Society Foundation was established in Hungary in 1984 to set up a training center. He later founded the Central European University in both Budapest and Prague and established a foundation called School of Public Policy. Soros continues to contribute millions of dollars to the university to this day. He finances persons who will cooperate with his plans. Soros states that his plan in Hungary was to help the country transform from a closed society to an open society. The Hungarian authorities first demanded that they have control on the foundation but later came to an agreement regarding representatives. Soros says one of his best projects involved offering photocopying machines, in exchange for local currency, to cultural and scientific institutions. The money was used for local grants to support unofficial initiatives. Before he distributed the copy machines they were under control of the government, but now they could be used to distribute information. He had a budget of $3 million and was able to influence the culture of the country better than the Ministry of Culture.

In 1986 he established foundations in Poland, China and the Soviet Union. In Poland he worked with the CIA backed Solidarity operation and the communist government and introduced Shock Therapy to help transform the country. The plan was for the communist government to allow Solidarity to take over the country which would instill confidence to the citizens. The second action was for the government to freeze wages, instigate extremely high interest rates, and withhold state credits to bankrupt the country's industrial and agricultural enterprises. After the country went bankrupt Soros promised his friends would purchase the state owned companies. He did this with the steel company Huta Warsawa. The government agreed to assume all debts of the company and then sold the debt free company for $30 million. To build a complex of that size would have cost $3 to $4 billion. Shock Therapy caused industrial output to fall over 30% in 2 years. The foundation he established Stefan Batory Foundation was run by Jeffery Sachs who advised and supervised the economic transformation. Sachs is a Harvard University economist who had expertise in transforming new economies. His expertise includes the advice he gave Bolivia in 1985, a country that was later taken over by those involved in the cocaine trade. (Sachs developed Shock Therapy, founded the Millennium Promise Alliance, and is a current special advisor at the U. N.). Soros now not only controlled the government but the media as well. He knew the loss of employment and the inability to purchase needed goods would cause unrest which is why he insisted Solidarity be involved with the plan; so they could deal with the problems. While Poland was in turmoil Soros and his friends made profits. This is his idea of capital enterprise.

Next he went to Russia. The Soviet Union was in financial trouble with the cost of the Afghanistan war, plus some republics were starting to declare sovereignty. Mikhail Gorbachov attempted to make reforms with 'perestroika' to reform the economy and decentralize the government and with 'glasnost' allowing public access to information. Soros befriended Raisa Gorbachov and with her help established the Cultural Initiative Foundation which provided the entire country with textbooks. The textbooks included Open Society propaganda to indoctrinate the Russian youth. Soros spent $250 million to control and dominate their media, education, and research centers. He spent another $100 million to establish the International Science Foundation and made payouts to 50,000 Russian scientists to get control of their scientific discoveries. He used the foundations to meet the people who were making policy in the top levels of the country. After Gorbachov left office Soros befriended Yeltsin.

Soros brought Sachs to Russia so the country could benefit from Shock Therapy in 1991. Sachs suggested that some of his friends come to Russia to be part of the plan; one of his friends that participated was Larry Summers from Harvard. The plan was to reach zero deficits within 3 months. To achieve this Yeltsin drastically cut state spending to both industry and agriculture. Credit to industry ended and inflation was out of control. The country plunged into chaos and hyperinflation as scientists and others fled the country seeking employment in the West. Now it was time for Soros and his friends to make money. Marc Rich bought aluminum with hard money for extremely low prices which he later 'dumped' into western markets causing a 30% decrease in the price of metal. He purchased so much aluminum from Russia that they had a shortage for their fish canneries. It is reported Marc Rich also attempted to control the export of West Siberian crude oil to western countries. Another friend, Shaul Eisenberg, was able to obtain exclusive contracts for textiles in Uzbekistan. In 1995 Soros' friend Fred Cuny disappeared in Chechnya while providing disaster relief in an area that was in the throes of violence as a result of a political destabilization campaign. Russia accused Cuny of being a CIA operative supporting the Chechen uprising. The Russian intelligence agencies have accused the Soros foundations of espionage in their country with the help of the Ford and Heritage Foundations, and the universities of Harvard, Duke and Columbia.

Soros was not well received in China. He tried for 3 years to break into the Chinese culture but was not successful. The Confucian ethic is, "If you give someone some support he becomes beholden to you, he looks to you to look after him for the rest of his life and he owes loyalty". The Chinese did not want to be beholden to Soros or his foundations and they did not trust him. He was accused of being a CIA operative and their secret police infiltrated his foundations.

The fall of the Soviet Union and with the Iron Curtain in Berlin being torn down caused the region to be in chaos. Soros certainly was not going to let a crisis go to waste. Romania had their revolution in December 1989. Nicolae Ceausescu led the country under a brutal communist police state. The people lived in poverty as agriculture and manufacturing were exported for cash to pay off the national debt. He controlled the messages that the public would hear, even the typewriters and copy machines were under police control. He controlled the media and created himself as a cult personality, offering two hours daily of television dedicated to him and his policies. These were the only programs televised as all other programming was illegal. What he could not control was the broadcasting from neighboring countries, which communities on the border could pick up on 'illegal' television and radio stations. The people watched Sky News and CNN and heard BBC and Radio Free Europe. When Ceausescu took a tour of the city of Timisoara he spotted a number of television satellite dishes. Later he found out they were not solar collectors as he was told, and he ordered them destroyed. He was not aware that his orders were not carried out and the dishes were left operating. Many people had video cassette recorders and news was able to spread throughout the country illegally. The public debt was paid off in early 1989, but the austerity programs continued and tensions got worse.

When riots broke out in Timisoara, after an attempted arrest of a religious leader, the news of the event was broadcast over BBC. Ceausescu sent workers from factories across the country with clubs to fight the protesters; but they joined the protesters instead. To show the country that Ceausescu was still popular he broadcast a show with people holding provided signs promoting his policies. What he did not expect was a large demonstration that broke out from the crowd that was televised across the country. The revolutionaries took over the television station and placed their command center in that building. The rebels won after one of the bloodiest revolts in history and Open Society Association of Romania opened in June 1990. Soros was actually in Romania on January 6, 1990 to set up a meeting with a leading dissident, Alin Teodoresco, to discuss the opening of foundations in the country. The focus of Open Society was public relations, civil society, and education with the programs led by Romanian citizens. Ion Iliescu, a communist, won the election in May 1990 under the National Salvation Front party and promptly took over the television and other media outlets. Romania is currently in an economic crisis with debt reaching 82% of its GDP. The country is selling off its state owned property to raise money and is welcoming foreign investors.

The Open Society Foundations seem to follow revolutions around the globe as Soros is attempting to change the world in his vision. He has Open Society Foundations in many other Soviet-bloc countries where he has introduced them to Shock Therapy economic policies and/or social justice programs. These countries include Armenia, Azerbaijan, Bulgaria, the Czech republic,

Estonia, Georgia, Latvia, Moldova, Slovakia, and the Ukraine. There are foundations in the Balkan countries of Albania, Macedonia, Montenegro, and Serbia. He also has foundations in Bosnia and Kosovo. He has foundations throughout Europe, Asia, the Caribbean, South America, Central America, and Africa.

Soros is the man who broke the Bank of England. He is a currency speculator and trader and who appears to manipulate currencies as he becomes more wealthy. In 1992 he speculated the British pound would depreciate because of economic conditions within the country, so he used a process call shorting. He borrowed billions of pounds and then converted them to Deutsch Marks and French Francs. When the pound depreciated, as he predicted, he repaid the loans at the lower value and made over $1 billion. In 1997 Southeast Asia experienced a financial crisis. Before the crisis hit Thailand and Indonesia, the countries were having a growth period with foreign investments due to the high interest rates they were paying. Soros predicted the economy would burst so he shorted their currency. As he expected their money depreciated and the financial crisis spread throughout the region. The International Monetary Fund lent funds with conditions which led to a prolonged crisis. The Malaysian Prime Minister accused Soros of sabotaging his country's currency and Soros was considered an "economic war criminal" in Thailand. It is suspected that the Soros run on the Euro through his hedge fund Quantum is what triggered the financial crisis in Europe.

The Managed Funds Association (MFA) was formed in 1991 as a lobby group for hedge funds or what they call the alternative investment community. Soros is one of the largest partners at Managed Funds Association. Wall Street is designed for people that create products to grow the economy which people and business invest in through general stocks and mutual funds. Hedge funds make money by short selling in the hopes of companies failing, countries collapsing, or commodities falling in price. The MFA authored the Chris Dodd finance reform bill in 2006 that removed safeguards for investors. It is estimated that hedge funds stole $11 trillion from the United States economy with the devalued home mortgages through short sales. Soros appears to have targeted our country for collapse and attempting to transform America from a Capitalist country to a Socialist country.

Hedge funds and short sales are being blamed for the collapse of Greece. In 2001 Greece wanted to join the European membership and be part of the Euro. The problem was to be eligible to join a country's debt needed to be below 3% of GDP and Greece was well above that number. Goldman Sachs made a secret deal to help Greece hide their true debt with currency swaps and other manipulations. Goldman Sachs is a member of MFA and shared the now not so secret deal with Soros and other hedge dealers. Goldman Sachs and Soros bet against Greece through short sales. Now that country's deficit is 12.7% of GDP and their debt is 125% of GDP. They are in financial ruin, poverty is growing, unemployment is expected to reach 16%, and there are riots in their streets. If the EU bails out Greece it will cause the EU deficit to grow and weaken the Euro. Hedge funds including Soros are expecting the EU to bail out Greece and are willing to gamble on that assumption. This could bankrupt and ruin the entire EU, but the hedge funds will make money.

The Open Society Institute (OSI) is the grant making foundation created in 1993 designed to promote democratic governance, human rights, plus economic, legal and social reforms. OSI develops civil society organizations to encourage participation in a democratic open society seeking social justice. Money that funds the numerous grass root organizations connected to Obama and Democratic causes originate at OSI.

Project on Death in America was formed by Soros in 1994 to promote euthanasia. The project is to train hospitals, nurses, and doctors the "proper" way to care for the dying by not using expensive life saving treatments and equipment.

International Crisis Group (ICG) was formed by Open Society in 1995 with a mission to prevent and resolve conflicts. The ICG offers advice to the United Nations, the European Union, and the World Bank. The organization supports the doctrine of the Responsibility to Protect which states the international community must protect civilians from mass atrocities. Founders of the organization were World Bank vice president Mark Brown, U.S. diplomat Morton Abramowitz, and Fred Cuny from Open Society Foundations. Board members and advisors include former National Security Advisor in the Clinton Administration Sandy Berger (he was caught stealing papers from the National Archives), former Deputy Secretary of State Richard Armitage, the U.N. Secretary-General from 1997 until 2006 Kofi Annan, and former National Security Advisor in the Jimmy Carter administration Zbigniew Brzezinski. Mohamed El Baradei was on the board but left in January 2011. He is the former Director General of the International Atomic Energy Agency (IAEA) that ran the weapons investigation in Iraq and determined Iran does not have an atomic bomb. He was quite busy in Egypt during 2011 stirring up demonstrations, volunteering to lead a transitional government after Mubarak was removed from office, and declared he was a candidate for the presidency of Egypt. The ICG has many offices and is active in Asia, Africa, Latin America, and Europe. Soros was asked if he had a foreign policy and he answered, "Yes, I have a foreign policy...my goal is to become the conscience of the world".

Soros uses Human Rights Watch as his mouthpiece to shape public opinion. They routinely ignore atrocities in Columbia and Cuba and report, sometimes exaggerate, atrocities in other countries. They supported the overthrow of Nortiega in Panama and Haiti's first elected leader Aristide. They shaped public opinion to endorse the bombing in Bosnia by overstating atrocities and are currently supporting Tibet to resist China's rule. The countries that get ignored are those that are opposed to neo-liberalism, which is the total lack of regulations for economic enterprise.

Human Rights Watch promoted to the media that Milosevic was involved in ethnic cleansing. It did not report that Open Society Foundations and the United States financially supported the opposition group Kosovo Liberation Army (KLA). The KLA was portrayed as "freedom fighters" not as terrorists that dealt in illegal drug trade, including the cocaine trade from Afghanistan. It did not report that the International Crisis Group (ICG), which advocated for NATO to use military force, had its eyes on the Trepca mines in the country. The Trepca mines have gold, silver, lead, zinc, crystals, plus many other metals and gems. The ICG advised NATO to take over the mines quickly and then have the mines closed claiming environmental problems. After bombing all of Kosovo's infrastructure to splinters the Trepca mines escaped without any damage. The U.N. Mission in Kosovo (UNMIK) took over control of Kosovo and closed the mines citing extreme levels of lead contamination. NATO troops evicted miners who did not want the mine closed and intended to sell to private investors. Soros has invested $350 million in the mines that have an estimated value of $5 billion and sought to purchase to mines. Title to the mine has been under continued investigation with many contesting ownership and multiple countries and investors attempting to take it over. Human Rights Watch did not report that Soros and Albanian billionaire Sahit Mujo showed interest in Kosovo coal reserves with an estimated value of over $300 billion dollars.

Very soon after Kosovo was destroyed the KLA was transformed into uniformed, civilian non-military organizations which were issued arms to provide protection and help with emergency relief. Kosovo declared independence in 2008 and the UN finally recognized the independence in 2010 and but international supervision continues. Hashim Thaci is the current Prime Minister elected in 2007. Thaci and Xhaviti Haliti were both leaders of KLA, both involved with the regulations set by UNMIK, and both accused of organized crime before and after the Kosovo take over.

Arab Spring began in December 2010 with the overthrow of Tunisian President Zine El Abine Ben Ali. The voice of the revolutionaries was Radio Kalima which was funded by OSI. Ben Ali led a corrupt police state. The revolutions was planned by the Open Society network and National Endowment for Democracy. Fighting erupted over frustration of high unemployment, high food prices, and brutal police actions. Elections held in October 2011 resulted in the moderate Islamic Nahada Party securing the majority of seats in the new parliament. They state Tunisia's new government will be modeled with Turkey's secular form of governance. As tourism is one of their industries the claim is that alcohol will not be banned and bikinis will be allowed on the beaches. Elections for Prime Minister will be held in 2012.

Egypt's revolutions started while their military leaders were in Washington discussing military equipment and payments with our military. Was that a coincidence? The United States knew an uprising was in the making as a group called The Alliance for Youth Movements (AYM) was formed by the U.S. Department of State. AYM held a summit in New York City at Columbia University in December 2008 with the help of Facebook, Google, YouTube, Howcast, and Access 360 Media. Speakers included Whoopi Goldberg, Dustin Moskowitz of Facebook, and Luke Russert from MSNBC. Conferences taught how to use social media to bring change to promote freedom and counter oppression. Hillary Clinton, in 2009, described the youth who attended the summit "the vanguard of a rising generation of citizen activism." AYM was the beginning of Movements.org organized by the Council of Foreign Relations to be able to send youth to "hot spots". The United States did not help Murbarak, an ally of Israel, by providing help or securing the Suez Canal but supported the protesters led by El Baradei from Soros' International Crisis Group. El Baradei is the face of the Muslim Brotherhood that wants to establish a caliphate across the region with Sharia Law. Since 2008 the International Crisis Group pushed Mubarak to include the Muslim Brotherhood to be part of Egypt's political system, but Mubarak refused to allow the militant group to get involved. Well now the Muslim Brotherhood is involved. The Soros funded group Arab Network for Human Rights helped to write a draft for a new constitution.

Libya was attacked by NATO using the Responsibility to Protect Act for justification. The Global Centre for the Responsibility to Protect is funded by Soros. What did Soros know and when did he know it. In 2009 he invested heavily in Western oil in Libya and sold off in late 2010 to purchase oil stock in Russia and China. I guess timing is everything when investing. But oil is not the only resource in Libya. They have gold; in fact they have 144 tons of gold. The new government has not been established (elections are pending) but they have created a central bank. Before Libya was invaded Khadafy wanted to establish the gold dinar and refuse to accept either the dollar or the euro as currency. This is not part of the one world order plan. Secondly, Europe owes Libya $200 billion and does not have the money to pay the debt. The International Monetary Fund may have less money than Libya and perhaps they may find a way to help Libya with their reform. The other asset they have is water in the desert. They have the largest and most extensive irrigation system which provides 70% of their drinking and irrigation water. The water comes from underground through the Nubian Sandstone Aquifer System developed by their government to provide for their people. Libyans were getting concerned that the NATO air strikes were getting close to the pipelines that provided water to their nation. Libya has resources which can be used to control lives.

Soros claims to want to bring Open Societies to former communist or dictatorships controlled countries because he does not like communism or closed societies. So how is it that so many of the countries he helps fall into communist rule or to brutal dictators? And how is it that when countries fall some people make money?

George Soros is an American citizen as he was naturalized in 1961. His Open Society Institute funds many organizations that present this country in a bad light saying America is racist, unfair and greedy. He has even funded faith based groups to forward his agenda. These organizations include:

- Catholic Alliance for the Common Good
- Sojourners
- People Improving Communities Through Organizing
- Catholics For Choice
- J Street

- Arab American Institute
- Bill of Rights Defense Committee
- Mexican American Legal Defense and Educational Foundation
- NAACP
- National Council of La Raza
- Sentencing Project
- Critical resistance
- Leadership Conference on Civil and Human Rights

Many organizations that support the Democratic Party objectives of social justice, progressive judicial system, green jobs, global warming, abortion rights, gun control, banning coal mining and oil exploration are funded by Soros. These include:

- Center for American Progress
- Center for Economic and Policy Research
- Economic Policy Institute
- Ella Baker Center for Human Rights
- Emma Lazarus Foundation
- Alliance for Justice
- American Constitutional Society for Law and Policy
- Justice at Stake
- Institute of Policy Studies
- New America Foundation

- Urban Institute
- Feminist Majority Foundation
- Ms. Foundation for Women
- National Partnership for Women and Children
- Health Care for America Now
- Center for Reproductive Rights
- National Abortion Federation
- NARAL Pro-Choice America
- Planned Parenthood
- Choice USA
- Jews for Racial and Economic Justice
- Violence Policy Center
- Gun Violence Prevention
- Earth Justice
- Green For All
- Natural Resources Defense Council
- Friends of the Earth
- Alliance for Climate Protection
- Earth Island Institute

Open Society Institute provides money to groups that recruit and train individuals in grassroot organizing skills seeking social change and social justice.

- Center for Community Change
- Gamaliel Foundation
- Ruckus Society
- American Institute for Social Justice
- Institute for America's Future
- People for the American Way
- Democracy for America
- Midwest Academy

Influencing the media and promotion of liberal ideology OSI supports:

- American Prospect, Inc
- Free Press Independent Media Institute
- AlterNet
- Nation Institute
- Pacifica Foundation – Pacifica Radio
- Media Watch for America
- Sundance Institute
- NPR
- Investigative News Network
- Media Matters
- ProPublica
- Center for Public Integrity

- Center for Investigative Reporting
- The Lens
- Columbia School of Journalism
- National Federation of Community Broadcasters
- National Association of Hispanic Journalists
- Committee to Protect Journalists
- PBS
- Organization of News Ombudsmen
- Wisconsin Institute for Computer Assisted Reporting
- Daily Kos
- Think Progress
- Democracy Now- radio and news program
- Media Consortium
- Brave New Foundation
- Project Syndicate
- Public News Service

Voting rights, voter registration, and voting reforms are funded:

- Project Vote
- ACORN
- Catalist
- Brennan Center for Justice

- Progressive States Network
- Progressive Change Campaign Committee
- America Coming Together
- Center for American Progress
- Media Fund
- MoveOn.Org

OSI supports numerous organizations that promote open borders, immigration reform, benefits for illegal aliens, oppose national security activities, defend terrorists, depict military actions by Americans as immoral, and advocate for reduced military budgets:

- American Immigration Council
- Casa de Maryland
- Immigration Legal Resource Center
- Migration Policy Institute
- Latino Justice
- National Immigration Forum
- National Immigration Law Center
- Human Rights Watch
- Constitution Project
- Lynne Stewart Defense Committee
- National Security Archive
- Center for Constitutional Rights

- American Civil Liberty Union
- Amnesty International
- Global Exchange
- American Friends Service Committee

George Soros supports the Tides Foundation which was founded by former SDS member Drummond Pike. Teresa Heinz Kerry contributes millions to this foundation. Tides will allow persons to contribute anonymously to organizations that they support but do not want to be made public. It also allows non-profit groups to donate to their profit making activities without a paper trail. The foundation basically launders money. Sitting on the board is Maya Wiley, the daughter of George Wiley, and the chairman of the board is Wade Rathke. Tides Foundation is the parent of the Apollo Alliance which Soros supports. Founders of Apollo Alliance are former member of SDS Carl Pope and the founder of the New Party Joel Rogers. Founding members include John Podesta (CAP), Van Jones (Green for All), and former SDS member Jeff Jones. The Apollo Alliance members Jeff Jones and Van Jones (no relation) wrote the stimulus bill that benefited many of their green projects, community organizations, and unions.

This list of organizations that OSI supports and funds is only a partial list as there are many, many more. Soros does not only want to affect American policies as he is a major supporter of the United Nations International Millennium Development Project. This project has lofty goals supporting social justice but other Soros projects across the globe have not worked out so well in many countries.

Often referred to as a Jewish philanthropist, Soros does not promote many Jewish or pro-Israel causes. He created J Street and the Progressive Jewish Alliance to counter AIPAC influence in Washington. Originally Soros hid his connection to J Street as he didn't want his influence to be an issue. The Progressive Jewish Alliance joined with Jewish Funds for Justice; another organization he helped establish. Jewish Funds for Justice supported the Obama position that Israel should return to 1967 borders and establish a country of Palestine.

The first known speech Soros gave before a Jewish audience was given in November 2003 at a conference for the Jewish Funders Network. He stated the rise in anti-Semitism in Europe was caused by the policies of the United States and Israel. He stated that if these policies would change "then anti-Semitism will diminish". He also talked about "regime change" in the United States and funding projects in the country of Palestine.

The International Crisis Group backed the uprising in Egypt that overthrew Murbarak and backs the Muslim Brotherhood and Mohamed El Baradei. In March 2011 Soros said, "The main stumbling block is Israel. In reality, Israel has as much to gain from the spread of democracy in the Middle East as the United States has. But Israel is unlikely to recognize its own best interests because the change is too sudden and carries too many risks". He continued, "Fortunately, Obama is not beholden to the religious right, which has carried on a veritable vendetta against him".

Soros is a member of the Council of Foreign Relations an international think-tank that discusses international policy. It is a resource for government leaders, journalists, civic leaders, and educators. Albright, Sandy Berger, Shirley Temple Black, Tom Brokaw, Zbigniew Brzezinski, George H.W. Bush, Jimmy Carter, Richard Cheney, Wesley Clark, Bill Clinton, Katie Couric, Mario Cuomo, Caroline Kennedy, Robert Kennedy Jr., Rashid Khalidi, Henry Kissinger, Anthony Lake, Scooter Libby, Richard Dreyfuss, Lawrence Eagleburger, Douglas Fairbanks, Dianne Feinstein, Tim Geithner, Mikhail Gorbachov, Gary Hart, Janet Napolitano, Colin Powell, Condoleezza Rice, Jeffrey Sachs, Carl Sagan, Edward Said, Lawrence Summers, and George Stephanopoulos.

The World Economic Forum is a non-profit foundation where political leaders, business CEOs, and journalists meet to discuss important issues such as health, environment, interfaith initiatives, and humanitarian aid. Corporations with membership normally have a yearly turnover of $5 billion. Soros is an active member of the foundation.

The Club of Rome is another organization Soros is active with which develop world agendas. One of their top priorities is to depopulate the world. In a 1981 report by Executive Intelligence Review (EIR) it was disclosed that the Club of Rome wanted to reduce global population by 2 billion people "by war, famine, disease, and any other means necessary". The report quoted one member saying, "There is a single theme behind all our work-we must reduce population levels. Either they (governments) do it our way, through nice clean methods or they will get the kind of mess that we have in El Salvador, or in Iran, or in Beirut. Population is a political problem. Once population is out of control it requires authoritarian government, even fascism, to reduce it". "El Salvador is an example where our failure to lower population by simple means has created the basis for a national security crisis. The government of El Salvador failed to use our programs to lower their population. Now they get a civil war because of it. There will be dislocation and food shortages. They still have too many people there". The official continued, "Civil wars are somewhat drawn-out ways to reduce population. The quickest easy to reduce population is through famine, like in Africa, or through disease like the Black Death.

The Club of Rome takes credit for developing the global warming reforms. Alexander King, a co-founder of the Club of Rome wrote the following in his 1991 book "The First Global Revolution". "The common enemy of humanity is man. In searching for a new enemy to unite us, we came up with the idea that pollution, the threat of global warming, water shortages, famine and the like would fit the bill. All these dangers are caused by human intervention and it is only through changed attitudes and behavior that they can be overcome. The real enemy then is humanity itself". Al Gore is a member of the Club of Rome and he said "I believe it is appropriate to have an over-representation of the facts on how dangerous it is, as a predicate for opening up the audience". Member and UN Assistant Secretary General, Dr Robert Muller said, "In my view, after fifty years of service in the United Nations system, I perceive the utmost urgency and absolute necessity for proper Earth government. There is no shadow of a doubt that the present political and economic systems are no longer appropriate and will lead to the end of life evolution on this planet. We must therefore absolutely and urgently look for new ways". He also said, "What an incredible planet in the universe this will be when we will be one human family living in justice, peace, love and harmony with our divine Earth with each other and with the heavens". Another member Maurice Strong said, "It is the responsibility of each human being today to choose between the force of darkness and the force of light. We must therefore transform our attitudes, and adopt a renewed respect for the superior laws of Divine Nature". Other members of the Club of Rome include; Mikhail Gorbachov, Kofi Annan, Dalai Lama, David Rockefeller, Bill Clinton, Jimmy Carter, Ted Turner, Tony Blair, Deepak Chopra, and Henry Kissinger.

Up and through the 2000 Presidential campaign Soros did not support or fund in any large way American politics although he did say that he worked with Bill Clinton "as a team". He got active leading up to the 2004 Presidential elections with the goal to defeat Bush and his war on terror policies.

Soros said about 9/11 in a December 2003 article in the 'Atlantic Monthly', "Hijacking fully fueled airliners and using them as suicide bombs was an audacious idea, and its execution could not have been more spectacular". He said the war on terror should not be guiding United States policy and said, "America under Bush is a danger to the world" and "I'm willing to put my money where my mouth is". Soros spent up to $26 million, diverted through MoveOn.Org and America Coming Together, to defeat Bush for a second term in office. This was when the Shadow Party was created. He met Obama and had a fund raiser for him at his home in June 2004.

Bush won re-election, so Soros met with 70 wealthy donors who shared his ideology to come up with a new plan for the next election. This group was called the Phoenix Group. In 2006 Soros met with Obama for about an hour and a few weeks later Obama announced his bid for President after serving only 143 days in office as a senator. Soros was able to raise $500,000 within 4 months towards the campaign. The McCain-Feingold Act allowed the Soros and his friends to be more creative in raising money. With the help of grassroot community organizations, newly formed PACs, bundlers using the internet, 527 groups, he raised enormous amounts of money for Obama. Former backers of Hillary Clinton were now behind Obama in his bid for the Presidency. Soros told Judy Woodruff, reporter from PBS, "Obama has the charisma and the vision to radically reorient America in the world". During the campaign Obama was put in the awkward position of having to once disagree with Soros publically. Soros wrote an article in the 'New York Review' stating the Democratic Party should "liberate" themselves from the pro-Israel lobby and pressure Israel to negotiate with a Hamas ruled Palestine.

Soros' groups attacked Sarah Palin the Republican V.P. candidate more than John McCain; perhaps it was because McCain has connections to Soros. When McCain started the Reform Institute, to promote government accountability and transparency, he accepted funding from both the Open Society Institute and the Tides Foundation. McCain had been a member of the Soros funded Americans for Gun Safety and it was Soros who helped fund groups defending his campaign finance law. Palin however was a different story as she presented herself as a proud patriotic American. Soros wants a one world order and nationalism to any country is a hindrance to his plans. The Soros funded group Citizens for Reform and Ethics in Washington (CREW) and other liberals constantly complained about her in every way possible. They criticized her lack of experience, her parenting skills, and CREW filed many ethics charges that got thrown out for lack of merit. One of the ethic charges was about the clothing the GOP purchased for her to wear during the campaign. Frivolous charges continued, even after the election, costing her and the State of Alaska time and money. The Alinsky types of attacks were so ongoing even the style and size of her American flag pins she wore were under attack.

Soros money and his grassroots organizations, as well as the media, produced a cult type following for Obama. None of his gaffs got much attention such as his announcement that he had visited 57 States with one more to go, or his referral to a tornado in Kansas that killed ten thousand people when only 12 died, and his statement to George Stephanopoulos that McCain has not referred to his Muslim faith. Busloads of people showed up for rallies with their preprinted signs and slogans to listen to his life story and promises of hope and change. Then there was Samuel J. Wurzelbacher "Joe the Plumber" who asked Obama about his economic policy and Obama's response was, "I think when you spread the wealth around its good for everybody". The media did not question Obama's agenda, but tried to demonize "Joe" by looking into all his personal information trying to find something to attack him with.

Soros backed Democratic causes during the 2008 election cycle in the amount of $5.1 million. Obama won and Democrats won the majority in both the House and Senate. Obama made sure all his personal records were sealed and then installed his cabinet and dozens of czars with connections to Soros funded organizations. Obama supported the Recovery and Reinvestment Act and signed the Stimulus Bill soon after taking office. Within the first 100 days he supported an equal pay bill that allowed increased lawsuits against employers, the tobacco bill that gives government control over tobacco companies, expanded child health care to an additional 4 million families, increased fuel standards on vehicles which will increase the cost by about $600 each, and introduced the Cap and Trade climate change bill in which Fannie Mae owns the patent.

When Cap and Trade didn't pass Obama signed an executive order to close off land for mining. About coal and energy costs he said, "If somebody wants to build a coal powered plant they can. It's just that it will bankrupt them" and that with his energy plan "electricity prices would necessarily skyrocket". This sounds very much like the Soros plans used in other countries to bankrupt them with government control and higher costs. In the 2½ years since Obama took office gasoline prices have doubled. The Chicago Tribune reported in June 2011 that electric bills are expected to rise 40% to 60%. The government took over General Motors and is promoting their unpopular and unprofitable Chevy Volt.

Obama used the oil spill disaster to stop drilling and exploration but offers our tax money to other countries. Soros invested $811 million in Brazil's oil company and Obama offers that company federal funds promising to be their best customer. Soros invests in and owns 11.9% of the InterOil company in New Guinea and Obama offers New Guinea our tax money to help with energy development. A bill pending in Congress, HR1380, is to subsidize alternative energy trucks (natural gas) to the tune of $5 billion dollars or $64,000 per vehicle. It just so happens that Soros owns 5% of the stock held in Westport Innovations Inc. and is the company's largest stockholder. The company is a global supplier of solutions to enable engines to run on clean burning fuels. Soros even started a new investment fund called Silver Lake Kraftwerk which leverages technology to improve energy efficiency, harness renewable energy, and reduce emissions. He hired Cathy Zoi to work at his new endeavor. Zoi is Obama's former Acting Under Secretary for Energy and the Assistant Secretary for Energy Efficiency and Renewable Energy.

Soros is a frequent visitor to the White House. Soros is a convicted felon. He was convicted on insider trading in France, but that is a minor detail it seems when you are a billionaire. How many times he visited is hard to tell as the White House is not very transparent with sharing their visitor logs. They have released less than 1% of the names of visitors in the first 8 months Obama was there. How many more plans and schemes are being developed is anybody's guess.

Soros has a long interest in mines, mining, and the products that come out of mines. He is still interested in the Kosovo mine, and has a history of investing in stocks and mines that produce gold, silver, potash, copper, uranium, platinum, etc. He buys, trades, and sells the commodities and his activities are watched by other investors. In June 2011, for example, he sold his gold stock but bought gold mines. He is investing in coal, especially since 2008. In March 2008 he bought Alpha Natural Resources the 3rd largest coal company in the United States and in November he purchased 2.9 million shares of Arch Coal and 833,658 shares of Consol Energy. Alpha Natural Resources bought Massey Energy in March 2011which was the largest mining company in the Appalachian area. Alpha Natural Resources now owns 110 mines and coal resources and is the world's 3rd largest coal mining company and controls 29% of our county's coal. Much of this coal is metallurgic coal which is needed in the production of iron and steel. China needs this coal for their production of iron and steel for buildings, cars, machinery and more. The world's supply of this type of coal has been reduced due to the floods in Australia that has hindered their mining. He now owns most of West Virginia's coal mines.

Soros is not done with reforming America to his open society utopian view. In the 2010 election cycle he supported the Secretary Of State Project (SOSP). SOSP was an effort to elect Democrats in the positions of Secretary of State throughout the country, as that is where the votes are counted. SOSP states electing Democrats to that position is one of the most effective ways for "progressives" to get a fair chance of winning elections. SOSP began in 2006 when Mark Ritchie of Minnesota, one of the persons backed by the organization, won. He was the person responsible for the numerous recounts in 2008 in the Senate race between Al Franken (D) and Norm Coleman (R). The initial count gave Coleman a 215 vote lead in November, but the recounts ended when Franken achieved a 312 vote advantage. Franken was finally sworn into office in July 2009. The money spent in the 2010 election cycle did not produce the victories anticipated as only 2 of the 7 candidates they supported won.

The Trilateral Commission met in Washington D.C., April 8th to the 11th, 2011. The first session of the conference was the titled United States Politics and Economy. Speaking on this subject was David Brooks from the New York Times, Senator Tom Coburn, and Chairman of the Council of Economic Advisors Austan Goolsbee. John Podesta, President of the Center of American Progress, spoke at the 3rd session on the U.S. economy. On the second day Lawrence Summers and Michael Froman, U.S. Deputy National Security Advisor, spoke about Global Governance. National Security Advisor Thomas Donilon spoke during lunch. The last day Henry Kissinger gave a speech regarding Afghanistan and Pakistan.

That same weekend Soros had a Bretton Woods II conference in New Hampshire. The first Bretton Woods conference was held in 1944 to decide the international finance system after World War II. The dollar at the time was backed by gold and was the standard all other money was tied to. John Maynard Keynes was in attendance at the first meeting promoting economic growth with macroeconomics encouraging debt-based money for ailing counties. Keynes, at that time, argued for a world currency that was not based on the gold standard, but he lost that fight. When Nixon took the country off the gold standard in 1971, countries around the world continued to recognize the dollar as the money standard.

Soros spent $50 million on Bretton Woods II to invite 250 leaders in education, business, and government to come together to be part of his new organization Institute for New Economic Thinking (INET). As Soros said, "Reorganizing the world order will need to extend beyond the financial system". Speakers at the conference included Lawrence Summers, Paul Volcker, and Gordon Brown. The INET web site states its partners are; The London School of Economics and Political Science, Centre for International Governance Information, and the Oxford Martin School at Oxford University. Jeffrey Sachs, director of the Earth Institute and former director of the UN Millennium Project is an advisory director of INET. Former SDS member and founder of the Tides Foundation, Drummond Pike is on the governing board. The executive director is Robert Johnson; he was a managing director at Soros Fund Management and is an international investor.

In June 2011 the Bilderberg organization had their annual conference in Switzerland. Soros is a member and may have attended, but attendance lists are not available. Membership includes 120 of the world's richest and most powerful people primarily from America, Canada and Western Europe. Members include David Rockefeller, Henry Kissinger, Bill Clinton, Gordon Brown, Alan Greenspan, Ben Bernanke, Lawrence Summers, Tim Geithner, Donald Rumsfeld, and Rupert Murdoch. Members also include those from the Council on Foreign Relations, IMF, World Bank, Trilateral Commission, EU, Federal Reserve, and Bank of England. Other members are presidential candidates, senators and congressmen, plus officials in the FBI, CIA, NSA, and other government agencies.

Known objectives of the Bilderbergs are to have one international set of universal values, the ability to control world public opinion, no middle class only rulers and serfs, manufacturing crises and perpetual wars. They also want to control of education, use of UN as a world government with a UN tax on world citizens, a universal legal system, and a welfare state where the obedient are rewarded and non-conformists are exterminated. David Rockefeller wrote, "Some even believe we are part of a secret cabal working against the best interests of the United States characterizing my family and me as 'internationalists' and conspiring with others around the world to build a more integrated global political and economic structure – one world, if you will. If that's the charge, I stand guilty, and I am proud of it".

Ken Adachi, a Canadian writer stated, "What most Americans believe to be 'Public Opinion' is in reality carefully crafted and scripted propaganda designed to elicit a desired behavioral response from the public".

Americans who are members of these groups may be in violation of the Logan Act which bans private U.S. citizens from being involved in making foreign policy. The Logan Act states, "Any citizen of the United States, wherever he may be, who, without authority of the United States, directly or indirectly commences or carries on any correspondence or intercourse with any foreign government or any officer or agent thereof, with intent to influence the measures or conduct of any foreign government or any officer or agent thereof, in relation to any disputes or controversies with the United States, or to defeat the measures of the United States, shall be fined under this title or imprisoned not more than three years, or both." It certainly would make for an interesting Supreme Court case.

Soros continues to be busy, as he is purchasing farmland that got flooded in the spring of 2011. His major competition for the land grabs is the government. Critics complain the government flooded the land, which occurred when the government blew up the levees at Birds Point Missouri on May 2, 2011 which sent strong torrents of water into 130,000 acres of prime farm land, and it did not have to happen. Landowners had asked that dams downstream be opened to ease water through the area much earlier, but their requests were in vain. The government said they had to save Cairo, Illinois which is a city that had been almost abandoned and is littered with vacant buildings including homes, schools and hospitals. The excess water was the result of record snowfall the previous winter, but the amount of snow melt was able to be calculated before there was an emergency with the rising water breaching the levees. The value of lost crops is estimated at $82.5 million. The total economic loss is estimated to be $156.7 million, as farmers lost their homes, and much of the land cannot be replanted for a year and maybe not for years to come.

The Federal government is offering to purchase the land they flooded. The Federal government already owns nearly half of the land in this country with most of it west of the Mississippi River. On June 9th Obama signed Executive Order 13575 which established the White House Rural Council which gives the government complete control of rural areas of public land for development. Some are concerned the executive order is in accordance with UN Agenda 21. Agenda 21 allows government, locally, federally, or globally to take control of all areas in where humans impact the environment. Members of the National Wildlife Federation and other environmental groups are quite happy that flood water in June was still waist level high and the bottom had a hard sand bottom. They have expectations the area will become a delta with marsh plants and not grain or other farm products to feed people which used to grow there.

Soros is investing in agricultural land both in the United States and across the globe. His companies are offering to purchase the flooded farmland of distraught landowners. Not only is he purchasing land but grain elevator companies. His purchase of DeBruce Grain in Kansas City makes his company Gavilon the third largest grain company in the United States. If only a few people control the growth of food and its processing the price of food will not be based on fluctuations of need or weather conditions but on the whim of the people in control.

Soros is in his eighties and he is still attempting to control everything. One of his newest project is Justice at Stake. He provided $45million dollars on his campaign to take the election process out of selecting judges. The plan is to create a merit system and the American Bar Association selects the judges. It has already started with Soros funded Pennsylvanians for Modern Courts claiming to want to take politics out of the judicial system. It is estimated that 95% of all civil actions take place in state courts. If the court system is taken out of the hands of the people somebody will make sure they control the judges. Soros does not invest his money unless he has a plan.

The Occupy Wall Street (OWS) group started in New York City protesting greed by corporations and banks. Occupiers of other cities have grown since then demanding everything from free life time education, guaranteed income (whether one works or not), guaranteed housing, removal of debt obligations and even guaranteed recreation time. They are demanding a utopian lifestyle with no input. They decry the rich but want to have everything the rich worked for. The Occupiers have set up tent cities in public spaces without needed sanitation and restroom facilities. The tent cities are not safe as violence has erupted within their community and rape free zones needed to be established. They protest by obstructing entrances to business and disrupting events. The idea for OWS and the Occupiers came from an article in the magazine 'Ad Busters' which is funded by the Tides Foundation. The article suggested America should have Arab Spring type demonstrations to demand change.

Who finances and supports these grassroots groups? The answer is many of the organizations that receive funding from George Soros and other well known groups. These include the Working Families Party, Planned Parenthood, Common Cause, Public Campaign, MoveOn.org., Black Panthers, Nation the Islam, CAIR and the Communist Party USA, plus many others. The Working Families Party even paid some people to attend the demonstrations.

Barack Obama, Joe Biden and Nancy Pelosi have expressed their support of the demonstrators. So have Hugo Chavez, the Iranian Revolutionary Guard and Hezbollah. Some people have profited very well using Capitalism and support the Occupiers. The list includes Yoko Ono, Russell Simmons, Roseanne Barr, Kanye West, Alec Baldwin, and Michael Moore.

Judge me by the people who surround me.

CHAPTER 30

★ ★ ★ ★ ★

So what do you think?

Obama did not select the family he was born into but he was influenced by them. He did select the people he wanted to associate with as an adult. There are so many of his friends and people he chooses to associate with who do not like America. Even his wife expressed how she had never been proud of this country.

Some of his friends don't like America because they were colonists. Did they forget that America was once a colony? Countries conquering other countries have been going on since ancient history as a means to expand their power.

Some of his friends don't like America because we had slaves. Slavery was common across the globe. In America, slaves were used in the fields before there was machinery to perform the jobs that are done now. It was America that fought against slavery because they recognized it was wrong. Slavery was common perhaps as early as 8000 B.C. There was slavery in Africa, Asia, Europe and South America. It is illegal in every country now, but is estimated that there are as many as 25 million people currently that are slaves. Sudan still has debt slaves that continue through generations.

Some of his friends believe America is greedy and our wealth needs to be distributed across the globe so everybody is equal. This will not lift the quality of life for most people but will diminish the quality of life for those that worked and saved to provide for themselves and their families. I think it is much better to teach people how to prosper than to take away from others. Some of Obama's friends believe Socialism is good and Capitalism is bad. Of course they believe they will be the elite and everyone else will have to live by their rules and regulations.

Some of his friends don't like America because Israel is our friend and ally.

They don't believe Israel has the right to exist and want to establish a country that has a goal of destroying everything Jewish.

Some of his friends want power and believe that if they take away the power of America they will be more powerful. Some of his friends want power so they can control others. Some of his friends attempt to control others by promoting class envy, getting the followers to act in a way that will benefit the controllers. Some of his friends want to control the world and America is in their way.

These are my conclusions. What do you think? I hope you will not just rely of the messages that are sent over the television and radio. Please take the time to look up information from various sources to back up your opinions. You may find facts that don't agree with my opinions or you may find additional facts that will. Have fun as you search the internet and any other sources of information.

Judge me by the people who I surround myself with you said;
and we will.

References

Chapter 1

emorywheel.com EmoryWheel 10/ 19/ 2009 David Giffin 'Judge Him By His Company'

answerdigger.com AnswerDigger 1/ 12/ 2011 'Should we judge Obama by the "people with whom I surround myself"?'

Chapter 2

garymcleod.org Gary McLeod 'Republic vs. Democracy'

wisegeek.com WiseGeek 'What is a Republican Form of Government?' 'What is a Monarchy?' 'What is an Oligarchy?' 'What is a Caliphate?'

merriam-webster.com 'Republic' 'Monarchy' 'Theocracy'

lexrex.com LexRex 'An Important distinction: Democracy versus Republic'

lectlaw.com 'Republic'

westillholdthesetruths.org William J. Bennett 'We Still Hold these

constitution.org 2/6/1788 "Independent Journal" James Madison 'The Federalist No. 51'

britannica.com 'Encyclopedia Britannica's Guide to American Presidents'

investopedia.com 'Keynesian Economics'

investorwords.com 'Keynesian Economics'

famousquotesandauthors.com 'Capitalism Quotes and Quotations'

quotelucy.com 'Socialism Quotes'

answers.com 'capitalism'

econlib.org Robert Hessen The Concise Encyclopedia of Economics 'Capitalism'

wsu.edu WSU 1996 Richard Hooker The European Enlightenment Glossary 'Capitalism' differencebetween.net 'Communism vs. Capitalism'

graphcomp.com 1995 Robert M. Free 'Comparisons: Capitalism vs. Communism Vs. Socialism' 'Economics Critique: Capitalism Critique: Communism'

ai-jane.org 8/25/ 1997 Walter E. Williams 'Capitalism and the Common Man'

anu.edu 1848 Karl Marx and Frederick Engels 'Manifesto of the Communist Party' 'Socialismvscommunism.org 'Communism vs. Socialism / Communism & Socialism Explained'

brainyquotes.com 'Communism Quotes'

slayerment.com 2/27/2010 Slayerment 'Communism VS Socialism VS Fascism VS Capitalism Table/ Chart'

allaboutphilosopy.org 'What is Communism'

auburn.edu Auburn Dr. Paul M. Johnson 'Communism: a Glossary of Political Economy Terms'

onlineschool.org 2011 Online Schools 'What is Communism?'

rense.com Rense 5/28/2003 Dr. Lawrence Britt 'Fourteen Defining Characteristics of Fascism'

finestquotes.com 'Fascism Quotes'

cyberlearning-world.com George Casutto's Cyberlearning 'Types of Government'

angelfire.com 'Quotes on socialism'

worldsocialism.org 'What is socialism?'

socialismvscommunism.org 8/13/2006 World Socialist Movement 'Socialism Vs. Communism

thinkexist.com 'Socialism'

fabians.org The Fabian Society 'Research The Fabian Society Where the British left thinks'

jstor.org June 1948 Thomas P. Jenkin University of California at Los Angeles 'The American Fabian Movement'

homepage.newschool.edu 'The Fabian Socialists'

nolanchart.com 8/4/2008 Republicae (libertarian) 'A Fabian Socialist Dream Come True' alor.org Australian League of Rights February 1964 Eric Butler 'The Fabian Socialist Contribution to the Communist Advance'

couplescompany.com 'Theocracy: Monarchy: Dictatorship: Marxism: Socialism and Democracy: Socialism and Communism:'

wordig.com 'Oligarchy' 'Dictatorship'

answer.yahoo.com 'Are there any countries that are under oligarchy?'

historyforkinds.org 'Oligarchy'

aynrandlexicon.com 'Dictatorship'

fact-index.com 'Dictatorship'

historylearningsite.co.uk 'Nazi Germany – Dictatorship'

wikipedia.org Wikipedia 'Oligarchy' 'Islamic Socialism' 'Caliphate' 'Muslim Brotherhood' 'Social Justice' 'History of the Democratic Party (United States)' 'Congressional Progressive Caucus'

stutzfamily.com 2002 'Descriptions of governments can be based on:'

wiki.answers.com 'What countries use Theocracy'

vftonline.org Vine & Fig Tree 'Theocracy and Anarcho-Theocracy'

mahalo.com Mahalo 'Islamic Socialism'

mzuhdijasser.com 2/6/2011 M. Zuhdi Jasser Pundicity 'Understanding Egypt: Islamic Socialism and the Left'

freerepublic.com FreeRepublic.com 2/3/2011 'News of the World'

examiner.com Examiner February 4, 2011 Bill Belew 'Is Islamic Socialism and the Muslim Brotherhood an Egyptian Solution?'

governmentgrantinfo.com 'Government Grants Information'

ikhwanweb.com Muslim Brotherhood 2/2/2011 'What the Muslim Brothers Want'

boncherry.com Boncherry 'Islamic Socialism Political System' 'Caliphate: Definition and History'

huffingtonpost.com 6/25/2012 AP Egypt Election Results

hawaii.edu 1997 R.J. Rummel 'Statistics of Democide: Genocide and Mass Murder Since

1990' 'R. J.Rummel'/ July 1997 'Rudolph Rummel Talks About the Miracle of Liberty and Peace' 'The Freeman: Ideas of Liberty and Peace'

mega.mu.ampp 3/13/2001 R.J. Rummel 'Freedom, Democracy, Peace, Power, Democide, and War

lp.org 'What is the Libertarian Party/ Introduction/Our History/Platform/ Issues'

gop.com 'Issues' 'What we believe'

gop.gov 'GOP Solutions For America

pledge.gop.gov 'The Pledge to America'

cprr.org 1860 Central Pacific Railroad Photographic History Museum 'Republican National Platform, 1860'

suite101.com Suite101 9/3/2008 Linda Sue Grimes 'Women and the Republican Party Suffrage Rights First Fought for by Republicans

nfrw.org National Federation of Republican Women 'The Party of Women'

oldgop.gop.com 'The Republican Party GOP History'

ushistory.org 'Republican Philadelphia- The Origins of the Republican Party'

american-conservativevalues.com 'Getting to the Heart of Republican Beliefs'

citizendium.org Citizendium 'U.S. Republican Party, History'

rsc.jordan.house.gov 1/4/2011 'What is RSC?'

rlc.org Republican Liberty Caucus 'Statement of Principles and Positions'

legal-dictionary.thefreedictionary.com 'Republican government'

encyclopedia.thefreedictionary.com 'Republic'

couplescompany.com Laura Dawn Lewis 'Citizenship Republic'

repconcaucus.com 'About the RNCC'

honda.house.gov 12/20/2010 'Congressional Asian Pacific American Caucus- Chairman's Message'

rnha.org The Republican National Hispanic Assembly 'About – Our Mission- Our History

garymcleod.org Gary McLeod 'Republic vs. Democracy/Rule by Law vs. Rule by Majority' democracy-building.info 2004 'A Short Definition of Democracy'

pursuingtruthinpolitics.wordpress.com 8/12/2009 'Forms of Government: Democracy vs. Republic'

observer.com Observer 1/5/2011 David Freedlander The New York Observer 'Senate Dems bolt Democratic Caucus'

lexrex.com LexRex 'An Important Distinction: Democracy versus Republic'

albatrus.org 'Democracy Versus Republic'

realdemocracy.com 'Are We a Democracy or a Republic?'

crowley.house.gov 1/2/2011 'New Democrats' Statement on the Announcement of William Daley as White House Chief of Staff' 'About the New Democrat Coalition'

esortment.com 'History of the Democratic Party'

hnn.us.com History News Network 'The Racist History of the Democratic Party'

rosshouse.gov 'Blue Dog Coalition'

arkansasgopwing.blogspot.com 10/8/2010 ARRA News Service 'The Blue Dog Coalition Myth of Being Fiscally Responsible Democrats'

usliberals.about.com About.com Deborah White 'Blue Dog Democrats, Fiscally Conservative House Members'

bluedogsdem.com 'Welcome to the Blue Dog Coalition Website'

thehill.com The Hill 11/16/2010 Vicki Needham 'Blue Dog Coalition announces new leadership'

newsobserver.com server Newsobserver 6/6/2008 Ryan Teague Beckwith 'Who are the Blue Dog Democrats?'

wsj.com Wall Street Journal 11/2/2010 'Election Thins Blue Dog Coalition'

pdamerica.org Congressional Progressive Caucus of the US Congress 'The Progressive Promise: Fairness For All' 'PDA Issue Organizing teams'

coms.gov 'House Caucuses

house.gov Sustainable Energy & Environment Coalition

dsusa.org Democratic Socialist of America 'The Organization' 'Where We Stand The Political Perspective of the Democratic Socialist of America' 'Analysis of the Progressive Caucus's Grades' grijalva.house.gov 6/15/2010 Raul M. Grijalva 'Letter to the President Regarding the Need for Comprehensive Immigration Reform' 'On reauthorization of the Elementary and Secondary Education Act' 11/7/2007 'CPC Official Position on US Policy towards Iran' 10/5/2007 'On Reforming the Foreign Intelligence Surveillance Act and Protecting Our Civil Liberties' 9/5/2007 'On International Trade Reform and US Trade Policy' 12/11/2009 'CPC Release Health Care Principles' 1/ 5/ 2011 'Caucus Member List'

dems.gov 'The Democratic Caucus' 'Issues'

dyn.politico.com Politico 3/15/2009 Chris Frates Politico 'Dems: Don't push health care too far'

usnews.com USNews 5/11/2006 Michael Barone 'Democratic Party Philosophy'

democrats.org 'What We Stand For'

chc.velazques.house.gov Congressional Hispanic Caucus web site

cbcfinc.org The Congressional Black Caucus Foundations Inc. 'Public Health' 'Vision/ Mission/ Goals' 'CPAR Center for Policy Analysis and Research' 'Leadership Development' 'Economic Development'

nytimes.com NY Times 1/5/2011 Ashley Southall 'Republican Allen West Joins Congressional Black Caucus'

unmillenniumproject.org 'UN Millennium Project' 'Millennium Development Goals' 'Millennium Villages'

aim.org Accuracy in Media 2/12/2008 Cliff Kincaid 'Obama's Global Tax Proposal Up for Senate Vote'

un.org UN 'United Nations Millennium Development Goals'

socialdemocratsuse.org Social Democrats Socialist Party 4/11/2009 'One in five Americans finds socialism superior, poll says' 'Party Within a Party' 'Declaration of Principles – adopted June 22, 2008, amended May 3rd 2009'

jeremiahproject.com JeremiahProject.com 'The Trashing of America' 'Socialist in the House'

people.ubr.com 'Norman Thomas Quote

newworldencyclopedia.org 'Norman Thomas'

wnd.com World Net Daily 8/115/2010 'How many socialist sit in Congress today?'

socialistparty-usa.org 2010 Socialist Party USA '2011 Platform' thecypresstimes.com The Cypress Times 8/9/2010 John G. Winder 'Congressmen Fail to Include "Democratic Socialists of America: Membership in the Election Campaigns'

holycoast.blogspon.com HolyCoast.com 3/25/2010 'Sen. Max Baucus: Obamacare Was An "Income Shift"'

hyscience.com 8/25/2010 Hyscience Developer Behind Ground Zero Mosque Was a Waiter Just A Few Years Ago (So where did he get the money?)

americanthinker.com American Thinker 8/14/2010 Rick Moran 'Socialist Party of America reveals 70 Democrats as belonging to their caucus'

dougpowers.com 8/14/2010 Doug Powers 'List of the 70 Democrat Members Who Are in The Socialist Party Caucus; "The Powers That Be"'

gatewaypundit.rightnetwork.com GateWayPundit 8/13/2010 Jim Hoft 'American Socialist Release Names of 70 Congressional Democrats In Their Ranks'

action.progressivecongress.org Progressive Congress 'About Us'

Chapter 3

discoverthenetworks.org Discover the Networks 'Saul Alinsky' 'George Alvin Wiley'

humanevents.com Human Events 3/9/2007 Jed Babbin 'Who was Saul Alinsky?'

progress.org The Progress Report Sanford D. Horwitt 'Saul Alinsky and the Industrial areas Foundation' 'Alinsky: More Important Now Than Ever'

crossroad.to.com Quotes and Excerpts from "Rules for Radicals" by Saul Alinsky 1971

hyscience.com Hyscience 8/26/2008 Richard Hyscience 'Michelle Obama Used Lines From Saul Alinsky's Book "Rules for Radicals" in Last Night's Speech'

canadafreepress.com Canada Free Press 9/2/2008 Judi McLeod 'Saul Alinsky's son: Obama learned his lesson well'

nea.org National Education Association 'Recommended Reading: Saul Alinsky, The American Organizer'

nndb.com NNDB 'Saul Alinsky'

washingtonpost.com Washington Post 3/25/2007 Peter Slevin 'For Clinton and Obama, a Common Ideological Touchstone'

psrf.org Public Service Research Foundation 'Labor Unrest and Public Policy' newzeal.blogspot.com NewZeal 6/27/2010 Trevor Loudon '1966 Cloward/Piven Strategy Unveiled at Socialist Scholars Conference'

americanthinker.com American Thinker 2/7/2009 Nancy Coppock 'The Cloward/ Piven Strategy of Economic Recovery' 11/23/2009 James Simpson 'Cloward /Piven Government'

thenation.com The Nation 12/22/2010 Frances Fox Piven 'Mobilizing the Jobless' 12/1/2008 Frances Fox Piven 'Obama Needs a Protest Movement' 5/8/ 1967 'Richard A. Cloward and Frances Fox Piven' 'Author Bios – Frances Fox Piven' 5/2/1966 Frances Fox Piven and Richard Cloward 'The Weight of the Poor: A Strategy to End Poverty'

theblaze.com The Blaze 12/31/2010 Jonathon M. Seidl 'Frances Fox Piven Rings In the New Year By Calling For Violent Revolution'

keywiki.org 'Frances Fox Piven'

gc.cuny.edu The Graduate Center Cuny 'Frances Fox Piven'

newsrealblog.com NewsRealBlog 1/8/2011 Matthew Vadum 'Marxist Frances Fox Piven Call For A Violent Uprising Against the American System'

wikipedia.org Wikipedia 'Cloward /Piven Strategy'

itmakessenseblog.com 8/5/2010 'Cloward – Piven Strategy Part 1'

backpast.org Backpast 'Wiley, George Alvin (1931 – 1971)'

georgewileycenter.org George Wiley Center 'About Us' 'Our Philosophy' 'Keep The Pressure On Keep Utilities On'

manhatton-institute.org 8/26/2006 Steven Malanga/Wall Street Journal 'Acorn Squash'

Chapter 4

usatoday.com USA Today 4/7/2008 Dan Nakaso 'Family precedent: Obama's grandmother blazed trails'

google.com 2/6/2009 Hugh Pickens 'President Obama's Mother and Grandparents lived in Ponco City, Oklahoma in Early 1950's'

everything2.com 'The CIA in the 1950's'

hawaiireporter.com Hawaii Reporter 8/11/2010 Duane Vachon 'Quiet Hawaii Hero Stanley Armour Dunham Had Chest Full of Medals and a Grandson Who Became President'

genealogy.about.com Kimberly Powell About.com 'Ancestry of Barack Obama' freerepublic.com FreeRepublic.com 12/14/2008 Free Republic 'Obamanism 101: The Stanley Ann and Madelyn Dunham factor'

obambi.wordpress.com 8/19/2010 Wayne Madsen 'Barry in the Company III'

info-wars.org 8/19/2010 Infowars Ireland 'Barack Obama conclusively outed as CIA creation

proliberty.com Idaho Observer July 2009 Don Harkins 'Aka BHO (et al) 'Who's your Daddy?' 4/25/2009 Don Nicoloff 'The Three Stooges go to Washington: Part 3' 4/25/2009 Don Nicoloff 'The Three Stooges go to Washington: Part 6' 9/ 2008 Don Nicoloff The Three Stooges go to Washington: Part 4'

opionion-maker.org WMR 11/17/2010 Wayne Madsen 'Obama's Hawaii Connection'

wordsforgood.org 12/6/2009 'Obama's Childhood Medallion & the Art of Genetic Engineering'

gray.com Susan Peters KAKE 10 ABC 'President Obama: From Kansas to the Capitol Part 1-4'

wnd.com World Net Daily 4/12/2010 Jerome R. Corsi 'FBI destroyed file on Obama's grandfather'

judicaryreport.com Judiciary Report 4/13/2010 'FBI Destroyed Terrible File on Obama's Grandfather'

familypedia.wiki.com 'Stanley Armour Dunham (1918 – 1992)'

washingtonexaminer.com Washington Examiner May 2009 Betsy Taylor and Randy Herschaft 'AP report: Obama's grandfather Stanley Dunham'

newforestpa.gov 2010 New Forest National Park 'In the footsteps of the President's grandfather'

poncacity.com 'History of the Marland Oil Company'

digital.library.okstate.edu Oklahoma Historical Society 'Marland Oil Company'

poncacitynews.com Ponca City News 9/18/1996 Louise Abercrombie Ponca City News 'Piper Cub 50th Anniversary Included Fly-In-Here Thursday''

uus.org Unitarian Universalism 'History'' Justice& Diversity' 'Theological Perspectives' 'Principles' 'Social Justice' 'Spiritual Practice' 'Life and Death' ' Existence of a Higher Power'

eastshoreunitarian.org Eastshore Unitarian 'About Us' 'Our Mission' 'Core Values' Statements of Purpose' 'History' 'Social Justice'' Peace Making Pledge' Inner Peacemaking' Social Peacemaking'/ Global Peacemaking' wikipedia.org 'History of Hawaii'

deephawaii.com 'A brief history of Hawaii 300 AD – 1900'

Chapter 5

obambi.wordpress.com 1/5/2010 'Who's Your Daddy? Who's Your Mama?'

fourwinds10.com 12/3/2009 Ken Adachi educate-youself.org 'Obama's Parentage and Nationality'

thepopulist.net The Populist 'The Rockefeller Family Secret? – Jews'

educate-yourself.org 2/24/2009 Dr. Orly Taitz ESQ 'The Fraud of Barry Soetoro (a.k.a. Barack Hussein Obama)'

atlasshrugs2000.typepad.com Atlas Shrugs 10/24/2008 Pam Geller Atlas Shrugs 'How could Stanley Ann Dunham have delivered Barack Hussein Obama Jr. in August of 1961 in Honolulu When...?'

atlasshrugs222.typepad.com Atlas Shrugs 7/20/2008 Pam Geller 'Atlas Exclusive Final Report on Obama Birth Certificate Forgery Change You Can Believe in'

hirecord.org. The Record 4/1/2010 Joe N. S. Indiana 'Original Obama birth certificate unearthed in Harvard Law School Library'

thenewamerican.com New American 3/24/2010 Rebecca Terrell 'Hawaii Denies Requests for Obama's Birth Certificate'

associatedcontent.com AssociatedContent/Yahoo 2011 B.L. Babb 'Is Obama a U. S. Citizen? This is About More Than a Birth Certificate'

wnd.com World Net Daily 1/18/2011 Jerome R. Corsi 'Hawaii governor can't find Obama birth certificate' 4/11/2010 Drew Zahn 'Kenyan Official: Obama born here' 8/2/2009 "Is this really smoking gun of Obama's Kenyan birth?' 10/27/2009 Aaron Klein 'Michelle contradicts Obama nativity story' 8/4/2009 Jerome R. Corsi 'Obama 'mama' : 15 days from birth to Seattle class' 11/9/2010 Jerome R. Corsi '62 letter from father ignores Obama, mom' 7/ 6/2009 Jerome R. Corsi 'Hospital won't back Obama birth claim' 11/2/2008 Jerome R. Corsi 'Doubts persist about Obama birth certificate' 8/17/2008 Aaron Klein 'Was young Obama Indonesian citizen?' 8/17/2008 'Obama's childhood records vindicate Corsi book'

americanthinker.com American thinker 2/7/2010 Jack Cashill 'Another Look at Obama's Origins'

hubpages.com HubPages Vraiavala 'Obama's Mother: Stanley Anne Dunham'

cashill.com Cashill 2/14/2010 'A Further Inquiry into Obama's Origins' thepostemail.com Post & Email 10/21/2009 John Carlton 'A Witness Steps Forward, History or Internet "Rumour" Documented' 9/5/2010 Sharon Rondeau 'Document allegedly Obtained in Kenya Sent to Every Member of Congress'

nigerianobservernews.com Nigerian Observer News November 2008 Solomon Asowata 'US Presidential Polls: Obama, McCain slug it out today'

allafrica.com 1/28/2007 All Africa 'Africa: Obama...'Is White House Beckoning on Africa?'

web.archive.org 6/27/2004 AP The Standard LTD 'Kenyan –born Obama all set for US Senate' 10/25/2008 Internet Archive 'Otunnu on Luo Tribe Member Being Elected President'

freerepublic.com FreeRepublic.com 10/18/2009 the Right Side of Life 'Historical News Articles and Fact Check Agree: Obama is Kenyan-born' 9/8/2010 Polarik 'Stanley Ann Dunham's Birth Certificate REVEALED' Trevor Loudon New Zeal 'Obama File 197 Neil Abercrombie, Yet Another Covert Socialist in the Obama "Orbit"'

cartaretnewstimes.com Cartaret County News/ Times 4/11/2010 'Kenyan born?'

aipnews.com AIP News 11/14/2009 AP 'June 27, 2004 Sunday Standard story described Obama as "Kenyan" born (other similar stories surface)'

npr.org NPR 10/9/2008 Ofeibea Quist-Arcton 'Trial and Triumph: Stories Out of Africa'

canadafreepress.com Canada Free Press2/22/2009 Joy Tiz 'Barry Soetoro: Profiles in Chaos'

israelnationalnews.com Arutz Sheva Israel National News 1/11/2009 Tamar Yonah 'Obama Born In Kenya? His Grandmother Says Yes'

therightperspective.org RightPerspective.org 1/1/2009 'Where In the World Was Barack Obama Born?'

thomhartmann.com 6/10/2010 Joe Kovacs 'Hawaii Elections clerk: Obama not born here'

indonesianmatters.com Indonesian Matters 11/ 6/2008 'Barry Soetoro Former Menteng student now US President'

righttruth.typepad.com RightTruth 10/25/2008 'October Surprise!!! Barack Obama Born in the Coast Provincial General Hospital at Mombass Kenya at 7:24 pm on August 4th in 1961?'

rense.com Rense 7/25/2008 Lame Cherry 'Obama's 'Birth Certificate''

politicalvelcraft.org 3/24/2010 'Obama Eligibility: Barry Soetoro's Sister May Soetoro, Born In Indonesia Has Here Hawaiian (COLB) /Certification of Live Birth Too' patriotnewsnetwork.org Patriot News Network 2/22/2010 John Spoony 'Citizen Kenya or Agent double-O Soul: WHO is he???'

capitol.hawaii.gov (S338-17.8) Certificates for children born out of State. (a) Upon application of an adult or the legal parents of a minor child, the director of health shall issue a birth certificate ...Vol. 06 Ch. 0321-1344

beforeitsnews.com 6/26/2010 BeforeItsNews 'Bombshell: Hawaii Official Janice Okubos's birth certificate was used to forge Obama's COLB, amended Obama's records, Got Politifact?' July 31, 2010 'Stanley Ann Dunham/Obama/ Soetoro-Passport Records Released Under FOIA, Earliest Passport Application No Longer Exists, Got Purged?'

politicalforum.com 7/1/2009 Political Forum.com 'Of Obama's birth certificate and COLB'

cbsnews.com CBS News Andrew C. McCarthy National Review 'Suborned in the U.S.A.'

youtube.com YouTube 2011 'Obama Birth Certificate in Adobe Illustrator – Prank of Test Layer... 'PROOF Birth Certificate FORGERY Layers' Alex Jones 2011 'Proof the Obama Birth Certificate is a fake'

seattletimes.com Seattle Times Jonathan Martin 'Obama's mother known here as "uncommon"'

reasearchandideas.com 'Stanley Ann Dunham'

thepoliticalcesspool.org PoliticalCesspool.org 10/24/2008 James Edwards 'Race, Politics and Hypocrisy in 21st Century 'Nude Photos of Obama's Mother'

astuteblogger.blogspot.com Astute Bloggers 10/22/2008 'Every Thing You Ever Wanted to Know About Barack Hussein Obama Soetero... But Were Afraid to Ask Naughty Obama Mamma'

libertasbigblog.com 'Nude Holiday Obama'

wiki.answers.com 'Are the nude photos of Obama's mother that are circulating around the internet for real and who did she make them for?

dailymail.co.uk Mail Online 4/21/2011 David Gardner ' 'Any nation will do': New book reveals Barack Obama wanted to be prime minister of Indonesia at tender age of 9'

military-money-matters.com 'Barack Obama's Mother'

squidoo.com Squidoo 'What You May Not Have Know About Barack Obama'

hawaii.edu Malamalama Magazine of University of Hawaii 1/14/2009 Paula Bender 'Legacy of the President's Mother' oilforimmigration.org 1/10/2009 David Crockett 'More on Stanley Ann Dunham death certificate Dr. Orly Taitz released'

librarieshawaii.org 'Passports'

hawaii.hi.us 'Driver Licensing General Information'

wikipedia.org Wikipedia 'Ann Dunham' 'Neil Abercrombie' 'Barack Obama Sr.'

sodahead.com SodaHead 2/2/2010 'Is Obama's Mother still alive?'

auburnjournal.com Auburn Journal 1/28/2011 Gold Penner 'Hawaii Health Director Quits 1 Week After Obama Birth Certificate Admitted "Does Not Exist"'

nydailynews.com NY Daily News 1/22/2011 Aliyah Sahid 'Neil Abercrombie, Hawaii governor drops mission to dispel birthers, prove Obama was born in state'

mediate.com Mediate 12/27/2010 Jon Bershad 'Hawaii Governor will try to end birther debate'

loatze.blogspot.com 1/25/2007 'An American Expat in Southeast Asia'

globalpolitician.com Ted Belman 'Obama's Muslim Connection'

en.metapedia.org Barack Hussein Obama, Sr.'

dy.politica.com 4/15/2008 Ben Smith and Jeffrey Ressner Politico 'Long – lost article by Obama's dad surfaces'

guardian.co.uk Guardian/UK 1/10/2008 Elana Schor 'The other Obama-Kennedy connection'

Chapter 6

voltairenet.org VoltaireNetwork 8/20/2010 Wayne Madsen "The Obama Story: All in the Company Part 1'

carolo43.newsvine.com 1/4/2011 'Obama's heritage'

freebase.com 'Barack Obama Sr.'

genealogy.about.com 'Ancestry of Barack Obama'

freerepublic.com FreeRepublic.com 4/8/2008 The News Now Network 'Obama's Paternal Grandfather Hussein Onyango Obama?' 8/8/2010 Ellie Velinska Big Bureaucracy 'Lolo Soetoro; the exchange student saga that brought Obama to Indonesia' 8/15/2004 'top 10 connections between John Kerry and 527s' iwulocal1142.org 3/12/2009 International Longshore and Warehouse Union 'Barack Obama Senior in 1962'

washingtonpost.com Washington Post 10/8/2010 Dinesh D'Souza 'Why Barack Obama is an anti-colonialist'

livejournal.com 8/11/2010 Wayne Madsen 'The US & Obama/Soetoro's CIA Pedigree'

dailymail.co.uk Mail Online 6/19/2010 Zoe Brennan, Paul Oregon 'The real reason President Obama loathes the British…' 4/21/1011 David Gardner 'Any nation will do New book reveals Barack Obama wanted to be prime minister…' 4/12/2011 'He WAS born in Hawaii' 4/26/2011 'Boost for birthers as poll reveals only 38% of Americans believe Obama was born in US'

usasurvival.org America's Survival Inc 'Investigators release reports on Obama's communist connections'

telegraph.co.uk Telegraph 2/14/2009 Tim Shipman 'Barack Obama sends bust of Winston Churchill on its way back to Britain'

worldcantwait.net 2/14/2010 Ann Wright 'U. Hawaii Protest Challenges CIA Recruitment on Campus'

eastwestcenter.org East West Center 'Mission and Organization Overview' 'Education Overview'

opinion-maker.org 11/17/2010 Wayne Madsen 'Obama's Hawaii Connection'

yourdictionary.com 'grant-n-aid'

investopedia.com 'Grant-in-Aid'

forbes.com Forbes 9/18/2010 Dinesh D'Souza 'Obama's Problem With Business'

indonesiamatters.com Indonesia Matters 10/4/2006 'Citizenship Law'

businessinsider.com Business Insider 4/22/2011 '45% of Republicans think Obama was born somewhere else'

cnn.com CNN 4/27/2011 Policalticker 'Certificate of Live Birth'

latimes.com LA Times 4/27/2011 'Obama birth certificate: Prominent birther still has doubts' 6/10/2010 Teresa Watanabe 'President's half sister speaks on her mixed-race experience'

alohareporter.com Aloha Reporter 2/18/2011 'Obama birth certificate not for sale' 3/18/2010 'Hawaii considering law to ignore Obama birthers' patriotactionnetwork.com Patriot Action Network 4/29/2011 Steve Cooper 'Certificate of live Birth birthplace Kenya; registered Honolulu...'

escapetyranny.com EscapeTyranny.com 5/1/2011 Ben Hart 'Here's the birth certificate that appeared in the Aloha Reporter that says Obama was born in Kenya'

obamareleaseyourrecords.blogspot.com 2/2011 Prof. Charles Rice 'Obama Eligibility'

thestatecolumn.com The State Column 22/18/2011 'Obama birth certificate bill dies in Hawaii'

politico.com Politico 2/15/2011 Andy Barr '51% GOP voters: Obama Foreign'

conservativebyte.com ConservativeByte 4/26/2011 'Shock Poll: Only 38% say Obama definitely born in USA'

expat.or.id/info The Jakarta Post 6/26/2004 Kurniawan Hari 'Revision to Citizenship Law Imposes More restrictions'

abovetopsecret.com AboveTopSecret 10/19/2008 'Obama (Barry Soetoro) has Dual Citizenship'

wikipedia.org Wikipedia May Soetoro-Ng

metapedia.org 'Lolo Soetoro Mangunharjo'

museumstuff.com 'Lolo Soetoro: Biography'

opinionmaker.org 1/19/2011 Raja Mujtaba 'Past Haunts Obama'

beforeitsnews.com BeforeItsNews 'Obama Stepfather Lolo Soetoro's U.S. Records Released, some Records...'

obamaforwards.com 4/8/2010 'Obama a Muslim'

redstate.com RedState 1/19/2010 'Top lies of President Obama!'

zimbio.com Zimbio 8/16/2010 'Previously unknown Obama stepsister dies'

firetown.com Firetown 11/7/2010 'Obama's adopted sister dies now right before meeting him?'

wtpotus.wordpress.com WTPOTUS 8/7/2010 'Lia Obama's Adopted Sister Died Suddenly'

kabarinews.com Kabari News 11/17/2008 Yayat Suratmo 'K-video: Kisah Orang-Orang Dekat Obama (1)' huffingtonpost.com Huffington Post 11/12/2008 Dan Nakaso 'Maya Soetoro-Ng: Meet Barack's Sister'

businessinsider.com Business Insider 4/12/11 Megan Angelo Business Insider 'WATCH: Al Roker Was clearly Only Allowed to Ask President Obama's Half-Sister One Birther Question'

nytimes.com NY Times 1/20/2008 Deborah Solomon 'All in the Family' 4/21/2011 Dalia Sussman, Marina Stefan 'Obama and the Birthers in the latest poll'

examiner.com Examiner 7/27/2009 Gregory Dail 'Did you know? Obama's half sister, born in Indonesia, has a Hawaiian Certification of Live Birth'

wnd.com World Net Daily 4/12/2011 Bob Unruh World Net Daily 'Obama's half-sister joins eligibility talk-show tour' 10/30/2008 Jerome R. Corsi World Net Daily 'Marxist mentor' sold drugs with Obama' 8/11/2010 Jerome R. Corsi 'Previously unknown Obama stepsister dies' politicalbelcraft.org 9/23/2010 'Obama's Step Sister Dies: Lia Soetoro & Barry Soetoro Both Were Indonesian Citizens' 4/29/2011 Obama's McCain resolution demand American parents' 10/27/2009 Chelsea Schilling 'Obama law tab up to $1.7 million' 6/5/2011 Jerome R Corsi 'Criminal complaint details birth-certificate forgery'

telegraph.co.uk Telegraph 8/22/2008 Toby Harnden 'Frank Marshall Davis, alleged Communist, was early influence on Barack Obama'

americanthinker.com American Thinker 10/30/2008 Paul Kengor 'Dreams from Frank Marshall Davis'

citizenwells.wordpress.com CitizenWells 10/22/2008 Andy Martin 'Andy Martin Hawaii, Obama not Barack Obama, FRANK MARSHALL DAVIS father,...'

newzeal.blogspot.com NewZeal 2/8/2010 'Obama File 96 coincidence? Obama, Frank Marshall Davis and Earl Durham Connection'

nationalreview.com National Review 10/5/2010 Paul Kengor 'Obama's Communist Mentor'

uncap.lib.uchicago.edu DuSable Museum 'Guide to the Frank Marshall Davis Collection 1935-1987'

nationalenquirer.com National Enquirer 10/20/2008 'Exclusive: Obama Sex Perv Scandal'

2. hawaii.edu Kathryn Waddell Takara, Ph.D. 'Frank Marshall Davis; Black Labor Activist and Outsider Journalist: Social Movements in Hawaii'

reformation.org Reformation.org 2008 Niall Kikenny 'President Frank Marshall Davis Obama!'

discoverthenetworks.org Discover the Networks 'Frank Marshall Davis' poets.org 2011 Academy of American Poets 'Frank Marshall Davis'

Chapter 7

eastchance.com 'Occidental College'

cies.org 'Fulbright Scholar Program'

educationnews.org EducationNews 11/6/2010 Jimmy Kilpatrick 'Uncovered: Obama's mystery college years'

blogs.abcnews.com ABC News 4/8/2008 'Obama's College Trip to Pakistan'

mikefrances.com 9/8/2008 'In 1981 Barack Obama visited Pakistan stayed with Mohammed Hasam Chandoo, who are the Chandoo Brothers?'

strategypage.com 'Osama Bin Laden – Timeline'

flickr.com Flickr 'Osama Bin Laden and Zbigniew Brzezinski'

atlasshrugs2000.typepad.com Atlas Shrugs 9/12/2008 'Obama's Paki Connection'

drkatesview.wordpress.com 10/19/2009 drkate 'Obama, Brzezinski and Pakistan'

nytimes.com NY Times 2/8/2008 Serge Kovaleski 'The Young Obama' 2/6/1900 Fox Butterfield 'First Black Elected to Head Harvard's Law Review' 11/17/2010 Charlie Savage 'Laurence Tribe is Leaving Justice Job' 4/2/1981 Deidre Cammody 'Brzezinski Renews his Columbia ties'9/15/1983 The New York Times 'Deposit Survey Puts Compliance at 82%' 3/26/1983 Sam Howe Verhivek 'Study Finds More New York Trash, Despite Crisis' 10/5/2001 'G.E. and the Hudson' 10/30/2007 Janny Scott 'Obama's Account of New York years often differs from what others say' 5/27/2004 Anthony DePalma 'Metro Briefing New York Cortland: Concern About Mercury Levels' 12/31/2010 Kareem Fahim 'Cuomo Names Developers of a Student Loan Center'

wnd.com World Net Daily 2/5/2011 Jack Cashill 'How Obama got into Harvard' 9/29/2008 Aaron Klein World Net Daily 'Is Obama hiding something from his college days?'

canadafreepress.com Canada Free Press 2/15/2010 Joy Tiz 'Finally! Somebody Remembers Obama at Occidental'

nicedeb.wordpress.com 10/23/2010 'Paul Kengor interview on The Glen Meakem Show'

newsmax.com Newsmax 2/8/2010 Ronald Kessler 'Obama Espoused Radical Views in College'

gulfcoastnews.com GulfCoastNews 5/3/2009 Perry Hicks 'The Long March'

pak-times.com Pakistan Times 7/10/2011 Azhar Masood 'Obama's larkana Connection' iaoj.wordpress.com Indus Asia Online Journal 11/16.2009 Khalid Hashmani 'Obama's Sindh connection'

wikipedia.org Wikipedia 'President of Pakistan' 'Zbigniew Brzezinski' Muhammad Mian Soomro' 'Gamaliel Foundation' 'Laurence Tribe' 'Lawrence Summers' 'Cass Sunstein' 'The Strawberry Statement' 'Business International Corporation'

cannonfire.blogspot.com 4/22/2009 'Obama, the passport scandal, and a murder'

timetotellthetruth.net 'Names of key people with influence into Obama's life'

americanthinker.com American Thinker 9/14/2008 Thomas Lifson 'Obama's mentor at Occidental College speaks'

abagond.wordpress.com 4/11/2008 'Obama at Occidental College'

urbanlegends.about.com David Emery 'Obama Citizenship case reaches Supreme Court'

directorblue.blogspot.com 10/23/2010 'exclusive transcript; Obama at Occidental was looking forward to an imminent..revolution, where the working class would overthrow the ruling class'

theurbangrind.net UrbanGrind.net 'On Obama's 1981 trip to Pakistan'

freerepublic.com Free Republic Pakistan International News 9/23/2008 'Soomro a host to Obama in Pakistan

gpr.hudson.org 11/15/2010 Ronald Radosh Hudson Institute 'The Obama Vision'

gamaliel.org Gamaliel 'About Gamaliel History' 'Mission'

illuninateurself.com 'Gamaliel Foundation'

romanticpoet.wordpress.com RomanticPoet 2/4/2011 Michael J. Gaynor 'Mary Gonzales of the Gamaliel Foundation' 'Gamaliel and the Barack Obama Connection by Gregory A. Galluzzo'

pittsburghlive.com Pittsburgh Tribune-Review 10/17/2010 Stanley Kurtz 'Obama's radical past'

blogcritics.org 'Walking the Edge of Immorality

indybay.org 9/25/2008 Michael Harris Indybay 'President Obama – Harvard Law Review'

politico.com Politico 8/22/2008 Ben Smith and Jeffrey Ressner 'Exclusive: Obama's lost law review article'

voices.washingtonpost.com Washington Post 10/28/2010 Al Kamen 'Laurence Tribe unfiltered on Sonia Sotomayor' keywiki.org 'Charles Ogletree' 'Zbigniew Brzezinski'

cyber.law.harvard.edu Berkman Center, Harvard 'Charles Ogletree'

breitbart.com Breitbart.com 3/7/2012 Dan Rielh 'Obama Mentor: We hid this throughout the 2008 campaign' 3/9/2012 'Ogletree's I was just kidding doesn't survive scrutiny' 'Video of Obama praising Prof. Derrick Bell'

patdollard.com Pat Dollard 3/8/2012 'Obama forced his students to read racist Professor Bell's…at Chicago Law School'

townhall.com Townhall 3/9/2012 Katie Pavlich 'Radical professor Obama embraced: I live to harass white forks'

salon.com Salon 5/7/2010 Guy Uriel, Charles Anupam Chander, Luis Fuetes-Rohwer and Angela Onwuachi-Willig Salon 'The White House's Kagan talking points are wrong'

associatedcontent.com AssociatedContent.com 9/18/2010 William Browning 'Obama Selects Harvard Professor Elizabeth Warren to Launch New Federal financial Protection Bureau'

nysun.com NY Sun 9/2/2008 Ross Goldberg 'Obama's Years at Columbia Are a Mystery'

weeklystandard.com Weekly Standard 7/25/2008 Jaime Sneider 'Obama's Missing Thesis'

metrogael.blogspot.com Metro Gael 6/2/2009 'Zbigniew Brzezinski and the Obama Doctrine'

mindfully.org Progressive Review 1/3/2009 'The Strange Rise of Obama'

expressindia.com Express India 9/3/2008 'Obama's mother may have spent 5 years in Pakistan'

columbia.edu Columbia University 11/5/2008 'Barack Obama, CC'83, first Columbia Graduate Elected President of the United States' Shira Boss-Bicak 'Barack Obama'83'

seattletimes.nwsource.com Seattle Times 5/15/2008 Adam Goldman, Robert Tanner 'Old friends recall Obama's years in LA, NY'

csis.org Center for Strategic & International Studies 'Zalmay Khalizad'

insightanalytical.wordpress.com 10/27/2008 'The Story Unfolds 2: Obama, Biden, Brzezinski, Carter…and the Trilateral commission?'

wikicu.com 'Barack Obama'

columbiabso.org 'Black Students Organization'

the7thfire.com David Allen Rivera 'Final Warning a History of the New World Order' onlinejournal.com Online Journal 8/19/2009 Wayne Madsen 'The Latin American policies of Richard Milhous Obama' 1/5/2010 Wayne Madsen 'Obama's White House Press Corps warned about asking certain questions' 9/24/2009 Wayne Madsen 'New details on Obama's CIA front employer'

veteranstoday.com Veteran'sToday.com 8/18/2010 Wayne Madsen 'Obama's CIA Connections, Part I and II'

debsimonforcongress.blogspot.com 12/8/2010 'Deb Simon for Congress'

everything2.com 'The Strawberry Statement (review)'

beatl.barnard.columbia.edu 'The Strawberry Statement" Notes of a College Revolutionary'

uk.answers.yahoo.com 'Why did Obama hide his links with BIC (CIA front)?'

engforum.pravda.ru 3/2/2009 'Barack Obama's CIA Employment'

spingola.com 3/13/2010 Deanna Spingola 'Barack Obama, Former CIA Agent'

nypirg.org New York Public Interest Research Group 'About Us' 'President Barack Obama's work History as an Organizer with NYPIRG'

examiner.com Examiner 4/6/2010 Anthony Martin 'Obama the invisible student at Columbia University?'

analyzethis.net 7/9/2005 Denko 'Barack Obama Embellishes His Resume'

Chapter 8

wikipedia.org Wikipedia 'Michelle Obama' 'Stokely Carmichael' 'Sidley Austin"

squidoo.com Squidoo 'Michelle Robinson Obama's Biography'

usatoday.com USA Today 12/5/2008 Liza Mundy 'Except from 'Michelle: A Biography'

chicagotribune.com Chicago Tribune 12/12008 Dahleen Glanton and Stacy St. Clair 'Michelle Obama's family tree has roots in a Carolina slave plantation'

nytimes.com NY Times 10/7/2009 Racheil Swarns, Jodi Kantor 'In first Lady's Roots, a Complex Path from Slavery' 10/26/2009 Damon Winter 'The Obamas' Marriage' 3/9/2009 Racheil Swarns 'Friendship born at Harvard Goes on to White House' 11/27/2009 Helene Cooper and Brian Stelter 'Obama's Uninvited Guests Prompt an Inquiry'

biography.com 'Michelle Obama Biography'

cnn.com CNN7/16/2009 Joe Johns, Justine Redman 'Tracking Michelle Obama's slave roots' famous-women-and-beauty-.com 'Michelle Obama'

danielpipes.org 8/28/2008 Lame Cherry 'Barack Obama through Barack Sr.'s Eyes'

atlasshrugs2000typepad.com Atlas Shrugs 10/13/2008 Pam Geller Atlas Shrugs 'Obama's Heritage'

foro.univision.com Univision.com 2/17/2009 Heritage 'Barack Hussein Obama's Family Were African slave Traders; his Mama's family owned!'

oneafricanow.com One Africa Now 'Tribal Violence in Africa; A History'

freerepublic.com FreeRepublic.com 2/17/2009 Shirley Madany 'Arabs and Slave Trade' 6/23/2008 'Michelle admits she grew up in Jesse Jackson house; Obamas seek advice from him' 8/5/2009 Chelsea Schilling World Net Daily 'What happened to Michelle Obama's law license?' 1/7/2010 Sudetenland 'Anybody Here Look familiar?' 9/22/2008 Hank Harwell 'ACORN links challenge Barack Obama's credibility' 8/10/2010 Ellie Velinska 'Michelle Obama vacation a Spain's Costa del Crime'

allafrica.com All Africa 8/15/2004 John Oywa 'Kenya: Special Report: Sleepy Little Village Where Obama Traces His Own roots'

patterico.com Patterico's Pontifications 10/6/2008 'Obama and Ayers, together Again'

ssa.gov 'National average wage indexing series 1951 -2009' 'National Average Wage Index'

wiki.answers.com 'Did Michelle Obama attend Princeton on a scholarship?'

eduinreview.com EDU in Review 10/23/2008 'Michelle Obama's College Record'

nationalreview.com National Review 10/7/2008 Ed Whelan 'Michelle Obama, Bernardine Dohrn, and Sidley & Austen' 8/22/2008 Stanley Kurtz 'Michelle, Anti-American Radicals, and U of C'

wsj.com Wall Street Journal 6/23/2008 'Campaign '08 Michelle Obama's Sidley Austin' 9/11/2010 Michael Barone 'The End of Chicago's Daley Dynasty' 8/8/2010 Adam Entous 'US to Sell F-15s to Saudis'

law.com Law.com 6/25/2008 Lynne Marek 'The 'Other Obama' Honed Her Skills at Sidley Austin'

suntimes.com Sun Times 10/5/2008 Lynn Sweet 'Michelle Obama book tells of her discontent at Chicago law firm' 7/27/2010 'Michelle Obama adds Spain to 2010 vacation schedule' 8/26/2008 Lynn Sweet 'Michelle Obama: Democratic Convention Speech, transcripts...' 2/9/2010 Lynn Sweet 'Michelle Obama's "Let's Move" obesity campaign program elements'

law.harvard.edu Harvard Law School 'Michelle Obama's commitment to public service began at HLS' nbcchicago.com NBC Chicago 1/19/2009 Rob Stafford 'A Friend to the First Lady'

life-in-spite-of-ms-.com 'Fraser Robinson III Michelle Obama's Father'

digitaljournal.com DigitalJournal.com 2/24/2008 Lew Waters 'The Chip On Michelle Obama's Shoulder'

dailymail.co.uk Mail Online 11/1/2008 David Jones 'Obama the chameleon-how he found a way to move seamlessly between different worlds' 2/23/2008 Sharon Churcher 'Mrs. O: the truth about Michelle Obama's 'working class' credentials'

everything2.com 7/12/2004 'Barack Obama'

midknightreviewpage3.blogspot.com Page Three 'Michelle Obama Her Philosophical Under-Pinnings'

muckety.com Muckety 3/11/2009 James Memmott 'Law school friendship brings Jocelyn Frye to the White House'

celebritybrideguide.com 1/19/2008 'Barack Obama and Michelle Robinson Obama Wedding'

lamecherry.com Lame Cherry 9/8/2008 'Community Organizer Obama'

chicagomag.com Chicago Mag June 2008 James L. Merriner 'Making Peace' Karen Springen 'First Lady in waiting'

wnd.com 12/23/2008 World Net Daily 'Michelle Obama's old law firm defends ACORN' 10/16/2008 Aaron Klein 'Michelle Obama organized event with Ayers, husband' 4/20/2011 Jerome R. Corsi 'Why do 3 supporters own Obama's home?'

verumserum.com VerumSerum 10/16/2008 'Crossing Paths Daily: Obama and Ayers Shared an Office'

chronicle.uchicago.edu University of Chicago Chronicle 6/6/1996 'Obama named first Associate Dean of Student Services' 11/6/1997 Jennifer Vanasco 'Close-up on juvenile justice'

uchospitals.edu University of Chicago Medical Center 'About UCSC/Our Unique History' 5/5/2005 'Michelle Obama appointed vice president for community and external affairs at the University of Chicago Hospitals' 11/8/2005 'South Side Health collaborative holds forum to help residents find a primary care home'

uchicago.edu 1/9/2009 Michelle Obama resigns Position at University of Chicago Medical Center'

minnesota.publicradio.org MPR News 8/12 2008 Cheryl Corley 'Michelle Obama: The Exec, Mom and Campaigner' huffingtonpoost.com Huffington Post 3/18/2005 Anya Strzemien 'Obama's Intricate Indonesian Wedding Band'

seattletimes.nwsource.com 10/19/2004 Laurie Goering/Chicago Tribune 'Obama's a local hero in Kenyan villages'

obamaprincetonthesis.wordpress.com 1985 Michelle LaVaughn Robinson 'Princeton Educated Blacks and the Black Community'

dyn.politico.com Politico 2/22/2008 Jeffery Ressner Politico 'Michelle Obama thesis was on racial divide'

ireport.cnn.com CNN iReport 11/3/2008 'Doubts Persist on Obama's Birth Place'

factcheck.org 'Q: Was Barack Obama really a constitutional law professor?'

time.com TIME 8/25/2008 Jay Newton-Small 'Michelle Obama's Savvy Sacrifice'

sourcewatch.org Source Watch 'Sidley Austin'

sidley.com Sidley Austin LLP 'Our Firm/History/Mission/Our People'

james4america.wordpress.com 10/4/2008 'Michelle Obama does not have a Law License in Illinois'

americanthinker.com American Thinker 5/19/2008 Ethel C. Fenig 'Friends in high places' 3/2/2009 David Catron 'Michelle Obama's Patient-dumping Scheme' 8/6/2010 Ethel C. Fenig 'Political fundraising courtesy of the mob' 7/27/2010 Ralph Alter 'Michelle Obama's luxury Spanish vacation'

punchng.com PUNCH/Nigeria magazine 11/8/2008 Harold Ayodo 'The Obama you don't know' Joe Ombour 'Obama's father and the origin of Muslim name Baraka Karama 'Why I agreed that Obama should marry Michelle, Obama's grandmother'

pajamasmedia.com PajamasMedia.com 10/25/2009 Patti Villacorta 'The Originators of Obama-speak: Public allies and the ABCD Institute'

abcdinstitute.org Asset-Based Community Development Institute 'Michelle Obama'

aletmanski.com 9/29/2010 Al Etmanski 'Which type of community organizer is Obama'

gatewaypundit.rightnetwork.com GatewayPundit 12.30.2010 Jim Hoft The Gateway Pundit 'Everyone Must Sacrifice…Obama's Vacation will cost Taxpayers $1,474,2000'

publicallies.org Public Allies 'Our Story'/ 'Fact Sheet About Allies and the Obamas' 5/12/2009 'Remarks by the First Lady at a Corporation for National and Community Service Event'

canadafreepress.com 3/11/2009 Canada Free Press Judi McLeod 'General in a sleeveless dress' 11/26/2009 Judi McLeod '"Party Crashers" had a five-year relationship with Obama before state dinner' 8/24/2010 Judi McLeod 'Michelle Obama made dusk visit to Great Mosque of Granada during Spanish trip'

ysa.org Youth Service America 'First Lady Michelle Obama is the Honorary Chair for Global Youth Service Day'

eaglerockschool.org 10/21/2009 'Eagle Rock School Kicks off iParticipate'

congress.org 1/26/2011 Senator John McCain 'Why is the First Lady Trying to Tutor America?'

investors.com Investors.com 9/5/2008 'Michelle's Boot Camps for Radicals'

theraiser.blogspot.com The Raiser's Razor 11/23/2008 'Obama's Plan for Partnering with Nonprofits'

washingtonpost.com Washington Post 7/25/2009 Peter Slevin 'In Chicago, a University Initiative Rethinks Health Care' 11/26/2009 Amy Argetsinger, Roxanne Roberts 'Off the list, but somehow on the South Lawn'

nationalreview.com National Review 2/29/2008 Byron York 'Michelle Obama: Don't Go Into Corporate America'

chitowndailynews.org CHI-Town Daily News 6/4/2009 Alex Parker 'Activists blast U of C on charity care' 6/3/2009 Lex Parker 'Rush calls for investigation a U of c for patient dumping allegations'

semp.us/publications3/13/2009 'University of Chicago Medical Center patient-care disaster delayed'

state-of-the-nation-.com 12/7/2010 Katherine Skiba/ Chicago Tribune 'Michelle Obama aide Susan Sher's pay from University of Chicago Medical Center in 2009: $511,000!!! For 19 days Work!!!'

hotair.com HotAir 7/23/2008 Ed Morrissey 'Video" Did Michelle Obama start a patient-dumping program?'

thepostemail.com Post & Email 8/24/2010 Sharon Rondeau 'Is Obama effecting an Islamic takeover of the United States?'

democraticunderground.com 10/4/2007 Christine Simmons 'Bush says U.S. stands with Muslims'

whitehouse.gov 8/14/2010 'President Obama Celebrates Ramadan at White House Itfar Dinner' 2/9/2010 First Lady Michelle Obama Launches Let's Move: America's Move to Raise a Healthier-Generation of Kids' 9/13/2010 'Remarks by the First Lady in address to the National Restaurant Association Meeting' pcah.gov President's Committee on the Arts and the Humanities 'About Us'

sundance.org Sundance Institute 2/16/2011 'Help save Funding for the Arts'

hawaiireporter.com Hawaii Reporter 12/28/2010 Malia Zimmerman 'Obama's Million Dollar Hawaiian Vacation: Costs to Taxpayers Detailed'

whitehousedossier.com White House Dossier 2/19/2011 Keith Koffler ' Michelle Obama Goes Skiing in Colorado'

thehill.com The Hill 7/26/2010 Jordan Fabian 'Michelle Obama to make private visit to Spain during president's birthday'

nymag.com NY Mag 2/25/2010 'The Michelle Obama Look'

harpersbazaar.com Harper's Bazaar 'Michelle Obama: Power Fashion'

cbsnews.com CBS News 8/5/2010 Brian Montopoli 'Michelle Obama Criticized as "Modern-day Marie Antoinette" Over Spain Vacation' 2/11/2009 Esther Breger 'Princeton Releases Michelle Obama's Senior Thesis'

wtpotus.wordpress.com WTPOTUS 8/9/2010 We The People of The United States 'Michelle Obama's trip to Spain was not "Tone Deaf", it was Pitch-Perfect'

theblacksphere.net The Black Sphere 8/6/2010 Kevin Jackson 'Obama- True black Royalty'

suzyrice.com 8/9/2010 Suzy Rice 'Michelle Obama says Spain is over; Pschew, its Hard Work being an egomaniac...'

jpost.com The Jerusalem Post 9/8/2010 'US to sell Saudis F-15 fighter jets'

marketwatch.com Market Watch 8/9/2010 Christopher Hinton 'US plans $30 billion F-15 sale to Saudi Arabia'

examiner.com Examiner 8/4/2010 Scott Paulson 'Obama celebrating 49th birthday at Graham Elliot Restaurant in Chicago' Thomas McAdam 'Why did the Obamas lose their law licenses?'

csmonitor.com Christian Science Monitor 4/1/2010 Natasha Metzler 'Michelle Obama expands the White House garden'

dailyfinance.com Daily Finance 7/9/2009 Alex Salkever 'Michelle Obama's toxic veggie nightmare: White House organic garden polluted with sludge'

abcnews.com ABC News 5/22/2007 Sunlen Miller 'Michelle Obama Cuts Ties with Controversial Wal-Mart Supplier' letsmove.gov 'Healthy Communities' 2/18/2011 'The Farmers Market Promotion Program is Feeding Healthy communities'

usatoday.com USA Today 5/11/2010 'Michelle Obama reveals goals of childhood obesity task force'

thestir.cafemom.com The Stir 5/12/2010 Suzanne Murray 'Michelle Obama Announces Childhood Obesity Guidelines'

washingtontimes.com Washington Times 12/18/2010 Gabriella Hoffman 'Nutrition bill is not all sunshine and lollipops'

foodproductdesign.com 2/9/2011 'Let's Move! Campaign Marks ! Year Anniversary'

restaurant.org Resturant.org 9/13/2010 Dawn Sweeney 'First Lady Michelle Obama praises industry's efforts'

acefitness.org Americas Council on Exercise 'The Fight Against childhood Obesity Enters the School Cafeteria'

conservativebyte.com ConservativeByte.com 4/11/2011 'Food Fight: Chicago School Bans Students From Bringing Own Lunches'

latimes.com L.A. Times 4/13/2011 Nicole Brochu 'Chicago lunch policy is a lesson on the nanny state, not good nutrition'

boston.com Boston Globe 2/9/2011 Deborah Kotz 'Michelle Obama's Super Bowl junk fest: really ok?'

guardian.co.uk The Guardian 2/18/2011 Ed Pilkington 'Michelle Obama's breastfeed plan attacked by Tea Party's leading ladies'

quotes and poem.com 'Michelle Obama Quotes'

citizenwells.wordpress.com CitizenWells 7/24/2008 'Barack Obama Illinois Bar Application, Obama lied?...'

factfirstok.blogspot.com 8/12/2008 'Bar, No more Anonymous complaints'

fellowshipofminds.wordpress.com Fellowship of the Minds 9/16/2010 'Barack & Michelle Gave Up Law License'

directorblue.blogspot.com 3/1/2010 'to be (a lawyer) or not to be…'

downrange.tv 3/2/2010 'Re: Obama, Lawyer and Professor'

slate.com Slate Magazine 3/19/2008 Bonnie Goldstein 'Obama on Racism 1990' npr.org NPR 1/20/2011 Michelle Ob ma partners with Walmart for healthy eating'

reuters.com Reuters1/20/2011 Jessica Wohl 'Walmart and Michelle Obama team up on healthy food'

telegraph.co.uk Telegraph 5/13/2007 Philip Sherwell 'Obama called hypocrite for wife's Wal-Mart link'

abc.go.com ABC News 1/20/2011 Tahman Bradley 'Michelle Obama and Walmart Join forces promoting healthy food'

Chapter 9

discoverthenetworks.org Discover the Networks 'Jeremiah A. Wright Jr.' 'Liberation Theology' 'James Cone'

chicagotribune.com Chicago Tribune 1/27/2007 Manya A. Brachear 'Rev. Jeremiah A. Wright Jr.: Pastor inspires Obama's 'audacity'' 3/28/2008 Manya A. Brachear 'Wright's sermons fueled by complex mix of culture, religion'

thehistorymakers.com 'Dr. Jeremiah A. Wright Biography'

newsweek.com Newsweek 5/3/2008 'Something Wasn't Wright'

nytimes.com The New York Times 4/30/2007 Jodi Kantor 'A Candidate, His Minister, and the Search for Faith' (undated) Times Topics 'Jeremiah A. Wright Jr.' 6/11/2009 Jim Rutenberg 'Rev. Wright Tries to Explain Away Remarks'

npr.org NPR 4/28/2008 Jerome Vaughn 'Rev. Wright: Critics are Attacking Black Church' 3/24/2008 'Understanding Rev. Jeremiah Wright' 3/18/2008 Barbara Bradley-Hagerty 'A Closer Look at Black Liberation theology' 3/31/2008 'Black Liberation Theology, in its founder's words'

newsbusters.org NewsBusters 12/8/2008 Tim Graham 'Rev. ABC, CNN, Time,...as Gates of Hell' 3/13/2008 Mark Finkelstein 'Obama's Spiritual Guide: God Damn America'

acton.org Acton Institute 4/1/2008 Anthony B. Bradley 'The Marxist roots of Black Liberation Theology'

dailycaller.com Daily Caller 7/20/2010 Jonathan Strong 'Documents show media plotting to kill stories about Rev. Jeremiah Wright'

nationalreview.com National Review 5/20/2008 Stanley Kurtz 'Left in Church'

canadafreepress.com Canada Free Press 4/1/2008 Lee Kaplan 'How Obama's church and associates link him to the ISM' abcnews.go.com ABC News 2008 Brian Ross, Rehabel-Buri 'Obama's Pastor: God Damn America, U.S. to Blame for 9/11' 4/27/2008 'Rev. Wright Delivers Fiery Address to NAACP'

newsmax.com News Max 4/13/2008 Ronald Kessler 'Obama's Rev. Wright Mythology'

trinitychicago.org Trinity Church 'Our History' 'The Black Value System' 'What we believe'

debbieschlussel.com Debbie Schlussel 3/13/2008 'Obama's Pastor's Views: Does B Hussein O Share This "Audacity of Ignorance"?' 4/25/2008 'Pan-Terrorist Arab Muslim Group Brags About Sponsoring Rev. Wright Speech'

thepostemail.com Post & Email 9/20/2010 Brigitte de Maubec 'Why does This "Christian" Always Flock To Hear The Muslim Message?'

mcclatchydc.com McClatchy Newspapers 3/20/2008 Margaret Talev 'Obama's church pushes controversial doctrines'

huffingtonpost.com Huffington Post 3/18/2008 'Obama Race Speech: Read the Full Text'

cnn.com CNN 3/14/2008 Alex Mooney 'Controversial minister off Obama's campaign'

beliefnet.com Beliefnet 3/28/2008 'Rev. Wright's retirement home…'

luxist.com Luxist 3/31/2008 Deidre Wollard 'Reverend Wright's Million dollar Retirement Home'

adc.org American-Arab Anti-Discrimination Committee 'About Us'

sweet-light.com Sweetness & Light Rhoda McKinney-Jones 'The Honorable Minister Louis Farrakhan'

bobmccarty.com 4/2/2008 Bob McCarty 'Obama Organized Farrakhan's Million Man March'

politifact.com 8/19/2010 'Obama a Muslim? No he's not. The evidence has not changed'

tradionalvalues.org 2008 'Senator Barack Obama's Faith: Is It Black Liberation Theology?'

religionlink.com 8/8/2005 'Liberation theology; a challenge to the church'

christendom-awake.org Fall 1984 Joseph Cardinal Ratzinger 'Liberation Theology'

landreform.org 'A concise History of Liberation Theology'

acton.org 4/1/2008 Acton Institute Anthony B. Bradley 'The Marxist Roots of Black Liberation Theology'

wfu.edu Wake Forest 'A Black Theology of Liberation'

americanthinker.com American Thinker 2/22/2008 Lee Cary 'Obama's Mentor's Mentor' 3/28/2011 Monte Kuligowski 'Did Obama forget to have a Gaddafi meeting 'Without Preconditions'?'

pbs.org PBS 'James Cone'

wnd.com 2/23/2011 World Net Daily Aaron Klein 'Obama's mystery links to Gadhafi uncovered'

pajamasmedia.com PajamasMedia.com 3/15/2011 Kyle-Anne Shiver 'Obama, Wright, Farrakhan, and Gaddafi'

religionfacts.com 'Jewish Beliefs about Human Nature'

jewishideas.org Jewish Ideas 10/2/2010 mdangel 'Created in the Image of God...'

Chapter 10

latimes.com LA Times 4/6/2008 Dan Morain 'Obama's law days effective, but brief'

freerepublic.com FreeRepublic.com 10/9/2008 ' Obama's Job Description at Illinois Project Vote-today's ACORN' PapaBear3625 'Obama's connections' 'William Ayers and his father Tom Ayers' 2/8/2009 'Khalid al-Mansour (aka Don Warden-Obama sponsor) 4/23/2007 Tim Novak, Chicago Sun Times 'Obama and his Rezko ties'

nationalreview.com National Review 6/10/2008 Jim Geraghty 'Obama's Book-Writing Sabbatical in Bali, Indonesia' 11/1/2008 Stanley Kurtz 'Senator Stealth' 9/8/2008 Byron York 'The Organizer' 10/13/2008 Greg Pollowitz 'More Chicago corruption in the News' 6/5/2008 Stephen Spruiell 'Rezko: Guilty'

americanthinker.com American Thinker 10/17/2008 Jack Cashill 'Evidence Mounts: Ayers Co-Wrote Obama's 'Dreams'' 3/10/2011 Lee Cary 'Obama's friends and Chicago's New Slums' 10/12/2008 Ed Lasky 'don't tell me – Another radical in Obama's background?'

projectvote.org Project Vote 'Our Mission'

wikipedia.org Wikipedia 'Project vote' 'Early life and career of Barack Obama' 'Local School Councils' 'Allison S. Davis' 'Operation board Games' 'Tony Rezko'

discoverthenetworks.org Discover the Networks 2005 Richard Poe. 'Project Vote: Extended Profile' 'The Agitator' by Ryan Lizza) 'Khalid Abdullah Tariq al-Mansour' 'Marilyn Katz'

wikisource.org 'Barack Obama's Iraq speech'

betsyspage.blogspot.com 7/31/2008 Betsy's Page 'Barack Obama at the University of Chicago' nytimes.com New York Times 7/30/2008 Jodi Kantor 'Teaching Law, testing Ideas. Obama Stood Slightly Apart' 10/11/2007 Jim Rutenberg 'Obama returns to 2002'

commonamericanjournal.com 3/28/2008 'Lynn Sweet: Obama did not 'hold the title' of a University of Chicago law school professor'

law.uchicago.edu University of Chicago Law School 'Media Inquiries'

chicagotribune.com Chicago Tribune 3/27/2009 Tom Hundley 'Ivory tower of power' 5/30/2008 Jeff Coen, Ray Gibson, and Bob Secter 'Rezko's gambling troubles' 5/26/2005 'John Chase 'Tony Rezko' 3/16/2008 'Barack Obama interview'

politifact.com 2009 'Rove claims Obama used to be a lawyer for ACORN'

sweetness-light.com Sweetness & Light "Social Policy" Winter 2003 issue 'Obama Taught ACORN 'Leadership Classes''

chicagomag.com Chicago Magazine January 1993 Gretchen Reynolds 'Vote of confidence'

breitbart.com/big government 5/15/2012 Joel B. Pollak "The Vetting"

atlasshrugs.2000.typepad.com Atlas Shrugs 8/20/2009 'Obama and Gamaliels Freak Show: Faith Hijacking Strategy'

therealbarackobama.wordpress.com RBO 6/25/2010 Brenda J. Elliott 'Is It Really Credible That Obama and Ayers Did Not Meet in 1987 or 1988?'

chicagoreader.com ChicagoReader.com 12/7/1995 Hank De Zutter 'What Makes Obama Run?'

atrueott.wordpress.com 7/22/2010 A. True Ott, PhD 'Obama –The Changeling'

huffingtonpost.com Huffington Post 7/8/2008 Markus Ziener 'Barack Obama: forensics on the Southside'

illinoisissues.uis.edu Illinois Issues March 2009 Phil Davidson 'Obama's mentor'

catalyst-chicago.org Catalyst Chicago 7/1/1995 'Local School Councils'

designsforchange.org DFC January 2002 Donald R. Moore and Gail Merritt 'Chicago's Local School Councils; What the research Says' 'Original Framework and Rationale for Chicago's Local School Councils'

cps.edu Chicago Public Schools 'The Chicago Board of Education'

keywiki.org Key Wiki 'Heather Booth' 'Marilyn Katz'

emergingcorruption.com Emerging Corruption 10/1/2009 Anita MonCrief 'A Leftist Love Story; Teamstergate' slate.com Slate Bonnie Goldstein re: Barack Obama (Harvard Law student) undated 'Top Student: What Kind of Minorities do Firms Want?'

canadofreepress.com Canada Free Press 12/28/2008 Warner Todd Huston 'Man Who told of Obama's Islamic Benefactor Passes Away' 9/17/2008 Andrew Walden Lehman brother: Obama's Rezko-Auchi conflict of interest'

ny1.com NY1 1/2/2010 'Local Leader Hold Radio Tribute For Percy Sutton'

newsmax.com Newsmax 9/4/2008 Kenneth R. Timmerman 'Who is Khalid al-Mansour?'

westernjournalism.com Western Journalism 5/27/2010 Caleb 'How Obama got into Harvard'

google.com/search 2/23/2009 'ACTS-Friend, adviser of Obama talks about segregation in Syracuse' Spring 2007 David Moberg 'Obama's Third Way'

wnd.com World Net Daily 1/30/2011 'Obama's money trail' 3/11/2011 Aaron Klein 'Marxists, socialists launched Obama?'

politico.com Politico 9/4/2008 'Obama camp denies Sutton story'

infoplease.com 'Federal Minimum Wage rates. 1955-2009'

the-classic-liberal.com The Classic Liberal 8/28/2008 Barack Obama, Are You Experienced?'

e-cytaty.com 9/19/2009 Nimmo-infowars 'Unearth! Obama's Twisted ACORN Roots'

maps.yahoo.com 'west98th St NYC' '339 E 94th St NYC'

countercurrents.org Counter Currents 4/7/2008 Evelyn Pringle 'Barack Obama: Operation Board Games For Slumlords'

cookrepublicanparty.com 6/8/2011 Tim Novak ' Another deal goes sour for Daley nephew'

chicagojournal.com Chicago Journal 6/9/2009 Micah Maldenberg 'Feds investigating firm that owns local buildings'

nalert.blogspot.com Newsalert 9/23/2007 'The Mayor Daley – Barack Obama – Pension Connection?'

chicagobreakingnews.com Breaking News Center 3/19/2009 'Pension probe; Inspector eyes Daley ties'

lewrockwell.com LewRockwell.com Kirk W. Tofte 'Obama-Rezko Redux' workinglife.org Working Life 1/27/2008 John Desiderio 'Obama and Rezko: CNN omits the Nub of the Story'

msnbc.msn.com MSNBC 2/20/2007 AP 'Obama got his start in civil rights practice'

dailykos.com Daily Kos 11/25/2007 'Remembering Harold Washington'

casinowatch.org CasinoWatch.org 2/17/2009 'Political Corruption'

fallbackbelmontblogspot.com The Belmont Club 2/23/2008 (Nick Cohen,2003 the Guardian) 'Rezko, Auchi and Obama'

abc.go.com ABC News 6/4/2008 'Political fundraiser Antion 'Tony' Rezko found guilty' 1/10/2008 Brian Ross and Rhonda Schwartz 'The Rezko Connection: Obama's Achilles Heel?'

metapedia.org Metapedia 'Tony Rezko'

hotair.com HotAir 8/2/2008 Ed Morrissey 'Giannoulias bank gave Rezko $22.75 million loan in 2006'

biggovernment.com BigGovernment.com 10/4/2010 Joel B. Pollack 'Schakowsky's Newest Bank Scandal Links to Blago, Rezko, Obama' 6/15/2010 Andrew Marcus 'The Progressive Jihad Against Israel'

salon.com Salon 2/1/2008 Edward McClelland 'How close were Barack Obama and Tony Rezko'

prnewswire.com PR Newswire 6/4/2008 'Obama and Rezko have had a Relationship for 20 years'

citizenwells.wordpress.com CitizenWells 10/3/2008 'Obama plan, Obama desperation to win…'

inthesetimes.com InTheseTimes 12/5/2003 Jeff Epton 'From Protest to Politics'

mkcpr.com MKCommunications 'Marilyn Katz, President' 'Clients: Not for Profit/for Profit/Government'

encyclopedia.chicagohistory.org 'Democratic Convention Protests, 1968'

marathonpundit.blogspot.com Marathon Pundit 10/26/2008 'Marilyn Katz: Another radical in Obama's circle'

romanticpoets.wordpress.com Romanticpoet Weblog (from NewZeal Trevor Loudon) 'Obama file 95 Concert or Coincidence?'

townhall.com Townhall 8/31/2008 Buy Benson 'Obama's Radical Delegate' newsbusters.org NewsBusters 9/20/2008 Noel Sheppard 'IBD: Carter More to Blame for Financial Crisis Than Bush or McCain'

spectator.org American Spectator 10/29/2008 Matthew Vadum 'ACORN's Food Stamp Mortgages'

clearinghouse.net Civil Rights Litigation Clearinghouse 'Buycks-Roberson v. Citibank Fed Sav. Bank'

law2unke.edu Douglas O. Linder 'The Chicago Seven Conspiracy Trial'

Chapter 11

pathlessland.net 4/17/2010 James R. Keena 'Meet the Ayers Family (Chapter 6)'

watch.pair.com "The Synarchy" Part III 'Thomas G. Ayers & Barack Obama'

monthlyreview.org Monthly Review March 2009 Bill Ayers and Bernardine Dohrn 'What Race Has to do With It'

wnd.com World Net Daily 10/14/2008 Brad O'Leary 'The Obama-Ayers incestuous money trail' 5/2/2010 'The Obama-Ayers meeting: What you haven't been told' 11/12/2009 Aaron Klein 'Ayers, Dohrn accuse Hillary of white supremacy' 3/11/2011 Aaron Klein 'Obama worked closely with terrorist Bill Ayers' 9/23/2009 Art Moore 'Author confirms Bill Ayers helped Obama write Dreams' 1/1/2010 Aaron Klein 'Ayers Dohrn stir chaos in Middle East' 9/18/2009 'New report adds to evidence against Dohrn' 5/4/2011 Aaron Klein 'Obama adviser: American freedom, equality are just myths'

stoptheaclu.com Stop the ACLU 10/6/2008 '"Guilty as Hell, Free as a Bird, America is Great..."'

jewishworldreview.com Jewish World Review 1/15/2010 Caroline b. Glick 'Ayers wife heads to Middle East with group to collaborate with Hamas'

bud-meyers.blogspot.com Bud Meyers 12/10/2010 'Pine Street Bomb Factory' ''Kathy Boudin'

wikipedia.org Wikipedia 'Thomas G. Ayers' 'Chesa Boudin'

bioneers.org Bioneers 'Our Mission'

zombietime.com ZombieTime 10/27/2008 'Barack Obama's Close Encounter with the Weather Underground'

time.com TIME 11/2/1981 Claudia Wallis, James Wilde, Pete Staler 'Bullets from the Underground thepostemail.wordpress.com Post & Email 9/26/2009 John Charlton 'Declassified FBI report exposes Communist seedbed for Obama Associates-Part I'

pibillwarner.wordpress.com 'PI Bill Warner'

usasurvival.org America's Survival, Inc. 'Prepared remarks of Larry Grathwohl October 21 America's Survival Inc. ...Conference'

freerepublic.com FreeRepublic.com 'The 1981 Weather Underground Black Liberation Army Brinks robbery' 3/22/2008 Obama attended UIC conference with Bill Ayers and Bernadine Dohrn!' 4/14/2008 'Weatherman'

hnn.us/articles HistoryNewsNetwork 12/02/2001 Kenneth Heineman 'Books: Bill Ayers Fugitive Days...'

stephen-diamond.com 8/15/2008 Stephen Diamond 'Chicago's "Citizen of the Year"? Obama, Ayers and Daley'

mikefrancesa.com 10/19/2008 'Obama reviewed William Ayers book, "A Kind and Just Parent"'

campus-watch.org Canada Free Press 3/29/2009 Joy Tiz 'Ayer'ed Out: Bill Ayers is influencing Your Kids'

weeklystandard.com Weekly Standard 9/23/2008 Mary Katharine Ham 'Obama and Bill Ayers Worked to get ACORN Teaching Schoolchildren in Chicago'

nationalreview.com National Review 8/18/2008 Stanley Kurtz 'Chicago Annenberg Challenge Shutdown?' 8/27/2008 Andrew C. McCarthy 'Bill Ayers: Unrepentant Lying Terrorist' 10/13/2008 Deroy Murdock 'Obama's Weathermen Pals Should Worry you'

infoplease.com 'Federal Minimum wage Rates, 1955-2009'

discoverthenetworks.org Discover the Networks 'Apollo Alliance(AA)' 'Bill Ayers' 'Bernardine Dohrn' 'Weatherman' 'Jeff Jones'

professionalsoldiers.com Professional Soldiers 9/7/2009 John Perazzo 'Jeff Jones, Marxist Revolutionary former Weatherman, Part 1'

wikipedia.org Wikipedia 'Jeff Jones' 'Kathy Boudin' 'Bill Ayers' 'Weather Underground' 'Bernardine Dohrn' 'Students for a Democratic Society' 'Free Gaza Movement' 'Working Families Party' 'Gaza flotilla raid'

nytimes.com NY Times 1/30/2008 Jennifer Lee 'Where Obama Lived in 1980s New York' 9/18/2003 Lisa W.Foderaro 'With Bouquet and a Wave, Boudin in Free 22 Years Later' 'Bill Ayers'

newsbusters.org NewsBusters 3/15/2011 Stanley Kurtz 'Barack Obama and Bill Ayers'

10/5/2008 Terry Trippany 'CNN Ignores Bernardine Dohrn's Terrorist Past While Defending Obama'

emperors-clothes.com 'The Weathermen Redeemed, Part 3'

csmonitor.com Christian Science Monitor 6/9/2010 Husna Haq 'You can rent President Obama's New York apartment for only $1,900 a month'

sharprightturn.wordpress.com 'Prairie Fire: William Ayers Weather Underground Manifesto'

noquarterusa.net NoQuartersUSA 5/29/2008 'Ayers, Obama, Philanthropy, Corruption: What Big Media…'

conservapedia.com Conservapedia 'Bernardine Dohrn'

city-journal.org City Journal 11/3/2008 Daniel J. Flynn 'The Ghosts in Grant Park' 4/23/2008 Sol Stern 'Obama's Real Bill Ayers Problem'

familysecuritymatter.org Family Security Matters 10/7/2008 John Howard 'William Ayers and Bernardine Dohrn – Friends of Barack Obama' 6/2/2010 'Global Muslim Brotherhood Heavily Represented on Gaza Flotilla'

nndb.com Notable Names Data Base 'Bernardine Dohrn'

powerlineblog.com Power Line Blog John Hinderaker, Scott Johnson Paul Mirengoff 'The Friends of Barack Obama Part 1'

politico.com Politico 2/22/2008 Ben Smith 'Obama once visited '60s radicals'

terrorism.about.com Any Zalman 'Bill Ayers-Profile of Bill Ayers the Weatherman'

aim.com Accuracy in Media 3/3/2009 Cliff Kincaid 'Justice for Victims of the Weather Underground' 8/12/2009 Cliff Kincaid 'Bill Ayers and Hugo Chavez: Blood Brothers in Terror'

patdollard.com Pat Dollard 10/22/2008 'Terrorist Bill Ayers-Barack Obama- Jew-hater Rashid Khalidi..'

nicedeb.wordpress.com Nice Deb 10/29/2008 FBI Report: Ayers/Weather Underground Aided by Cuba'

chinaconfidential.bloggerspot.com China Confidential April 2005 'IBD on Obama's real Bill Ayers Problem'

msnbc.msn.com MSNBC News 2/27/2007 AP 'Obama got his start in civil rights practice'

slate.com Slate 10/10/2008 David S. Tanenhaus 'Barack, Bill, and Me'

chicagomag.com Chicago Magazine August 2001 Marcia Froelke Coburn 'No Regrets' npr.org NPR 11/18/2008 'Which Way The Wind Blows: Bill Ayers On Obama'

cnn.com CNN 10/7/2008 Drew Griffin and Kathleen Johnston "Ayers and Obama crossed paths on boards, records show'

uic.edu University of Illinois at Chicago 'Bill Ayers'

abc.net Australian Broadcasting Corp. 3/30/2009 'The influence and significance of Barack Obama as writer'

usnews.com US News 8/22/2008 Michael Barone 'Obama Needs to Explain his Ties to William Ayers'

backyardconservative.blogspot.com Backyard Conservative 10/6/2009 Anne Leary 'Bill Ayers No Dream'

americanthinker.com American Thinker 10/9/2008 Jack Cashill 'Who Wrote Dreams from My Father?' 10/17/2008 Jack Cashill 'Evidence Mounts: Ayers Co-Wrote Obama's Dreams' 6/13/2010 Benyamin Korn 'What about Egypt's blockade of Gaza?'

mediamatters.org Media Matters 9/23/2009 'Hannity, Andersen advance discredited claim that Ayers helped Obama pen his autobiography'

pajamasmedia.com PajamasMedia.com 9/23/2009 Rod Radosh 'An Old Claim Arises Once More: Did Barack Obama Write Dreams from My Father?' 5/20/2009 Mary Grabar 'Ayers and Dohrn Embark on US Bashing Book Tour' 9/24/2010 'Sirhan Sirhan dedication backfires on Bill Ayers 36 years later'

lincolntribune.com Lincoln Tribune 2/7/2011 Jim Kouri 'Obama linked to 'Egyptian Muslim Brotherhood'

adl.org Anti-Defamation League 'Israel's Action in Gaza Spurs Anti-Israel Rallies'

israeli-occupation.org 12/31/2009 Josh Stump 'Gaza Freedom March Madness Day Three'

palsolidarity.org Palsolidarity 1/1/2010 Sayed Dhansay 'Gaza Freedom March activists target Egypt's complicity'

foundingbloggers.com 6/15/2010 'The Progressive Jihad Against Israel'

democracynow.org Democracy Now 1/16/2009 'Bloody Israeli assault on Gaza enters fourth week…'

bigpeace.com Big Peace 1/30/2011 Ben Barrack 'Underground Uprising in Egypt'

grendelreport.posterous.com Grendel Report 6/6/2010 Brenda J. Elliott 'Ayers Dohrn top Terrorists in Gaza flotilla group' washingtonexaminer.com Washington Examiner 6/1/2010 Barbara Hollingsworth 'Ayers, Dohrn helped organize flotilla group'

globalmbreport.org Global Muslim Brotherhood Daily Report 3/8/2011 'Former Al-Aqsa Foundation Leader Issues Press Statement…'

clubofrome.org The Club of Rome 'About Us'

pbs.org PBS 'The Weather Underground'

globalnewsdaily.com Global News Daily 8/31/2008 Jim Kouri 'Resume of a Terrorist: Obama's Buddy Ayers'

fbi.gov FBI 1/24/2004 '1975 Terrorism flashback state Department Bombing'

time.com TIME 10/7/2008 Claire Suddath 'The Weather Underground'

chicagotribune.com Chicago Tribune 9/24/2010 'Really!?! Sirhan Sirhan is or even was a political prisoner?'

chicagobreakingnews.com 9/223/2010 'Ayers denied emeritus status after plea from Chris Kennedy'

humanevents.com Human Events 4/29/2008 Allan H. Ryskind 'Obama and His Weatherman Friends'

barksdale.uta.edu Barksdale Dana Zakrzewski 'Students for a Democratic Society'

keywiki.org 'Adam Kline'

antiauthoriarian.net '"Osawatomie" Summer 1975 no.2 Weather Underground Organization'

irseview.org International socialist Review October 2003 Geoff Barley 'The rise and fall of SDS'

studentsforademocraticsociety.org 'SDS/History' 8/18/2010 'University of Minnesota SDS reports back on Arizona Freedom Summer'

markrudd.com Mark Rudd 1/3/2002 'The Death of SDS'

2iath.virginia.edu 'Port Huron Statement'

uruknet.info Uruknet.com 1/1/2010 Xinhua 'Israeli Warplanes, Tanks Strike Eastern, southern Gaza strip'

gazafreedommarch.org 5/31/2010 'Urgent Call for Action: global Day to Break Israeli Siege' 12/5/2010 'Compilation of Wikileaks Relating to Israel & the Palestinians' 'Gaza flotilla protest Saturday 5th June 2010 London Lifeline' imemc.org International Middle East Media Center 5/29/2010 Saed Bannoura 'Israel Dubs Its Planned Attack On Gaza Ships As Operation Sky Winds'

occupiedpalestine.wordpress.com Free Gaza Movement 6/1/2011 'Passenger List U.S. Boat to Gaza'

maannews.net Ma'an News Agency 8/14/2011 On board the Freedom Flotilla Passenger List'

pacificfreepress.com Pacific Free Press 5/29/2010 Lauren Booth 'Mainstream' Media "Silence Meets Gaza Flotilla'

biggovernment.com Big Government Kristinn Taylor and Andrea Shea King 'Code Pink Democrats Aid and Abet...' Kristinn Taylor and Andrea Shea King 'Obama Funder Jodie Evans Provokes Crisis in Egypt...'

caabbs.com 10/22/1010 Bob Unruh 'FBI informant to Congress: Investigate Ayers, Dohrn now...'

aim.org Accuracy in Media 9/27/2010 Cliff Kincaid 'Will the Truth Catch up to Bill Ayers and his comrades?' 10/26/2010 Cliff Kincaid 'Terrorist Ayers Endorses Stewart Colbert Rallies'

frontpagemag.com FrontPageMag 3/19/2003 Michael Tremoglie 'Not In Our Name and the World Wide Terrorism Web'

ifconews.org 'About IFCO Pastors for Peace'

rantcollective.net Rant 'Rant Trainers Collective'

trainersalliance.org 'Alliance of Community Trainers'

Chapter 12

patriotactionnetwork.com Patriot Action Network 7/26/2010 'A trail of money that leads straight to BHO'

joycefdn.org The Joyce Foundation 'About Us' 'Grant List' 'Environment' 'Money and Politics' 'CCX' 'History' 4/30/2010 Sandy Williams 'The Joyce Foundation, firearms Research Digest Now Online'

woodsfund.org Woods Fund of Chicago 'History of the Fund' 'Core Principles'

discoverthenetworks.org Discover the Networks 'Woods Fund of Chicago'

rezkowatch.blogspot.com 4/9/2008 'Follow the Money: Who's Howard Stanback...?'

mediacircus.com Media Circus 10/19/2010 'The ShoreBank Heist...all about money' us-aaa.com USA Political Conservative News 8/26/2010 'Obama's connections with Shorebank Cap & Trade'

americanthinker.com American Thinker 7/7/2008 Richard Henry Lee 'Obama and the Woods Fund of Chicago'

wnd.com World Net Daily 2/24/2008 Aaron Klein 'Obama worked with terrorist'

wikipedia.org 'Joyce Foundation' 'Joel Rogers'

examiner.com Examiner 4/27/2010 Gregory Dail 'Scandal: Obama, Gore, Goldman, Joyce Foundation CCX partners to fleece USA'

problembanklist.com 8/21/2010 Bill Zielinski 'Politically connected ShoreBank of Chicago Fails and reincarnated at Taxpayer expense'

vdare.com VDare 5/20/2010 Michelle Malkin 'The "Chicago Way and the Shady ShoreBank Bailout'

whatreallyhappened.com 'The ShoreBank. Obama, Chicago Climate Exchange Scam!'

chicagotribune.com Chicago Tribune 8/20/2010 Becky Yerak 'Chicago's ShoreBank fails, is bought by investors'

cdobs.com Chicago Daily Observer 5/18/2010 'Crony Capitalism Shores up ShoreBank'

biggovernment.com Big Government 'ShoreBank Bailout: The Ties that Bind'

centralillinois912project.com 3/11/2010 Ira Visit Shorebank: the First "Green" Bank' 3/16/2010 Darla June 'The Star Players in the ShoreBank Story'

foxnews.com FOX News 5/21/2010 'Glenn Beck: ShoreBank's Tangled Web 11/8/2009 Ed Barnes 'Collapse of Chicago Climate Exchange Means a Strategy Shift on Global Warming Curbs'

washingtonexaminer.com Washington Examiner 8/4/2010 'SIGTARP agrees to audit Chicago's politically connected ShoreBank'

pr-inside.com PR Inside 5/20/2010 'Andy Martin links Barack Obama to the growing ShoreBank Scandal in Chicago'

emergingcorruption.com 8/29/2010 Ann "Babe" Huggett 'Chicago's ShoreBank morphs into…'

crainsdetroit.com Crain's Detroit 8/22/2010 AP 'ShoreBank fails; will be reincarnated as Urban Partnership Bank'

canadafreepress.com Canada Free Press 3/26/2009 Judi McLeod 'Obama's involvement in "Chicago Climate Exchange and the rest of the story' nytimes.com NY Times 1/3/2011 Nathanial Gronewold 'Chicago Climate Exchange Closes Nation's First Cap-and-Trade System but Keeps Eye to the Future'

chicagoclimatex.com Chicago Climate Exchange 'Overview' 'Chicago Climate Exchange Announces Paula DiPerna to become Executive Vice President'

meetup.com 'The CCX Scandal, Pt 1: CCX is Born' 'Pt 2: The Fannie Mae Connection' 'Pt3: Emerald Cities' 'Pt 4 A Progressive Crime Family'

carboncapitalist.com 11/14/2010 Christopher Porto 'Chicago Climate Exchange Set to Close: What went wrong?'

inotruth.com 11/11/2010 'Gore Pocketed $18 Million from Now-Defunct Chicago Climate Exchange'

thecypresstimes.com The Cypress Times 5/10/2010 'More on Obama, Al Gore, & Crime Inc...'

cows.org Center on Wisconsin Strategy 'Emerald Cities Collaborative'

emeraldcities.org Emerald Cities Collaborative 'Board of Directors' 'Board Members' 'Goals' 'Mission statement'

findarticles.com Progressive October 1996 John Nichols 'Joel Rogers a founder of the New Party Crashing the Parties'

thenation.com The Nation 'Joel Rogers, contributing editor'

newzeal.blogapot.com NewZeal 5/1/2010 Trevor Loudon 'Joel Rogers and the Obama movement'

law.wisc.edu University of Wisconsin Law School 'Joel Rogers'

appinsys.com Applied Information Systems 'Carbon Monetization The Insiders'

onlygunsmoney.com 8/9/2010 'New Joyce Foundation Anti-Gun Rights Grants'

noquarter.com No Quarter 4/20/2008 'Obama on board That Funded Handgun Bans'

pajamasmedia.com Pajama's Media 10/6/2008 David T. Hardy 'Obama and the Attempt to Destroy the Second Amendment'

georgiapacking.org 'Anti-Gun Links'

politico.com Politico 4/19/2008 'Obama linked to gun control efforts'

wtpotus.com WTPOTUS 5/26/2010 'Obama and Joyce foundation Pay to Influence the Supreme Ct.'

offshoredrillingjobs.org 9/9/2010 'Obama is so worried about deep water drilling why'd he give Brazil & Mexico 4 bil to drill ...'

capitalresearch.org Foundation Watch November 2008 "Philanthropy Notes?" 'ACORN: Who funds the Weather Underground's Little Brother'

dailytell.com The Daily Tell 4/28/2010 Byron Butler 'Joyce Foundation awards $10 million in grants'

pnd.com Philanthropy News Digest 7/30/2010 'Joyce foundations announces $15 Million in Grants

prnewswire.com PR Newswire 7/28/2010 Joyce Foundation announces $15 million in summer 2010 grants'

Chapter 13

capitalresearch.org Capital Research Center 'Our Profile of the Massive Waste of Money Know as the Annenberg Challenge

therarealbarackobama.wordpress.com RBO 9/17/2008 Brenda J. Elliott 'Obama, Ayers, Karanja the Chicago Annenberg Challenge and the Chicago School Reform Collaborative'

nationalreview.com National Review 9/23/2008 Stanley Kurtz 'Obama's Challenge' 8/18/2008 Stanley Kurtz 'Chicago Annenberg Challenge Shutdown?'

wikipedia.org Wikipedia 'Chicago Annenberg Challenge' 'New Party' 'UFO religion' 'Million Man March' 'Alice Palmer' 'Quentin Young'

mediamatters.org Media Matters 6/2/2008 'CNN report accusing Obama of getting a little dirty'

conservapedia.com Conservapedia 'Alice Palmer'

talkleft.com Talk Left 5/29/2008 Obama and Alice Palmer Back in the News'

latimes.com LA Times 4/26/2008 'Once Obama's mentor, Alice Palmer now campaigns for Clinton'

renewamerica.com RenewAmerica.com 5/26/2008 Wes Vernon 'Barack Obama's communist connections'

newzeal.blogspot.com NewZeal 2/11/2010 Obama's mentor Quentin Young; Radical abortionist' 11/26/2009 'Obama File 90 Alice Palmer Re-examined-Was Obama's First Political Boss a soviet "Agent of Influence"?'

democracynow.org Democracy Now 3/11/2009 Dr. Quentin Young, Longtime Obama Confidante...'

romanticepoets.wordpress.com RomanticPoet 'Obama and the Weissbourds Was There a Frank Marshall Davis Connection?'

phhp.org Physicians for a National Health Program 'Fresh Air Interview Quentin Young, M.D.

mypetjawa.mu.nu The Jawa Report 10/8/2008 'Democratic Socialists of America Founded the New Party ...Claims Obama Was a Member'

freerepublic.com 'web archive of New Party website 1990s 'Principles of the (Socialist) New Party...'

salon.com Salon 9/12/2010 'Barack Obama sought the New Party's endorsement..'

keywiki.org 'New Party' 'Quentin Young'

wnd.com World Net Daily 10/24/2008 Aaron Klein 'Newspaper shows Obama belonged to socialist party'

newsbusters.org NewsBusters 10/8/2008 P.J.Gladnick 'Will MSM report on Obama Membership in Socialist New Party?' 2/23/2008 John Stephenson 'Will the Media report Obama's Terrorist Connection?' 10/7/2008 Matthew Balan 'Alice Palmer CNN's Drew Griffin Does a real fact-check on Obama/Ayers connection'

humanevents.com Human Events 6/10/2008 Erick Erickson 'Obama and the New Party'

americanthinker.com American Thinker 10/8/2008 Thomas Lifson 'Archives prove Obama was a New Party member'

arabamericanactionnetwork.wordpress.com 12/22/2010 '15th Anniversary Event with Helen Thomas' 9/13/2010 'Helen Thomas to Keynote AAAN Fundraiser'

worldtribune.com World Tribune 11/29/2010 2010 Cliff Kincaid 'Helen Thomas Honored by Group Raided by FBI'

zubfrcom.net 2/15/2011 Carl Horowitz 'Chicago SEIU Local Leaders Probed for Terror Links'

chicagotribune.com Chicago Tribune 9/24/2010 Andy Grimm and Cynthia Dizkes 'FBI raids anti-war activists' homes' 2/27/2011 Becky Schlikerman 'Farrakhan: Revolution imminent in U.S.'

huffingtonpost.com Huffington Post 9/27/2010 Steve Karnowski 'FBI Protests: Hundreds Rally Against Raids...' 2/25/2011 Sophia Tareen 'Nation of Islam Convention to Include UFO Talk'

chicago.indymedia.org 'SOLIDARITY VIGIL Against FBI Raids on Activists' hickeysite.blogspot,com 9/26/2010 'FBI Terror Suspects- The Professor and SEIU...'

indybay.org 9/24/2010 'Obama's Justice Dept Attacks Peace Groups as "Terrorist"

oyez.org 'Timmons v. Twin Cities Area New Party'

discoverthenetworks.org Discover The Network 'Louis Farrakhan' 'New Party' 'Alice Palmer'

foxnews.com FOX News 10/14/2005 'Farrakhan's Take on the Breaching of the New Orleans Levees'

jewishvirtualilibrary.org 'Minister Louis Farrakhan In His Own Words'

adl.org Anti-Defamation League 2/26/2006 'Farrakhan Again Spews Hate in Saviour's Day Speech' 3/5/1996 Spewing Hate in Saviour's Day Speech...Condemns America and the Jews'

newsmax.com News Max 3/21/2006 'Wicked Jews in Hollywood'

noisd.org Nation of Islam 'History of Saviour's Day'

therealbarackobama.wordpress.com RBO 3/4/2011 Brenda J. Elliott 'Klein: Farrakhan, Gadhafi supported US terrorist group'

roblorinov.wordpress.com 2/23/2011 'Obama-Khadafi Mystery SOLVED!!'

aim.org Accuracy in Media 11/2/2002 Reed Irving & Cliff Kincaid 'The Nation of Islam and Violence'

gatewaypundit.rightnetwork.com GatewayPundit 4/2/2008 Jim Hoft 'Wright & Obama Helped Organize March with Louis Farrakhan'

suntimes.com Sun Times 3/4/2011 Kim Janssen 'Louis Farrakhan says Moammar Gadhafi has always been a friend'

dailycaller.com Daily Caller 7/17/2010 Caroline May 'Farrakhan sends letter asking Jews for reparations'

hardford-hwp.com May 29/1995 'The Assassination of Malcolm X'

stanford.edu 1/171995 'Farrakhan helped build climate for Malcolm X's death'

cbsnews.com CBS News 5/10/2000 'Farrakhan Admission on Malcolm X'

tampabay.com St. Petersburg Times 10/18/2010 Shelley Rossetter and Thomas C. Tobin 'Louise Farrakhan renews call for self-determination...'

freedomeden.blogspot.com 9/24/2010 'Ahmadinejad UN Speech (9/23/2010) Transcript'

nypost.com NY Post 9/26/2010 Brad Hamilton 'A'jad monster's ball'

standbyliberty.org 9/27/2010 'Mahmoud Ahmadinejad has New Friends in America...'

zoa.org Zionist Organization of America 7/6/2010 Morton A. Klein 'Obama Should condemn Farrakhan's New Anti-Semitic Letter...'

finalcall.com NOI 9/7/2010 Cedric Muhammad 'response to Morton Klein's letter'

Chapter 14

discoverthenetworks.org Discover the Networks Richard Poe 'ACORN: History', Activities, and Agendas' 'ACORN; view list of all groups' 'ACORN backgrounder' 'Wade Rathke' 'George Alvin Wiley' 'Bertha Lewis'

acorn.org ACORN 'Mission Statement' 11/2/2010 'The end of an era: ACORN files Chapter 7 bankruptcy'

capitalresearchcenter.org Capital Research Center Mathew Vadum 'Who funds the Weather Underground's Little Brother?' 11/10/2009 Matthew Vadum 'Citigroup Executive Pulls Out of Sham ACORN Panel...'

city-journal.org City Journal Spring 2003 Sol Stern 'ACORN's Nutty Regime for Cities' Winter 2003 Steven Malanga 'How the "Living Wage' Sneaks Socialism into Cities'

ballotpedia.org 'ACORN' 'Wade Rathke'

thehill.com The Hill 7/19/2007 Karen Hanretty 'ACORN cried foul over minimum -wage hike; what would Edwards do?'

freerepublic.com FreeRepublic.com 10/31/2004 Meghan Clyne 'ACORN sued for minimum wage exemption' 7/31/1997 Jim Allen 'ACORN leader Madeline Talbott arrested Obama contact storms city council' 5/11/2011 YouTube video: 'Bertha Lewis sings Walmart Sucks!'

washingtontimes.com Washington Times 1/3/2006 'Minimum wage ACORN roots'

patriotactionnetwork.com Patriot Action Network 3/18/2009 'Voter fraud organization ACORN to assist Globama and his sidekick Rahm Emanuel in the 2010 census'

spectator.org Spectator 10/22/2008 Peter Ferrara 'Voter Fraud' 3/2/2010 Matthew Vadum 'ACORN Housing Boom' 9/11/2009 Paul Chesser 'Okeefe's Acorn Expose' Moves to DC' Matthew Vadum 'Wrathful Wade Rathke' Matthew Vadum 'ACORN founder Wade Rathke wanted terrorist Attack on Republican Convention to Succeed' Matthew Vadum 'Glenn Beck on ACORB and Drummond Pike's Tides Foundation' prnewswire.com PR Newswire 'Illegalities, fraud and contradictions detailed in Report...' 'Walmart creates over 125.000 new jobs in 2005...'

pajamasmedia.com PajamasMedia.com 10/14/2008 Jim Hoft 'The Complete Guide to ACORN Voter Fraud'

manhattan-institute.org The Wall Street Journal 10/26/2006 Steven Malanga 'Acorn Squash'

americandaughter.com 11/8/2006 Jim Simpson 'ACORN Alert'

wnd.com World Net Daily 112/1/2000 Kenneth R. Timmerman 'Coup behind closed doors' 5/20/2009 Phyllis Schlafly 'Remove ACORN from federal trough' 6/12/2011 'Just when you thought America was purged of this evil'

commondreams.org Common Dreams 11/13/2000 Rich Cowan '13 Myths about the results of the 2000 election'

rense.com Rense 11/19/2000 Tory Briggs 'Statistical Evidence of Florida Democratic Vote Fraud'

pbs.org PBS 11/15/2000 Betty Ann Bowser 'Florida Recount' transcript of News Hours Show

cnn.com CNN 11/10/2000 'Bush leads Gore by 327 votes in Florida recount AP reports' 9/23/2009 'ACORN sues filmmakers;

boston.com Boston Globe 11/24/2000 Lynda Gorov and Anne E. Kornblut 'Gore to challenge results'

consortiumnews.com 8/5/2002 Robert Parry 'Bush's Conspiracy to Riot'

wikipedia.org Wikipedia 'Florida election recount' 'James O'Keefe' 'Wade Rathke' 'Madeline Talbott'

dailykos.com Daily Kos 8/4/2009 'GOP Returns to 2000 Dade County Recount Playbook'

democrats.com 4/19/2006 'Rove's Replacement Brags About "Brooks Brother Riot"...'

washingtonexaminer.com 'The Washington Examiner on ACORN:'

univision.com Univision 10/15/2008 'Wade Rathke, Obama and ACORN'

americanthinker.com American Thinker 1/17/2010 James Simpson 'How to Lock Democrats in Power' 'Barack Obama and the Strategy of Manufactured Crisis'

reviewjournal.com ReviewJournal.com 10/8/2008 Adrienne Packer and Molly Ball 'Alleging fraud, authorities raid voter group' rottenacorn.com 'Recent Fraud'

epionline.org Employment Policies Institute 'Rotten ACORN America's Bad Seed'

westernexperience.wordpress.com 9/15/2009 'ACORN: The poison nut that is getting cracked'

trustreagan.com 10/7/2008 Stanley Kurtz 'The Sordid History of ACORN and the Ties to the Financial Meltdown'

eppc.org Ethics and Public Policy Center Stanley Kurtz 'Planting Seeds of Disaster'

nypost.com NY Post 9/29/2008 Stanley Kurtz 'O's Dangerous Pals'

wordiq.com 'Omidyar Network – Definition'

goa.gov Government Accountability Office 6/14/2010 'Preliminary Observations on Funding...'

thenewamerican.com New American 11/2/2008 Gregory A. Hession, J.D. 'ACORN: No business Like Poverty like Poverty Business' 10/31/2008 'ACORN: War on the Poor'

npr.org NPR 10/15/2008 'ACORN's Money Tree Has Many Branches' 10/1/2009 Pam Fessler ACORN Donations Dwindle in Wake of Videos' 1/20/2011 'Michelle Obama Partners with Walmart for Healthy Eating' 3/23/2010 Deborah Tedford "CEO says ACORN 'Isn't Dead Yet'"

telegraph.co.uk Telegraph 5/13/2007 Philip Sherwell 'Obama called hypocrite for wife's Wal-Mart link'

politico.com Politico 10/11/2008 Alexander Burns 'ACORN gives GOP new line of attack' 'Bertha Lewis' 4/21/2010 Video 'ACORN Bertha Lewis proudly declares "I'm A Socialist" 6/10/2010 'ACORN's Lewis plans Black Leadership Institute to focus on Immigration'

realclearpolitics.com Real Clear Politics 9/15/2009 Rich Lowry 'ACORN's Lawlessness Exposed'

commondreams.org Common Dreams 11/15/2006 'ACORN joins international forces against Wal-Mart' 2/2/2007 ACORN Applauds Senate Move on Minimum Wage Increase'

therealacorn.blogspot.com 7/11/2007 'Dangerous and unfair Work Conditions? Walmart? Try ACORN!!'

independent.org 5/8/2007 Richard K. Vedder Ken Jacobs 'Is Wal-Mart Good or Bad for America?'

wiki.dickinson.edu Dickinson College Wiki 'The Living Wage'

adaction.org Americans for Democratic Action 'Living Wage No. 353'

townhall.com Townhall 3/19/2002 Bruce Bartlett 'The truth about the so-called living wage'

acorncracked.com 'Funding Sources'

hud.gov HUD 10/24/2002 'Bush Administration Awards $22 million in self-help grants ...' 'Self-help Homeownership Program (SHOP)'

nhi.org National Housing Institute 'Homesteading Program, Chicago

housingfinance.com 2/23/2006 'Housing zeitgeist, late night edition'

latimes.com LA Times 6/21/1991 AP House 'Banking Panel votes Protection for Poor Areas'

biggovernment.com BigGovernment.com 'Anonymous Donors, Liberal Foundations and Labor Unions Fuel renamed Acorn affiliates' 'ACORN's Roots Watered by Taxpayers' 'Commerce Department's Rejection of ACORN Application belies Alternative Funding Sources' 10/27/2010 Warner Todd Huston 'ACORN's Get-Out-The-Vote operative under state felony charges' 11/9/2010 AP 'Auditor: ACORN owes government $3.2 million' 5/25/2010 Morgen Richmond 'Bertha Lewis Arrested at immigration protest' 1/4/2010 'White House visitors Log: ACORN, CEO Bertha Lewis...' 1/4/2010 Andrew Breitbart 'White House spokeswoman says different Bertha Lewis on Visitor's log

msnbc.msn.co MSNBC News AP 9/11/2009 'Census Bureau Cuts Its Ties With Acorn'

judicialwatch.org Judicial Watch 5/28/2009 Census Bureau refuses to partner with 'Hate Groups, Law...'

abcnews.go.com ABC News 3/9/2011 Ron Claiborne, Ben Forer 'James O'Keefe Ensnares Liberal Groups with Actors and Hidden Camera' 1/20/2011 Tahman Bradley 'Michelle Obama and Walmart Join forces promoting healthy food' 9/20/2009 George Stephanopoulos 'Obama on ACORN: "Not something I've followed closely" won't commit to cut federal funds'

hispanicpundit.com 2/3/2006 'The Benefits of Wal-Mart'

nypost.com NY Post 9/14/2009 Jeremy Olshan '"Pimp & Hooker" catch B'klyn staff'

townhall.com Townhall 10/27/2008 Amanda Carpenter 'ACORN Owes Millions in taxes'

emergingcorruption.com 1/3/2011 Michael Gaynor 'ACORN's Rathke and Talbott: Just Believe What Obama Say About Himself'

law.com 8/16/2010 Mark Hamblett 'Congress De-funding of ACORN is constitutional' crainsnewyork.com Crains NY 11/3/2010 Daniel Massey 'Acorn files for bankruptcy' 10/17/2010 'Local Acorn remnant revives activism'

sourcewatch.org Source Watch 'Wade Rathke'

chieforganizer.org 'Wade Rathke, Organizer'

socialpolicy.org Social Policy: Organizing for Social and Economic Justice Winter 2011 Wade Rathke 'Publisher's Note' 'About Us'

noquarterusa.net NoQuarterUSA 10/17/2008 Bud White 'Wade Rathke: ACORN's Founder, Ayers compatriot'

romanticpoet.wordpress.com RomanticPoet 5/22/2009 Web of Deceit: Wade Rathke/ ACORN/SEIU/ and Possibly Obama?'

deathby1000papercuts.blogspot.com 9/223/2009 'Weather Underground, ACORN and Obama…'

findarticles.com 5/7/2001 'bills set state for battle between labor, business'

foxnews.com FOX News 11/10/2010 AP 'government Audit Says ACORN should pay back $3.2.Million in Federal Funds'

iidnet.org Initiatives for International Dialogue' 'Beginnings'

nlpc.org National Legal and Policy Center 11/23/2010 Carl Horowitz 'HUD report reveals misspending by ACORN affiliate' 2/27/2010 'Senate Committee approves radical Obama NLRB nominee; filibuster likely'

pittburglive.com Pittsburgh Tribune-Review 11/5/2010 Walter F. Roche Jr. 'ACORN, affiliates owe state $750,000'

masslive.com 10/24/2009 Jack Flynn 'ACORN founder Wade Rathke returning to Western Mass…'

nytimes.com NY Times 7/9/2008 Stephanie Strom 'Funds misappropriated at 2 nonprofit groups' 11/7/2009 AP ACORN offices in New Orleans are raided' 3/4/2010 Stephen Witt AY starts off an economic boom for Brooklyn contractors'

mediacircus.com MediaCircus.com. 10/3/2008 'Obama sued Citibank under CRA to force it to make bad loans'

madelinetalbott.com 'Action Now'

theeprovocateur.blogspot.com 5/28/2009 'The Embezzlement of Dale Rathke'thenextright.com 10/30/2008 Dayton 'Is Obama connected to the ACORN-Rathke embezzlement scandal?'

canadafreepress.com Canada Free Press 9/302009 'ACORN founder Wade Rathke was fired from ACORN last year'

libcom.org 7/12/2008 ACORN's Wade Rathke steps down after revelation of Brothers theft and Rathke instigated coverup'

nola.com Times Picayune 3/26/2010 'ACORN International puts down roots in South Korea, Egypt'

newzeal.blogspot.com NewZeal 2/14/2011M Michael Gaynor/Emerging Corruption 'What did Wade Rathke Know about Egypt that the CIA didn't and what will Obama do now?

bostonreview.net Boston Review Madeline Talbott 'Where Do We Begin?'

pumabydesign001.wordpress.com 2/22/2010 ACORN crime family shutting down nation-wide: Launching renaming effort'

netrightdaily.com 3/28/2011 'Rebranded ACORN network will target battleground States in 2012' 11/1/2010 Matthew Vadum 'ACORN lives! The Ban on Federal Funding Expires'

pelicaninstitute.org Pelican Institute 11/12/2010 Kevin Mooney 'Renamed ACORN affiliates are well positioned for 2012 election in Key States'

actionnow.org Action Now 6/30/2009 Aileen Kelleher 'New foreclosure mediation program in the Cook county Courts!' 'Action Now recent reviews'

nonprofitlist.org 'Chicago Illinois Non-profit organizations'

confederateyankee.mu.nu 9/29/2008 'Love the financial crisis? Thank your local "Community Organizer"

examiner.com Examiner 5/6/2009 Martha R. Gore 'Obama connection to ACORN and voter fraud investigation' 4/21/2010 J.P. Freire 'Fmr ACORN head calls Tea Parties 'bowel movement' and claims 'they're coming after you'

theatheistconservative.com 'Moment of decision'

observer.com NY Observer 4/22/2010 Eliot Brown 'Martha Lewis, ACORN CEO, not happy for Daniel Goldstein'

mycrains.crainsnewyork.com Crain's 9/16/2007 Bertha Lewis 'A believer fights the good fight'

verumserum.com VerumSerum 4.20.2010 'Video: ACORN CEO Bertha Lewis attacks conservatives, promotes socialist''

whorungov.com WhoRunsGov 'Bertha Lewis Why She Matters'

medill.northwestern.edu 11/11/2009 Paul Takahashi 'Chief judge to propose $3 million amendment to Cook County budget'

chicagobreakingbusiness.com 2/6/2011 Alejandra Cancino 'Ill. Senate bill on minimum wage gets more support'

ctunet.com Chicago Teachers Union 8/6/2010 'Teachers to lobby Aldermen to put TIF money back into schools'

humanevents.com Human Events 7/10/2011 Matthew Vadum 'ACORN sprouting fresh branches' 7/18/2010 John Howting 'The Old Mistaken Identity Play'

r8ny.com Room Eight NY 5/31/2009 Hildy Johnson 'Brad Lander and the Acorn/rather Atlantic yards conspiracy'

atlanticyardsreport.blogspot.com 'Atlantic Yards Report'

stopforeclosurefraud.com 7.9.2010 John Atlas 'New Yorkers to Wall Street; Help with foreclosures or well move out money to banks that will'

vaughnweberlaw.com 2/9/2011 Cara Buckley 'NY Unions want Chase to modify mortgages'

sadhillnews.com 2/10/2011'Change that matters ACORN sprouts new roots under NYCC name'

nycommunities.org "The Nation" 7/15/2010 Katrina vanden Heuvel 'Move Your BIG Money' 'About NY Communities for Change' 2/2/2011 'Press Releases'

brownstoner.com 2 /14/2011 'Wal-Mart foe call possibility of chain landing in ENY a Bait and Switch'

observer.com NY Observer 1/20/2011 Matt Chaban 'Even Michelle Obama Will shop at Walmart'

dnainfo.com 5/4/2011Patrick Hedlund 'Walmart foes warn lower East Side about chain store "Virus"

aipnews.com AIPNews 9/21/2009 Breitbart TV 'Obama: "I didn't even know that ACORN was getting a whole lot of federal money" 9/22/2010 Erick Erickson 'A review of ACORN CEO Bertha's Lewis's Rolodex suggests strong White House ties'

allbusiness.com AllBusiness.com 'Left for dead, local Acorn remnant revises activism'

newshounds.us.com 1/4/2010 Gretchen Carlson promotes bogus Bertha Lewis White House Visit Story on Fox 7 Friends'

Chapter 15

counterpunch.org CounterPunch 3/5/2002 Edward Said 'Thoughts About America' jcpa.org Jerusalem Center for Public Affairs 1/23/2003 'The Anti-Israel Agenda of MIFTAH'

miftah.org MIFTAH 'About Us' 9/27/2003 Ziad Asali 'Remembering Edward Said'

aljazeerah.info Al-Jazeerah 1/9/2003 Richard Melson 'Radicalization Processes'

yesmagazine.org Yes!Magazine.org 9/17/2001 'Diverse Coalition of Americans speak Out Against War'

matrixmatters.com MatrixMatters 3/13/2003 'Edward Said miscellaneous thoughts'

progressive.org The Progressive November 2001 David Barsamian 'Interview with Edward W. Said'

discoverthenetworks.org Discover the Networks 'Edward Said: Profile' 'Rashid Khalidi' 'Arab American Action Network (AAAN)' 'Ali Abunimah'

english.emory.edu 'Orientalism'

wikipedia.org Wikipedia 'Edward Said' '1948 Palestinian exodus' 'Nabka Day' 'Rashid Khalidi' 'Bobby Rush' 'Huwaida Arraf' 'International solidarity Movement'

electronicintifada.net Electronic Intifada 'Nabka, the Palestinian catastrophe (1948)' 'EI Team'

cnn.com CNN 'In the Area blogs 2/25/2011 'Foreign policy experts Bret Stephens and Rashid Khalidi discuss what a post-Gadhafi Libya might look like' 7/9/2008 'Jackson apologizes for crude Obama remarks'

antiwar.com 2/22/2011 Scott Horton 'Rashid Khalidi'

mideast.foreignpolicy.com 2/24/2011 Rashid Khalidi 'Reflections on the revolutions in Tunisia and Egypt'

debbieschlussel.com Debbie Schlussel 1/30/2008 'Obama's Nation of Islam Staffers, Edward Said...'

campus-watch.org CampusWatch 7/25/2010 Ma'an News Agency US Boat to join Gaza Flotilla' April 2005 Andy Humm 'Academic freedom, Intimidation and Mayoral Politics: The case of Rashid Khalidi' 9/29/2010 WND Aaron Klein 'FBI terror probe target group funded b Obama (incl. Rashid Khalidi) 10/9/2008 'Columbia's Arafat Stooge (on Rashid Khalidi)' 2/24/2008 WND Aaron Klein 'Obama worked with terrorist' 7/20/2007 Winfield Myers 'Rashid Khalidi appeals for funds for ship to run Israeli Blockade of Gaza'

sourcewatch.org Source Watch 'American Task Force on Palestine'

gatewaypundit.rightnewtork.com GatewayPundit 11/28/2009 Jim Hoft 'White House Party

Crashes linked to Obama's Radical Pal Rashid Khalidi' 4/2/2008 'Ruh-Roh...Obama's links to Radical Islamic-Marxist Group reported'

bittenandbound.com 12/3/2009 'Michaele Salahi Washington Redskins Cheerleader Fraud' 11/25/2009 Therese Lisieux 'Michaele Salahi Playboy...'

nytimes.com NY Times 'Rashid Khalidi' 1/7/2009 Rashid Khalidi 'What You don't know about Gaza' 9/9/2007 Janny Scott 'In 2000 a streetwise veteran schooled a bold young Obama'

meforum.org 8/25/2003 Jonathan Calt Harris NY Post 'Anti-Israel U.'

townhall.com Townhall 8/31/2010 David Limbaugh 'Obama's appalling mistreatment of Israel' 10/29/2008 Katie Favazza 'What you should know about Rashid Khalidi and Barack Obama'

noquartersusa.net NoQuartersUSA 2/18/2008 Larry Johnson 'More on Rashid Khalidi and the Risks for Obama'

jewishpolicycenter.org Focus Quarterly Winter 2008 Cinnamon Stillwell 'Rashid Khalidi, campus Watch and Middle East Studies'

columbia.edu Columbia University 'Rashid Khalidi'

americanthinker.com American Thinker 5/3/2008 Rick Moran 'Obama's good friend Rashid Khalidi' 8/5/2010 Lauri Regan 'Us to Gaza: A charade that must be stopped'

latimes.com LA Times 4/10/2008 Peter Wallsten 'Allies of Palestinians see a friend in Obama'

familysecuritymatters.com Family Security Matters 10/24/2008 Rachel Neuwirth 'Barack Obama's Anti-Israel Alliances'

associatedcontent.com 10/26/2008 Mark Whittington 'Rashid Khalidi is another Barack Obama Scary Friend'

newsmax.com Newsmax 10/27/2008 David A. Patten 'Obama: Constitution is "Deeply flawed"

wsj.com Wall Street Journal 10/28/2008 Steven G. Calabresi 'Obama's Redistribution Constitution'

Chapter 16

chicagoreader.com Chicago Reader 1/15/2009 Edward McClelland 'Is Bobby Rush in Trouble?'

salon.com Salon.com 2/12/2007 Edward McClelland 'How Obama learned to be a natural' chicagotribune.com Chicago Tribune 1/22/1995 Sharon Honaker 'American Jewish Congress to Honor Bettylu Saltzman'

keywiki.org 'Bettylu Saltzman'

usatoday.com USA Today 10/24/2007 Christopher Wills 'Obama learned from failed Congress run'

sweetness-light.com Sweetness& Light Illinois Issues August/September 1998 'Obama on organizing after Saul 'Alinsky'

richardlandlive.com 8/23/2008 Doug Carlson 'Fact Sheet: Barack Obama and the Born-Alive Infants Protection Act'

lifesitenews.com LifeSiteNews8/11/2011 Gudrun Schultz 'Planned Parenthood reports record $882 million income $63 million profit' 1/29/2010 Steven Ertelt 'International Planned Parenthood pushes Sexual Rights…'

freerepublic.com FreeRepublic.com7/14/2008 Sean Robins 'Obama on Illinois "Born Alive Bill (2001)'

wikipedia.org Wikipedia 'Bobby Rush'

nrlc.org National Right to Life 8/28/2008 Douglas Johnson and Susan T. Muskett 'National Right to Life White paper'

jillstanek.com 2.9/2008 'Links to Barack Obama's votes on IL's Born Alive Infant Protection Act'

factcheck.org 8.25.2008 'The facts about Obama's votes against Born Alive bills in Illinois'

taxfoundation.org 4/4/2008 'Comparing Charitable Giving of Clinton and Obama'

taxprof.typepard.com 3/25/2008 'Obama releases 2000-2008 Tax Returns'

ramallahquakers.org 'Friends International Center in Ramallah September 2010 Newsletter'

hyscience.com Hyscience 8/9/2008 'From Obama's 'Audacity of Hope: 'I will stand with the Muslims should the political winds shift in an ugly direction"

gazafreedommarch.org 'A benefit for the US Boat to Gaza' 7/22/2010 Diaa Hadid 'Gaza flotilla has roots in pro-Palestinian group'

jewishpeacenews.blogspot.com 11/7/2010 'Deepa Kumas: The US to Gaza Initiative and the Hillel Controversy at Rutgers'

chicago.indymedia.org 5.31.2010 'Emergency Rally at Israeli consulate to Protest Attack on Humanitarian ships' socialistworker.org 6/4/2010 'Standing against Israel's war crimes'

thestrategycenter.org The Strategy Center 11/24/2008 'Ali Abunimah, Huwaida Arraf & Amal Sabawi: The crisis in Gaza'

palsolidarity.org Palsolidarity 1/1/2009 Sayed Dhansay/Electronic Intifada 'Gaza Freedom March activists target Egypt's complicity'

commentarymagazine.com Commentary 1/29/2008 Eric Trager 'Obama and American Jews'

israelnationalnews.com Israel International News 3/23/2008 Gil Ronen 'Arab-American Activist says Obama Hiding Anti-Israel Stance'

talkleft.com TalkLeft.com 4/17/2008 'Obama and Ayers: The Khalidi Question'

wnd.com World Net Daily 2/25/2008 Aaron Klein 'Obama raised funds for Islamic causes'

israpundit.com Israpundit 2/12/2011 Bill Levinson 'International Solidarity SM movement Hopes Americans will be Killed in Gaza Flotilla' 10/9/2007 Electronic Intifada's Nigel Parry: Proven Liar'

palestinenote.com 6/5/2010 'Israel arrests released SM co-founder'

israelmatzav.blogspot.com 4/3/2008 'Barack Hussein Obama and the International Solidarity Movement'

canadafreepress.com Canada Free Press 4/1/2008 Lee Kaplan 'How Obama's church and associates link him to ISM'

pajamasmedia.com PajamasMedia.com 9/13/2008 Jennifer Rubin 'Obama and the Woods Fund'

commondreams.org Common Dreams 2/3/2002 Ali Abunimah 'U.S. Approach Hurts All Parties'

friendsofsouthasia.org Ali Abunimah 'One Country'

aliabunimah.posterous.com 3/7/2011 Ali Abunimah 'Israel's negative rating rise sharply in US, Uk...'

cnsnews.com CNS News 2/10/2010 Edwin Mora' International Planned Parenthood pushes sex for 10-year olds...'

lifenews.com Life News 1/29/2010 Samantha Singson 'International Planned Parenthood pushes Sexual rights...'

msnbc.msn.com MSNBC News Molly Masland 'Carnal knowledge The sex-ed debate'

Chapter 17

answers.com ‘Jesse Jackson, Jr.’

sourcewatch.org SourceWatch ‘Jesse Jackson Jr.’

chicagogop.com 11/19/2009 Isaac C. Hayes ‘Apollo Alliance: Home to Van Jones, Jesse Jr.’

sodahead.com SodaHead ‘The Apollo alliance…Hijacking America’

nowpublic.com 7/16/2008 ‘Jesse Jackson, used the N-word, saying “Obama tells N****s how to behave” on Fox’

articles/cnn.com CNN 7/9/2008 Jackson apologies…’

israelnationalnews.com Israel National News 10/14/2008 Gil Ronen ‘Jesse Jackson: ‘Zionists control US…’

skepticalbrotha.wordpress.com ‘Jackson Jr. informed on Blagojevich’

newsone.com NewsOne.com Casey Grane-McCalla ‘Jesse Jackson Kr. Says he is not an informant’

abc.go.com ABC News 12/10/2008 ‘Rep Jesse Jackson Jr. is Senate Candidate No.5’

suntimes.com Sun-Times Media 5/27/2011 Natasha Korecki ‘Rod Blagojevich denies Jesse Jackson Jr.’s extortion allegation’

huffingtonpost.com Huffington Post ‘Jesse Jackson Jr. is Senate Candidate 5 (video)’

nytimes.com NY Times ‘Rod Blagojevich’

csmonitor.com Christian Science Monitor 7/8/2010 Mark Guarino ‘Blagojevich trial…’

npr.org NPR 8/25/2008 ‘Transcript: Jesse Jackson Jr.’s Speech’

jessejackson.org ‘Jackson’s Organizations’

blacpast.org Black Past ‘Jackson, Jesse Louis Jr.’

ilga.gov Illinois General Assembly ‘Senator Emil Jones, Jr.’

zimbio.com Zimbio 4/17/2008 Illinois state Senate Leader Emil Jones: Obama’s Kingmaker’ 8/6/2010 Former Illinois State Senate President Emil Jones Jr. Joins Zimek technologies Advisory Board

chicagotribune.com Chicago Tribune 6/10/2010 ‘Monk: Deal would have given Emil Jones Obama’s Senate seat’ 9/9/2008 Eric Zorn ‘Obama’s foes fire same old cheapshot’ talkleft.com TalkLeft 3/23/2008 'Obama, Emil Jones and Earmarks'

austinweeklynews.com Austin Weekly News 12/12/2007 Delores McCain 'Ministers endorse Barack

chicagodefender.com Chicago Defender 11/5/2008 Emil Jones an early backer of Obama White House bid'

wikipedia.org Wikipedia 'Jesse Jackson Jr.' 'Emil Jones, Jr.' 'US Senate career of Barack Obama'

nbcchicago.com NBC News 6/11/2010 Edward McClelland 'Why Emi Jones Jr. took a bullet for Obama'

cbsnews.com CBS News 3/31/2008 AP 'Obama's political Godfather in Illinois'

ilga.gov Illinois General Assembly 'Senator Emil Jones Jr.'

townhall.com Townhall 4/19/2011 'On Libya and Budget President Obama votes Present'

factcheck.org 'How many times did Obama vote present…'

nbcchicago.com NBC/Chicago 'Why Emil Jones Jr. Took a bullet for Obama'

vvdailypress.com High Desert Daily Press 3/29/2011 Steve Williams 'The yellow button'

Chapter 18

discoverthenetworks.org Discover the Networks 'Michael Pfleger'

chicagotribune.com Chicago Tribune 5/3/2007 Ray Long, Ray Gibson, David Jackson 'State port to Obama's district included allies, donors' 4/21/2011 AP 'Meeks considers resigning from Ill. Senate'

frontpagemag.com Front Page Mag10/9/2008 Tom Fitton 'Obama's Earmark for Fr. Pfleger'

abcnews.com ABC News 5/29/2008 'Priest and Obama Ally Mocks Clinton's Tears from Obama's Church's Pulpit'

dallassouthblog.com 5/30/2007 'Min .Louis Farrakhan visits Father Michael Pfleger and St. Sabina'

chicago.cbslocal.com CBS Chicago 3/15/2011 Father Pfleger's future at St. Sabina in question'

nbcchicago.com NBC Chicago 4/19/2011 Mary Ann Ahem 'Francis Cardinal George on His, Pfleger's futures' suntimes.com Sun Times 4/18/2011 Mark Konkol 'Cardinal, Pfleger discuss him possibly leaving St. Sabina'

abclocal.co.com ABC News 6/3/2008 'Fr. Pfleger takes temporary leave;

wikipedia.org 'Michael Pfleger' 'James Meeks;

sbcoc.org Salem Baptist Church of Chicago 'Rev. James T. Meeks' 'About Us'

chicagoreader.com Chicago Reader 1/25/2007 Mick Dumke 'The Church of Clout' Hank De Zutter 'What Makes Obama Run?'

newsbusters.org NewsBusters3/20/2008 Tom Blumer 'Another Close Religious Adviser to Obama Old Media has Ignored'

atlasshrugs.2000.typepad.com Atlas Shrugs 3/24/2008 'The Wright Stuff: Obama & James Meeks show me your friends'

towlerroad.com 9/14/2010 'Anti-gay Chicago Mayoral hopeful James Meeks would address gay rights if he got bored enough'

huffingtonpost.com Huffington Post 4/26/2011 'James Meeks: White Women shouldn't get Affirmative Action from City' 4/26/2011 Karen Hawkins, Sophia Tareen 'James Meeks Drips Out of Chicago Mayor's Race'

anythingblog.com 4/1/2008 'James Meeks: Obama's Other Bigoted Spiritual Leader...'

christianitytoday.com Christianity Today 11/11/2008 Steve Waldman 'Obama's fascinating interview with Cathleen Falsani' 2/1/2004 Bob Smietana 'Mega Shepherd'

cbsnews.com CBS News 6/2/2008 Stanley Kurtz/National Review Online 'Obama's Radical-Left Ties Broad and Deep'

todaysdrum.com '17 couples take Rev. James Meeks up on challenge, tie the knot'

christianvisionproject.com November 2006 'Redeeming a Needy Neighborhood'

james-meeks.co.tv 'James Meeks'

substancenews.net 10/20/2009 George N. Schmidt 'The biggest gang problem in Chicago is the Chicago Teachers Union'

chicago.cbslocal.com CBS News 12/23/2010 'Meeks withdraws from Mayor's race'

Chapter 19

chicago.indymedia.org 2/14/2007 'Barack Obama's Crown Dynasty Connection' judicialwatch.org Judicial Watch 3/14/2008 'Obama Earmarks for wife's employer, big donor'

thenextright.com TheNextRight 4/30/2010 Eric Ames 'The Paula Crown Affair, Part 2'

gather.com 3/14/2008 'Obama and the Crown Dynasty (General Dynamics)

turcopolier.typepad.com 'Lester Crown and Barack Obama'

uchicago.edu UChicagoNews 2/12/2009 'James Crown to step down as Chairman of the Board of Trustees' August 1996 R. Bruce Dold 'Dissenting Opinion'

aspeninstitute.org Aspen Institute 'James Schine Crown'

forbes.com Forbes 'James S. Crown'

jewishaz.com Jewish News of Greater Phoenix 10/10/2008 Pauline Dubkin Yearwood 'Barack Obama

ynetnews.com YNET News Yitzhak Benhorin 'Obama targeted in smear campaign' 4/22/2010 'Obama to US Jews; peace cannot be imposed;

suntimes.com Sun Times 9/22/2007 Lynn Sweet 'Post High Holidays, Obama and Clinton woo big Jewish donors...' 4 /28/2008 Obama's billionaire finance chair Penny Pritzker's failed bank lost money for 1,400 customers' 8/6/2009 Obama taps Martha Minow, John G. Levi for Legal Service Corporation Board' 4/22/2010 'Ann Williams, Martha Minow on Obama Supreme Court short list...' 6/16/2008 'Warren Buffett to headline $28,500 per person "'private dinner" for Obama...' 7/13/2009 'Chicago's Alan Solow, Jewish leaders meet with Obama today'

wnd.com World Net Daily 10./20/2008 Brad O'Leary 'Obama's money trail'

mondoweiss.net Mondoweiss 8/10/2010 Philip Weiss 'Did Billionaire Lester Crown get to Obama on Israel?'

engology.com 'Lester Crown'

powerbase.info 'Lester Crown'

militantislammonitor.org Militant Islam Monitor 12/8/2008 'Has Philanthropist Lester Crown been Duped by Islamists?'

wikipedia.org Wikipedia 'Lester Crown' 'Penny Pritzker' 'Abner J. Mikva' 'Newton N. Minow' 'David Axelrod' 'Alan Solow' 'American Israel Public Affairs Committee'

salon.com Salon 8/12/2010 Justin Elliott 'Did top Obama donor carry Israeli message to W.H.?'

zimbio.com Zimbio 11/24/2009 'List of White House state dinner guests' penny-pritzker.com 'Penny Pritzker'

huffingtonpost.com Huffington Post 11/19/2008 'Penny Pritzker: Commerce Secretary?' 11/6/2008 'David Axelrod: Obama's Senior Adviser?"

thecrimson.com The Harvard Crimson 6/5/2006 Madeline W. Lissner 'Penny Pritzker'

gdaeman.blogspot.com 2/21/2008 GDAE Man 'Who is Penny Pritzker and Why is She Obama's Campaign Finance Chair?'

chicagojewishnews.com Chicago Jewish News 10/224/2008 'Obama and the Jews'

lsc.gov 'Laurie Mikva'

nytimes.com NY Times 6/25/2010 John Schwartz 'In a Mentor, Kagan's Critics see Liberal Agenda' 5/1/2008 1Becker, Christopher Drew 'The Long Run' 10/27/2008 Jeff Zeleny 'Long by Obama's side...'

legalblog.typepad.com 6/11/2009 Robert J. Ambrogi 'Minow named Dean of Harvard Law'

chicagotribune.com Chicago Tribune 6/11/2009 Ameet Sachdev 'New dean at Harvard Law' 3/17/2011 Melissa Harris 'Newton Minow, 50 years into the vast wasteland' 1/30/2011 Exit Interview: David Axelrod...' 3/21/2010 Melissa Harris 'Chicagoan to head pro-Israel group' 5/2/2009 Josh Meyer 'US to drop espionage-related charges against ex-AIPAC lobbyists'

vanityfair.com Vanity Fair 10/29/2008 Todd S. Purdum 'Meet Newton Minow, Adlai Aide and Obama Mentor'

sidley.com Sidley Austin LLP 'Newton N. Minow'

pbcchicago.com Public Building Commission 'Bryan s. Traubert, M.D'

bloomberg.com Bloomberg Billionaire donors split with Obama on Law that may hurt hotels'

spectator.org Spectator 9/26/2008 Edward Sisson 'Obama in the Tank for Pritzker'

24ahead.com 6/17/2009 'Tom Brokaw, Wesley Clark...others on White House Fellowships Commission'

whorungov.com WhoRunsGov Robert S. Rivkin's World'

floydreports.com 2/24/2011 Ben Johnson 'Obama's Economic Advisers International Socialists, Union thugs NBC Execs...'

whitehouse.gov 'White House Fellows'

biography.com 'David Axelrod Biography'

newzeal.blogspot.com 10.30/2008 Obama 'File 46: ...Who is behind the man behind Obama?'

romanticpoet.wordpress.com RomanticPoet 3/5/2008 'Who Is David Axelrod Obama's Political Advisor' 8/18/2009 Michelle Malkin 'Axelrod's profits: un who's on the take from the drug lobby again?!?!'

hubpages.com Chris Chen 'Did Obama...Create a Cult of Personality to win the Presidency?'

inthesetimes.com InTheseTimes 8/23/2008 Laura S. Washington 'The Whole World Was Watching'

aipnews.com AIPNews 9/11/2009 'David Axelrod's Communist Associations'

the obamaclub.com 'Are These the only people Obama knows?'

chicagomag.com Chicago Mag September 2011 Daniel Libit 'David Axelrod's Last Campaign'

tabletmag.com Tablet 3/18/2010 Allison Hoffman 'The Go-Between'

americanthinker.com American Thinker 7/24/2009 Leo Rennert 'National Jewish Leader Turns against Obama' 8/7/2008 Rick Moran 'Obama faked 2002 anti-war speech for ad...'

noquarterusa.net NoQuarter 3/26/2008 Susan UnPC 'The staged Iraq war speech & more...'

haaretz.com Haaretz 12/21/2008 Bradley Burston 'Key Obama backer, confidante Alan Solow tipped to head US Jewry's top body' 1/29/2008 Shumuel Rosner 'Obama slams ugly smears from Jewish Community'

conferenceofpresidents.org 'Alan Solow, Chairman'

washingtonexaminer.com Washington Examiner 4/14/2010 AP 'World Jewish Congress confronts Obama on White House double-standard on Israel and Palestinians' juf.org Jewish United Fund Joel Schatz 'Jewish leader Robert M. Schrayer dies at 75'

pumabydesign001.wordpress.com 3/30/2011 'World Jewish Congress confronts Obama on Obama's Betrayal...'

worldjewishcongress.org World Jewish Congress 'About the World Jewish Congress Foundation'

the jewishweek.com Jewish Week 4/26/2011 'Alan Solow'

jpost.com Jerusalem Post 4/27/2010 'Obama' Ties with Israel Unshakable' cjnews.com Canadian Jewish News 4/8/2011 Ron Kampeas 'Obama and the Jews'

freerepublic.com FreeRepublic.com 1/24/2008 Robert Kandelman/Chicago Jewish News 'The Real Barack Obama'

forward.com Jewish Daily Forward 1/7/2008 Ron Kampeas 'Obama has courted Jews from beginning'

radioislam.org Radio Islam '2008 US Presidential candidate Sen. Barack Obama dances to Jewish tunes'

jweekly.com JWeekly 8/6/2004 Ron Kampeas 'Obama, Democrats rising star; known for harmony with Jews'

electronicintifada.net Electronic Intifada 3/9/2007 Harold Brackman 'Obama and the Jews'

chicagojewishnews.com Chicago Jewish News 'Robert M. Schrayer'

moveoverapac.org 'Join us in DC this May to expose AIPAC and usher in a new foreign policy!' Statement about Helen Thomas and Move Over AIPAC'

aipac.org AIPAC 'What is AIPAC' 'Lee Rosenberg Why He Matters'

israelnationalnews.com' Israel National News 3/21/ Tzvi Ben Gedalyahu 'Former Obama Aide new Head of AIPAC'2010

Chapter 20

wikipedia.org Wikipedia 'Danny K. Davis' 'Lane Evan' Jan Schakowsky' 'U.S Senate election in Illinois, 2004' 'Alan Keyes' 'Joseph Bruno' 'Zeituni Onyango' 'The Audacity of Hope' 'Logan Act'

police-brutality-dwb.net/ 11/20/2007 'Driving While Black or Brown'

b12partners.net 11/24/2007 'Congressman Sees Bias in Chicago Traffic Stop'

firedoglake.com FireDogLake 11/29/2008 Teddy Partridge 'Is the Next Illinois Senator Danny Davis?'

redstate.com Redstate 'congressman Danny Davis and the Tamil Tigers (terrorists)

srilankaguardian.org Sri Lanka Guardian 12/29/2010 Hassina Leelarathna 'Congressman Danny Davis calls Tamil Tigers "freedom fighters", Sinhalese "slave owners"'

abc.go.com ABC News 12/31/2010 'Rep. Danny Davis drops out of mayoral race' AP 'Obama's Kenyan Aunt says US is obligated to make her citizen'

sourcewatch.org Source Watch 'Lane Evans'

fec.gov 6/28/2005 Friends of Lane Evans Committee Agrees to Pay $185,000 civil penalty'

progressillinois.com 11/10/2008 Josh Kalven 'Obama Invited Lane Evans to Election Night Suite'

nndb.com 'Jan Schakowsky'

discoverthenetworks.org Discover the Networks 'Jan Schakowsky'

americanthinker.com American Thinker 10/31/2010 Stella Paul 'Why doesn't everyone know Jan Schakowsky's husband wrote ObamaCare in Jail?' 7/12/2009 Jack Cashill 'Who wrote Audacity of Hope?"

jstreet.org JStreet 'Rep. Jan Schakowsky, Democrat'

weeklystandard.com Weekly Standard 9/28/2010 Daniel Halper 'Candidates Associated with JStreet come under fire'

thejewishweek.com NY The Jewish Week 11/2/1020 James Besser 'Schakowsky wins easily in Ill. In JStreet-shadowed contest'

israelmatzav.blogspot.com 10/16/2010 'JStreet Jan won't return her Soros money'

gatewaypundit.rightnetwork.com GateWayPundit 10/19/2010 Jim Hoft 'Top Socialist Democrat Jan Schakowsky Won't Condemn Gaza Flotilla Terrorists to Pesky Bloggers (Video)'

huffingtonpost.com Huffington Post.com 3/16/2011 Lucia Graves 'Jan Schakowsky introduces/bill to raise taxes for wealthiest Americans'

nytimes.com NY Times 8/9/2004 'Keyes vs. Obama in Illinois Race' 3/7/2007 Mike McIntire, Christopher Drew 'In '05 Investing, Obama took same path as donors' 11/8/2008 Gardiner Harris, Abby Goodnough 'Obama was unaware of Aunt's Status, Aides Say' 3/7/2007 Jeff Zeleny 'Obama Offers explanation of Stock Purchases' 8/26/2006 Jeffrey Gettleman 'Obama gets a warm welcome in Kenya'

freerepublic.com 8/23/2008 'Does anyone remember Jack Ryan and Obama's Senate run four years ago?' 11/7/2010 Aaron Klein/WND "Communist Party covers up support for Obama' 11/30/2010 Breitbart T V 'Obama in 2006 exalts dem take-over of congress; warns Bush not to be stubborn'

mediamatters.org Media Matters 8/12/2008 'Wash. Post Mag mischaracterized Obama's account of 2004 DNC invitation...' 7/23/2010 'McCarthy's book promotes false claim that Obama campaigned for Kenyan candidate'

chicagomag.com Chicago Mag June 2007 David Bernstein 'The Speech' usliberals.about.com Deborah White Barack Obama's Inspiring 2004 democratic Convention Speech'

wnd.com World Net Daily 2/21/2009 Drew Zahn 'Alan Keyes: Stop Obama or U.S. will cease to exist'

the postemail.com Post & Email 10/21/2009 John Charlton 'Obama concedes he's not a NBC in Obama vs. Keyes 2004 Debate' 7/15/2010 Sharon Rondeau 'Tanzanian Newspaper declares 'Obama born in Kenya

chicagotribune.com Chicago Tribune 6/24/2004Liam Ford, Rudolph Bush 'Ryan quits race'

ballot-access.org 11/16/2008 Richard Winger 'Alan Keys files lawsuit over Obama eligibility'

fistfulofeuros.net Pedantry 11/5/2004 'Why can't more republicans be like Alan Keyes?"

therealbarackobama.wordpress.com RBO 6/17/2008 'Once again, Sen. Obama, it's that appearance of impropriety that irritates'

thecapitolpressroom.org 12/82009 'Strike 1 Hiram Strike 2 Joe Strike 3 Albany'

virtualglobetrotting.com 'Jared Abbruzzese's House'

timesunion.com Times Union 11/23/2009 'Jared Abbruzzese'

nydailynews.com NY Daily News 5/6/2010 Kenneth Love, Glenn Blain 'Former Senate Majority Leader Joseph Bruno gets two years in federal prison'

bfeldman68.blogspot.com 4/16/2009 B. Feldman 'Obama's $1.7 million Bookgate Scandal contract revisited'

theoraclegroup.net The Oracle Group 11/16/2008 'Obama will release children's book Of Thee I Sing out'

newsone.com News One 9/14/2010 AP 'Barack Obama will release children's book...'

investopedia.com 'Blind Trust'

slate.com Slate 12/14/2006 John Dickerson 'Barackwater'

newsbusters.org NewsBusters 9/18/2008 P.J. Gladnick 'Fannie Mae CEO to Democrats you are our Family and Conscience'

hollywoodgrind.com HollywoodGrind 'Fannie Mae CEO thanks Barack Obama in 2005'

spectator.org American Spectator 11/3/2008 'Aunt Zeituni's Protectors' reuters.com Reuters 4/1/2009 'Judge extends Obama's aunt's stay in United States' 10/13/2011 Felix Salmon 'On George Soros, Occupy Wall Street and Reuters'

bostonherald.com Boston Herald 2/4/2010 'Obama's auntie still freeloading'

ethiopianreview.com Ethiopian Review 10/6/2008 Bwendimu 'Found in a rundown Boston estate: Barack Obama's aunt Zeituni Onyango'

masslive.com MassLive.com 9/21/2010 AP 'Obama's aunt Zeituni Onyango says U.S. obligated to make her citizen'

cbsnews.com CBS News 9/20/2010 'Obama's Aunt Zeituni Onyango: The system took advantage of me' 6/14/2006' Barack Obama Interview'

advanceindiana.blogspot.com 1/20/2009 'Illegal Alien Obama Aunt Enjoys Inaugural Activities'

james-4america.wordpress.com 1/27/2009 Aunt Zeituni attended Inauguration and Balls with the blessings of ICE

washingtonpost.com Washington Post 11/2008 Matthew Mosk 'Obama Campaign to return Aunts donations' 12/17/2006 Peter Slevin 'Obama says he regrets land deal with fundraiser'

politifact.com PolitiFact 12/29/2007 'Obama sworn in on his Bible' 'Is Obama a hypocrite on reconciliation?' 8/20/2008 'Obama did not take sides in Kenya'

realclearpolitics.com Real Clear Politics 11/16/2009 (video) 'Obama says KSM will get Full Military Trial'

bluegrasspundit.com BlueGrassPundit 9/8/2009 '2006 Obama: Raising the debt ceiling (Bush) show a failure of leadership 2009 Obama: We need to raise the debt ceiling'

calvarykenya.org 'Kenya: Some background information'

sacred-destinations.com 'Religion Demographics'

onejerusalem.com One Jerusalem 2/23/2008 'Barack's Israeli Experience'

obamaspeeches.com 'January 2006 Middle East Trip Podcast transcript'

worldproutassembly.org WorldProutAssembly 12/29/2008 'Obama's 2005 and 2006 voting record'

sweetness-light.com Sweetness & Light 'Barack Obama's letter to the Daily Kos'

centuryinstitute.org Century Institute Peter Osnos 10/30/2006 'Barack Obama and the Book Business' time.com TIME 4/18/2005 Perry Bacon Jr. 'Barack Obama' 'The 2005 TIME 100'

americandaughter.com AmericanDaughter 10/13/2008 Nancy Matthis 'Corsi escapes Kenya with Obama-Odinga Emails'

wnd.com World Net Daily 10/10/2008 Bob Unruh 'Proof Obama backed Odinga'

think-israel.org Think-Israel 'Barack Hussein Obama and Raila Odinga describe themselves as Agents of Change'

israpundit.com Israpundit 10/18/2008 Ted Belman 'Obama the community organizer orchestrated a coup in Kenya'

atlasshrugs2000.typepad.com Atlas Shrugs 1/4/2008 'Kenya, Islam and Barack Hussein Obama'

citizenwells.wordpress.com CitizenWells 10/10/2008 'Obama Kenya visit 2006 video...'

newamerican.com New American 10/5/2011 Alex Newman 'Big Money linked to Occupy Wall Street

humanevents.com Human Events 10/21/2011 Matthew Vadum 'George Soros funds Occupy Wall Street'

occupywallst.org Occupy Wall Street 1/17/2012 'About' 'America occupies the Capitol'

librarygrape.com 12/1/2011 'Occupiers finally make their demands'

forbes.com Forbes 12/13/2011 T. Scott Gross 'Occupy Wall Street : Ask for the impossible'

theblaze.com The Blaze 11/1/2011 Mike Opelka 'This is the comprehensive list of those supporting Occupy Wall St.' 10/13/2011 Tiffany Gabbay 'Top ten richest celebrities supporting Occupy Wall Street'

electronicinfada.net Electronic Infada 5/25/2011 Ali Abunimah 'Why Sasha Gelzin disrupted Netanyahu at AIPAC'

occupyaipac.org Occupy AIPAC 5/24/2011 'Moveover AIPAC protester disrupting Netanyahu in US Congress arrested in hospital'

truthtellers.org Truth Tellers 5/19/2011 Rev. Ted Pike 'Heckling inside AIPAC conference will sabotage free speech'

Haaretz.com Haaretz 5/5/2011 Natasha Mozgovaya 'Left wing hecklers interrupt Netanyahu's speech as AIPAC'

Chapter 21

newsbusters.org NewsBusters 10/20/2009 Candance Moore 'Anita Dunn: How we created Obama's cult of personality'

politico.com Politico 10/22/2009 Michael Calerone 'Who joined Maddow, Olbermann at the White House" 4/27/2010 'Stern, Dunn hit speaking circuit' 11/13/2009 Kenneth P. Vogel 'Bauer pick panned, praised' 10/2/2010 Mike Allen, Josh Gerstein 'Gibbs eyed for DNC chairman 4/20/2011 Jennifer Epstein 'Gibbs's status: No Facebook gig' 8/6/2009 Carrie Budoff Brown 'WH to Dems: Punch twice as hard' 5/16/2010 Interview: Melody Barnes' 4/8/2009 Ben Smith 'common Purpose'

wnd.com World Net Daily 10/18/2009 Aaron Klein 'White House boasts: We control news media' 8/13/2009 Chelsea Schilling 'Town halls burst with Obama plants' 5/10/2010 Chelsea Schilling 'Obama waives ethics rules for eligibility lawyer' 4/22/2009 Chelsea Schilling 'Is Obama campaign cash quashing eligibility suits?' csmonitor.com Christian Science Monitor 10/22/2008 Dave Cook 'Who is Anita Dunn?' 11/10/2009 Susan Walsh 'Dan Pfeiffer to replace Anita Dunn…' 9/11/2009 Bob Unruh 'Eye-popper: Is Nancy Pelosi in on the eligibility cover-up?'

hotair.com HotAir 10/21/2009 Allahpundit 'Revealed Who else was at that secret Obama briefing with Olby and Maddow?' 11/17/2010 Ed Morrissey 'Podesta advises Obama to ignore voters, bypass Congress through agency action'

nytimes.com NY Times 10/12/2009 Brian Stelter 'Fox's Volley with Obama Intensifying' 2/1/2007 Adam A. Gourney, Jeff Zeleny 'Obama formally enters presidential race' 1/16/2007 Jeff Zeleny 'Obama takes big step toward 2008 bid' 11/24/2008 Helene Cooper 'Cassandra Q. Butts' 6/20/2009 Rachell Swarns 'Vows Melody Barnes and Marland Buckner Jr.' 3/27/2011 Andrew Ross Sorkin 'Facebook may hire Robert Gibbs…' 1/5/2011 Jeff Zeleny 'Gibbs to Leave as White House Press Secretary' 4/4/2011 'Jim Messina' 123/2008 Michael Luo 'In banking, Emanuel made money and connections'

huffingtonpost.com Huffington Post 10/9/2009 'Anita Dunn: Fox News an outlet for GOP propaganda 4/10/2011 'Donald Trump for President? David Plouffe says there's no Chance he'd ever he hired' 4/1/2011 Robert Creamer 'Jim Messina is a perfect choice to be Obama's campaign manager' 10/27/2011 Luke Johnson 'Robert Gibbs: Obama can win re-election despite economy'

wsj.com Wall Street Journal 10/21/2009 John Fund 'From Mao to Obama'

wikipedia.org Wikipedia 'Anita Dunn' 'Greg Craig' 'Robert Bauer' America Coming Together' 'America Votes' 'Cassandra Butts' 'Security through Regularized Immigration and a Vibrant Economy Act of 2007' 'Robert Gibbs' 'David Plouffe' 'William M. Daley' 'Melody Barnes' 'EMILY's List' 'Executive Order 12958' 'Center for American Progress' 'Rahm Emanuel'

swamppolitics.com 12/2/2007 John McCormick 'Obama: Hope fund is not a slush fund' suntimes.com Sun Times 5/3/2007 Lynn Sweet 'Obama's Illinois operation campaign to launch Camp Obama'

opencongress.org 'Contributions to campaign endorses Barack Obama'

sourcewatch.org Source Watch 'Barack Obama's contributions to campaign endorsers' 'Dan Shapiro' 'Center for American Progress' 'America Coming together' 'Robert Gibbs' 'Common Purpose Project'

leadingauthorities.com 'Anita Dunn'

washingtonpost.com Washington Post 3/26/2010 Anne E. Komblut 'A profile of Bob Bauer: Is this the counsel Obama keeps?' 1/9/2012 David Nakamura 'White House Chief of Staff William Daley resigns; Budget chief Jacob Lew fills post'

motherjones.com Mother Jones Suzy Khimm 'Watchdogs worry about Obama's New Ethics Czar'

sagepub.com 9/2/2007 'Top Down or Bottom Up?'

2012obama2012.com 'Fired Up & Ready To Go!'

gop.com GOP November 2009 'Who Is Bob Bauer?'

theobamafile.com 'Robert Bauer'

judicialwatch.org Judicial Watch 'Bob Bauer named new White House counsel'

opensecrets.org Open Secrets.org 'Perkins Coie' 'Buckner, Marland lobbyist'

freerepublic.com FreeRepublic.com 10/22/2009 Chuck Justice 'Robert Bauer and Anita Dunn A match made for Obama's White House' 7/30/2009 'Obama's first act as President Executive Order 13489…'

obamareleaseyourrecords.blogspot.com 4/29/2011 'Obama's half-sister raises birth-certificate doubts'

visiontoamerica.org Vision to America 6/16/2011 Ex-CIA; Forged document released as birth certificate'

island-adv.com 11/15/2010 Michelle Malkin 'Open-borders One America Votes operated illegal political committee'

americavotes.org America Votes 'About'

legaltimes.typepad.com 4/27/2011 David Ingram 'Perkins Coie got Obama's birth certificate'

npr.org NPR 8/4/2008 Will Evans 'Profile: America Votes' 11/19/2007 Audie Cornish 'Rare national buzz tipped Obama's decision to run' 6/1D/2007 David Schaper 'Camp Obama trains campaign volunteers' 11/6/2008 David Schaper 'Emanuel could return to the White House'

nationalreview.com National Review 8/3/2005 Byron York 'America Coming Together comes apart'

discoverthenetworks.org Discover the Networks March 2005 'America coming Together (ACT) Backgrounder' 'John Podesta'

pumasunleashed.wordpress.com 1/31/2009 'Obama's new attorney, DC insider, Bob Bauer'

electionspeeches.com '3/2/2008: AIPAC Obama says all the right things to Jewish group...'

forward.com 8/29/2008 'Denver 2008: Boosters, Power Brokers and Money Men...' 8/19/2008 Nathan Guttman 'Obama campaign appoints adviser to coordinate Jewish Outreach'

washingtonrealist.globspot.com 2/13/2008 Nikolas Gvosdev 'Obama's foreign policy approach; Who call the shots?'

punditpress.blogspot.com 2/24/2011 Thomas Ferdousi 'Surprise: White House secretly meeting with lobbyists'

uspolitics.tribe.net 8/20/2008 'Daniel Shapiro'

politifact.com 'Tougher rules against revolving door for lobbyists and former officials'

obamawatch.wikidot.com 1/25/2009 'Lobbyists won't work in my White House'

jpost.com Jerusalem Post 10/3/2011Hillary Leila Krieger 'Dan Shapiro named next US ambassador'

mondoweiss.net 4/26/2009 Philip Weiss 'Former Israel lobbyist stands at policy crossroads...'

americanrhetoric.com 1/16/2007 Barack Obama announces presidential exploratory committee'

txcn.com TXCN Texas Cable News 10/6/2008 Gromer Jeffers Jr. 'Texas volunteers learn ropes at Camp Obama in Dallas'

wired.com 10/29/2008 Sarah Lai Stirland 'Obama's secret weapons; Internet, databases and psychology'

whitehouse.gov 11/6/2009 President Obama taps Cassandra Butts as Senior Advisor at the Millennium Challenge corporation' 'Domestic Policy Council' mcc.gov Millennium Challenge Corporation 'About MCC'

whorunsgov.com 'Cassandra Butts' Greg Sergeant 3/10/2009 'Center for American Progress launching big war room to drive Obama agenda'

metapedia.org 'List of Barack Obama's friends and associates'

commonamericanjournal.com Washington Times 1/12/2010 'A must read: Annotated Panther timeline'

dakotavoice.com Dakota Voice 7/13/2010 Bob Ellis 'Trail of dropped Black Panther case may lead to White House'

democracythatdelivers.com 'Cassandra Q. Butts'

wonkette.com 4/29/2011 Jack Stuef 'Sensitive Obama bans reporter who took embarrassing video of him'

americanprogress.org American Progress CAP 8/8/2005 Cassandra Q. Butts 'Celebrating and Strengthening the Voting Rights Act' 'Campus Progress' 8/16/2010 Ken Gude 'Upholding Our American Values'

onbingablacklawyer.com 'Obama Posse List (Cassandra Butts & Melody Barnes)'

muckety.com Muckety 10/21/2008 Carol Eisenberg 'John Podesta and Cassandra Q. Butts oversee Obama's transition' 'Marland Buckner Jr.'

thinkprogress.org ThinkProgress.org 11/24/2008 Faiz Shakiron 'Obama to appoint Melody Barnes as head of Domestic Policy Council' 'About Think Progress'

gsp-llc.com Global Strategic Partners 'About'

articlesbase.com 4/19/2011 'Green Collar Economics: Quantifying the labor demands of the low carbon future'

socialpulse.com 'Robert Gibbs Profile'

newser.com Newser 10/22/010 John Johnson 'Robert Gibbs may be next DNC Chair'

absoluteastronomy.com 'Robert Gibbs'

prweekus.com 8/28/2008 Beth Krietsh 'Obama's communications chief gets enforcer label'

abcnews.go.com ABC News 4/20/2011 Joshua Miller 'Obama advisor David Plouffe: budget cuts both draconian and historic' 11/7/2008 Brian Ross, Rhonda Schwartz 'Emanuel was director of Freddie Mac during Scandal' gatewarypundit.righnetwork.com 4/10/2011 Jim Hoft 'Nice...David Plouffe bashes Fox News viewers on Fox News Sunday (video)'

the atlantic.com The Atlantic 1/27/2011 Chris Good 'David Plouffe: The man who will re-make the White House'

sunlightfoundation.com Sunlight Foundation 2/12/2010 Paul Blumenthal 'The legacy of Bill Tauzin: The White House-PhRMA /deal'

post-gazette.com Post Gazette 6/4/2010 Josh Gerstein/Politico 'White House's Mr. Fixit has own mess to fix'

thenation.com The Nation 3/20/2011 Air Berman 'Jim Messina, Obama's Enforcer'

washingtonexaminer.com Washington Examiner 5/23/2010 David Freddoso 'Why Sestak's allegations matter'

markbittman.com 5/26/2010 Tom Laskawy 'Let's Move needs to get real with the food industry'

obamafoodorama.blogspot.com 2/8/2011 'Let's Move" Year 1...Progress Report'

presidentialufo.com 'John Podesta: Clinton's X-Files Man'

cnn.com CNN 10/22/2002 Richard Stenger 'Clinton aide slams Pentagon's UFO secrecy'

freedomforum.org 3/17/1999 Harry F. Rosenthal Top Clinton aide: Find balance between secrecy, openness'

youtube.com YouTube 'Clinton White House Chief John Podesta on UFO disclosure'

latimes.com LA Times 7/28/2010 'John Podesta writes probing foreword for new book on UFOs.

bibliotecapleyades.net 2002 Leslie Kean 'Project Moon Dust and Operation Blue Fly'

ufocasebook.com 7/3/2010 'Podesta's reversal on UFOs is mystifying'

dailymail.co.uk Daily Mail 4/19/2011 'Was JFK killed because of his interest in aliens? Secret memo...'

abc15.comC News 4/19/2011 Katrina Schaefer 'John F. Kennedy requested UFO files 10 days before his assassination'

unexplained-mysteries.com 4/19/2011 'Secret memo reveals JFK interest in UFOs'

climateprogress.org 'About Climate Progress'

center-for-american-progress.co.tv CAP 'History and Mission'

tunein.com 'The Bill Press Show'

clearchannel.com 'Clear Channel Radio'

campaignfreedom.org Center for Competitive Politics 4/5/2011 Sean Parnell 'Center for American Progress releases latest lame attack on Koch brothers'

hyscience.eom Hyscience 3/31/2011 'Hillary to Congress: Obama would ignore your war resolutions'

politics4all.com 3/9/2009 Mike Davis 'Obama: Let Mexican trucks roll! ...defies unions, ignores congress'

marketplace.publicradio.org 3/4/2011 Nancy Marshall Genzer Obama makes deal to let Mexican trucks on US highways'

conpats.blogspot.com 4/20/2011 Donald Strong 'Obama snubs Issa on subpoena for ATF documents' 4/11/2011 'Obama ignores congress again; refuses to deport illegal aliens!'

lmliberty.us 4/19/2011 Lake Minnetonka Liberty 'Obama ignores congress'

usatoday.com USA Today 4/18/2011 Catalina Camia 'GOP blasts Obama for ignoring Congress on czars'

independent.co.uk 11/7/2008 Leonard Doyle 'Obama chooses" Rahmbo" as chief of staff'

salon.com Salon 11/7/2008 'Obama's designated a—hole'

suntimes.com Chicago Sun Times 3/9/2011 Abdon M. Pallasch "Rahm Emanuel's $18.5 million paychecks; How did he do it?'

advanceindiana.blogspot.com 2/8/2011 'How Rahm Emanuel made $18.5 million in investment banking without any experience'

bollyn.com Christopher Bollyn 'Who Runs the Obama White House?'

inforwars.com InfoWars 11/10/2008 Kurt Nimmo 'Obama Consigliere 'Rahmbo" Emanuel sent dead fish to foe'

reason.com Reason 2/2/2010 Peter Suderman 'White House Adviser Rahm "Rahmbo" Emmanuel apologizes for calling liberals Retarded...'

thecrimson.com Harvard Crimson 10/11/2006 Abe J. Riesman 'Tome Raider The Plan: Big Ideas for America' chicagotribune.com Chicago Tribune 3/26/2009 Bob Secter, Andrew Zajac 'Rahm Emanuel's profitable stint at mortgage giant'

dailycaller.com Daily Caller 1/26/2010 Jon Ward 'Progressives' anger grows against White House chief of staff Rahm Emanuel'

wsj.com Wall Street Journal 11/21/2008 Gerald F. Seib 'In crisis, opportunity for Obama' 1/28/2009 'A 40-year wish list'

examiner.com Examiner Jerome Tuccille 'Obama's chief of staff choice favors compulsory universal service'

chicago2011.org 'Meet the Mayor-Elect'

mediate.com Mediate 1/8/2012 Josh Feldman 'Axelrod confirms that Robert Gibbs did curse Michelle Obama' book "The Obamas'

Chapter 22

wikipedia.org Wikipedia 'Valerie Jarrett' 'List of US executive branch czars' 'Rainforest Action Network' 'color of Change' 'Oligopoly' 'Robert W. McChesney' 'Talk radio' 'Mark Lloyd' 'Samantha Power' 'A Problem from Hell' 'Carr Center for Human Rights Policy

discoverthenetworks.org. Discover the Networks 'Valerie Jarrett' ''Robert McChesney

theeveningpost.com Evening Post 'Who is Valerie Jarrett?'

time.com TIME 11/11/2008 M.J. Stephens, Claire Suddath 'Valerie Jarrett'

whitehouse.gov 'Senior Advisor Valerie Jarrett'

newmediajournal.us New Media Journal 6/8/2011 Trevor Loudon 'Valerie Jarrett, her father-in-law and the Communist Party'

spectator.org Spectator 9/8/2009 'Valerie Jarrett's Show'

michellemalkin.com 9/18/2009 Michelle Malkin 'Olympic-sized boondoggle: What Valerie Jarrett and Michelle Obama are up to'

cnsnews.com CNS News 11/12/2009 Fred Lucas 'Ethics Watchdog seeks records on White House Officials, failed Olympics Bid'

boston.com Boston Globe 6/27/2008 Binyamin Appelbaum 'Grim proving ground for Obama's housing policy'

nytimes.com NY Times 11/6/2008 Jodi Kantor 'Valerie Jarrett' 3/29/2011 Sheryl Gay Stolberg 'Still crusading, but Now on the Inside' change.gov 8/27/2011 Valerie B. Jarrett'

huffingtonpost.com Huffingtonpost.com 8/5/2011 Valerie Jarrett' Why I'm proud to be part of President Obama's team' 3/25/2011 Jameel Jaffer 'The surveillance memos, and a suggestion for Jack Goldsmith' 12/ 21/2007 Green-Collar Jobs: Energy Bill includes Christmas present for nation's job seekers' 5/6/2011 Brad Johnson 'Van Jones at Power Shift 2011:...' 3 /6/2008 Samantha Power resigns over Hillary Monster remark'

sheikyermami.com 8/31/2009 Sheik Yermani 'Destroying America from within'

lawiscool.com 8/30/2009 'Jameel Jaffer of ACLU is a Canadian!'

aclu.org ACLU 2/24/2009 'About the ACLU's National Security Project'

latimes.com LA Times 4/6/2011 Jameel Jaffer 'National security; When secrecy is a weapon'

pbs.org PBS 3/27/2008 Tavis Smiley Show 'Van Jones interview' 3/11/2005 'Samantha Power'

examiner.com Examiner 7/17/2009 Kathy Shaidle 'Van Jones green jobs Czar a self-described communist arrested during Rodney King Riots'

ellabakercenter.org Eller Baker Center 'Van Jones, esq.'

aim.org Accuracy in Media 9/7/2009 Cliff Kincaid 'The blogger who nailed Van Jones' 12/22/2009 'The $50 Billion New Socialist Media' 6/28/2010 'Hugo Chavez, Oliver Stone give Socialism a bad name'

usasurival.org USA Survival 9/4/2009 Cliff Kincaid 'Van Jones Mystery solved?' 10/21/2009 'Damaging disclosures in Van Jones scandal' 9/10/2009 'The true Identity of Van Jones' 9/15/2009 'Soros money financed Communist Van Jones'

wiki.answers.com 'How much salary do the Obama czars earn?'

bejohngalt.com Be John Galt 9/7/2009 'Czars in the shadow of executive privilege'

freerepublic.com FreeRepublic.com 8/14/2009 Glenn Beck/glennbeck.com 'List of Obama's Czars'

wnd.com World Net Daily 8/30/2009 Aaron Klein 'Czar: Spread the wealth! Change the whole system' 5 /19/2010 'Soros-funded group urges media run by government' 9/3/2005 "Radio host urges poor to loot'

washingtonpost.com Washington Post 9/6/2009 Scott Wilson, Grance Franke-Ruta 'White House advisor Van Jones resigns amid controversy over past activism' 2/24/2010 Juliet Eilperin 'former White House adviser Van Jones lands new DC gig at liberal think tank' cnn.com CNN 96/2009/Obama did not order Van Jones' resignation, adviser says'

climateprogress.org 2/24/2010 'Van Jones rejoins American Progress to lead Green Opportunity initiative'

dailycaller.com Daily Caller7/24/2010 Chris Moody 'Van Jones: Stop worrying about the deficit. The government can just take more money from rich companies' 10/14/2010 John Rossomando 'Republicans plan January takedowns of Obama's czars'

reidreport.com Reid Report 9/8/2009 People '"The truth about Van Jones'

mediamattersaction.org Media Matters 9/7/2009 'Smear; Van Jones is an avowed communist'

sodahead.com SodaHead 6/12/2010 'STORM revolution handbook shuts down Glenn Beck's servers'

glennbeck.com Glenn Beck 'STORM handbook "Reclaiming Revolution", spring 2004'

notalemming.wordpress.com 5/1/2010 'Crime inc. Obama, Van Jones & Joel Rogers in Climate Collusion'

ran.org Rainforest Action Network 'About RAN' "If a tree falls in the forest, we make noise'

bioneers.org Bioneers 'Our Mission'

apolloalliance.org Apollo Alliance3/10/2009 'Apollo board member Van Jones accepts White House post'

worldtribune.com World Tribune 10/221/2009 'Valerie Jarrett and the resignation of Van Jones'

dakotavoice.com Dakota Voice 9/4/2009 Bob Ellis 'Van Jones: Exposed and Condemned by his own words'

homelesstates.com 'Is Van Jones a communist?'

gov.ca.gov 3/16/2009 'California Green Corps: Putting federal Economic Stimulus Dollars to work...'

spectator.org American Spectator 8/29/2009 Matthew Vadum 'Van Jones and his STORM troopers denounced America the night after 9/11' 1/26/2010 Mark Hyman 'The FCC's war on broadcasting'

beaufortobserver.net Beaufort Observer 9/1/2009 'Van Jones and STORM should scare the daylights out of every American' undueinfluence.com 'Van Jones'

nysut.org 'Van Jones'

talkingpointsmemeo.com TPM 7/23/2010 'Van Jones to Netroots: Quit beating up on Obama'

theblaze.com The Blaze 11/17/20 Madeleine Morgenstern 'Van Jones on the future of Occupy Wall St.: You Haven't Seen Anything Yet'

thenewamerican.com New American 12/1/2020 Raven Clabough 'The unintended, or intended, effects of Wikileaks?'

gatewaypundit.rightnetwork.com GateWayPundit 1/6/2011 Jim Hoft 'republicans introduce bill to eliminate Obama's 39 czars'

bigjournalism.com Big Journalism 4/27/2011 'Former White House advisor thinks rocks should have human rights'

moonbattery.com Moonbattery 4/26/2011 Van Helsing 'Van Jones pushes to install Mother Earth as global communist dictator'

educationnews.org 11/17/2009 'Who is behind the media reform movement?'

stkarnick.com 8/11/2009 S.T. Karnick The Marxist founder of Free Press and the group's agenda…'

newsreal.blog.com NewsReal10/12/2009 Matthew Vadum 'Robert McChesney's war on the First Amendment'

newwaveslave.com 6/2/2010 'FREE PRESS funded by George Soros wants State Controlled Media'

redstate.com Red State 6/24/2009 Neil Stevens 'Free Press: too radical even for Obama officials'

biggovernment.com Big Government 2/1/2010 Phil Kerpen 'Congress must stop FCC's internet regulations'

washingtonpost.com Washington Post 10/30/2009 Robert W. McChesney, John Nichols 'Yes, journalist deserve subsidies too'

wsj.com Wall Street Journal 12/21/2010 John Fund 'The Net Neutrality Coup'

romanticpoet.wordpress.com Romantic Poet RBO 3/22/2011 Brenda J. Elliott 'Lying Liars: Media Access Project'

foxnews.com Fox News 5/6/2010 Phil Kerpen 'The FCC goes for the nuclear option' 3/24/2010 Steve Forbes 'Could a Chavez-style media crackdown be coming our way?'

americansfortaxreform.com 11/2/2009 Christopher Butler 'Why does the left want net neutrality regulation of the internet?'

dailykos.com Daily Kos 5/7/2006 'Progressive talk radio a failure??'

npr.org NPR 1/21/2010 Frank James 'Air America radio goes silent, makes bankruptcy filing'

weeklystandard.com Weekly Standard 8/6/2007 Philip Terzian 'Radio Free America'

politico.com Politico 2/18/2011 Eliza Krigman 'FCC: Diversity czar not a czar at all' 11/2/2010 Laura Rozen 'Obama NSC meets with Egypt democracy advocates'

thinkprogress.org Think Progress 'The right-wing smear campaign against Mark Lloyd'

therealbarackobama.wordpress.com RBO 8/17/2009 'Mark Lloyd: redistribution of wealth czar at the FCC'

thelibertyjournal.com Liberty Journal 8/25/2009 'FCC's diversity czar Mark Lloyd's effort to silence free speech'

wheredidmyamericago.com 7/22/2007 Michael Solomon 'To build a better mousetrap'

tuninginradio.blogspot.com 4/7/2010 'Conservative talk dominates the airwaves'

thehill.com The Hill 5/6/2011 Debbie Siegalbaum 'Republican leaders blast disclosure order as blatant assault on free speech'

mcr.org Media Research Center 10/31/2007 'No fairness Doctrine for PBS'

charlestonteaparty.org Toccata '1/22/2011 'Dead Air'

newsbusters.org NewsBusters 8/6/2009 Seaton Motley 'New FCC chief Diversity Officer co-wrote ...'

broadcastwebblog.com 11/24/2010 Brenda Holland 'FCC releases multiple items implementing rules for Satellite Television Extension and Localism act (STELA)'

benton.org Benton 'Broadcast Localism: An informed public plays a vital role in helping stations...'

brainyquote.com 'Mark Lloyd quotes'

thenationalscene.com The National Scene 9/24/2009 'FCC's Diversity Czar Mark Lloyd makes racist comments and praises Hugo Chavez'

about.com Corey Deitz 'Mark Lloyd the FCCs' chief Diversity Officer'' netcaucus.org 'Mark Lloyd'

freepress.net 'Mark Lloyd'

iraqsinconvenienttruth.com 4/26/2011 'A statement from the Pachamama Alliance'

pachamama.org Pachamama Alliance 'About Us'

awakeningthedreamer.org 4/27/2011 'Together, we are a genius'

commentarymagazine.com Commentary 2/19/2008 Noah Pollak 'Samantha Power: The Salon interview'' 1/27/2008 'Obama and Israel It gets worse'

newsrealblog.com NewsReal 3/23/2011 Chris Queen 'Samantha Power: The troubling woman behind the curtain of Obama's Libya policy' 3/28/2011 Jeff Dunetz 'Samantha Power, The Obama administrations' anti-Israel rising star'

thedailybeast.com The Daily Beast 3/23/2011 Tara McKelvey 'Samantha Power's case for war on Libya'

slate.com Slate 3/21/2011 Tom Scocca 'Samantha Power is the New President of Libya'
abcnews.com ABC News 11/28/2008 'The Return of Samantha Power'

romanticpoet.wordpress.com 4/26/2011 Aaron Klein WND 'Obama aid uses war to achieve radical values?'

americankafir.wordpress.com American Kafir 3/21/2011 Frank Gaffney 'The Gaddafi Precedent'

yidwithlidblogapot.com 2/3/2008 'Samantha Power another Barak Obama Israel Hating advisor'

worldjewishdaily.com World Jewish Daily 5/7/2011 'Will America's next Secretary of State support armed intervention against Israel?'

nationalreview.com National Review 4/5/2011 Stanley Kurtz 'Samantha Power's Power'

hks.harvard.edu Harvard Kennedy School 'Samantha Power on US Foreign Policy' 'Carr Center'

jewishindy.com Jewish Indy 3/23/2011 Aaron Klein/WND 'Soros fingerprints on Libya bombing'

thepartyofknow.com 3/29/2011 'What is Samantha Power thinking?'

realizingrights.org Realizing Rights 2/8/2008 'Global Centre for the Responsibility to Protect'

globalr2p.org CR2P documents' 'About'

responsibilitytoprotect.org 2/1/2011 'Ban urges implementation of responsibility to protect by force if needed' 'Founding purposes'

ikhwanweb.com Muslim Brotherhood English website 'Breaking news' 11/5/2010 Obama NSC meets with Egypt democracy advocates'

notable-quotes.com 'Samantha Power'

prophecynewswatch.com Prophecy News Watch WND 'Responsibility to Protect sets tome for one World Order'

americanthinker.com American thinker 3/20/2011 Ed Lasky 'The rise of Samantha Power and the risks for the American-Israel relationship'

msnvc.msn.com MSNBC News AP 3/7/2008 Obama adviser resigns; called Clinton monster'

latimes.com LA Times 2/10/2011 Peter Nicholas, Christi Parsons 'Obama's advisors split on when and how Mubarak should go'

carnegieendowment.org Carnegie Endowment 11/2/1010 'Working group on Egypt meets with NSC staff'

canadafreepess.com Canada Free Press 2/5/2011 Daniel Greenfield 'Pulling back the Egyptian veil'

mediate.com Mediate 2/11/2011 Colby Hall 'Lawrence O'Donnell: Obama administration divided over how to deal with Egypt'

Chapter 23

vegancrowd.com 'Cass Sunstein'

lanternsoflibertyus.com 'Cass Sunstein quotes'

knowthelies.com 10/12/2009 'Absolute Insanity!...Cass Sunstein...Harvest organs from helpless patients without consent!'

papers.ssm.com 1/6/2008 Cass R Sunstein, Adrian Vermeule "Conspiracy Theories"

wikipedia.org Wikipedia 'Cass Sunstein' 'Ezekiel Emanuel' 'John Holdren' 'Kathleen Sebelius' 'Margaret Sanger' 'Planned Parenthood'

consumerfreedom.com 1/15/2009 'Exposed: The secret animal rights agenda of America's next regulatory czar'

wnd.com World Net Daily.com 1/14/2010 Aaron Klein 'Top Obama czar; Infiltrate all conspiracy theorists' 10/9/2009 Jerome R. Corsi 'Holdren; Ice age will kill 1 billion' 4/27/2009

US regulatory czar nominee wants Net Fairness Doctrine' 9/6/2010 'Fraud charges plaguing Planned Parenthood'

aclj.org American Center for Law & Justice 8/24/2010'Victory against Planned Parenthood stands'

papers.ssrn.com 1/17/2008 Cass R. Sunstein, Adrian Vermeule 'Conspiracy Theories'

bostonreview.net Boston Review Summer 2001 Cass Sunstein 'The Daily We'

salon.com Salon 1/15/2010 Glenn Greenwald 'Obama confidant's spine-chilling proposal' 11/10/2010 'Wikileaks disgusting hypocrisy!!' 12/19/2010 Glenn W. Lafantasie 'How the South rationalizes secession'

examiner.com Examiner 9/23/2010 Anthony Martin 'Obama czar Cass Sunstein says we're too dumb to make right choices' 12/8/2010 Donna Anderson 'Alex Jones: Wikileaks attacking Hillary Clinton, freedom of speech is next'

knowthelies.com 12/12/2009 'Cass Sunstein…Harvest Organs from helpless patients without consent!'

law.harvard.edu Anthony Lux 'Free speech in the age of the internet'

nhteapartycoalition.org 'Cass Sunstein regulatory czar'

washingtontechnology.com 12/2/2010 Alice Lipowicz 'Cass Sunstein remembers a special date'

veteranstoday.com VeteransToday.com 4/24/2009 Webster Tarpley 'Nihilists of The Word Unite; Wikileaks is the cognitive infiltration operation demanded by Cass Sunstein' 12/14/2010 John Allen 'Cass Sunstein, Wikileaks and the public right to know'

infowars.com INFOWARS12/10/2010 Paul Joseph Watson 'Wikileaks founder: bigger bombshells on the way'

elliswashingtonreport.com 2/3/2011 Ellis Washington Cass Sunstein and his Lady Macbeth'

yourdaddy.net Your Daddy's Politics 4/7/2011 Notalemming 'Word Bank; The end of Israel close at hand'

abovetopsecret.com AboveTopSecret 1/12/2010 'The man behind the NOW curtain'

English.ruvr.ru The Voice of Russia 12/8/2010 'Julian Assange believes he could rebuff allegation'

itmakessenseblog.com 12/5/2010 'Georg Soros is the money behind Wikileaks'

daily.pk Pakistan Daily W. Madsen 'CIA, Mossad and Soros behind Wikileaks' huffingtonpost.com Huffington Post 12/2/2010 Jack Mirkinson 'Beck: Wikileaks tied to Soros Conspiracies'

ironicsurrealism.blogivist.com 5/25/2010 'Uncovered Audio Obama's regulatory czar Cass Sunstein big Gov power Grabbing…' (Sunstein WBEZ interview)

pacificfreepress.com Pacific Free Press 12/11/2020 Scott Creighton 'Wikileaks and Cognitive Infiltration'

truthiscontagious.com 8/3/2010 Washington Post reprint 'Cass Sunstein in Wikileaks (2007)…'

mortgagegrapevine.com 12.8/2010 Dr. Branker 'Did Cass Sunstein start Wikileaks? With the intent to regulate the press?'

washingtonpost.com Washington Post 2/24/2007 Cass R. Sunstein 'A Brave New Wikiworld'

stevescomments.wordpress.com 12/1/2010 Doug Hagmann 'Wikileaks: a staged crime scene'

patriotactionnetwork.com Patriot Action Network 12/3/2020 Joan McDaniel 'Soros and Wikileaks; time to Investigate their connection'

guardian.co.uk The guardian 12/10/2010 Steven Morris 'Julian Assange lawyers preparing for possible US charges'

patdollard.com Pat Dollard 11/30/2010 'Wikileaks founder Julian Assange tells TIME; Hillary Clinton should resign'

myteapartychronicle.blogspot.com 12/10/2010 'Assange: Hero or villain'

birdflu666.wordpress.com 12/3/2010 Julian Assange forced to chat on Guardian as web options close'

prisonplanet.com 'Assange under mansion arrest exposing a direct connection to George Soros'

the daily beast The Daily Beast 8/30/2010 Philip Shenon 'Accused leaker to fight charges'

defsi.typepad.com Deafening Silence august 2008 'Under the skin of health care reform Dr. Ezekiel Emanuel in his own words pt2'

bioethics.nih.gov department of Bioethics 'Ezekiel J. Emanuel, MD, PhD'

nytimes.com NY times 4/17/2009 Robert Pear 'A hard-charging doctor on Obama's team' 12/20/2007 Raymond Hernandez, Christopher Drew 'It's not just ayes and nays…'

vanityfair.com VanityFair.com 3/2008 Todd Purdum 'Raising Obama' healthblog.ncpa.org 7/22/2009 'Rationing Health Care'

washingtonmonthly.com Washington Monthly June 2005 Ezekiel Emanuel, Victor R. Fuchs 'Solved"

thelancet.com The Lancet 1/31/2009 Govind Persad, Alan Wertheimer, Ezekiel J. Emanuel 'Principles for allocation of scarce medical interventions'

kaiserhealthnews.org KHN 1/6/2011 Christopher Weaver Zeke Emanuel, adviser on health reform leaves White House'

washingtonexaminer.com Washington Examiner 7/23/2009 David Freddoso 'Obama's science czar suggested compulsory abortion, sterilization'

canadafreepress.com Canada Free Press 22/24/2009 Tim Ball, Judi McLeod 'Obama's Science Czar John Holdren involved in unwinding climategate scandal'

associatedcontent.com 9/16/2010 Mark Whittington 'John Holdren Obama science czar advocated de-development of the United States'

freerepublic.com 3/9/2010 Terresa Monroe-Hamilton 'Science Czar John Holdren national security risk' 11/12/2010 Townhall/ Mona Charen 'Obamacare hits the most vulnerable'

newzeal.blogspot.com NewZeal 3/8/2010 Security Risk? Obama science Czar john Holdren and the Federation of American Scientist'

sciencemag.org ScienceInsider 12/24/2010 Eli Kintisch 'an interview with John Holdren part 2'

kavlifoundation.org Kavli Foundation 9/6/2010 2010 Kavli Prize science forum keynote address John P. Holdren…'

climatesciencewatch.org 12/28/2010 Climate Science Watch 'text of John Holdren's talk at the Stephen Schneider ….12/s2/2010'

masterresource.org Master Resource 12/30/2010 Robert Bradley Jr. 'John Holdren's big science…'

renewamerica.com 8/12/2009 Phill Kline 'Obamacare' not a slippery slope, but a cliff'

about.com Robert Longley 'Kathleen Sebelius Secretary of Health and Human Services'

dailycaller.com Daily Caller 9/30/2010 Jon Ward 'Sebelius: Obamacare is salvation for private insurance market' 2/4/2011 Mike Riggs 'Issa investigating allegations the GAO destroyed evidence gather during investigation of for-profit colleges' 10/12/2010 Caroline May 'Komen breast cancer charity provides funding…'

abcnews.com ABC News 8/30/2010 Steven Portnoy 'Sebelius: time for Reeducation on Obama Health Care Law' abcnews.go.com 6/28/2012 Matt Negrin Supreme Court Health care Ruling: The Mandate can Stay

whorunsthegov.com WhoRunsTheGov 'Kathleen Sebelius'wizbanglob.com 9/10/2020 Kim Priestop 'Kathleen Sebelius threatens to shut Obamacare critics out of health care system'

weeklystandard.com Weekly Standard 12/25/2010 Jeffrey H. Anderson 'Sebelius and Holder admit that Obamacare is fundamentally about coercion'

nydailynews.com NY Daily News 12/23/2010 Andrea Tantaros 'More Obamacare insanity...'

investors.com Investors 6/8/2010 Merrill Matthews 'America's most powerful woman...'

spectator.org American Spectator 4/26/2010 'What Lies Beneath' 8/2/2010 Philip Klein 'Sebelius makes false claim about double-counting of Medicare savings'

reason.com 2/18/2011 Peter Suderman 'Kathleen Sebelius, Tooth Spy?

foxnews.com Fox News 5/3/2011 John Brandt 'House Republicans pass piecemeal health care repeal bill'

thomas.loc.gov 'HR3200' HR3590' 'HR4872'

politico.com Politico 5/5/2011 J. Lester Feder 'Sebelius; Die sooner with GOP plan'

paywizard.org 'Kathleen Sebelius'

nypost.com NY Post 3/8.2011 S.A. Miller, Geoff Earle 'Sebelius hit for BamCare trick'

cbsnews.com CBS News 3/22/2010 Tucker Reals 'Sebelius; Americans will embrace health reform'

theconservativediva.net 2/23/2011 Planned Parenthood's latest annual report...'

prolife.com 'Planned Parenthood'

latimes.com LA Times 3/8/2008 Charles Ornstein 'Cost of the pill inflated?'

plannedparenthood.org 'Planned Parenthood'

newsbusters.org NewsBusters 6/30/2010 Nathan Burchfield 'Media ignore Planned Parenthood's $1.3 billion federal funding discrepancy'

thenewamerican.com 2/10/2010 Raven Clabough 'Planned Parenthood advocates for sex education for 10-year olds'

lifesitenews.com LifeSiteNews.com Canadian MP launches Petition to stop Federal funding...' 10/12/2010 Steven Ertelt 'Komen for the cure donated $730K...'

catholicforum.com 3/9/2007 'Planned Parenthood Find out how much $$ your state gives'

sjr.com SJ-R.com 2/22/2009 G. Jeffrey MacDonald 'Abortion opponents target Planned Parenthood funding'

prolifemc.org 'Planned Parenthood boycott list'

aclumich.ort ACLU 'Think Twice before giving to the United Way'

usatoday.com USA Today 9/11/2009 Sharon Jayson 'Obama budget cuts fund for abstinence-only sex education'

smartgirlpolitics.ning.com SGP 2/16/2011 Barbara Howard 'The politics of blackness...'

med.studentsforlife.org 'Abortion-Racism link'

citizenreviewonline.org 5/10/2001 Tanya L. Green 'The Negro Project'

dianedew.com 'Margaret Sanger in her own words'

blackgenocide.org Citizen magazine 1/20/1992 'The truth about Margaret Sanger'

cappsonline.org CAPPS online 4/11/2022 Mark Hyman 'Washington Examiner Inside the biggest GAO scandal you never heard about'

rhrealitycheck.org 7/20/2009 Amy Dempsey 'Surgeon General's view on abortion'

docs.house.gov/rules Affordable Health Care for America Act 10/29/2009 HR 3962

federaltimes.com Federal Times 11/30/2010 Sean Reilly 'Senate panel approves Dodaro nomination'

opposingviews.com 7/15/2009 Thomas Peters 'Is surgeon general pick Regina Benjamin pro abortion?'

Chapter 24

americanthinker.com American Thinker 4/10/2008 Ed Lasky 'Obama's new foreign policy advisor Daniel Kurtzer 8/26/2007 Slater Bakhtavar 'Jimmy Carter's human rights disaster in Iran'

princeton.edu Woodrow Wilson School of Public and International Affairs 'Daniel C. Kurtzer'

pjvoice.co Philadelphia Jewish Voice April/May 2008 'Ambassador Daniel Kurtzer' 5/15/2011 'National Security Advisor Tom Donilon at the Washington Institute for Near East Policy' jewishvirtuallibrary.org Jewish Virtual Library 'Daniel Kurtzer'

washingtonpost.com Washington Post 6/14/2009 Daniel Kurtzer 'The facts on Israel's settlements' 6/29/2008 Ivo Daalder, Philip Gordon 'Talking to Iran is our best option' 11/21/2008 Brent Scowcroft, Zbigniew Brzezinski 'Middle East Priorities for Jan 21'

yahoo.com 3/9/2011 Barry Schweid 'Obama to nominate top adviser to Israel envoy post'

politico.com Politico 2/22/2011 'Obama to nominate Dan Shapiro to be envoy to Israel' 3/23/2011 Lawrence Korb 'Obama helps U.S. interests in Libya' 10/8/2010 Ben Smith, Glenn Thrush, Laura Rozen 'James Jones never made it to President Obama's inner 10/8/2010 Josh Gerstein, Abby Philip 'Fannie Mae on Donilon's resume' 10/22/2010 Mike Allen 'Obama promotes McDonough'

wnd.com World net Daily 8/20/2008 Aaron Klein 'Obama adviser travels to Syria' 5/19/2011 'Gadhafi fall means ascent of Muslim Brotherhood'

israelnationalnews.com Israel National News 2/22/2011 Tzvi Ben Gedalyahu 'Obama to name Dan Shapiro as new ambassador to Israel'

wikipedia.org Wikipedia 'Daniel B. Shapiro' 'Balkans' 'Ethiopia' 'Meles Zenawi' 'Lawrence Korb' 'Jonathan Pollard' 'Joseph Cirincione' 'New Start' 'Iran hostage crisis' 'Ian Brzezinski' 'Thomas E. Donilon' '2010-2011 Middle East and North Africa protests' 'Mahmoud Jibril' 'Denis McDonough' 'Susan Rice'

uspolitics.tribe.net Tribe net 8/20/2008 'Daniel Shapiro'

turkey.usembassy.gov Embassy of U.S. Philip H. Gordon 'The Obama administration's vision for southeastern Europe'

state.gov U.S. Dept of State 'Philip H. Gordon'

insideislam.wisc.edu Inside Islam 'Easter Europe, Central Asia and Russia'

brookings.edu Brookings Institution 5/331/2006 Ivo Daalder 'The Iran Talks' 'Ivo H. Daalder'

nato.int NATO 'Ivo H. Daalder'

boston.com Boston Globe 7/24/2008 Ivo Daalder, Anne Marie Slaughter 'America's new global challenge'

enoughproject.org Enough Project 'Gayle Smith, co-founder' 'About Us'

huffingtonpost.com 5/6/2009 Matthew Kavanagh 'Obama's global health plan's missing the money' 4/19/2010 Goldman hires Greg Craig…' 6/10/2008 MSNBC News 'veteran James Jones surfaces on Obama VP list' 4/29/2011 'Carla Marinucci in hot water with White Hose over protest song video' 5/20/2011 'Obama Cairo speech: Call for new Beginning…' (video/full text) 1/15/2012 Sarah El Deeb 'El Baradei pulls out of Egyptian Presidential race' devex.com International Development 2/17/2011 Ma. Rizza Leonzon 'Gayle Smith in Obama's inner circle…' 3/17/2009 David Francis 'Gayle Smith joins National Security Council'

momocrat.typepad.com s MOMocrats 9/3/2008 'DNC 08 A look at Obama's foreign policy team'

facilegestures.com Facilegestures 3/20/2011 John McMahon 'Libya, "Obama's Women" and absurd gender narratives'

modernghanna.com Modern Ghana 5/5/2011 Thomas C. Mountain 'West funds full blown genocide in Ethiopia'

countercurrents.org Count Currents 12/1/2010 Thomas c. Mountain 'Guerilla mistress to Obama confidant'

nazret.com Nazret.com 10/28/2008 F. Hager 'Obama and the prospects for democracy in Ethiopia'

nytimes.com NY Times 5/26/2010 'Premier's party sweeps Ethiopian vote' 9/16/2008 Brian Stelter 'McCain spars with Morning Joe co-host' 11/8/2008 Neil A. Lewis 'Gregory B. Craig' 11/7/2008 Helene Cooper 'Anthony Lake' 11/24/2008 Michael Cooper 'Denis McDonough'

latimes.com LA Times 12/10/2008 David R. Rivkin Jr. 'Our military is still in demand use it wisely' 2/11/2009 Paul Richter 'For Obama campaign advisors there's no sure thing'

amconmag.com American Conservative 12/22/2010 Philip Giraldi 'Holiday Hijinks'

theglobalist.com The Globalist 'Joseph Cirincione, President Ploughshares Fund' 'Mark Brzezinski partner McGuire Woods LLP'

newsrealblog.com 11/21/2010 Chris Queen '5 lesser known but equally insidious recipients of George Soro's money'

ploughshares.org Ploughshares Fund 'Our Impact'

jewishindy.com Jewish Indy 2/25/2008 'Who is Zbigniew Brzezinski?'

yidwithlid.blogspot.com 5/28/2008 Jeff Dune 'Obama adviser Brzezinski says Jewish lobby practices McCarthyism'

barenakedislam.wordpress.com 2/3/2011 Michael Savage, Greg Lewis 'Barack Obama, George Soros and Zbigniew Brzezinski behind the fall of Egypt…'

nysun.com NY Sun 2/12/2008 Eli Lake 'Obama adviser leads delegation to Damascus'

bariumbles.com 'Dystopian visionary quotes from Brzezinski' book "Between Two Ages" written in 1970'

4rie.com 'Trilateral Commission'

bibliotecapleyades.net Zbigniew Brzezinski, Robert Gates/ Council on Foreign Relations 2004 'Iran Time for a New Approach'

crisigroup.org 'About Crisis Group'

abovetopsecret.com AboveTopSecret 8/4/2009 'Lets list Obama's speech inconsistencies'

newworldorderreport.com Jonathan Elinoff 'Zbigniew Brzezinski,...admitted...that unelected private interests, think tanks and power brokers circumvent the system and write policy...'

israelinsider.net Israel Insider 2/7/2011 'Evidence mounts that Obama and confederates are subverting Egypt and Israel with Soros and Brzezinski'

globalresearch.ca Global Research 5/16/2011 Andrew Gavin Marshall 'global political awakening and the New World Order' 9/21/2001 "Clinton Administration supported the Militant Islamic Base'

conservativebyte.com Conservative Byte 5/5/2011 'Panetta confirms waterboarding led to Bin Laden, left freaks out'

commondreams.org Common D reams 10/18/2002 Stephen Zunes 'Carter's less known legacy'

findarticles.com Political Science Quarterly spring 1992 Paul E. Masters 'Carter and the Rhodesian Problem'

jstor.org Political Science Quarterly Spring 1992 Martha L. Cottam 'The Carter administrations' policy toward Nicaragua...'

srpska-mreza.com Republican Policy Committee 1/16/1997 'Extended Bosnia mission endangers US troops'

dailypaul.com Daily Paul 10/29/2009 'Marxist Zbigniew Brzezinski's sons are both advisors to both McCain and Obama'

avascentinternational.com Avascent International 'Ian J. Brzezinski'

sunlightfoundation.com Sunlight Foundation 'Brzezinski Group for Central Europe Energy Partners'

whitehouse.gov 11/16/2010 'President Obama announces more key administration posts' 5/13/2011 'Readout of NSA Donilon's meeting with Dr. Mahmoud Gibril' 5/12/2011 NSA Tom Donilon to welcome Dr. Mahmoud Gibril and Delegation from the Libyan Transitional National Council'

atlantic-community.org Atlantic Community Mark Brzezinski 'Obama's Global Approach' nsnetwork.org National Security Network 4/8/2010 'Mark Brzezinski says start enhances US security'

prweb.com PRWeb 4/15/2008 'New book ...Guru Brzezinski seeks Global showdown'

washingtonpost.com Washington Post 11/19/1998 Lloyd Grove, John F Harris 'Crisis Quarterback Gregory Craig is calling the plays on Clinton's team' 1/7/2012 Leila Fadel 'Islamists secure lead in Egypt elections'

time.com TIME 11/19/2009 Massimo Calabresi, Michael Weisskopf 'The fall of Greg Craig...'

discoverthenetworks.org Discover the Networks 'Anthony Lake' 'Pol Pot'

thenewamerican.com New American 4/23/2010 William F. Jasper 'Security risk Anthony Lake to head UNICEF'

politicsdaily.com Politics Daily 10/8/2010 David Wood 'James Jones, Obama's National Security Advisor resigns'

inteldaily.com Inteldaily 5/3/2010 Rick Rozoff 'Atlantic Council Securing the 21st Century for NATO'

nationalsecurityforum.net 10/10/2010 'Jones a Failure as NSA?'

outsidethebeltway.com Outside the Beltway 10/8/2010 Jim Jones steps down; Tom Donilon new NSA'

abcnews.com ABC News 5/27/2009 Luis Martinez 'NSA James Jones: Obama's decisions make US more secure' 10/10/2010 Mathew Mosk 'Tom Donilon's revolving door'

abc.go.com ABC News 3/27/2011 'Biden team apologizes to reporter for sticking him in closet'

whorunsgov.com WhoRunsGov 'Thomas Donilon' 'Denis McDonough'

ntcliby.org 'Founding statement of the Interim Transitional National Council (TNC) 5/13/2011 Mahmoud Gebriel Warfally 'What the Libyan resistance Needs'

bigpeace.com Big Peace 3/2/2011 D.I. Adams 'Arab spring 2011 Hopes and Fears'

bbc.co.uk BBC 3/11/2009 Murad Batal al-Shishani 'Are Libyan rebels an al-Qaeda stalking horse?'

therunagatesclub.blogspot.com 4/3/2011 'Wikileaks hints US planned the war in Libya long before...'

niqnaq.wordpress.com 3/31/2011 Vijay Prashad 'Libya; oodles of entrepreneurial spirit' gowans.wordpress.com 4/17/2011 Gowanson 'In Libya, protecting profits from an outbreak of peace'

iranica.com Encylopaedia Iranica 'Richard Cottam'

foxnewss.com FOX News 3/30/2011 'Obama authorizes covert operation in Libya...' 3/3/2011 'Flickers of Al-Qaeda in Libya aren't new' 3/27/2011 'Biden aide apologizes after reporter kept in storage closet...'

zunguzungu.wordpress.com Zunguzungu 'Meet Mahmoud Jibril'

tripolipost.com Tripoli Post 12/5/2011 Morgan Strong 'Summary of the American and International press on the Libyan Revolution'

conservativedailynews.com Conservative Daily News 3/29/2011 'Who is really behind the Libyan rebel movement?'

feb7info.com 5/11/2011 Libyan Revolution Central 'Mahmud Jibril; Libya is one country, one history, one future, capital in Tripoli'

entrepreneur.com Entrepreneur 'APS review downstream trends'

voanews.com VOA 5/5/2011 'Contact group to discuss funding Libya Rebels'

redicereeations.com 3/10/2011 Edward Cody/Washington Post 'France officially recognizes Libyan rebel group'

irishtimes.com Irish Times 5/6/2011 Paddy Agnew '$250m pledged to help Libyan rebel groups'

highbeam.com High Beam Research 2/22/2007 'Launch of the Libyan Economic Development Board'

johnbatchelorshow.com John Bachelor Show 3/28/2011 'Schedules'

news1.ghananation.com Ghana Nation News 5/13/2011 'Libya; Obama approves covert aid to Opposition'

scoop.co.nz Scoop 5/16/2011 Dan Lieberman 'Critical analysis of the Libyan interim Prime Minister'

c-spanvideo.org C-Span 5/12/2011 Brookings Institute 'Future of Libya'

thehill.com The Hill 5/18/2011 Sam Youngman 'President will call for a new chapter of support for Arab Spring'

theweek.com The Week 3/1/2011 'Are Libyan rebels being led by a CIA plant?'

morningliberty.com Morning Liberty 4/6/2011 'top 4 NOW pawns helping al-Qaeda take down Qadhafi'

familysecuritymatters.com Family Security matters 3/23/2011 'More Global Muslim Brotherhood updates'

globalmbreport.org Global Muslim Brotherhood Daily Report 'Recommended reading Energized Muslim brotherhood in Libya eyes a Prize' 'Qaradawi says Arab leaders should recognize Rebel Council'

frontpagemag.com FrontPageMag 5/11/2006 Patrick Poole 'The Muslim Brotherhood Project;

sanfransico.cbslocal.com KCBS News 4/29/2011 'White House, SF Chronicle in conflict over reporter's video'

slate.com Slate Magazine7/12/2010 Jack Safer 'The man who wasn't there'

potusphere.com Potusphere 7/12/2010 Amy Greene 'Times profile of Obama confidante Denis McDonough

christianaction.org Christian Action Network 3/14/2011 'Deputy National Security Advisor speaks at Brotherhood-tied Mosque'

mccarthycenter.blogspot.com Eugene J McCarthy Center 2/15/2011 'Denis McDonough'

atlasshrugs2000.typepad.com Atlas Shrugs 5/1/2011 'Obama Chavez-style media thuggery…'

escapetyranny.com AP 4/30/2011 'White House says reporter and San Francisco Chronicle will be punished' 'Carney says San Francisco Chronicle broke the rules'

conservativetimes.org Conservative Heritage Times 3/29/2011 Harrison Bergeron 'Obama finds his inner Neocon'

aolnews.com AOL News 10/22/2010 'Denis McDonough, Obama's New Deputy National Security Adviser; 5 key facts'

bostonherald.com Boston Herald 5/18/2011 Hillary Chabot 'White House shuts out Herald scribe'

thenewpolitical.com New Political 4/25/2011 Frank Bumb 'White House press relationship sours'

mediate.com 3/29/2011 Tommy Christopher 'Jon Stewart wonders why White House Reports put up with being shoved in a closet' (video)

yahoo.com Daily Caller 5/2/2011 Mike Riggs 'San Francisco Chronicle accuses White House of lying about banned reporter' pbs.org PBS NewsHour 3/23/2022 'Denis McDonough: We're not talking about an exit strategy in Libya/transcript'

rightwingnews.com RightWingNews.com Kathleen McKinley 'Free Press? Not at this White House'

jkshows.wordpress.com 1/31/2011 jkshaws 'Obama's Muslim brotherhood links deserve second look'

cbsnews.com CBS News 3/7/2011 AP White House: We need US Muslims' help'

newsbsters.org NewsBusters 3/26/2011 Tom Blumer 'Drudge: Reporter confined in a closet at Biden-Nelson event'

abcactionnews.com ABC News 3/28/2011 'Reporter put I closet during veep visit'

npr.org NPR 5/19/2011 Michele Norris 'What is Obama's Middle East Peace Doctrine' Rice interview

tnr.com The New Republic 5/13/2011 Gal Beckerman 'The Real Rice'

gatewaypundig.rightnetwork.com Gateway Pundit 2/24/2011 Jim Hoft 'Good Grief! Obama Ambassador Rice skips UN meeting on Libya' 1/17/2012 Culture of corruption update NY Democrats go on trial for massive voter fraud case'

biggovernment.com Big Government 1/22/2010 Richard Grenell 'Where has Susan Rice, our UN Ambassador, been this past year?'

americansituation.com American Situation 3/20/2011 'The idea behind the war on Libya: R2P'

frontpagemag.com FrontPage Magazine 4/18/2011 Rick Moran 'The misguided tenure of Susan Rice'

newsmax.com News Max 12/22/2011 'Four NY Democrats plead Guilty to voter fraud felony charges'

Chapter 25

wikipedia.org Wikipedia 'Hillary Rodham Clinton' 'Rose Law Firm' 'Jim McDougal' 'White House FBI files controversy' 'Legal Services Corporation' 'National Lawyers Guild' 'White House travel office controversy' 'Suicide of Vince Foster' Vince Foster' 'Quadrennial diplomacy and Development Review' 'Fairness and Accuracy in Reporting' 'New World Foundation' New Left' 'Waco siege' 'Clinton health care plan of 1993' ''Liberal Party of New York' 'Working Families Party' 'Media Matters for America' 'Arizona Proposition 200 (2004) 'Arizona Public Program Eligibility Act, Proposition 300 (2006)' 'Leon Panetta' 'Muslim Brotherhood' 'Robert Gates' US Strategic Command' bfeldman68.blogspot.com 6/17/2007 Bob Feldman 'Hillary Clinton's Rose Law Firm clients'

celsias.com 2/19/2008 Linn Cohen-Cole 'Open letter to Hillary Clinton from a Wellesley College alumna'

washingtonpost.com Washington Post 'Whitewater time line' 5/27/1994 Charles R. Babcock 'Hillary Clinton Futures Trades detailed' 2/27/1995 Toni Locy 'For White House Travel Office, a two-year trip of trouble' 9/4/1999 Ruth Marcus 'Clintons home loan deal raises questions' 6/25/2006 John Pomfret 'At front line of immigration debate' 'US Congress votes database/Leon Panetta' 5/14/2009 Chris Cillizza ''Pelosi fuels fire on Interrogations' 5/16/2009 Perry Bacon Jr. Joby Warrick 'CIA Chief Panetta rebuts Pelosi' charges on interrogation briefings' 6/10/2011 Greg Jaffe, Michael Birnbaum 'Gates rebukes European allies in farewell speech'

hillary-rodham-clinton.org 'Whitewater Hillary and Bill Clinton's roles' 'First Lady Hillary Clinton' 'Senator Hillary Clinton'

pbs.org PBS Rick Young 'The castle grande deal' 6/6/1996 'FBI Files transcript' 'Tracking the rose law firm records' 6/26/1996 'The paper trail transcript' June 2000 'Chris Bury 'Leon Panetta interview transcript'

cbsnews.com CBS News 4/11/2008 'Bill resurrects Hillary's Bosnia blunder'

biography.com 'Hillary Clinton'

freerepublic.com 12/26/2002 John Elvin/Insight Mag 'Hillary hides her Panther Fling' 3/20/2009 'Hillary Clinton, George Soros, ACORN tied to Working Families Party...'

geoffmetcalf.com 6/5/2003 'A Whitewater Chronology'

carlbernstein.com 5/2/2008 Carl Bernstein 'the question of Hillary Clinton's guilt by association tactics'

newfoundations.com New foundations F/4/2008 Sheneka T. Soloman 'The educational theory of Marian Wright Edelman'

learningtogive.org Megan E. Ray 'Children's Defense Fund'

childrensdefense.org 'Our History'

discoverthenetworks.org Discover the Networks 'Marian Wright Edelman' 'Shadow Party' 'Guide to the George Soros Network' 'Hillary Rodham Clinton'

iai.it/pdf London School of Economics International Spectator April/June 2000 Karen E. Smith 'The End of Civilian Power EU: A welcome demise or cause for concern?'

renewamerica.com 12/12/2007 Carey Roberts 'Hillary Clinton, cultural Marxist' sptimes.com St. Petersburg Times 2/16/2008 Robert Farley 'E-mail on Clinton twists the facts'

mega.nu AMPP 'Filegate'

wnd.com World Net Daily 1/9/2000 Jon e. Dougherty 'Judicial Watch finds another White House whistleblower' 9/8/2009 Les Kinsolving 'Media Matters targets Dobbs and me' 6/18/2011 Aaron Klein 'Panetta keynoted pro-Soviet group's conference' 6/29/2004 Michael Evans 'Saddam's WMD are in Syria...'

judicialwatch.org Judicial Watch 'Cara Leslie et al vs. FBI, et al US District Court District of Columbia' 11/16/2010 'Napolitano may exempt Muslims from airport pat-downs'

whatreallyhappened.com 'Partial list of the persons whose FBI files were illegally obtained...' 'The death of Vincent Foster'

nytimes.com NY Times 7/26/1996 Neil A. Lewis 'Documents tie hiring of aide in files case to First Lady' 12/16/2000 Hillary Clinton book advance, $8million, is near record' 2/24/2010 AP 'Ban on women on submarines ends' 11/9/2006 Scott Shane 'Robert Gates, a cautious player for a past Bush Team'

tech.mit.edu 6/26/1996 The Tech Robert L. Jackson, Ronald J. Ostrow/LA Times 'Documents are handed over to House in FBI files probe'

newsmax.com News Max 10/19/2000 'Ray: Hillary lied about Travelgate' 10/20/2010 'Soros gives $1 million to target Fox News'

prorev.com Progressive Review Richard. L. Franklin 'The Vince Foster Case'

rense.com Rense 4/30/2008 Pat Shannon 'Vince Foster was murdered Suicide was fixed' 2/14/2008 Robert Morrow 'Hillary ordered the final Massacre at Waco' 7/17/2000 Sherman H. Skolnick 'The murder of John F. Kennedy, Jr. an update'

highbeam.com High Beam Research 1/10/2000 Washington Post 'Ex-White House worker claims Hillary hired political staff' Monterey County Weekly 11/13/2002 'Panetta Protégés; Monterey's favorite son will head facility ...to teach how to get things done'

cnn.com CNN 7/25/1996 'Documents suggest Hillary know Craig Livingstone' 4/15/2009 'Napolitano defends report on right-wing extremist groups;

salon.com Salon Andrew Ross 'Investigative reporter paints a damaging portrait of scheming First Couple'

nationalreview.com National Review 6/13/2003 Byron York 'Hillary's False Testimony'

canadafreepress.com Canada Free Press 'Dick Morris: Bill Clinton personally orchestrated the 1993 Waco Texas tragedy'

serendipity.li Carol Moore 'Waco questions Congress refuses to answer' rickross.com 3/3/1993 Mark England, Darlene McCormick 'The Sinful Messiah'

nstarzone.com Nstar Zone 'The Clinton Death List'

allfaith.com 2/28/2009 'Never forget what the US government did at Waco!'

carpenoctem.tv 'What happened in Waco'

biggovernment.com Big Government 2/22/2011 Tom Fitton 'Judicial Watch Get Hillarycare Docs…after 5-year legal battle'

findingdulcinea.com Finding Dulcines 7/8/2009 Jill Marcellus 'Revisiting HillaryCare: What it proposed and why it failed'

cmpa.com Center for Media and Public Affairs 2/1/2008 'Media boost Obama, bash 'Billary'

about.com 'Sexism in Media Coverage of Hillary Clinton's campaign' Deborah White 'Profile of Janet Napolitano…' 1/22/2011 'Leon Panetta' Amy Zalman 'Profile of Leon Panetta, CIA Director'

newsbusters.org NewsBusters 110/1/2007 Noel Sheppard 'Hillary Clinton told yearly Kos Convention she helped start Media Matters' 9/18/2007 Tom Blumer 'American prospect: Hillary 1990' Health Plan role is mythology'

workingfamiliesparty.org 'About Working Families'

zillow.com 'Famous homes of US Presidents'

relistr.com 5/10/2008 Presidential candidates from their house to the White House'

politifact.com PolitiFact 12/1/2008 Robert Farley Angie Drobnic Holan 'Hillary's travels as First Lady'

pittsreport.com Pitts Report 2/2/2011 'Bill and Hillary Clinton's mess in Haiti'

cbnews.com CBS News 2/11/2009 'Hillary calls for end to Electoral College'

nydailynews.com NY Daily News 6/9/2011 Corky Siemaszko 'Secretary of State Hillary Clinton to run for World Bank president: report' 12/28/2009 Richard Sisk, Helen Kennedy 'Homeland Security's Janet Napolitano claims the system worked after terrorist attack foiled'

presscore.ca Press Core 9/18/2008 'Classified until 2015 Clintons, George HW Bush, George W. Bush named in JFK Jr. assassination'

govtrack.us 'Hillary Clinton

tomflocco.com Tom Flocco 'Who killed John-John?'

foxnews.com FOX News 10/2/2007 John Gibson 'Online slime machine Media Matters co-founded by Hillary Clinton' ...'5/19/2009 'Panetta urges CIA staff to focus on mission' 4/15/2010 'Panetta left to fend for himself...' 2/10/2011 'Obama Administration corrects Clapper's claim that Muslim Brotherhood is Secular'

hollywoodreporter.com Hollywood Reporter 5/18/2011Paul Bond 'Media Matters launches campaign urging advertiser boycott of Fox News Channel' 7/10/2007 John Perazzo 'Media Matters; Hillary's Lap Dogs' 5/19/2011 Paul Bond 'Orbitz backs Fox News Channel amid Media Matters Smear Campaign'

dropfox.com DropFox 6/20/2011 'Latest Posts'

dailycaller.com The Daily Caller 2/10/2012 Alex Pappas 'Religious Broadcasters want IRS Investigation of Media Matters' 2/17/2012 David Martosko 'Left-wing foundation lavish millions on Media Matters' 2/12/2012 'Inside Media Matters'

theblaze.com The Blaze 2/14/2012 Christopher Santarelli 'New details in Media Matters Investigation...' 2/16/2012 Tiffany Gabbay Pat Buchanan: I was blacklisted by MSNBC...'

frontpagemag.com Front Page Mag 10/6/2004 David Horowitz, Richard Poe 'The Shadow Party:Pt1'

google.com 9/25/2009 'Clinton unveils US food security initiative'

state.gov U.S. Dept of State 'Office of Global Food Security'

theatlantic.com The Atlantic 1/2011 Jeffrey Goldberg 'Hillary Clinton: Mubarak regime is stable'

vanityfair.com Vanity Fair 6/2011 Jonathan Alter 'Woman of the World'

dailycampus.com University of Connecticut 10/19/2009 Samantha Stafford 'Hillary Clinton discusses global hunger'

huffingtonpost.com Huffington Post 6/11/2009 'Attacking hunger at its roots' 11/19/2008 'Robert Gates: Obama's Defense Secretary'

cbsnews.com CBS News 12/3/2010 Mary Dooe 'Hillary Clinton: Secretary of State is my last public position'

hungercenter.org International Fellows Program 'Roadmap to end global hunger'

wwwlabour.ie Labour 6/15/2011' Eamon Gilmore meets with Hilary Clinton in Tanzania to discuss global hunger' realclearpolitics.com 9/25/2009 Hillary Clinton 'Secretary Clinton's Remarks at the Clinton Global Initiative'

spartacus.schoolnet.co.uk Spartacus Educational 'Robert Gates'

airforcetimes.com AirforceTimes.com 6/4/2011 Robert F. Dorr 'Robert Gates deserves a lot of credit'

defense.gov 'Dr. Robert M Gates'

motherjones.com Mother Jones 12/4/2006 'CIA Veteran: How Robert Gates cooked the Intelligence'

cia.gov CIA Robert Gates Preemptive Reform'

businessweek.com Bloomberg Businessweek 6/23/2011 Viola Gienger, Jonathan Ferziger 'Israel may use great force in response...'

nndb.com NNDB 'Robert M Gates'

time.com TIME Mark Halperin 'Grading the Obama Administration'

reuters.com Reuters 2/23/2010 Pentagon oks lifting ban on women in submarines'

voanews.com VOA News 3/24/2011 US pushes for peace talks despite Israeli-Palestinian unrest'

diggersrealm.com DiggersRealm 11/10/1006 'Arizona Governor Napolitano says will not follow resident's wishes on Immigration...'

wsj.com Wall Street Journal 11.20/2008 'Arizona's Napolitano being vetted for Homeland Security Job' 5/16/2009 Siobhan Gorman, Naftali Bendavid 'CIA Chief rebuts Pelosi on briefings' 5/2/2011 'CIA Director Panetta's statement on Bin Laden Death'

hispanic7.com Hispanic News 6/1/2006 -7/6/2007 archive Napolitano blasts Feds'

history.com 'Janet Napolitano'

townhall.com Townhall 12/8/2008 Star Parker 'CNN's Brown on Rendell recalls Napolitano, Anita Hill and Clarence Thomas

slatė.com Slate 11/20/2008 Dana Goldstein 'The long history of Janet Napolitano'

justoneminute.typepad.com 11/20/2008 ''Arizona Gov. Janet Napolitano to head Homeland Security'

politicsdaily.com 6/22/2009 Walter Shapiro 'Janet Napolitano on Immigration Reform, enforcement and Killer Pumpkins' sfgate.com 4/26/2011Carla Marinucci 'Janet Napolitano clarifies immigration program'

abcnews.go.com ABC News 2/0/2011 Jason Ryan, Devin Dwyer 'Terror threat Most Heightened since 9/11' 5/1114/2009 'Nancy Pelosi: CIA lied to me'

cbc.ca CBC News 4/21/2009 'Canada more lax than US about whom it lets in, Napolitano says'

spiegel.de Spiegel 3/16/2009 'Interview with Homeland Security Secretary Janet Napolitano'

americaswatchtower.com America's Watchtower 3/22/2009 Steve Dennis 'Janet Napolitano refuses to use the term Terrorist'

rasmussenreports.com Rasmussen Reports 3/11/2011 '47% have unfavorable view of Napolitano'

thehill.com The Hill 11/21/2010 Judy Yager 'Next step for tight security could be trains, boats, metro'

humanevents.com Human Events 112/17/2998 Rep. Lamar Smith 'Napolitano poor on immigration and border security'

dwkcommentaries.wordpress.com 5/22/2011 'The Sanctuary Movement case'

jstor.org Yale Law & Policy Review Spring/Summer 1987 Julie A. Mertus 'Ecclesiastical Sanctuary: Worshippers' legitimate expectations of privacy'

fas.org Dept of Homeland Security 1/6/2009 '(U/FOUO) Leftwing Extremists Likely to Increase Use of Cyber Attacks over the Coming Decade

abolitionistapproach.com Dept of Homeland Security 4/7/2009'(U/FOUO) Rightwing Extremism: Current Economic and Political climate Fueling Resurgence in Radicalization and Recruitment'

washingtontimes.com Washington Times 4/16/2009 Audrey Hudson, Eli Lake 'Napolitano stands by controversial report' 5/23/2009 Kara Rowland 'Pelosi refused queries on CIA dispute' 8/16/2004 'Saddam agents on Syria border helped move banned materials'

theatlanticwire.com The Atlantic Wire 12/27/2009 Benjamin f. Carlson 'Janet Napolitano: The system worked'

2wsls.com WSLS10 News 6/23/2011 'Napolitano's claim on number of pat down searches'

usatoday.com USA Today 11/14/2010 Janet Napolitano 'Scanners are safe, pat-downs discreet'

rawstory.com Raw Story 12/26/2010 David Edwards 'Napolitano: Pat-downs are here to stay' examiner.com Examiner 12/27/2010 Joe Newby 'Airport pat-downs to continue while some foreigners allowed to bypass security'

shtfplan.com 2/15/2011 SHTFplan Mac Slavo 'Police State Update: TSA pat-downs , Bag searches After passengers get off trains (video)

abc4.com ABC4 5/28/2010 'Utah lawmaker's proposal to ban TSA pat-downs in Utah'

presstv.ir PressTV 6/1/2011 'Americans tired of TSA pat-downs'

gcn.com GCN 6/2/2011 Michael Protos 'TSA might back down some on pat-downs'

transportationnation.org 6/22/2011 Todd Zwilich 'Sen. Paul: TSA Clueless on Passenger Pat-downs'

island-adv.com 5/27/2011 Jim Kouri 'Supremes torpedo Obama's Arizona lawsuit on illegal aliens'

panettainstitute.org 'The Panetta Institute for Public Policy' 'Study and Research by Invitation'

miamiherald.com Miami Herald 5/30/2011 Michael Doyle 'Leon Panetta will bring a lifetime of service to the Pentagon'

thenewamerican.com New American 6/1/2011 Christian Gomez 'Leon Panetta and the Institute for Policy Studies'

washingtonexaminer.com Washington Examiner 11/6/2010 Sara A. Carter 'Panetta says CIA will probe Wikileaks document release'

usasurvival.org America's Survival 4/9/1983 Cliff Kincaid 'The IPS and the Media: Unholy Alliance' 'What is the Institute for Policy Studies' 'Leon Panetta and the Marxist Institute for Policy Studies'

keywiki.org 'Lucy Haessler'

americanthinker.com American Thinker Thomas Lifson 'Who donated millions to Leon's Panetta's foundation?'

washingtonmonthly.com Washington Monthly 6/27/2010 Steve Benen 'CIA Director Panetta tries to explain what victory in Afghanistan would look like'

washingtontimes.com Washington Times 11/17/2010 Rowan Scarborough 'Under Panetta, morale up at CIA'

outsidethebeltwary.com Outside the Beltway James Joyner 'Leon Panetta Speaking fees scandal?'

saudinewstoday.com Saudi News Today 6/10/2011 'CIA: Gaddafi staying in power could undermine Arab Spring'

whorunsthegov.com WhoRunsTheGov 'James R. Clapper' 'Robert Gates'

nationalcorruptionindex.org National Corruption Index 5/16/2009 'James Clapper'

af.mil US Air Force 9/1/1995 'Lieutenant General James R. Clapper Jr.'

abcnews.com ABC News 2/10/2011 Jonathan Karl 'Director of National Intelligence James Clapper: Muslim Brotherhood Largely Secular'

gatewaypundit.com 10/23/2010 Jim Hoft 'Wikileaks's papers reveal US Troops did find WMD in Iraq'

Chapter 26

changegov.com Change 'President-elect Barack Obama establishes President's Economic Recovery Advisory Board'

rawstory.com The Raw Story 11/7/2008 'Obama emphasizes economic proposals in first press conference'

newsweek.com Newsweek 6/3/2008 Council on Foreign relations 'Obama's Brain Trust'

politico.com Politico 11/6/2008 'Obama's economic advisers'

mackinac.org Mackinac Center 2/3/2010 Michael LaFave 'State of the State: Blown Away'

nrtwoc.org National Right to Work Committee 5/3/2011 'Former Michigan Governor Jennifer Granholm makes the case for Right to Work Laws'

abcnews.go.com ABC News 11/8/2008 Lee Ferran 'Gov. Granholm; Obama Economic Insider'

abcnews.com ABC News 2/16/2011 Jake Tapper 'Steve Jobs, Eric Schmidt and Mark Zuckerberg to meet with President Obama Thursday in San Francisco'

wikipedia.org Wikipedia 'Jennifer Granholm' 'Laura Tyson' 'David Bonior' 'Antonio Villaraigosa' 'Warren Buffett' 'Carbon dioxide' 'Carbon' 'Anne M Mulcahy' 'Eric Schmidt' 'William M Daley' 'Penny Pritzker' 'Robert Rubin' 'Robert Reich' 'New America Foundation' 'Roger W Ferguson Jr.' 'Paul Volcker' Glass-Steagall Act' 'Carbon Tax'

investigativeproject.org 3/27/2008 Steven Emerson 'Exclusive photos show Al-Hanooti's political clout'

wsj.com Wall Street Journal 5/28/2008 'Granholm's tax?' warning' 1/6/2011 'Bill Daley's Banking Track Record' rightgrrl.com Rightgrrl 2/16/1999 Carolyn Gargaro 'Newt Gingrich Cleared! Now how about a refund'

familysecuritymatters.org Family Security Matters 3/17/2011 Steve Emerson 'Ex-CAIR official faces sentencing'

arabamericannews.com Arab American News 3/26/3022 Ahmed Ghappour 'From a spy to a patriot: Muthanna al-Hanooti'

pbs.org PBS News Hour 8/26/2008 'Denver offers testing ground for Obama-nomics'

nytimes.com NY Times 8/28/2010 Laura Tyson 'Why we need a second stimulus'

americanrightsatwork.org Americans Rights at Work 'David Bonior , chair'

foxnews.com FOX News 3/27/2008 'Michigan man accused of helping Saddam set up prewar visit to Iraq by US lawmakers'

thecuttingedgenews.com The Cutting Edge 10/13/2008 Armstrong Williams 'Killing fields of California's Sanctuary Cities'

laweekly.com LA Weekly 5/25/2020 Jill Stewart, Tibby Rothman 'Antonio Villaraigosa free tickets are worth…list of 80 free events…'

npr.org NPR 10/22/2008 'Former SEC Chairman: Greater regulation needed'

law.harvard.edu Harvard Law School 1/8/2010 Obama names Hauser and Campos to Intelligence Advisory Board'

sec.gov Securities and Exchange 'Commissioner Roel C. Campos' 'Concurring views of Commissioner Roel c. Campos at Open Commission Meeting commission response to remand by Court of Appeals'

notablebiographies.com 'Parsons, Richard'

about.com Joshua Kennon 'Warren Buffett Biography'

warrenbuffett.com 'Who is Warren Buffett'

jewsagainstobama.wordpress.com 8/17/2008 via Debbie Schlussel 'More on "Republican" Obama supporter Rita Hauser'

nysun.com NY Sun 8/113/2008 'Obama's Republicans'

nydailynews.com NY Daily News 5/21/2009 George Rush 'Citigroup's Richard Parsons has love child with model MacDella Cooper'

time.com TIME 1/21/2009 'Citigroup Chairman Richard Parsons' thenation.com The Nation' 9/8/2010 'Laura Tyson: Tax the Rich, Spend for Jobs'

americanprogress.org Center for American Progress 'Laura Tyson, Senior Fellow'

newamerica.net New America Foundation 9/6/2010 Laura Tyson 'The case for a multi-year infrastructure investment plan'

chemicool.com 'Carbon Element Facts'

education.jlab.org Jefferson Lab 'The Element Carbon'

cityfile.com 'Anne Mulcahy'

reuters.com Reuters 2/26/2010 Steve Eder, Dan Wilchins 'Citi board; Armstrong, Mulcahy out, Zedillo in' 4/6/2010 'Volcker: Taxes likely to rise eventually to tame deficit'

forbes.com Forbes 4/30/2008 'CEO compensation #166 Anne M Mulcahy'

investors.target.com 'Anne M Mulcahy Chairman of the Board of Trustees, Save the Children Federation. Inc.'

investor.jnj.com 10/22/2009 'Xerox Chairman Anne M Mulcahy appointed to Johnson & Johnson board of directors'

cnn.com CNN 'Anne Mulcahy's tarnished resume' '1/31/2008 'Robert Rubin; What meltdown?'

washingtonpost.com Washington Post 8/1/2007 David S Hilzenrath 'Some charges dismissed from lawsuits against Fannie Mae directors' 1/22/2010 David Cho, Binyamin Appelbaum 'Obama's Volcker Rule shifts power away from Geithner'

rbj.net Rochester Business Journal 9/30/2009 Andrea Deckert 'Former Xerox workers file suit over benefits'

huffingtonpost.com Huffington Post 5/25/2009 'Xerox targets retirees: Can today's workers be far behind?' 5/23/2011 'Eric Schmidt, Sean Parker among moguls investing in Raine' 11/2/2009 Robert Reich 'Health care reform is critically important, getting Americans back to work is more so' 5/10/2011 Robert Reich 'Why we need to rein in Government contractors that use taxpayer money for political advantage'

allthingsd.com 10/24/2008 John Paczkowski 'Xerox CEO: Get me 3,000 copies of this pink slip, pronto'

telegraph.co.uk Telegraph 2/5/2011 Kamal Ahmed 'Google's Eric Schmidt predicts the future of computing...'

gigaom.com GigaOM 9/9/2008 Katie Fehrenbacher 'Google's Eric Schmidt details energy plan...'

instituteforenerbyresearch.org 'Piggybacking on the bailout plan is a good way to frame a bad idea'

11thhouraction.com Atraction 11/1/4/2009 'Google's CEO Eric Schmidt shows enthusiastic support for Smart Grid'

smartgridnews.com SmartGridNews 2/9/2009 Jesse Berst 'Google jumps into Smart Grid'

muktware.com Muktware 1/20/2011 Neil Richards 'Larry Page to replace Eric Schmidt as Google CEO'

searchenginewatch.com Search Engine Watch 4/28/2009 Nathania Johnson 'Eric Schmidt and Craig Mundie named to President's Council of Advisors on Science and Technology'

cnet.com CNET News 10/1/2008 Stephen Shankland 'Google CEO: How to fix US energy problems'

bettereconomics.blogspot.com 5/20/2011 'Eric Schmidt wants to fix the Post Office'

theregister.co.uk The Register 3/19/2011 Rik Myslewskiin 'Eric Schmidt's next gig: Obamaman?'

engadget.com 5/22/2011 Tim Stevens 'The Protect IP Act Google's Eric Schmidt squares off ...'

latimes.co LA Times 12/14/1997 'William Daley interview'

hponline.org Harvard Political Review 1/9/2011 Sandra Korn 'The Daley Dilemma'

thedailybeast.com The Daily Beast 8/19/2009 Charlie Gasparino 'Robert Rubin's Agony' 1/5/2011 Charlie Gasparino 'Paul Volcker's Resignation Volcker Rule is a Sad End to a brilliant career'

cfr.org Council on Foreign Relations. 'Robert E Rubin'

michellemalkin.com 1/22/2009 Michelle Malkin 'Robert Reich: Keep stimulus money away from skilled workers and white male constructions workers'

commoncause.org 'About Common Cause'

forums.macnn.com nnforums 10/14/2008 'Robert Reich reveals brutal health care truths...'

firstthings.com 11/13/2009 Wesley Smith 'Obamacare: Robert Reich tells the truth about the downsides of health care reform'

salon.com Salon 8/10/2009 Robert Reich 'The White House deal with Big Pharma undermines democracy' federalreserve.gov Federal Reserve System 2/22/2007 Press Release' 'Roger W Ferguson Jr. submitted his resignation'

nndb.com NNDB 'Group of Thirty'

investopedia.com 'New Keynesian Economics' 'Keynesian Economics'

tiaa-cref.org TIAA-CREF 'Who we are' 'Who we serve'

campaignforliberty.com 11/26/2008 'Paul Volcker Wiki Page tell all'

marketswiki.com 'Paul A Volcker'

infowars.wikia.com 'Paul Volcker'

fedupusa.wordpress.com 1/15/2011 'Group of Thirty'

nationalreview.com National Review 6/14/2004 Bruce Bartlett 'Volcker and Reagan got the job done'

group30.org Group of 30 'About'

usinflationcalcutator.com 'Historical Inflation rates 1914 – 2011'

critiqueofcrisistheory.wordpress.com 'Paul Volcker's banking reform proposals and Socialist Revolution'

amconmag.com The American conservative Sheldon Richman 'Keynesian Cons'

goldnews.bullionvault.com Bullion Vault 10/312008 'Volcker vs. Bretton Woods'

telegraph.co.uk The Telegraph 5/24/2011 'Google's Eric Schmidt clashes with Nicolas Sarkozy at G8'

Chapter 27

foxbusiness.com FOX business 1/13/2009 Kathryn Elizabeth Tuggle 'Bernanke: Obama stimulus would lift economy'

wikipedia.org Wikipedia 'Ben Bernanke' 'Macroprudential policy' 'Federal Reserve System' 'Timothy Geithner' '1997 Asian financial crisis' 'Troubled Asset Relief Program' 'American Recovery and Reinvestment Act 2009' 'Kissinger Associates' "Lawrence Summers' 'History of Lithuania' 'Alan Goolsbee' 'Christina Romer' 'David Romer' 'D.E. Shaw & Co.' 'Peter R Orszag' 'Jacob Lew' 'Hedge Fund'

federalreserve.gov Federal Reserve System 'Ben S Bernanke' '5/5/2011 Ben S Bernanke speech 'Implementing a Macroprudential approach to supervision and regulation' 'The Board of Governors of the Federal Reserve System' pragcap.com Pragmatic Capitalism 10/10/2010 Cullen Roche 'Northern Trust: QE1 failed, why will QE2 work?'

calculatedrisk.blog.com Calculated Risk 10/3/2010 'A QE1 timeline'

informedtrades.com Informed Trades 11/7/2010 'QE2 explained'

dallasnews.com Dallas News 11/10/2010 Cheryl Hall 'What is Fed's QR2, and what will it do?...'

csmonitor.com Christian Science Monitor 12/13/2010 Paul McDonnold 'Bernanke's bold QE2 finally explained with burgers and fries'

economicpolicyjournal.com Economic Policy Journal 2/5/2011 'The interest rate spoke since QE2 explained' 3/17/2009 Robert Wenzel 'Who is Timothy Geithner?'

forbes.com Forbes 1/22/2011 Robert Lenzner 'Bernanke's QE1 andQE2 have paid off big-time in higher stock prices'

investopedia.com 'Core Inflation'

bls.gov 'Consumer Price Index'

wealthcycles.com Wealth Cycle Principle 1/25/2011 'Investors love Bernanke but hate his policies'

economicpopulist.org The Economic Populist 5/23/2011 'Ben Bernanke loses control of the Fed'

biggovernment.com Big Government 5/2/2011 Chriss W Street 'Ben Bernanke's failure as a talk show host'

finance.yahoo.com 4/15/2011 Dirk van Dijk 'Core Inflation still tame'

editorialexpress.com 4/29/2011 John Junggun Oh 'design of Macroprudential Regulations and their effects on Economic Stability'

imf.org International Monetary Fund 2/15/2011 Christopher Crowe, Giovanni Dell'Ariccia, Deniz Igan Pau Rabanal 'Policies for Macrofinancial Stability: Options to Deal with Real Estate Booms'

aei.pitt.edu University of Pittsburg Ivo Maes 'On the origins of the BIS macro-prudential approach to financial stability...'

investopedia.com 'Macroprudential Analysis' 'Private Equity'

the-priateer.com 'Long-term $US 5x3 gold chart since 2004'

federalreserveonlone.org 'The Federal Reserve System Online'

cnbc.com CNBC 10/18/2010 Bill Isaac 'Geithner's TARP myths'

huffingtonpost.com Huffington Post 1/13/2009 Nico Pitney 'Timothy Geithner housekeeper status unchecked, taxes unpaid' 10/17/2008 'Tim Geithner, Treasury Secretary Housekeeper Problem?" 1/7/2010 'Geithner's New York Fed pushed AIG to keep Sweetheart Deals secret' 6/7/2011 'Austan Goolsbee Exit: Adviser leases behind frustration, political dysfunction' 8/6/2010 AP Christina Romer resigning...' 2/14/2011 Jacob Lew The 2012 Budget' 9/21/2010 Shahien Nasiripour Jacob Lew, Obama Nominee and former Citigroup executive...'

hubpages.com 'Tim Geithner Child to Treasury Secretary'

abcnews.com ABC News 'A rocky road for Treasury Secretary-Designee Geithner?'

wsj.com Wall Street Journal 1/22/2009 'Geithner's Tax Code' 1/14/2009 Jonathan Weisman 'Geithner's Tax History muddles confirmation' 4/5/2009 John D McKinnon, TW Farnam 'Hedge Fund paid Summers $5.2 million in past year'

americanthinker.com American Thinker 3/7/2009 Rick Moran 'The Geithner: Boy Genius myth exploded'

newyorkfed.org Federal Reserve Bank of New York 'Timothy F Geithner' 'Actions related to AIG'

usasurvival.org America's Survival 1/16/2009 Cliff Kincaid 'The Big Money behind Tim Geithner...'

rense.com Rense 4/26/2009 'Geithner Group of 30 Servant, Change Agent'

rightpulse.com Right Pulse 3/28/2009 'Tim Geithner and two former treasurers'

foxnews.com FOX News 3/3/2009 'Geithner touts tackling tax evaders after failing to pay own taxes'

network.deas.org Hendri Saparini, PhD 'Policy Response to Overcome Crisis; A Lesson from Indonesian Case'

businessreview.com Business Review 12/20/2010 'All About'

time.com TIME 6/1/2009 Bill Powell 'Geithner's Asia background shows on his China trip

marketwiki.com 'Bank stress test'

baselinescenario.com Baseline Scenario 7/15/2010 Simon Johnson 'Tim Geithner's ninth political life' abc.go.com ABC News 5/13/2009 Matthew Jaffe 'Geithner announces bailout repayments will be resused for smaller banks'

theshriverbrief.org Shriver Center 3/7/2011 Karen K Harris 'Bank closures hit harder in poor neighborhoods'

latimes.com LA Times 2/3/2009 Jonah Goldberg 'democrats are hypocrites when it comes to paying taxes'

washingtonexaminer.com Washington Examiner 9/2009 'The clock is ticking on tax cheat Charlie Rangel'

snooperreport.com 5/6/2009 Mark 'Snooper' Harvey 'It takes a tax cheat to catch a tax cheat?'

scrappleface.com 3/3/2009 Scott Ott Business, US News 'Geithner to catch global tax cheats by going undercover'

startthinkingright.wordpress.com 3/22/2011 Michael Eden 'Claire McCaskill joins the ranks of hypocrite Democrat tax cheat

moonbattery.com Moonbattery 2/8/2009 'Al Franken: Yet another tax cheat Democrat'

joshuapundit.blogspot.com 4/1/2009 'Another Democrat tax cheat!'

whorunsgov.com Washington Post 'Timothy Geithner'

newhomessection.com 2/10/2009 'Treasury and Federal Reserve announce TARP 2 details...'

telegraph.co.uk The Telegraph 1/23/2009 Malcolm Moore 'timothy Geithner currency manipulation accusation angers China'

treasury.gov Office of Financial Stability October 2010 Katalina Bianco, J.D. "A Retrospective of the Troubled Asset Relief Program" 5/9/2011 'Remarks by Treasury Secretary Tim Geithner 2011 US-China Strategic and Economic Dialogue...'

arsipberita.com Indonesian News 3/31/2011 'Timothy Geithner seeks uniform exchange rate policy'

marketwatch.com Market Watch 12/16/2010 Ronald D. Orol 'Geithner: Only TARP costs will be from housing'

truetaxfacts.com True Tax Facts 1/27/2009 'Geithner blames his tax woes on Turbo Tax'

financialreformwatch.com Financial Reform Watch 19/4/2010 'Obituary: TARP (Born 19/3/2008; Died October 3/2010) nafcu.org National Association of Federal Credit Unions 1/22/2009 'Geithner pledges TARP reform at Treasury'

mainjustice.com Main Justice 3/30/2011 David Stout 'Departing TARP watchdog say banks benefited too much'

openleft.com Open Left 3/17/2009 Chris Bowers 'Bonus Scandal: Four questions on Geithner and Summers'

waysandmeanshouse.gov Apollo News Service 2/10/2009 Keith Schneider 'Apollo Weekly Update'

allbusiness.com All Business Salt Lake Tribune Matt Canham 'Bennett get $50M Utah water project in stimulus bill...'

recovery.gov 'The Recovery Act'

cnnmoney.com CNN 2/1/2009 Jeanne Sahadi Stimulus: Now for the hard part'

insidescience.org Inside Science 10/28/2009 Philip F Schewe 'Funding a greener grid'

npr.org NPR 2/9/2009 Brian Naylor 'Stimulus bill gives shovel-ready projects priority'

politico.com Politico 3/4/2010 Erika Lovley 'Democrats pull tax cheat bill' '11/28/2008 Lisa Lerner 'Who is Christina Romer?' 6/21/2010 Mike Alan 'Orszag to bail next month' 6/3/2011 Darren Samuelsohn 'House GOP blames Obama regs for jobs rate'

publicintelligence.net Public Intelligence 10/20/2009 'Kissinger Associates, Inc'

dollars and sense.org Dollars & Sense 11/22/2008 Chriss Starr 'Geithner and Kissinger Associates pt1'

newworldorderreport.com 'Inside the Global Banking Intelligence Complex, BCCI Operations'

thenation.com The Nation 8/6/2010 William Greider 'The AIG bailout scandal' 11/10/2008 Mark Ames 'The Summers Conundrum'

salon.com Salon 5/17/2011 Andrew Leonard 'Beyond the debt ceiling barrier' 5152011 Jonathan Easley 'A performance review for Timothy Geithner' 9/25/2010 Maxwell Strachan 'The Larry Summers hall of shame'

portfolio.com Portfolio 112/9/2009 'Geithner extends TARP'

propublica.org ProPublica 1/14/2009 Jeff Gerth 'How Citigroup unraveled under Geithner's watch' 6/2/2011 Paul Kiel 'Shoddy bank practices continue even after mortgage mods' cbsnews.com CBS News 12/11/2008 The Early Show 'After Rescue; Bonuses still flow at AIG'

nypost.com NY Post 1/9/2010 Mark DeCambre, Paul Tharp, John Aidan Byrnne 'Time for Tim to go!'

siecus.org Siecus 'Comprehensive Sexuality Education'

abcnews.com ABC News 2/11/2011 Tahman Bradley 'Treasury Sec. Tim Geithner's plan to wind down Fannie Mae and Freddie Mac'

kansascity.com McClatchy Newspapers 5/30/2011 Kevin G Hall 'Defaulting on US debt dangerous even to consider'

michaelsavage.wnd.com 5/12/2011 Cliff Kincaid/AIM 'Connection between Timothy Geithner and George Soros'

cnsnews.com CNS News 6/3/2011 Terence P Jeffrey 'China has divested 97% of its holding in US Treasury Bills' 1/16/2011 Susan Jones 'Obama order review of business-stifling regulations…'

publicbraodcasting.net WUKY Reuters 5/25/2011 'Future crises unlikely as severe as last: Geithner'

lawrencegmcdonald.com 3/4/2011Washington Insight 'Geithner predicts US dollar to remain world reserve currency'

itmtrading.com ITM Trading 3/17/2011 Timothy Geithner welcomes a new world reserve currency'

foxnews.com FOX News 2/17/2011 'Geithner rocked at Senate hearing, forced to admit the truth about Obamanomics'

totalbankruptcy.com 4/5/2011 'Geithner defends HAMP'

lexisnexis.com Lexist Nexis News 4/30/2011 The Houston Chronicle 'Around the Nation'

banksandtheeconomy.blogspot.com 2/10/2011 ABA voices concern for Community Banks to Geithner and Woodruff'

fdic.gov FDIC 'Failed Bank List'

sourcewatch.org Source Watch 'Larry Summers'

usnews.com US News 11/24/2008 Jennifer O'Shea '10 things you didn't know about Lawrence Larry Summers' 3/24/2009 Kenneth T Walsh 'Larry Summers Obama's designated thinker in a troubled economy' counterpunch.org Counter Punch 6/15/1999 Jim Vallette 'Larry Summers war against the earth'

whitehouse.gov Council of Economic Advisers 'About CEA' Office of Management and Budget 'Jacob J Lew, Director'

americanfreepress.net American Free Press December 2008 Victor Thorn a Change? Obama inner circle filled with Bilderbergers'

boston.com Boston Globe 11/29/2009 Beth Healy 'Harvard ignored warnings about investments' 1/19/2005 Marcella Bombardieri Harvard women's group rip Summers'

bloomberg.com Bloomberg 12/18/2009 Michael McDonald, John Lauermanand, Gillian Wee 'Harvard swaps are so toxic even Summers won't explain (update 3)' 5/12/2011 Roger Runningen 'Obama says he's identified business regulations for elimination'

msn.com MSN 11/30/Kim Peterson 'Harvard's investment flubs'

uk.reuters.com Reuters 11/29/2009 Felix Salmon 'How Larry Summers lost Harvard $1.8 billion' 4/6/2009 Roberta Rampton 'Hedge fund paid Obama adviser Summers $5.2 million'

washingtonpost.com Washington Post 1/19/2005 Michael Dobbs 'Harvard Chief's comments on women assailed' 10/4/2007 George F Will 'The Democratic Economist' 3/24/2011 Ezra Klein 'Romer: You care about the deficit be because it allows you...' 9/6/2010 Greg sergeant 'Bush tax cuts'

nytimes.com NY Times 2/21/2006 Alan Finder, Kate Zernike 'Embattled President of Harvard to step down at end of semester' 4/6/2009 Louise Story 'A rich education for Summers (after Harvard) 12/20/2010 'Jacob J Lew' 1/19/2011 Jackie Calmes 'Obama asks for review of rules stifling jobs' 1/16/2011 Sheryl Gay Stoleberg 'Obama orders review of Business regulations'

crooksandliars.com Crooks and Liars 11/7/2008 Nicole Belle 'Larry Summers for Treasury Secretary?'

hks.harvard.edu JFK School of Government Harvard 'Lawrence H Summers'

softpanaorama.org Softpanorama September 2010 'Harvard Mafia, Andrei and the Economic rape of Russia'

larouchpub.com Executive Intelligence review 4/10/2010 Rachel Berthoff Douglas 'Summers hated in Russia for his 1990s record'

imf.org International Monetary fund August 1996 David D Driscoll 'The IMF and the World Bank How do they Differ?'

conservapedia.com Conservapedia 'Larry Summers corrupt and Incompetent Chief Economic Advisor to Obama' wanghutner.com 'Larry Summers Biography'

bayesianheresy.blogspot.com Bayesian Heresy 3/27/2008 "Larry Summers time at the Work Bank'

curiouscapitalist.blogs.time.com TIME 4/12/2011 Rana Foroohar 'Larry Summers: No regrets on deregulation'

economist.com the Economist 12/13/2010 'The legacy of Larry Summers'

newyorker.com The New Yorker 10/12/2009 Ryan Lizza 'Inside the Crisis'

ecomonistpopulist.org The Economist Populist 9/ 2/1008 Robert Oak 'Goolsbee-Obama's Economic Adviser It's all in your head'

seekingalpha.com Seeking Alpha 6/9/2011 Rorty Bomb 'The changing nature of confidence in the Administration's economic policy'

usatoday.com USA Today 9/1/2010 Mimi Hall 'Christina Romer: recession terrifying and so difficult to cure' 2/21/2011 Jacob Lew 'Opposing view; Social Security isn't the problem'

astuteblogger.blogspot.com The Astute Bloggers 8/5/2010 Kirk Victor 'I think Christina Romer is quitting because she favors extending...'

econlib.org Library of Economics and Liberty Christina D Romer 'Business Cycles'

businessweek.com Bloomberg Businessweek 6/9/2011 Hans Nichols, Vivien Lour Chen 'Romer resigns in second exit for Obama Economy team'

healthreform.mckinsey.com McKinsey & Co. 4/1/2011 'Administration releases proposed rules for Medicare Accountable Care Organizations'

brookings.edu The Economists' Voice 2005 Peter A Diamond, Peter Orszag 'Saving Social Security: The Diamond-Orszag Plan'

peterorszagsite.net 4/3/2011 'Peter Orszag at the Brookings Institution'

tobinproject.org 'About the Tobin Project'

jewishvirtuallibrary.org 'Peter Orszag'

lonelyconservative.com Lonely Conservative 1/5/2011 'Obama's new regulations on business cost $28 billion'

newsweek.com Newsweek 1/5/2011 Daniel Gross 'The lure of the big Citi'

dailycaller.com Daily Caller 4/11/2011 Daniel Keylin 'Peter Orszag reveals Obama White House is full of drama' senate.gov Senate Budget Committee 2/15/2011 'Conrad remarks at hearing on President's FY 2012 budget proposal'

c-span.org 2/15/2011 'House Budget Cmte. Hearing with OMB Director Jacob Lew'

Chapter 28

abcnews.go.com 6/20/2012 Devin Dwyer Committee Votes Attorney Gereral Eric Holder in Contempt of Congress After Obama asserts Executive Privilege

forbes.com 6/11/2012 Todd Ganos Alleged White House Leaks

newsmax.com 6/7/2012 Ronald Kessler Pattern of White House Leaks Threatens Nations Security

huffingtonpost.com 6/9/2012 Pete Yost White House Leaks: Eric Holder appoints 2 Prosecutors to Lead Investigation youthtoday.org Youth Today 11/19/2008 John Kelly AGto- be Eric Holder: What we know' 6/28/2012 Jennifer Bendery Eric Holder contempt resolution over Fast and furious Passes House

galeschools.com Gale Schools 'Eric Holder Jr.'

zimbio.com Zimbio 11/19/2008 Sultan Knish 'Eric Holder, Obama's crooked pick for attorney general Terrorists and Crime'

discoverthenetworks.org Discover The Networks 'Eric Holder' 'Andrew Stern' 'Richard Trumka' 'Joe Biden' 'Harold Koh' 2005 Jacob Laksin 'Jim Wallis; Expanded Profile' 'Jim Wallis'

wikipedia.org US Department of Justice' 'Public Integrity Section' 'Extraordinary rendition by the US' 'David Petraeus' 'Andy Stern' 'Craig Becker' 'Joe Biden' 'Ahmed Aboul Gheit'

time.com TIME 2/13/2001 Jessica Reaves 'The Marc Rich Case' A Primer' 3/29/2010 Massimo Calabresi 'Eric Holder's Trials and Tribulations'

nytimes.com NY Times 11/24/2008 George Larderner Jr. 'A pardon to remember' 1/22/2011 Sheryl Gay Stolberg, Anahad O'Connor 'Obama picks GE chief for board as focus turns to jobs' 1/22/20 'Immelt to succeed Volcker as Obama Economic Adviser' 4/14/2010 Steven Greenhouse 'Andy Stern to step down as chief of politically active union' 6/26/2012 'Supreme Court Decision on Arizona Immigration Law'

wnd.com World Net Daily 9/27/1999 J.R. Nyquist 'Clinton's sympathy for Marxist terrorists' 10/13/2009 Chelsea Schilling 'Obama: We're going to paint the nation purple with SEIU' 10/12/2010 David A Noebel 'The communists within' 3/15/2010 Aaron Klein 'Not again! Meet Obama's new controversial pastor' 6/14/2010 Bob Unruh 'Egypt official: US president claims to be Muslim'

fas.org 'Armed Forces of Puerto Rican National Liberation'

dailykos.com Daily Kos 11/18/2008 'So who is Eric Holder?'

latimes.com LA Times 1/9/2009 Josh Meyer, Tom Hamburger 'Eric Holder pushed for controversial clemency'

humanevents.com Human Events 4/9/2011 'Top 10 reasons Eric Holder should not be Attorney General' 4/9/2011 'Khalid Sheikh Mohammed military trial; Sanity trumps Eric Holder' 3/3/12010 Rabbi Aryeh Spero 'Obama's Rev. Jim Wallis misreads the Bible'

nypost.com NY Post 5/12/2010 Mike Rogers 'Fighting terror like it's 1993'

usatoday.com USA Today 4/1/2009 Kevin Johnson , Matt Kelley 'Holder urges Ted Stevens' conviction reversed' 4/28/2011 'Petraeus' war legacy befits his future post as CIA'

newyorker.com New Yorker 2/15/2010 Jane Mayer 'The Trial'

theatlanticwire.com The Atlantic Wire 4/14/2010 Max Fisher''6 Controversies addressed at Holder Senate Hearing'

prorevnews.blogspot.com Undernews 2/10/2011 'Eric Holder: One reason Obama waffled on Egypt'

politics daily.com 2/16/2010 Ria Misra 'Eric Holder taps Susan Carbon for Violence against Women Post'

whorunsgov.com 'Susan Carbon'

justice.gov US Department of Justice 2/23/2011 'Statement of the Attorney General on Litigation involving the Defense of Marriage Act'

cnn.com CNN 5/9/2010 Holder: Feds may sue over Arizona immigration law' 6/23/2011 David Gergen 'Why didn't Obama listen to Petraeus?'

foxnews.com FOX News 5/14/2010 'Holder admits to not reading Arizona's immigration laws despite criticizing it'

cbsnews.com CBS News 4/27/2010 'Holder: US may fight Arizona Immigration law' '5/16/2011 Lucy Madison 'In letter CIA chief undercuts role of torture in search for Osama bin Laden'

abcnews.com ABC News 5/9/2010 Holder: AZ immigration law not racist' 4/27/2011 Jake Tapper 'Gen. David Petraeus will take helm of CIA after Leon Panetta moves to Pentagon'

abc.go.com ABC News 12/13/2007 Christine Brozyna 'Get to know Joe Biden'

newser.com Newser 7/6/2010 Kevin Spak 'Us files suit against Arizona immigration law' pajamasmedia.com Pajamas Media 6/14/2011 Bob Owens 'Gunwalker under fire' 1/31/2011 Ed Driscoll 'GE's Jeff Immelt and Obama's antipathy to free markets'

americanthinker.com American Thinker 3/5/2011 Phil Boehmke 'Bloody Fast and Furious program approved by Holder's DOJ'

reasonedpolitics.blogspot.com Reasoned Politics 6/21/2011 'Hillary, Eric, Wikileaks and the BATFE Scandal: An overview and timeline'

defense.gov US Department of Defense 'General David H. Petraeus' 9/10/2007 General David H Petraeus 'Report to Congress on the Situation in Iraq'

capitolhillblue.com Capitol Hill Blue 5/3/2011 CIA ran bin Laden operation'

freedomslighthgouse.net Freedom's Lighthouse 5/3/2011'CIA Director Leon Panetta confirms that Waterboarding was used on detainees…led to Bin Laden'

huffingtonpost.com Huffington Post 11/28/2011 Siga Technologies Center of small pox contract dispute threaten HuffPost with lawsuit' 9/28/2010 Sam Hananel 'FBI investigating prominent labor leader Andy Stern in corruption probe at SEIU' 3/25/2010 Jim Wallis 'A million Christians for Social Justice'

hotair.com HotAir 11/25/2011 Ed Morrissey 'McCaskill call for probe into small pox vaccine boondoggle'

newsbusters.org NewsBusters 4/22/2009 Noel Sheppard GE shareholders meeting: the crowd was very upset with MSNBC'

examiner.com Examiner 6/30/2009 James Hyde 'By putting NBC News in bed with Obama is GE pandering for payback?' 2/27/2011 Dan Spencer 'Obama and SEIU flashback Obama: SEIU's agenda is my agenda'

washingtonexaminer.com Washington Examiner 7/1/2010 Timothy P Carney 'The GE-Obama affair, and Jeff Immelt's harsh words'

newsroomamerica.com NewsRoomAmerica 10/12/2010 Jon E Dougherty 'GE got $25 million in Stimulus Funds'

ft.com Financial Times 1/18/2011 Ed Crooksin 'GE to sign slew of China deals in jobs boost' 4/29/2011 'Jeff Immelt resigns from NY Fed's board'

forbes.com 'Jeffrey R Immelt' '11/10/2009 Richard A Epstein 'The tussle over Craig Becker'

ge.com GE 'Jeff Immelt, CEO'

tuck.dartmouth.edu Tuck School of Business 'Jeff Immelt D'78 at Tuck' wsj.com Wall Street Journal 6/12/2011 Jeff Immelt, Ken Chenaulty 'How we're meeting the job creation challenge' 5/14/2009 'Andy Stern's go-to guy'

cbsnews.com CBS News 3/30/2011 Brian Montopoli 'Liberals want GE CEO Jeff Immelt out of Obama administration'

gatewaypundit.rightnetwork.com 9/16/2007 Jim Hoft 'Barak Hussein Obama picks Anti-Israel foreign advisor'

connectusfund.org Connect US Fund 'Barack Obama Foreign Policy Advisors'

newsweek.com Newsweek 6/2/2008 'Obama's Brain Trust'

foxnews.com FOX News 12/14/2009 Maxim Lott 'Obama's Safe Schools Czar tied to lewd readings for 7th graders' 3/31/2009 'Koh, No? Critics decry Obama nominee for State department Legal Adviser' 4/9/2008 John R Lott Jr. , Sonya D Jones 'Abortion rate among black women far exceeds rate for other groups'

biggovernment.com Big Government 6/21/2011 'Good Riddance Obama's radical safe schools czar hits the skids' 11/16/2009 Brian Johnson 'How Andy Stern got around Obama's No Lobbyist policy; He just didn't register' 2/3/2010 Brian Johnson 'Why you should know about Craig Becker (and why you need to be worried)'

msnbc.msn.com MSNBC News Molly Masland 'Carnal knowledge; The sex-ed debate'

factoidz.com 'The facts of Comprehensive Sex Education'

siecus.org Siecus 'Comprehensive Sexuality Education'

avert.org Avert 'Sex education that works'

newsweek.com Newsweek 10/27/2009 Sarah Kliff 'The future of abstinence'

blackchristiannews.com Black Christian News 5/12/2009 'Abstinence funding to end...'

ncfpc.org North Carolina Policy Council 4/23/2009 'Planned Parenthood abortions outweigh adoptions'

cnsnews.com CNS News' International Planned Parenthood pushes sex-ed for 10 year olds'

aipnews.com AIP News 5/23/2011 'Obama's safe Schools Czar Kevin Jennings to leave US Dept. of Education...'

sternburgerwithfries.blogspot.com SternBurger 12/13/2011 'Andy Stern in hot seat over Siga bid-rigging' 12/30/2011 'Court sentencing SEIU officials in Illinois' 6/11/2011Stern in hot seat as Congress probes Siga's $2.8 billion contract'

siga.com 6/21/2010 'Andy Stern joins SIGA's Board of Directors' stevenbirnspeacks.wordpress.com 4/8/2011 Steven Birn 'Former SEIU President Andy Stern attacks Constitution'

nlpc.org National Legal and Policy Center 11/18/2009 Carl Horowitz 'SEIU President Andrew Stern is frequent White House visitor, may have violated lobbying laws'

washingtonpost.com Washington Post 6/22/2004 Thomas B Edsall 'Union Leader urges AFL-CIO reform' 7/26/2005 Thomas B Edsall 'Two top unions split from AFL-CIO'

thenunionews.blogspot.com The Union News 10/2008 'NPR exposes ACORN-SEIU $$ connection'

maverick-strategies.com Maverick Strategies 7/1/2008 Bret Jacobson 'ACORN's troubling ties to US labor'

findarticles.com Find Articles/Reason 11/2000 Michael McMenamin 'Labor lost declining influence of labor unions'

cnn.com CNN 7/25/2005 'Teamster, SEIU quit AFL-CIO' 6/25/2012 Mike Ahlers 'Official: Obama administration will enforce its priorities, not Arizona's'

frontpagemag.com FrontPageMag 10/11/2004 David Horowitz , Reich Poe 'The Shadow Party; Part III'

washingtontimes.com Washington Times 4/23/2010 Vernuccio: Andy Stern's debts'

nrtwc.org National Right to Work Committee 6/24/2011 SEIU, Andy Stern, Obama & the $2.8B no-bid

newsbusters.org NewsBusters 9/21/2009 Tom Blumer 'ACORN Independent Advisory Council member Andy Stern lets loose on ACORN's critics, press mum'

cnsnews.com CNS News 6/7/2010 Penny Starr 'Andy Stern: A member of Obama's fiscal responsibility commission says Worshipping the Market has failed America'

heritage.org Heritage Foundation 4/13/2010 Conn Carroll 'Morning Bell Andy Stern's America' 3/26/2010 Ryan O'Donnell 'Craig Becker: Big Labor's Big Ally'

smallbusiness/house.gov 6/14/2919 Eamon Javers CNBC: House panels probing contract awarded to Perelman-Affiliated Company'

political.com Politico 2/9/2010 Meredith Shiner 'Senate blocks Labor Board nominee'

lonelyconservative.com The Lonely Conservative 2/26/2011 'Richard Trumka advised President Obama to raise national gas tax'

washingtonwatch.com Washington Watch 12/15/2010 'The Epicenter $48,000,000,000' aflcio.org AFL-CIO 'Richard L Trumka, AFL-CIO President'

whitehouse.gov 'Vice President Joe Biden'

danielpipes.org Daniel Pipes 3/30/2009 'Harold Koh, Promoter of Shari'a?'

tomgrossmedia.com Tom Gross Mideast Media Analysis 8/28/2008 'Sot on Iran: Serious concerns in Israel about Joe Biden'

law.yale.edu Yale Law School 'Harold Hongju Koh'

pres-outlook.com Outlook 3/15/2005 'Monologue of the Religious Right, over Jim Wallis tells LPTS'

thinkexist.com 'Jim Wallis quotation'

thechristianworldview.com The Christian Worldview 3/26/2009 Dr. David Noebe 'Jim Wallis: Obama's Red Spiritual Adviser'

blog.sojo.net Sojourners 6/21/2011 'Jim Wallis' 6/21/2011 Jim Wallis 'This is Not Enough' 'Mission/History'

lewrockwell.com The LRC Blog 8/19/2010 Bill Anderson 'Jim Wallis and Sojourners; Clients of George Soros'

ewtnnews.com EWTN News 8/15/2010 'Sojourners took George Soros money, Rev. Jim Wallis acknowledges'

politicsofthecrossresurrected.blogspot.com 8/22/2010 'Jim Wall admits taking donations from Soros after calling…a liar for telling the truth'

ironicsurrealism.com 11/2/2009 'Controversial New Video of Obama's Pastor/AIM' 3/24/2010 'Obama's Marxist advisor Rev. Jim Wallis: advocate of redistribution of wealth and social justice'

worldviewweekend.com Worldview Times 2/19/2008 David A Noebel Tony Campolo, Jim Wallis: The Marxist delusion and a Christian Evangelist'

christianledershipallianc.org Christian Leadership Alliance 2/5/2010 Stanley Carlson 'President's faith-based advisory council makes recommendations'

christiancrusade.com Christian Crusade Newspaper July 2010 'Why did Egyptian foreign Minister Ahmed Abul Gheit say Obama confided he's still a practicing Muslim?'

westernjournalism.com Western Journalism 5/31/2011 'Egyptian Foreign Minister Ahmed states Obama told him…he was still a Muslim' mediamatters.org Media Matters 6/16/2010 Kate Conway 'Right-wing runs with dubious claim that Obama admitted I am a Muslim'

atlasshrugs2000.typepade.com Atlas Shrugs 6/12/2010 'I am a Muslim, Obama tell Egyptian Foreign Minister...'

eutimes.net EU Times 6/14/2010 'Egyptian minister says Obama told me he is a Muslim'

Chapter 29

georgesoros.com 6/22/2011 George Soros 'My Philanthropy' '10/5/2010 'The sovereign Debt Problem' 'George Soros'

soro.org Soros Foundation Romania 'General Overview' 'Open Society Foundations'

wikipedia.com 'George Soros' 'Kosovo' 'Hashim Thaci' 'London School of Economics' 'First 100 days of Barack Obama's presidency' 'Global Poverty Act' 'Jeffrey Sachs' 'World Economic Forum' 'International Crisis Group' 'Fred Cuny' Central European University' 'Soviet Union' 'Quantum Group of Funds' 'The Open Society and Its Enemies by Karl Popper' 'US Senate election in Minnesota, 2008' 'Secretary of State Project' 'Move.On.org ad controversy'

wsj.com Wall Street Journal 4/2011 US, Soros' Foundation providing financial and military aid to the KLA on Kosovo war'

wnd.com World Net Daily 2/12/2008 Jerome R Corsi 'John McCain funded by Soros since 2001' 4/4/2011 Aaron Klein 'Will Bretton Woods shock US economy?' 2/8/2011 Aaron Klein 'Soros group: Normalize Muslim Brotherhood'

huffingtonpost.com Huffington Post 4/10/2008 Sam Stein 'McCain camp lashes Soros after McCain took his money' 11/12/2010 'Randy Scheunemann, Sarah Palin adviser, bankrolled by Georg Soros' 11/6/2008 'Sarah Palin's Clothes: GOP lawyer dispatched to Alaska to retrieve some' 10/2/2008 'Palin wearing flag pin The Size of a Child's Fist' 5/24/2011 Steve Clemons 'New America Foundation acquires Google CEO'

answers.com 'When did George Soros become an American citizen?'

wsws.org World Socialist Web Site 6/28/2001 Paul Stuart 'The Trepca mining complex': How Kosovo's spoils were distributed'

emperors-clothes.com 2/28/2000 Diana Johnstone 'How it is done Taking over the Trepca mines: Plans and Propaganda'

anarchitext.wordpress.com AnarchitexT 12/9/2003 Heather Cottin 'Soros: Philanthropist? Spook? Or Philanthropist spook?' 4/'17/2011 'US Dept of State: Press release on alliance of Youth Movements Summit, Dec 3-5'

larouchepub.com Larouche Publications 8/22/2008 Hector Rivas 'Soros's Nazi roots are showing' 7/4/2008 Ed Hamler 'George Soros buys the nomination; Obama borrows it'

unitypublishing.com Unity Publishing 3/14/2010 Richard Salbato 'Did Soros cause the 2008 crash?'

aim.org Accuracy in Media 4/1/2010 Zubi Diamond 'The Dodd financial Reform Bill lets Soros off the hook' 4/23/2008 Cliff Kincaid 'With Obama, It's the Communism, Stupid'

humanevents.com Human Events 9/9/2010 Buzz Patterson 'The Obama-Soros Connection' 4/2/2011 'Top 10 reasons George Soros is dangerous' 10/221/2011 Matthew Vadum 'George Soros funds Occupy Wall Street'

fromthewildernesspublications.com From the Wilderness Publications 4/7/1999 Michel Chossudovsky 'Kosovo Freedom Fighters Financed by Organized Crime'

unmikonli9ne.org UN Mission In Kosovo 'UNMIK media reports'

jta.org Jewish Telegraphic Agency 11/10/2003 Uriel Heilman 'In rare Jewish appearance, George Soros says Jews and Israel cause Anti-Semitism'

thirdworldtraveler.com Third World Traveler 12/7/2008 Tom Burghardt 'Kosovo: A European Narco State'

balkanblog.org Balkanforum 9/10/2001 Michel Chossudovsky 'Washington behind terrorist assaults in Macedonia'

newskosovo.wordpress.com News Kosovo 11/6/2011 'Kosovo PM Thaci to be investigated on Marty Report allegations'

discoverthenetworks.org Discover the Networks 10/2004 'George Soros Backgrounder' 'Open Society Institute' 'Tides Foundation and Tides Center' 'Institute for New Economic Thinking (INET)' 'Additional information on the Institute for New Economic Thinking' 10/16/2011 Organizations funded directly by George Soros and his Open Society Institute' 'Tides Foundation and Tides Center'

songfacts.com Song Facts 'Give Peace a Chance/John Lennon'

about.com 'Judaism Do we have to listen when the billionaire speaks?'

history-of-macedonia.com History of Macedonia '112/9/2003 Heather Coffin 'George Soros: Everything you want to know about him'

free-invest.com 2/20/2011 'LUKOIL's investments into Romania economy have exceeded 1 billion…'

wiki.answers.com 'Is Romania a communist country?'

findarticles.com Journal of Broadcasting & Electronic Media Winter 1998 Thomas A Mollison 'Television broadcasting leads Romania's march toward on open democratic society'

alina_stefanescu.typepard.com 3/8/2009 'Romania revealed The letter of the Six from 1989'

word.world-citizenship.org "1000Peace Nobel 2005' 8/15/2007 'Cristina Guseth/Romania'

carnegie.ru Carnegie Moscow Center Sept-Oct1996 Thomas Carothers 'Aiding post-Communist Societies: A better way'

cnn.com CNN 4/29/2009 Christiane Amanpour 'Obama's 100 days of foreign affairs' 11/4/2009 George Soros 'In revolutionary times the impossible becomes possible' 4/28/2000 Jennifer Karchmer 'A shakeup at Soros funds'

history-of-macedonia.com 10/10/2008' History of Macedonia George Soros Everything you want to know about him'

righttruth.typepad.com Right Truth 2/15/2008 "Obama's Poverty Bill

2.lse.ac.uk 'LSE history'

sweetness-light.com Sweetness & Light 8/15/2008 Bloomberg 'Soros invests $811million in Brazilian Oil'

americanthinker.com American Thinker 6/13/2011 Ed Lasky 'Crony Capitalism and Obama's anti-coal crusade' 9/11/2010 Ed Lasky 'Soros' latest gambit' 3/28/2011 Ed Lasky 'Soros wins under Obama's Energy Policies'

usatoday.com USA Today 7/18/2008 Ken Dilanian 'Obama shifts stance on environmental issues' 5/12/2008 David J Lynch 'Soros sees Reflexivity theory of economic as life's work'

zimbio.com Zimbio 5/5/2010 'Fannie Mae owns patent on residential cap and trade exchange' 6/15/2011 'George Soros is funding effort to remove conservatives from local judgeships' 2/5/2011 'Atheist George Soros: The main stumbling block is Israel…'

nytimes.com NY Times 6/22/2009 Jeff Zeleny 'Occasional smoker 47 signs tobacco bill' 5/2/2011 A.G. Sulzberger 'Army Corps blows up Missouri levee' 3/26/1998 Market Place; Buffett likes silver; Soros, a silver mine'

abcnews.go.com ABC News 1/28/2009 Claire Shipman 'Obama signs equal pay for equal work bill'

real-world-news-org. 'The Global Warming Hoax in the words of The Club of Rome'

nysun.com NY Sun 3/21/2007 Eli Lake 'Obama rebuffs marketswiki.com 'Managed Funds Association' 'World Economic Forum' educate-you self.org Educate-Yourself 3/10/1981 Lonnie Wolfe 'World Depopulation is Top NSA Agenda: Club of Rome The Haig-Kissinger depopulation policy'

scribd.com/doc Scribd 1992 Alexander king, Bertrand Schneider "The First Global Revolution: A Report by the Council of the Club of Rome'

leftbusinessobserver.com Left Business Observer 8/2005 'The long strange career of Jeffrey Sachs'

investopedia.com Investopedia 'Merchant Bank' 'Hedge Fund'

nowtheendbegins.com Now the End Begins 'George Soros, Obama's Puppet Master'

richardsilverstein.com 10/12/2006 'George Soros to fund progressive Jewish lobby to counter AIPAC'

jewishjustice.org Jewish Justice 'History'

newsrealblog.com NewsReal Blog 1/16/2011 Jeff Dunetz 'Jewish Funds for Justice's racist collective guilt teaching behind its Glenn Beck attacks'

jstreet.org JStreet 5/19/2011'J Street commends President Obama's Middle East Speech' 2/23/2011 'With World's eyes on the Middle East 2000+ gather for 2nd Pro Israel, Pro-Peace Conference'

thejc.com Jewish Chronicle 9/28/2010 Jessica Elgot 'Israel lobby lied about George Soros cash'

canadafreepress.com Canada Free Press 11/14/2010 Daniel Greenfield 'The Jewish People vs George Soros'

crf.org Council on Foreign Relations 2/22/2012 Membership Register' 'Mission Statement'

recyclewashingtonwordpress.com Recycle Washington 4/29/2010 Savant Noir 'Unraveling the Club of Rome (part 1)

washingtonpost.com Washington Post 2/3/2011 Jennifer Rubin 'Soros blames Jews for Egypt' 11/7/2008 Kathleen Parker 'The Empress' clothes'

ineteconomics.org Institute for New Economic Thinking 'Bretton Woods Conference'

digitaljournal.com Digital Journal 6/2/2009 'George Soros behind ethics complaint against Gov Sarah Palin'

tides.org Tides 'History'

the libertyjournal.com The Liberty Journal 8/10/2008 'Communist linked, Tides Foundation funded, Apollo alliance helped write Obama's Stimulus' apolloalliance.org Apollo Alliance 1/15/2009 Keith Schneider 'Clean energy is foundation of proposed Stimulus'

mrc.org 5/25/2011 Dan Gainor 'Soros-funded Lefty Media reach more than 300 million every day' 5/18/2011 'Soros spends over $48 million funding media organizations'

thestockmarketwatch.com StockMarket Watch 6/27/2011 'The truth about George Soros' gold Position, Fed, & GPXM News'

mineweb.com Mineweb 5/21/2011 Julian DW Phillips 'The Soros gold sale. Has it signaled the end of the gold and silver market?' 11/25/2008 'Soros and other finds buy major coal equities at fire sale prices'

whitehousedossier.com White Hose dossier 4/13/2011 Keith Koffler 'White House Visitor Log Scam is Revealed'

theblaze.com The Blaze 2/24/2011 Meredith Jessup 'Business New Soros investment fund to profit from Obama Green Agenda' 6/15/2011 Billy Hallowell 'Faith why is atheist George Soros giving money to a Faith project?' 11/9/2010 'Read the updated Beck TV background guide to George Soros' 11/1/2011 Mike Opelka 'This is the comprehensive list of those supporting Occupy Wall Street' 10/13/20111 Tiffany Gabbay 'top ten richest celebrities supporting Occupy Wall Street'

thestreet.com The Street 8/5/2010 Eric Rosenbaum 'Why George Soros is buying Westport Innovations'

opencongress.org OpenCongress 4/5/2011 'H.R. 1380 New Alternative Transportation to give Americans Solutions Act of 2011'

crisisgroup.org 'About Crisis Group'

examiner.com Examiner 1/3/2011 Kenneth Schortgen Jr. 'George Soros says that America must give up the dollar and accept world currency' Anthony Martin 'Soros meddles in courts, attempts to buy Leftwing judges'

anationbeguiled.wordpress.com 6/8/2011 Jon Christian Ryter 'The Global Currency War'

questionsquestions.net 11/1/1996 William Engdahl 'The Secret Financial Network behind Wizard George Soros'

usasurvival.org America's Survival, Inc 11/14/2009 Cliff Kincaid 'Atheist Soros funds Catholic Groups'

lycos.com Lycos Retriever 'George Soros: Quantum Fund'

washingtonexaminer.com Washington examiner 11/14/2011 Mark Hemingway ' Soros uses his billion to undermine democracy' 1/30/2011 Timothy P Carney 'The Kochs vs. Soros: Free markets vs. state coercion' foxnews.com FOX News 3/23/2011 Dan Gainor 'Why are the Media ignoring plans by George Soros to remake the entire Global Economy?'

streetstories.com StreetStories 7/10/1990 Stephen Taub, David Carey, Amy Barrett, Richard J Coletti, Jackie Gold 'George Soros in the Wall Street Top 100...'

telegraph.co.uk The Telegraph 9/13/2002 David Litterick 'Billionaire who broke the Bank of England'

plato.stanford.edu Stanford Encyclopedia of Philosophy 'Karl Popper'

esperanto.org Esperanto 'The International Language'

olesiafx.com Olesia 4/2006 'Soros and his foundation faced continuing mistrust on the part of the government'

thomas.loc.gov Library of Congress 'H.R, 1380 Bill summary & Status 112th Congress'

sharpeinvesting.com Sharpe Investing '8/6/2007 'Theory of Reflexivity'

tammybruce.com Tammy Bruce 6/24/2011 'Obama Boss George Soros ready to Profit from Oil Disaster'

escapetyranny.com Escape Tyranny 6/13/2011 Ben Hart 'Electricity prices to soar 40-60% as coal plants close (due to Obama's anti-coal policies)'

washingtontimes.com Washington Times 6/23/2011 Chuck Neubauer 'Soros and liberal groups seeking top election posts in battleground states'

radioviceonline.com RadioViceOnline.com 7/15/2009 'Andree McLeod: Palin's personal stalker'

citizensforethic.org 10/23/2008 CREW files FEC complaint against Gov Palin ...'

thespeechatimeforchoosing.wordpress.com A Time For Choosing 6/4/2009 'Following up on Soros, CREW, Palin, and Obama'

plunderbund.com Plunderbund 8/31/2008 'Sarah Palin's Unamerican Flag Pin'

wvnews.net Western Voices World News 2/2/2008 John Young 'John McCain: George Soros' Best Friend'

zerohedge.com ZeroHedge 4/13/2011 'Libya: All about Oil, or All About Banking?'

truthistreason.net Truth is Treason 2/18/2011Tony Cartalucci/ BlackListed News 'Want to Understand the Egypt Issue? George Soros is writing Egypt's Constitution'

nogw.com 'Barack Obama Zionist Wolf in Sheep's Clothing'

trilateral.org Trilateral Commission 'Program of the 2011 Annual Meeting'

globalresearch.ca Global Research ca 6/2/2009 Stephen Lendman 'Review of Daniel Estulin's book "The True Story of the Bilderberg Group and what they may be planning now'

onwardjames.blogspot.com Onward James 2/4/2011 'Barack Hussein Obama, George Soros, Egypt, Muslim Brotherhood Conspiracy?'

freerepublic.com FreeRepublic.com 2/4/2011 Terresa Monroe-Hamilton/ Noisy Room. net 'Youth, High Tech and the Fundamental Change that is Revolution' 6/24/2011 Ann Barnhardt/Capital Management, Inc. 'Double red alert ('Soros buying up farmland)' 5/21/2010 Raven Clabough 'Shorebank Another Example of Cronyism ...'

un.org UN 'Agenda 21'

republicbradcasting.org Tony Cartalucci 'George Soros and Egypt's New Constitution'

washingtontimes.com Washington Times 9/10/2010 Dan Pero George Soros vs. Judicial elections'

time.com TIME 4/12/2011 Rana Foroohar "Larry Summers: No regrets on deregulation' 11/221/2008 M.J. Stephey 'Bretton Woods System'

batr.org 'Bretton Woods II The final enslavement of mankind'

americanfreepress.net Pete Papaherakles 'Soros convenes Bretton Woods II'

brettonwoodsproject.org Bretton Woods Project 4/17/2011 'Spring meetings 2011 communiques coverage'

deltadispatches.org Delta dispatches 7/7/2011 Elizabeth Skree 'As flood waters recede, New land appears in West Bay '

dcexposed.com dcxposed 7/5/2011 Sheila F 'Coincidence or conspiracy in Missouri farmland flood'

searshomes.org 5/1/2011 'Farmland 0, Cairo 1'

commercialappeal.com Commercial Appeal 6/26/2011 Tom Charlier 'Mississippi River levees took quite a hit from floods

reuters.co.uk Reuters 6/12/2011 Barton Lorimor 'Midwestern farmers await levee decision to rebuild' 10/13/10`` Felix salmon 'On George Soros, Occupy Wall Street and Reuters'

farmlandgrab.org Farmland Grab.org 6/4/2011 Tom Webb 'Big money moves into the Midwest grain trade' foodfreedom.wordpress.com Food Freedom 4/24/2011 Ann Barnhardt 'Feds buying up farmland they flooded, Soros in on it'

topstockanalysts.com Top Stock Analysts 6/4/2011 David Sterman 'George Soros just spent $455 million on these two stocks'

therealrevo.com The Real Revo 4/5/2011 'Soros' Gavilon buys AWB, Union elevator to become 3ed largest grain company on earth'

seekingalpha.com Seeking Alpha 6/29/2011 Zvi Bar 'How Soros's 2011 transactions have worked out so far' 1/28/2011 Todd Campbell 'Two metallurgical coal stocks to satisfy china's import appetite'

coal.energy-business-review.com Energy Business Review 6/16/2011'Arch coal acquires International Coal Group'

usactionnews.com US Action News 1/2011 'Obama's war on coal and your electricity'

uncoverage.net Uncoverage.net 2/16/2011 Carolyn Greenberg/Conservative Outlooks 'Obama energy policy now a 4-alarm fire'

firebasefreedom.ning.com Firebase Freedom 2/2/2011David L Huffman Esquire 'George Soros Proud new owner of most of West Virginia's coal'

investmentmoast.com Investment Moats 8/20/2008 'George Soros: Distress buying of mining companies'

parkersburgwvteapary.ning.com Parkersburg Tea Party 1/30/2011 Mario Parker, Zachary R Mider 'Alpha Natural (Soros company) agrees to buy Massey Energy…'

gainerstoday.com Gainers Today 'Alpha Natural Resources, Inc'

mineweb.com Mineweb business-mongolia.com Mongolia Business News 7/31/2008 Dorothy Kosich 'Soros Foundation releases Mongolian mining, exploration license statistics'

english.albeu.com/Albania Albeau News 7/11/2011 'Soros requires the mines of Kosovo'

english.aljazeera.net Aljazeera 3/6/2011 'Egypt PM appoints new key ministers'

guardian.co.uk 2/10/2011 Guardian Chris McGreal 'Egyptian foreign minister rejects US intervention' 11/21/2011 Tunisia's election winners form interim government after uprising'

foreignpolicyjournal.com Foreign Policy Journal 1/18/2011 Dr. K.R. Bolton uprising planning by Opens Society Network and National Endowment for Democracy'

almasryalyoum.com AlMasryAlYoum English edition 2/3/2011 FM call revolution one of most important in history' npr.org NPR 1/29/2009 Adam Davidson, Alex Blumberg 'Obama gives Keyes his first real-world test'

mrc.org 6/25/2011 Jeff Poor 'CNBC personalities explain $787 billion stimulus not implemented correctly...'

cato.org Cato Institute 1/29/2009 Ike Brannon, Chris Edwards 'Barack Obama's Keynesian Mistake'

conservativedailynews.com Conservative Daily News 7/12/2010 John smith 'Obama: Keynesian economics or Cloward-Piven strategy'

frontpagemag.com Front Page Mag 8/8/2005 John Perazzo 'Left-Wing Monster: Pol Pot' 10/11/2004 David Horowitz, Richard Poe 'The Shadow Party Part III'

bloomberg.com Bloomberg 10/5/2004 Katherine Burton 'George Soros hands control of money management firm to his sons'

abovetopsecret.com Above Top Secret 'Is Obama Considering another Perseus Exec for his campaign?'

snopes.com Snopes 'Advice and Descent'

brookings.edu Brookings 'Quality Independence Impact'

newsbusters.org NewsBusters 3/29/2011 Dan Gainor 'Soros adds more lefty supports to event aiming to remake economy' 3/29/2011 'Soros adds more lefty supporters to event aiming to remake economy'

pittsburghlive.com Pittsburgh Tribune-Review 7/30/2006 Bill Steigerwald 'Illuminating the Shadow Party'

jewishworldreview.com Jewish World Review 10/15/2010 Caroline B Glick 'Now it's the Israel Left fearing a destruction of the American-Israel bond'

thefortworthpress.com The Fort Worth Press "Obama and JStreet vs Israel, again'

redstate.com Red State 4/21/2010 'Don't let Soros and the Secretary of State Project take over your state'

lonelymachines.org 6/9/2008 'The real powers behind this election'

franklincountypatriots.com Franklin County Patriots 7/26/2010 'Deceiving America by popular vote'

bbc.com BBC 10/27/2011 'Islamists win Tunisia's Elections'

thenewamerican.com The New American 10/5/2011 Alex Newman 'Big money linked to Occupy Wall Street'

forbes.com Forbes 12/13/2011 T Scott Gross 'Occupy Wall Street: Ask for the impossible'

allianceforglobaljustice.org Alliance for Global Justice 'Marrying donations supports anti-war and anti-Israel orgs.'

CPSIA information can be obtained at www.ICGtesting.com
Printed in the USA
VOW021541230712
5939BV00002B/3/P